Business Law
in Canada

FOURTH EDITION

RICHARD A. YATES

British Columbia Institute of Technology

Prentice Hall Canada Inc.
Scarborough, Ontario

Canadian Cataloguing in Publication Data

Yates, Richard
  Business law in Canada

4th ed.
ISBN 0–13–293119–2

1. Commercial law — Canada. I. Title.

KE919.Y37 1995   346.71'07   C94–931187–1
KF889.3.Y37   1995

Prentice-Hall, Inc., Englewood Cliffs, New Jersey
Prentice-Hall International (UK) Limited, London
Prentice-Hall of Australia, Pty. Limited, Sydney
Prentice-Hall Hispanoamericana, S.A., Mexico City
Prentice-Hall of India Private Limited, New Delhi
Prentice-Hall of Japan, Inc., Tokyo
Simon & Schuster Asia Private Limited, Singapore
Editora Prentice-Hall do Brasil, Ltda., Rio de Janeiro

ISBN 0–13–293119–2

Acquisitions Editor: Jaqueline Wood
Developmental Editor: Maurice Esses
Copy Editor: Mia London
Production Editor: Dawn du Quesnay, Mary-Ann Field
Production Coordinator: Anna Orodi
Permissions/Photo Research: Karen Taylor
Cover Design: Olena Serbyn
Cover Image: Damir Frkoyic/Masterfile
Page Layout: Jerry Langton

4 5 RRD 99 98 97 96

Printed and bound in the United States

Disclaimer: The names used throughout the text are fictitious.
The examples and cases in which they appear in
no way typify the actions of any ethnic group.

Contents

Chapter 3: Formation of Contracts   82

Chapter 4: Formation of Contracts (continued)   106

Chapter 10: Agency   291

Chapter 11: Business Organization: Sole Proprietorship and Partnership   314

Chapter 12: Business Organization: Part II   335

Chapter 13: Negotiable Instruments   365

Chapter 14: Personal and Intellectual Property and Insurance   395

Preface to the Fourth Edition

As we bring out this fourth edition of *Business Law in Canada* we appreciate the positive response the book has received from students and instructors alike. At the outset, we had anticipated the need for a book designed specifically for one-term introductory courses in business law, and we have been gratified at its reception. Over the years, we have made a number of alterations to the text in response to the changing nature of business law courses and the helpful suggestions of instructors across Canada. This edition incorporates a great many changes that may not be apparent at first glance. Effort has been made to retain the original book's focus on legal concepts in language accessible to students and to make only those changes that clarify or update the information. In addition, at the recommendation of instructors using the text, we have revamped and moved the second chapter. Charter law and constitutional law have been incorporated into Chapter 1 and the portion of Chapter 2 that deals with administrative law has been added to the last chapter in this edition. A significant portion of the new Chapter 16 is devoted to environmental law and the business community's growing concern with the regulatory environment within which it must function.

An ongoing concern has been to keep the text as brief as possible without sacrificing the content needed to support the various business programs for which it is used. The introductory material is limited to one chapter and the second chapter is devoted to the law of torts. The important area of contract law is covered in the next four chapters. These chapters are intended to form the nucleus of any business law course, and I suggest that none be excluded from an introductory course. The remaining ten chapters of the text are devoted to discrete legal topics which can be used or deleted as the instructor deems appropriate. For instance, an instructor may feel that negotiable instruments or real estate law is not necessary for his or her course and will choose to leave out this material. Even within chapters this flexibility is possible. Chapter 7 has been divided into two distinct parts so that only one section need be covered. Similarly, in Chapter 9 (Employment Law), some instructors will choose not to include the material provided under the heading of Collective Bargaining, and any of the three components comprising chapter 14, intellectual property, personal property or insurance, can be deleted as need dictates. It should also be mentioned that, since these chapters have been designed to stand alone, the order in which they appear in the text is to some extent arbitrary. Thus, an instructor may prefer to use Chapter 8 (Securing Debt and Collections) as the final topic of a course or may wish to deal with business organizations before covering employment law. It should be noted, however, that the chapters devoted to Agency (Chapter 10), Partnership (Chapter 11) and Corporations (Chapter 12) are intended to be studied in sequence.

Out of necessity some compromises have been made in the text. For example, Chapter 15, devoted to real property matters, is little more than an introduction to that specialized and important area with minimal attention given to the variety of provincial laws in place. The assumption is that those who need a more thorough grounding will be supplied with supplementary materials or will take a follow-up course.

Each chapter begins with a short case study. At the end of each chapter, questions help students test their understanding of the materials covered in the chapter. Similarly, summaries of actual, reported cases have been included to allow students to apply legal principles to real situations. The actual citations in these cases will be included in the *Instructor's Manual* so that the instructor can choose whether to have the students look them up. The *Instructor's Manual* now includes reproductions of various legal forms of the type formerly included in the text.

Icons like the ones in the margin appear beside paragraphs in the text to refer the reader to corresponding sections in *Business Law in Canada Casebook* (D'Anne Davis, ISBN 0-13-295106-1). The large icon alerts the reader to actual extracts of relevant cases from law reports, while the smaller icon refers to summaries of cases from other, secondary literature.

Also included at the end of each chapter are a number of issues designed to facilitate class discussion. The instructor can also use these issues to encourage students to examine concepts that go beyond the material contained in the text or to provide an impetus for further research. Appended to each chapter are summaries of relevant legislation which will assist students in determining which statutory provisions apply in their particular jurisdictions. Marginal notes have been included in the body of each chapter to assist students' review and to facilitate the quick location of information, but care should be taken with their use. While an attempt has been made to make them accurate and comprehensive, abbreviations such as these can be misleading. They should be used only in conjunction with the text material. A *Study Guide and Workbook* designed to facilitate students' access to the text is available as well as a test bank for instructors' use, which is also available in computerized format.

While many of the concepts that apply to the common law provinces apply to Québec as well, no attempt has been made in the text to deal specifically with the differences in the law between Québec and the common law provinces of Canada. I must also emphasize that this text and the material contained within it are designed to facilitate the teaching of general business law principles and concepts, and not to provide specific, accurate and detailed legal information. It has been necessary in many instances to leave out important details or to generalize concepts and ideas to facilitate the teaching process and to avoid becoming bogged down in detail. While every effort has been taken to make the information as accurate as possible, such information can quickly grow out of date because of amendments and other changes in the law of the various jurisdictions. The reader is cautioned not to use the material in this text as a substitute for legal advice when faced with a specific problem. In such circumstances, the reader should go to a lawyer who will provide appropriate legal advice for the problem at hand.

I hope, however, that exposure to these materials will make the reader a more sophisticated client.

I would like to thank the reviewers, publishers' representatives and users of the first three editions for their helpful suggestions as well as those who responded to a questionnaire on the third edition. I would also like to acknowledge the tireless and painstaking efforts of the editors who have been associated with the text at Prentice Hall Canada. I would also like to thank my students and colleagues at the British Columbia Institute of Technology and at Simon Fraser University who have given many useful suggestions and assisted in the tedious task of locating and correcting the various errors and mistakes that managed to creep into the previous editions.

Richard A. Yates
1995

Table of Statutes

Table of Cases

1

INTRODUCTION TO THE LEGAL SYSTEM

Objectives of the Chapter

- to develop a workable definition of the term "law"
- to distinguish between common law and civil law
- to outline Canadian constitutional history and the workings of the parliamentary system
- to describe the court system in place in Canada today
- to explain the litigation process and consider various alternatives to it

WHAT IS LAW?

We live in a complex world in which our success depends largely on how effectively we interact with one another. An understanding of the legal concepts and principles that govern personal and commercial relationships is essential for orderly progress in our society. Most of us readily recognize the rules and regulations that are considered law, but it is difficult to establish a satisfactory, all-inclusive definition. Philosophers have been trying for centuries to determine just what is meant by law, and their theories have had an ongoing effect on the development of our legal system.

Philosophical Basis of Law

In ancient times, the prevalent moral code determined whether any given rule was a law or not. Thus, a mad king's order that all children under the age of three be put to death would not be considered law since carrying out the order would be immoral. The legal philosophy that supports this interpretation of rules is called

natural law theory, and reflects the quality and nature of individual rules. The problem with this approach was that it depended on the moral code established by the dominant religious body of the time.[1] When reform movements took exception to established codes, governing institutions could not tolerate the conflicting ideas of what constituted right and wrong behaviour.

Legal positivism, which quickly overshadowed natural law theory, examined the status rather than the quality of the rule and recognized a rule as a law only if the person or body enacting it had the authority to do so. Legal positivists recognize as valid the rules laid down by even a mad king and are bound by them.

A more practical approach, called **legal realism,** developed in the United States from the teachings of Oliver Wendell Holmes. In this system, a rule is only recognized as a law when the courts are willing to enforce it. It makes no difference whether the rule is moral or who passed it; if the courts will enforce it, it is a law. These three philosophies define law in terms of what is morally justifiable, who makes the law or whether the law is enforced. There are many other approaches to legal philosophy, each with a different definition of law. This brief discussion simply illustrates why it is so difficult to give a concise, simple and workable definition of law.

No wholly
satisfactory
definition of law

From Theory to Practice

To understand the problems involved in applying these ideas, it is worthwhile considering the dilemma facing the German courts and the war crimes tribunals, set up by the victorious Allies, at the end of World War II. Both the German courts and the Allied tribunals had to deal with people who had committed unjust acts that were not contrary to Nazi law. The Third Reich was a lawfully constituted government, Hitler came to power legally, and the changes made to the German Constitution were properly passed. The legal realists had to acknowledge that the laws passed in Nazi Germany were real laws in that the courts enforced them. The legal positivists had a similar problem since an authorized body passed the laws. Only the largely discredited natural law theory provided a philosophical basis for the trial of war criminals. The judges at the Nuremberg war trials found that the acts for which the defendants were being tried were so despicable and so terrible that no rules or no amount of authority could justify them. The acts were wrong by their very nature. More significantly for our discussion, after the war the German court system convicted people who had committed unjust acts during the Nazi regime on the same philosophical basis. When the defendants argued that they had only done what was legal and permitted under Nazi law, the court's response was that their acts were "contrary to the sound conscience and sense of justice of all decent human beings" and therefore unlawful.[2] One suspects that the courts merely searched for a philosophical basis to support what they had decided to do in any case.

[1] Oliver Wendell Holmes, "The Path of the Law," *Harvard Law Review* (1897) p. 457.
[2] H.L.A. Hart, "Positivism and the Separation of Law and Morals," *Harvard Law Review* (1958) p. 593.

Problems
applying theory

These examples are not presented to support the validity of the natural law theory, but rather to demonstrate that there is no simple answer to the question of what law is. Knowing that various theories have contributed to the development of our legal system helps us to appreciate the complexities involved in the administration of that system.

A Workable Definition

Definition

For our study of law at this introductory level, it is helpful to be able to use a simplified definition of law. **Law is the body of rules which can be enforced by the courts or by other government agencies.** We are exposed to many rules in our daily activities. Courtesy demands that we do not interrupt when someone else is speaking. Social convention determines that it is improper to enter a restaurant while shirtless or shoeless. Private clubs usually have rules or bylaws governing procedures for meetings. Universities and colleges often establish rules of conduct for their students and faculty. None of these rules falls into our definition of law because the courts cannot enforce them. But when there is a disagreement over who is responsible for an accident, a question of whether a crime has been committed or a difference about the interpretation of the terms of a contract or a will, the participants may find themselves before a judge. Rules which can be enforced by the courts govern these situations; thus they are laws within the definition presented here.

A person dealing with government agencies such as labour relations boards, the Workers' Compensation Board, or city and municipal councils must recognize that these bodies are able to try matters in dispute before them, and render decisions that affect the rights of the parties. The rules enforced by these bodies are also laws within this definition. The unique problems associated with government agencies and regulatory bodies will be discussed in the last chapter of this text.

ORIGINS OF THE LAW

Québec—civil law;
all other
provinces—
common law

Nine of the ten Canadian provinces have adopted the common law system developed over the last thousand years in England. Québec's legal system is based on the French Civil Code. Although this text focuses on common law, understanding it may be assisted by briefly examining the basic differences between the two systems.

Civil Law

Civil law originated in Rome when Emperor Justinian had Roman law codified for use throughout the Roman Empire. Its most significant modification occurred early in the nineteenth century when Napoleon revised and recodified it, and saw that it was established throughout Europe and the French colonies. The most important feature of French civil law is its central code, a list of rules stated as broad principles of law. Under this system, people wanting to know their legal rights or obligations refer to the civil code. For example, if a person were to suffer injury in Québec because of the careless acts of an employee delivering fuel oil, the victim would turn to the Québec Civil Code to determine his or her rights. Articles 1457 and 1463 of the most recent Code state the following:

> 1457. Every person has a duty to abide by the rules of conduct which lie upon him, according to the circumstances, usage or law, so as not to cause injury to another. Where he is endowed with reason and fails in this duty, he is responsible for any injury he causes to another person and is liable to reparation for the injury, whether it be bodily, moral or material in nature.

He is also liable, in certain cases, to reparation for injury caused to another by the act or fault of another person or by the act of things in his custody.

> 1463. The principal is liable to reparation for injury caused by the fault of his agents and servants in the performance of their duties; nevertheless, he retains his recourses against them.

Civil Code
provides
predictability

Québec courts rely on the Code for guidance and solutions. Civil law judges are influenced by decisions made in other cases and lawyers will take great pains to point out what other judges have done in similar situations, but the key to understanding the civil code system is to recognize that ultimately the Code determines the principle to be applied. While the decisions of other judges and the opinions expressed by learned people discoursing on the law can be very persuasive, they do not constitute binding precedents in a civil law jurisdiction. A new Québec Civil Code has been developed and came into effect January 1, 1994, a very significant event in the evolution of the law of Québec.

Common Law

Common law
grew from
struggle for
power

As Roman civil law was taking hold in Europe, relations between the existing English and French kingdoms were frequently strained. It has been suggested that this strain is the reason England maintained its unique **common law** system of justice rather than adopting the more widely accepted Roman civil law. The Norman conquest of England in 1066 is considered a significant event in the development of English common law, not because of any great changes brought about in the legal system at that time but because of the centralization of power that took place under King William.

The development of the English legal system was further affected by the ongoing struggle for power between the king and the nobility and between later kings and parliament. William the Conqueror was a strong king who had no difficulty controlling the nobles whom he had brought with him to England. Rather than giving them land outright, he restricted them to merely holding it under the very precise terms of the feudal system. William was followed by several weak kings who lost much of this power. Stronger kings who followed in turn set out to regain control and influence.

One of the great rulers of this succession was Henry II. Before his rule, people with disputes had to go to local lords, barons or sheriffs whose concepts of justice were often arbitrary and capricious. These courts often resorted to barbaric practices such as trial by battle or ordeal.

In trial by battle, the litigants or their chosen champions participated in armed combat. The theory was that God would ensure that the survivor of the conflict would be the one in the right. Trial by ordeal involved a test such as being forced to hold a red hot iron bar. If the bandaged wound festered after a week, it was assumed that the person was in the wrong. If the wound was clean, God was presumed to be protecting that person and the truth of his or her statements was verified.

Henry II establishes courts

King Henry was responsible for establishing travelling courts which provided a more acceptable method of resolving disputes between citizens of the kingdom. His royal judges were less likely to be biased, incompetent or corrupt, and their judgments were more reasonable and predictable. The more just Henry and those who followed made the courts, the more popular they became and eventually the courts of the nobles fell into disuse. The royal courts did not impose any particular set of laws. Their purpose was to administer justice, but justice was defined in terms of what the local population considered to be just and fair. Rather than imposing rules created by the king or his advisers, the travelling courts simply discovered the laws that were already in place in the form of local customs or traditions of the communities they visited. The judges also began to look to each other for rules to apply when faced with new situations.

Judges follow each others' decisions

STARE DECISIS. Gradually, a system of justice developed in which the judges followed each other's decisions. This process is called ***stare decisis***, or following precedent. Another factor that affected the development of *stare decisis* was the creation of appeal courts. Although appeal courts as such are a relatively modern development, the rudiments of an appeal structure existed during the early phases of the development of common law. When a decision made by a lower court judge was overturned on appeal, the reason for the reversal was stated and made available to the rest of the legal community and the lower court judge was declared to be in error. To avoid this kind of embarrassment, judges would simply follow the principles laid down by the appeal court. Eventually, the practice of following precedent became institutionalized. The most significant feature of our legal system today is that the decision of a judge at one level is binding on all other judges in that system who function in a court of equal or lower rank, providing facts in the two cases are similar. Strictly speaking, a judge is not bound to follow decisions made by other judges in a court at the same level in that province. However, the practical effect is the same since these judges must follow their colleagues' decisions, "...in the absence of strong reason to the contrary."[3]

[3] Rex Ex Rec. *McWilliam v. Morris*, [1942] O.W.N. p. 447 at p. 449 High Court of Justice.

Thus today, a judge considering a case in the Court of Queen's Bench for Alberta would be required to follow a similar decision laid down in the Court of Appeal for Alberta or the Supreme Court of Canada, but would not have to follow a decision involving an identical case from the Court of Appeal for Manitoba. Such a decision would be merely persuasive since it came from a different jurisdiction. Because the Supreme Court of Canada is the highest court in the land, its decisions are binding on all Canadian courts.

Stare decisis plays the same role in the English common law system as the civil code does in the French system. It allows the parties to predict the outcome of any litigation and thus avoid going to court. However a significant disadvantage of following precedent is that a judge must follow another judge's decision even though social attitudes may have changed. The system is anchored to the past and bound to it with only limited capacity to adapt and change to meet the needs of modern circumstances. A judge will often be confronted with several conflicting precedents presented by opposing legal representatives to support their arguments. The judge's job is to analyze the facts in the precedent cases and compare them to the case at hand. Since no two cases are ever exactly alike, this gives the judge some flexibility in deciding whether or not to apply a particular precedent. Judges often try to avoid applying precedent decisions to cases in which they feel such a finding would be unjust. A judge will usually be able to find essential differences between the two cases if he or she does not want to apply the precedent. This process is referred to as distinguishing the facts of opposing precedents.

Stare decisis provides predictability

Results in an inflexible system

SOURCES OF LAW

Common Law

At an early stage in the development of common law, three great courts, the **court of common pleas**, the **court of king's bench** and the **exchequer court**, referred to collectively as the common law courts, were created. The rules developed in the courts were called "the common law" because the judges, at least in theory, did not create law but merely discovered it in the customs and traditions of the people to whom it was to be applied. However, the foundation for a complete legal system could not be supplied by local custom and tradition alone, so common law judges borrowed legal principles from many different sources. Roman civil law gave us our concepts of property and possessions. Canon or church law contributed law in relation to families and estates. Another important European system that had an impact on the common law was called the law merchant. Trading between nations was performed by merchants who were members of guilds (similar to modern trade unions or professional organizations) which developed their own rules to deal with disputes between members. As the strength of the guilds declined, common law judges found themselves dealing increasingly with disputes between merchants. The law merchant was then adopted as part of the English common law and it included laws relating to negotiable instruments such as cheques and promissory notes.

Customs and traditions major source of common law

Roman Law

Canon Law

Law merchant

Equity

Common law courts had some serious limitations. Parties seeking justice before them found it difficult to obtain fair and proper redress for the grievances they had suffered. Because of the rigidity of the process, the inflexibility of the rules applied and the limited scope of the remedies available, people often went directly to the king for satisfaction and relief. The burden of this process made it necessary for the king to delegate the responsibility to the chancellor who in turn appointed several vice-chancellors. This body eventually became known as the **Court of Chancery**, or Court of Equity. It dealt with matters that for various reasons could not be handled adequately or fairly by the common law courts.

The Court of Chancery did not hear appeals from the common law courts; rather, it provided an alternative place to go. If people seeking relief knew that the common law courts could provide no remedy or that the remedy was inadequate, they would go to the Court of Chancery instead. The advantage of the Court of Chancery was that it was not hampered by the great body of formal and technical rules that was the heritage of the common law courts. Initially, at least, the chancery judges did not have to follow precedent, nor were they restricted by rigid procedures; rather, they decided a case on its merit or by what was morally fair or just.

The system of law developed by the courts of chancery became known as the **law of equity**. The most significant asset of equity was also one of its greatest drawbacks. Each decision of the courts of chancery appeared arbitrary; there was no uniformity within the system and it was impossible to predict the outcome of a given case. The common law judges resented the fact that the judges in the courts of chancery could ignore the great body of law that had been developed and could arbitrarily follow their own consciences. Inevitably, conflict arose. Although a truce was reached during the reign of James I, the friction was only completely eliminated when the courts were amalgamated by the *Judicature Acts* of 1873-75. Part of the resolution of this dispute was that whenever the principles of equity and common law conflicted, equity would prevail. Another outcome of the friction between the common law judges and chancery judges was that the courts of chancery adopted many of the formal rules of common law courts including the following of precedent. Eventually, courts of chancery became as formal and rigid as the common law courts.

The rules of equity were designed to meet the objectives of fairness and justice, but as society's concept of right and wrong has changed, the principles of equity have been unable to make corresponding changes. Today, equitable principles must be viewed as a body of rules developed by the courts of chancery which may or may not be consistent with today's concepts of right and wrong. When modern judges are asked to apply equitable principles, they are not being asked to be fair and just but to apply the rules developed by the chancery court. It is hoped, however, that the application of equitable principles will accomplish that objective. Equity serves as a supplement to rather than a replacement of the common law. The courts of chancery have been instrumental in developing such new principles in law as the trust (in which one party holds property for another) and have also provided several alternative remedies, such as injunction and specific performance, which we will examine later in this text.

Margin notes:

Common law rigid

Courts of chancery provide relief

Conflict results in rigidity in chancery as well

Equity today does not simply mean fairness

As part of the general reform movement in English law in the nineteenth century, the common law courts, the courts of chancery and several minor English judicial bodies were abolished and replaced by a single system of courts, divided into several trial divisions and a separate appellate court.[4] The common law Canadian provinces also adopted this system. The separate bodies of law created by the common law and chancery courts, however, remain distinct to this day and a judge may be asked to apply common law principles in one case and equitable principles in another. Of course, judges must always be alert to the fact that any applicable parliamentary statute will override both.

Statutes

In many situations, justice was not available to litigants in either the common law or chancery courts and the parties had to turn to yet another source for satisfaction. The English Civil War of the seventeenth century firmly established the principle that Parliament rather than the king was supreme and from that time, Parliament handled any major modification to the law. Parliamentary enactments are referred to as statutes and take precedence over judge-made law whether based on common law or equity.

Statutes and regulations override judge-made law

When we speak of the government, we must differentiate between the legislative, the judicial and the executive branches of government. Parliament legislates or creates the law, the judicial branch is the court system, and the executive branch and its agencies implement that law. Organizations such as the RCMP, the Unemployment Insurance Commission and the military are all part of the executive branch of government. Most of these bodies have been given the power by statute to regulate themselves. Therefore, when legislation is considered as a source of law, regulations passed by government agencies must be included.

THE LAW IN CANADA

Confederation

Canada came into existence in 1867 with the formation of a federation of Upper Canada, Lower Canada, Nova Scotia and New Brunswick. Other provinces followed, with Newfoundland being the most recent to join Confederation. Every jurisdiction except Québec adopted the English common law system before joining Confederation. Québec elected to retain the use of the French Civil Code system for matters falling within provincial jurisdiction.

Confederation was accomplished when the British Parliament passed the *British North America Act*, now referred to as the *Constitution Act (1867)*. The *Act*'s primary significance is that it created the Dominion of Canada and determined the func-

---

[4] *Judicature Acts*, (1873–75) 31 Geo. III.

BNA Act created
Canada and
divided powers

tions and powers of the provincial and federal levels of government. Most of the basic rights and protections established under the American Constitution are not present in the *Constitution Act (1867)*. The preamble to the *Act* says Canada has a constitution "similar in principle to that of the United Kingdom." That is, we claim as part of our constitution all of the great constitutional institutions of the United Kingdom such as the *Magna Carta* and the English *Bill of Rights*. Also included are such unwritten conventions as the rule of law which recognizes that, although Parliament is supreme and can create any law considered appropriate, until it does so, citizens are protected from the arbitrary actions of government. In addition, our constitution includes those acts passed by both the British and Canadian Parliaments subsequent to the *Constitution Act (1867)* that have status beyond mere statutes, such as the *Statute of Westminster (1931)* and the *Constitution Act (1982)* which includes the *Charter of Rights and Freedoms*. In fact, the *Constitution Act (1982)* sets out a list of enactments that have constitutional status.

More to
Canadian
Constitution than
BNA Act

Constitution and Division of Powers

In Canada, as in Britain, Parliament is supreme and traditionally has had the power to make laws that cannot be overruled by any other body, although the *Charter of Rights and Freedoms* and the *Constitution Act (1867)* place some limitations on this supremacy. This supremacy must be contrasted to the American system where a painstakingly established system of checks and balances ensures that no government institution has absolute power. In England and Canada, parliamentary bodies until recently had the power to pass any form of legislation, subject only to the realities of the political system in which they functioned. Unlike the United Kingdom, though, Canada has a federal form of government with eleven different legislative bodies, each claiming the supreme powers of Parliament. The powers of the federal government are set out in Section 91 of the *Constitution Act (1867)*, and those of the provincial governments in Section 92 (see Appendix 1-1). The federal government has power over such matters as banking, printing currency, the postal service, criminal law (although not its enforcement) and the appointment of judges in the higher level provincial and federal courts. The provinces have jurisdiction over such matters as hospitals, education, the administration of the courts and commercial activities carried on at the provincial level. It is important to note that these areas of jurisdiction cover the nature of the legislation that can be passed, rather than the individuals or things that can be affected. Thus, while the federal government has the power to pass legislation dealing with banks, it can deal not only with the banks themselves but with anything to do with the banking process, including interest rates, the amounts that must be kept on deposit and how those deposits can be invested. Similarly, the federal government can enact legislation dealing with all aspects of criminal law or the military and the provinces have been given power to enact legislation dealing with anything to do with education.

On occasion, one level of government disguises legislation to hide its attempt to infringe on another area. For example, municipal governments have tried to control

Constitution Acts
and Charter limit
power of federal
and provincial
governments

*Constitution Act
(1867)* divides
powers between
federal and
provincial
goverments

prostitution or pornography using their zoning or licensing power when, in fact, these matters are controlled by criminal law, a federal area. To keep prostitutes out of the west end of Vancouver, the city used its zoning power to prohibit that activity. The courts struck down this bylaw stating that it was an attempt to pass criminal law since it was designed to control moral conduct. This type of legislation is called colourable legislation, and the court simply looks at what the governing body is really trying to do as opposed to what it claims to be doing and asks whether or not it has that power.

The powers of the federal and provincial governments can overlap considerably. For example, the Alberta government passed legislation prohibiting the production and sale of the hallucinogenic drug LSD shortly after it came on the market. This legislation was valid under the province's public health power. Subsequently, the federal government passed similar legislation under its criminal law power which was also valid.

When provincial and federal law conflict follow federal

When overlap does take place, the principle of **paramountcy** requires that the federal legislation be operative and that the provincial legislation go into abeyance and no longer apply. If the overlap between provincial and federal legislation is merely incidental, both are valid and both are operative. An individual must obey both by adhering to the higher standard, whether provincial or federal. It is only when the laws are such that only one can be obeyed that a true conflict exists. The doctrine of paramountcy requires that the federal legislation be obeyed in such circumstances.

Since neither the federal nor the provincial levels of government are considered inferior legislative bodies, both are supreme parliaments in their assigned areas. Over the years, for various reasons, these bodies have sometimes found it necessary to transfer the power given to them to the other level of government. However, direct delegation between the federal and provincial governments is prohibited. For example, during the 1930s' depression it became clear that a national system of unemployment insurance was needed. The provinces, which have jurisdiction in this area, attempted to delegate their power to the federal government. The court held that they could not do so as it was an "abdication" of the "exclusive powers" given to the provinces under the *Constitution Act (1867)*. To make unemployment insurance an area of federal responsibility, the British parliament needed to amend the constitution. This amendment is now incorporated in section 91, subsection a, of the *Constitution Act (1867)*.

Direct delegation prohibited

Although direct delegation is prohibited, it is possible for the federal and provincial governments to delegate their powers to inferior bodies such as boards and individual civil servants; in fact, this is usually the only way that governmental bodies can conduct their business. It is also possible for the federal government to delegate its power in a particular area to a provincial board or a provincial civil servant. Similarly, a province can give power to federal boards since these are also inferior bodies. In this way governments overcome the prohibition against delegation.

Statutes

Government-made laws, legislation, statutes, acts or bills, when published and made available to the public are called **statutes**. The Government of Canada publishes a compilation of these statutes annually; they can be found in most libraries under *Statutes of Canada.* The federal government summarized and published all current statutes in the *Revised Statutes of Canada* in 1985, cited as *R.S.C.* (1985). Indexes and guides are provided to assist in finding federal legislation.

Federal and provincial statutes published and summarized

Similarly, each province annually publishes the statutes passed by its legislative assembly. Each province also provides a compilation of all current legislation in the form of revised statutes. Unfortunately, there is no uniformity in the timing of the revisions, and each province has revised and summarized its statutes in a different year. A summary is provided in Appendix 1-3 of the most recent revision in each province at the time of writing. Reference will be made to these statutes throughout the text. It must be remembered that the effect of such statutes (passed within the power of the respective governments as set out in the *Constitution Act (1867)* and other constitutional provisions) overrides any previous law in place, whether judge-made law (common law or equity) or prior legislation.

Judges interpret and apply statutes

A trial judge required to deal with a statute must first determine what it means. This task is not always simple since the legislation is not usually drafted by someone who knows all of the situations in which it will be applied or who understands all of the legal implications of the wording. The judge must then determine whether or not, under the *Constitution Act (1867)* and other constitutional provisions, the legislative body that passed the statute in question had the power to do so. If the Ontario government passed a statute making it a crime to perform an abortion it would be declared *ultra vires* (beyond the power of the body that passed it), because the power to enact criminal laws under Section 91, Subsection 27, of the *Constitution Act (1867)* is given exclusively to the federal government. When a judge interprets and applies a statute, that decision becomes a precedent and henceforth the statute must be interpreted in the same way by courts lower in the provincial or federal court hierarchy.

Decisions create precedent

Charter of Rights and Freedoms

The *Constitution Act (1982)* made a significant addition to the Canadian Constitution in the form of the *Canadian Charter of Rights and Freedoms.* Although the provisions of the common law created an essentially free society, many felt that the protection provided by an unwritten constitution was inadequate, especially since the principle of supremacy of parliament allowed the provincial and federal governments to interfere at will with civil rights through legislation. One need look no further than the way Japanese Canadians were treated during World War II to conclude that Canadians might find it dangerous to leave the protection of their basic rights to the political process. All provinces and the federal government passed various forms of human rights legislation before 1980, many of which were effective in protecting civil liberties. But since this legislation was merely statutes, they could be repealed, amended or overruled by the legislative bodies which passed them if that course of action became politically expedient.

Common law did not provide adequate protection of personal freedoms

The effect of including the Charter of Rights and Freedoms in our Constitution is two-fold. First, neither the provinces nor the federal government has the power to change, modify or otherwise interfere with the basic rights set out in the Charter except through constitutional amendment. The provisions are said to be entrenched in the Constitution. Second, the burden of protecting those rights has shifted from the politicians to the judges. Now, an individual who feels that his or her rights have been interfered with by legislation or other forms of government action can seek redress in the courts, relying on the Charter provision as a statement of the current law of Canada. Thus, the doctrine of parliamentary supremacy has been modified.

A brief summary of the types of rights and freedoms Canadians now enjoy because of the Charter of Rights and Freedoms follows. It must be emphasized that the following is no more than an indication of the kinds of matters within the scope of the Charter. The Charter sets out several rights which are available in some cases to citizens of Canada and in other cases to everyone in the nation. The extent of the rights and freedoms set out in the Charter, their meaning and the limitations on those rights are now being defined by the great amount of litigation that is taking place in our courts. It should also be noted that the Charter refers only to public matters; it controls all government agencies and bodies including municipalities, providing they are exercising statutory authority. Private matters between individuals, corporations or even government-funded bodies acting in a private capacity, such as schools and hospitals, are covered by local human rights legislation. Recourse is available in the courts if these declared rights are interfered with by legislation, regulations, laws or the acts of public servants.

Types of rights protected under Charter

PERSONAL FREEDOMS. The Charter first declares certain underlying, fundamental freedoms available to everyone in Canada. These are freedom of conscience and religion, freedom of belief, opinion and expression, and freedom of peaceful assembly and association.

DEMOCRATIC RIGHTS. These provisions are designed to protect the democratic institutions of the nation, such as the right to vote and the requirement that elections be held at regular intervals.

MOBILITY RIGHTS. This section ensures that Canadians can travel and live both within the geographic limits of Canada, and enter and leave the country. It also ensures that all Canadians have the right to earn a livelihood in any part of Canada.

LEGAL RIGHTS. These rights are life, liberty, security and the right not to have these rights taken away except in accordance with the "principles of fundamental justice," which is similar to the American concept of due process. This section also prohibits such activities as unreasonable search and seizure and arbitrary imprisonment, and provides for the right to be informed of the reason for an arrest, the right to retain counsel, the right to be tried within a reasonable time, the presumption of innocence, the right not to be tried twice for the same offence and the right not to be subjected to any cruel or unusual punishment.

EQUALITY RIGHTS. The equality rights set out in Section 15 of the Charter prohibit discrimination on the basis of sex, religion, race, age or national origin, and ensure that all people in Canada have the same claim to the protection and benefits of the law. In addition to these specific provisions, general provisions in the Charter state that the equality of males and females is guaranteed (Section 28) and that the Charter in no way affects the aboriginal and treaty rights of the Native Indians of Canada (Section 35).

LANGUAGE RIGHTS. The part of the Charter headed *Official Languages of Canada*, outlined in Sections 16-22, ensures that French and English have equal status and protects the rights of minorities to use those languages. Minority Language Educational Rights are outlined in Section 23 and guaranteed for the citizens of Canada, thus ensuring that those whose first language is English or French or who received their primary education in English or French have the right to have their children educated in that language.

LIMITATIONS. There are two important limitations on the entrenchment of these basic rights. Section 1 of the Charter of Rights and Freedoms states that the listed rights and freedoms can be interfered with if doing so could be "demonstrably justified in a free and democratic society." This provision gives the courts the power to ignore the provisions of the Charter when enforcing them might lead to an unreasonable result. However, problems arise when individual judges have to determine what is reasonable and what is not.

The second limitation is contained in Section 33. It allows each of the provinces and the federal government to override the basic rights contained in Section 2 and Sections 7-15 of the Charter simply by stating that the new legislation "operates notwithstanding" the specific provision of the Charter that would otherwise make the legislation inoperative. These sections include such provisions as freedom of conscience and religion; freedom of thought and belief, opinion and expression; freedom of assembly and association; the right of life, liberty, security of person and property, and security against unreasonable search and seizure, arbitrary imprisonment, and detention; the right not to be discriminated against on the basis of sex, age, religion, race and colour; and the guarantee of equality before the law.

It would appear that Section 33 weakens the Charter of Rights and Freedoms considerably. Supremacy of parliament seems to have been restored, at least in relation to those sections, and reliance again switched to politicians to protect basic rights and freedoms. The original hope was that most provinces would not find it politically expedient to override the Charter and so would refrain from doing so. This hope has proved unfounded. Québec, for example, has shown little hesitation in using Section 33 to pass language legislation restricting the use of English on business signs in that province. Without using Section 33, this legislation clearly violates the Charter. This provision does not apply to any of the other sections, such as those guaranteeing the right to vote, to elect members to Parliament and legislative assemblies, to enter and leave Canada or to use both official languages. In addition, the rights of Native Indians and the rights guaranteed to both sexes cannot be overridden by either the federal or provincial governments through the application of the "notwithstanding" qualification in Section 33.

Government cannot interfere with basic rights and freedoms except—

—if reasonable to do so

—if legislature so declares

The significance of these 1982 additions to the Canadian Constitution cannot be overemphasized. These provisions, and especially the Charter of Rights and Freedoms will affect and shape the development of Canadian law over the next century. Canadian courts had adopted the position that their function was to apply the law as it existed. If the law needed to be changed, the judiciary left that job to the legislative assemblies and parliament. It is likely that one of the significant changes which will take place in our legal system as a result of the enactment of the Charter is that the courts will be forced to play a more active role and create new law through their interpretation and application of the provisions of the Charter.

The *Constitution Act (1982)* also abolished the requirement that any major change involving Canada's constitution has to be made by an act of the Parliament of Great Britain. Because the original *BNA Act* was an act of the British Parliament, any changes to it had to be made by that body. When the provinces and the federal government agreed on a formula for amending the constitution, the British Parliament passed the Canada Act, making Canada completely independent of Britain. Québec, however, did not approve this agreement. Since then, another important agreement, known as the Meech Lake Accord, was drawn up which attempted to change this amending formula. The Meech Lake Accord did not receive the required unanimous provincial approval within the specified time limit. Its failure and the failure of the subsequent Charlottetown Accord has created a constitutional crisis in Canada. At the time of writing this crisis continues.

It should be emphasized that although Canada's ties to the British parliament have been severed, our relationship with the monarch remains. The Queen remains the Queen of Canada, just as she is the Queen of England, Australia and other independent nations.

The Courts

As a general rule, Canadian courts are open to the public. Justice must not only be done but must be seen to be done; no matter how prominent the citizen and no matter how scandalous the action, the procedures are open and available to the public and the press. There are, however, important exceptions to this rule. When juveniles are involved or when the information coming out at a trial may be prejudicial to the security of the nation, the courts will hold **in-camera** hearings which are closed to the public. Publication of other evidence and information may be prohibited to ensure a fair trial.

The hearing or trial must be fair. The parties to the action must have notice of the matters in dispute and an opportunity to present their side of the case. The actual procedure involved is discussed later in this chapter. The courts in Canada preside over criminal prosecutions or adjudicate in civil disputes. While civil matters are the major concern of this text and criminal law is only incidentally discussed, it should be noted that important differences exist between civil and criminal actions. In civil actions, two private persons use the court as a referee to adjudicate a dispute and the judge, or in some cases judge and jury, chooses between the two positions put before him or her. The decision will be made in favour of the side advocating the more probable position. The judge in such circumstances is said to be deciding the matter on the balance of probabilities.

Criminal prosecutions are quite different. When a crime has been committed, the offence is against the state and victims of the crime are merely witnesses at the trial. The government pursues the matter and prosecutes the action through a crown prosecutor. The person charged is called the accused. Since the action is taken by the government (the crown) against the accused, such cases are cited *R v. Jones*. (The R stands for either Rex or Regina depending on whether a king or queen is enthroned at the time of the prosecution.) While a civil dispute is decided on the balance of probabilities, in a criminal prosecution the judge (or judge and jury) must be convinced beyond a reasonable doubt of the guilt of the accused. This test is much more stringent; even when it is likely or probable that the accused committed the crime, the charge must be dismissed if any reasonable doubt remains about guilt.

Both trial and appellate functions

TRIAL COURTS. The courts have two primary functions in the judicial process. The one most people are familiar with is the trial function. The trial court is often called the court of first instance, or the court of original jurisdiction, meaning the court that first hears the matter. It is before this court that the parties first appear and testify, witnesses give evidence and, in the case of a jury trial, the jury deliberates upon the findings of the court and makes its decision. If one of the parties is dissatisfied with the outcome or with the procedure of the case, it may appeal that decision. Then the second, or appellate, function comes into play.

Questions of law only can be appealed

APPEAL COURTS. The court exercising an appellate jurisdiction does not hold a new trial. Rather than have all the witnesses and the parties testify again, the appeal court will read the record made in the trial court and deal with the specific objections to the trial judge's decision. Only the lawyers appear in court to make their arguments to a panel made up of three or more judges. As a general rule, an appeal is limited to questions of law, not questions of fact. Questions of fact are questions regarding the details of an event. For example, was Erasmus at the corner of Portage and Main in the city of Winnipeg at 7:00 a.m. on March 5, 1989? Did a portion of the building owned by Washington fall on Erasmus? Was he paralyzed as a result of his injury? Was Washington aware of the danger? Had she taken steps to correct it? Questions of law, on the other hand, concern the rules or laws that are to be applied in the situation. For example, was Washington obliged to keep the outside of her building in good repair? How would the obligation be affected if Washington was unaware of the danger? The individuals best qualified and in the best position to determine questions of fact are the judge or judge and jury who hear all the evidence presented by witnesses. Therefore, a claim that a lower court judge made a mistake must be based on questions of law to be considered by an appeal court.

PROVINCIAL COURTS. The nature and structure of these courts vary from province to province. At the lowest level, all provinces have courts variously referred to as magistrate's courts, provincial courts, small claims courts and family courts. As their names suggest, the family courts deal with the enforcement of family relations matters, including custody, maintenance and in some cases youth offences. Small claims courts deal with civil matters that involve relatively small amounts of money. These amounts vary from province to province but usually are no more than $10 000. Magistrates have jurisdiction over the less important criminal matters assigned to them by the Criminal Code of Canada. In many provinces, these various functions have been amalgamated into one court structure called the provincial court.

Until recently, most provinces had an intermediate level court called the County or District courts. These have now been abolished in all provinces.

Low, intermediate, superior and appellate level courts

The highest trial level court, and thus the superior court of the provinces, is called the Supreme Court, High Court, Court of Queen's Bench or, in the case of Québec, the Provincial Court. This court has an unlimited monetary jurisdiction in civil matters. The highest court in each province is the Court of Appeal. In some provinces, it is a separate court altogether. This court's only function is to hear appeals from the other courts of the province. It must hear an appeal before a matter can go to the Supreme Court of Canada. Currently, the judges of these superior courts are appointed by the federal government from a list of candidates supplied by the provinces. Some provinces have also retained specialized provincial courts, referred to as surrogate or probate courts, dealing with the administration of wills and estates. See the chart on pp. 18–19 for a summary of the provincial courts.

FEDERAL COURTS. Two courts affect all Canadians. The first is the Supreme Court of Canada which is the highest court in the land and has a strictly appellate function as far as private citizens are concerned. There are nine judges chosen from throughout Canada and typically three or five of them will sit on an appeal. The court's judgment is binding on all courts in Canada. The court hears criminal and civil cases and is sometimes asked to rule directly on constitutional disputes involving federal and provincial governments.

Supreme Court of Canada

The Federal Court of Canada is quite different from the Supreme Court and can be more appropriately compared to a provincial Superior Court. The Federal Court is divided into a trial and an appellate division. The trial division hears matters that fall within the federal sphere of power such as disputes dealing with copyrights and patents, disputes against federal boards and commissions as well as disputes involving federal lands or money, disputes arising out of contracts with the federal government and claims against the Federal Court. The appeal division of the Federal Court hears appeals from the trial division as well as appeals from decisions of federal regulatory bodies and administrative tribunals such as the Unemployment Insurance Commission. An appeal from the Federal Court, Appeal Division, will go directly to the Supreme Court of Canada.

Federal Court and Federal Court of Appeal

There is another specialized federal court, the Tax Court of Canada, established in 1983 exclusively to hear disputes concerning federal tax matters. This body hears appeals from assessment decisions made by various federal agencies enforcing taxation statutes.

In addition to the courts discussed above, bodies called administrative tribunals may look and act like courts but are not courts in actual fact. Administrative tribunals are part of the executive branch of government at the federal, provincial and municipal levels and they, along with all government bureaucrats empowered to make deci-

Government tribunals are not courts

sions affecting our lives, must exercise those powers within restricted boundaries. These government decision makers can be every bit as important as the courts within their areas, however, and it is important to be aware that we all have certain rights when we are affected by their decisions. These rights will be discussed in the last chapter.

THE PROCESS OF CIVIL LITIGATION

Should try to settle dispute

Some variations from province to province

Most of this text deals with matters of substantive law, that is, law that summarizes rights and obligations of the "thou shalt" or "thou shalt not" variety rather than procedural law which deals with the process by which we enforce those rights and obligations. But it is important to be familiar with the procedures involved in bringing a dispute to trial, if only to understand the function of lawyers and the reasons for the expense and delays involved. Before a decision is made to sue someone, all avenues for settling the dispute outside of court ought to be exhausted. The procedures may vary somewhat from province to province, but they are substantially the same in all common law jurisdictions and they apply to most superior courts. The procedure set out below is taken from the system used in British Columbia. One of the distinguishing characteristics of small claims courts is that this procedure has been streamlined significantly, eliminating many of the steps described below.

Pre-trial

The lawyer of the plaintiff (the person bringing the action) begins an action by drawing up a writ of summons, referred to as a Notice of Action in several provinces. The clerk of the court puts official authorization on several copies of the document and then the plaintiff's lawyer has the writ served on the defendant (the person being sued). There are other methods of initiating a court action, depending on the nature of the dispute and the remedies sought, but the writ of summons is the most common. The writ contains the names of the parties and their addresses as well

Writ of summons

as those of the plaintiff's lawyer. It also contains a very brief summary of the nature of the plaintiff's claim. In some jurisdictions, notably Ontario, the writ of summons has been eliminated and an action is now commenced by issuing a statement of claim and serving that document on the defendant.

Appearance

Once this document has been served, a defendant who wants to dispute the claim is obligated to file an appearance, usually within a week of receiving the writ. This simply indicates that the action will be defended. An appearance is a very important document; if the defendant fails to file it, the plaintiff can usually short-circuit the rest of the procedure and ask for a summary judgment. Once the appearance has been filed with the court clerk and a copy sent to the plaintiff's lawyer, the plaintiff must then draw up a statement of claim. This document sets out

Statement of claim

The Provincial Courts

	Alberta	British Columbia	Manitoba	New Brunswick	Newfoundland
Appellate Court (Superior Court)	Court of Appeal	Court of Appeal	Court of Appeal	Court of Appeal	Supreme Court – Appeal Division
Highest Trial Court **(Superior Court)**	Court of Queen's Bench	Supreme Court of B.C.	Court of Queen's Bench – Family Divison – Special Small Claims Procedure	Court of Queen's Bench – Trial Division – Family Divison	– Trial Division
Intermediate Trial Court			– Special Probate Procedure		
Lower Trial Court	Provincial Court – Criminal Division – Youth Divison – Family Division – Civil Division	Provincial Court – Small Claims Court – Family Court – Criminal Court	Provincial Court – Criminal Division – Family Division	Provincial Court – Criminal Division – Family Division	Provincial Court – Criminal Division – Civil Unified Family Court

Nova Scotia	Ontario*	Prince Edward Island	Québec	Saskatchewan	Northwest Territories	Yukon Territory
Supreme Court Appeal	Court of Appeal	Supreme Court of P.E.I. – Appeal Division	Court of Appeal	Court of Appeal	The Court of Appeal of the Northwest Territories	Court of Appeal
Trial Division	Ontario Court of Justice General Division :– Div. Court :–Small Claims Court	–Trial Division – Estates Section – Family Section –Small Claims – General Section	Superior Court	Court of Queen's Bench	Supreme Court of the Northwest Territories	Supreme Court
Provincial Court – Small Claims – Criminal – Family	Provincial Division	Provincial Court – Criminal	Court of Québec –Civil Division – Criminal and Penal Division –Youth Division –Expropriation Division – Municipal Courts	Provincial Court – Criminal – Family –Small Claims	The Territorial Court of the Northwest Territories	Territorial Court of Yukon Justice of the Peace Court of Yukon Small Claims Court

* Note proposed changes to Ontario courts — see appendix 1–4

Statement of
defence

in more detail the plaintiff's dispute with the defendant and notifies the defendant
of the nature of the claims against him or her. The statement of claim must be
filed with the court clerk and sent to the other party. After receiving the statement
of claim, the defendant is obligated to file a statement of defence in which he or she
provides answers to the claims of the plaintiff and returns it to the plaintiff.

If the defendant not only feels he has a good defence but that he was in fact the
victim, he can include in his statement of defence a counterclaim. This initiates a
claim against the plaintiff and is treated as a statement of claim by him or her. It
should be noted that the exchange of these documents is not the process of arguing
and justifying the two positions; rather, the parties are merely stating the positions
which give rise to the dispute between them. If one of the parties feels that the documents do not make his or her position completely clear, further documents may pass
between them, replying to statements, and/or demanding more information.

Once the pleadings (the statements of claim and defence etc.) have been closed,
the parties have the right in many jurisdictions to initiate the process of discovery.
Discovery can be divided into two parts:

Discovery

(a) discovery of documents—the lawyers of the parties have the right to arrange
for the inspection of any document in the possession of the other party which may
be used in the trial as evidence;
(b) examination for discovery—the parties and their lawyers meet before a court
reporter and under oath are asked detailed questions about the problem to be tried.

The process varies between jurisdictions, but in general the parties are required
to answer these questions fully and truthfully. Anything that is said is recorded and
may be used later at the trial. Note that this process of examination for discovery
generally applies only to the parties to the action, not to witnesses. Once the discovery process has been completed, either party can arrange a time for trial with
the court registry and give notice to the other party. In some jurisdictions, before
the trial takes place a pre-trial conference must be held in which the lawyers go before a judge to see if there is any chance of settling the matter without a trial or to
determine whether the issue is triable. All of these procedures are designed to
provide as much information as possible to the parties before trial and to encourage the parties to settle the matter before an actual trial has to take place. In
fact, most private disputes are settled during this pre-trial process.

Payment into
court

Another tool often available to parties before a trial is payment into court. A defendant being sued for damages, may admit liability but think that the amount being
demanded by the plaintiff is too high. When Resnick, for example, fails to perform the
terms of his contract with Wong, he may freely admit his liability and be willing to
pay $15 000 but balk at Wong's claim for $25 000 damages. Resnick can deposit
$15 000 with the court and notify Wong of the payment. Wong can either take the
money, thus ending the action, or ignore the payment and proceed to trial in the hope
of getting the additional $10 000. But in doing so, she takes the risk of not only los-
ing the $10 000 but also the award for damages which would have covered her court
and legal fees. In making a decision on the case, the judge is unaware of the pay-

ment and if the judgment is for less than the amount deposited by the defendant, the plaintiff will not be compensated for any of the costs incurred after the payment was made. The plaintiff had an opportunity to accept a fair settlement and any costs incurred after her failure to do so must be borne by her. If the amount awarded is more than the payment into court, the defendant's payment was obviously not fair and the plaintiff will be able to claim compensation for any costs that have been incurred. This system encourages the defendant to make a fair offer of payment and the plaintiff to accept it and not risk unrecoverable expenses. Payment into court, then, is an example of another mechanism to persuade the parties to settle the matter before trial.

In some provinces a related provision exists for the plaintiff to file an offer to settle which has a similar effect. If the plaintiff sues for $25 000 but is willing to settle for $15 000, he or she can make the offer and file it with the court and notify the defendant. If the defendant refuses to accept the offer and insists on a trial, he or she runs the risk of the judgment being for more than the offer to settle. If this happens, the defendant will be required to pay double the plaintiff's costs incurred after the offer to settle was made. If the judgment is less than what was offered, of course, the defendant will only have to pay the costs of the plaintiff in the normal way.

If at this stage the dispute between the parties is still not settled, the next step is to go to trial. This part of the civil procedure is open to the public and readers are urged to attend both civil and criminal actions at a local courthouse to see the justice system in action.

The Trial

The trial usually proceeds in the following manner. The plaintiff presents his or her case and witnesses first. The plaintiff's lawyer will assist witnesses in their testimony by asking specific questions, but the types of questions which can be asked are restricted. For example, the plaintiff's lawyer is prohibited from asking leading questions in which the answer is suggested: "You were there on Saturday, weren't you?" When the plaintiff's lawyer completes this direct examination of the witness, the defendant's lawyer is given the opportunity to cross-examine the witness. In cross-examination, the defence lawyer is permitted more latitude in the type of questions asked; he or she is also permitted to ask leading questions. When the opposing lawyer feels that the lawyer questioning the witness is abusing the process by asking prohibited questions, he or she will object to the question and the judge will rule on the objection and decide whether to permit the question or order the lawyer to withdraw it. The rules governing the type of testimony that can be obtained from witnesses and all other types of evidence to be submitted at a trial are called the rules of evidence. (These rules are complex and beyond the scope of this text.) If anything new comes from the cross-examination, the plaintiff's lawyer can re-examine witnesses on those matters. After both sides have finished calling witnesses, the plaintiff's lawyer and then the defendant's lawyer are allowed to summarize the evidence and make arguments to the court. Again, if anything new comes up, the other party is given a chance to respond to it.

Judgment and its Enforcement

If a jury is involved, which is not common in civil cases, after the lawyers' summaries the judge will make a submission and give instructions to the jury. The jury then retires to consider the case and returns to announce its decision to the judge. The function of the jury in such cases is to decide questions of fact; the judge decides the questions of law. If the matter is being heard by a judge alone, the judge retires after hearing the arguments of the lawyers and returns when ready to give a decision. In a civil action this decision is reached "on the balance of probabilities." In the case of a superior court trial, it is more common for the judge to hand down a judgment in writing some time later. The judge will include reasons for his or her decision as part of the judgment. These reasons can form the basis for an appeal.

The process of initiating an action to sue a debtor is usually very expensive and creditors may decide to write off a debt rather than incur this expense. In most provinces the cost of court services is minimal but the cost of obtaining legal services is often prohibitive. This is one reason small claims courts have been introduced in most common law jurisdictions. In small claims courts, the presence of a lawyer is the exception rather than the rule. But even when the creditor's complaint qualifies as a small claims action, unless the creditor is willing to appear personally, the services of a lawyer must be obtained. Although the parties have the right to represent themselves, lawyers are generally the rule in higher level courts.

The creditor has to pay for the lawyer even when the suit is successful. If the amount of the claim is large enough to qualify for superior court, the successful claimant will obtain judgment from the debtor for the amount owed and for costs as well. That is, that the debtor will be required to compensate the successful creditor for a portion of the legal expenses. As a general rule, the creditor will face some legal expenses even when successful and, of course, there is always the risk of losing and having to bear all the costs.

ENFORCEMENT. Even when the judgment is obtained, there is no guarantee that the debt will be paid. The judgment normally eliminates any dispute over the debtor's liability, but the creditor must take further steps to enforce that judgment if the debtor still refuses to pay. If the debtor is unable to pay, the judgment is called a dry judgment. Thus, a creditor (plaintiff) who has apparently been successful may still be required to bear his or her own costs because of the debtor's inability to satisfy the judgment. The debtor may have no assets to satisfy the judgment at the time. However, if his or her prospects for being able to do so in the future are brighter, it may be wise for the creditor to proceed to judgment in order to enforce it some time in the future. Such a judgment remains enforceable for a considerable period of time, up to twenty years in many cases. The creditor must take into consideration all of these factors as well as the risk of losing the action when deciding to proceed with a civil action against a debtor.

IMPRISONMENT OF THE DEBTOR. In Charles Dickens' times, failure to pay debts frequently resulted in imprisonment. Such a drastic course of action is rarely taken these days and the use of imprisonment in matters of debt has been severely restricted. An order for imprisonment can only be obtained when the debtor has been ordered by the court to pay the judgment and refuses to do so (as opposed to being unable to pay) or when the debtor attempts to avoid payment through fraud or by leaving the jurisdiction. But in these circumstances, the punishment is for being contemptuous of the court's authority rather than for failing to honour a debt.

Imprisonment of debtor only for contempt of court

ENFORCING JUDGMENT. Once judgment has been obtained, most provinces provide for a further hearing, usually called an examination in aid of execution, to determine which of the debtor's assets are available to satisfy the judgment. During this process, the creditor is able to question the debtor, who is under oath, about his or her wealth, assets, employment, bank accounts, safety deposit boxes and so on. The creditor can also ask about any property transfers in which the debtor may have been involved. At the conclusion of the process, the creditor can ask the court for an order to execute against a particular property or garnishee any funds owing, such as wages, bank accounts and rental or mortgage payments.

Hearing to aid execution

SEIZURE OF PROPERTY. The execution process involves seizing the debtor's property to satisfy the judgment. The court order is given to a sheriff (private bailiffs cannot enforce court orders) who then seizes the property in question. Under common law, the proceeds of any subsequent sale of assets went only to the creditor who initiated the process. Other creditors were left without remedy. Most jurisdictions have now introduced legislation like Ontario's Creditor's Relief Act which states that any property seized by the sheriff in the process of enforcing a judgment must be used for the benefit of all creditors. If there are insufficient funds to satisfy all the claims, the unsecured creditors are paid an equal percentage. There also might be some system of priority based on security, builders' liens and so on in relation to a specific property.

Property seized by sheriff

Proceeds of sheriff's sale shared by all creditors

Some properties are exempt from execution in this form. This varies with the jurisdiction but food, clothing, bedding, furniture, tools needed to perform a trade, fuel, motor vehicles used in the course of employment and goods under a certain value usually cannot be seized. The property must be kept in the sheriff's possession for a specified period after seizure to allow all the creditors to make claims against the property. This time also gives the debtor a chance to reclaim the property by satisfying the judgment. Once this period is expired, the sheriff is free to sell the property, usually at a public auction. The sheriff distributes the proceeds to the creditors on a pro rata, or percentage of claim, basis after subtracting a fee to cover the costs of the seizure and sale. Any excess goes to the debtor. It should be noted that in addition to secured creditors and builders' liens holders, local legislation may also create other priorities among the creditors. For example, wage earners in situations not covered by builders' lien legislation and landlords to whom rent is owed are often given preference. It is only after these claims have been satisfied that the sheriff will disperse the remaining funds to the other creditors.

Some property is exempt from seizure

When a security is involved, that is, when the debtor has given the creditor an interest in some property to ensure repayment of the debt, the priority of the creditor is restricted to the specific goods used as security. It should be noted that real property (land and buildings) can be seized to satisfy a judgment, but the method employed varies with the jurisdiction. Often, registering the judgment against the property is enough to pressure the debtor to pay.

GARNISHMENT. If the judgment is executed by seizing a bank account, wages or other outstanding claims, the process is called **garnishment**, or sometimes the **attachment of debt**. Some provinces have incorporated their legislation controlling the attachment of debt into one statute dealing with execution generally. Other provinces have retained separate statutes covering the different aspects of the enforcement of judgments, such as Manitoba's *Garnishment Act* and Saskatchewan's *Attachment of Debts Act*. The exemptions to the garnishment process are the most significant provisions of this legislation. In every province where the garnisheeing of wages is permitted, not all of the debtor's earnings are available to the creditor to satisfy the a judgment. The statutes typically set out a certain amount that must remain with the debtor in order to permit survival. This amount varies depending on the debtor's earnings and number of dependents. In Ontario, for instance, only 20 percent in total of the wage earner's net income can be garnisheed. Garnishment is an effective tool in enforcing judgment because the garnishment process allows the creditor to intercept funds that would normally be paid to the debtor. Once the garnishee order is served on the person making payments to the debtor, that person pays those funds into the court which then supervises their disbursement.

JUDICIAL REMEDIES BEFORE JUDGMENT. Although most methods of execution require first the obtaining of a judgment, some judicial remedies are available to the creditor even before that judgment is obtained. Property, other than money owed, can be seized to satisfy a debt before judgment only if the debtor flees the jurisdiction of the court to escape the debt. Even then, it is necessary in most provinces to get a court order before the property can be seized. It should be noted that this court order is not the judgment referred to above, but merely an order allowing the seizure of the property before the trial takes place. Who is actually entitled to the property will be determined at the trial. When the debtor is owed money, most jurisdictions allow for the attachment of available funds even before judgment to ensure that the funds will be available to satisfy the judgment at the time of the trial. This remedy is limited, however, since most jurisdictions will not permit the seizure of wages due or debts due, but only bank accounts and other forms of savings. New Brunswick and Nova Scotia do not permit garnishment at all before the judgment.

Another remedy available in some situations is to make a request to the court for an injunction to prevent a third party from paying out money owed to the debtor. This does not direct these funds to the creditor, but it does prevent them from going to the debtor who may abscond with or dissipate them. The process of collection and enforcement of judgment as described here may appear cumbersome, but it is quite effective because of the diversity of options available. However, the process can be quite expensive and may not be justifiable economically depending on the amount

Funds owed to debtor can be seized pursuant to judgment

Prejudgment remedies limited

of the debt and the likelihood of recovery. Note that when an agreement provides that specific property will be used as security, that agreement will usually also provide that, in the event of a failure to pay, the property can be seized without recourse to the courts. Such agreements are valid although the creditor's rights may be severely restricted by legislation, especially when personal property is involved. This topic will be discussed further in Chapter 7.

Limitation Periods

If court action could be initiated for an indefinite period after the act complained of had taken place, potential defendants could be left in a state of uncertainty for the rest of their lives. Furthermore, prolonged delay in bringing an action can make it much more difficult to arrive at a fair outcome: witnesses become un-available, memories dim and documents get destroyed. For these reasons, all provinces have introduced legislation requiring that legal proceedings commence within a relatively short period of time. Usually such legislation is called a **statute of limitations**. In Ontario, for example, a person who is owed money from a sim-ple sale of goods transaction and wishes to sue for the debt must bring an action against the debtor within six years of the failure to pay the debt. An action is ini-tiated by filing a writ of summons (in Ontario, a statement of claim) with the ap-propriate court. Failing to fulfil that step within the limitation period means that the plaintiff will be barred from pursuing the action. This time limitation will vary according to the nature of the complaint involved and may be embodied in several different statutes in a province.

Expiration of limitation period prohibits suing

With the expiry of the limitation period and the threat of court action removed, the potential defendant is not likely to settle out of court and the plaintiff is left with no recourse. Thus, it is important for a person involved in a potential lawsuit to get the advice of a lawyer as quickly as possible. Once the matter is put into the lawyer's hands, the responsibility to act within the limitation period rests with the lawyer. Failure to commence the action within the time limit specified can result in the lawyer being sued for negligence. The client can claim what would have been awarded had the action proceeded as it should have. Limitation periods vary not only with the nature of the action but also from province to province.

Alternatives to Court Action

Recently there has been an upsurge of interest in alternatives to court action for solv-ing disputes between parties. In family matters, it is becoming more common to involve mediators to help the parties come to an out-of-court settlement. While me-diators cannot impose a decision on the parties, they can reduce the adversarial at-mosphere which predominates in a courtroom and enhance the possibility of an amicable agreement. The use of such mediators has for years been an option in labour disputes and the process has been institutionalized in that field. Mediation

Mediation

is also becoming more common in business areas that involve ongoing contractual relationships.

Arbitration

Arbitration is another alternative to court action. The disputing parties select an independent body to make a decision and agree that the decision will be binding on them. Arbitration is used for collective bargaining when there are disputes over the meaning of contracts already in place. It has the advantage of allowing the parties to choose an independent arbitrator who has expertise in the area in dispute and who understands the needs and practices of the industry involved. This may lead to a faster and more satisfactory resolution of the dispute and has become a viable alternative to expensive and time-consuming court action.

SUMMARY

There are many different definitions of law but a simple and useable one is, "that body of rules that can be enforced by the courts or other government agencies." Québec uses a legal system based on the French Civil Code while the other provinces base their legal systems on the English common law. The common law is founded on decided cases and is composed of common law, equity and statutes which, because of parliamentary supremacy, override common law and equity when they are properly passed.

The *Constitution Act (1867)*, formerly called the *British North American Act*, created Canada from several British colonies and divided powers between the federal and provincial levels of government. In 1982, the last ties between the British and Canadian parliaments were severed with the passage of the *Constitution Act (1982)* which also contained the Charter of Rights and Freedoms. Supremacy of parliament is limited by the requirements of the *Constitution Act (1867)* and the Charter of Rights and Freedoms. The meaning of an ambiguous statute is determined by the courts using certain rules of interpretation. The Charter limits the power of government at all levels and protects personal freedoms; democratic, mobility, legal and equality rights; and language rights. These rights are qualified by Section 1 of the Charter which allows reasonable exceptions and Section 33 which allows both federal and provincial governments to opt out of the operation of several important sections.

The court systems of the provinces vary but most have a lower level trial court, an upper level trial court, and an appeal court. The Supreme Court of Canada is the highest court in Canada and the Federal Court and Federal Court of Appeal have been established to hear matters within the jurisdiction of the federal government. There are also many administrative tribunals created within various government departments to deal with disputes arising within them.

The lengthy civil litigation process is designed to give both parties as much information as possible and to encourage settlement before trial. Once a judgment has been obtained it can be enforced through seizing property and garnisheeing wages and bank accounts. Today two alternatives to the litigation process, mediation and arbitration, are becoming more popular.

QUESTIONS

1. Why is it difficult to come up with a satisfactory definition of law?
2. Where do we look to predict the outcome of a legal dispute
   a) in a common law system?
   b) in a civil law system?
3. Explain how the use of previous decisions differs in civil law and common law jurisdictions.
4. Describe what is meant by the following statement: "Common law judges did not make the law, they found it."
5. Explain the advantages and the disadvantages of the system of *stare decisis*.
6. Explain which disadvantages in the common law system led to the development of the law of equity.
7. Explain what was accomplished by the *Judicature Acts* of 1873-75.
8. Explain what is meant by the phrase "the supremacy of parliament."
9. Explain what effect a properly passed statute will have on inconsistent judge-made law (cases).
10. Using the principles of *stare decisis*, explain how judges determine whether or not they are bound by another judge's decision in a similar case.
11. What is included in Canada's constitution?
12. Explain how the Constitution Act (1982), including the Charter of Rights and Freedoms, affects the doctrine of supremacy of parliament.
13. Give examples of democratic rights, mobility rights, legal rights and equality rights as protected under the Charter. Give examples of three other types of rights protected under the Charter.
14. What is the effect of Sections 91 and 92 of the *British North America Act, The Constitution Act (1867)*?
15. How did the *Constitution Act (1867)* limit the power of the federal and provincial governments? How is it possible, given that division of powers, to have identical provisions in both federal and provincial legislation and have both valid? Explain what is meant by the doctrine of paramountcy. When does the doctrine apply?
16. Describe the limitations on the federal or provincial governments' power to delegate their authority to make laws.
17. Distinguish between questions of law and questions of fact and explain why this distinction is significant.
18. Distinguish between administrative tribunals and courts and explain why this distinction is significant.
19. How does the discovery process take place and what is its significance in civil litigation?
20. Explain how a payment into court can affect the judgment award made by the court to the plaintiff.

21. Why might a creditor be reluctant to sue a debtor even when he or she can be sure of successfully obtaining a judgment? What advantage might there be to obtaining a dry judgment?

22. Under what circumstances can a debtor be imprisoned in Canada today?

23. Explain what an examination in aid of execution is and describe its value in the execution process.

24. How can a judgment be enforced against a debtor who is trying to avoid payment?

25. Explain the value of an injunction as a prejudgment remedy. Discuss other prejudgment remedies available to aid in the collection of debt.

26. What is a limitation period and what effect can it have on the right of parties to litigate a matter in dispute?

ISSUES

1. When commenting on the practice of *stare decisis*, Oliver Wendell Holmes said: "It is revolting to have no better reason for a rule of law than that it was laid down in the time of Henry IV. It is still more revolting if the grounds upon which it was laid down have vanished long since and the rule simply persists from blind imitation of the past." If you were a proponent of *stare decisis*, how would you meet this criticism?

2. Consider the phrase "justice delayed is justice denied," and apply it to the process of civil litigation in Canada. The complex procedure in civil litigation is designed to encourage the parties to reach a settlement, but does the process created serve or defeat the ends of justice?

3. Fundamental to the American system of government is the principle of checks and balances. In the U.S. constitution, care has been taken to divide power equally among the judiciary (courts), the legislative branch (congress) and the executive branch (president and cabinet). In England, because the principle of supremacy of parliament is firmly in place, the final say in the creation of law belongs to the legislative branch. In Canada, until recently, we followed the English approach but with the new constitutional provisions embodied in the Charter of Rights and Freedoms, the courts have been given a much more prominent role, to the point that they may be able to overrule the will of parliament. Discuss the advantages and disadvantages of the two approaches to government. Which do you feel is the more appropriate for Canada?

4. Chief Justice Burger of the U.S. Supreme Court has said that the American judicial system has been considerably hampered by too much unnecessary litigation promoted by over-enthusiastic lawyers. Similar comments have

been made about the Canadian judicial system. The response to such accusations is usually that one person's technicality is another person's justice. Does the complexity of the Canadian legal system facilitate or hinder the objective of justice? Is the legal profession part of the problem or part of the solution?

5. Generally creditors must proceed to judgment in order to collect the amount due from debtors who refuse to pay. Because this process can be quite expensive, the cost will often persuade a person with a legitimate claim not to sue. From this arises the allegation that our system of civil justice favours the wealthy and is inequitable and prejudicial. Discuss the validity of this allegation. Consider not only the factors that make the process expensive and risky but also any steps that have been taken to overcome this problem.

6. The principle of supremacy of parliament is traditional in Canada. It is based on the fact that the power to make all types of law rests with the elected legislators who have few, if any, restrictions on their powers. However, the Charter of Rights and Freedoms introduced significant limitations on the power of such parliamentary bodies in Canada. The power has shifted to the courts which can now declare some legislation as beyond the power of any legislator to enact. Is this shift in power more consistent with our concept of freedom and democracy than the more traditional approach of supremacy of parliament? In your answer, consider the benefits derived from the Charter of Rights and Freedoms such as certain standards which cannot be interfered with by legislators. As well, consider the reasons for the development of the principle of supremacy of parliament and the safeguards present in the system, such as the rule of law. Are they sufficient to protect minorities from abuses of parliamentary power? Consider the power to opt out included in the Charter which allows a legislative body to declare that, for a particular statute, the provisions of the Charter will not apply. Does this provision destroy the value of the Charter of Rights and Freedoms?

7. The *Constitution Act (1867)* divides power between the federal and provincial governments. Two separate levels of government were created, each of which is supreme in its own jurisdiction. This equality has caused a considerable amount of difficulty for the courts in determining which level of government has power in a given situation, and a significant part of our constitutional law is devoted to the interpretation of the Act, especially Sections 91 and 92. Would Canada be better off if we had followed the British model and created one supreme parliament with the provincial legislative assemblies clearly subordinate to it? Consider the arguments for each side of this proposition.

LEGISLATION

Alberta
Court of Appeal Act, R.S.A. (1980) c. C-28
Judicature Act, R.S.A. (1980) c. J-1
Limitations of Actions Act, R.S.A. (1980) c. L-15
Provincial Court Act, R.S.A. (1980) c. P-20
Provincial Court Judges Act, S.A. (1981) c. P-20.1

British Columbia
Court of Appeal Act, S.B.C. (1982) c.7
Limitation Act, R.S.B.C. (1979) c.236
Provincial Court Act, R.S.B.C. (1979) c.341
Small Claims Act, R.S.B.C. (1979) c.387
Supreme Court Act, R.S.B.C. (1979) c.397

Manitoba
Court of Appeal Act, R.S.M (1987) c. C-240
Court of Queen's Bench Act, S.M. (1988-89) c.4
Garnishment Act, R.S.M. (1987) c. G-20
Limitations of Actions Act, R.S.M. (1987) c. L-150
Provincial Court Act, R.S.M. (1987) c. P-275
Court of Queen's Bench Small Claims Practices Act, R.S.M. (1987)c. C-285
Court of Queen's Bench Surrogate Practices Act, R.S.M. (1987) c. C-290

New Brunswick
Judicature Act, R.S.N.B. (1973) c.J-2
Juvenile Courts Act, R.S.N.B. (1973) c.J-4
Limitation of Actions Act, R.S.N.B. (1973) c.L-8
Provincial Court Act, R.S.N.B. (1973) c.P-21

Newfoundland
Provincial Court Act, R.S.N. (1974) c.77
Small Claims Act, S.N. (1979) c.34
Supreme Court Judgments, (1976) Act, S.N. (1975-76) c.41
Unified Family Court Act, S.N. (1977) c.88
Limitations of Actions (Personal & Guarantees) Act, R.S.N. (1970) c.206
Limitations of Actions (Realty) Act, R.S.N. (1970) c.207

Nova Scotia
County Court Act, R.S.N.S. (1989) c.106
County Court Judges Criminal Courts Act, R.S.N.S. (1989) c.108
Family Court Act, R.S.N.S. (1989) c.159
Judges of Provincial Magistrates Court Act, R.S.N.S. (1989) c.238
Judicature Act, R.S.N.S. (1989) c.240
Limitation of Actions Act, R.S.N.S. (1989) c.258
Small Claims Court Act, R.S.N.S. (1989) c.430

Ontario
County Court Judges Criminal Court Act, R.S.O. (1980) c.99
County Courts Act, R.S.O. (1980) c.100
County Judges Act, R.S.O. (1980) c.101
Courts of Justice Act, (1984) S.O. c.11
Creditor's Relief Act, R.S.O. (1980) c.103
Judicature Act, R.S.O. (1980) c.223
Limitations Act, R.S.O. (1980) c.240
Provincial Court (Civil Division) Act, R.S.O. (1980) c.397
Provincial Courts Act, R.S.O. (1980) c.398
Small Claims Act, R.S.O. c.476
Surrogate Courts Act, R.S.O. c.491

Prince Edward Island
Provincial Court Act, R.S.P.E.I. (1988) c. P-5
Statute of Limitations, R.S.P.E.I. (1988) c. S-7
Supreme Court Act, R.S.P.E.I. (1988) c. S-10

Québec
Charter of Human Rights and Freedoms, R.S.Q. (1977) c.C-12
Courts of Justice Act, R.S.Q. (1977) c.T-16

Saskatchewan
Attachments of Debt Act, R.S.S. (1978) c.B-8
Court of Appeal Act, R.S.S. (1978) c.C-42
Limitations of Actions Act, R.S.S. (1978) c.L-15
Provincial Court Act, R.S.S. (1978) c.P-30.1 (SUPP)
Queen's Bench Act, R.S.S. (1978) c.Q-1
Small Claims Enforcement Act, R.S.S. (1978) c.S-51
Unified Family Court Act, R.S.S. (1978) c.U-1.1 (SUPP)

Northwest Territories
Judicature Act, R.S.N.W.T. (1974) c.J-1
Limitation of Actions Act, R.S.N.W.T. (1974) c.L-6
Territorial Court Act, S.N.W.T. (1978)(2) c.16

Yukon
Court of Appeal Act, R.S.Y. (1986) c.37
Judicature Act, R.S.Y. (1986) c.96
Limitation of Actions, R.S.Y. (1986) c.104
Supreme Court Act, R.S.Y. (1986) c.165
Small Claims Court Act, R.S.Y. (1986) c.160

Federal
Federal Court Act, R.S.C. (1985) c.F-7
Supreme Court Act, R.S.C. (1985) c.S-26
Constitution Act, R.S.C. (1985) Appendix II
Canadian Charter of Rights and Freedoms, R.S.C. (1985) Appendix II

APPENDIX 1-1

The British North America Act
Sections 91 and 92*

VI.—DISTRIBUTION OF LEGISLATIVE POWERS.

Powers of the Parliament.

Legislative
Authority of
Parliament of
Canada

91.   It shall be lawful for the Queen, by and with the Advice and Consent of the Senate and House of Commons, to make Laws for the Peace, Order, and good Government of Canada, in relation to all Matters not coming within the Classes of Subjects by this Act assigned exclusively to the Legislatures of the Provinces; and for greater Certainty, but not so as to restrict the Generality of the foregoing Terms of this Section, it is hereby declared that (notwithstanding anything in this Act) the exclusive Legislative Authority of the Parliament of Canada extends to all Matters coming within the Classes of Subjects next herein-after enumerated; that is to say,

1.   The amendment from time to time of the Constitution of Canada, except as re-gards matters coming within the classes of subjects by this Act assigned ex-clusively to the Legislatures of the provinces, or as regards rights or privileges by this or any other Constitutional Act granted or secured to the Legislature or the Government of a province, or to any class of persons with respect to schools or as regards the use of the English or the French language or as regards the requirements that there shall be a session of the Parliament of Canada at least once each year, and that no House of Commons shall continue for more than five years from the day of the return of the Writs for choosing the House: provided, however, that a House of Commons may in time of real or apprehended war, in-vasion or insurrection be continued by the Parliament of Canada if such con-tinuation is not opposed by the votes of more than one-third of the members of such House. (39)

1A.   The Public Debt and Property. (40)

2.   The Regulation of Trade and Commerce.

2A.   Unemployment insurance. (41)

3.   The raising of Money by any Mode or System of Taxation.

4.   The borrowing of Money on the Public Credit.

5.   Postal Service.

6.   The Census and Statistics.

7.   Militia, Military and Naval Service, and Defence.

8.   The fixing of and providing for the Salaries and Allowances of Civil and other Officers of the Government of Canada.

---

* Reproduced by permission of the Minister of Supply and Services Canada.

9. Beacons, Buoys, Lighthouses, and Sable Island.
10. Navigation and Shipping.
11. Quarantine and the Establishment and Maintenance of Marine Hospitals.
12. Sea Coast and Inland Fisheries.
13. Ferries between a Province and any British or Foreign Country or between Two Provinces.
14. Currency and Coinage.
15. Banking, Incorporation of Banks, and the Issue of Paper Money.
16. Savings Banks.
17. Weights and Measures.
18. Bills of Exchange and Promissory Notes.
19. Interest.
20. Legal Tender.
21. Bankruptcy and Insolvency.
22. Patents of Invention and Discovery.
23. Copyrights.
24. Indians, and Lands reserved for the Indians.
25. Naturalization and Aliens.
26. Marriage and Divorce.
27. The Criminal Law, except the Constitution of Courts of Criminal Jurisdiction, but including the Procedure in Criminal Matters.
28. The Establishment, Maintenance, and Management of Penitentiaries.
29. Such Classes of Subjects as are expressly excepted in the Enumeration of the Classes of Subjects by this Act assigned exclusively to the Legislatures of the Provinces.

And any Matter coming within any of the Classes of Subjects enumerated in this Section shall not be deemed to come within the Class of Matters of a local or private Nature comprised in the Enumeration of the Classes of Subjects by this Act assigned exclusively to the Legislatures of the Provinces.

Exclusive Powers of Provincial Legislatures.

Subjects of
exclusive
Province
Legislation

92.   In each Province the Legislature may exclusively make Laws in relation to Matters coming within the Classes of Subject next herein-after enumerated; that is to say, —

1. The Amendment from Time to Time, notwithstanding anything in this Act, of the Constitution of the Province, except as regards the Office of Lieutenant Governor.
2. Direct Taxation within the Province in order to the raising of a Revenue for Provincial Purposes.
3. The borrowing of Money on the sole Credit of the Province.
4. The Establishment and Tenure of Provincial Offices and the Appointment and Payment of Provincial Officers.

5. The Management and Sale of the Public Lands belonging to the Province and of the Timber and Wood thereon.

6. The Establishment, Maintenance, and Management of Pubic and Reformatory Prisons in and for the Province.

7. The Establishment, Maintenance, and Management of Hospitals, Asylums, Charities, and Eleemosynary Institutions in and for the Province, other than Marine Hospitals.

8. Municipal Institutions in the Province.

9. Shop, Saloon, Tavern, Auctioneer, and other Licences in order to the raising of a Revenue for Provincial, Local, or Municipal Purposes.

10. Local Works and Undertakings other than such as are of the following Classes:

    (a) Lines of Steam or other Ships, Railways, Canals, Telegraphs, and other Works and Undertakings connecting the Province with any other or others of the Provinces, or extending beyond the Limits of the Province;

    (b) Lines of Steam Ships between the Province and any British or Foreign Country;

    (c) Such Works as, although wholly situate within the Province, are before or after their Execution declared by the Parliament of Canada to be for the general Advantage of Canada or for the Advantage of Two or more of the Provinces.

11. The Incorporation of Companies with Provincial Objects.

12. The Solemnization of Marriage in the Province.

13. Property and Civil Rights in the Province.

14. The Administration of Justice in the Province, including the Constitution, Maintenance, and Organization of Provincial Courts, both of Civil and of Criminal Jurisdiction, and including Procedure in Civil Matters in those Courts.

15. The Imposition of Punishment by Fine, Penalty, or Imprisonment for enforcing any Law of the Province made in relation to any Matter coming within any of the Classes of Subjects enumerated in this Section.

16. Generally all Matters of a merely local or private Nature in the Province.

APPENDIX 1-2

The Constitution Act (1982)
Charter of Rights and Freedoms*

SCHEDULE B
CONSTITUTION ACT, 1982

PART 1   CANADIAN CHARTER OF RIGHTS AND FREEDOMS

Whereas Canada is founded upon principles that recognize the supremacy of God and the rule of Law:

Guarantee of Rights and Freedoms

Rights and
freedoms in
Canada

1. The *Canadian Charter of Rights and Freedoms* guarantees the rights and freedoms set out in it subject only to such reasonable limits prescribed by law as can be demonstrably justified in a free and democratic society.

Fundamental Freedoms

Fundamental
freedoms

2. Everyone has the following fundamental freedoms:
   - *(a)* freedom of conscience and religion;
   - *(b)* freedom of thought, belief, opinion and expression, including freedom of the press and other media of communications;
   - *(c)* freedom of peaceful assembly; and
   - *(d)* freedom of association

Democratic Rights

Democratic
rights of citizens

3. Every citizen of Canada has the right to vote in an election of members of the House of Commons or of a legislative assembly and to be qualified for membership therein.

Maximum
duration of
legislative bodies

4. (1) No House of Commons and no legislative assembly shall continue for longer than five years from the date fixed for the return of the writs at a general election of its members.

Continuation in
special
circumstances

   (2) In time of real or apprehended war, invasion or insurrection, a House of Commons may be continued by Parliament and a legislative assembly may be continued by the legislature beyond five years if such continuation is not

*Reproduced by permission of the Minister of Supply and Services Canada.

opposed by the votes of more than one-third of the members of the House of Commons or the legislative assembly, as the case may be.

Annual sitting of legislative bodies

5. There shall be a sitting of Parliament and of each legislature at least once every twelve months.

Mobility Rights

Mobility of citizens

6. (1) Every citizen of Canada has the right to enter, remain in and leave Canada.
(2) Every citizen of Canada and every person who has the status of a permanent resident of Canada has the right:

Rights to move and gain livelihood

(a) to move to and take up residence in any province; and
(b) to pursue the gaining of a livelihood in any province.
(3) The rights specified in subsection (2) are subject to
(a) any laws or practices of general application in force in a province other than those that discriminate among persons primarily on the basis of province of present or previous residence; and

Limitation

(b) any laws providing for reasonable residency requirements as a qualification for the receipt of publicly provided social services.

Affirmative action programs

(4) Subsections (2) and (3) do not preclude any law, program or activity that has as its object the amelioration in a province of conditions of individuals in that province who are socially or economically disadvantaged if the rate of employment in that province is below the rate of employment in Canada.

Legal Rights

Life, liberty and security of person

7. Everyone has the right to life, liberty and security of the person and the right not to be deprived thereof except in accordance with the principles of fundamental justice.

Search or seizure

8. Everyone has the right to be secure against unreasonable search or seizure.

Detention or imprisonment

9. Everyone has the right not to be arbitrarily detained or imprisoned.

10. Everyone has the right on arrest or detention
(a) to be informed promptly of the reasons therefor;

Arrest or detention

(b) to retain and instruct counsel without delay and to be informed of that right; and
(c) to have the validity of the detention determined by way of *habeas corpus* and to be released if the detention is not lawful.

Proceedings in criminal and penal matters

11. Any person charged with an offence has the right
(a) to be informed without unreasonable delay of the specific offence;
(b) to be tried within a reasonable time;
(c) not to be compelled to be a witness in proceedings against that person in respect of the offence;

(d) to be presumed innocent until proven guilty according to law in a fair and public hearing by an independent and impartial tribunal;

(e) not to be denied reasonable bail without just cause;

(f) except in the case of an offence under military law tried before a military tribunal, to the benefit of trial by jury where the maximum punishment for the offence is imprisonment for five years or a more severe punishment;

(g) not to be found guilty on account of any act or omission unless, at the time of the act or omission, it constituted an offence under Canadian or international law or was criminal according to the general principles or law recognized by the community of nations;

(h) if finally acquitted of the offence, not to be tried for it again and, if finally found guilty and punished for the offence, not to be tried or punished for it again; and

(i) if found guilty of the offence and if the punishment for the offence has been varied between the time of commission and the time of sentencing, to the benefit of the lesser punishment.

Treatment or punishment

12. Everyone has the right not to be subjected to any cruel and unusual treatment or punishment.

Self-incrimination

13. A witness who testifies in any proceedings has the right not to have any incriminating evidence so given used to incriminate that witness in any other proceedings, except in a prosecution for perjury or for the giving of contradictory evidence.

Interpreter

14. A party or witness in any proceedings who does not understand or speak the language in which the proceedings are conducted or who is deaf has the right to the assistance of an interpreter.

Equality Rights

Equality before and under law and equal protection and benefit of law

Affirmative action programs

15. (1) Every individual is equal before and under the law and has the right to the equal protection and equal benefit of the law without discrimination and, in particular, without discrimination based on race, national or ethnic origin, colour, religion, sex, age or mental or physical disability.

(2) Subsection (1) does not preclude any law, program or activity that has as its object the amelioration of conditions of disadvantaged individuals or groups including those that are disadvantaged because of race, national or ethnic origin, colour, religion, sex, age or mental or physical disability.

Official Languages of Canada

Official languages of Canada

16. (1) English and French are the official languages of Canada and have equality of status and equal rights and privileges as to their use in all institutions of the Parliament and government of Canada.

Official languages of New Brunswick

Advancement of status and use

Proceedings of Parliament

Proceedings of New Brunswick legislature

Parliamentary statues and records

New Brunswick statutes and records

Proceedings in courts established by Parliament

Proceedings in New Brunswick courts

Communications by public with federal institutions

Communications by public with New Brunswick institutions

Continuation of existing constitutional provisions

Rights and privileges preserved

(2) English and French are the official languages of New Brunswick and have equality of status and equal rights and privileges as to their use in all institutions of the legislature and government of New Brunswick.

(3) Nothing in this Charter limits the authority of Parliament or a legislature to advance the equality of status or use of English and French

17. (1) Everyone has the right to use English or French in any debates and other proceedings of Parliament.

(2) Everyone has the right to use English and French in any debates and other proceedings of the legislature of New Brunswick.

18. (1) The statutes, records and journals of Parliament shall be printed and published in English and French and both language versions are equally authoritative.

(2) The statutes, records and journals of the legislature of New Brunswick shall be printed and published in English and French and both language versions are equally authoritative.

19. (1) Either English or French may be used by any person in, or in any pleading in or process issuing from, any court established by Parliament.

(2) Either English or French may be used by any person in, or in any pleading in or process issuing from, any court in New Brunswick.

20. (1) Any member of the public in Canada has the right to communicate with, and to receive available services from, any head or central office of an institution of the Parliament or government of Canada in English or French, and has the same right with respect to any such institution where

(a) there is a significant demand for communications with and services from that office in such language; or

(b) due to the nature of the office, it is reasonable that communications with services from that office be available in both English and French.

(2) Any member of the public in New Brunswick has the right to communicate with, and to receive available services from, any office of an institution of the legislature or government of New Brunswick in English or French.

21. Nothing in sections 16 to 20 abrogates or derogates from any right, privilege or obligation with respect to the English and French languages, or either of them, that exists or is continued by virtue of any other provision of the Constitution of Canada.

22. Nothing in sections 16 to 20 abrogates or derogates from any legal or customary right or privilege acquired or enjoyed either before or after the coming into force of this Charter with respect to any langauge that is not French or English.

Minority Language Educational Rights

23. (1) Citizens of Canada

Language of
instruction

Continuity of
language
instruction

Application where
numbers warrant

(a) whose first language learned and still understood is that of the English and
French linguistic minority population of the province in which they reside, or
(b) who have received their primary school instruction in Canada in English or
French and reside in a province where the language in which they received
that instruction is the language of the English or French linguistic minority
population of the province, have the right to have their children receive
primary and secondary school instruction in that language in that province.
(2) Citizens of Canada of whom any child has received or is receiving primary
or secondary school instruction in English or French in Canada, have the
right to have all their children receive primary and secondary school instruction in the same language.
(3) The right of citizens of Canada under subsections (1) and (2) to have
their children receive primary and secondary school instruction in the language of the English or French linguistic minority population of a province
(a) applies wherever in the province the number of children of citizens who
have such a right is sufficient to warrant the provision to them out of
public funds of minority language instruction; and
(b) includes, where the number of those children so warrants, the right to
have them receive that instruction in minority language educational facilities provided out of public funds.

Enforcement

Enforcement of
guaranteed rights
and freedoms

Exclusion of
evidence bringing
administration of
justice into
disrepute

24. (1) Anyone whose right or freedoms, as guaranteed by this Charter, have been
infringed or denied may apply to a court of competent jurisdiction to obtain
such remedy as the court considers appropriate and just in the circumstances.
(2) Where, in proceedings under subsection (1), a court concludes that evidence was obtained in a manner that infringed or denied any rights or freedoms
guaranteed by this Charter, the evidence shall be excluded if it is established
that, having regard to all the circumstances, the admission of it in the proceedings would bring the administration of justice into disrepute.

General

Aboriginal rights
and freedoms not
affected by
Charter

Other rights and
freedoms not
affected by
Charter

25. The guarantee in this Charter of certain rights and freedoms shall not be construed so as to abrogate or derogate from any aboriginal, treaty or other rights
and freedoms that pertain to the aboriginal peoples of Canada including
(a) any rights or freedoms that have been recognized by the Royal Proclam-
ation of October 7, 1763; and
(b) any rights or freedoms that may be acquired by the aboriginal peoples of
Canada by way of land claims settlement.

26. The guarantee in this Charter of certain rights and freedoms shall not be construed
as denying the existence of any other rights or freedoms that exist in Canada.

27. This Charter shall be interpreted in a manner consistent with the preservation and enhancement of the multicultural heritage of Canadians.

28. Notwithstanding anything in this Charter, the rights and freedoms referred to in it are guaranteed equally to male and female persons.

29. Nothing in this Charter abrogates or derogates from any rights or privileges guaranteed by or under the Constitution of Canada in respect of denominational, separate or dissentient schools.

30. A reference in this Charter to a province or to the legislative assembly or legislature of a province shall be deemed to include a reference to the Yukon Territory and Northwest Territories, or to the appropriate legislative authority thereof, as the case may be.

31. Nothing in this Charter extends the legislative powers of any body or authority.

Application of Charter

32. (1) This Charter applies
  (a) to the Parliament and government of Canada in respect of all matters within the authority of Parliament including all matters relating to the Yukon Territory and Northwest Territories; and
  (b) to the legislature and government of each province in respect of all matters within the authority of the legislature of each province.
(2) Notwithstanding subsection (1), section 15 shall not have effect until three years after this section comes into force.

33. (1) Parliament or the legislature of a province may expressly declare in an Act of Parliament or of the legislature, as the case may be, that the Act or a provision thereof shall operate notwithstanding a provision included in section 2 or sections 7 to 15 of this Charter.
(2) An Act or a provision of an Act in respect of which a declaration made under this section is in effect shall have such operation as it would have but for the provision of this Charter referred to in the declaration.
(3) A declaration made under subsection (1) shall cease to have effect five years after it comes into force or on such earlier date as may be specified in the declaration.
(4) Parliament or the legislature of a province may re-enact a declaration made under subsection (1).
(5) Subsection (3) applies in respect of a re-enactment made under subsection (4).

Citation

Citation

34. This Part may be cited as the *Canadian Charter of Rights and Freedoms*.

Recognition of existing aboriginal and treaty rights

PART II   RIGHTS OF THE ABORIGINAL PEOPLES OF CANADA

35. (1) The existing aboriginal and treaty rights of the aboriginal peoples of Canada are hereby recognized and affirmed.

Definition of "aboriginal people of Canada"

(2) In this Act, "aboriginal peoples of Canada" includes the Indian, Inuit and Métis peoples of Canada.

APPENDIX 1-3

The Revised Statutes for the Provinces

1. Revised Statutes of Alberta (1980)
2. Revised Statutes of British Columbia (1979)
3. Revised Statutes of Manitoba (1987)
4. Revised Statutes of New Brunswick (1973)
5. Revised Statutes of Newfoundland (1970)
6. Revised Statutes of Nova Scotia (1989)
7. Revised Statutes of Ontario (1980)
8. Revised Statutes of Prince Edward Island (1988)
9. Revised Statutes of Québec (1977)
10. Revised Statutes of Saskatchewan (1978)
11. Revised Statutes of the Northwest Territories (1974)
12. Revised Statutes of the Yukon (1986)

APPENDIX 1-4

The Courts of the Provinces

Alberta
1. The Provincial Court of Alberta
   • Criminal Division
   • Youth Division
   • Family Division
   • Civil Claims Division (civil matters not exceeding $4000)
2. The Court of Queen's Bench for Alberta
   • Superior level trial court for the province
   • Criminal and civil matters
3. The Court of Appeal for Alberta
   • Appellate court for the province
   • Appeals to the Supreme Court of Canada

British Columbia
1. The Provincial Court of British Columbia
   • Criminal Court
   • Family Court
   • Small Claims Court (civil matters not exceeding $10 000)
2. The Supreme Court of British Columbia
   • Superior level trial court for the province
   • Civil and criminal jurisdiction
3. The Court of Appeal for British Columbia
   • Appellate Court for the province
   • Appeals to the Supreme Court of Canada

Manitoba
1. The Provincial Judges Court
   • Criminal Division
   • Family Division (including young offenders)
2. Her Majesty's Court of Queen's Bench for Manitoba
   • Superior level trial court for the province
   • Civil and criminal jurisdiction
   • Special procedures for small claims (under $5000) and probate
   • Family division
3. The Court of Appeal for Manitoba
   • Appellate Court for the province
   • Appeals to the Supreme Court of Canada

New Brunswick
1. The Provincial Court

- Criminal Court
- Family Division (including young offenders)
2. The Court of Queen's Bench for New Brunswick
   - Trial Division (superior level trial court for the province with criminal and civil law jurisdiction)
   - Family Division (trial level function for all types of family matters including young offenders)
3. The Court of Appeal for New Brunswick
   - Appellate Court for the province
   - Appeals to the Supreme Court of Canada

Newfoundland
1. The Provincial Court of Newfoundland
   - Criminal matters
   - Family Division (including juvenile matters)
   - Small claims (civil matters not exceeding $3000)
2. Unified Family Court
   - Family matters (including juvenile)
3. The Supreme Court of Newfoundland
   - Trial Division (superior trial court for the province with civil and criminal jurisdiction)
   - Court of Appeal (Appellate Court for the Province. Appeals to the Supreme Court of Canada)

Nova Scotia
(Note changes have been enacted but not proclaimed at the time of writing)
1. Provincial Court
   Small Claims Court
   - Adjudicator presides
   - Civil matters (not exceeding $3000)
   Family Court
   - Family Matters (including young offenders)
   Criminal Court
   - Criminal matters
2. The Supreme Court of Nova Scotia
   (superior trial level court for the province)
   - Appeal Appellate Court for the province, appeals to the Supreme Court of Canada)

Ontario
1. Ontario Court of Justice
   General Division
   - Civil matters, serious criminal matters, estates and wills. This is the superior level court of the province in both civil and criminal matters
   Divisional Court

• Hears limited appeals in matters (e.g., less than $25 000.00)

Small Claims Court

• Civil disputes involving moderate amounts

Provincial Division

• Criminal matters, young offenders, family matters, provincial offenses and civil matters up to $6000

Note: Unified Family Court

• Deals with family disputes over property, support, maintenance payments, the use of the family home, etc. (Criminal powers to deal with young offenders but only in one judicial district.)

2.   Court of Appeal

• The appellate court of the province (Appeals go to the Supreme Court of Canada.)

Prince Edward Island

1.   The Provincial Court
• Criminal jurisdiction
• Judge has powers of a magistrate

2.   The Supreme Court of Prince Edward Island — Trial Division
• Estates Section (deals with wills and estate matters)
• Family Section (including juvenile)
• General Section (superior trial level court of the province with criminal and civil jurisdiction).
• Small claims section deals with civil matters.
• Appeal Division of Supreme Court (Appellate Court for the Province, appeals to the Supreme Court of Canada)

Québec

1.   Municipal Courts
2.   Court of Québec
• Civil Division
• Criminal and Penal Division
• Youth Division
3.   The Superior Court
• Criminal and civil jurisdiction
• Some appeals from lower courts
4.   The Court of Appeal
• Appellate Court for the province
• Appeals to the Supreme Court of Canada

Saskatchewan

1.   The Provincial Court of Saskatchewan
• Criminal jurisdiction (powers of magistrate)
• Family matters (including youth)
• Small claims civil matters not exceeding $5000

   • Appeal to Court of Queen's Bench
2.   Her Majesty's Court of Queen's Bench for Saskatchewan
   • Superior trial level court for the province
   • Criminal and civil matters
   • Surrogate Court (presided over by judge of the Court of Queen's Bench, deals with wills and estate matters)
   • Unified Family Court (presided over by a local judge of the Court of Queen's
   • Bench, deals with family disputes and juvenile matters)
3.   The Court of Appeal for Saskatchewan
   • Appellate Court for the province
   • Appeals to the Supreme Court of Canada

Northwest Territories
1.   The Territorial Court of the Northwest Territories
   • All powers of a magistrate under the criminal code
   • Civil jurisdiction not to exceed $5000
   • Youth Court (Offenses under federal Young Offenders Act)
2.   Supreme Court of the Northwest Territories
   • Unlimited criminal and civil jurisdiction
3.   The Court of Appeal of the Northwest Territories (to hear appeals from the Supreme Court)

Yukon Territory
1.   Small Claims Court (maximum $3000)
2.   Territorial Court of Yukon (Judges have power of magistrate under the criminal code, including the powers of a youth court judge under the Young Offenders Act. No civil jurisdiction)
3.   Supreme Court of the Yukon Territory (no limit on jurisdiction.)
4.   Court of Appeal.

2 THE LAW OF TORTS

Objectives of the Chapter

- to define torts and describe various types of tortious conduct
- to distinguish between careless and negligent conduct
- to determine whether or not a duty of care is owed
- to set out the standards of care expected

While washing their truck at a service station, the parents of a four-year-old boy allowed him to play without supervision behind the station. Unknown to the parents, there was an open cesspool there. It was unmarked and its opening was flush with the ground. Their son fell in and although rescued became very ill, required hospitalization and suffered significant physical problems as a result of the accident. The parents brought an action against both the oil company that owned the station and the operators who leased it. The judge found that the defendants were negligent and liable under the Ontario Occupier's Liability Act since they had known of the open cesspool. By doing nothing about it, they had failed to take reasonable steps to protect the little boy from its dangers.[1]

[1] *Vachon et al. v. Roy et al.*, Ont. Dist. Ct., Jan. 1987, 642-009.

Not only in our businesses, but also in our personal lives we constantly run the risk of carelessly or wilfully causing injury to others or to their property. When injuries do result from our negligent or wilful conduct, under the law of torts we are liable to compensate the victims for the injuries they suffer.

INTRODUCTION

When people engage in commercial activities, conflicting interests or simple interactions often lead to the commission of torts. There is no wholly satisfactory definition for torts because there is considerable disagreement over whether there is one underlying principle governing all types of tortious activity or whether there are many different torts, each governed by different rules. Some general principles, however, do apply. Tort law mediates situations in which an individual's conduct interferes with another's person, property or reputation. If the interfering conduct falls below a minimum social standard and causes injury or loss, a tort has been committed and the victim has the right to sue for compensation. For this reason, torts can be defined as social wrongs other than crimes or breaches of contract. *Because the resulting court action is civil rather than criminal, such torts are usually called civil wrongs*.

Conduct so serious that it poses a threat to society generally is said to be criminal in nature. The object of the courts in dealing with criminal activity is to punish the wrongdoer, not to compensate the victim. With many crimes, the victim retains the right to sue for tort. Thus, wrongful conduct is often both a crime and a tort.

A tort must also be distinguished from a breach of contract. An act that breaches a contract may not be inherently wrong, but the contractual relationship makes the violation of its terms unacceptable. A tort on the other hand is inherently wrongful conduct that falls below a minimum acceptable social standard that is judicially imposed. The court determines who should bear the loss for the injuries suffered and the amount that will adequately compensate the victim.

Two major categories of tortious activities will be considered in this chapter: intentional or deliberate acts, and careless or negligent acts that cause another to suffer loss or injury. It is important to keep the concept of **vicarious liability** in mind while studying these categories of tort. Often a person involved in a wrongful act which gives rise to the right to sue for tort is functioning in a master/servant (employment) relationship. An employer can be held liable for the tortious act an employee commits during the employment. This liability is limited to torts committed while carrying out the employee's employment responsibilities. The employer will not be vicariously liable when the employee is "on a frolic of his or her own." The importance of vicarious liability in the business world cannot be over-emphasized. A detailed examination of the master/servant relationship and vicarious liability can be found in Chapter 9, Employment Law.

A tort is a civil or social wrong

tort/breach of contract

Torts may involve intentional or inadvertent conduct

INTENTIONAL TORTS

Assault and Battery

Fear of contact
• assault
Actual contact
• battery

Assault and battery (or trespass to person) is intentional physical interference with another. An action which makes a person think that he or she is about to be struck is an **assault.** If someone takes a swing and misses, points a gun or picks up a stone to threaten another person, an assault has been committed. A **battery** takes place when someone is in actual physical contact with another person. Since battery almost invariably involves an assault and since the legal remedies are the same, the term assault is usually used to refer to both assault and battery.

It is not necessary to show that any actual injury was suffered to be successful in an action. In the case of *Cole v. Turner* [2] the judge declared that, "the least touching of another in anger is battery." Normal, unavoidable contacts we all experience in social situations such as tapping someone on the shoulder to gain attention or brushing against another person in a crowded hallway do not constitute battery. Assault and battery involves intentional conduct by the offending party and the application of physical force to the victim. Negligence involves inadvertent conduct and will be discussed below.

In considering whether an action amounts to assault, it is not necessary for the victim to be fearful of imminent harm, only that unwelcome contact is expected. When a person threatens to kiss another, there may be no fear involved but the action may still constitute an assault. The action complained of must be a physical gesture and not only words, although words accompanying the action can turn the conduct into an assault. A person rushing towards you might seem to be an assault were it not for the words, "How nice to see you again." Thus, the words and the action must be considered together. The words accompanying the action might make an innocent action an assault or might take the threat away from a threatening gesture. It is not necessary that the person committing the assault or battery have an evil or malicious goal. A doctor, with the best of intentions, might operate to save the life of a protesting patient. Such an act, when consent is denied, may nevertheless constitute a battery. [3]

Intent to harm not required

Consent is a defence

Normally, doctors escape liability for their actions when operating or otherwise treating patients through the principle of consent. Essentially, a person who consents, either expressly or by implication, to conduct that would otherwise constitute an assault or battery, loses the right to sue. This is the reason injured boxers cannot sue their opponents. The consent must be informed consent; people must know what they are consenting to. Some people for religious reasons resist medical intervention, even when it would save their lives. Refusal is their right. The doctor who persists in treating them after being told of their refusal has committed a technical battery and is liable to the victim. [4] Of course, if the person's condition is not ag-

---

[2] *Cole v. Turner*, (1705) 87 E.R. 907 (Kings Bench Div.).

[3] This right may not extend to others within their care. When parents refuse treatment needed to save the lives of their children for religious reasons, the courts are often willing to interfere by taking custody of the children away from the parents and ordering treatment.

[4] *Mulloy v. Hop Sang*, (1935) 1 W.W.R. 714.

gravated but helped by the treatment, the court will not be inclined to award significant damages.

One way an assault can become a problem for the business person is when an uncooperative patron needs to be ejected. The general rule is that when a patron becomes a trespasser by violating the rules of the establishment, the occupier or servant of the occupier is justified in asking the patron to leave. If the patron refuses, the occupier then has the authority to use as much force as is necessary to eject the trespasser. However, if excessive force is used and the patron is injured, the operator will be held liable for those injuries.

In the case of *Cottreau v. Rodgerson*,[5] the plaintiff was a patron in the defendant's establishment and became intoxicated. When he refused to leave, the bartender ejected him into the back lane. The bartender turned and was walking back to his establishment when he thought he saw the patron lunging toward him. The bartender turned and struck him a severe blow in the face, causing a serious injury. The plaintiff sued, claiming the bartender had used excessive force. The court held that the bartender had acted properly in asking the patron to leave, then, when his request was refused, by removing him forcibly. But the court held that even if the patron had been lunging to assault the defendant in the lane, a blow of such force was not needed to subdue the patron because of his intoxicated condition. The defendant was liable, therefore, to compensate the victim.

SELF-DEFENCE. The law entitles people who are being attacked or think that they are about to be attacked to use as much force as is necessary to defend themselves. The test is reasonable force. When one person attacks another with a clenched fist and the person being attacked shoots the attacker with a gun, such a response is considered excessive, and the injured party has the right to sue for assault and battery. Of course, when someone with no experience in responding to violence is threatened by someone twice his or her size, the person being attacked might have difficulty in measuring exactly how much force is necessary to subdue the other party. The court will take this lack of experience into consideration in determining if the amount of force used in the response was reasonable. The test the courts use is what a reasonable person with the same skills, knowledge and background as the person being attacked would have done in the circumstances.

It is important to note, however, that the victim can use the concept of self-defence as a defence only while being attacked. Once the danger has passed, self-defence cannot be used to support later acts of vengeance. It is not the responsibility of private citizens to punish perpetrators of tortious or criminal acts. Court action provides a substitute for personal retaliation.

Trespass to Land

Trespass to land involves someone who goes onto another person's property without having either the lawful right or the owner's permission to do so. Some individuals

---

[5] *Couttreau v. Rodgerson*, (1965) 53 D.L.R. (2d) 549, (Nova Scotia Supreme Court).

Margin notes:

Reasonable force permitted to eject trespasser

Reasonable force to defend permitted

On land without authority

have statutory authority empowering them to enter private property for specific purposes. Municipal inspectors, meter readers, police officers and other officials have the lawful right to be on private property, and cannot be charged with trespass if their purpose in being there is in keeping with their official duties. Permission to enter private property for anyone other than those legally empowered to be there may be expressed or implied. If an owner or occupier has knowledge that people have been using his or her property for some time, but has done nothing to discourage them, they may be said to have implied permission or license to be on the property and cannot successfully be sued for trespass.

Trespass to land is an intentional tort to the extent that a person who is voluntarily on another's land without lawful right or permission has committed trespass. It is only necessary that the person be there of his or her own volition. A trespasser cannot avoid liability by claiming ignorance of where the property line is.

However, when a person is found on the property of another through no act of his or her own, it is not a case of trespass. In the early case of *Smith v. Stone*,[6] the defendant was carried onto private property by the violent acts of other people. The judge determined that the trespass was committed not by the defendant but by the people who carried the defendant onto the property. This case also illustrates the point that the defendant need not come onto the land to commit a trespass. It is also trespass when objects are thrown or placed on another's property. A vandal who throws a rock through a window has committed a trespass.

Trespass can be indirect

Trespass is actionable even if no injury or loss has taken place. The "mere bruising of the grass" is said to be enough to support a trespass action. In such cases, the courts are usually reluctant to award anything but nominal damages, but a trespass has been committed nonetheless. More significantly, the occupier of property has the right to use as much force as is necessary to eject a trespasser. Typically, this right means that the occupier can demand that the trespasser leave; if the trespasser refuses, the occupier then has the right to use reasonable force to eject the trespasser without being liable for assault and battery.

Trespassers who cause damage while on private property bear responsibility for any injury or loss caused, whether it was foreseeable or not. In cases where a person is suing for injuries suffered while on private property, it can be important for the defendant to show that the injured person was a trespasser. Though there is some confusion today about the exact nature of the duty an occupier owes to a trespasser, it does seem clear that such a duty is minimal.

CONTINUING TRESPASS. Continuing trespass is involved when a party puts up a building or other structure that encroaches on the property of another. In the case of *Gross v. Wright*,[7] the owners of two adjoining properties agreed to establish a common wall on the property line. The wall was to be twenty-four inches at its base and taper as it went up. The finished wall was twelve inches on each side at the base as agreed, but as it tapered up towards the top, the builder made

---

[6] *Smith v. Stone*, (1647) 82 E.R. 533 (Kings Bench Div.).
[7] *Gross v. Wright* [1923] 2 D.L.R. 171 (Supreme Court of Canada).

sure that the full width of twelve inches was maintained on the property of his neighbour and that all the tapering took place on his side. The wall at the top was entirely on the property of the neighbour in violation of the agreement. When the neighbour discovered this, he took the defendant to court. The court decided that a continuing trespass was taking place and issued an injunction ordering that the continuing trespass cease. An injunction is an equitable remedy whereby the court orders that a condition or activity in violation of the law be stopped or corrected. In this case, the court suspended the operation of the injunction to give the defendant time to make adjustments so that the wall would conform to the agreement. One can readily see the kinds of problems this might cause for structures such as the multistoried buildings now located in most urban areas.

Injunction available to remedy continuing trespass

3. False Imprisonment (非法拘禁)

False imprisonment (also a form of trespass to person) as a cause of action occurs when people are unlawfully and intentionally restrained against their will. The restraint may take place in a prison cell or in any completely confined room. There is no imprisonment if people are barred from crossing a bridge or going down a passageway because they can go back the way they came. Nor is there imprisonment if it is possible to slip out through an unnoticed door or an open window. This does not mean that imprisoned victims have to use heroic means to obtain their freedom. It is not necessary for people confined in a ship to jump into the water to free themselves.

Restraint without lawful excuse— false imprisonment

Imprisonment may also take place when the person being imprisoned submits to another's control through recognition of authority or a threat. When a police officer orders someone to remain in a particular location and the person complies thinking there is no alternative, there has been a submission of will to the authority of the police officer and therefore imprisonment. If a person goes voluntarily with the police officer, no imprisonment has taken place, but the willingness to cooperate with the officer must be real. If the person accompanies the officer to avoid embarrassment or because of fear that refusal would result in being forced to comply, then an imprisonment may have taken place. For a person to be imprisoned, there must be a true submission of will.

Submission to authority can constitute imprisonment

In the case of *Bahner v. Marwest Hotel Company Ltd., Muir et al.*,[8] the defendant, a patron in a Vancouver restaurant, was unfamiliar with the provincial liquor laws when he ordered and obtained a bottle of wine at 11:30 p.m. The waiter opened the bottle and left it on the table. At a few minutes to twelve, the waiter told Bahner that he would have to drink the wine before midnight. The customer replied that he could not do that without becoming intoxicated and suggested that he take the bottle with him. The waiter said that was not permitted and Bahner refused to pay for the wine. When he got up to leave after paying for the meal but not the wine, a security guard ordered him to stay while the police were called. When the police arrived, Bahner was taken to the police station where he had to spend the night before

---

[8] *Bahner v. Marwest Hotel Company Ltd., Muir et al.*, (1969) 6 D.L.R. (3d) 322 (B.C.S.C.).

being released. Bahner sued the restaurant for false imprisonment. At the trial, the restaurant argued that, because there were other ways out of the restaurant, the plaintiff had not been imprisoned. The court decided that this was a situation in which the customer had submitted his will to the command of the security guard so there had been an imprisonment. The judge said,

> The plaintiff, commanded by the security officer to stay and prevented by the officer from leaving by the ordinary exit, behaved with admirable restraint in making no forcible attempt to pass the security officer. After what the officer had said and done he could reasonably expect to be restrained by force if he tried to leave by any exit and he was not required to make an attempt to run away.[9]

There are two factors to consider when examining this kind of action. First, it must be clearly demonstrated that there was an imprisonment and, of equal importance, that such imprisonment was false or without authority. Once it had been established that there had been imprisonment, the court had to deal with the second point: whether or not the plaintiff had done something for which he could be imprisoned, that is, refusing to pay for the wine. Since the plaintiff had intended to pay for the wine when he ordered it, the only recourse left to the restaurant was to sue for breach of contract. Had the restaurant demonstrated that the customer had never had any intention of paying for the wine, that would have amounted to a crime and the imprisonment would have been justified even when made by a private citizen or security guard. In fact, the police, security guards and even the owners of property being threatened have greater powers to arrest than the ordinary citizen.

Imprisonment is false—where no authority

This case also illustrates the circumstances under which courts will award punitive damages. The primary object of tort law is to compensate victims of actionable wrongs for the injury or loss they suffer. When the plaintiff can show that expenses have been incurred or that specific, calculable losses, called **special damages**, have resulted, the victim will be compensated for them. When it is not possible to place an actual value on the loss, as in the case of pain and suffering, harm to reputation or future loss of earnings, the court will assess the loss and award general damages.

The main object of tort law is to compensate people for wrongful injury or loss, not to punish wrongdoers. Only on rare occasions will a court order the defendant to pay damages to the plaintiff in excess of any injuries suffered. Such an award serves to punish the wrongdoer rather than compensate the victim and is referred to as **punitive damages**. In the *Bahner v. Marwest Hotel* case, the judge considered the action of the hotel employees sufficiently objectionable to award significant punitive damages in addition to the general and special damages awarded as compensation.

A charge of false imprisonment is a significant risk for any business involved in serving the public, including restaurants, hotels, retail stores and bars. This risk is especially strong when, either because of store policy or inexperienced staff, customers are detained whenever they are suspected of wrongdoing. The managers of many establishments which serve the public discourage their employees from apprehending shoplifters. Their reasoning is that the potential loss from goods stolen

---

[9] *Ibid.*, p. 325.

is far outweighed by the danger of losing a false imprisonment action. This is one area in which training staff to know when they can detain a person and when they cannot is a well-justified expense.

④ Private Nuisance 妨害罪

The tort of **private nuisance** is committed when a person uses property in such a way that it interferes with a neighbour's use or enjoyment of his or her property. Such interference is usually ongoing and continuous. The most common complaint arises from the escape of polluting or dangerous substances such as noise, odours, smoke, water or falling debris. If a smokehouse is set up in a back yard and the resulting smoke and odour make it impossible for neighbours to use their yards, they could have an action for nuisance. Similarly, when a factory emits pollutants into the air that destroy paint on neighbouring cars and buildings, there could be cause for action.

Private nuisance—use of property interferes with neighbour

There are certain limitations to this principle of law; the offending neighbour must be using the property in an unusual or unreasonable way and the problem caused must be a direct consequence of this unusual activity. A person living in an industrial section of a city cannot complain when a factory begins operating in the neighbourhood and emits noise, smoke and dust. It is also doubtful that residents of a rural area could successfully complain about the smells escaping from a neighbouring farmer's property when they are the normal odours associated with farming.

Until recently problems giving rise to complaints had to emanate from reasonably close or adjoining properties, but in the Alberta case of *Motherwell v. Motherwell*[10] the judge made a significant departure from this tradition. In this case, the defendant persistently used the telephone to harass the plaintiffs. The judge determined that this was a private nuisance even though there was no adjoining property. Because the harassment interfered with the plaintiffs' enjoyment of their property, they were successful in their action.

A more recent development with personal nuisance is the suggestion that a person will be found liable only when injury to the plaintiff is reasonably foreseeable, as with a negligence action. Negligence will be discussed below. Because nuisance often involves offending substances, it has become important as a tool of environmental protection. The law of the environment is one of the subjects that will be discussed in the final chapter.

⑤ Defamation （誹謗）

Defamation is a published false statement about a person which is detrimental to his or her reputation. If a statement is true, no matter how derogatory, the victim has no complaint. Strictly speaking, a statement is defamatory if it can be shown to be detrimental to a person's reputation. The court presumes that the statement is false.

[10] *Motherwell v. Motherwell*, (1977) 73 D.L.R. (3d) 62 (Alta. S.C. Ap. Div.).

Defamation—
detrimental
statement

Thus, once a person establishes that such a detrimental statement has been made, it is not necessary to prove that it is false as well. Of course, if the defendant demonstrates that the statement is true, this is an absolute defence to the action.[11] When the statement complained of is untrue but not derogatory, there is no defamation. If a professor said a student was the smartest student at the university, that student could not successfully sue for defamation even if it could be demonstrated that the statement was false. The case of *Youssoupoff v. Metro-Goldwyn-Mayer Pictures Limited*[12] determined the test of what amounts to a defamatory statement: "Statements which are calculated to bring under hatred, ridicule or contempt...or causes them to be shunned or avoided...." On appeal, Lord Justice Scrutton said that he preferred the test, "...a false statement about a man to his discredit."[13]

Statement must
be published

Innuendo

To succeed in a defamation action, the plaintiff must prove that the offending statement is detrimental, that it refers to the plaintiff and that it was published. In this situation, "to publish" means that the statement had to be communicated to a third party. Publication could have occurred in a newspaper, in the broadcast media or simply by word of mouth. It is sufficient publication if just one other person hears the defamatory statement. Another important factor to consider is that statements often contain innuendo: implied or hidden meanings. A statement may appear perfectly innocent on the surface but, when combined with other information, it may take on a different meaning. To say that Mary Navarro had a baby yesterday could be an innocent remark, but if one of the hearers of that statement knows that Mary Navarro is a very religious, unmarried fifteen-year-old committed to living a chaste life, the remark takes on a sinister air and might be defamatory. It is no excuse to say that the person making the statement thought it was true or did not know of the special facts that created the innuendo. Such a mistake is no defence, and the offending party can be held liable for the defamatory remark. Because of the constitutional protection of the press in the U.S., mistake is an effective defence when the media are involved. This appears not to be the case in Canada, although the question is still open due to the freedom of the press provision found in Section 2 (b) of the Charter of Rights and Freedoms.

Mistake no
excuse

Newspapers and the broadcast media often find themselves in serious difficulty because of such mistakes. In the case of *E. Hulton & Co. v. Jones*,[14] a newspaper published a fictitious story lampooning the double standards of the English upper-middle class. In the story, a man named Artemus Jones was depicted frolicking on the continent in the company of "a woman who was not his wife." It was clear that the author and publishers of the story thought they were creating entirely fictitious characters. Unfortunately for them, there really was an Artemus Jones who fit the description of the character in the story, and his friends and acquaintances thought the article was about him. He sued for defamation. Even though the author and publishers had no idea of Mr. Jones' existence, he succeeded in the action against them.

[11] *Elliott v. Freison et al.*, (1984) 6 D.L.R. (4th) 338 (Ontario Court of Appeal). Affirming (1982) 136 D.L.R. (3d) 281 (Ontario High Court) Leave to Appeal to S.C.C. refused.
[12] *Youssoupoff v. Metro-Goldwyn Mayer Pictures Limited*, (1934) 50 T.L.R. 581
[13] *Ibid.*, p. 584.
[14] *E. Hulton & Co. v. Jones*, [1910] 26 T.L.R. 128 (House of Lords).

Libel written/slander spoken

LIBEL AND SLANDER. Defamation can be either **libel,** which is written defamation, or **slander**, which is spoken defamation. One important aspect of the distinction between the two lies in the area of proof. Libel is of a more enduring nature, is easier to prove and supposedly causes more harm than slander. However, with modern means of mass communication, the rationale for this distinction is beginning to break down. Spoken defamation on television or radio is easy to prove and does at least as much damage as the same words published in a newspaper. The significance of finding a defamatory remark to be libelous rather than slanderous is that with libel it is not necessary to establish some actual proof of a specific loss. General damages will be awarded when the plaintiff has suffered some form of harm even though it is not calculable. In most actions for slander, the awarding of special damages depends on the plaintiff submitting a statement of actual expenses incurred, supported by bills. In some exceptional circumstances, an action of slander can be successful without proving special damages. For example, people who are accused of committing crimes or other actions that would make them unfit for their jobs might be successful in an action even without such proof of specific loss. In many provinces the distinction between libel and slander has been eliminated by legislation that deals with defamation that has been broadcast.[15]

Slander and special damages

DEFENCES. Once it has been established that a defamatory statement has been made, several defences are available to the defendant. **Truth**, sometimes called the defence of justification, is an absolute defence. But even when a statement is technically true, it can still be derogatory if it contains an innuendo or if it is capable of being interpreted as referring to another person about whom the statement is false.

Truth is an absolute defence

The second method of defence is called **absolute privilege**. Anything discussed in certain defined situations cannot give rise to a defamation action no matter how malicious, scandalous or derogatory. Any statement made on the floor of any provincial legislative assembly or in parliament in Ottawa as part of the proceedings of that body is immune from defamation actions. Similarly, executive communications between high level officials are protected from defamation actions. In these situations, no matter how false and damaging a statement is, no matter how much malice is involved or the motivation behind it, the person being defamed cannot successfully sue. The same principle applies to testimony given in court. If a witness on the stand lies viciously about another, there can be no defamation action. Of course, other methods are used in these situations to discourage the abuse of this privilege. Legislative bodies have their own rules to control the conduct of members on the floor and the courts can charge a witness with perjury for false statements.

Absolute privilege

Another defence which is often raised and has a broad application, is **qualified privilege**. This defence can be used when a person makes a defamatory remark about another in the course of fulfilling a duty or an obligation. As long as people are fulfilling their duties and their motives are sincere, with no knowledge of falsehood and without malice, they are protected and will not be held liable for losses

Qualified privilege, requires duty

[15] *Libel and Slander Act*, R.S.O. (1980) c.237 s.2.

resulting from defamatory remarks. For example, if, during an examination, an instructor thinks a student is cheating and reports this to a supervisor, the student could not succeed in a defamation action against the instructor even if the accusation was false. In fact, the instructor is in the examination room for the express purpose of ensuring that no cheating takes place. As long as the instructor thinks that the accusation is true and has no other motive, the remark is not defamatory. However, a person can lose the protection of qualified privilege by making accusing statements to a larger audience to whom no responsibility is owed or to a reporter who broadcasts the information.

Fair comment

The final defence available in the field of defamation is the defence of **fair comment**. When someone becomes a public figure by publishing a book, producing a movie or becoming involved in politics, they create the right for people to express uncomplimentary opinions about their work or character. The evidence, such as the movie, book or voting record, must be available to the public and the comments complained of must relate to the work. Even if everyone else thinks the work is exceptionally good, it is possible for a critic to state a negative opinion as long as that opinion is drawn from the facts available. This principle applies to all public figures, but the law does not permit abuse. If malice or another unjust motive can be demonstrated, the defence of fair comment is lost.

When dealing with the subject of defamation it must be remembered that the courts have tried to balance the democratic concepts of free speech and individuals' rights to have their prestige and reputation spared from unjustified assault. Because of this and historical anomalies in the separate development of the laws of slander and libel, these rules have become cumbersome and inefficient and many jurisdictions have passed legislation summarizing, and in many cases, significantly modifying, the common law.

NEGLIGENCE

Negligence— careless conduct causing another injury

The second general category of torts includes **negligent** or inadvertent conduct that causes injury to another person or damage or loss to property. One of the most common causes of court action is the suit for damages arising out of accidental or careless conduct. Careless behaviour must be unintentional and result in injury or damage to another person to qualify as negligence and to be recognized by the courts as cause for action. The court's duty is to establish the standard of care required of the defendant and whether or not that standard was met. The plaintiff must prove that a duty to be careful was owed, that there was a failure to act at the level of care required, that actual injury or loss was suffered and that the conduct complained of caused the injury.

Defendants may raise several factors in their defence. They may argue that the injury suffered was too remote from the offending conduct or that the plaintiff contributed to the injury through his or her own negligence. Defendants may also suggest that the plaintiff was ineligible for compensation as the risk of injury was voluntarily assumed.

The Reasonable Person Test

Reasonable person test establishes standard

The reasonable person test helps courts establish the standard for measuring socially acceptable behaviour. The concept of the **reasonable person** is used in various ways throughout our legal system. This hypothetical character has become a point of reference to help courts make decisions without imposing rigid standards. Faced with the problem of having to decide if certain conduct is socially acceptable, the judge or members of the jury simply ask themselves, "What would a reasonably prudent person, in possession of all the facts of the case, have done in this situation?"

Reasonably prudent is better than average

A common misunderstanding is that courts using the reasonable person concept require people to live by an average standard. This is not so. Since the test asks what a reasonably prudent person would have done in the circumstances, it is measuring the conduct of a person who is being particularly careful or considerably better than average. On the other hand, the conduct is not required to be perfect since even reasonably prudent people can sometimes make mistakes. The conduct of the reasonable person falls somewhere between average and perfect.

A good comparison is "par" in golf. A standard score, called par, is established for each of the eighteen holes found on a golf course. If par for a hole is three, it does not mean that the average score for that hole is three strokes but that the average score is four or five strokes. On the other hand, three is not the best possible score. Rather, par is the score you would expect from a good golfer playing well. Similarly, the reasonable person test represents the standard of care expected from a prudent person who is being careful.

Determining the Existence of a Duty

For a litigant to sue successfully in a negligence action, it is necessary to establish that the defendant owed a duty to be careful. The court uses a variation of the reasonable person test, referred to as the **reasonable foreseeability test,** to determine whether or not such a duty exists. If it were reasonably foreseeable that the conduct complained of would cause harm to the plaintiff, a duty to be careful exists. In other words, if the likelihood of injury would have been apparent to a reasonable person had he or she considered who was put at risk by his or her conduct, then the defendant owed a duty.

Reasonable foreseeability establishes duty

The case of *Palsgraf v. Long Island Railroad Co.*[16] illustrates this point. During rush hour, a man attempted to board a train at a station in New York. Two employees of the railway company tried to help him onto the train but caused him to drop the bag he was carrying onto the tracks below. The bag contained fireworks which exploded on impact. The blast caused a heavy object mounted on the station wall several yards down the track to fall on and injure Mrs. Palsgraf who sued the railroad company and the two employees for negligence. The court was faced with the question of whether or not the employees of the railroad company owed a duty

[16] *Palsgraf v. Long Island Railroad Co.*, (1928) 248 N.Y. 339 (New York Court of Appeal).

to be careful to Mrs. Palsgraf. The court found that the railway employees owed no duty to Mrs. Palsgraf because they had no knowledge of the fireworks. They did owe a duty to be careful to the person they were assisting onto the train, and they may have failed to live up to that duty. However Mrs. Palsgraf could not rely on the failure of duty to support her action. A duty had to be owed directly to her and that duty had to be based on the principle of reasonable foreseeability. Duty was not owed because the employees could not be expected to reasonably anticipate that she was at any risk.

The result would probably have been different, however, if Mrs. Palsgraf had sued the passenger carrying the fireworks. Again, the court would have had to determine if he owed her a duty to be careful. The test would be the same. Would the possibility of injuring someone several metres away be apparent to a person carrying explosives? The answer would be yes, since the man ought to have known that what he was carrying was dangerous and could cause injury to those even at some distance if dropped. The court would then have to determine whether he had failed to live up to the appropriate standards.

One of the most significant cases concerning torts in this century is *Donoghue v. Stevenson.*[17] Two women went into a café where one ordered a bottle of ginger beer for her friend, Mrs. Donoghue. After consuming some of it, Mrs. Donoghue discovered part of a decomposed snail at the bottom of her bottle. She became very ill as a result of drinking the contaminated beverage. In the process of suing she discovered that she had some serious problems. She could not successfully sue the café that had supplied the ginger beer for breach of contract because she had no contract with the establishment as her friend had made the purchase. Similarly, she could not successfully sue the café for negligence since the beer was bottled in an opaque bottle and served to her in the bottle. There was no opportunity for the café to discover a problem in the product and, therefore, no negligence on their part.

Since it was obvious that the snail had entered the bottle at the point of manufacture, the plaintiff sued the manufacturers for negligence. In their defence, the manufacturers claimed that they owed no duty to the victim because they could not be expected to anticipate who would consume their product or anything that might happen to it in the meantime. This is not as ridiculous as it sounds because manufactured products go through several stages before reaching the consumer. At any of those stages the product could be inspected, modified or otherwise interfered with. To hold the producer responsible for damage done at any stage could place an undue hardship on manufacturers. Indeed, it was generally accepted before this case that a manufacturer had no duty to be careful to the ultimate consumer. It was also generally accepted, because of the way the law of negligence had developed, that the duty was owed only to those in the immediate vicinity. In this case, however, the plaintiff pointed out that the drink was bottled and capped with the idea that no intermediate inspection or interference would take place, and hence the bottle of ginger beer would get into the consumer's hands in the same condition in which it left the factory. In fact, the design of the product ensured this result. The Court of

[17] *Donoghue v. Stevenson*, [1932] A.C. 562 (House of Lords).

Appeal took an important step forward in the area of negligence when it decided that the manufacturers of the ginger beer did owe a duty to be careful to Mrs. Donoghue. Lord Atkin, the judge in the case, made the following classic statement when discussing how to determine to whom we owe a duty:

> The rule that you are to love your neighbour becomes in law, you must not injure your neighbour; and the lawyer's question, Who is my neighbour? receives a restricted reply. You must take reasonable care to avoid acts or omissions which you can reasonably foresee would be likely to injure your neighbour. Who, then, in law, is my neighbour? The answer seems to be—persons who are so closely and directly affected by my act that I ought reasonably to have them in contemplation as being so affected when I am directing my mind to the acts or omissions which are called in question.[18]

Duty owed to anyone who could foreseeably be harmed

We owe a duty, then, to anyone we can reasonably anticipate might be harmed by our conduct. Over the years, the decision of the court in *Donoghue v. Stevenson* has had a tremendous impact on the law of negligence both in England and in Canada. But problems arose when this test was applied to special situations such as negligent misstatement (as opposed to negligent conduct) and cases in which there was no physical damage, only economic loss. In 1977, the English *Anns* case[19] further developed the *Donoghue v. Stevenson* test by establishing that the court should go through a two-stage process in determining whether a duty to be careful existed. The first question to ask is whether there was a degree of neighbourhood or proximity between the parties such that if the person being sued had thought of it he or she would have realized that his or her actions posed a risk of danger to the other. Essentially this question restates the *Donoghue v. Stevenson* reasonable foreseeability test. The second question, however, is whether there was any reason that the duty should be not imposed, that the scope of the duty be reduced, that the class to whom the duty is owed be limited or that the damages be reduced. This question allows the court to consider social policy rather than strict legal rules when looking at special situations and relationships such as when negligent words are involved and when the damage complained of is only economic loss. The principles developed in the Anns case have been abandoned in England but appear to be still accepted as good law in Canada (the *Jervis Crown Case*).[20] Today, then, at least in this important area, the law of Canada and England seems to be diverging. It is enough to understand the principle that duty is established by the reasonable foreseeability test set out in *Donoghue v. Stevenson* and developed in the *Anns* case adopted by the Supreme Court of Canada.

This discussion of duty should not end without observing that as a practical matter the question of whether a duty is owed seldom comes up in actual court cases. In most situations the existence of duty is obvious and not the subject of litigation unless the action involves negligent misstatement or the loss is only economic. Usually the court is dealing with physical damage or injury and is asked only to

---

[18] *Ibid.*, p. 580.
[19] *Anns v. Merton, London Borough Council*, [1977] 2 All E.R. 492 (H.L.).
[20] *Canadian National Railway Co. v. Norsk Pacific Steamship Co.*, (1992) 91 D.L.R. (4th) 289 (S.C.C.).

determine whether the conduct of the person being sued fell below the standard imposed by that duty or to determine what monetary compensation ought to be paid. Still establishing a duty of care is the important first step in determining liability for negligence.

In addition to developing a general test to determine the existence of a duty to take care, *Donoghue v. Stevenson* also introduced the principle of product liability into English and Canadian tort law. Historically, because there were several intervening steps between the manufacturer and the ultimate consumer, it was accepted that the manufacturer owed no duty of care to the ultimate consumer. This case established, however, that if a product is designed in such a way as to get into the hands of the consumer without intervening inspection or modification, a duty of care does exist. When it can be shown that the manufacturer breached that duty through carelessness, a negligence action can be successfully brought against the manufacturer.

It must be emphasized, however, that the action must be based on negligence rather than strict liability. Although the result of *Donoghue v. Stevenson* may have made it easier for the plaintiff to prove negligence in such cases, negligence must still be shown. In the United States, the courts have imposed a much greater responsibility on manufacturers by only requiring injured consumers to demonstrate that a defect in the product caused the injury. There is no need to establish negligence by demonstrating the existence of a duty or the existence of a failure to live up to a standard of care.

This strict liability approach to product liability has not yet been adopted in Canada. In this country it is still necessary for a plaintiff to establish that the defendant was negligent. The courts in Canada, however, have relied on the principle of *res ipsa loquitur* in such cases, which goes some distance in making it much easier for the plaintiff to succeed in such an action. This principle is discussed below under the heading of "*Res Ipsa Loquitur.*" It should also be noted that it is becoming increasingly rare, especially when a civil jury is involved, for the manufacturer not to be found liable when its product causes injury. Whether this reflects a raising of the standard imposed, a move toward adopting strict liability, or a decision to place the liability on the party likely to have insurance remains to be seen.

MISFEASANCE AND NONFEASANCE. The law imposes a duty on people to be careful in carrying out their activities so that they will not cause harm to others. The courts will provide a remedy in a case of **misfeasance**, that is, when a person acts in a socially undesirable way. But the courts are very reluctant to provide a remedy in a case of **nonfeasance** (when a person fails to do something) unless it can be established that a particular relationship existed, such as in the case of a swimmer and lifeguard, or a child and guardian. People who see a child drowning have no duty in tort law to rescue that child unless they happen to be lifeguards. But if a person were to initiate and then abandon a rescue attempt, it is no longer a case of nonfeasance but a case of misfeasance. The would-be rescuer would have failed to live up to a socially imposed duty and the conduct would be actionable. There are many other situations in which a person can assume an obligation or a duty where there was previously no duty. When someone attempts to repair a car, there

Marginal notes:

To sue manufacturer negligence must be established

Unacceptable action— misfeasance

Failure to act— nonfeasance

is no duty in tort law requiring a friend to help. But if a friend does start to help, responsibility to act carefully is assumed. If lack of care results in damage to the car, the owner of the car would be able to sue for the damage caused, even though the work was performed for free.

Usually no duty

Like any other private citizen, a medical doctor has no legal obligation to render assistance at an automobile accident. On the other hand, if a doctor does start to help, he or she has an obligation to render assistance measuring up to the standard of a reasonable doctor in the circumstances. If the treatment given is lower than this high standard and further injury results, the doctor could be sued for negligence and would be liable for the resulting loss. In an attempt to alleviate such harsh consequences, some jurisdictions have introduced legislation designed to protect such rescuers from liability for injuries arising out of their rescue efforts. Without such legislation, the law would discourage people from helping because of the risks involved.

Doctor must give care up to a reasonable doctor's standard

Standard of Conduct

Once it has been established that a duty is owed, the court will determine the nature and extent of that duty, that is, what standard of care the defendant in the case was required to exercise. The reasonable person test is applied in a slightly different context: "What would a reasonable person have done in the circumstances?" If a reasonable person would have responded in the same way the defendant did, there is no negligence. However, if a reasonable person would have been more careful, then the defendant's actions fall below the standard accepted by society and he or she would be liable for any injury or loss resulting from the conduct.

Reasonable person test determines standard of care

The standard imposed by the court can vary depending on several different factors. The element of risk is an important consideration. A case heard in the English Court of the Exchequer in 1856 asked just how careful a person should be. In *Blyth v. Birmingham Water Works, Co.*,[21] the plaintiff's home was flooded when a water main serving a fire-plug froze and burst during a severe winter cold spell. The pipe had been installed 25 years before at a level deep enough to avoid freezing under normal conditions. The plaintiff's claim was that the pipe should have been placed deeper. The court decided in favour of the water works company because the weather that provoked the incident was the worst the city had experienced in 50 years. The court held that a reasonable person would not have incurred the significant additional expense involved in placing the pipe deeper. The standard of care was satisfied and there was no liability. The judge in the case said:

Risk of injury affects standard

> Negligence is the omission to do something which a reasonable man, guided upon those considerations which ordinarily regulate the conduct of human affairs, would do, or doing something which a prudent and reasonable man would not do.[22]

Negligence determined by what a reasonable person would do

---

[21] *Blyth v. Birmingham Water Works, Co.*, (1856) 156 E.R. 1047 (Court of Exchequer).
[22] *Ibid.*, p. 1049.

Risk can play a role in determining the standard of care required in other ways. A person driving a car is expected to be more careful than a person driving a wagon, not only because the risk of an accident is greater, but also because the potential for damage is greater. The greater the risk of injury, the higher the standard of care required. Similarly, the greater the potential for severe damage, the higher the standard imposed. The courts have shown that they will take into consideration the cost involved in reducing the risks and weigh them against the potential value of the loss resulting from the failure to reduce those risks. The point to remember is that a person must take steps to protect those who would be placed at unreasonable risk as a result of his or her conduct. It is reasonable to expect the areas of the Grand Canyon frequently visited by tourists to be fenced off, but it would be unreasonable to expect that a fence be placed around the whole canyon. Similarly, the courts are a lot more likely to regard the actions of the driver of a firetruck racing to a fire as reasonable than the same conduct exhibited by a person testing a new sports car.

Res Ipsa Loquitur

Res ipsa loquitur requires defendant to prove no negligence

To establish liability in a negligence action, it is usually necessary for the plaintiff to prove not only that the injury took place and that it was caused by the defendant, but also that the defendant was "careless" in that the conduct fell below an accepted standard of care. In some situations, however, such "carelessness" is apparent from the injury. For example, if a piano were to fall into the street from a fourth-floor apartment, injuring a passerby, those facts by themselves seem to say more eloquently than anyone could that the people who were handling the piano were careless in the way they moved it. In such circumstances, *res ipsa loquitur* is applied. This means, in essence, that the matter speaks for itself. Instead of the plaintiff having to prove that the defendant was careless, the obligation is shifted to the defendant to show that he or she was not negligent. This concept applies to negligence generally and may be raised in any negligence action where it is appropriate to do so. In Canada, it has become significant recently in the area of product liability. While U.S. courts have adopted a strict liability approach, in Canada it is still necessary for the plaintiff to establish that the defendant was negligent in the production of the product. This application of *res ipsa loquitur* means that, at least in the more blatant defective product cases, the plaintiff will not be required to prove carelessness on the part of the defendant. Instead, the defendant will be required to show that he or she was not careless in order to avoid liability.

Special Situations

Although great reliance has been placed on the reasonable person test in determining negligence, there are some situations in which the court will abandon that standard. Perhaps the most visible example is the degree of care demanded from the owner or occupier of property in relationship to the people who use that property.

Occupiers owe special duty

The obligation toward people using the property lies with the occupiers, or those in possession of the property, rather than the owners. In a rental situation, the obligation to keep the property free from dangers lies with the tenant, not the landlord. If a visitor is hurt while on the premises, the tenant, not the landlord, is normally responsible. Depending on the nature of the landlord/tenant relationship, the tenant might have some recourse to the landlord for compensation for loss suffered as a result of being sued.

Traditionally, a distinction was made between various kinds of visitors when assessing an occupier's liability. People who visited for business purposes or for some other mutually beneficial reason were said to be invitees and the occupier was required to take steps to protect them from any unusual dangers that existed on the property. Thus, if there were an obvious danger such as an open elevator shaft, the occupier would have a duty to fence it off to protect invitees. However, if the people were on the property out of sufferance, they were mere licensees (for example, people who habitually cut across the property with permission), and the duty was considerably less. The occupier was only obligated to warn licensees of any hidden danger. If an old mine shaft was near the path, the occupier would fulfil any obligation to licensees by putting up a warning sign.

Because of a Supreme Court of Canada decision, however, the nature of these distinctive duties has been cast into doubt.[23] The Ontario courts have gone so far as to declare that the distinction between the duty owed by an occupier to an invitee and the duty owed to a licensee has been abolished altogether.[24] The importance of this case is significantly reduced, however, due to the passage in Ontario of the *Occupiers' Liability Act* which eliminates the distinction between the nature of the duty owed to different classes of visitor using such property.[25] Other provinces have also eliminated this distinction through legislation. In Manitoba, for example, the *Occupiers' Liability Act*[26] imposes a duty on occupiers to take such care as is reasonable to protect the person or property of guests whether they are invitees, licensees or trespassers. Thus, in the case introducing this chapter, the garage proprietors were liable for the injuries the boy suffered because they had failed to take reasonable steps to protect him from the danger of the open cesspool, as required by the provincial act.

Invitee/licensee question may no longer be important

A similar problem exists when determining what duty is owed to trespassers. Again, the traditional approach is that the only duty occupiers owe is to refrain from wilfully or recklessly causing harm to trespassers. Thus it can be said that the trespassers take the property as they find it. If there are dangers, whether hidden or obvious, the trespassers take the risk and if they are injured, the occupier is not liable. However, because of the cases discussed above and because of a lack of specific provisions dealing with trespassers in the occupiers' liability legislation, there is confusion about the nature of the duty owed to trespassers. Whatever the situation,

---

[23] *Mitchell et al. v. Canadian National Railway Co.,* (1974) 46 D.L.R. (3d) 363 (Supreme Court of Canada).

[24] *Urzi v. North York Board of Education,* (1981) 116 D.L.R. (3d) 687 (Ontario High Court) Aff'd. (1982) 127 D.L.R. (3d) 768 (Ontario Court of Appeal).

[25] *Occupiers' Liability Act,* R.S.O. (1980) c.322.

[26] *Occupiers' Liability Act,* R.S.M. (1987) c.0.8.

it may well be that the duty is lower unless the occupiers have some reason to expect trespassers or someone else on the property.

Special duties of innkeepers

An even more onerous duty is imposed on occupiers when an inn or hotel is involved. Innkeepers owe a duty to their guests to provide protection from the wrongful acts of others even when the innkeeper or servant is not at fault. This is a much higher duty than would normally exist. It is only when the damage or loss to a guest's property is caused by his or her own negligence that the innkeeper is relieved of responsibility. Most provinces have reduced the common law liability of innkeepers through legislation but only when the provisions of that legislation are properly followed by the innkeeper.[27]

Modification imposed by statute

LEGISLATION. Because of the concept of supremacy of parliament, all of the standards that have been developed and imposed by the courts can be and often are modified by legislation. Motor vehicle acts, innkeepers' acts and occupiers' liability acts are a few examples of legislated changes in the common law standard of care. When reading these statutes one must be careful to determine whether they really do establish a different standard of care. If the statute applies to an area in which a common law obligation of tort is already in force, such as occupiers' liability, then the existence of legislation may increase or decrease that standard. However, when a statute prohibits some conduct traditionally not considered a tort, such as racial discrimination, that legislation will not create a new type of tort action unless specifically provided for in the legislation. For this reason, whenever human rights legislation is breached, victims must rely on the enforcement provisions set out in the statutes, rather than on bringing tort actions. Many statutes, especially in consumer and environmental protection areas, specifically create such a right of action for the victims.

The trend away from fault

Tort law generally, and negligence in particular, is a system based on the imposition of liability by the assessment of fault. Either one person or the other bears the loss, although this loss can be shared in some circumstances (see the discussion of contributory negligence below). In situations, however, where the potential of devastating loss exists, a system based on fault breaks down. Large judgments can be ruinous to the person found at fault or the victim may be left without compensation when the judgment debtor is unable to pay. This problem has become particularly pronounced when motor vehicles are involved, prompting several provinces to pass legislation requiring that all drivers have their cars insured against personal liability for accidents. Many consider compulsory insurance schemes to be only a partial measure. Ontario has gone further. It initially required that most accidents be dealt with on a no-fault basis. Only the more serious accidents with extensive personal injuries could be litigated and damages were awarded based on the fault of the participants. Recently Ontario has imposed a complete no-fault system even in the most serious accidents, the idea being that the loss is then distributed among all of the driving public in the form of compulsory insurance. Several other provinces have indicated an intention to follow suit.

[27] For example, *Hotel Keepers Act*, R.S.M. (1970) CCSM c.H-150.

Negligent Misstatement and the Liability of Professionals

The courts have always been reluctant to award damages when the only injury was economic loss unaccompanied by physical injury to person or property. This was especially true when the injury was caused by negligent misstatement and no contractual duty, fiduciary duty or fraud was present. It has only been in the past thirty years that the courts have granted compensation for this kind of loss. In 1963, the House of Lords was faced with this question in the case of *Hedley Byrne & Co. Ltd. v. Heller and Partners, Ltd.*[28] An advertising firm asked its bank to enquire into the financial condition of a client. The bank stated that the client was in a good financial position but disclaimed any responsibility for the statement. It turned out that the client was in very poor financial shape and, as a result, the advertising company lost a substantial amount of money. The advertising company sued the bank that had misled them. The House of Lords held that it was possible to award compensation for the victim of a negligent misstatement even if there had been no contract, no fiduciary duty and no fraud. But it also concluded in this particular instance that the bank's disclaimer absolved it of any responsibility and, therefore, the bank was not liable.

Since this decision, there have been many cases in which the courts have held defendants liable for the losses caused by their negligent words. The Supreme Court of Canada was faced with this problem in the case of *Haig v. Bamford et al.*[29] An accounting firm negligently prepared financial statements for a company knowing that the statements would be used to encourage investors. Mr. Haig purchased a number of shares, but found them to be considerably less profitable than the incorrect financial statements had led him to believe. As a result, he suffered a financial reversal.

In this case there was no direct relationship between Mr. Haig and the negligent accounting firm. The firm was negligent in the performance of its services to the firm of which Mr. Haig was merely a potential investor. Previously, the imposition of liability depended on the negligent conduct causing physical injury or damage. In this case, there was no physical contact and no physical loss. Mr. Haig lost money when he relied on the financial statement. This case is significant because, for the first time in Canada, liability for the tort of negligence was extended to pure economic loss caused by negligent words spoken by experts. As a result such experts find themselves responsible not only to their immediate clients, but to others who suffer loss because of their careless statements. The case of *Donoghue v. Stevenson* discussed above established that the test to be used to determine whether a duty of care exists in a negligence action is the reasonable foreseeability test.

Many argue vigorously, however, that this test is much too broad for determining liability when mere words are involved and only economic damage has been suffered. In fact, the judges in the Haig case did not go so far as to adopt this test but said only that a duty of care was owed when the person making the misleading statement knew it was to be used by a limited class of people. The *Anns* case discussed

Negligent words causing economic loss actionable

[28] *Hedley Byrne v. Heller* [1963] 2 All E.R. 575 (House of Lords).
[29] *Haig v. Bamford* (1976) 72 D.L.R. (3d) 68 (Supreme Court of Canada).

above has been welcomed in Canada because it retains this general reasonable fore-seeability test but provides a framework for dealing with negligent misstatement and mere economic loss on a more restrictive basis. The first question in *Anns* established duty based on the injury being reasonably foreseeable, but the second question allowed for this duty to be diminished or limited where considerations warranted the duty to be restricted to a specific class or the damages to be reduced. Haig clearly established that we can be held liable for our careless words but there has always been a question of where to draw the line. Now there seems to be some clarification: liability will be restricted to those situations where we knew (or should have known) that our words would be relied on by an individual or by someone who was a member of a group that we knew would be relying on the statement. It also seems clear that when only economic loss results from other forms of negligence, there are similar restrictions. It is still open for the Supreme Court of Canada to expand this definition and impose liability whenever careless words cause loss that is reasonably foreseeable, but given the conservative approach taken in England and shown by the lower courts in this country, it is doubtful they would go in this direction.

Pure economic loss recoverable

In the past, professionals and other experts only faced liability for shoddy work to their clients on the basis of contract law and to their colleagues and clients on the basis of a breach of a fiduciary duty. (Contract law will be covered in the following chapter and fiduciary duty will be described in the chapters devoted to business relationships.) Only experts such as architects and engineers whose services resulted in a physical structure were subject to liability if their negligence caused the structure to collapse. Today all professed experts who cause injury by their negligent misstatements may be held responsible for their words not only to their clients but to others hurt because they followed the advice. Whether the liability is for careless conduct or careless words, the standard of care imposed on professionals is very high.

Another problem in applying the reasonable person test to determine the standard of care required arises when dealing with people who have special skills and abilities. Essentially, they are required to have the skills and abilities that one would expect an expert or professional in the field of professed expertise to have. They are required to exercise that skill with a degree of care that would be expected from a reasonable person with the same expertise. The level of care expected from children and the mentally disabled reflects their degree of maturity or the extent of their disability.

Reasonable person in the circumstances

In assessing liability, the court determines what a reasonable person, possessed of the same skills and abilities as the defendant, would have done in the circumstances giving rise to the complaint. For a doctor, the test is that of a reasonable doctor; for an accountant, a reasonable accountant; and for a lawyer, a reasonable lawyer. It must be emphasized that a client or patient is not required to tolerate ineptitude on the part of professionals because of inexperience. It may be true that a doctor or mechanic in the first month of employment is more likely to make a mistake, but these people have represented themselves as proficient members of their profession and so must live up to the level of skill and competence one would expect of a normal member of their profession functioning in a reasonably prudent manner.

In addition, simply showing that the conduct complained of was common practice among a group of professionals will not necessarily absolve the defendant of liability for negligence. The test is that of a reasonable person, not an average person. Although one hopes that the average standard of practice in the skilled professions and the practice one would expect from a reasonable person would coincide, this is not always the case. When it is obvious that the common practice is dangerous or careless, then such sloppy practice will not be tolerated. The court, in such circumstances, is not reluctant to declare that the common practice falls below the standard of a reasonable person and is therefore negligent.[30] It is clear, however, that to find such negligence in the face of common practice in a profession would only happen in extraordinary circumstances.

Material Loss

Damage or injury must be present

In addition to establishing that the defendant owed a duty to be careful and failed to live up to that duty, the plaintiff must also show that some sort of loss to either person or property has been suffered. When the driver of a motor vehicle operates it in such a careless manner that it skids, narrowly missing another vehicle, it is obvious the driver has failed to live up to a standard of care. But since no damage has been done, there is no right to sue. However, if the driver of the vehicle that was almost struck suffered a heart attack because of the incident or a pregnant passenger miscarried, these would be tangible, physical injuries which would provide grounds for an action. If the driver of the second vehicle swerved to avoid the skidding vehicle and hit a tree, an action for damages could be brought. But without some sort of injury or damage, there is no claim.

In the past, the courts refused to grant compensation if the injury suffered had only an emotional or mental impact on the victim unless it was accompanied by physical symptoms such as vomiting, miscarriage, ulcers or heart problems. Similarly, the courts traditionally refused to find liability if the only injury suffered was economic loss due to loss of income. Today, there is no question that a victim can be compensated for economic loss, although what limits will be placed on the availability of purely economic loss is still in the process of development. Canadian courts have also shown a willingness to compensate victims if the result of the negligent conduct is a recognizable mental disorder such as depression or schizophrenia. Canadian courts are still reluctant to give an award if only mental distress such as anger or anxiety is claimed.

Causation

The injury complained of must be a direct result of the careless conduct. If the operator of a motor vehicle knowingly drives at night without tail-lights, the driver can be said to be careless. However, if the vehicle is involved in a head-on collision, the driver of the other car could not rely on the first driver's failure to have tail-lights

---

[30] *Chasney v. Anderson* (1950) 4 D.L.R. 223 (Supreme Court of Canada).

Conduct must be cause of injury

to support a negligence action. The test usually applied in such situations is called the **but for** test. The plaintiff must prove to the court's satisfaction that but for the complained-of conduct, no injury would have resulted. In this illustration, the plaintiff cannot say that but for a failure to have properly functioning tail-lights no collision would have occurred.

In the Ontario case of *Kauffman v. Toronto Transit Commission*,[31] two boys were scuffling on an escalator and bumped into a man causing him to fall against the plaintiff who in turn fell down and was injured. She sued the Toronto Transit Commission, claiming that they had been negligent in not supplying proper handrails. The court found that the Toronto Transit Commission had not been negligent. Mrs. Kauffman failed to prove that the lack of a handrail had anything to do with her injuries. The court was satisfied that she would have been injured no matter what handrail had been supplied. The plaintiff was unable to establish that, but for the negligent conduct of the Toronto Transit Commission, she would not have suffered an injury.

Defences

Once the plaintiff has established that the defendant owed a duty to be careful to the plaintiff, that the defendant's conduct fell below the standard of care required in the situation and that the conduct complained of caused some injury or loss to the plaintiff, negligence is established. Still there may be some matters the defendant can raise in defence. These are summarized below.

Problem of remoteness

REMOTENESS. It is clear that when the injury complained of is a direct result of negligent conduct, there is a right to sue for negligence. Where the connection between the conduct complained of and the injury is only tenuous, the defendant may be able to avoid liability. One of the most difficult problems in the law of negligence is when the connection between the damage suffered and the conduct complained of is remote or indirect, or when the resulting injury is out of all proportion to what one would have expected from the negligent conduct. Again, it is important to realize that the decision about where to draw the line is often no more than an application of social policy. In the case of *Abbot v. Kasza*,[32] Justice Clement of the Alberta Court of Appeal recognized the difficulty of developing any hard and fast rules in this area.

> The common law has always recognized that causation is a concept that in the end result must be limited in its reach by a pragmatic consideration of consequences; the chain of cause and effect can be followed only to the point where the consequences of an act will be fairly accepted as attributable to that act in the context of social and economic conditions then prevailing and the reasonable expectations of members of the society in the conduct of each other.[33]

---

[31] *Kauffman v. Toronto Transit Commission* (1959) 18 D.L.R. (2d) 204 (Ontario Court of Appeal).
[32] *Abbott v. Kasza*, (1977) 71 D.L.R. (3d) 581 (Alberta Supreme Court, Appellate Div.).
[33] *Ibid.*, p. 588.

Remoteness is an issue in those unique situations that we tend to regard as bizarre accidents. But when the problem does arise, the courts do little more than make policy decisions which have been variable and uneven. It was originally thought that whenever there was a direct cause and effect relationship between the conduct complained of and the injury, there was liability no matter how unusual that injury.[34] Subsequently, in a case referred to as *Wagon Mound #1*, which dealt with the problem of a spark from a welder's torch that fell on some floating cotton which ignited and caused a spill of bunker oil to catch fire, the English Privy Council adopted a different test. The court decided that a defendant is liable only if the injury itself is reasonably foreseeable.[35] But this position caused some unacceptable results and English courts continued to vacillate over the appropriate test to apply in this area.[36] The position in Canada is somewhat different from the present state of the law in England and is summarized by Mr. Justice Dickson in *The Queen v. Coté*.

> It is not necessary that one foresee the "precise concatenation of events"; it is enough to fix liability if one can foresee in a general way the class or character of injury which occurred.[37]

Foreseeability of type of injury sufficient

If it can be shown that the general type of injury suffered was reasonably foreseeable, that is enough to impose liability in Canadian law. It is easy to confuse this test for determining remoteness with the reasonable foreseeability test used to determine the existence of a duty in the first place. The distinction is that, when determining whether a duty exists, the court asks whether a reasonable person would have anticipated injury in any form as a consequence of the conduct. With remoteness, however, the test is whether a reasonable person would have anticipated the general nature of the injury suffered. Although the issue of remoteness relates to the existence of a duty of care, it is dealt with here because it is conceptually easier to deal with after the basic elements of negligence have been established.

Although there is much confusion in the application of these principles, there is one area of certainty when the nature but not the extent of a personal injury was reasonably foreseeable. The rule is simply that we take our victims as we find them. If a person has a weak heart, a tendency to a particular disease or a physical condition such as having a skull as thin as an eggshell, we cannot avoid responsibility by claiming that we could not reasonably be expected to foresee the special condition. If a person experiences greater injury from our conduct than would be expected because of a unique physical condition, there is nonetheless a responsibility to compensate for all consequences of the injury. This principle is often referred to as the **thin skull rule**. In the case of *Smith v. Leech Brain*,[38] the defendant's employee was hurt when he was struck on the lip by a drop of molten metal. Because of a pre-cancerous condition existing in the employee, this burn developed into cancer

---

[34] Re *Polemis v. Furness, Withy*, [1921] 3 K.B. 560 (Court of Appeal).
[35] *The Wagon Mound* (No. 1), [1961] A.C. 388.
[36] *The Wagon Mound* (No. 2), [1967] A.C. 617 (p.c.).
[37] *The Queen v. Coté* (1974) 51 D.L.R. (3d) at p. 252 (Supreme Court of Canada).
[38] *Smith v. Leech Brain* [1961] 3 All E.R. 1159 (Queen's Bench Division).

which eventually killed him. Although this consequence of the injury was in no way reasonably foreseeable, the employer was held liable for the death of the employee because the original accident was caused by the employer's negligence.

Contributory Negligence

When the plaintiff is partially responsible for his or her own loss, the defendant can raise this contributory negligence to reduce liability. Historically, whenever carelessness on the part of plaintiffs contributes to their injuries, they are considered to be the authors of their own misfortune and the defendant cannot be held responsible for the injury. For example, if a driver fails to stop at a stoplight and a second driver fails to notice the car coming into his path because he is busy adjusting his radio, he would not be able to recover for any injuries suffered in the resulting accident.

In this case, it is clear that the second driver was being careless by not being fully aware of what was happening on the road; this conduct at least contributed to the accident and completely bars the second driver from recovery of damages. Because this approach is rather harsh, it was somewhat modified by the **last clear chance doctrine**. This means that the person who had the last opportunity to avoid the accident is responsible for all of the loss. In the example given, the second driver could have avoided the accident if he had been paying attention. He must assume responsibility for the loss because he had the last chance to avoid the accident. This is a little fairer but also results in some unjust decisions, and legislation has been passed to alleviate this problem.

The *Negligence Act* in Ontario is a typical example.[39] The problem with the traditional common law approach of the last clear chance doctrine is that it is all or nothing. The *Negligence Act* permits the court to apportion responsibility between the two parties and then orders that compensation be paid in proportion to that assigned responsibility. In the example above, the first driver was at fault for driving through the stoplight and the second driver contributed to the accident through lack of attention. The courts would apportion liability and require both to bear some responsibility for the losses suffered.

Negligence of victim may reduce or eliminate award

Statute allows apportionment of responsibility

Voluntarily Assuming the Risk

When people voluntarily put themselves into positions where there is obviously risk of injury, the person in control of the dangerous situation may be able to avoid responsibility for injuries suffered by the volunteers. For example, if a passenger entered a motor vehicle knowing that the driver was intoxicated, he or she may be said to have voluntarily assumed the risk (*volenti non fit injuria*) and may be barred from recovery for injuries suffered in an accident caused by the intoxicated driver. But the risk must be obvious and there must be a clear indication from the conduct

[39] *Negligence Act*, R.S.O. (1980) c.315.

of the parties not only that they knew the risks and participated voluntarily, but also that they were giving up any claim against the driver if injury resulted. When a person puts himself or herself in harm's way like this, he or she is completely barred from recovering any damages. This is an all or nothing situation and the courts are now backing off from this approach. Now, for a claim of voluntary assumption of risk to bar recovery in a negligence action, the victims must make it clear that they are not only assuming the physical risk but the legal risk as well. They must make it clear that they are absolving the other party of any responsibility for any injuries or damage that results. Because, in fact, this rarely, if ever, happens, it is not likely today that a claim of voluntary assumption of risk will be successful. The courts now deal with such foolhardy behaviour under the heading of contributory negligence and this in turn permits the courts to apportion the loss between the parties—a much more satisfactory result.

The margin note: **The law will not assist volunteers**

The margin note: **But assumption of legal risk must be clear**

When a rescuer is involved, he or she cannot be said to have voluntarily assumed the risk. The person causing the danger should have anticipated the possibility of an attempted rescue. If the rescuer is injured, the author of the danger cannot escape liability by claiming the rescuer voluntarily assumed the risk. The person who caused the danger must pay compensation to both the victim and the injured rescuer.[40] Similarly, the principle does not apply to work-related accidents even if the work being performed is inherently dangerous.

Strict Liability

There are some situations in which the standard imposed is so high that there is liability no matter how cautious or careful the person responsible has been. The case of *Rylands v. Fletcher*[41] established a rule applicable in such instances. Rylands had a reservoir built on his property but was unaware of a shaft leading to a coal mine being operated by his neighbour. The accumulated water escaped, causing damage to the plaintiff's mine. It was clear from the facts that Rylands had not been negligent, nor was there any intentional wrongdoing. Nevertheless, the court held Rylands responsible for the damage done to his neighbour's mine. The principle adopted was that if something inherently dangerous is brought onto property and it escapes, the occupier is responsible for any consequence whether or not there is negligence or any other form of fault. The House of Lords supported Mr. Justice Blackburn's decision which said,

The margin note: **Strict liability imposed when dangerous substances escape**

> The true rule of law is, that the person who, for his own purposes, brings on his land and collects and keeps there anything likely to do mischief if it escapes, must keep it at his peril; and if he does not do so, is *prima facie* answerable for all the damage which is the natural consequence of its escape.[42]

[40] *Videan v. British Transport Commission* [1963] 2 All E.R. 860 (Court of Appeal).
[41] *Rylands v. Fletcher* (1868) L.R. 3 H.L. 330.
[42] *Ibid.* p. 339.

This principle may at first appear redundant given the rules of nuisance discussed above. There are, however, several distinctions between the rule of *Rylands v. Fletcher* and private nuisance. Private nuisance requires interference with the plaintiffs' use and enjoyment of their property whereas with dangerous activities it is only necessary to show an escape of the dangerous substance from the land of the defendant. Thus, even a passerby could sue if injured by the escaping substance. As well, a nuisance is usually an ongoing, continuous activity whereas the rule of *Rylands v. Fletcher* can be applied even when the event complained of has happened only once. In addition, the modern position appears to be that a defendant cannot be successfully sued for private nuisance unless some injury or harm was reasonably foreseeable, whereas the rule of *Rylands v. Fletcher* is both the origin and embodiment of the concept of strict liability.

Strict liability
involves escape
of dangerous
substance

Strict liability, that is, liability without fault, is also imposed when an employer is held liable for torts committed by employees during the course of their employment. The employer is without fault and yet is held liable for the wrongful acts of employees. This will be covered in Chapter 9 under the heading of Employer Liability. When dangerous products, processes or animals are involved, the standard of care required is high because the risk of injury is great. The obligations of persons in control approach strict liability. Food handlers, for example, find themselves in this unenviable position.

Other Business Torts

People involved in business activities can find themselves faced with tortious liability for their conduct in all of the categories of torts listed above. Businesses that deal directly with the public, especially in the service industries such as restaurants, hotels and retail merchandising, are often faced with their employees becoming involved in altercations with customers in the course of their employment. Such altercations can result in actions against the business based on vicarious liability for assault and battery, negligence, trespass and even false imprisonment. When business premises visited by customers or the public are involved, there can be actions for negligence based on occupiers' liability. Much more likely, however, are actions for negligence for injury or damage caused by improper performance of the service supplied. Even if only careless words are involved and the business is restricted to giving advice and opinions, there can now be liability to both clients and third parties who suffer financially from relying on those words. And if those words cause damage to someone's reputation, the business can be sued for defamation.

In addition to the categories of torts discussed in this chapter, there are a number of additional areas of tort liability that can be important to businesses. These business-related torts are primarily the following: inducing breach of contract, deceit, conversion, passing off, and defamation with respect to a product, called injurious falsehood.

Inducing breach
of contract
actionable

Inducing breach of contract usually involves an employer persuading an employee of another business to leave that employment and work for him. This practice is common when that employee has special knowledge about trade secrets or customer lists, or has a special relationship with customers enabling her to bring them with her to her new employment. If she is contractually committed to stay in that position of employment for a period of time or not to disclose the secret information, she will breach that contractual obligation if she does so. For the other employer to persuade her to do so, usually with financial incentives that make it worth the risk, violates a duty not to intervene in that relationship. The new employer may face the tort action of inducing breach of contract as a result. This type of tort can also be committed when one business induces another to breach contractual relations with someone else, as when a supplier is persuaded to abandon one customer in favour of a competitor.

Fraud or deceit actionable

The tort of deceit involves the fraudulent and intentional misleading of another person causing damage. This is a common wrong committed in business and will be dealt with in a subsequent chapter under the heading of Fraudulent Misrepresentation.

Coversion actionable

Conversion involves one person intentionally appropriating the goods of another person for his or her own purposes. Theft of goods, in addition to being a crime, is also actionable under the tort of conversion. When someone wrongfully disposes of goods belonging to someone else, such as by selling them, there is a conversion. Conversion also takes place when a person acquires possession of goods through deceit and the goods are damaged or destroyed to the extent that they are no longer of any value to the rightful owner. The courts in such circumstances will usually award damages as a remedy, the person converting the goods in effect being forced to purchase them. The courts also have the power to order the return of the goods if that is a more appropriate remedy. Of course, any direct intentional interference causing damage to the goods of another is a trespass to chattels, and other remedies may be available as a result.

Passing off actionable

A passing off action is appropriate when a business or product is presented to the public in such a way as to lead the public to believe that the product is being provided by another. When imitation Rolex watches are sold as the real thing or when a restaurant adopts the golden arches logo leading the public to believe it is part of the McDonald's chain when it is not, the tort of passing off has been committed. This will be discussed in more detail under the heading of Intellectual Property.

Injurious falsehood actionable

The tort of injurious falsehood will also be discussed under that heading. This tort takes place when one person attacks the reputation of another's product or business. When a person spreads a false rumour that the wine manufactured by a competitor is adulterated with some other substance or that his business is about to become bankrupt, she has committed an injurious falsehood. Although this tort is often called trade slander or product defamation, it must be distinguished from the tort of defamation which involves injury to the personal reputation of the injured party. Injurious falsehood deals with the reputation and value of a person's property.

SUMMARY

The law of torts protects people from intentional or unreasonable interference with their person, property or reputation. Assault and battery, trespass to land, false imprisonment and defamation are the most common examples of intentional torts. Consent or self-defence can be an adequate defence to assault and battery actions but when self-defence is used, only reasonable force can be involved. Trespass requires someone to enter directly or indirectly onto another's property without authority or permission. Trespass can take the form of a temporary intrusion, such as when someone comes onto the property or places some object onto it, or it can be a permanent intrusion, such as when a building or other structure is built on the property. For false imprisonment to be actionable the plaintiff must not only establish that there was an imprisonment, which can take a physical form with restraints or a mental form when someone submits to the authority of another, he or she must also establish that the imprisonment was done falsely, without authority. Defamation takes place when a false statement is made about a person to his or her discredit. Libel is written defamation and slander is spoken. Defences that may be available to defamation are absolute privilege, qualified privilege, truth, and fair comment.

Negligence is the most common form of tort action today. It involves inadvertent conduct falling below an acceptable standard of behaviour. To succeed in a negligence action the plaintiff must first establish that a duty of care was owed to the plaintiff. The test of reasonable foreseeability is used to establish that such a duty of care was present. In addition, to succeed, the plaintiff must show that the defendant's conduct fell below the level of conduct which would be expected from a reasonable person in the same circumstances, that material damage resulted from the conduct complained of, that the injury or damage was not too remote, and that the victim had not voluntarily assumed the risk. Historically, contributory negligence would also have absolved the defendant of any responsibility for the loss, but today statutes have been enacted in most jurisdictions that allow the courts to apportion the losses between the parties where contributory negligence is present.

QUESTIONS

1. Explain what is meant by the statement, "A tort is a civil wrong."
2. How do the courts usually determine what standard people must meet to avoid being declared negligent?
3. Distinguish between an assault and a battery.
4. How do doctors avoid liability for the tort of assault and battery when operating on, or otherwise treating, patients?
5. What limitations are there on the right of self-defence when people are defending themselves against an assault?
6. Describe the situations in which battery may be justified.
7. What are the necessary elements that must be present for a person to be classified as a trespasser?

8. Imprisonment can take the form of confinement, arrest or submission to authority. Explain.

9. What must be established to sue successfully for false imprisonment?

10. Distinguish between libel and slander and explain the significance of the distinction.

11. Define the terms innuendo and qualified privilege.

12. List and explain what a plaintiff must establish to succeed in a negligence action.

13. What test do courts use to determine whether the defendant owed a duty to be careful to the plaintiff?

14. What problem normally faced in product liability cases was overcome by the decision made in *Donoghue v. Stevenson*?

15. Distinguish between misfeasance and nonfeasance and explain the significance of the difference in tort law.

16. Explain how the test used to determine the standard of care required from professionals is different from the test used to determine the standard of care required generally.

17. Explain how the standard of care that an occupier must exercise to a person using the property has changed in recent years.

18. How does the *but for* test help to satisfy the requirements of causation?

19. Why is the case of *Hedley Byrne v. Heller* considered so important in the recent development of tort law?

20. Explain how the effect of the presence of contributory negligence has been modified in recent years.

CASES

1. *Chaytor et al. v. London, New York and Paris Association of Fashion.*
   The plaintiffs were employed by a competing department store and went to the defendant's place of business to compare prices. The defendant accused them of being spies, some angry words were exchanged, and the defendant called the store detective and told him to, "Watch these people." The defendant shouted at the plaintiffs to get out of the place and then telephoned the police. Two constables arrived shortly afterward and escorted the plaintiffs out of the store. When one of the plaintiffs started to go in another direction, the police took him by the arm and said, "You must come with us." The plaintiffs claimed they were falsely imprisoned but the police claimed they went with them voluntarily. Discuss.

2. *MacDonald et al v. Sebastian.*
   The plaintiffs, Mrs. MacDonald and several other tenants, lived in premises owned by the defendant landlord (Mr. Sebastian). Unfortunately, the

drinking water on the premises was contaminated by arsenic. The acceptable limit is .05 milligrams per litre of water and these premises had .36. The result was that Mrs. MacDonald and several members of her family became ill. What are the causes of action they may have against Mr. Sebastian? Outline any arguments that he may be able to raise in his own defence. Would your answer be affected if you were aware that Mr. Sebastian knew of the contamination before he rented the premises? If successful, can the victims get punitive damages?

3. *Van der Zalm v. Times Publishers, Bierman, McClintock and Underhill.*
The plaintiff was the Minister of Human Resources for the government of British Columbia and had been responsible for initiating some significant changes in the province's welfare programs. Many people in the province were very critical of what they perceived to be a restrictive and retrogressive approach to welfare. The defendants published in their newspaper a cartoon depicting the plaintiff "gleefully pulling wings from flies." The defendants claimed that since the plaintiff had carried on his duties as cabinet minister in a way that inflicted suffering on those who could not protect themselves, their depiction of him as cruel and thoughtless was fair comment. The evidence before the court, however, indicated that the minister had carried out his duties in good faith and there was no evidence to show that he was a person of cruel or sadistic character who enjoyed inflicting suffering. The court was left with the problem of deciding whether the message contained in the cartoon was fair comment. Discuss the probable outcome.

4. *Croker v. Sundance Northwest Resorts Ltd.*
As part of the festivities associated with an event called the Sundance Spring Carnival, the defendants, who were operators of a ski slope, put on an inner tube race. This race was run on the regular ski slopes in a section where there were "moguls" that caused the tubes and the people on them to bounce around like "rag dolls." A videotape of the event showed the contestants "falling off these tubes, being bounced off, releasing their grip, chasing after the tubes and generally having what was described by the plaintiff's co-contestant as a "blast." The plaintiff (Croker) signed up for the race and in the process signed, without reading, a release absolving the defendant of all responsibility for any injuries he might suffer as a result of the race. The plaintiff and his co-contestant, in a festive mood, went down the slope once with only minor injury and won their heat. By the second heat it was clear that Croker had been drinking and the manager of the facility suggested that he should not go down the hill. Croker went anyway and in the process fell off the tube, breaking his neck. The consequence of this injury was that he became a paraplegic. The plaintiff sued the defendant for compensation for the injuries received. Discuss the liability of the parties.

5. *Mallet v. Shulman et al.*

   Mrs. Mallet, a Jehovah's Witness, was in a serious automobile accident. She was taken to the hospital in an unconscious state where Dr. Shulman determined that a necessary part of the treatment that she needed to preserve her life was a blood transfusion. Before it was given, the nurse discovered a card which stated that she was a Jehovah's Witness and under no circumstances was she to be given a blood transfusion. The doctor went ahead and gave her a blood transfusion anyway. Her daughter was contacted and even when her daughter insisted that the transfusion be stopped the doctor continued with it. Mrs. Mallet eventually recovered and sued the doctor and the hospital. What is the nature of her complaint? Explain the arguments supporting the positions of both parties and the likely outcome. Would your answer be different if it could be clearly established that she would have died without the transfusion? How would your answer be affected if the patient had been fifteen years old?

6. *Dixon v. Deacon Morgan McEwan Easson*

   Mr. Dixon was an investor who chose to invest $1.2 million in National Business Systems when the share price was $12.89 per share. These shares went up in price somewhat but, before he could sell, the Securities Commission suspended trading. When trading resumed the shares sold at about $3. Dixon had invested on the strength of financial statements, including one marked "Consolidated Statements of Income and Retained Earnings (Audited)" which had been audited by the defendants. In fact these statements were based on fraudulent information supplied by the management of National Business Systems to indicate annual profits of $14 million when the company had lost $33 million. There is no question that the accounting firms involved in the audit were negligent for not detecting the inaccuracy. Mr. Dixon sued the accounting firm for negligence. Nothing on the document indicated who the auditors were and the statements had been prepared without the auditors knowing that they would be used by an investor such as Mr. Dixon. The question the court had to determine was whether the auditor owed a duty to Mr. Dixon to be careful. If the auditors had known that the statements were being prepared to attract investors, would this affect your answer?

7. *Nicholson v. John Deere Ltd.*

   The plaintiffs purchased a second-hand riding lawnmower manufactured by the defendant, John Deere Ltd. Before using the mower one day, Mrs. Nicholson opened the hood to fill up the gas tank. She took off the cap and placed it on the tank and started to pour in the gas. She had to stop to retrieve the gas cap when it rolled off the tank. She again placed it on the hood and continued to pour gas into the tank. The cap rolled away again; this time it hit the battery and caused a spark that ignited the gasoline fumes. As the fire started, she spontaneously dropped the gasoline can she was holding, spilling the gas. The resulting fire destroyed both the garage and her home. (Note that there was a decal on the gas tank and a note in the owner's manual warning of this potential danger.) Mrs. Nicholson sued the manufacturer for compensation for the losses she had suffered. Discuss the grounds for her complaint and the defences which might be available to John Deere Ltd. Consider how this discussion is affected by the knowledge that John Deere recognized the danger associated with their product and manufactured a battery-covered safety kit to solve the problem. They also took steps to warn the users of their mower of the danger and of the availability of the safety kit.

ISSUES

1. It is possible for wrongful conduct to be both a tort and a crime. Defendants may find themselves in the unpleasant position of having to appear in court to answer a criminal charge while also being on trial in another court for a tort action arising from the same conduct. Some jurisdictions feel that this is inappropriate and have passed legislation denying the right to proceed with a civil action once a criminal prosecution has begun in cases of assault and battery. Is it appropriate to permit a person who has engaged in wrongful conduct to be prosecuted criminally and also be required to answer for his or her conduct in a civil tort action?

2. Plaintiffs in slander actions are usually required to show that they have suffered some sort of special damages such as lost wages, medical expenses or some other type of expense for which bills can be produced. In a libel action, however, it is sufficient to show general damages such as loss of reputation, loss of future income, etc. Is it appropriate for the courts to require different standards of proof in actions for slander as opposed to libel actions?

3. Many types of prohibited conduct are included under the heading of torts and each has a different test, standard of behaviour and remedy. Many people have tried to reconcile these differences. The question for discussion is: Would our legal system be more effective with one consistent approach to wrongful conduct, no matter what category of tort it falls into, or is justice better served by recognizing that these are diverse human activities and each needs unique and individual treatment?

4. Tort law is designed to provide compensation for injury or damages suffered. There are some situations, however, in which the courts will award a remedy

even when no injury has been inflicted. In a trespass action, the mere bruising of the grass is enough to entitle the victim to a remedy. For some kinds of tortious conduct, such as defamation and assault, the courts will often award punitive or exemplary damages to the plaintiff, thus shifting their attention from compensating the victim to punishing the wrongdoer. This remedy is not available for other tortious conduct such as negligence. The questions for discussion are: Is it appropriate for the civil court to abandon the principle of compensation and award damages where no loss has been suffered by the person suing? Should the types of remedies vary with the different types of torts committed?

5. A strict liability approach has been developed in product liability cases in the United States. In Canada, however, a person seeking compensation for damages suffered from the use of a product when no contract exists must show not only that the product was defective in some way but must also demonstrate that the manufacturer or manufacturer's employee was negligent. Should these requirements be abandoned?

6. The reasonable person test is used to determine negligence and is used in many other areas of the law. This test allows the court to impose an objective standard of behaviour that is higher than the level of conduct one would expect from the average person. Is it appropriate, especially in the area of negligence, to assess fault and assign liability based on a test that requires the exercise of such a high level of care by the defendant in these circumstances?

7. The normal method of determining whether a duty exists in tort law to be careful to another person is the test developed by Lord Atkin in *Donoghue v. Stevenson*, referred to as the **good neighbour test**. Under this test, defendants owe a duty to anyone they can reasonably foresee might be harmed by their careless conduct. Before 1963, it was thought that if the injury suffered was only economic loss for negligent misstatement, no remedy was available. This was changed by the House of Lords in *Hedley Byrne v. Heller*. The judges in this case were careful, however, to point out that the normal reasonable foreseeability test for determining whether a duty is owed was too broad when dealing with negligent misstatement and they considerably narrowed the concept in these circumstances. The Canadian Supreme Court broadened the principle in *Haig v. Bamford*, but many still argue that they did not go so far as to reintroduce the reasonable foreseeability test used for other negligence cases. Is it appropriate for the courts to be restrictive in determining to whom a duty is owed for pure economic loss caused by negligent misstatement but to allow the much broader approach of reasonable foreseeability to be used when physical injury is involved? When only economic losses are involved, is it ever justified to impose liability on the negligent party without some sort of explicit or implied voluntary assumption of responsibility?

LEGISLATION

Alberta
Contributory Negligence Act, R.S.A. (1980) c.C-23
Fatal Accidents Act, R.S.A. (1980) c.F-5
Innkeepers' Act, R.S.A. (1980) c.I-4
Occupiers' Liability Act, R.S.A. (1980) c.0-3
Tortfeasors Act, R.S.A. (1980) c.T-6

British Columbia
Hotel Keepers Act, R.S.B.C. (1979) c. 182
Libel and Slander Act, R.S.B.C. (1979) c.234
Negligence Act, R.S.B.C. (1979) c.298
Occupiers' Liability Act, R.S.B.C. (1979) c.303
Privacy Act, R.S.B.C. (1979) c.336
Trespass Act, R.S.B.C. (1979) c.411

Manitoba
Defamation Act, R.S.M. (1987) c.D-20
Fatal Accidents Act, R.S.M. (1987) c.F-50
Hotel Keepers Act, R.S.M. (1987) c.H-150
Nuisance Act, R.S.M. (1987) c.N-120
Occupiers' Liability Act, R.S.M. (1987) c.0-8
Petty Trespassers Act, R.S.M. (1987) c.P-50
Privacy Act, R.S.M. (1987) c.P-125
Tortfeasors and Contributory Negligence Act, R.S.M. (1987) c.T-90

New Brunswick
Contributory Negligence Act, R.S.N.B. (1973) c.C-19
Defamation Act, R.S.N.B. (1973) c.D-5
Fatal Accidents Act, R.S.N.B. (1973) c.F-7
Innkeepers' Act, R.S.N.B. (1973) c.I-10
Tortfeasors Act, R.S.N.B. (1973) c.T-8
Trespass Act, R.S.N.B. (1973) c.T-11.2

Newfoundland
Contributory Negligence Act, R.S.N. (1990) c.C-33
Defamation Act, R.S.N. (1990) c.D-3
Fatal Accidents Act, R.S.N. (1990) c.F-6
Innkeepers' Act, R.S.N. (1990) c.I-7
Petty Trespass Act, R.S.N. (1990) c.P-11
Privacy Act, R.S.N. (1990) c.P-22

Nova Scotia

Contributory Negligence Act, R.S.N.S. (1989) c.95
Fatal Injuries Act, R.S.N.S. (1989) c.163
Innkeepers' Act, R.S.N.S. (1989) c.229
Occupiers of Land Liability Act, R.S.N.S. (1989) c.322
Tortfeasors Act, R.S.N.S. (1989) c.471

Ontario

Innkeepers' Act, R.S.O. (1990) c.I.7
Libel and Slander Act, R.S.O. (1990) c.L.12
Negligence Act, R.S.O. (1990) c.N.1
Occupiers' Liability Act, R.S.O. (1990) c.D.2
Trespass to Property Act, R.S.O. (1990) c.T.21

Prince Edward Island

Contributory Negligence Act, R.S.P.E.I. (1988) c.C-21
Defamation Act, R.S.P.E.I. (1988) c.D-5
Fatal Accidents Act, R.S.P.E.I. (1988) c.F-5
Innkeepers Act, R.S.P.E.I. (1988) c.I-2
Occupiers' Liability Act, R.S.P.E.I. (1988) c.0-2
Trespass to Property Act, R.S.P.E.I. (1988) c.T-6

Saskatchewan

Contributory Negligence Act, R.S.S. (1978) c.C-31
Fatal Accidents Act, R.S.S. (1978) c.F-11
Hotel Keepers Act, R.S.S. (1978) c.H-11
Libel and Slander Act, R.S.S. (1978) c.L-14
Privacy Act, R.S.S. (1978) c.P-24

Northwest Territories

Contributory Negligence Act, R.S.N.W.T. (1988) c.C-18
Defamation Act, R.S.N.W.T. (1988) c.D-1
Hotel Keepers Act, R.S.N.W.T. (1988) c.H-5

Yukon

Contributory Negligence Act, R.S.Y. (1986) c.32
Defamation Act, R.S.Y (1986) c.41

CHAPTER

3 FORMATION OF CONTRACTS

Objectives of the Chapter

- to list and describe the requirements of a valid contract
- to show the necessary conditions for an offer and an acceptance to be effective
- to explain the requirements of consideration in a contract
- to describe the principles of promissory estoppel and *quantum meruit*
- to show when a seal is required to validate a contract

Mr. and Mrs. McIntyre decided to purchase a house being offered for sale by the Pietrobons. They signed an interim agreement and paid a deposit of $10 000. The interim agreement contained a standard provision, which stated "Subject to purchaser obtaining satisfactory personal financing." The McIntyres didn't obtain financing; they didn't even try. They simply changed their minds and wanted their $10 000 deposit back. The Pietrobons would not return the money because they claimed that the McIntyres had breached their contract and had forfeited their right to it. The McIntyres sued. The judge held that since the clause was so vague there was no agreement, and ordered the return of the money.[1] The terms of a contract must be certain and show that there is in fact agreement between the parties over what their obligations are. While this decision may yet be challenged as an accurate summary of the law in this area, it does illustrate the need

[1] *McIntyre v. Pietrobon* (1987) 15 B.C.L.R. (2d) 350 (BCSC).

for people working in real estate and other industries to be well versed in the law and very careful when drawing up such agreements. Contracts are the subject of this and the following three chapters.

THE CONTRACTUAL RELATIONSHIP

A knowledge of contract law is vital to all business people because most commercial transactions have contracts at their base. A general understanding of the principles upon which contracts are made is important to anyone who enters a store, buys a drink, purchases a postage stamp, rides a bus, invests in a car or buys a house. **A contract is a voluntary exchange of promises, creating obligations which if defaulted on, can be enforced and remedied by the courts.** A contract may be written, verbal or implied. It creates a relationship in which the contracting parties establish a world of law unto themselves. The modern principles of contract law developed at a time when laissez-faire was the dominant economic principle so the courts have adopted a hands-off approach to the contractual relationship, often referred to as freedom of contract. Thus, for the most part, courts do not concern themselves with the social desirability or fairness of the contract but simply enforce the rights and obligations the parties have assumed in their agreement.

Contracts may be written, verbal or implied

Ingredients of a Contract

Agreements are enforceable in our courts if they meet certain basic qualifications. These are:

1. CONSENSUS. Parties to a contract must reach a mutual agreement to commit themselves to a certain transaction. They are assumed to approach the agreement from equal bargaining positions, free to enter it as they choose. The process by which this agreement is reached involves an offer and an acceptance.

2. CONSIDERATION. There must be a commitment on the part of both parties to do something or to abstain from doing something. The consideration is the price each is willing to pay to participate in the contract.

3. CAPACITY. Parties to a contract must be legally capable of understanding and entering into the bargain. Limitations in contracting capacity have been placed on infants, insane or intoxicated persons, aliens and, in some instances, Native peoples and corporations.

4. LEGALITY. The object and consideration involved in the agreement must be legal and not against public policy.

5. INTENTION. Both parties must be serious when striking the bargain and both must intend that legally enforceable obligations will result from it.

WRITING. Although the general rule is that an agreement reached verbally between parties is every bit as binding as a written one, legislation has been passed requiring that certain types of contracts be supported by evidence in writing before they can be enforced in the courts.

Terms and Definitions

Before addressing these elements of a contract in more detail, it is necessary to outline some basic terminology used in the discussion of contractual obligations.

FORMAL OR SIMPLE CONTRACTS. A formal contract is one under seal. A modern seal is usually a paper wafer affixed to a document by the party to be bound. Simple contracts, sometimes called parol contracts, may be verbal or written but are not under seal.

EXPRESSED OR IMPLIED CONTRACTS. An expressed contract is one in which the parties have stated their agreement either verbally or in writing. An implied contract is inferred from the conduct of the parties. When people deposit coins in vending machines, it can be inferred that they intend to create a contractual relationship and thus an implied contract is in force. Portions of an expressed contract may also be implied.

VALID, VOID AND VOIDABLE CONTRACTS. A valid contract is one which is legally binding on both parties. A void contract does not qualify as a legally binding contract because of some missing ingredient. If the parties to a void contract thought they were bound and followed the agreement, the courts would try to put the parties back to their original positions. A voidable contract does exist and has legal effect, but one of the parties has the option to end the contract. This distinction between void and voidable can have important implications for outsiders to the contract who have acquired an interest in the subject matter.

UNENFORCEABLE AND ILLEGAL CONTRACTS. An example of an unenforceable contract is one that is required to be in writing under the Statute of Frauds, and is not. It may be good and valid in all other respects, but the courts will not help either party to force the other to perform such a contract. As well, if it has been performed, the courts will not help either party get out of it. An illegal contract is one that has as its objective the performance of an unlawful act. It is void and the parties to such an agreement cannot be required to perform it. If the contract has been performed or partially performed, the court, because of the moral taint, normally will not assist either party to undo it by returning them to their original positions as would usually be the case in a void contract. For example, when a deposit has been paid, the court will not order its return nor will it require property to be returned even when one of the parties has been enriched at the other's expense. The status of these two types of agreement then is quite different. The unenforceable contract is valid and the illegal contract is void, but they are handled in a similar fashion by the court. However, the courts are more sympathetic where an unenforceable contract is involved and are more likely to help the parties when disputes arise than is the case with an illegal contract.

BILATERAL AND UNILATERAL CONTRACTS. A bilateral contract is one in which both parties assume obligations before performance. There is no exchange of promises in a unilateral contract. A promise is made by only one party without a corresponding commitment from the other. Only when the other party voluntarily does what has been requested does the contract comes into effect. A reward is an example of a unilateral contract. It is not until the lost item is returned that the offer is accepted and the contract created.

Consensus

The essence of a contract is, at least in theory, the meeting of the minds of the contracting parties. Both parties must have a common will in relation to the subject matter of their negotiations and they must have reached an agreement. They must share an understanding of the bargain struck and be willing to commit themselves to the terms of the contract. However, if people were bound only to the terms of contracts they fully understood, there would be few enforceable contracts. Few people thoroughly read the major contracts they enter into, such as insurance policies, leases and loans, and of those who do, few fully understand the specific meaning of the documents. The law does not recognize the excuse that one of the contracting parties did not read the contract or that he or she did not understand it. Both parties must have had an opportunity to read and understand the contract for it to be valid. That is, the terms of the contract must be unambiguous, so that if they are read with the help of a lawyer a reasonable person could understand the meaning of the terms. If the meaning of the terms is ambiguous, then the court will decide that there has been no consensus between the parties and the contract may be declared void. This was the problem with the agreement used to introduce the chapter. Because of the vague nature of the terms, the would-be purchasers were successful in getting back their deposit—there was no contract.

Obviously, mistakes happen and some very complex rules, which we will discuss later, have been developed to handle them. Nevertheless, contract law is based on the assumption that the culmination of the bargaining process is when one party states its position in the form of an offer in the expectation that the other party, through acceptance, will make a similar commitment to be bound by the terms of the offer.

Agreement reached— bargain struck

Terms must be clear and unambiguous

Offer

Offer—tentative
promise

The offer contains all of the terms to be embodied in the contract; all that is required of the other party is to give its consent or denial. The offer is a tentative promise on the part of one party to do something if the other party is willing to do whatever the first party requests. When a person offers to sell a car to someone for $500, the offer is a tentative promise by the first party to make a commitment to deliver the car contingent on the second party's willingness to promise to pay $500. The process of making an offer is the communication of a willingness to be bound and the terms and conditions upon which the intention is based.

This aspect of the offer often confuses those involved in commercial activities. People borrowing money, acquiring insurance and so forth frequently have a form placed before them by a salesperson who says, in effect, "This is our contract; sign here." In fact, the document is not a contract at all but only an offer. Once accepted and signed by the customer, the document embodies the terms and conditions of the contract. The offer must contain all significant terms of the contract. The courts do have the power to imply into contracts many of the insignificant terms the parties may not have considered, such as time of delivery, time of payment and so on. Such terms must be incidental to the central agreement, but consistent with the apparent intention of the parties. In fact, it is possible for the courts to infer the entire contract from the conduct of the parties but if important terms are left out, there can be no contract and it will be declared void.

The case of *Rossdale v. Denny*[2] involved a long-term lease in the possession of Major Denny for a property known as Marble Arch. After some negotiation, Rossdale made an offer to purchase the lease that contained the term, "This offer is subject to a formal contract to embody such reasonable provisions as my solicitors may approve." Major Denny accepted the offer, but subsequently, the parties had a disagreement and Major Denny refused to go through with the agreement. The court held that there had been no contract and that Rossdale could not successfully sue Major Denny since what was purported to be the offer contained terms indicating that the parties were to agree upon important items later. Thus, when parties either neglect to include important terms in their agreement or agree to leave something to be negotiated later, they have not entered into a contract.

Offer—must
include all
important terms

Some types of contractual relationships, often referred to as quasi-contracts, must be viewed as exceptions to this rule. Parties seldom agree in advance on the precise cost of the services of doctors, lawyers, mechanics, builders, etc. Although this is a significant term that has not been agreed upon, there is still an obligation to pay. To attempt to evade a mechanic's repair bill on the basis that there was no indication of the ultimate cost is unfair and the courts would not recognize such a claim. Although there is no question that there is an obligation to pay for the service, the precise amount of the bill can be disputed. The courts would apply the reasonable person test. The customer who has requested the services is only obligated to pay a reasonable amount for them. However, if the customer pays the bill or in

Note exception
for service
contracts.

[2] *Rossdale v. Denny* [1921] 1 Ch. 57 (Court of Appeal).

some other way indicates acceptance of the amount the total charge is no longer open to question. This exception may be imposed by statute as well. For example, provincial sale of goods acts require a reasonable price to be paid for goods where no price was agreed on.

INVITATION TO TREAT. An offer is usually made to an individual or a group of people but it is also possible to make an offer to the world at large, such as a newspaper ad offering a reward for the return of a lost item. Generally, however, newspaper advertisements are called invitations to treat and are simply invitations to engage in the process of negotiation. It is sometimes difficult to distinguish between an offer and an invitation to treat. An ad in the newspaper which says, "Automobile tires for sale, two for the price of one," is not an offer at all. The potential customer must go to the shop, look at the tires and determine the value of the deal. The ad is simply an invitation to the reader to visit the place of business and make an offer to purchase some tires. Catalogues and personal ads in the classified section of a newspaper are also invitations to treat. To identify an invitation to treat as an offer and saddle the person making the invitation with the responsibilities entailed by that offer would short-circuit the whole process. If a merchant were to advertise a one only item for sale and it was accepted by ten people, this would create an impossible situation.

Invitation not an offer

Goods displayed on the shelves of stores, even though the prices of items are clearly marked, are only an invitation to the customer to pick up the desired item, take it to the checkout counter and make an offer to purchase it at the price marked.

Display is an invitation, not an offer

There is still some controversy over this point, but most jurisdictions have accepted the principle established in *Pharmaceutical Society of Great Britain v. Boots Cash Chemists (Southern), Ltd.*[3] In this case, the English Court of Appeal was faced with the problem of deciding whether a statute controlling the sale of certain types of drugs had been violated. The court had to determine whether clearly priced goods displayed on the shelf of a self-service merchandising operation were being offered for sale. The court determined that such a display was an invitation to treat and not an offer.

Another English case, *Fisher v. Bell*,[4] demonstrates the significance of the distinction between an offer and an invitation to treat. A shopkeeper displayed a prohibited type of knife in his window and was charged with "offering for sale" a prohibited weapon. He was acquitted because the display of the knife was not an offer but rather an invitation to treat.

Since the display of an item is merely an invitation to treat, some people might be tempted to make any offer they want. They might take a grease pencil to the store, change the price and make their own offer. However, the principle is that shoppers are being invited to make the offer indicated by the price on the product. If they want to make any other offer, they must bring this fact to the attention of the vendor. Otherwise, such misleading price alteration can qualify as a crime.

---

[3] *Pharmaceutical Society of Great Britain v. Boots Cash Chemists (Southern), Ltd.* [1952] 2 All E.R. 456 Queen's Bench Div. (Aff'd. by Court of Appeal [1953] 1 All E.R. 482).
[4] *Fisher v. Bell* [1960] 3 All E.R. 731 (Queen's Bench Div.).

Offer may be
implied from
conduct

OFFER BY CONDUCT. A customer in a self-serve store brings the goods to be purchased to a cashier and places the goods and money on the counter. This is an offer by conduct. When a person hails a cab, the gesture of raising a hand and calling "Taxi" constitutes an offer. An auctioneer's comment, "Do I hear $50?" is merely an invitation to the customer to make an offer. When a person in the audience raises a hand or makes some other acceptable gesture, that is the offer, and the auctioneer is free to accept or reject it. A further question, "Do I hear $60?" is an invitation for more offers. The statement, "Sold" is an acceptance of the customer's offer.

COMMUNICATION OF AN OFFER. Before offers can be accepted, they must first be communicated to the offerees; people cannot accept offers they know nothing about. If a lost dog is returned by someone who is unaware that a reward had been offered, he or she has no right to claim the reward since the offer has not been communicated. Another situation in which the communication of an offer can present a problem is when two offers cross in the mail. If one party sends a letter to another offering to sell a car for $500 and the person to whom the offer is sent, unaware of the first letter, sends another letter offering to purchase the car for the same price, there is no contract. Even though the parties are of a similar mind, neither is aware of the other's offer when the letters are sent and so neither could be called an acceptance. If the owner of the vehicle sells it to a third party, the other party would have no complaint. Similarly, if a person fails to bring all the terms of the offer to the attention of the offeree, the uncommunicated terms do not form part of the contract and are not binding on the offeree.

Offer must be
communicated

A merchant will often try to include as part of a contract a term exempting or limiting liability for improper performance of the contract. At a parking lot, for example, there is usually a sign disclaiming responsibility for theft or damage to cars or contents left on the lot. A ticket granting admission to a racketball court or to use a ski lift often includes a term disclaiming responsibility for injury, damages or loss of personal property by theft. In both cases the term is only binding where it has been reasonably brought to the attention of the patron at the time the contract is made. The sign in the parking lot must be placed in a well-lit, strategic spot where the driver will see it before or at the time the contract is made. If a ticket is involved and the terms are listed on the back, there must be a reference on the front of the ticket drawing the patron's attention to it. The ticket must be given at the time the contract is made, not afterwards.

Only person(s) to
whom offer is
made can accept

Only the person to whom the offer is made can respond to it. If the offer is made generally, anyone fulfilling the terms can respond. If the offer is made to a group, anyone in the group satisfying the terms can respond to the offer. But if the offer is made to a specific person, no one else can accept it.

THE END OF AN OFFER. For the acceptance of an offer to be effective, the offer must be in force at the time of the acceptance. There are several ways for an offer to come to an end before acceptance.

1. *End of a specified time.* If the offer contains a term specifying when the offer will come to an end, the expiration of that time will end the offer. The time

Offer ends when specified

limit may be a specific date or a period of time. The offeror can end the offer before the expiration of that date by communicating to the offeree that the offer is revoked. In order to guarantee that an offer be left open until the expiration date, the offeree must give the offeror something extra just to hold the offer open until the specified time. This separate contract is called an option.

—at a reasonable time

2. *The expiration of a reasonable time.* If no time is specified for the offer to end, it will expire at the end of a reasonable time. The answer to the problem of determining what is a reasonable time is provided by examining the circumstances. Thus, one would expect an offer to sell a ship to be held open longer than an offer to sell a load of ripe peaches.

—at death of offeror

3. *Death or insanity of offeror.* If the offeror dies or becomes insane to the extent of being incapable of understanding what he or she is doing, the offer automatically ends and cannot be accepted. This is the case even if the offeree is unaware of the death or insanity.

—when revoked

4. *Revocation of offer.* The offeror may revoke an offer any time before acceptance. For such revocation to be effective, it must be communicated. Thus, revocation is accomplished, very simply, when the offeror tells the offeree that he or she is no longer willing to enter the contract. However, if the offeree accepts the offer before learning of the revocation, there is a valid, binding contract. To make sure, the offeror should specifically revoke the offer and not do anything with the goods involved until it is certain that the revocation has been communicated.

Revocation must be communicated

In the case of *Dickinson v. Dodds*,[5] Mr. Dodds offered to sell Mr. Dickinson some property and stated that the offer had to be accepted before 9:00 a.m. the following Friday. During the week, Dodds sold the property to a third party. Dickinson found out about this and took steps to ensure that an acceptance was in Dodds' hands before the deadline. The court was asked to decide if Dodds had effectively revoked the offer before acceptance. The court held that because Dickinson knew "beyond a shadow of a doubt" that Dodds had changed his mind, there was an effective revocation implied in the sale of the property to the third party. It is important to realize that if Dickinson had not learned of the sale before he accepted, Dodds would have been in serious difficulty. This case also illustrates the point that even if an offeror promises to keep an offer open for a specified time, he or she is free to revoke it before that time expires if no option has been purchased.

REJECTION AND COUNTEROFFER. During the bargaining process, several different proposals may be put forward, rejected and then followed by counter-proposals. If each proposal and counter-proposal remained in effect, the purpose of the bargaining process would be defeated because none of the parties involved would know where they stood. To solve this difficulty, the courts have developed the principle that whenever an offer is put forward and rejected or a counter-proposal is put forward, which by implication is a rejection, the first offer is brought to an end. For example, if somebody offers to sell a car to another person for $500 and that person replies, "I'll give you $450," a counteroffer has been made and, by implication,

---

[5] *Dickinson v. Dodds* (1876) 2 Ch. 463 (Court of Appeal).

the original offer has been rejected. If the seller rejects the counteroffer, it is too late for the purchaser to reconsider and accept the original offer; it no longer exists. Under such circumstances, an attempt to accept the original $500 offer constitutes a new offer which the seller is free to accept or reject.

Sometimes it is difficult to tell what constitutes a rejection or a counteroffer. When the offeree is merely requesting information or clarification, that does not constitute a counteroffer or a rejection and the offer remains in force. If the purchaser in the preceding example had asked, "Does the car have whitewall tires?" the courts would interpret the question as a request for information which would have no effect on the original offer. On the other hand, if the purchaser had asked, "Will you take $450?", even though it was worded as a request for information, it is clearly a counteroffer and the original offer would end.

The existence of an offer can be affected by other factors as well. For example, the offer will be ended if the activity contemplated by the contracting parties becomes illegal before acceptance or if the goods forming the subject matter of the contract are destroyed without the parties being aware of it.

STANDARD FORM CONTRACT. The law assumes that both parties to an agreement are in equal bargaining positions and that both parties will negotiate the terms of the agreement until a consensus is reached which represents a fair bargain. But any passenger who tried to negotiate with an airline over the terms of a ticket to travel, would not meet with much success. Many large businesses are in a position to impose almost any terms they wish on their customers. They have developed specific non-negotiable terms to be included in their agreements or standard form contracts. These clauses, intended to limit the liability of one of the parties, are called exculpatory or exemption clauses. If customers do not like the terms, they are invited to go elsewhere. If they do accept the terms, they are bound by them because the common law assumes that both parties are in equal bargaining positions.

To alleviate some of the unfairness of this practice, all jurisdictions in Canada have passed statutes such as the Sale of Goods Act. This statute and various forms of consumer protection legislation will be discussed in Chapter 7. The courts have also tried to relieve some of the harshness of the common law approach by treating exculpatory clauses in standard form contracts very restrictively. Any business which includes in its contracts terms disclaiming responsibility for damage to goods left on the premises would still be held responsible for goods stolen from its premises. Exemption clauses must be very explicit. The theory that the offer is part of a negotiating or bargaining process is sometimes misleading.

Acceptance

At the heart of contract law is the concept of consensus and mutual commitment. The manifestation of an intention to commit on the part of the offeror is found in the offer; the offeree's intention to commit is found in the acceptance. The key to understanding acceptance is that the commitment must be total. If a condition or qualification is put on the acceptance, it then becomes a counteroffer, not an acceptance. If a person offers to sell a car for $500 and the response is, "I accept, but you must include new tires," the response is a counteroffer and the seller is now in a position to accept or reject the new offer. Nor is it possible to accept only part of an offer. If a person offers to sell a house and its furnishings at a stipulated price for each, the purchaser cannot say, "I accept your offer, but I only want the furniture." For an acceptance to be valid, it must be an all or nothing proposition.

Acceptance must be unconditional

A problem arises when an offer contains ambiguous wording which becomes part of the contract on acceptance. Under normal circumstances, the court will do all it can to interpret the ambiguities in such a way as to give effect to the intention of all the parties. In the process, the courts will apply the reasonable person test, but will not go so far as to strike a bargain on behalf of the parties. In the English case of *Scammel v. Ouston*,[6] the parties had referred to a hire-purchase agreement, but had failed to include the terms of that agreement in their negotiations for the purchase of a van. A hire-purchase agreement is a device to use the item being purchased as security for payments spread over a period of time. Lord Wright of the House of Lords declared that the parties "...never got beyond negotiations." Here the parties "...never in intention or even in appearance reached an agreement."[7] No matter how definite the acceptance, it will not overcome the defect of an incomplete or otherwise defective offer.

Acceptance will not cure defective offer

COMMUNICATION OF ACCEPTANCE. Usually, acceptance of an agreement is accomplished by communicating it to the offeror. However, it is possible for an offer to be accepted by conduct. If the offeror has indicated particular conduct to specify acceptance, the offeree must comply with that stipulation for it to be effective. If a person offers to sell a car for $500 and specifies that if the offeree wants to accept, he or she should come and get the keys from the offeror's landlord and drive the car away, paying the offeror upon return from vacation, full compliance with those directions amounts to acceptance. If the offeree acquires the keys from the landlord and drives the vehicle away, the offer has been accepted by conduct and neither of the parties can change their minds.

Offer may be accepted by conduct where specified

A unilateral contract is accepted by performance of the act specified in the offer. A firm in England offered a large sum of money to the first human-powered aircraft to fly across the English Channel. The principals of that firm would not have been impressed by someone planning to perform the feat coming to them to accept the offer. Starting the flight would not constitute acceptance either. For an acceptance to be effective, the cross-Channel flight would have to be completed. This poses a problem because an offer can be revoked at any time before the point of acceptance. Thus, in the period of time between the beginning of performance and its completion, the offeror could legally revoke the offer. For example, a representative of the firm offering the reward for the cross-Channel flight theoretically could have stood on the shore just before completion and shouted, "I revoke." Such an action would be morally repugnant and there is some debate as to whether such conduct

Unilateral contract accepted by completion of performance

---

[6] *Scammel v. Ouston* [1941] A.C. 251 (House of Lords).
[7] *Ibid.*, p. 269.

would be legally permissible. The American approach is that the offeror is not allowed to revoke once performance has begun.

A selling practice has recently developed in which a merchandiser sends a product to the home of a potential customer with a note saying that if the goods are not returned within ten days, the customer will have purchased them. The general rule, however, is that acceptance will not be inferred from silence, even when such silence is specified as the mode of acceptance in the original offer. The common law position is that the offeree is not obligated to respond when unsolicited goods arrive on the doorstep. The recipient is free to ignore the offer or to dispose of the products sent. It is vital to note that if the offeree uses the product in any way, acceptance is complete and the offeree would be bound in contract to the offeror. Many jurisdictions have passed legislation to curb these practices.

Although silence will not normally be taken as acceptance, the courts adopt a different approach when there has been a long history of dealings between the parties. If an offeror says, "If I don't hear from you by Monday, I'll assume we have a deal," the offeree would normally be free to ignore the offer without fear that a binding contract would result. However, if the event in question is just one of a continuing series, the courts are willing to recognize the offeree's failure to respond as requested as an acceptance resulting in a binding contract.

Acceptance must be communicated to the offeror to be effective unless it is accomplished by conduct. The result flowing from this general rule is that a contract comes into existence where the offeror learns of the acceptance rather than where it is made by the offeree. If someone in Halifax offers to sell a car to someone in Winnipeg and the offeree accepts over the telephone, the contract comes into existence in Halifax since that is where the offeror heard the acceptance. This has quite an impact since it may determine whether Nova Scotia or Manitoba law will apply. In addition, the acceptance becomes effective and a contract is formed at the time the acceptance is communicated.

THE POSTBOX RULE.
Difficulties arise when parties deal with each other over long distances using non-instant forms of communication. Because neither party can be absolutely sure of the other's state of mind at a given time, there can be no certainty of the contract's status. The postbox rule was developed to solve this problem.

When an acceptance is mailed and the use of the postal service is a reasonable means of communication in the circumstances, that acceptance is effective as soon as it is deposited in the mailbox. This is a clear exception to the general rule discussed above where an acceptance is not effective until the offeror learns of it. The postbox rule eliminates the difficulties of finding the point of consensus when the parties are communicating at a distance but it also leads to other problems. The biggest difficulty created when the postbox rule comes into play is that for a period of time, while the letter of acceptance is still in the mail, the offeror is bound in contract but is unaware of that fact.

When the original offer is sent by mail, there is usually little question about a response by mail being appropriate, and thus the postbox rule applies. The difficulty that arises when the acceptance is handled in some other way is illustrated in

Unsolicited offer not accepted by silence— exception

Acceptance must be communicated to be effective

Mailed acceptance effective when and where dropped in postbox

Henthorne v. Fraser.[8] The plaintiff, Mr. Henthorne, went to the defendant's office where he was offered some property, the offer to be left open for fourteen days. He took the offer home to think about it and after several days posted a letter of acceptance. In the meantime, the defendant, Mr. Fraser, sold the property to another party and wrote a letter to Henthorne revoking the offer. The two letters crossed in the mail. The court had to decide when, if at all, the acceptance was effective. It decided that a reasonable person would have responded by mail even though the offer had been handed to him, and therefore the acceptance was effective when it was placed in the postbox. The postbox rule has also been extended to include telegrams. The courts have, however, shown great reluctance to extend it to other forms of communication, such as telex and fax machines.

SPECIFIED MEANS OF ACCEPTANCE. A usual effect of the postbox rule is that for a period of time after the acceptance is mailed, the offeror is bound in contract without knowing it until the acceptance is actually received. If this uncertainty poses a problem, the offeror is free to stipulate another means of acceptance, and the problem can be readily overcome. The offeror is always free to stipulate how the offer is to be accepted and has the right to do this even when the means specified are unreasonable. If the offer states that the acceptance must be by mail, by phone or by telegram, and all other means of communication are prohibited, the offeree must comply if the acceptance is to be effective. If the offeror states that acceptance is to be by mail but does not prohibit other means of acceptance, the offeree can use a faster means of communication, such as the telephone or a telegram, but if a telegram is used, it will not be effective until received. If the offeror is silent as to the means of acceptance to be employed, a reasonable person test is used to determine if the method used is appropriate. It is usually appropriate to send an acceptance using the same method by which the offer was communicated. Thus, if the offer was mailed, the response should be by mail; if by fax, the acceptance should be given in the same manner.

COMMUNICATION OF A REVOCATION. The postbox rule does not apply to a revocation. For a revocation to be effective, it must be communicated to the offeree. If a person offers to sell something to one person, he or she cannot then sell it to someone else with the idea that the sale eliminates any claim the original offeree has to the goods. If a person makes an offer to sell something to someone and then sells it to a third person without revoking the offer to the first, there is a legal obligation to sell the item to both parties, if both accept the offer. This is true even when a letter of revocation has been mailed, but not yet received at the time of acceptance. This was Fraser's position in the case of *Henthorne v. Fraser* discussed above. The important point here is that the offer must be revoked by communicating the fact to the offeree. Once the offeree is aware of the revocation, the offer is no longer open and cannot be accepted. Suppose Chan offers to sell Phillips her car in a letter, the offer to remain open for a week, and the next day she sells it to

---

[8] *Henthorne v. Fraser* [1892] 2 Ch. 27 (Court of Appeal).

Only applies where response by mail appropriate

Postbox rule extended to telegrams

Postbox rule does not apply to revocation

someone else. She must let Phillips know she has changed her mind. If she mails the letter of revocation, that letter will not be effective until it is received. If Phillips mails the letter of acceptance before receiving the letter of revocation, according to the post-box rule, acceptance will be effective when it is dropped in the mailbox and there will be a contract. In such circumstances, Chan will find herself in the position of being bound by two different contracts to sell her car.

CONSIDERATION

Consideration—
the price one is
willing to pay for
a promise

Consideration—
not necessarily
money

Central to contract law is the bargaining process in which people trade promises for promises and all parties derive some benefit from the deal. That benefit, essential to the existence of a contract, is called consideration and is defined as the price one promises to pay for the promise of another. Consideration is not restricted to the exchange of money. A bargain may involve the exchange of anything the parties think is of value. For example, if the parties to a contract agree to exchange a car for $500, there is valid consideration on both sides. The promise to deliver the automobile is a valid consideration as is the promise to pay $500. Thus, before the parties actually exchange the automobile for the cash, they are still bound in contract because the consideration given is the exchange of commitments or promises. If one of the parties fails to honour that commitment, the other can successfully sue for breach of contract.

Consideration—
can be benefit or
detriment

Courts will not
enforce one-sided
contract

Because it is sometimes difficult to determine the value a person is getting from a deal, it is often better to look at what the parties are giving or paying. For example, Ali agrees to clean up a public park in exchange for Barbeau's promise to pay $500. Even though this commitment might have been made out of a sense of civic responsibility and results in no personal benefit, Barbeau is still obligated to pay. Similarly, the contract is just as binding if the consideration involved is a commitment not to do something as opposed to a promise to do something. For example, if someone promises to pay another $500 to quit smoking, such an arrangement is a valid, binding contract. The consideration on the one side is the promise to pay $500 and the consideration on the other side is the promise to refrain from doing something the party has a legal right to do, that is, smoke. Consideration is a benefit or a detriment flowing between the parties to an agreement as the result of a bargain struck. If the agreement is one-sided and only one of the parties is getting anything from the deal, it is called a gratuitous promise and the courts will not enforce it. However, once the gift has been given, the courts will not assist the giver in getting it back.

Sum Certain

It is not necessary that the consideration be fair to both parties. Contract law rests on the foundation that both parties are free to bargain. Once they reach an agreement, the court will assist them in enforcing the resulting contract but will not release either of them from a bad deal. If a person agrees to sell someone a brand new Cadillac

Consideration—
need not be fair
but must be
specific

for $100, this becomes a valid, binding contract. Although the consideration paid does not need to be fair, it must have some material value. In the case of *White v. Bluett*,[9] a father agreed to give his son money if the boy would stop bothering him. It was held that such a promise had no intrinsic value and therefore was not consideration. Similarly, if a person agrees to give love and affection in return for a promise of money, that is not sufficient consideration. Whatever the parties have bargained for must have some material value for the courts to enforce the bargain.

—particularly if
money is involved

When two parties strike a bargain, they must agree to a specific consideration or price. Suppose someone agrees to exchange a car for another's promise to "do some work around the house." Such a promise would not be enforceable because the work to be done is not specified. This problem becomes acute whenever a monetary consideration is involved. It is not sufficient to promise to give "some money" as payment for the promise of another. Such a commitment must refer to a specific amount of money. However, there have been cases which establish that there is sufficient consideration if the parties agree to pay the "market value" of an item or where some other objective method of pricing a product at some time in the future is used.[10]

Existing Duty

The adequacy of consideration becomes important whenever there is an existing duty to do the thing contracted for. For example, Olsen agreed to paint Chang's house for $500 and then said to Chang when the painting was three-quarters finished, "I will not finish unless you promise to pay me another $200." Even if Chang were to agree to this extra payment, it would not be binding because Chang would receive nothing in exchange for the promise to pay the extra $200. Olsen was obligated to finish painting the house before the promise to pay the extra $200 was made. After the promise to pay the extra $200 was made, the obligation remained the same. Olsen's legal position did not change, so therefore there was no consideration.

A new bargain
requires new
consideration

When a duty to act exists but that duty is owed to a third party, a promise to do the same thing for someone else is enforceable. In the situation above, if Adams, a potential tenant, realized that Olsen's reluctance to finish the job would delay possession of the premises, and thus cause greater expense, and Adams promised to pay Olsen the extra $200, that agreement would be binding. Before Adams' promise to pay the extra $200, Olsen was legally obligated to Chang to finish painting the house. After the promise to Adams, Olsen is now legally obligated to Adams as well as Chang to paint the house. Olsen's legal position has changed because Olsen now runs the risk of having to pay Adams' damages as well as Chang's if the contract is breached. There is a valid consideration here and the contract is binding.

Whenever the existing duty involves a police officer, firefighter or other public servant, there can be no further promise to do what they are already legally obligated to do. A firefighter cannot arrive at a blaze and extract a promise from the

---

[9] *White v. Bluett* (1853) 23 L.J. Ex. 36 (Court of Exchequer).
[10] *Folley v. Classique Coaches* (1934) 2 K.B. 1 (Court of Appeal).

victim to pay an extra $500 to put out the fire. Such a contract would be against public policy and unenforceable.

Past Consideration

There are situations when consideration appears to be present but in fact is not. One of these is when the consideration was given in the past. That is, the bargain is struck after the price agreed on has been paid. The classic example of this is when a person rescues someone from drowning and the grateful victim promises to give the rescuer $100. Although it may appear that both parties have given something; (the rescuer has performed a service and the other party has promised to pay), such a promise is not enforceable. The key to this problem is in the timing. When the promise to pay the $100 was made, the rescue had already taken place, so where is the bargain? The legal obligation of the rescued party to the rescuer has changed by the promise to pay the $100 but the legal position of the rescuer is unchanged. In fact, the rescuer, since the rescue has already been performed, is in exactly the same legal position before the promise as afterwards. Thus, it is often said that "past consideration is no consideration."

Paying Less to Satisfy a Debt

Another situation in which consideration appears to be present, but often is not, is when people who are obligated to pay a certain sum of money negotiate with their creditors to accept lesser amounts in full payment of the debt. Suppose a debtor who owes a creditor $500 payable on or before June 10th on June 11th approaches the creditor and says, "I can't pay you the $500 I owe you. If you will take $300 in full satisfaction of the debt, I will pay you that instead." What is the position of the creditor who takes this money? Can the creditor still sue for the remaining $200? In fact this is a gratuitous promise. The creditor has received nothing for his promise to take less in full satisfaction of the debt. Under the common law, it was quite clear that where such a one-sided promise was made, it was not binding. Even when partial payment was actually taken, the creditor could then turn around and sue for the remainder.[11] But as a practical business matter, in many situations, such an arrangement to take less is beneficial to the creditor as well as the debtor. The creditor might otherwise have to sue to recover and get nothing. Today all provinces have passed legislation providing that when a creditor has agreed to take less in full satisfaction of a debt and when the creditor has actually received the partial payment agreed on, the creditor is bound and cannot sue for any deficit.[12] When the creditor has only agreed to take less, however, and the payment has not yet been made, the creditor is still free to change his or her mind and insist on the entire amount being paid. Of course, when the debtor has agreed to pay the lesser amount

[11] *Foakes v. Beer* (1884) 9 App. Cas. 605 (House of Lords).
[12] *Law and Equity Act*, R.S.B.C. (1979) c.224 s.40.

early or do something in addition to the payment, such as clean up the creditor's property, there is consideration on both sides to support the new arrangement and the creditor is bound by the promise to take less.

Settlement Out of Court

Consideration not a factor in out-of-court settlements

Using this reasoning, it is possible to assume that when disputes are settled out of court, as they often are, there is no consideration and therefore the parties are not bound by the settlement. It has been argued that if one party receives considerably less than it would have won in a court action, there is really no consideration to support the agreement to take less. In fact, the court will not entertain such an argument. It may be difficult to see what each party has received, but it is clear that both have given up something pursuant to the agreement. In the settlement process, both parties have given up the right to have the matter brought before the court and tried, and that is something of value to each party. Hence, there is consideration on both sides.

Illegal Consideration

Illegal or impossible consideration is no consideration

There are some policy restrictions on what constitutes good consideration. If a person agrees to pay another to kill a third, such an agreement is not enforceable since the consideration given for the promise of payment is a commitment to perform an unlawful act. In addition, for consideration to be valid, it must be possible to perform the consideration promised. If a person were to promise to bring back someone's relative from the dead in exchange for the payment of $5000, such a promise would be unenforceable due to the impossibility of performance.

Request for Services

One situation in which it is difficult to determine consideration at the point of contract is when one party requests the performance of a service before the parties have agreed on a specific payment. When a lawyer or mechanic is hired, often no attempt is made to determine the ultimate price of the job. Even though no consideration has been agreed on in these circumstances, the court will enforce the obligation to pay. If the parties cannot come to an agreement on the amount, the courts will determine what reasonable amount must be paid for the service.

The courts are usually reluctant to enforce any promises when consideration is not present because no bargain has been struck. However, the bargaining nature of the arrangement is present in a request for services; it is just that the parties have not agreed on a specific consideration. Therefore, the courts are willing to enforce an implied promise to pay a reasonable amount.

Must pay reasonable amount for services

This is an application of the principle of *quantum meruit*. When goods or services are supplied but the parties have neglected to set out a price, the courts are willing to assess the value of those goods or services and impose an obligation to pay a reasonable price on the person who benefits. *Quantum meruit* means "as much as is deserved," and the courts have shown a willingness to use this principle as a basis of payment in other situations as well. Thus, if a contract involving services is breached by the person benefiting from the services, that person can be required to pay for what has been done. It is likely that recovery on a quantum meruit basis will be denied, however, if the person claiming is the one who breached the contract or if the contract requires the performance of some as yet unmet condition before payment is to be received. This principle has also been applied to the sale of goods by provincial statute.

Promissory Estoppel

Another exception to the rule that a promise is only enforceable if consideration is present is based on the principle of **promissory estoppel**, sometimes referred to as **equitable estoppel**. Someone who makes a gratuitous promise to do something for another person is not usually jeopardized if that promise is not performed. Such gratuitous promises are usually not enforceable. But there are situations in which the promisee incurs expenses or other obligations in anticipation of the promise being performed. Unique remedies have been developed to compensate for significant loss.

Gratuitous promises usually not enforcable

In the United States it is possible to sue for compensation when a person relies on such a one-sided promise and suffers a loss, but in England and Canada such an unfulfilled promise can only be used as a defence to an action initiated by the person who made the promise. In London, England, just before the war, High Trees House Ltd. rented an apartment building from Central London Property Trust Ltd. under a 99-year-lease with the intention of renting out the individual flats in that building. The two parties agreed to a set yearly rent of £2500. Because of the outbreak of the Second World War, it soon became apparent that High Trees would not be able to rent out all of the flats and so in 1942 the property owners agreed to lower the yearly rent to £1250. After the war they changed their minds and demanded payment of the entire rent including back rent for the portion that had not been paid since 1942. The court agreed that for the period after the war, High Trees had to again pay the full rent, but as far as the back rent was concerned, the property owners were bound by their promise to take the lower amount.[13] High Trees was not suing to enforce the promise,; rather the property owners were suing for the higher amount in spite of their promise. High Trees used the plaintiff's promise as a defence to its claim. Thus, in Canada and England the principle of promissory estoppel is remedial in nature. In the famous case of *Combe v. Combe*, Lord Denning made it clear that, "It does not create new causes of action where none existed before,"[14] and Lord Asquith, in his concurring judgment, said that promissory estoppel could only be used as a "shield but not as a sword."[15]

[13] *Central London Property Trust, Ltd. v. High Trees House, Ltd.* [1947] K.B.130.
[14] *Combe v. Combe* [1951] 1 All E.R. 767 (Court of Appeal) p. 769.
[15] p. 772. Recent legislation in British Columbia may have the effect of allowing a person to sue for compensation (use as a sword) when such promises are relied on as found in that province's Law and Equity Act, R.S.B.C. (1979) c.224 as modified by the Law Reform Amendment Act, S.B.C. (1985) c.10.

Although there is some dispute about it, promissory estoppel is effectively limited to use as a defence in Canada. In the High Trees case, if the company had paid the higher rent by mistake despite Central London's gratuitous promise to take less, High Trees would not have been successful had it tried to sue to retrieve the excess it had paid. This would have been using Central London's promise to take less as a "sword" which it cannot do. In fact, in almost every case where promissory estoppel has been made available as a defence, there was an existing contractual relationship which was modified by the promise. To raise this defence successfully, the victim must also demonstrate reliance on the promise and injury suffered as a result of that reliance.

Promissory estoppel can only be used as a defence

Sealed Documents

Sealed documents do not require consideration

The last major exception to the requirement of consideration is the use of the seal. Seals were originally made by placing some melted wax on a document and impressing a signet ring in it, thus lending authenticity or authority to the document. Different rules came into play when the parties took the trouble to perform this act. The parties to such a sealed agreement were bound by the contract whether or not any consideration was involved. This practice was implemented before modern contract law had developed and before consideration became a requirement. As the modern law of contract came into being, the practice of sealing some documents was retained. A paper wafer has replaced the formal seal and signet impression, although the seal can be almost any form of marking on the document which the parties have identified as a seal. These types of contracts are now considered formal contracts or deeds, and the court will not entertain any suggestion that the promise contained in the document is not supported by consideration. Although it is not necessary to look for consideration when a seal is present, it is important to realize that the existence of the seal does not do away with the other requirements of a valid contract.

There must be some form of valid consideration in the form of a benefit or detriment flowing between the parties for a legally binding contract to exist. Only when the document embodying the agreement is sealed, or on those rare occasions when the promise of the promisor is being raised as a defence by the promisee will the court not require consideration to be established.

SUMMARY

A contract is an exchange of promises or commitments enforceable in court. All of the essential terms of the contract must be contained in the offer which is a tentative promise by the offeror contingent upon an acceptance by the offeree. Non-essential terms will be implied. The offer will end at a specified time, but it may be revoked earlier simply by notice to the offeree, unless an option agreement has been entered into. In the absence of a specified time limit, the offer will lapse after a reasonable time. A counteroffer, rejection, or the death or insanity of the offeror will also cause an offer to lapse.

The acceptance is merely an indication of a willingness to be bound and must be communicated to be effective. The postbox rule is an exception. It provides that, when use of the mail system is appropriate, the acceptance is effective when and where it is dropped in the mailbox. Offer and acceptance lead to consensus, the first element necessary for the existence of a contract.

The second requirement is consideration. Gratuitous promises are not enforceable. Consideration is the price paid by one party to a contract for the promise of the other. Both contracting parties must have experienced some benefit or detriment pursuant to the bargain. The consideration given must be both specific and legal. Past consideration is no consideration. When the agreement is only for the performance of an already existing contractual obligation, there is no consideration. In many provinces, when a person agrees to take less in full satisfaction of a debt, and in fact takes the money, it is legally binding despite the lack of consideration.

A one-sided promise is generally not enforceable. It may, however, be possible to raise the promise as a defence in an action being brought by the promisor under the principle of promissory or equitable estoppel. When there is a request for services with no agreement as to the amount, a reasonable price must be paid under the principle of *quantum meruit*. When there is a seal, there can be no question about the presence of consideration.

QUESTIONS

1. What is meant by "freedom of contract"? Explain the impact of this principle on the development of contract law.
2. List and explain the elements that must be present for an agreement to qualify as a contract.
3. At what stage in the process of forming a contract are the terms of the contract clearly set out?
4. Explain what is meant by an implied term in a contract.
5. What circumstances might prompt a court to imply terms into a contract?
6. Distinguish between an offer and an invitation to treat.
7. List and explain the various ways an offer can come to an end.
8. What is the effect of the offeror stating in an offer that the offer will remain open for acceptance until a specific date?
9. Explain what is meant by an option.
10. What risks are faced when a person offers to sell certain goods to A and then sells them to B? How can this problem be avoided?
11. What qualities must an acceptance demonstrate to be effective?
12. Explain how a unilateral offer is accepted.

13. Explain the effect of the postbox rule on the principles governing acceptance.
14. How do the courts determine when the postbox rule should be applied?
15. Define consideration and explain what is meant by the term "the exchange of consideration."
16. What difficulty might be faced by a person who has already agreed to do a specific job and then extracts a promise of more pay from the other party?
17. Explain why a contract dispute settled out of court is considered binding even though one party would have obtained more if the action had been taken to court.
18. Explain a person's obligation regarding payment when he or she has requested a service without specifying a particular fee.
19. Describe what is meant by promissory estoppel and the circumstances in which it will arise in contract disputes.
20. How does the presence of a seal affect the requirement that consideration must be present in a contract?

CASES

1. *Regina v. Dawood.*
   Mrs. Dawood had been shopping in a department store and came to a display rack containing children's jumpers and blouses. On some of the hangers the jumpers and blouses were combined to make an outfit on sale for a single price, while some of the hangers contained individually priced jumpers and blouses. Mrs. Dawood took a blouse from one of the two-piece outfits and put it on its own hanger with a jumper from one of the individual hangers and took the outfit she had made to the cash register. She had removed any indication of price from the blouse so that the clerk was led to believe that the price from the jumper was the price for the whole outfit. The cashier charged her the lower price which she paid. It is important to note that there was no attempt to hide the blouse in any way but the effect was that she paid for only the jumper. Mrs. Dawood was subsequently charged with theft and the problem for the court was to determine if a crime had taken place.

2. *Courtney and Fairburn, Ltd. v. Tolaini Brothers (Hotels) Ltd.*
   Tolaini owned some property on which he wanted to build a hotel. He approached Mr. Courtney, a contractor, for that purpose. Courtney said that he would supply someone to lend Tolaini sufficient funds for the undertaking if he could have the job of building the hotel. The letters exchanged between the two confirmed this commitment and stated that if Tolaini reached an acceptable agreement with the people providing financing he would then turn to

the contractor, Mr. Courtney, and negotiate "fair and reasonable contract sums with respect to each of the three projects as they arise." In other words, Courtney would actually be used in the construction of the hotel. Courtney responded by referring to that correspondence and stating that he "...agreed to the terms specified therein." In fact, Courtney did find somebody willing to provide financing which Tolaini took advantage of. But when Tolaini refused to engage him, Courtney sued for breach of contract. The problem facing the court was to determine whether there actually was a contract capable of being enforced.

3. *Calgary v. Northern Construction Ltd.*
   The city of Calgary advertised for tenders for a construction project. One of the terms of the advertisement was that once submitted the bid could not be revoked. Northern Construction submitted the low bid on the job. They then examined their bid and realized they had made an error in their calculations. They showed these documents to Calgary's representatives who agreed that they had made an error. Northern Construction then requested that they be released from their bid. Calgary, however, would not release them from the bid and then accepted it as the winning one. Northern Construction refused to honour the contract and Calgary was forced to go with the second lowest bid. They then sued. Explain the legal arguments available to both sides and the likely outcome of the action.

4. *Michaud v. Grand Falls Golf Course Inc.*
   Michaud was a contestant in a golf tournament which offered a prize of a new Toyota automobile for a hole in one scored on the second hole. Because this was a nine hole course and the tournament was for eighteen holes, it was necessary for all golfers to go around the course twice. A shotgun start was used for the tournament which meant that the various golfers started on different tees spread throughout the golf course. To facilitate this set-up, each tee had two numbers; at the second hole, the numbers 2 and 11 were posted on a flag beside the tee. Michaud started on Tee #3 and played his eighteen holes by playing from #3 to #9, then around the nine holes a second time, finally playing 1 and 2 again to end the game. It was on the last hole he played, the hole marked #2, that he scored a hole in one and as a result claimed his prize.
   The Grand Falls Golf Course claimed that for him hole #2 was only #2 the first time around. The time he scored the hole in one, it was hole #11 and so he was not entitled to the prize. The general rules of golf state that where a shotgun start is used, the contestant will start at the tee assigned, carry through the eighteen holes, and then go back and make up the original holes missed. Explain the legal arguments on both sides as to whether he is entitled to the car or not. How would your answer be affected if he had scored a hole in one on the preceding two holes and, just before he swung on this hole, the appropriate official of the golf course announced that the offer was revoked.

5. *Scheckford v. B.C. Winegrowers Ltd.*
   In this case, the defendant, B.C. Winegrowers Ltd., sent a letter to the plaintiff offering to purchase a specified lot of fresh loganberries. The offer was mailed on April 22 and arrived on April 23 or 24. The plaintiff waited six days and mailed an acceptance on April 30. The problem facing the court was whether the offer was capable of being accepted on April 30 when the acceptance was sent. Discuss the arguments on both sides.

6. *Re 6781427 Holdings and Alma Mater Society of U.B.C.*
   The holding company in this case leased an area from the Alma Mater Society in the Student Union Building where it operated a cookie shop with a three-year lease containing an option to renew. The renewal provision of the lease required that notice of renewal be given to the landlord in writing before midnight, July 31, 1986. In fact, the holding company approached the general manager of the Alma Mater Society to see if they could expand the area that they were using. The manager could not give a response right away but said he would probably know by September.

   When September came the manager said he would not know until December. As a result the holding company missed the July 31 deadline while waiting for a response to their request. In September the Alma Mater Society ordered it to vacate the premises. Explain the arguments available to both parties to explain their positions.

ISSUES

1. Contract law is based on the assumption that both parties to a contract are in an equal bargaining position. The courts' refusal to interfere with the provisions of the contract, even when unfair advantage has been taken of one of the parties, is based on this assumption. In many situations, however, one of the parties may not be in an equally free bargaining position to negotiate the terms of an agreement, for example, users of railroads, ferries and telephone services. Is this assumption of freedom of contract a hindrance or a help in contract law? Would it be more appropriate for the courts to get involved in evaluating the fairness of the terms of a contract? In your answer, examine specifically the effect of this approach on the courts' attitude toward fair consideration.

2. The distinction between an offer and an invitation to treat is easy enough to understand when the communication involved is designed to attract the attention of the customer and to encourage a discussion of the merits of the product, for example, an advertisement or a window display. The distinction between the two is sometimes difficult to determine because it often appears that the

distinction is not based on the conceptual definition of an offer but on a pragmatic facilitation of commerce. The pharmaceutical case discussed in this chapter, which gives support to the declaration that the display of goods on a shelf in a self-service merchandising situation was an invitation to treat rather than an offer, is a good example of this problem. The question is whether the present distinction between an invitation to treat and an offer is appropriate. Direct your attention specifically to self-service merchandising.

3.   Students are often surprised to discover that if they have offered something for sale to several people and sell it to one of them, they still have to revoke their offer to the others to avoid the obligation of selling the same thing to more than one person. The mere selling of the subject of the offer is not enough to end the offer; a revocation must be communicated to the other offerees. The question is, is it appropriate to have such rules when common understanding and accepted practice cause the parties to act in a way inconsistent with those rules? Would it be more appropriate to have the offer end automatically once the item has been sold? A related question is whether a rejection or counteroffer should be taken as automatically ending the original offer. Many people are surprised to find out that once their counteroffer has been rejected they cannot turn around and accept the original offer without the consent of the original offeror.

4.   An acceptance must be received for it to be effective. The postbox rule must be viewed as an exception to this general rule. Under the postbox rule, an acceptance is effective where and when it was mailed if the post is an appropriate means of communication. Given modern communication techniques, would it not be more appropriate to abolish the postbox rule altogether? If the postbox rule is to be retained, should it not be extended to include other matters such as rejection offers, revocations and counteroffers? Similarly, should the rule be extended beyond the mail and telegrams to include other methods of communication such as the telephone, and telex and fax machines?

5.   Offer and acceptance are viewed by the courts as essential steps in the establishment of a consensus between the parties. In fact, there are many situations in which consensus clearly exists but in which it is difficult to clearly identify a specific point of offer and acceptance. Often when there have been protracted negotiations between the parties, the courts face a difficult task in identifying which communication is the offer and which is the acceptance. For example, in some of the relationships governed by contract law, such as a membership in a club or association governed by bylaws or a constitution, it is difficult to evaluate the relationship in terms of offer and acceptance. If the relationship between the parties is based on an implied contract, it does not make sense to look for an offer or acceptance. Has contract law become distorted by putting so much emphasis on an offer and acceptance? Would it be more appropriate to concentrate on some other feature, such as consensus?

6. Although consideration is now treated as a separate ingredient necessary for the existence of a contract, many argue that consideration merely meets the court's need to be satisfied that the parties were serious and that the intended legal consequences flow from their agreement. The development of the principle of promissory estoppel and the court's requirement that a reasonable price be paid when services are performed even when there is no agreement as to price indicates that there are many situations in which the courts are uncomfortable with the requirement of consideration. In fact, some have argued that the requirement of consideration is a historical oddity which ought to be abolished. Should the separate requirement that consideration be demonstrated to establish a contract be abolished? Should the presence or absence of consideration be treated merely as evidence establishing the intention of the parties to be legally bound? Your answer should consider similar arguments directed at the use of the seal in contract law. Consider also the effect of such an abolition on the principle of promissory estoppel.

4

FORMATION OF CONTRACTS (continued)

Objectives of the Chapter

- ■ to describe the various conditions under which people are limited in their capacity to enter into contracts
- ■ to explain what constitutes illegal contracts and those that are against public policy
- ■ to consider the role of intention in determining whether a person is bound in contract
- ■ to illustrate the various forms a contract can take
- ■ to explain when writing is required

When Mr. Guzzo sold his retail fruit market, he signed a written agreement that included the term that he would not become involved in a similar business within five miles of the one he sold for a period of five years. Within a year of the sale, a similar business was opened up by Mr. Guzzo's son within the prohibited five-mile radius. The purchasers suspected that it was really Mr. Guzzo's new business and sued for breach of the non-competition clause in the purchase agreement. The judge decided that the clause was valid, that the arrangement for the new business was no more than a "sham" and that Mr. Guzzo himself was at least indirectly involved in it in violation of the non-competition covenant. The plaintiff was awarded damages of

$20 000.[1] Such non-competition covenants are valid only if they are reasonable and in the public interest; otherwise they are void. That the terms of the contract be legal is only one requirement of a legally binding contract which will be discussed in this chapter.

The previous chapter examined consensus and consideration as requirements of a legally binding contract. This chapter will discuss the other elements that must be present in order to have an enforceable contract. They are capacity, legality, intention and the requirement that some contracts be evidenced in writing.

CAPACITY

Our lawmakers have always recognized that some people are more vulnerable than others and thus require special protection. Over the years, several categories of people have been protected by having their freedom to enter into contracts severely restricted or, in some cases, eliminated completely.

Infants

The age of majority or the age at which a person is considered to be an adult is twenty-one in common law. The age at which a person becomes an adult in Canada today is controlled by statute and varies from province to province (either eighteen or nineteen in most provinces). In common law, people who are under the age of majority have always had their freedom to enter into contracts severely limited for their own protection. In some jurisdictions, such as B.C., this protection is governed by special statute.

Age of majority
varies with
provinces

The general principle in all jurisdictions is that infants (persons under the age of majority) who enter into contracts are not bound by the agreements although the adults with whom they contract are bound. The application of this principle has proven to be quite complicated because there are two opposing factors to be weighed by the courts. The first objective is to protect infants from their own inexperience in business matters and the second is to avoid placing undue hardship on the other parties to the contracts. The law of infancy tries to balance the protection of infants against harm resulting to merchants when infants abuse this protection.

It is important to distinguish between the artificial incapacity imposed on the youth who is a functioning member of society and the actual incapacity of the child who is incapable of understanding what is happening. Most problems arise when

[1] *The Lawyers Weekly*, April 7, 1987, pp. 1 and 8.

dealing with young people who are approaching the age of majority. The test for infancy is objective. When an adult deals with a customer who is under the age of majority, it makes no difference if the adult was under the impression that the other party was an adult. The court is only concerned with the fact that the person was under the statutory age of majority. As a general rule, whenever an infant enters into a contract with an adult, the adult is bound by the contract but the infant can escape. The contract, therefore, is voidable. For example, an adult named Myers offers to sell a car for $500 to a minor called Prokop who accepts the offer. Myers would be bound by the contract but Prokop would be free to either honour the agreement and purchase the car or refuse to go through with the deal.

Infants not bound by contract, but adults are

Infants are bound by contracts for the acquisition of necessaries. **Necessaries** are things required to function in society, such as food, clothing, transportation or lodging. For an adult to enforce a contract with an infant, it must be demonstrated to the court that the goods sold to the infant could be classified as necessaries and that the infant needed them. This point is often quite difficult to prove since the merchant has to produce evidence showing that the infant did not already have an adequate supply of the goods. Although transportation can be a necessary, the courts are extremely reluctant to find that the purchase of a car qualifies as a necessary. The courts have held that medical, dental and legal services, toiletries, uniforms and even a house can be necessaries in different situations. What is or is not a necessary has varied with the social status of an infant. For example, fine jewellery was held to be a necessary for a wealthy man's son in the nineteenth century.[2] This distinction is of less significance now. If the merchant succeeds in establishing that the contract was for a necessary, the contract will be binding on the infant. However, the infant is only required to pay a reasonable price for the necessary. If it can be demonstrated that the merchant has charged an exorbitant amount, the infant will not be required to pay the contracted amount but only that which is deemed fair and reasonable under the circumstances.

Infants bound to pay reasonable prices for necessaries

The question arises as to whether an infant can refuse delivery when necessaries have been ordered. It is clear that when educational, medical or legal services are involved, the contract is binding on the infant even if the services have not yet been delivered. However, it is not yet clear in Canadian common law whether the same principle applies to goods. *The Sale of Goods Act* does require infants to pay a reasonable price for necessaries in the form of goods that have been sold and delivered.

Infants must repay money borrowed for and used for necessaries

Another problem arises when money is loaned for the purchase of necessaries. Is a contract to repay the money binding on the infant? When the borrowed money has actually been used by the infant for the purchase of a necessary, the creditor can insist on repayment. However, if the infant declares that the money will be used for necessaries but in fact uses it for a different purpose, the creditor cannot enforce repayment. Thus, money loaned to an infant to pay for school tuition cannot be recovered by the creditor if it is used for gambling. Government student loans are exceptions because they are supported by legislation requiring repayment regardless of what the money is used for.

2 *Peters v. Fleming* (1840) 6 M & W 42.

BENEFICIAL CONTRACTS OF SERVICE. A contract in which an infant agrees to do something for someone else is binding if it can be demonstrated that taken as a whole the contract is for the benefit of the infant. The classic example of this is an apprenticeship agreement. In the case of *Roberts v. Gray*,[3] an infant entered into a contract with a well-known billiards player to be his assistant and, in the process, be taught to play the game. This contract was held to be binding on the infant since it was beneficial to him. However, in the case of *DeFranesco v. Barnam*,[4] in which a young girl had agreed to be an apprentice to a dancing master, the contract was determined to be not binding. The court ruled that the girl had been taken advantage of by having to provide significant labour for the dancing master with little or no commitment on his side to teach anything. The contract was held to be not in her best interest and was therefore not binding. These common law provisions are of less significance today because provincial and federal governments have passed legislation covering apprenticeship arrangements which override common law provisions.

Infants bound by contracts of service which substantially benefit them

It is often difficult to assess when contracts of service are binding on infants. It is clear that contracts involving infants' services as part of a business or trade, or contracts made by infants to facilitate a business or trade are not binding on the infants. For example, if an infant were to purchase a truck to facilitate a delivery business, that contract would not be binding on the infant. But most simple employment contracts are considered beneficial contracts of service and thus the infant is bound by them.

INFANTS' VOIDABLE CONTRACTS. The voidable nature of an infant's contract means that the infant can get out of the contract. But when the infant reaches the age of majority, he or she can ratify the contract, either in writing or by implication. The process of ratification breathes new life into old agreements, making them binding. For example, if an infant agrees to pay $500 for an automobile, this contract is voidable. If, however, on coming of age, the infant makes a written statement or indicates by actions that he or she intends to be bound by the contract, it is binding.

Infant can ratify contract at age of majority

Some types of contracts are voidable at the option of the infant. These contracts require positive steps on the part of the infant to overcome their effects. The infant must take action shortly after reaching majority to indicate that he or she will no longer be bound by the agreement if the subject of the contract is a continuing benefit. Continuing agreements include acquired interest in land through lease arrangements, partnership agreements or holding shares in a company. Infants who have agreed to marriage settlement arrangements are bound by them unless they are repudiated at the age of majority. There are some types of contracts, however, that are not binding on the infant under any circumstances. If a contract contains a clause amounting to a penalty against the infant or if the contract, taken as a whole, can be said by the court to be prejudicial to the interests of the infant, the contract is simply void.

---

[3] *Roberts v. Gray* [1913] 1 K.B. 520 (Court of Appeal).
[4] *DeFrancesco v. Barnam* (1890) 45 Ch.D. 430 (Court of Appeal).

Although these principles may seem reasonably straightforward, their application has created a good deal of confusion. To appreciate the reasons for this, it is necessary to think of the contractual relationship progressing through prescribed stages. At the first stage, when the parties have entered into the agreement but the infant has not yet obtained any benefit from it and has not yet paid, the infant can definitely get out of the agreement. This is an executory contract. If the infant has received the goods but has not yet paid for them, he or she is not necessarily bound by the agreement. This is a partially executed contract. When the goods are in the infant's possession, the infant will be required to return them or pay for them. If the infant has passed those goods on to a third party or the goods have been destroyed, the merchant will not be entitled to repayment nor can the merchant insist that the party to whom the goods have been given return them.

Conflict may arise when the contract has been **executed**. Can infants change their minds once they have obtained the benefit under the contract and insist on the return of their money? In Canadian law, the conclusion seems to be that infants are bound by the agreement unless it can be demonstrated that what was received was of no value at all. An infant can insist that payment be returned if there is total failure of consideration or if the infant gained nothing from the deal.

Where contract bestows no benefit infant can escape even executed contract

Parents not responsible for infant's contracts except where authorized

PARENTS' LIABILITY. There is a popular misconception that liability will rest with the parents if a child fails to pay a debt. Parents are not responsible for the torts of their children, nor are they responsible for their contractual obligations in the absence of specific legislation creating such a responsibility. If an infant enters into a contract, it is that infant's responsibility alone. The adult contracting with the infant cannot turn to the parents if the infant does not live up to the contract. The parents are in no way obligated to honour the infant's defaulted promises whether or not those promises are binding on the infant. Only when the merchant is under the impression that he or she is dealing with an infant who is the agent of the parents may the parents be liable for the agreement. This is a simple question of agency and the infant's authority to bind parents as agents will be dealt with in a subsequent chapter. Merchants can overcome this difficulty by having the parent guarantee the infant's obligation at the time the contract is entered into. A guarantee is a written commitment whereby the guarantor agrees to pay the debt if the debtor does not. Since the very purpose of the guarantee is to encourage the merchant to go through with the contract, these guarantees have been held to be binding on the parents in Canadian law.

LEGISLATION. To bring a sense of order to the complicated aspects of infancy law, the British Parliament passed the *Infants Relief Act* in 1874 which purported to make some sweeping changes. The most significant of these changes states that any contract for the loan of money or supply of goods for non-necessaries, either now or in the future, is "absolutely void." Although this appears to be a significant modification of the common law, the British courts have interpreted these provisions very liberally. As a result, the rights and responsibilities of infants in contract are not that much different than under common law in Canada. If the provisions of this statute had been interpreted to their full effect, adults as well as infants could escape these void contracts. As well, anyone purchasing goods from infants would face the problem of the infant not having title to convey the goods because the contract by which the goods were obtained was void. These results have been avoided because of the generous interpretation given the statute by the British courts.

Infants Relief Act causes confusion

Of the Canadian provinces, only British Columbia has adopted this English statute in the form of the *Infants Act*.[5] To avoid the difficulties associated with the term "absolutely void," British Columbia has amended its *Infants Act*[6] so that such infants' contracts are declared unenforceable against the infant but enforceable against the adult. It remains to be seen how the courts will interpret the wording of this new statute, but it appears that the intention is to bring the law in B.C. with regard to infants more in line with the rest of Canada. It should be noted that in B.C., all infants' contracts, including those for necessaries, are unenforceable. The B.C. *Act* has recently been further amended to allow guardians to enter into contracts on behalf of infants involving up to $10 000 (more with the approval of the court). Although other provinces have statutes which relate to infants, none of these attempt to make the kinds of significant changes included in the British Columbia and British legislation.

INFANT'S LIABILITY FOR TORTS. The law of infancy is advantageous to infants but it often puts merchants in very vulnerable positions. In response to this, merchants have been tempted to try to avoid the protection given to infants in contract law by suing them in tort. Tort liability is a completely different type of action based on different principles and responsibilities. It is a basic tenet of tort law that an infant is as liable as an adult for torts committed although the standard of behaviour expected may differ. Once it has been established that an infant has failed to live up to the level of responsibility society deems appropriate, the infant will be held responsible for those inappropriate actions.

It is true that an infant cannot be sued for breach of contract when non-necessaries are involved. However, many of the situations classified as breaches of contract would be, except for the existence of the contract, considered torts. If an infant cannot be sued for breach of contract, why not sue for negligence instead?

Adult cannot avoid protection given to infant by suing in tort

The courts will not allow adults to change to a tort action just to get around the incapacity problem in contract law. If it is appropriate to sue for breach of contract then the plaintiff must do so and if the infant is protected by the defence of incapacity, then that is the end of the matter.

On the other hand, if the infant used the subject matter of the contract in some way completely beyond the contemplation of the contract and carelessly caused injury or damage to those goods, the adult would be able to sue for negligence since the act complained of was not anticipated in the contractual relationship. For example, if an infant rents an automobile and then damages it while trying to plough a field, the merchant would be able to sue the infant for negligence since the use to which the automobile was put was completely outside what was anticipated in the contract.

---

[5] *Infants Act*, R.S.B.C. (1979) c. 196.
[6] *Infants Act* R.S.B.C. (1979) c. 196 as amended by *Law Reform Amendment Act* S.B.C. (1985) c.10.

However, if the infant had an accident while driving the rented automobile on the highway, the adult could not sue for tort even if the infant were clearly negligent because that activity could have been anticipated by the contract. In short, the adult cannot circumvent the protection afforded to the infant in contract law by suing for tort instead. It should be further noted that an infant is responsible for other tortious conduct as well. If a tort such as fraudulent misrepresentation is involved, the adult may have another avenue to pursue in seeking redress from an infant with whom he or she has contracted.

Except where tort arises independent of contract

Insanity and Drunkenness

The law extends its protection to those incapacitated because of insanity in a way similar to the protection given to infants. To qualify for this protection, it must be shown that the person could not understand the nature of the act being performed. For example, if a man is under the impression that he is Napoleon and thinks he is selling his horse when in fact he is selling his car, he would be declared insane because he does not understand that he is selling his car. To escape contractual liability on the basis of insanity, the insane person or a representative must prove not only insanity but that the person he or she was dealing with knew or ought to have known of the incapacity.

Insanity applies if person did not understand

In the case of *Hardman v. Falk*,[7] a real estate agent was trying to acquire land for the development of an industrial estate. He approached two sisters because he thought that they owned the particular parcel of land he wanted to acquire. After some tough negotiating, the two sisters agreed to give him an option on the land and he agreed to pay a substantial sum for the purchase of the land on behalf of his clients. Only later did he realize that the sisters did not own the land. He then explained the deal to the actual owner of the property, their invalid mother. She was old and feeble and had difficulty signing the documents but appeared to understand what was happening when he explained the nature of the transaction. However, when the real estate agent exercised the option to purchase on behalf of his clients, the two daughters refused to go through with the transfer of the land, claiming that their mother's mind was gone at the time she signed the contract. In this case, the mother was undeniably insane at the time of the contract but, because the agent was not in a position where he knew or should have known of the insanity, the agreement was held binding on the mother and the property was sold at the agreed-upon price.

—and if other party knew or ought to have known of incapacity

It should be noted that this approach is considerably different from the approach taken with infants. It makes no difference whether the adult knew the other party was an infant or not—the infant is still protected. In cases of insanity, however, even when it has been demonstrated that the person was insane, there can be a binding contract if the other party was not aware of the insanity.

Once a person has been committed to a psychiatric institution, all contracts entered into are considered void and are not binding on either party whether they are

---

[7] *Hardman v. Falk* [1955] 1 D.L.R. 432 (B.C. Supreme Court). Aff'd [1955] 3 D.L.R. 129.

Provincial
legislation applies
to people
committed to
institutions

Drunkenness
treated like
insanity

Must repudiate
upon becoming
sober

Bound by
purchase of
necessaries

for necessaries or otherwise. To understand the precise rights and obligations of such patients and the care and use of the patient's property, the appropriate provincial legislation should be carefully examined.

People who lose their ability to reason through intoxication are treated in the same way as the insane. Such intoxication is usually caused by alcohol but the same principles apply for other intoxicants, such as drugs. For a defence of intoxication to be considered, it must be demonstrated that the person was so incapacitated that he or she could not understand the nature of the transaction and that the other person knew or ought to have known of the incapacity. The person trying to escape a contract on the basis of drunkenness must be able to show that, on reaching sobriety, the contract was repudiated. An intoxicated person who purchases shares is not permitted, on becoming sober, to wait and see whether the stocks go up or down before repudiating the contract. Hesitation to repudiate makes the contract binding. This requirement of repudiation also applies to insane people who regain their sanity. Usually an insane person will be held responsible for contracts for necessaries, but, as was the case with infants, will only be obligated to pay a reasonable price for them.

A person who is of weakened intellect or otherwise vulnerable but not insane is still to some extent protected. Unconscionable transactions, the legal principle providing this protection, will be discussed below.

Native Indians

Status Indians
still protected
under *Indian Act*

The capacity of Native Indians living on reserves (status Indians) is still limited to some extent by the *Indian Act*.[8] It is likely that such paternalistic provisions will not long survive, given current attempts at reform.

Corporations

Corporation—
seperate legal
person

There are several situations in which the law recognizes the existence of an artificial person or legal entity separate and apart from the individuals who make it up. The most common example of such an artificial body is a modern business corporation or limited company. In fact, the corporation as a person does not really exist. It is a legal fiction, albeit a convenient one, for the world of commerce. Whenever we deal with a corporation, and most consumer activities do involve sales transactions with corporations, we are dealing with a fictional person who is considered to be a separate legal entity. When we purchase something from a department store such as The Bay, our contract is with The Bay itself and not with The Bay's shareholders. Company law will be dealt with in a subsequent chapter. At this point the problem to be considered is the method by which corporations enter into contracts.

The method of incorporation varies from province to province and in some provinces the power or capacity of corporations to enter into contracts has been

---

[8] *Indian Act* R.S.C. (1985) c.I-5.

limited. This was a significant feature of company law in many provinces in the not very distant past. This lack of capacity is much less important in Canadian company law today because several provinces have recently changed the method of incorporation used or have otherwise reformed their company law legislation with the effect that such corporations have the capacity of a natural person.[9] Incorporation under federal and provincial legislation will be examined in depth in Chapter 12.

Corporate capacity—usually no longer a problem

It must be emphasized, however, that there are many special corporations and other government bodies in Canada, including crown corporations, created by specific provincial or federal legislation which are intended to carry out government policy. The Canadian National Railway, Canada Post, Petro-Canada, Air Canada and Canada Mortgage and Housing Corporation are some examples. The normal rules of contract law apply to these bodies but their powers are often limited by specific legislation, and outsiders dealing with them must be alert to their limited capacity. In the absence of such statutory provisions, the merchant is free to assume that the government body or corporation in question has the power to do whatever it has agreed to do. Legislation will override any common law contractual principle, so anyone dealing with a crown corporation or government body must always check the legislation which created it.

Capacity of government bodies and crown corporations limited by legislation

Aliens

Any contract with a citizen of a country against which war has been declared is void under common law if it can be shown to have a detrimental effect on Canada. A citizen of an enemy country, whether a resident of Canada or of a hostile territory, is classed as an enemy alien. Most frequently the people concerned would be foreigners doing business in Canada when war breaks out. If the effect of the contract is not detrimental to the country in any way, the contract is merely suspended for the duration of the hostilities; otherwise, it is void. The Canadian government usually passes legislation to cover this area of law which overrides the common law provisions whenever hostilities break out.

Capacity of enemy aliens limited in times of war

Contracts with foreign governments or their representatives were traditionally thought to be unenforceable even in times of peace because of a foreign government's immunity from prosecution in Canadian courts. This immunity is based on the fact that the sovereignty of the foreign government would be lost if subjected to the jurisdiction of our courts. This provision was particularly important when dealing with matters of state that were of diplomatic importance. However, since foreign governments are now more frequently involved in simple commercial enterprises that have nothing to do with matters of state, the courts have been willing to treat them as any other party to commercial transactions. Legislation has recently been passed embodying these principles in statute law.[10] Representatives of foreign governments, such as ambassadors and their families, have traditionally been immune

---

[9] *Business Corporations Act* (1982) S.O. (1982) c.4 s.15.
[10] *State Immunity Act*, R.S.C. (1985) c.S-18.

from prosecution in our criminal courts and continue to be. A court will not issue a writ against such a person in a civil matter and their property is immune from seizure. Of course, these representatives can waive this immunity if they wish, but anyone dealing with people with diplomatic immunity ought to be aware of the protection they have been given.

Married Women

Capacity of married women no longer limited

In the past, married women were incapacitated in much the same way as infants and the insane under the common law. However, legislation has abolished these common law restrictions. Married women now have the same legal capacity to enter into contracts as any other adult person.

Unions

Trade unions have capacity to contract for union activities

Historically, unions were denied the capacity to enter into contracts because of their illegal status, but modern legislation in all provinces has given trade unions the capacity to enter into contracts relevant to their union responsibilities. Trade unions in many jurisdictions are, with some qualifications, considered legal entities much like corporations and can sue or be sued in their own capacity.

Bankrupts

People who have filed for or been placed in bankruptcy also have their contractual capacity significantly limited before they are discharged. Bankruptcy will be discussed in a subsequent chapter.

LEGALITY

The objectives of an agreement must be legal and not contrary to the public interest for the agreement to qualify as a binding contract. It is easy to understand that a contract to commit a crime would be void, but there are many other types of activities that, while not illegal, are considered immoral or contrary to the public interest. The courts have taken several different approaches when faced with the problem of immoral or illegal contracts.

Illegal Contracts

Illegal contracts—courts will not assist parties

At one extreme are contracts involving blatantly unacceptable conduct that can be characterized as illegal, such as an agreement to purchase a prohibited drug. Under

Response of
court varies
according to
violation

normal circumstances, the courts will help the parties return to their original positions if a contract is found to be void. This may include the refund of deposits or the return of property. With illegal contracts, however, not only is the contract declared void, the courts will refuse to deal with the parties. If money or property has changed hands, the court will not assist the parties to get it back. However, if one of the parties to an illegal contract has acted innocently, the courts will help that person to recover what has been lost.

Contracts can be jeopardized because they are inconsistent with either federal or provincial statutes. Workers' compensation legislation is designed to provide for safer working conditions and to compensate workers injured on the job. Any agreement between the worker and employer that circumvents the provisions of this legislation would be void. Much consumer protection legislation is designed to prevent unacceptable sales tactics and prohibit contracts that try to override these protective mechanisms.

Statute may
set out
consequences

Statutes which restrict the right of parties to contract often contain provisions setting out the rights of the parties in the event of a violation of the statute. Unfortunately, many statutes do not state the consequences of such violations. In such instances, the courts are left to apply the common law provisions related to illegal contracts. The courts have developed a flexible attitude when violations occur because of the variation in the degree of acceptability of the violations. Depending on the severity of the infraction, the courts may declare the contract void and assist the parties to return to their original positions. In some circumstances, the courts may enforce the contract. For example, most cities have legislation requiring that tradespeople such as roofers and painters acquire licences to practise. When work has been performed by a tradesperson who does not have a licence and the courts determine that the object of the bylaw is merely to generate revenue, they may enforce the contract and simply require that the tradesperson acquire the licence after the fact. If the purpose of the bylaw is to protect the public from the unqualified or the unethical, however, the unlicensed tradesperson will not be able to enforce the contract. If the legislation itself sets out the consequences of an infraction, this will override any discretion available to the court.

Contracts against Public Policy

Contracts
determined not
to be in
public's
best interest may
not be binding

There is little difficulty in applying these principles when a crime is involved or a statute exists that prohibits certain conduct or types of contracts. However, some types of agreements have been treated as not binding because they are not considered to be in the public's best interests. These agreements may not violate any law. They may vary in seriousness from those not in the public interest but not particularly immoral to those most members of the public would find offensive. Contracts that are not particularly offensive but which the courts feel should be set aside in the best interest of the public are simply declared void. If a deposit has been paid, money has been advanced or property has changed hands, the parties will be able to recover their expenditure. The parties to such contracts have not committed a crime for which they could be arrested or sued, but the courts simply refuse to promote activities they have determined should not be encouraged by enforcing such agreements. The very offensive agreements are treated in the same way as an illegal contract. The courts not only declare them void but will not help the parties return to their original positions. Of course, conduct that is criminal or is otherwise prohibited by statute is included as being against public policy.

Examples of contracts against public policy

The following is a list of some of the types of contracts that have been determined to be against public policy.

1. *Contracts to commit a crime or a tort.* For example, if Mullins offered Nowak $100 to claim that Abercromby did a poor job of repairing his house, that would be defamation.

2. *Contracts involving immoral acts.* For example, although prostitution is not illegal in Canada, a prostitute could not expect the courts to enforce a bargain made with a client because the act is considered immoral.

3. *Contracts that obstruct justice.* If the effect of the contract is to interfere with the judicial process, it is against public policy. For example, suppose Sawchuk is sent to jail for producing illegal alcohol. Fischer had promised to pay him a salary of $1000 per month if he was sentenced to jail. That contract would be deemed to be against public policy and therefore void. Sawchuk could not force payment from Fischer for the time he spent in prison. Enforcing such a contract would defeat the whole purpose of the jail term.

4. *Contracts that injure the state.* An example of this would be a contract to sell steel to Germany during World War II.

5. *Contracts that unduly restrain trade.* Business people often enter into contracts with provisions that prohibit certain types of business activities. If such a provision is reasonable and necessary to protect the interests of the parties, it is enforceable, but if the provision is unreasonably restrictive, that provision of the contract is void. For example, Beaudoin purchases a barbershop from Ahmed for $50 000. A considerable portion of the purchase price may be for the customer relations established by Ahmed. If Ahmed then opens another barbershop next door, it would destroy the "good will" aspect of the contract. It would be reasonable for the buyer to include a provision in the contract prohibiting the seller from carrying on a similar business for a specified time (for example, three years) and within a specified geographical area (for example, five kilometres). This would be classed as a reasonable restraint of trade and the contract would be valid. In the example used to introduce this chapter, the agreement prohibiting Mr. Guzzo from opening a similar business within five years was held by the court to be a reasonable restraint of trade. His violation of this clause cost him $20 000.

Restraint of trade contracts particularly important

Essentially, some interest must need to be protected, the restrictions must be no greater than necessary to protect that interest, and the restrictions must not be against the interests of the public. It is possible to separate the restrictive covenant from the rest of the agreement, making it the only part of the contract that is void, if it unduly restrains trade. That is, if the restrictive covenant were found to be unduly restrictive, it is the only part of the contract made void. The purchase price and all other terms of the agreement would be the same but the seller would have no restrictions at all and would be free to open a similar business anywhere. In the example above, if the provision in the contract for the purchase of the barbershop prohibited Ahmed from opening another shop anywhere in Canada or imposed an unreasonably long period of time such as ten years, this provision of the agreement would be void. Ahmed would then be free to open a new barbershop wherever or whenever he wanted.

Restrictive covenants can also be imposed if the success of a business depends to some extent on the loyalty of its employees. If the employees could do the business considerable harm either by taking away customers when leaving employment or by revealing trade secrets to new employers, the employer will often impose a restraining term in the contract of employment. Again, such a restriction must be reasonable in nature and not against the public interest.

6. *Contracts that restrict competition.* The federal *Competition Act*[11] specifically prohibits agreements which have as their primary purpose or objective the restriction of competition. Thus, if two merchants agreed not to sell a particular commodity below a certain price, that act would be prohibited and the contract void.

7. *Contracts that are bets and wagers.* This area is covered by statute and varies from province to province. Horse track betting, provincial lotteries, bingo games, etc., are permitted if the appropriate permission or licence is obtained. But activities such as off-track betting, poker games in which the house takes a cut and other types of gambling activities are usually prohibited.

It should be noted that provisions prohibiting gambling have application beyond games of chance. For example, insurance policies are special types of wagers. When a person insures a property, it is really a wager that the property will be destroyed. If the property is destroyed, the person who carries the insurance wins and collects on the wager. That is the difference—to win, the victim must lose. The intent of insurance is not to give a person a windfall but to provide a method of spreading the risk of loss. Therefore, it is necessary to show that the party insuring the property has an insurable interest in the subject of the policy and has something to lose if the anticipated event takes place. An insurance policy taken out on one's own house is valid and, if the house burns down, the owner is compensated for the loss. But if an individual takes an insurance policy out on someone else's house and has nothing to lose if it burns down, that person would not be permitted to collect on the policy since it is only a wager. The terms of the policy are void because there is no insurable interest. Contracts for the sale of shares suffer the same problem. If the contract merely requires the parties to pay each other the difference if the share price goes up or down, it is void as a wager. To avoid this problem, the contract must provide that the share will actually change hands.

[11] *Competition Act*, S.C. (1984-85-86) c.91.

8. *Contracts that promote litigation.* The courts have always been careful to ensure that they are used only to fulfil their declared public purpose: to settle disputes between the parties who come before them. Entering into agreements to use the courts for an ulterior motive is illegal. One party paying another to proceed in a court action against a third party would be an illegal and unenforceable agreement. If Chase carelessly drove over Park's foot and Roscoe were to offer to pay Park to sue Chase because of a dislike for Chase, such an agreement would be unlawful because it is against public policy. If a person approached the victim of an accident and offered to pay all of the legal fees in exchange for a promise of half of the eventual court award, such an agreement would be unlawful.

Contingency fee arrangements permissible because they make courts accessible

Lawyers, however, quite often enter into contingency fee arrangements with their clients whereby the lawyer agrees to bear the burden of the cost of the action and the risk of loss if the client will agree to pay a certain percentage of the award. This agreement appears to be permissible because it does not promote litigation but serves to make the courts more accessible to those who normally could not afford to proceed.

9. *Contracts injuring public service.* An example of this type of contract is if someone tried to pay a politician to vote a certain way in the legislature.
10. *Contracts in restraint of marriage.* Any contract that has as its object the prevention of marriage is against public policy. An agreement to pay someone $100 000 in return for a promise never to marry would not be binding.

These are some of the categories held to be against public policy. This list is neither complete nor exhaustive and it may well be that new types of activities made possible by changing technology could also be declared against public policy.

INTENTION

Parties must have intended legal consequences from agreement

Another element necessary to establish the existence of a binding contract is the requirement that the parties must have intended that legal obligations and rights would flow from their agreement. If a person invited a friend over for dinner who failed to show up for some reason, the delinquent guest would probably be quite surprised if the would-be host were to sue for breach of contract. In such a social relationship, neither party intended to create a legal responsibility.

Courts will enforce reasonable expectations

The statement that the parties must have intended to be bound is a little misleading, however, in that the court is less concerned with whether the promisor intended to be bound than with whether the promisee's reasonable expectations have been protected. The test is objective. It is no defence for promissors to state that they were just kidding or even to produce evidence to the court to support the contention that they did not think the contract would be binding. The courts will direct their attention to the person who is being promised something and ask whether that person should have known that the other party was not serious. Only if the court concludes that the promisee should have realized there was no serious intent to be legally bound will the agreement not be enforceable. In the example above, the guest invited to dinner would not normally expect a binding contract to be in place to force an appearance. The following situations illustrate instances in which this problem arises and indicate the courts' probable responses.

1. *Stated intention of the parties*. If the parties clearly state that they do not wish to be legally bound by their agreement, the court will grant this wish. Such a statement must be embodied in the terms of the contract and be very clear as to the intention. An example of a case in which the courts have honoured such a desire is *Rose and Frank Co. v. J.R. Crompton and Bros. Ltd.*[12]

Courts will accept stated intention

2. *Commercial relations*. If the relationship between the contracting parties is primarily commercial in nature, the courts will presume that the parties intended to be legally bound by their agreement. The contract will be binding on them in the absence of any evidence to the contrary.

Courts will presume intention in commercial transactions

3. *Domestic and social relations*. When an agreement involves members of a family, there is a presumption that the parties do not intend legal consequences to flow from the agreement. This is probably the result of a policy of non-interference in family disputes, but the effect is to make such agreements not binding in the absence of clear indication that the parties intended otherwise. If members of a family informally agree to make payments to each other, such as a child agreeing to pay room and board, the courts would assume that there is no intention to be legally bound and would not enforce the agreement. However, if the parties had gone to the trouble of having a lawyer draw up a formal contract, then the court would be satisfied that the parties did intend that legal consequences would flow from their agreement and would enforce the contract. The courts will presume there is no intention to be legally bound in purely social relationships.

Courts will presume no intention in domestic and social relations

4. *Social and business relations*. Problems arise when the relationship involved is a mixture of social and commercial, such as when people jointly enter a contest and dispute over the distribution of the prize. This problem could become more prevalent in Canada with the proliferation of lotteries with large prizes. In such cases, the court must treat each situation on its individual merit. In fact, the courts turn to the reasonable person test to determine whether it is reasonable for the parties trying to enforce the agreement to think that a legally binding contract had been created.

Reasonable person test applies where social and business mix

5. *Exaggerated claims*. Another area in which the problem of intention arises is when exaggerated claims are used to sell goods. Often the adviser or salesperson will say something like, "This is the best product in Canada," or "This is the best deal in the city." Most people expect dealers to exaggerate the qualities of their products and the defence is often raised that these claims are mere advertising "puffs" and that there was never any intention that they should be taken seriously. Many of these situations are now controlled or prohibited by statute.

—and when dealing with exaggerated claims

[12] *Rose and Frank v. Crompton* [1923] 2 K.B. 261 (Court of Appeal).

When an exaggerated claim forms part of the contract, the court must determine the intention of the parties. Again, the courts turn to the reasonable person test and simply ask if a reasonable purchaser would have recognized the claim to be an exaggeration. In the case of *Carlill v. Carbolic Smoke Ball Company*,[13] the defendant manufacturers made a product which they claimed would protect users from influenza. They offered £100 to anyone who used their product as prescribed and still contracted influenza. They stated in an advertisement that £1000 had been deposited in the Alliance Bank, Regent's Street, which showed their sincerity in the matter. Mrs. Carlill used the product and got influenza. She claimed the money but the company reneged, stating that the advertisement was an advertising puff that merely indicated some enthusiasm for the product and was not meant to be taken seriously by the public. The court held that depositing money to back up the claim had taken it out of the category of an advertising puff. It was determined that a reasonable person would have thought the advertisement was serious, so the offer was valid. There was intention, and Mrs. Carlill's use of the product and contracting the illness were appropriate forms of acceptance; thus there was a valid contract.

FORM OF THE CONTRACT

We have established that the essential ingredients of contracts are consensus, consideration, capacity, legality and intention. Nevertheless, the courts must consider an additional factor before they will enforce a contract. Historically, the form of the contract was very important. Promises were enforceable because they were contained in sealed documents or deeds. The seal is significant now because it eliminates the need to show consideration. As a general rule, in the common law system today there are no **formal** requirements that must be met for a contract to be enforceable although many jurisdictions have set out in statute specific situations when the documents used must be sealed.

Verbal contracts binding but writing advised

People are often surprised to find that verbal agreements are every bit as binding on them as those in writing. While there is some truth in the old saying that a promise is worthless if it is not in writing, it cannot be overemphasized that a verbal agreement has the same legal status as a written one as long as it meets the requirements described in this and the previous chapter.

The importance of the written document is practical, not theoretical. It is always a good idea to put the terms of an agreement in writing so that if a dispute arises something permanent establishes the terms to which the parties agreed. In the absence of such a document, it is surprising how differently people remember what they have agreed to. If the dispute between the parties does end in litigation, the parties will be in a better position to prove their case if they can produce written evidence to support their claim. In some circumstances, however, a contract **must** be evidenced in writing for it to be enforceable.

---

[13] *Carlill v. Carbolic Smoke Ball Co.* [1892] 2 Q.B. 484; [1893] 1 Q.B. 256 (Court of Appeal).

Statute of Frauds

During the reign of Charles II in the seventeenth century, many unscrupulous land dealers cheated others out of their property by perjuring themselves in court. To prevent this abuse, parliament enacted the *Statute of Frauds* which required that certain types of transactions be evidenced in writing before the courts would enforce them. The Statute has remained in force in Britain over the years and has become part of the law of most of the common law provinces in Canada. Because of the illiteracy prevalent at the time the Statute was enacted, it led to much abuse and caused as many problems as it solved. Significant modification to the Statute has been made in the United Kingdom, British Columbia and Manitoba, but in the rest of Canada the *Act* has remained essentially as passed. British Columbia recently repealed its *Statute of Frauds* altogether and included those provisions that were retained in the *Law and Equity Act*.[14] Manitoba has similarly repealed its *Statute of Frauds*; there is no general writing requirement in that province.[15] It must be emphasized that failure to comply with the Statute does not invalidate the contract; it merely prevents the parties from using the courts to enforce it.

Writing required to enforce some contracts

Statute of Frauds requires writing for enforcement in courts

The following is a discussion of the types of contracts generally included under the *Statute of Frauds* in Canada.

1. *Contracts not to be performed within one year.* When the terms of the agreement make it impossible to perform the service stipulated in the contract within one full year from the time the contract is entered into, there must be evidence in writing for it to be enforceable. For example, if Sasaki agrees to paint Monette's house one year from the following Monday, that contract must be evidenced by writing to be enforceable. Failure to have evidence in writing will make it no less a contract but the courts will refuse to enforce it. British Columbia has abolished the inclusion of this category altogether in its repeal of the *Statute of Frauds*.

When contract cannot be performed in one year

2. *Land Dealings.* Any contract that affects a party's interest in land must be evidenced in writing to be enforceable. It is often difficult to determine just what types of contracts affect interest in land, or ownership, and what types do not. Any sale of land or part of it, such as the creation of a joint tenancy in land, must be evidenced in writing. Any creation of an easement or right of way or estate, such as a life estate, is also covered by the Statute. But contracts for services to the land which do not affect the interest to the land itself are not covered. For example, if a carpenter agrees to build a house, such an agreement may affect the value of the land but not the interest in the land itself and so need not be evidenced in writing to be enforceable. Similarly, when permission is given to someone to come on the land (licensee) or when someone is lodging in another's home, these types of agreements need not be evidenced in writing. This provision of the *Statute of Frauds* has also been modified in

When the title to land is involved

---

[14] *Law Reform Amendments Act*, 1985 Bill 42 (British Columbia) 1985, Sect. 7.
[15] *An Act to Repeal the Statute of Frauds*, L.M. (1982-83-84) c.29.

some jurisdictions. In British Columbia, a lease for three years or less is exempt from the legislation but longer leases are treated just like any other interest in land and must be evidenced in writing to be enforceable.

When guarantee is involved

3. *Guarantees and Indemnities*. When moneylenders are not satisfied with the credit worthiness of a debtor, they may insist that someone else sign as well. This means that the creditor wants another person to add his or her credit to the transaction and assume responsibility for the repayment of the debt. The arrangement can be in the form of a guarantee or an indemnity. If the third party incurs a secondary liability for the debt, it is called a guarantee. The guarantor promises that if the debtor fails to pay the debt, he or she will assume the responsibility and pay. Note that in this type of transaction the obligation is secondary or contingent; there is no obligation on the guarantor until the debtor actually fails to pay the debt.

An indemnity describes a relationship in which the third party assumes a primary obligation for the repayment of the debt or other obligation along with the debtor. As a result, both owe the debt and the creditor can look to either for repayment. When a third party says, "I'll see that you get paid," there is an assumption of a primary obligation and the promise is an indemnity. The distinction between the two is important because, in most provinces, the *Statute of Frauds* requires that a guarantee be in writing but not an indemnity. If the court classifies the nature of the third party agreement as an indemnity, there is no requirement of writing. The distinction can be vital when a person has made only a verbal commitment to pay the outstanding loan of the debtor. In British Columbia, the *Law and Equity Act* requires that both indemnities and guarantees be evidenced in writing to be enforceable.

When promise is given in consideration of marriage

4. *Promises in Consideration of Marriage*. It is not necessary that a promise to marry be evidenced in writing to be enforceable. This provision covers those situations in which a promise is contingent on another's commitment to marry. Thus, a parent's promise to give a child a new car upon marriage would have to be evidenced in writing to be enforceable. This provision has been abolished in British Columbia.

When an executor promises to meet the debts of an estate out of own pocket

5. *The Promise of an Executor*. The Statute states that when the person appointed to look after the distribution of the assets of a person after death, known as the executor of the estate, promises to pay for a debt of the deceased out of his or her own pocket, there must be evidence in writing for the agreement to be enforceable. The executor is often a member of the family of the deceased and may feel a moral obligation to pay some of the debts even though no legal obligation exists. There are often considerable delays in paying out the debts of the deceased and such a promise may be given to avoid unpleasant pressure from creditors. This provision has also been abolished in British Columbia.

When goods sold over specific value

6. *Others*. The original *Statute of Frauds* required that whenever the purchase price of goods sold exceeded a specified minimum, there had to be evidence in writing for the sale to be enforceable. This provision has been included in the *Sale of Goods Act* in many jurisdictions in Canada but not in British Columbia. It is

usually sufficient evidence in writing if a receipt or sales slip has been given or if delivery of the goods has been accepted. The definition of goods and the sale of goods generally will be discussed in Chapter 7. Parliament and the provincial legislatures have passed many statutes which require the transaction itself to be in writing to be valid. Some examples are the *Bills of Exchange Act*, insurance legislation, consumer protection legislation, some of the legislation dealing with employment relations and the carriage of goods and passengers.

WHAT CONSTITUTES EVIDENCE IN WRITING. It is not necessary that the entire contract be in writing to satisfy the *Statute of Frauds*; the courts have held that only the main or essential terms must be evidenced in writing. This usually means a description of the parties to the agreement, a description of the property involved and a statement of the price paid. It must be remembered that if the parties have included any other unusual or essential terms in their agreement, those terms must also be evidenced by writing. Care has been taken throughout this presentation to avoid saying that the contract itself has to be in writing. It does not. The only thing that the Act requires is that there be some evidence in writing.

Writing must contain all essential terms

This evidence can come into existence after the contract. If someone is trying to avoid responsibility under an agreement because it is not "in writing," it would be unwise to write a letter to the other party to that effect. Such a letter may qualify as the required evidence in writing and thus defeat the objective of getting out of the deal. The Statute also requires that the evidence in writing be signed but only by the person who is trying to deny the existence of the obligation. The written evidence need not be in a single document but can be contained in a compilation of documents, the whole of which indicates the existence of the contract.

—and may arise after agreement

—and be signed by party to be charged but need not be in the same document

For example, if a person agreed to sell a house to another for $100 000 and the seller then refused to go through with the deal, it would be necessary for the purchaser to produce a document signed by the seller which identified the property, the purchaser, the amount of money involved and any other unique or essential terms. It is only when all of these requirements are satisfied that there is sufficient evidence in writing to satisfy the Statute and thus make the contract enforceable in the courts. (See Box 4.1, "Agreements enforceable without formal contracts".)

EFFECT OF THE STATUTE. It is vital to remember that under the *Statute of Frauds*, a contract is not void if it is not evidenced in writing, it is merely unenforceable. This means that the contract is still binding on the parties, but the courts will not assist the parties to enforce it. If the parties have already performed, or if there is some other remedy available that does not require the court's involvement, the contract will still be binding, even in the absence of evidence in writing. The courts will not assist a person who has performed to get out of a contract when a person has paid money in such circumstances. Nor will the court order the return of money even when there is no evidence in writing of the contract. In effect, the party only did what was required under the contract. Similarly, when there is a lien (a right to seize property) or when there is a right to set off a debt against the obligations established within the contract, the parties themselves are in a position to enforce it

Contract still valid even where no writing, just unenforceable

Box 4.1

Agreements enforceable without formal contracts

Businesses may be bound by agreements even if the parties don't sign formal contracts.

In Silvio Construction Co. vs. 678192 Ontario Ltd., Madame Justice Jean MacFarland decided that, even though the defendant had agreed that a formal contract should be prepared and that contract was never signed, the agreement was still binding.

Owned by Louis Meier, 678192 bought a large tract of land in Aurora, Ont. The idea was to build a subdivision called Hunters Hill Estates.

In the summer of 1987, Silvio Construction Co., owned by Domenic Lombardi, was asked to tender on the construction of roads, sewers and watermains for the project. After some preliminary negotiations, he submitted a bid of $1,093,889.

Early in January 1988, Lombardi was told he had the job and he agreed to a small reduction in the price.

When he heard nothing further, Lombardi wrote to Meier in March to demand that the contract be signed immediately.

In the first week of April, the construction company wrote again, saying that since the work was seasonal it had to begin right away.

Meier agreed to meet at his offices. At the meeting it was agreed Silvio would do the job.

Most of the agreement had been set out in the April letter, so a notation was made at the bottom of the letter.

This read: "I, the undersigned president and director of 678192 Ontario Ltd., do hereby agree to the above condition in principle, subject to a contract agreement prepared by Ray Floyd."

There was still a question of the final price, as the Town of Aurora had changed some of its requirements.

According to Mark Klaiman, the Toronto litigation lawyer who represented Silvio at trial, the formal contract was prepared by Floyd, who headed the consulting engineering firm on the project.

Lombardi signed it but Meier refused.

At trial, Meier claimed he had "made an agreement to make an agreement," so there was nothing legally binding.

He said many details were not settled, such as start and completion dates, final cost and terms of payment.

The judge did not accept his evidence.

"One would think on Mr. Meier's version of the meeting that he must have attended a different meeting," she said.

"All the essentials were set out in Lombardi's letter, save the starting date.... There were no additional terms to be left to the formal contract; the essentials were agreed upon.

"The formal contract was nothing more than a standard form into which the essential particulars agreed to at the April meeting would be inserted."

Lombardi was awarded $65,000 in damages, based on the justice's estimate of his lost profit.

The principle in the case according to Klaiman is that "if all the essential terms are agreed to, that is sufficient for a binding contract. The parties do not need a more formal contract document."

But although Meier lost the case, all was not lost for him.

During negotiations, a buyer offered to buy the property, netting Meier more than $2 million profit.

Source: James Carlisle, "Agreements enforceable without formal contracts," The Financial Post, Oct. 26, 1993, p. 17. James A. Carlisle is a partner in the litigation firm of Beard, Carlisle.

without the help of the courts and in that sense the contract is binding even though there is no evidence in writing.

PART PERFORMANCE. The court will waive the requirement of writing if the parties can produce evidence to show that the contract has been partially performed. There are some important limitations to this principle. The part performance must be

When part
performance
consistent with
contract—
writing not
required

evidence of the existence of the contract and consistent only with the existence of the contract. The payment of money owed under the contract will not be acceptable as proof of part performance because the payment of money is consistent with any number of different obligations.[16] However, when land has been sold and construction has been started, the permission to enter onto the land and start building is consistent with the sale of the land and so the part performance will be accepted by the courts as sufficient evidence to support the contract. It should be noted, however, that the remedies available in such situations are limited to equitable remedies such as specific performance, which means the court ordering the parties to go through with the contract rather than receive monetary compensation. This remedy is discussed in more detail in Chapter 6.

SUMMARY

Contracts with infants in most provinces are voidable except for contracts for necessaries and beneficial contracts of service. In British Columbia, by statute, all contracts with infants are unenforceable except those that are specifically made enforceable by legislation such as government student loans. Insanity or drunkenness will only cause a contract to be invalid when the person was so insane as to not know what was happening and when the other contracting party knew or ought to have known of that incapacity. Corporations, enemy aliens in time of war, trade unions, government agencies, bankrupts and even Native Indians under some circumstances may have their capacity to enter contracts limited to some extent.

Contracts that are illegal or against public policy may also be invalid or unenforceable. Agreements to commit crimes or immoral acts, to obstruct justice, to injure the state, to promote litigation, to injure public service, to restrain marriage and, in some circumstances, bets or wagers may be held to be illegal or against public policy. Contracts that restrict competition, such as price fixing, are prohibited, but contracts to restrain trade, such as when one party agrees not to carry on business in competition with another, are valid if they can be shown to be reasonable in terms of the interests of the parties and the public.

Both parties must intend to be legally bound by their agreement. In family and other social relationships there is a presumption of no intention but this can be challenged by evidence that shows an intent to be bound. In commercial relationships, intention is presumed. In unusual situations, the reasonable person test is used to determine intention.

Contracts dealing with land that will not be performed within one year (except leases for three years or less), and contracts involving guarantees, in consideration of marriage, and by the executor of an estate to personally pay a debt are examples of contracts that, under the *Statute of Frauds*, must be evidenced

---

[16] In B.C., the requirements to satisfy part performance are not as stringent, and part payment is acceptable.

in writing to be enforceable. This statute has been repealed or modified in several jurisdictions. When part performance is established, such agreements are enforceable.

QUESTIONS

1. Explain the circumstances in which an infant may escape liability for a contract and the circumstances in which an infant is bound by a contract.
2. What is the significance of an infant's contract being designated as a beneficial contract of service?
3. What is the responsibility of parents for the actions of their infant children in both tort and contract law?
4. What are the rights and obligations of the parties involved when an infant makes a contract with an adult for non-necessaries?
5. Explain the circumstances in which an infant can be sued for tort even though a contract between the parties is involved.
6. What must an insane or drunk person establish to escape liability under a contract?
7. Describe how the provisions of the *Indian Act* limit the capacity of status Indians to enter into contracts.
8. Explain what care business people must exercise when entering into contracts with crown corporations or government bodies.
9. Describe how the courts treat a contract to commit a crime.
10. Give five examples of contracts deemed by the courts to be against public policy and describe the effect of such a designation.
11. Are all contracts which restrain trade unlawful? Explain.
12. Explain how the courts' treatment of domestic agreements differs from their response to commercial transactions when the question of intention arises.
13. Describe tests the courts will use in determining whether the parties were serious in their statements.
14. What is the significance of a written document in contractual relations?
15. Explain why some people have suggested that the *Statute of Frauds* has led to more frauds than it has prevented.
16. Give examples of the types of contracts currently included under the *Statute of Frauds*.
17. What must be evidenced in writing to satisfy the requirements of the *Statute of Frauds*?
18. Under what circumstances will a contract falling under the jurisdiction of the *Statute of Frauds* be enforceable even though it is not evidenced by writing?

CASES

1. *Fannon v. Dobranski.*
   The infant plaintiff purchased a second-hand automobile from the defendant for $300 which, after being driven for 119 kilometres, broke down. Because the transmission needed replacing, which would have cost $200, the plaintiff simply towed the car to the home of the defendant, returned the keys and repudiated the contract. The infant then brought an action to recover the purchase price. Explain the probable outcome. Would your answer be different if the car had not broken down but the plaintiff had simply decided against buying the car?

2. *Osorio et al. v. Cardona.*
   Osorio and Cardona went to the horse races together. Both had recently come to Canada from Colombia. On July 10 a wagering scheme known as the sweep six was offered at the race-track. This wager involved betting on six races and predicting the winners. Both Osorio and Cardona had tickets on the sweep six and after the third race it was clear that both tickets were still in the running. At that time they entered into an agreement to the effect that if either of them won, the winner would pay the other 30 percent (this was later modified because of the odds involved so that if Cardona won, Osorio would only receive 20 percent but if Osorio won, Cardona would win 30 percent). In fact Osorio's horse was knocked out in the next race but Cardona's ticket went on to win $735 403.

   After several days of trying to avoid Osorio, Cardona finally told him that he would have to take $60 000 or nothing (the 20 percent share would have been $147 000). There was some threat involved in that Cardona indicated that he would leave the country and go back to Colombia. Osorio agreed to take the $60 000. This was given to him and then he sued for the remainder. Explain the arguments available to both sides as to whether he ought to be successful in obtaining judgment for the remaining $87 000.

3. *Merritt v. Merritt.*
   A husband and wife had a significant mortgage on their house which they paid off over the years. There was only £180 owing on the mortgage when the husband ran off with another woman. The husband agreed to pay the wife, who was employed, £40 per month out of which she had to maintain the payments on the house. The wife persuaded the husband to sign a document stating that, when the mortgage was completely paid of, he would sign over his interest in the title of the house to her. When the mortgage was fully paid off, he reduced his monthly payments to £25 and refused to give her the title of the house. The wife brought an action to obtain a court order to force the con-

veyance of the husband's interest to her. What arguments could he raise in his defence? Explain the outcome.

4. *Whitfield v. Canadian Marconi Co.*
    The plaintiff, an employee of the Marconi Co., was on duty in the north. While there, he developed an acquaintance with a young Inuit woman who lived in a nearby village. His employment contract contained a "non-fraternization" clause which prohibited him from associating with Native people. He was warned to discontinue seeing the woman, refused to do so and was fired. He brought an action seeking damages for wrongful dismissal. Explain the outcome. Do you think the Charter of Rights and Freedoms and other human rights legislation would have any impact on the case if it were to happen today?

5. *Canadian American Finance Corp. v. King.*
    The Canadian American Finance Corporation markets a registered scholarship savings plan for profit. King was employed to market the plan as director of agencies. King set up a separate company to market the plan. The agreement between the Canadian American Finance Corporation and King included a non-competition clause which said that once the relationship was terminated King could not enter into competition with the corporation for a period of two years in Canada or Bermuda. King eventually quit and went to work for a rival company in the provinces of Alberta and British Columbia. Comment on the arguments available to both parties as to the validity of this non-competition clause.

6. *Fairgrief v. Ellis.*
    The plaintiff agreed to be a housekeeper for the defendant on the understanding that his house would go to her when the defendant died. This agreement was never put down in writing but it is clear that this was the understanding of both parties during the course of their association. The defendant's wife arrived and the plaintiff was required to leave, but the defendant promised to pay her $1000 to replace the previous agreement. The plaintiff agreed to this and when the money was not paid, she sued for $1000. Explain the likely outcome. Would her suit have succeeded if she had sued on the original agreement?

7. *Performance Systems Inc. v. Pezim.*
    The defendant was involved in promoting a restaurant chain in Canada which required buying a franchise from a similar American company. The American company loaned the Canadian company $50 000 on the strength of a promissory note guaranteed by the defendant. There was some dispute about whether the agents who consented to the guarantee on behalf of the defendant were authorized to do so, but it was held that the defendant could not deny that he had guaranteed the promissory note. However, the guarantee was

not signed until several months after the $50 000 was advanced. When the Canadian company ran into difficulties and was unable to repay the loan, the American company demanded that the defendant honour the guarantee. What arguments would the defendant raise in defence of this action? Explain the likely outcome.

ISSUES

1. A person must demonstrate not only that he or she was insane but that the other party to the agreement knew of the insanity in order to escape a contract because of insanity. In a case of infancy, however, it is only necessary to demonstrate that the contracting party was under the age of majority. Merchants who deal with infants, therefore, are in a considerably different position than they would be if dealing with the insane and are considerably more at risk. The question for discussion is: Is this difference in the approach of the courts when dealing with infancy as opposed to insanity justified? Will merchants be any more likely to take advantage of infants if this provision is changed? A related problem for the merchant is that the infant is not liable for the purchase of what would normally be necessaries if the infant can demonstrate that he or she already has an adequate supply. The merchant, of course, has no way of knowing about the status of the infant's supply unless the infant actually tells the merchant. Would it not be more appropriate in both these circumstances to put the onus on the infant to show that the merchant knew or ought to have known of the infancy and should have known the infant had an adequate supply of the goods purchased?

2. Insane people are completely relieved of most contractual obligations when it can be demonstrated that they meet the established tests for incapacity. If they fall slightly short of that standard, however, they must honour contractual obligations. Infants just under the age of majority are protected while adults who may be only a few days older are fully obligated under the contract. These are all or nothing rules. The question for discussion is: Would it not be more appropriate for the courts to impose at least some obligation that increases as the youth approaches the age of majority and that varies with the degree of maturity, independence or lucidness of the person claiming the protection?

3. Vicarious liability is imposed on employers for the acts of their employees but not on parents for the acts of their children. Parents are not obligated for damages caused by their children either in tort or in contract. Would it

not be more appropriate to extend the general responsibility parents have for their children and create a vicarious liability for the damage caused by infant children either through tort or through breach of contract? Would it not be more appropriate for the parents to bear at least some of the loss rather than the innocent victim of the tort or breach of contract?

4. There is little disagreement with the courts' power to refuse to enforce a contract that embodies as a requirement the breach of some law or the commission of a crime. There are many circumstances, however, in which the courts will refuse to enforce a contract in which no breach of law or commission of crime is involved. These unenforceable contracts involve activities considered to be against public policy because they are of an immoral or otherwise unacceptable nature. For example, although prostitution is not illegal in Canada, access to the courts will be denied to prostitutes who wish to use the courts to enforce contracts made in their professional activities. The question for discussion is: Would it not be more appropriate to limit the courts' power to refuse to enforce contracts to those situations in which it can be clearly demonstrated that the contract requires the breach of some law or the commission of a crime? If it is necessary to discourage an activity by refusing recourse to the courts, surely that activity ought to be made illegal? This would allow the courts to avoid the criticism that judges merely impose their middle-class concept of morality on people who do not necessarily agree with it. Would this approach be more consistent with the concept of freedom of contract?

5. When dealing with the application of the *Statute of Frauds*, the courts first determine whether a valid, binding contract exists and then turn their attention to whether the requirements of the Statute have been met. If the court is satisfied that there is a valid contract, is there ever a justification for refusing to enforce the contract merely because some formal requirements imposed by the Statute have not been met? If not, the Statute is contributing to injustice rather than alleviating fraud as it was originally designed to do. The question for discussion is: Do the provisions of the *Statute of Frauds* facilitate justice or hinder it? Is there any justification for retaining the Statute in our present law? In your response, consider the history of the Statute and the reforms that have taken place, especially in the United Kingdom and British Columbia.

LEGISLATION

Alberta
Age of Majority Act, R.S.A. (1980) c.A-4
Dependent Adults Act, R.S.A. (1980) c.D-32

British Columbia
Infants Act, R.S.B.C. (1979) c.196 as amended by the *Law Reform Amendment Act*, S.B.C. (1985) c.10
Law and Equity Act, R.S.B.C. (1979) c.224 as modified by the *Law Reform Amendment Act*, S.B.C. (1985) c.10-S7

Manitoba
Age of Majority Act, R.S.M. (1987) c.A-7
Mental Health Act, R.S.M. (1987) c.M-110
Statute of Frauds Repeat Act, S.M. (1982-83-84) c.34

New Brunswick
Age of Majority Act, R.S.N.B. (1973) c.A-4
Statute of Frauds Act, R.S.N.B. (1973) c.S-14
Mental Health Act, R.S.N.B. (1973) c.M-10

Newfoundland
Minors (Attainment of Majority) Act, R.S.N. (1971) c.71

Nova Scotia
Age of Majority Act, R.S.N.S. (1989) c.4
Incompetent Persons Act, R.S.N.S. (1989) c.218
Statute of Fraud Act, R.S.N.S. (1989) c.442

Ontario
Age of Majority and Accountability Act, R.S.O. (1980) c.7
Mental Incompetency Act, R.S.O. (1980) c.264
Statute of Frauds, R.S.O. (1980) c.481

Prince Edward Island
Age of Majority Act, R.S.P.E.I. (1988) c.A-8
Statute of Frauds, R.S.P.E.I. (1988) c.S-7

Saskatchewan
Infants Act, R.S.S. (1978) c.I-9
Mental Health Services Act, S.S. (1984-85-86) c.M-13.1
Mentally Disordered Persons Act, R.S.S. (1978) c.M-14

Northwest Territories
Age of Majority Act, R.S.N.W.T. (1974) c.A-1
Infants Act, R.S.N.W.T. (1974) c.I-1

Yukon
Age of Majority Act, R.S.Y. (1986) c.2

Federal
Indian Act, R.S.C. (1985) c.I-5
State Immunity Act, R.S.C. (1985) c.S-18

5

FACTORS AFFECTING THE CONTRACTUAL RELATIONSHIP

Objectives of the Chapter

- to describe the nature and effect of a mistake in a contract
- to explain misrepresentation and its consequences on a contract
- to consider the implications of duress and undue influence
- to outline the rules governing privity and assignment

Mr. Hoy purchased a fifty-year-old house from Mr. and Mrs. Lozanovski after having a builder friend inspect it and indicate that it was sound. Soon after he moved in, he discovered that the house was infested with termites; it had to be completely renovated at a cost of $25 000 before he could live in it. Mr. Hoy sued the Lozanovskis, claiming damages in this amount for fraudulent misrepresentation. The judge held that there was no fraud since the Lozanovskis did not know of the termites when they sold the house. Even if they had, the judge said, they would not be liable since they were silent (they had made no statements that the house was free from such infestation) and the purchaser had not relied on any representations from them but had had his own builder inspect the house. To obtain damages, Mr. Hoy not only had to demonstrate that the misrepresentation was fraudulent rather than innocent but also that he had relied on the representation in question. In this case, not only was there no reliance on the representation, there was no representation at all.[1] Misrepresentation is just one of the factors to be considered in this chapter that can affect the rights of the parties to a contract.

The two previous chapters examined the process of forming contracts. This chapter will discuss the extent of the responsibilities and obligations of the original parties to an agreement, what happens when the parties disagree as to the nature and effect of the contract, and how those obligations are affected when an innocent third party or a stranger to the contract becomes involved.

MISTAKE

Misunderstanding that destroys consensus results in void contract

Mistake must be part of agreement, not just affect agreement

Mistake must relate to nature of agreement, not the law

Mistake must be serious

Consensus is an important aspect of a legally binding contract. As the term is used here, consensus may be actual or implied from the conduct of the parties. The test is objective and an actual meeting of the minds is not required. Thus, consensus may be missing if either party mistakes the nature of the agreement. Precise rules have been developed to deal with misunderstandings between the parties and to govern the court's interpretation of the terms of any contract. The contractual mistakes affecting the legal obligations of the parties to be dealt with here are mistakes concerning the agreement itself, not the effect of the agreement. If a person buys a property in the belief that a new highway will soon be built nearby and it turns out that the purchaser was mistaken in this belief, that mistake would not be grounds for claiming that the contract should be set aside. The purchaser made an incorrect assumption, but there is no problem with the agreement or its terms. However, if a purchaser thought that he or she was buying certain property, Blackacre, when in fact it was different property all together, Greenacre, this would be a mistake as to the nature of the agreement itself and could be raised as a defence when being sued for breach of contract.

A simple mistake in law is no defence. If either party misunderstands the legal effect of the agreement, he or she will not be able to escape the contract on the basis of mistake. Generally, the courts will not interfere with a contract unless it can be demonstrated that the mistake claimed is a very serious one. It must be a factual mistake as to the subject matter or the identity of the parties, or a misunderstanding of the agreement that is so fundamental it destroys the element of consent. Thus, a mistake involving the parties must concern the existence or identity of those parties and a mistake involving the subject matter must concern the identity or existence of the subject matter.

---

[1] *Hoy v. Lozanovski*, 648-015, *The Lawyers Weekly*, Apr. 3, 1987.

The three categories of mistake and how the courts deal with them will now be examined. It should be noted that the terms **common mistake**, **mutual mistake** and **unilateral mistake** are terms of convenience, and that many authors and judges use them in ways slightly different from their use here. It should also be noted that a voidable contract does exist and has legal effect, but one of the parties has the option of declaring the contract to be at an end.

A void contract is no contract at all. An innocent third party acquiring goods which are the subject of a voidable contract would have a valid claim to them, but if the contract were void, the third party would lose the goods.

Common Mistake (Shared Mistake)

A **common mistake** is made when the two parties are in complete agreement but they have both made the same mistake regarding a fundamental aspect of the subject matter of the contract. There are two circumstances in which the courts will declare such contracts to be void. The first is when the subject matter of the agreement does not exist at the time the parties enter into the contract.[2] Thus, if the parties enter into an agreement for the sale and purchase of the cargo of a ship without knowing that the cargo had been destroyed the night before, the contract is void because of common mistake. The second situation is when the vendor is in no position to convey title to goods because the prospective purchaser already has title. In the case of *Cooper v. Phibbs*,[3] a contract was held void because, although both the vendor and the purchaser thought the vendor had title to a fishery, it turned out that the purchaser already owned it. The contract was void because of this shared false belief about the subject matter of the agreement.

The court will not allow the careless party to escape responsibility when a shared mistaken belief about a fundamental aspect of the contract is the result of negligence on the part of one of the parties. This principle was clearly established in *McRae v. Commonwealth Disposals Commission*,[4] and legislation has been passed incorporating this provision into the *Sale of Goods Acts* in all the common law provinces in Canada. But these common law provisions apply to many situations other than the sale and purchase of goods.

When the parties make a mistake about only the value of what they are dealing with, it normally will not affect the enforceability of the contract. For example, if both vendor and purchaser think that they are dealing with some ordinary furniture and, in fact, a rare and valuable Hepplewhite table is included, the contract would be binding nevertheless.

Fundamental shared mistake about subject matter—void

Careless party responsible when mistake is result of negligence

---

[2] *Couturier v. Hastie*, (1852) 8 Ex. 40 (Court of Exchequer).

[3] *Cooper v. Phibbs* [1867] L.R. 2 H.L. 149 (House of Lords). In the case of *Hyrsy v. Smith*, the Ontario High Court of Justice has taken this principle even further. In that case, both the vendor and the purchaser of land thought the vendor had title to all of the land that was the subject matter of the contract. But the vendor had title to only part of the land and thus only that part was conveyed to the purchaser. In the subsequent action, the court held that a common mistake going to the "root of the contract" had taken place, the contract was void, and rescission was granted. *Hyrsy v. Smith* [1969] 2 O.R. 360.

[4] *McRae v. Commonwealth Disposals Commission* (1951) 84 C.L.R. 377 (High Court of Australia).

RECTIFICATION. If the written document does not reflect the common intention of the parties to the contract, the courts are willing to correct or rectify the document. For example, if two parties had agreed to the sale of land for $50 000 and a clerical error made the document read $5000, the court would add the missing zero and require the parties to perform the corrected agreement. The parties had entered into the contract. The written document was merely evidence of the contract. Therefore, the court is free to rectify the written document. However, there must be the clearest evidence that both of the parties agreed to something different from what was embodied in the written document to obtain rectification by the courts. The onus of proof rests on the party asking for rectification and it may be difficult to prove.

Courts may correct a mistake in recording agreement

When the shared mistake goes to the legal effect of what the parties have agreed to in the written document rather than the terms themselves, the courts will not rectify the agreement. Thus, if the parties include the term "barley" in a contract, each incorrectly thinking that the term refers to "hops," the court will refuse a request to rectify the written document because it is in fact a correct record of their agreement. It is important to remember that the courts are not rewriting the agreement during rectification. They are simply correcting a written document so that it corresponds to the demonstrated intention of the two parties.

Mutual Mistake (Misunderstanding)

A **mutual mistake** occurs when the parties have a misunderstanding about the terms of the agreement itself and neither party is aware of the other's different understanding of the agreement. When one party to an agreement thinks that the agreement is to do something else, the courts will usually apply the reasonable person test to determine which interpretation of the contract is more reasonable. The court will then adopt the more reasonable position as the correct interpretation of the contract. This point is discussed below in more detail under the heading "Rules of Interpretation." Only if the error is a serious one and the court cannot choose between the two positions because both are equally reasonable will the contract be declared void. For example, if there is an agreement to buy a 1984 Chrysler and the purchaser thinks this term means a 1984 Chrysler sailboat when the item for sale is a 1984 Chrysler automobile, a misunderstanding about a fundamental term of the agreement has taken place. The court will examine the relationship between the parties, including the comments made at the time of the agreement, to determine if one interpretation is more reasonable than the other. If the parties discussed the condition of the motor and the transmission, and what gas mileage was obtained, the position of the seller would seem more reasonable since such comments would normally be associated with a car rather than with a sailboat. But if, after examining all the factors, it is still not possible to choose one position as the more reasonable, the court would probably find that there is no contract. If the error is serious, involving an important term of the agreement, and the interpretations are equally reasonable, consensus is not present and there will probably be no contract between the parties.

Misunderstanding may void contract if serious enough

Unilateral Mistake (One-Sided Mistake)

Contract may be void when one party makes a fundamental one-sided mistake

If one of the parties makes a mistake in relationship to the contract and the other party is aware that this mistake is being made, this is called a **unilateral mistake**. Relief will be given to the person who makes the mistake only if it goes to the very root of the contract, involving some fundamental element. Thus, if a purchaser is under the impression that the car being purchased is equipped with a V8 engine when in fact it has only a four-cylinder engine and the seller is aware of the purchaser's misconception, the seller is under no legal obligation to disabuse the purchaser of any incorrect assumptions. This is an example of the principle of *caveat emptor* (let the buyer beware). But if the seller has misled the purchaser into believing that the car is equipped with a V8 engine, the situation is quite different and the principles of misrepresentation or breach of contract apply. It should be noted, however, that when the offeror makes an obvious error in relation to his or her offer, the purchaser will not be allowed to take advantage of this obvious error and snap up the offer. Thus, if a vendor intended to offer her property for $22 500 and wrote $12 500 instead, the court would hold that the resulting agreement was not enforceable. The purchaser should have realized that the vendor was making a mistake and the courts will not allow the purchaser to take advantage of it.

Caveat emptor applies when purchaser misleads himself or herself

Another situation in which a unilateral mistake can occur is in the incorrect identification of one of the parties to a contract. If the person claiming that a mistake has taken place actually thought the deal was with someone else and can demonstrate that identity was an important aspect of the agreement, the court will declare the contract to be void. However, if the party using mistaken identity as a defence was just in error about some attribute of the other party, this will not affect the existence of the contract. For example, if a vendor thought that jewellery was being sold on credit to Ms. Paré, a wealthy movie star, and in fact Ms. Paré was not associated with the movie industry at all, the contract would be binding and title would go to the purchaser. If the jewellery is resold, the ultimate purchaser would acquire good title. Of course, the seller would still have recourse against Ms. Paré if she did not pay for the jewellery. But if the seller thought that the purchaser was Ms. Paré, a wealthy and well-known movie star, and in fact the purchaser was Ms. Capozzi, a waitress, a mistake has been made about the identity of the person with whom the seller is dealing, and there would be no contract. In the first instance, the seller knew whom he was dealing with but was mistaken about some of the person's qualities or attributes; in the second situation, the seller was fooled into thinking the purchaser was somebody else entirely. Therefore, there is no contract.[5] If the reason for the mistake is a false representation by one of the contracting parties that misleads the other, an action for misrepresentation may be brought. If a mistake is made in the actual performance of a contract with, for example, more paid than is owed, the court can order the excess returned because the creditor has been unjustly enriched.

If mistake about attributes—valid contract

If mistake about identity—void contract

[5] *Cundy v. Lindsay* (1878) A.C. 459 (House of Lords).

NON EST FACTUM. Whenever it is clear that one of the parties, even though he or she was careful, was unaware of the nature of the contract, the courts have the right to declare the agreement void on the basis of *non est factum* (it is not any act). In these cases, the defendants hold that the signed documents do not represent what they thought they were signing, thus, there is no consensus. For this defence to succeed and the contract to be void, it must be shown that the mistake about the document went to the very nature of that document rather than merely to its terms. It is unlikely today that such a defence will be successful unless it can be shown that the error was caused by misrepresentation. For example, if Ms. Paré was fooled into thinking she was signing an autograph when in fact it was a mortgage on her property, that mistake would be significant enough to give rise to the defence of *non est factum* and the agreement would be void. Even when an innocent third party acquired the rights under the mortgage, she would not be bound by it. However, if she thought she was signing a mortgage document requiring 14 percent interest when in fact she had signed one requiring 20 percent interest, she would not be able to rely on the defence of *non est factum.* However, a personal remedy against the person who misled her, such as rescission or misrepresentation, may be available to Ms. Paré. Such remedies would, however, be of no value against an innocent third party who acquired these mortgage rights. When it can be demonstrated that a person was in any way careless in signing a document, he or she would not be permitted to rely on the defence of *non est factum.* Negligence on the part of the person claiming *non est factum* when the other party is clear of any wrongdoing may be a bar to this defence. Failure to read the document will likely be enough to constitute such negligence but this must be determined case by case.[6]

If misled about nature of document signed—void

—but not where negligence present

Rules of Interpretation

The test to determine whether a mistake has taken place or not is objective. The courts are not concerned with what the parties thought they were agreeing to but rather with what the parties should have been aware of when they made the agreement. In such instances, the courts use the reasonable person test. Instead of declaring the contract void because one of the parties has made a mistake about the meaning of a term, the courts will look at the wording to determine what a reasonable person would have understood the term to mean. In those rare circumstances in which there is no reasonable interpretation of the agreement or the positions taken by the two parties are equally reasonable, the courts will declare the contract to be void. In the case of *Raffels v. Wichelhaus,*[7] the contract concerned a crop being transported on a particular ship called *The Peerless.* It happened that there were two ships by this name both leaving the same port but at different times. The seller intended one of these two ships and the purchaser had in mind the other. There was no way of applying the reasonable person test to this case and,

Reasonable person test applies when misunderstanding is not fundamental

[6] *Marvco Color Research Ltd. v. Harris et al.* (1983) 141 D.L.R. (3rd) 577 (S.C.C.)
[7] *Raffels v. Wichelhaus* (1864) 2 H. & C. 906 (Exchequer Division)

since the disagreement was fundamental, the contract was declared void. In the vast majority of cases, however, the courts will simply impose a reasonable interpretation on the agreement.

Whenever there is a dispute involving the meaning of a specific term, the courts have a choice of applying the literal meaning of the term or adopting a more liberal approach by trying to determine the parties' intent. The courts will apply the literal meaning of the wording chosen by the parties if there is no ambiguity. If the term is ambiguous, the court will look at what was behind the agreement and apply the most reasonable meaning of the term to the contract.

Determining the literal meaning of the words is not as simple as it might first appear. Even dictionaries often have several different meanings for particular words. Determining the intention of the parties may also be difficult because of the conflicting positions taken by the parties to the dispute. The court will often look at how the terms are normally used in the particular industry involved. The court will also look at past dealings between the parties as well as their dealings at the time the contract was formed to determine what they intended by the words they used. The key to the court's approach to such ambiguous terms in an agreement is to choose the most reasonable interpretation. But whenever the courts are faced with a choice of two equally reasonable interpretations, one of which will result in a declaration that there is no contract and the other giving life to the contract, the courts have a preference for the term that will keep the contract alive.

Another rule courts use in these situations is the **parol evidence rule**. This rule states that when the written term of a contract is clear and unambiguous, the parties will not be permitted to introduce evidence outside of the contract to contradict that clear meaning. For example, if a seller agreed to sell a 1984 Chrysler automobile and that specific clause was used in the contract, the purchaser would not be permitted to introduce outside evidence later to show that the agreement concerned a 1984 Chrysler sailboat. Had the parties agreed to use the term 1984 Chrysler instead, the statement would be ambiguous and the court would be free to consider outside evidence brought in by the purchaser, as discussed above. An ambiguous term is just one of the exceptions to the parol evidence rule.

Another situation in which the courts will allow outside evidence despite the terms of the contract is when the evidence to be introduced is of a fraud or some other problem associated with the formation of the contract. Other exceptions to the parol evidence rule include evidence of a condition precedent (a condition that has to be met before the obligations set out in the contract are in force); evidence of a collateral contract (a separate contractual obligation that can stand alone, independent of the written one); evidence of a subsequent agreement entered into by the parties after the written one, or when there never was an intention that all of the contract would be embodied in the written document. When the evidence contradicting the terms of the agreement falls into one of these categories, the court can be persuaded to hear it, despite the parol evidence rule.

It does not occur to most contracting parties to provide terms in their offer for every possible eventuality. In such circumstances, the courts will imply terms to the contract which the parties may have overlooked or neglected to include. For

Courts apply literal meaning to specific wording

Ambiguous wording interpreted liberally

Courts will not permit outside evidence to contradict clear wording

example, if a seller offers to sell an automobile for $500 and a purchaser accepts the offer without coming to terms about the date of delivery or when payment is due, the two parties would probably assume it was implicit in the agreement that the car would be delivered in a reasonable time and that payment would take place upon delivery. The courts will not make an agreement for the parties; they will simply imply insignificant terms the parties would have included if they had thought of them.

Courts will imply terms where appropriate

The courts are willing to imply such terms when there is a considerable amount of tradition associated with a particular industry. When parties within the industry enter into agreements with each other, the courts are willing to imply terms to the contracts that are consistent with the practices of their trade. Some terms may be implied automatically by statute. The *Sale of Goods Act* has set down in rule form the terms that must be included in a contract for the sale of goods when the parties have not addressed them. As well, some consumer protection legislation imposes terms in contracts whether or not the parties have agreed to them.

Statutes may imply terms into contract

EQUITY. There are other circumstances in which the chancery courts have developed ways to handle disputes involving mistakes between the original two parties to a contract. The courts can actually use the principles of fairness and equity to justify the imposition of new terms on the parties even though the contract is declared void. Such imposition happened in the case of *Cooper v. Phibbs*[8] discussed under common mistake. In that case, a vendor sold a fishery to a purchaser without realizing that the purchaser already owned it. In fact, the vendor had done a considerable amount of work to prepare the property for sale but since the agreement was void he received nothing for his work. The court, however, applied the principles of equity, granted the would-be vendor a lien against the property and ordered the owner to pay him for the work he had done. The courts have maintained the right to set the contract aside when justified by either of the parties' conduct even if the mistake involved does not affect the foundation of the agreement and the contract is valid.

Equity may be used to settle mistakes in contracts

MISREPRESENTATION

Misrepresentation is a false statement of fact that persuades someone to enter into a contract. The concepts of misrepresentation and mistake frequently overlap. The rules of misrepresentation come into effect when one party can show that the mistake was a direct result of being misled by the other party. Remedies are available to victims of misrepresentation which are unavailable to those suffering from mistake. It is necessary to show that the mistake destroyed the very foundation of the contract to escape a contract on the basis of mistake. But the person claiming misrepresentation needs only to show that he or she had been misled about some

Misrepresentation is a misleading statement that induces a contract

[8] *Cooper v. Phibbs* [1867] L.R. 2 H.L. 149 (House of Lords).

material or important aspect of the contract to receive a remedy. Some other qualifications to this principle must also be considered.

Allegation of Fact

The statement that forms the basis of the misrepresentation must be an allegation of
fact. Only statements made about the current state of things which prove to be incorrect can be considered misrepresentation. A promise to do something in the future
or a statement of opinion will not normally qualify as misrepresentation. For example, the promise to paint a neighbour's house and then not doing so, or the statement
that the neighbour's house is the nicest in the area are not actionable under misrepresentation. Even though they are misleading, they involve statements of promise or
opinion rather than statements of fact. However, if someone promises to do something
in the future and it can be shown that he or she had no intention of fulfilling that
promise at the time of making it, a misrepresentation has taken place. The person
will be held liable for the promise. When an expert in the area covered by the contract

gives an opinion on the matter being dealt with and the other party relies on this special knowledge, the opinion will be taken as an allegation of fact and will lead to a misrepresentation action. If a real estate appraiser states incorrectly that a home is worth
more than any in the neighbourhood, such expert opinion can be misrepresentation.

Silence or Non-disclosure

Silence or non-disclosure is not usually actionable, but in some special situations, a duty
to disclose information does exist . For example, insurance contracts require the parties acquiring insurance to disclose a great deal of personal information that affects the
policy. People who apply for life insurance are required to disclose if they have had heart

attacks, whether or not the question is specifically asked. If the terms require that the
parties disclose all information to each other as a condition of the agreement, the contract can be rescinded if they fail to do so. Professionals have an obligation to disclose certain information at their disposal that might affect the actions of their clients.

   Actions for misrepresentation may be available when one of the parties to a contract does something to hide the facts. A person anxious to sell a car might be tempted
to hide a noisy transmission by using a heavier grade of oil, but such an act might well
invite a claim of misrepresentation. It is not necessary that the statement be written or
verbal; misrepresentation can occur even if the method of communicating it is a gesture such as a nod of the head. Misrepresentation is normally only available as a
cause of action when an actual representation has been made. When individuals mislead themselves, *caveat emptor* applies and there is no cause for complaint. It is for
this reason that the action against the vendors of the property infested by termites
failed in the example used to introduce the chapter. Mr. Hoy, the purchaser, went to
considerable trouble to inspect the property and so, in effect, misled himself about its
condition. The vendors had made no representation in relation to it.

STATEMENT OF LAW. A misleading statement about the law, for example, a statement describing the legal relationship of the parties or their obligations under the agreement, is not misrepresentation. The misleading statement must be an allegation of fact to qualify as misrepresentation. It is often difficult to distinguish between a statement of law and a statement of fact and the courts have a tendency to find that the statement involved is one of fact whenever possible.

Misrepresentation must be of fact, not law

False Statement

It is not only necessary to demonstrate that the misleading comment qualifies as an allegation of fact but it must also be shown that the statement is incorrect and untrue. Even when a person technically tells the truth but withholds information that would have created an entirely different impression, this can amount to misrepresentation. For example, if a used car salesperson tells a potential purchaser that the transmission of a particular car has just been replaced but fails to say it was replaced with a used transmission, this partial truth can be misrepresentation.

Partial disclosure may be misrepresentation

Statement Must be Inducement

A victim of misrepresentation must show that he or she was induced into entering a contract by a false statement. If the victim knew that the statement was false and entered into the agreement anyway, either because he or she did not believe the statement or it did not make any difference, the misrepresentation is not actionable. Similarly, if the person thought the statement was true but would have entered into the contract even if he or she had known it was false, there is no misrepresentation. The false statement must affect the outcome of the agreement and the victim must have been misled into doing something that he or she otherwise would not have done for there to be an actionable misrepresentation.

Misrepresentation must have misled victim

As a Term of the Contract

If the misleading statement complained of has become a term of the agreement, the normal rules of breach of contract apply. If Osterman agreed to sell Nasser a 1957 Ford Thunderbird for $10 000 but the car turned out to be a 1957 Ford Fairlane, Nasser is free to sue Osterman for breach of contract. But if a person bought a particular property because the vendor said that the municipal council had voted to build a new highway nearby, it would be a rare contract indeed that would include such a provision as a term of the agreement. Because the statement is an inducement to buy, not a term of the contract, the victim must rely on the rules of misrepresentation to obtain a remedy. The remedies available will depend on whether the statement was made inadvertently, fraudulently or negligently.

Breach of contract action may be appropriate if misleading term in contract

Innocent Misrepresentation

Unintentional
misrepresentation
—remedy is
rescission

An innocent misrepresentation is a false statement which the person who made it honestly believes to be true. The only recourse available to the victim is to ask for the remedy of rescission. As soon as the victim realizes what has happened, he or she can either choose to ignore the misrepresentation and affirm the contract or rescind the contract.

RESCISSION. Rescission returns both parties to their original positions; the subject matter of the contract must be returned to the original owner and any monies paid under the contract must also be returned. The courts will also require the party who is returning the subject matter of the contract to return any benefit derived from the property while it was in his or her possession. Similarly, a person can be compensated for any expenses incurred. Damages are not available as remedies because both parties are innocent. Although rescission is an important remedy, because it is an equitable remedy, it is quite restricted in its application. Rescission is not available in the following situations:

Rescission not
available if
contract affirmed

—restoration
impossible

—or it will affect
third party

1. *Affirmation.* Victims of misrepresentation who have affirmed the contract are bound by the affirmation and cannot later insist on rescission.
2. *Impossible to restore.* The remedy of rescission is not available if the parties cannot be returned to their original positions because the subject matter of the contract has been destroyed or damaged. Since neither party is at fault with innocent misrepresentation, the court will not impose a burden on either one of them but will simply deny a remedy.
3. *Third party involvement.* Rescission will not be granted if it will adversely affect the position of a third party. When the subject matter of the contract has been resold by the purchaser to a third party who has no knowledge of the misrepresentation and otherwise comes to the transaction with clean hands, the courts will not interfere with that person's possession and title to the goods.

Fraudulent Misrepresentation

Recission and/or
damages
for torts
are
remedies
for intentional
misrepresentation

If a misrepresentation of fact is intentional and induces another person to enter into a contract, the victim of the fraud can sue for damages under the tort of deceit in addition to seeking the remedy of rescission. The problem with fraudulent misrepresentation is to determine just how intentional the false statement has to be. In the case of *Derry v. Peek*,[9] it was established that fraud has taken place when the false statement was made, "1) knowingly, or 2) without belief in its truth or 3) recklessly careless whether it be true or false."[10] There have been some difficulties over the years in interpreting just what these words mean, but essentially it is fraud if it can be demonstrated that the person who made the false statement does not honestly believe it to be true. The persons making the statement cannot avoid responsibility by claim-

---

[9] *Derry v. Peek* (1889) 14 App. Cas. 337 at p. 374 (House of Lords).
[10] *Ibid.*, p. 374.

ing they did not know that what they said was false or because they did not bother to find out the truth. Even if the victim of the misrepresentation could have found out the truth easily but relied instead on the statement of the defendant, there is still fraud. There is no onus on the victim of the misrepresentation to check the truthfulness of the other party.

When a person innocently makes a false statement and later discovers the mistake, he or she must inform the other person of the misrepresentation. Failure to do so is a fraud. A person who, during the process of negotiating the terms of a contract, makes a statement which was true but, because of changing circumstances, later becomes false must correct the statement upon finding out the truth.

Once it has been established that the false statement was intentional and thus fraudulent, the courts have the following options:

Remedy for fraudulent misrepresentation rescission, damages

1. *Rescission or Avoidance*. The victim of fraudulent misrepresentation retains the right to have the parties to the contract returned to their original positions and to be reimbursed for any out-of-pocket expenses.
2. *Damages for Deceit*. The victim of fraudulent misrepresentation can demand monetary compensation for any loss incurred as a result of the fraud. The courts try to put the victim in the position he or she would have been in had the contract not been entered into. Note that no property is being returned and that the courts are not attempting to return both parties to their original positions, as with rescission. Rather, the courts try to compensate the victim financially for the loss suffered; this payment is made at the expense of the person who is at fault. A victim of fraud can seek damages even after the contract has been affirmed. The victim does not lose the right to demand monetary compensation simply by giving up the right to claim rescission. On rare occasions the victim of a fraudulent misrepresentation can seek punitive damages, that is, damages intended to punish the wrongdoer rather than compensate the victim.

Contract void when consensus destroyed

Whether the misrepresentation is innocent or fraudulent, the contract itself can be considered void if the misrepresentation is serious enough to cause the victim to make a mistake that goes to the very foundation of the agreement and destroys consensus. For example, if the false statement causes the victim to make a mistake about the identity of the other party or the nature of the agreement, the contract can be declared void. A void contract means that there never was a contract. If the contract involved the sale of property to a third party, it will be returned to the original owner because the person from whom it was obtained did not have title to convey.

Negligent Misrepresentation

Until relatively recently, it was thought that negligent misrepresentation when fraud was not involved must be treated the same as innocent misrepresentation. Thus the remedies were limited to rescission.

Negligent damages may be available in cases of misrepresentation

However, since the decisions of the House of Lords in *Hedley Byrne & Co. Ltd. v. Heller & Partners*, Ltd.,[11] the Supreme Court of Canada in the case of *Haig v. Bamford*,[12] and subsequent related cases, it appears that if it can be shown that the parties should have known what they said was false even though they honestly believed it was true, then the rules and remedies discussed in Chapter 3 under the tort of negligence apply and damages will be available. Even when the negligent statement becomes a term of the contract or arises out of a contractual relationship, the plaintiff may have a choice about whether to sue in contract or sue in tort for negligence. The Supreme Court of Canada in a recent decision made it clear that such "concurrent liability" may exist although with some important limitations, such as not permitting the plaintiff to circumvent the protection provided in an exemption clause by suing in tort instead.[13] Of course, when the misrepresentation has become a term of the contract and a breach results, damages as well as other contractual remedies are available.[14] It should also be noted that if a breach of contract can be established, damages are one of the remedies available. Thus, it appears that only when the misrepresentation is truly innocent and without fault is the victim restricted to the remedy of rescission.

DURESS AND UNDUE INFLUENCE

Duress

Duress involves threats of violence or imprisonment— contract voidable

When people are forced or pressured to enter into contracts against their will by threats of violence or imprisonment, duress is present and the contracts are voidable. The person who used duress is bound by the contract but the injured party may have the contract set aside. Originally, the definition of duress was limited to situations in which there were actual threats of violence or imprisonment, but the courts of chancery expanded this definition to include threats of criminal prosecution and threats to disclose embarrassing or scandalous information. In Canada, duress has been expanded further to include threats to a person's goods or property. A person who is unlawfully in possession of property belonging to another and uses that possession as a lever to force the rightful owner of the property to enter a disadvantageous agreement would find that the resulting contract is voidable due to duress. If O'Rourke threatened to run a lawnmower borrowed from Tong over rocky ground unless Tong sold him a particular plant he had grown, this would qualify as duress in Canada. To succeed, it is necessary to show that the threat was the main inducement for entering into the agreement although it is not necessary to show that the threat of violence or imprisonment came from the other party to the contract or his or her agent. If O'Rourke's relative threatened to damage the lawnmower if

---

[11] *Hedley Byrne v. Heller* [1963] 2 All E.R. 575 (House of Lords).

[12] *Haig v. Bamford* (1976) 72 D.L.R. (3d) 68 (Supreme Court of Canada).

[13] *Central Trust Co. v. Rafuse et al.* (1986) 31 D.L.R. (4th) 481 (S.C.C.). and *B.G. Checo v. B.C. Hydro* (1993) 99 D.L.R. (4th) 577.

[14] *Beaufort Realties v. Chomedey Aluminum Co.* (1981) 116 D.L.R. (3d) 193 (N.B.C.A.).

Tong refused to sell the plant, this is duress even though the threat did not come from O'Rourke.

Economic advantage not enough

Even though the threat of loss of employment and other financial losses can amount to economic duress, it is important not to mistake the normal predicaments in which we all find ourselves for improper pressure or duress. If a person has no choice except to use a particular taxi because it is the only one on the street or has to deal with the only airline or telephone company that services a particular area, these accepted conditions of the marketplace do not amount to duress. Even the threat of suing when the person doing so has a legitimate right to sue is not duress. Rather, it is the legitimate exercise of the rights of that person.

Voidable contract cannot affect third parties

A third party's position cannot be jeopardized if the victim of duress seeks a remedy. Thus, if a purchaser improperly pressures someone into selling a gold watch and then resells that watch to an innocent third party, the watch cannot be retrieved. Because a voidable contract is still a contract, the title is passed on to the third party. Had the watch been stolen from the original owner and then sold to an innocent third party, the original owner would not have given up title to the watch and could, therefore, retrieve it.

Undue Influence

Undue influence involves undue pressures— contract voidable

The types of pressure brought to bear on people are often more subtle than those described by duress. When pressure from a dominant, trusted person makes it impossible to bargain freely, it is regarded as undue influence and the resulting contract is voidable. Because it is sometimes difficult to prove that a person was improperly pressured to enter into a contract, the courts have developed rules to establish the existence of undue influence. Certain categories of relationships result in a presumption of undue influence and if the presumption is not rebutted the contract will be set aside. These categories are

Undue influence presumed in certain relationships

1. adult contracting with infant child or adult contracting with senile parent.
2. solicitor contracting with client.
3. doctor contracting with patient.
4. religious advisor contracting with parishioner.
5. trustee contracting with beneficiary.
6. guardian contracting with ward.

As a general rule, parents contracting with adult children or husbands and wives contracting with each other are excluded from these categories.

Of these relationships, the religious relationship seems to be one of the most suspect in the opinion of the courts. In the case of *Allcard v. Skinner*,[15] a woman entered a religious order and gave it all her property. The court determined that there had been undue influence when the contract was entered into and would have set the contract aside except that she had affirmed the contract after leaving the relationship. It

[15] *Allcard v. Skinner* (1887) 36 CH.D. 145 (Court of Appeal).

is interesting to note that in this case there was clear evidence that there had been no overt attempt on the part of the religious order to influence this woman, but the court decided that the situation itself had robbed her of her ability to act voluntarily.

If the relationship involved does not fall into one of the protected classes listed above, there must be further evidence to establish undue influence, as in the case of a husband and wife relationship. The courts then attempt to determine whether the surrounding circumstances cast doubt on the voluntariness of the agreement, in which case the court may presume undue influence. If the court makes that presumption, it falls on the party trying to enforce the contract to show that there was no domination or unfair advantage taken of the other party. When the relationship does not fall into the special categories or it is not possible to presume undue influence, parties trying to escape contracts must present evidence to satisfy the court that influence was exerted and that they were coerced. Undue influence can be difficult to prove since the victim must show that a relationship of trust developed because of the special relationship between the contracting parties, and that that trust was abused. When it can be shown that the person trying to enforce the contract took advantage of the fact that he or she was being relied on for advice, the courts may find that there was undue influence. Even when undue influence has been established, the contract will be binding if the person trying to enforce the contract can show that the undue influence was overcome and that the victim either affirmed the contract or did nothing to rescind it after escaping the relationship. The courts may refuse a remedy if the person trying to escape the contract is not altogether innocent of wrongdoing.

It is advisable for contracting parties who are concerned with this problem to get legal advice before entering into an agreement. When it can be demonstrated that the potential victim followed independent legal advice, it is very likely that the courts will enforce the agreement. It must be stressed that the terms of the agreement must be reasonable in such circumstances. The courts will not enforce a contract that conveys great advantage to one of the parties, whether or not legal advice has been taken. It should be further noted that, unlike duress, the undue influence must be exerted by the other party to the contract and not an outsider or stranger.

Unconscionable Transactions

The concept of **unconscionable transactions** has received a greater acceptance by courts in recent years. This is an equitable doctrine that permits the court to set aside a contract in which one party has been taken advantage of because of factors such as desperation caused by poverty or intellectual impairment that falls short of incapacity. To escape from such a contract, it must be shown that the bargaining positions of the parties were unequal, that one party dominated and took advantage of the other, and that the consideration involved was grossly unfair. There is some overlap between the principle of unconscionable transactions and undue influence. Although legislation has been passed in most common law provinces prohibiting unconscionable transactions, in most instances it is limited to loan transactions. The re-

In other relationships, more evidence is needed for undue influence

Independent legal advice desirable, but contract must be fair

Contract may be unconscionable and voidable if parties in unequal bargaining positions

cent acceptance of this equitable doctrine developed by the courts makes the defence of unconscionability available when the contracts in question do not involve the loan of money.

PRIVITY OF CONTRACT AND ASSIGNMENT

Privity

Contract only affects parties to it

When two parties enter into a contract, they create a world of law unto themselves. Contracting is a bargaining process and only those participating in the bargain can be affected by it. It is a fundamental principle of contract law that the parties to a contract do not have the power to impose benefits or obligations on third parties or outsiders who are not parties to the contract. The contracting parties have created a private agreement and outsiders to it can neither enforce it nor be bound to perform its terms. This principle is called privity of contract.

The case of *Donoghue v. Stevenson*[16] referred to in Chapter 2 illustrates the application of the privity principle. In that case, a woman bought a bottle of ginger beer with a decomposed snail in it for her friend. Because the person who bought the ginger beer was not the person who consumed it, the victim could not sue the owner of the café for breach of contract since there was no contract between them. Under normal circumstances, merchants can be sued for breach of contract for selling faulty products even though they are unaware of the problem. If there is no contract, the victim must turn to the manufacturer. If an action is to be maintained against the manufacturer in these circumstances, it must be done in tort for negligence.

Exceptions—Apparent and Real

Original party to contract can enforce it where benefit to be bestowed on outsider

These principles are perfectly compatible with the concepts developed by contract law through its bargaining nature. However, privity has caused some severe difficulties in normal commercial relationships and, therefore, there are several exceptions, both real and apparent. If contract law is based on the idea that people can enforce their reasonable expectations from a bargain, a degree of dissatisfaction would be expected if it were not possible to enforce those terms, especially when a third party stands to benefit. Our law clearly establishes that the original two parties to the contract can enforce the terms when they bestow benefit on a third party; the third party cannot enforce the contract. Thus, if Aguilar agrees with Balzer to mow Carriere's lawn, Carriere cannot enforce the agreement but Balzer certainly can. The court will either provide damages or money compensation calculated on the basis of what it would cost

---

[16] *Donoghue v. Stevenson* [1932] A.C. 562 (House of Lords).

to have somebody else mow the lawn or it will order the contracting party to perform the obligation under the agreement. This is called specific performance.

The original contracting parties are also free to enter into a new agreement which changes the terms of their original contract. This is called **novation** and typically involves the substitution of one party for another. For example, if a store owner has a contract with a wholesaler to supply commodities and then sells the store to another party, the purchaser will usually be substituted and the resulting contract will be between the original supplier and the new owner. Novation is not a true exception to the privity rule because there is no continuation of the original agreement; a new contract has just been substituted for the old one. To create this new contract, consensus as well as all of the other elements required to form a contract must be present. The new owner of the business cannot be unilaterally substituted into the agreement. When the new contract is substituted for the old, consent is often implied by the conduct of the parties but consent in some guise must be present. The old contract is then discharged and a new one substituted. If the new owner can show that the wholesaler continued to deliver goods after discovering that the business had changed hands, this would probably be sufficient to establish the required consent and existence of a new contract.

Neither of these situations is a true exception to the privity of contract rule. The original party to a contract who enforces its terms to benefit a third party is merely carrying out the agreement and, in the case of substituting a new party, a new contract has been formed. There are several other situations that have made it necessary to move away from strict adherence to the privity of contract rule.

LAND. Although interests in land are usually created by contractual arrangements, the resulting property rights are not limited by contract law principles. Because the relationships created are based on property law principles, the concept of privity does not apply. Some property rights run with the land. Restrictions and obligations tied to the property, even those which have been entered into by contract with some other outside party, are binding on the new purchaser when property is transferred or sold. An easement, the right someone has to cross or be on the property, is binding on any subsequent owner of that property. Similarly, even if the purchaser of a building is unaware of a tenant occupying a leased apartment, the purchaser is bound by that lease and cannot evict the tenant. Much of this area of land law is now covered by provincial statutes which impose obligations to register these interests.

AGENCY. Agency involves the creation of contractual relations between a principal and third party through the services of a go-between called an agent. Although all of the arrangements may have been made by the agent, the contract is created between the principal and the third party so this is not a true exception to the privity rule. For example, when a person goes to a department store to buy a jacket, the purchase will be arranged by a sales clerk. The clerk will write down the terms of the agreement and receive payment for the merchandise, but the contract is between the store and the individual buying the jacket. The sales clerk merely acts

Novation involves new agreement

Where interest in land involved, rights run with land

Obligation to register interest

Agents create contracts between principal and third party

as an intermediary or an agent. However, if the clerk tried to sell the store, the contract would not be binding because such an action would be beyond the authority given to the clerk. If dissatisfied, the third party or customer would sue the principal, or the department store. The only circumstance in which the third party can sue the agent is when the agent has gone beyond his or her authority.

—but limited by authority

In unusual circumstances, agents will contract with third parties on behalf of their principals without disclosing the fact that they are acting as agents. Providing the agents act within their authority, the principals and third parties must honour the contracts unless personal services, such as in an employment relationship, are required by the third party. If any of the terms of the contract are violated, the third party has the choice of suing either the agent or, upon determining the existence or identity of the principal, the principal for breach of contract. However, once the choice is made to sue either one, it is binding. In these rare circumstances, all three parties—principal, agent and third party—have acquired rights and obligations under the contract and can therefore sue and be sued.

Third party may seek redress from undisclosed principal or agent

TRUSTS. A difficult problem to resolve under common law was a situation in which someone wanted to transfer the benefits of a property to a third party while conveying the property itself to someone else. The courts of chancery created the concept of **trust** to deal with such situations. A trust involves three people: the person conveying the property, called the settlor; the person looking after the property, or the trustee; and the person benefiting from the trust, often called the beneficiary. Trusts allow people to bestow benefits on third parties through contracts which have been created with other parties. There is little difficulty in the third party (beneficiary) enforcing trust arrangements as long as the terms are specific.

Trusts allow a third party to benefit from the property of another

In certain instances called **constructive trusts**, the courts are willing to imply the creation of a trust from the surrounding circumstances and conduct of the parties. If the use of the constructive trust argument had become general, it would have been a very effective way to get around the rules of privity of contract. The courts, however, have been extremely reluctant to accept the existence of constructive trusts because they would have to determine that the original owner of the property had given up all claims and rights to that property through the creation of the trust relationship. If the two original contracting parties changed their minds, they would not be able to renegotiate the contract. Such a decision has always been considered a severe restriction on the freedom to create contractual relationships, so the courts will only accept the existence of a constructive trust in those rare circumstances where it is very clear that the settlors intended to completely divest themselves of the property in question, retaining no rights in relationship to it.

The effect of a trust, whether it is expressed or constructive, is that the beneficiaries will be able to enforce their rights under that trust. Beneficiaries can force their trustees to make appropriate payments. Trusts are often created by people who want to ensure that their family is adequately taken care of after their death. Under the rules of privity, trustees would be in a position to keep the property which they had been given only to take care of once the creator of the trust died. The third party, or outsider to the agreement, would not be able to enforce that agreement. This

Beneficiary can enforce trust agreement against trustee

would be an entirely unfair result. An exception to the privity rule was created and beneficiaries are able to enforce trusts.

A similar situation exists with life insurance policies. No property changes hands with insurance contracts but, in exchange for the payment of a fee, the insured is assured that payment will be made to a designated beneficiary in the event of the insured's death. This arrangement would be unworkable if the rules of privity applied and the third party or beneficiary could not force the insurance company to pay the agreed-upon amount. Statutes have been passed to create beneficiary rights to enforce such insurance agreements.

Beneficiary can enforce insurance contract

The Supreme Court of Canada has recently created another potentially important exception to the privity of contract rule. It is clear that, even when the relationship involved is based on contract, an injured party can sue for breach of contract as well as in tort for negligence when the circumstances are appropriate. It is normal for the parties to a contract to include terms in their agreement called exculpatory clauses that have the effect of limiting their liability. This limitation would apply if one party was suing the other party to the contract for breach of contract or for negligence by the other party. This was the case in *London Drugs Ltd. v. Kuehne & Nagel International Ltd.*[17] In this case, a clause in the contract limited liability to only $40 maximum. Kuehne & Nagel had contracted to store a large transformer and, because of mishandling by their employees, that transformer suffered significant damage. It was clear that the plaintiff could not recover from Kuehne & Nagel because of the $40 exculpatory clause and so sued their employees instead in tort for negligence since they were the ones who had actually caused the damage. Applying the privity principle, the $40 exculpatory clause could be used to limit the liability of the other party to the contract, Kuehne & Nagel, but not their employees who were not party to the contract. The Supreme Court had to decide whether it would make an exception to the privity rule and extend the protection created by this exculpatory clause to the employees of Kuehne & Nagel. The decision of the Supreme Court of Canada to override the privity rule and give the employees the protection of an exculpatory clause in a contract to which they were not a party is a significant departure and may become even more important if this is in an indication of a willingness on the part of the Supreme Court to depart from privity in other circumstances as well.

Employees protected by exculpatory clauses

Assignment

The discussion so far has focused on third parties being given rights under the terms of a contract. What happens when one of the parties to a contract tries to sell or transfer the rights obtained under it? People often resell goods they have purchased in a contract, but here we are dealing with the sale (called assignment) of rights or claims (called choses in action) rather than goods. Instead of asking whether the parties to a contract can bestow their rights on an outsider, the question to be examined is: Once a party to a contract has acquired rights or obligations

---

[17] *London Drugs Ltd. v. Kuehne & Nagel International Ltd.* [1993] 1 W.W.R. 1 (S.C.C.)

under it, can they be transferred to another? What kind of rights or obligations can be transferred? The historical doctrine developed by the common law courts is consistent with the rules of privity of contract. It was impossible to assign or sell rights that have been obtained under a contractual relationship. It was found, however, that this restrictive approach was neither practical nor appropriate in many situations. The courts of equity allowed the rights associated with trusts or legacies, such as inheritances, which were clearly within the equity area of law to be transferred by beneficiaries to strangers to the contract and enabled those strangers to enforce them, but those matters within the purview of the common law courts were a different matter. Although the courts of chancery could not directly interfere with the principles established by the common law courts, they often accomplished indirectly what they could not do directly. When legal rights under the jurisdiction of the common law courts were involved, such as debts or the sale of goods and services, the courts of chancery determined that, although outsiders to the contract could not enforce those rights, they could force the original party to the contract to enforce them. If Gabor owed Ozawa money and Ozawa assigned that claim to Brown, Brown could not sue Gabor for payment. Brown could, however, force Ozawa to sue Gabor to get payment. Thus, assignees of contractual rights that fell under the jurisdiction of the common law courts could enforce these rights only by joining the assignors as participants in their actions against the original contracting debtors.

Contracting party can assign rights

To overcome the cumbersome nature of this approach, the *Judicature Acts*, which joined the English courts of chancery and common law courts into one common court system, include provisions which allowed for **statutory assignment**. The statute simply states that when certain qualifications are met, the assignee of the contractual rights has the right to enforce that claim directly against the debtor rather that having to join the assignor in the action as a party to it. The qualifications that must be met are

1. The assignment must be absolute and unconditional. This means that if the assignor is owed $500 by the debtor, the entire $500 must be assigned to the assignee, not part of it. The assignment must also be complete; it cannot be used merely as a security.
2. The assignment must be in writing with adequate identification of the parties, the amounts involved and the signature of the assignor.
3. Proper notice of the assignment in writing must be given to the original debtor and that notice must contain all the pertinent information including the names of the parties.

Qualifications for statutory assignment

When these qualifications are met, the assignee can sue the debtor directly. The common law provinces of Canada have all adopted a version of this legislation.

The legislation creating statutory assignment did not abolish completely the original approach to assignment developed in the courts of chancery. If any one of these qualifications is not met, assignees can still enforce their claims but they must go through the assignor to do so. In other words, the assignor must be made a party to the action. This is called an equitable assignment. For example, Chadha owes

Ace Rental Co. $500 for the use of equipment. Ace Rental Co. is not really in the business of lending money so assigns that $500 debt to Wolanski Finance Co. This process is called factoring of accounts receivable. If the assignment is complete, meaning the entire $500 debt has been assigned, and the assignment is in writing, is signed by the appropriate officer of Ace Rental Co. and written notice has been given to Chadha, Wolanski Finance Co. can enforce the debt directly. Thus, Wolanski Finance Co. can sue Chadha in its own right if he fails to make his payments. But if these requirements are not met, Wolanski Finance Co. is not able to sue Chadha directly in the event of default. Rather, it would be forced to join with Ace Rental Co. as a party to the action and, in effect, ride on the coattails of Ace Rental's suit to force Chadha to pay. Great care should be taken in business transactions of this nature to make sure all the qualifications are met because it is much easier to proceed with a statutory assignment. One of the reasons statutory assignment is possible, in the face of the privity of contract doctrine, is because the contract itself is not being assigned; rather, the rights derived under the contract are being transferred to a stranger or outsider.

Some things cannot be assigned

Some things, by their very nature, cannot be assigned. Any claim for maintenance or alimony which might cause the assignor to become destitute and certain claims against government bodies cannot be assigned. In other circumstances, the contract itself may prohibit assignment. In these cases, the assignee has obtained no rights under the contract and the debtor would be well advised to pay the money to the court and let it decide who should receive the funds.

—the right to sue

Another important area of prohibited assignments developed out of the concept of **champerty**, or selling the right to sue. In an attempt to discourage wholesale litigation and abuse of court procedures, laws were established to discourage people from buying and selling the right to sue. The assignment of the right to litigate is invalid. For example, a person whose foot has been run over by another cannot sell the right to sue to a third person but would have to proceed with the action personally. However, the award of damages set out in the court order does create an assignable debt which can be assigned.

—or in the case of skilful performance

In some situations, the consent of the other contracting party must be obtained before an assignment can be made, especially when personal skill and knowledge are involved in the performance of the contract. It is important to note that only the advantages or rights obtained under a contract can be assigned, not the obligations. If one party has obtained a contract to paint a house, the payment to be derived under the contract may be assigned but the obligation to paint the house remains the responsibility of the contracting party. That is not to say, however, that it must be performed personally. In many situations, it does not matter whether the person who contracted performs the contracted duties personally or not. For example, a builder may subcontract many construction jobs such as framing, brick-laying, plumbing or electrical work. This is called vicarious performance and is permissible as long as the contract is of such a nature that personal performance is not required. However, if an impresario contracted with a famous performer to appear at the National Arts Centre and that performer sent an understudy instead, the impresario would be able to sue, even if it could be demonstrated that the understudy was just as good. In such circumstances, personal performance by the contracting party is required.

It is vitally important to realize that the assignee is in no better position than was the original party to the contract, whether the assignment is statutory or equitable. The expression used to describe this circumstance is that the assignee is subject to the equities between the original parties. If the right or claim that the original party to the contract had was tainted in some way, then the assignee obtains tainted rights. If a fraud involved in the original agreement would have given the original debtor a good defence if sued by the assignor, the debtor has the same defence when sued by the assignee. If the assignor has committed fraud or failed to perform the contract properly, or if the original debtor can establish another independent claim against the assignor's claim, these issues can all be raised as defences against the assignee's claim as well. Being subject to the equities between the original parties is a significant limitation on the power of the assignee to enforce any claims on the contract.

To eliminate the possibility that any subsequent claims might arise between the original parties and unfairly undercut the position of the assignee, a qualification has been developed to provide more equitable results. The general rule is that the rights or equities the assignee is subject to are determined when the debtor receives notice of the assignment. Any subsequent rights or claims arising between those parties, except those dealing with the performance of the contract itself, will not affect the rights or claims of the assignee.

A return to the example of the Ace Rental Co.'s assignment of Chadha's $500 debt to Wolanski Finance Co. will illustrate this point. Suppose Chadha defaulted on the debt and is sued by Wolanski Finance Co. and his defence is that he did not pay because the equipment rented did not live up to Ace Rental Co.'s guarantee. Wolanski Finance Co. would not be able to enforce the debt against Chadha. Chadha's defence against Ace Rental Co. is good because the company failed to fulfil its contractual obligation. The claim Ace Rental has against Chadha is tainted. Wolanski Finance has obtained tainted rights and is in no better position to enforce the debt than Ace Rental would have been.

If, after the notice of the assignment of the debt to Wolanski Finance, Chadha did some work for Ace Rental for which he was not paid, Chadha could not raise this as a defence when sued by Wolanski Finance for the original $500. Chadha's claim for wages arose after he received notice of the assignment and, therefore, will not affect the position of Wolanski Finance. On the other hand, if a debtor chooses to ignore a notice of assignment, he or she assumes the risk of having to make all future payments to the assignee. If the debtor continues to pay the original assignor, he or she will still be required to pay the entire amount owing to the assignee. Notice of assignment should never be treated lightly.

The notice given by the assignee to the debtor serves another important purpose. A company in financial difficulty might be tempted to fraudulently assign the same claim against a debtor to several different assignees. In such circumstances, priority is determined by the order in which the debtor receives the notices. A qualification on this rule is the principle that one assignee cannot gain

Assignee subject to equities at time of notice of assignment

Subsequent claims do not affect assignee

Debtor must pay first who gives notice of assignment

priority over another by giving notice while knowing of the existence of a prior claim. Only assignees who are ignorant of any other attempts to assign can obtain priority by giving notice to the debtor of the assignment.

The principles discussed so far relate to voluntary assignments. There are some circumstances in which the assignment of rights can take place involuntarily. For example, rights and obligations are automatically transferred to the administrator or executor of the estate when a person dies. This representative steps into the deceased's shoes and is not restricted by the privity of contract rule unless the terms of the contract require personal performance by the deceased. The second situation of involuntary assignment is when a party to a contract goes bankrupt. Under bankruptcy legislation, all of the bankrupt's assets are transferred to a trustee called the receiver who will then distribute them to pay the creditors as much as possible.

Negotiable Instruments

Another exception to the privity of contract rule recognizes the commercial realities of modern business. As commerce developed, it became necessary to devise a method to freely exchange and pass on claims for debt which had been incurred in the process of business. When these claims met certain qualifications, they were defined as **negotiable instruments** and through them unique rights were bestowed on the parties.

These rights will be discussed in Chapter 13 but in essence they were two-fold. The negotiable instrument could be freely passed from one person to another, conveying with it all the rights associated with the original agreement between the parties, and no notice of the transaction would be required. This flexibility is completely inconsistent with the doctrine of privity of contract and a clear exception to it. The most significant innovation of negotiable instruments was that better rights or claims than those held by the initial parties could be passed on. As discussed under assignment, it was clear that even when it was possible to assign contractual rights, the assignee was subject to whatever equities existed between the original two parties. Thus, a defence such as fraud would be available against the assignee as well as the original party to the contract. This is not the case with negotiable instruments. Even when a defence of fraud is available against the initial party to a transaction, a third party to a negotiable instrument who satisfies the qualifications to be a "holder in due course" can enforce the contract despite the existence of the fraud.

SUMMARY

For a mistake to affect the validity of a contract, it must go to the nature of the agreement or the existence of the subject matter, not just to the effect of the agreement when performed. When both parties are making a common error as to the existence of the subject matter at the time the contract is made, there is no contract.

If an error is made in recording the terms of the contract, it can be corrected by rectification. When the mistake is not shared but there is a misunderstanding between the parties, the court will adopt the most reasonable interpretation of the contract. When the mistake is one-sided (a unilateral mistake), *caveat emptor* applies unless the mistake is so fundamental as to destroy consensus between the parties.

When a person is induced to enter into a contract by a false statement, such a misrepresentation is actionable. When the misrepresentation is innocent, the remedy is rescission. When the misrepresentation is fraudulent, the victim may sue for damages for the tort of deceit. Damages may also be available when negligence can be demonstrated. When duress or undue influence is involved, the contract is voidable.

Under privity of contract, only the original parties to the contract are bound. Any benefit going to a third party must be enforced by the original party to the agreement. A novation is when a new party is substituted for one of the original parties and is enforceable only when there has been agreement by all. Contracts dealing with interests in land create rights that flow with the land. Agency arrangements involve contracts between the principal and a third party, the agent acting merely as a go-between. The trust is a true exception to the privity rule because the beneficiary can enforce it even though he or she is not a party to the original agreement. Under assignment, only the benefits in a contract can be sold (assigned) to a third party and those benefits must be enforced through the original contracting party, the assignor. Only when it qualifies as a statutory assignment can the assignee enforce the assigned rights directly.

QUESTIONS

1. Distinguish between a mistake about the effect of a contract and a mistake about its nature. Explain the significance of this distinction.
2. Distinguish between common mistake, mutual mistake and unilateral mistake.
3. What approach will the courts usually take when the mistake involves disagreement about the meaning of the contract?
4. What bias will the court display in choosing between two equally reasonable interpretations of vague wording in a contract?
5. Explain the parol evidence rule.
6. What must a party to a contract show to obtain rectification of a document?
7. Under what circumstances will a unilateral mistake cause a contract to be a nullity?
8. Under what circumstances would a person raise a claim of *non est factum*? What restrictions are there on its availability?
9. Explain what is meant by *caveat emptor*. What is this principle's significance in relation to unilateral mistake?

10. What happens when a misrepresentation becomes a term of the contract?
11. What is the distinction between fraudulent, negligent and innocent misrepresentation? Why is the distinction important?
12. Under what circumstances can silence or a statement of opinion become misrepresentation?
13. What factors may affect the availability of the remedy of rescission?
14. Describe the relationship between misrepresentation and mistake.
15. What is the significance of determining whether a contract is voidable rather than void?
16. Distinguish between duress and undue influence and give examples of each.
17. What is meant by privity of contract?
18. Explain what is meant by the term novation.
19. Explain the relationship of the privity principle to land transactions, agency, trusts, assignment and the position of employees.
20. What qualifications must be realized before there can be a statutory assignment?
21. What limitations are placed on the rights and obligations of the assignee when a contract is assigned?
22. What is meant by "the assignee takes subject to the equities"? When is it appropriate to determine these equities?
23. What is the significance of a negotiable instrument in terms of the rights conveyed to third parties?

CASES

1. *Solle v. Butcher.*
   The plaintiff and the defendant collaborated over the renovation of a house containing five apartments. The plaintiff spent a considerable sum of money on alterations and changes. Both parties thought that the changes and the redecoration would cause the apartments to be outside the rent controls that were then in effect. The relationship between the parties broke down and, when he discovered the apartments were subject to rent control, the plaintiff demanded repayment of the excess amount he had paid. Describe the probable outcome.

2. *Lindsey v. Heron & Co.*
   The plaintiff said to the defendant, "What will you give me for 75 shares of Eastern Cafeterias of Canada?" The defendant replied, "I'll let you know." The defendant company's manager later phoned the plaintiff and said, "I'll give you $10.00 per share for your Eastern Cafeterias." The plaintiff replied,

"I accept your offer," delivered the Eastern Cafeterias of Canada Ltd. shares and received a cheque. The defendant then claimed that he intended to purchase Eastern Cafeterias Ltd. shares, not Eastern Cafeterias of Canada Ltd. shares, a completely different company, and refused to honour the cheque. The plaintiff Lindsey sued for the value of the cheque. Explain what factors the court would consider in reaching a decision. Predict the probable outcome.

3. *Hayward v. Mellick.*
   Mellick had 145 acres of land that he wanted to sell. In the process of negotiations with Hayward, he represented to Hayward that the farm had approximately 65 acres of workable farmland. Relying on this representation, Hayward purchased the farm and later learned that the farm had only 51.7 workable acres. In fact, Mellick had never measured the farm and it was only his own personal belief that it had 65 workable acres. But he never told Hayward that he was not sure. Hayward sued for compensation. Discuss the legal position of the parties. How would your answer be affected by the knowledge that the written contract included an exemption clause that stated, "it is agreed that there is no representation, warranty, collateral agreement or condition affecting this agreement or the real property or supported hereby other than as expressed herein, in writing?"

4. *Junkin & Junkin v. Bedard & Bedard.*
   Mr. and Mrs. Junkin hired an agent to sell their motel and told the agent that their gross revenue for the previous year was $16 000 and the net profit was $9700. The judge found that Mrs. Junkin knew this information was false and that she had given it to the agent to persuade prospective purchasers. This information was given to the Bedards who relied on it when they decided to purchase. When they discovered that it was incorrect, they sued the Junkins asking for damages. Explain the likely outcome.

5. *Pettit & Johnston v. Foster Wheeler Ltd.*
   Roderick Ashley Ltd. was supplying materials for Foster Wheeler Ltd. at a project at the University of Alberta in Edmonton. Mr. Pettit had supplied $14 000 worth of financing to Roderick Ashley Ltd. Pursuant to that agreement, Pettit took an assignment of all accounts of Roderick Ashley. Notice of this assignment was given to Foster Wheeler Ltd. who was told to make all payments to Mr. Johnston, Pettit's lawyer, who would hold the money in trust for him. Some payments were made, but on December 27 the Bank of Nova Scotia sent a letter to Foster Wheeler Ltd. stating that it had received a general assignment of book debts of Roderick Ashley as collateral security for a debt and that any payments to be made to Roderick Ashley should now be paid to the Bank of Nova Scotia. Accordingly, Foster Wheeler immediately paid the $7345 outstanding to the Bank of Nova Scotia instead of paying to Pettit and Johnston. Pettit and Johnston then sued Foster Wheeler

for this amount, claiming that it should have been paid to them. Explain the likely outcome.

6. Re *Royal Bank of Canada and Gill et al.*

   The younger Mr. Gill was fluent in English and a sophisticated businessman who had worked in a credit union for a number of years as well as managing his father's berry farm. To take advantage of a business opportunity, he arranged with the Royal Bank to borrow $87 000. During the negotiations, it became clear that he could get a more favourable rate of interest if his father guaranteed the loan. In fact, the son had done a considerable amount of banking on behalf of his father who was also a customer of the same bank. The elder Mr. Gill could not read, write or speak English and relied on his son in all his business dealings. The documents were prepared and the son brought his father to the bank to sign. At no time did he explain to his father that he was signing a personal guaranty and the evidence is clear that the father had no idea what he was signing other than that it was a document associated with a loan transaction. Mr. Gill, senior, exercised implicit faith in his son's handling of his business affairs. Mr. Gill, junior, on the other hand was so excited about the deal that he apparently never explained the nature of the documents to his father. It is clear in this situation that at no time was there any misrepresentation to the father or the son on the part of the bank. When the loan was defaulted, the bank turned to the father for payment. Explain the arguments of the father and the bank as to whether Mr. Gill, senior, should be held responsible for this debt and the likely outcome.

7. *Stott v. Merrit Investment Corp.*

   Stott was a sales representative working in the securities business for the defendant. He was approached by a customer who wanted to start an account to speculate in gold futures, a very risky business. The account was started and some successes were achieved but then the market reversed itself and the customer lost heavily. The customer ended up indebted to the company for $66 000. Stott was called into his supervisor's office and asked to sign an agreement stating that Stott would be fully responsible for that amount if the customer could not pay. He suggested that he should have legal advice and was told, "You are probably right but if you don't sign, it won't go well with you at this firm and it would be very difficult for you to find employment in the industry." Stott signed the document and continued to work for Merrit. Deductions were taken off his income for this debt over the employment period. Several months later, he said that he had received legal advice and offered to settle the debt for 25 percent of the outstanding amount. Even when he resigned two years after the event, it was clear that he felt some obligation under the agreement. Some time after he left and obtained other employment, he refused any further responsibility and sued Merrit for the amount that had been deducted from his income to pay this debt. Merrit countersued for the amount still outstanding. What are the legal arguments to support each position. Would your answer be different if you were to learn that it was the practice in the industry to hold sales representatives responsible to some extent for such bad accounts?

ISSUES

1. The courts look primarily at the nature of the mistake itself to determine the availability of remedies when they deal with questions of mistake. If the mistake is serious and goes to the foundation of the relationship between the parties, the courts are more likely to allow one of the parties to escape from the agreement. If the mistake is caused by carelessness, such as failure to read a document before signing, this has not been a significant consideration until recent times. The question for discussion is: Should the courts be concerned with the conduct of the parties and the reasons for error rather than with the seriousness of the resulting mistake when determining the availability of remedies?

2. It makes little difference to the nature of the injuries suffered by the victims of false statements if they were misled intentionally or inadvertently. However, it makes a significant difference to the remedies available to the victims if they were misled intentionally or innocently. The victims of intentionally false statements can sue for damages; the victims of inadvertently false statements cannot. Should a distinction be drawn between innocent misrepresentation and fraudulent misrepresentation in determining the availability of damages as a remedy? In your response, consider the appropriateness of all the remedies available for misrepresentation in any form. Consider also the growing area of negligent misstatement and how it should be applied here.

3. The concept of *caveat emptor* is used to justify the lack of obligation of contracting parties to correct errors made by the other party even though they are aware of them. Nor is there any obligation to disclose information which might persuade the other party not to complete the deal. Should there be an obligation for contracting parties to correct errors made by the other party when they are aware of them? Should they be forced to disclose information when it is obvious that the other party is making a mistake? Should not failure to disclose information or correct misunderstandings be considered misrepresentation just as much as overt misleading statements? Why should it be possible to swindle people by silence? Consider the thrust of most modern consumer protection legislation in your response.

4. The principle of privity of contract limits the effect of the agreement to those two parties entering into it. Strangers to the agreement cannot be given rights or obligations under that contract. Over the years, many exceptions have been created to the privity of contract rule. The questions for discussion are: Does the rule of privity of contract serve any purpose in our legal system? Is the principle consistent with the concept of freedom of contract? Why can parties not be free to create rights to serve other parties if they so wish? Considering the number of exceptions and the preoccupation of the courts in developing them, it is clear that this is a rule with no modern justification for its existence. Discuss the validity of this evaluation, examining the advantages and disadvantages of the principle of privity of contract.

5. When rights under a contract are assigned and the contract is later breached by the assignor, the original contracting party and the assignee can be affected by the breach. The rule respecting assignment in such situations could be to the advantage of the original contracting party since the agreement is subject to the equities between the original two contracting parties. It can be argued that the debtor is less innocent than the assignee because he or she has provided the opportunity for the assignor to cheat the assignee and the assignee ought therefore to be given the advantage. Is the approach currently taken by the courts in relationship to assignments and the rights of the parties appropriate or would the ends of justice be better served by giving the advantage in such circumstances to the assignee?

6

THE END OF THE CONTRACTUAL RELATIONSHIP

Objectives of the Chapter

- to describe the various degrees of performance and their effect on contractual obligations
- to summarize the various conditions that constitute a breach of contract
- to outline the process of discharging by agreement
- to define frustration in contractual terms
- to list the remedies available to the victim of a breach of contract

Mr. and Mrs. Wright wanted to buy a particular house but, before they did so, they wanted to make sure that their new home would be in a telephone exchange area that would not require their having to pay long distance charges for calls to the local town. They talked with the local Bell Canada representative, showed a map with the location of the house and were assured that it was within the proper exchange. Before the transaction was finalized, they obtained a card from Bell Canada stating that the house was within the 666 exchange. As it turned out, their home was not located within the 666 exchange area, and they were billed for their long distance calls to the local town. They ran up a considerable bill and sued Bell Canada for the charges. The judge decided that in this case it was clear that a term of the service contract was that there would be no long distance charges on calls because the house was within the 666 exchange and therefore the charges represented a breach of contract. The judge ordered Bell to pay the Wrights $508 in damages and indicated that there would be a continued breach for each new period in which the long distance charges were levied.[1] Breach of contract is just one of the ways in which a contract can be discharged that will be discussed in this chapter.

Contractual obligations can come to an end or be discharged in four ways. These are by performance, breach, agreement between the parties to end or modify, and frustration. This chapter will examine each of these.

PERFORMANCE

Contractual obligations are discharged and a contract is ended when each party satisfactorily performs or completes its part of the bargain. Historically, the failure of one party to perform the terms of a contract relieved the other party of any obligation to perform its part of the bargain since the obligations of the parties were interdependent. If a lump sum payment was to be made for services rendered, no payment would be due unless that service was performed exactly as specified in the contract. Thus, a person who agreed to paint a building in exchange for payment upon completion would not be entitled to anything if only a portion, even if it was a major portion, of the building were painted. The obligation to pay was dependent on the completion of the painting. This was a harsh rule and over the years several exceptions to it have developed.

Substantial Performance

Contract discharged when contract substantially performed

When a party has performed most of the obligation under the agreement but has left out some element of performance that is trivial in its effect on the contract, the courts will treat the contract as performed. For example, if Jones contracts to deliver 1000 boxes of tomatoes to Sharif but delivers only 999 boxes, the contract is substantially performed and Jones is discharged from the obligation to deliver tomatoes to Sharif. However, Sharif has the right to deduct the value of that one undelivered box or to get it from somebody else and seek compensation from Jones for the expense of doing so.

But some contracts must be performed exactly

There are some types of contracts in which only complete and exact performance will suffice. For example, if Aarons has a contract to drill a water-producing well for Parada and drills 29 dry holes, this will not qualify as substantial performance

[1] *Wright v. Bell Canada* 714-009 Ont. Prov. Ct., June 15, 1987, *The Lawyers Weekly*, July 3, 1987.

because those dry holes are worthless to Parada. Only the delivery of a producing well will qualify as performance. Payment is said to be conditional on the exact performance as required in the contract.

Tender of Performance

When performance is refused or made impossible—that constitutes breach

The general rule in common law is that when a person has tendered performance of a contract, it counts as if the contract had been performed. This means that if a person is ready, willing and able to perform a contractual obligation and attempts to do so, but the other party refuses to accept it or prevents it, the first party is taken to have completed the contractual obligation and is discharged from it. The person who has attempted performance is then in a position to sue the other party for damages. Tendered performance means that the person performing must actually attempt to deliver the specified goods or attempt to perform the specified service. It should be noted that in many service arrangements, the service does not have to be provided personally; vicarious performance will suffice. If Watson contracts to clean Nyberg's windows and his employees are refused entrance by Nyberg when they show up to do the job, performance has been tendered and the contract is discharged. There are some types of contracts for which personal services are required and sending a substitute would not be an appropriate tender of performance. The compensation granted for refusal to accept delivery or service will cover only the damages suffered, not the cost of goods or services since these costs have not been incurred.

Where debt owed and money refused—money still owed but creditor bears expense

The effect of tendering proper payment of debt does not extinguish the debt but simply relieves the debtor of the obligation to seek out the creditor to make payment. It thus becomes the creditor's responsibility to ask the debtor for payment and to bear the cost of doing so. Even if it becomes necessary for the creditor to sue, the costs of the court action are the creditor's responsibility if it can be shown that the debtor properly attempted to pay the debt.

Payment must be in legal tender

Proper performance of a contractual obligation in which the payment of money is involved requires the tendering of cash. Cheques, even certified cheques, are acceptable only when the parties have agreed to allow cheques to be used to pay debts. This may be an actual agreement between the parties or it may be an accepted business practice. If there is any question about the acceptable form of payment, it is advisable to present cash. If the contract requires a specified amount to be given, exactly that amount must be tendered. The person paying does not have the right to demand that the other party produce change. A creditor need only accept a limited number of coins in payment of debt. The *Currency and Exchange Act*[2] states that creditors need only accept up to 25 pennies, five dollars worth of nickels and ten dollars worth of any larger coins. There is no limit on what qualifies as legal tender when gold coin or paper money is offered as long as official Canadian bank notes are used.

---

[2] *Currency and Exchange Act*, R.S.C. (1985) c.C-52.

The delivery of money, goods or services must be tendered at a reasonable time and place. Usually this means during normal business hours at a person's place of business, unless it has been otherwise specified in the contract. Thus, if Jones has a contract to deliver five tonnes of ripe tomatoes to Sharif's packing house by July 10, Jones would be expected to make that delivery to Sharif's packing house rather than to Sharif's home or office. The delivery should also take place during the usual working day. Sharif would not be obligated to accept delivery at six o'clock on Saturday evening unless such time was permitted in the contract. The general rule is that if a condition of the contract specifies a time for performance, the time specified is absolute. Failure to perform within that specified time will be fatal to the contract. If a person had an option to purchase property that must be exercised by July 30 and attempts to exercise that option on August 2, it would be too late. Rights under the option agreement would have expired.

In circumstances in which the parties have not specified a time for performance, they are obligated to perform within a **reasonable time**. The definition of reasonable time will vary with the nature of the agreement, the parties and the type of goods or services involved. A reasonable time would be shorter for an agreement to buy shares in a company trading on the stock exchange than for the purchase of a farm. If the time has not been specified and one of the parties feels that the other has been delaying too long, the appropriate action is to serve notice on the delaying party that performance must take place within a specified but reasonable length of time and that failure to perform in that time will discharge the agreement.

The courts of equity have developed a more lenient approach towards specific time requirements in the contract. The courts are much less likely to find that the contract has been discharged because of a failure to perform on time when the parties are seeking an equitable remedy, such as specific performance or injunction. These and other remedies for breach of contract will be discussed below.

Independent Obligations

In most contractual relationships, the obligation of one party is dependent on the performance of the other party to the contract. If one person agrees to sell another a car for $500, the obligation of the purchaser to pay the $500 will not arise until the car is delivered. If there is no delivery, there is no obligation to pay the $500. Similarly, if the purchaser is not willing to hand over the $500, there is no obligation on the part of the seller to hand over the car. In some relationships, however, the contractual obligations borne by the parties are independent or severable from each other. This means that if one of the parties fails to perform an obligation under the agreement, the other party will not be relieved from the obligation to perform. The tenant of leased property has an obligation to pay rent and the landlord has an obligation to make repairs when they become necessary. If the tenant notifies the landlord that certain repairs have to be made and the land-

Delivery must be at a reasonable time and place

May be obligation to perform despite breach

lord fails to make those repairs, the tenant is not relieved of the obligation to pay rent. This obligation is independent of the landlord's obligation to make repairs. This condition can be overcome by specifying in the contract that the obligations are interdependent.

Performance by instalments

A similar result occurs when the contract requires delivery in several instalments. For example, if a supplier has an obligation to deliver a tonne of coal per month for a year, that contract can be treated as a series of individual contracts, one for each instalment. If the supplier fails to make one delivery, the other contracting party is not relieved of the obligation to pay for the deliveries received. Again, the parties can specify in the contract that the obligation to pay is concurrent or dependent on the other party's complete performance of all the other provisions of the contractual relationship. In some situations, however, a supplier's failure to deliver an instalment is so important that failure to deliver it would undermine the whole contractual relationship. This failure would amount to a repudiation of the contract and there would be no obligation to accept any further deliveries. But even in these circumstances, the purchaser is obligated to pay for the instalments that have already been received.

BREACH

Breach of contract involves the failure of the breaching party to perform properly its contractual obligations (see Box 6.1, "Fast food fight heats up"). In the example used to introduce this chapter, Bell Canada was clearly in breach of its agreement with Mr. and Mrs. Wright and so were held liable for the extra charges levied against the Wrights. Such a breach may be either a major or a minor infraction.

Conditions and Warranties

Breach of condition— party relieved

Breach of warranty— performance required

Breach accepted— performance required

Terms essential to the substantial performance of a contract are called **conditions**. Terms which are insignificant or peripheral to the central obligation of the contract are called **warranties**. The failure to perform a condition of the contract generally permits the other party to treat his or her obligation as ended and sue for breach of contract. But the improper performance of a warranty does not relieve the other party of the obligation to fulfil his or her side of the agreement. The victim of such a failure to perform has the right to sue the other party for whatever it costs to overcome the deficiency in performance.

Although the breach of a condition will normally allow the victim of the breach to treat the contract as discharged, there is an obligation to perform if the partial performance is accepted. Acceptance means that the party has accepted some benefit under the agreement, knowing that the agreement has been breached. For example, if Beaman has a clear obligation to deliver to Singh a portrait of Singh's mother and delivers a landscape painting instead, this would normally be a breach

Box 6.1

Fast food fight heats up

Chicken Chicken seeks $25-million in damages in suits against Pizza Pizza

Chicken Chicken Inc. has served up another legal entrée in its fast food fight with Pizza Pizza Ltd.

The upstart Toronto chicken chain, created by former Pizza Pizza president John Gillespie, yesterday launched two lawsuits seeking a total of $25-million in damages against the pizza company and its senior officers.

Chicken Chicken and Mr. Gillespie maintain that Toronto-based Pizza Pizza's continuing $11-million lawsuit against them is, among other things, an abuse of process.

That court action, according to Mr. Gillespie, has seen Pizza Pizza and its chairman. Michael Overs, make "wild and reckless accusations" about Mr. Gillespie's conduct.

"I can't have (Mr. Overs) running around doing the things he's doing and saying the things he's saying," Mr. Gillespie said in an interview.

In a separate but related court application yesterday, Mr. Gillespie is also seeking a court order appointing a receiver to wind up Pizza Pizza. Mr. Gillespie is making the application as a Pizza Pizza creditor owed more than $2-million. The money represents the remaining installments of a $4-million settlement signed in 1988 after Mr. Gillespie had left Pizza Pizza. In addition, Mr. Gillespie wants a court order setting aside any contracts between Pizza Pizza and Cara Operations Ltd. concerning the sales and home delivery of Cara's Swiss Chalet brand chicken.

Lorne Austin, a spokesman for Pizza Pizza, called the Chicken Chicken actions "totally without merit."

Last spring, Pizza Pizza launched a suit against both Chicken Chicken and Mr. Gillespie, alleging that Mr. Gillespie had breached a non-competition pact and misused confidential information.

The Supreme Court of Ontario, however, rejected Pizza Pizza's motion for a temporary injunction against the chicken chain's continued growth until a full trial.

In his decision, Mr. Justice David Henry said the non-competition pact simply bars Mr. Gillespie from opening a pizza parlor. The judge also said Pizza Pizza would have "an uphill battle" proving that Mr. Gillespie used confidential information about Pizza Pizza's operations.

Mr. Gillespie, who joined Toronto's Pizza Pizza in 1978 and later became its president, left the company in 1987 in the wake of a bitter court fight with Mr. Overs over control of the firm. As part of a settlement. Mr. Gillespie agreed not to compete with Pizza Pizza "in the pizza business" until next July.

Last December, Mr. Gillespie launched Chicken Chicken, which, like Pizza Pizza, has a central phone number for ordering and offers home delivery within 30 minutes or the meal is free. Seventeen franchises have been sold in the Toronto area, 10 of which are now operating. Pizza Pizza has more than 100 outlets in and around Toronto.

In one of the two legal actions launched yesterday in the Supreme Court of Ontario, Chicken Chicken alleges that Pizza Pizza's senior employees have actively discouraged potential Chicken Chicken franchises and engaged in a "concerted malicious" campaign to damage Mr. Gillespie's reputation.

In the related application for a court order winding up Pizza Pizza Mr. Gillespie alleges that "Pizza Pizza is in a precarious financial position" as a result of its expansion into Montreal and the Kitchener/Waterloo and Guelph areas of Ontario.

"That's absurd," Pizza Pizza's Mr. Austin said. "Our sales have never been stronger. We are profitable." Because Pizza Pizza is a private company, he said he could not provide more details on its financial position.

In February and March, 1989, Pizza Pizza failed to make monthly payments to Mr. Gillespie required by the 1988 settlement, according to Mr. Gillespie's application. The settlement, as a result, was restructured to provide Mr. Gillespie's payment on the second Tuesday of each month, rather than on the first of each month.

> But Mr. Austin said the changed dates for the $80 000 payments was a question of cash flow, and had "nothing to do with financial condition." Pizza Pizza makes $1-million in lease payments at the start of each month, he said.
>
> Mr. Gillespie's application maintains that the lawsuit Pizza Pizza launched against Chicken Chicken earlier this year, as well as Pizza Pizza's joint venture with Cara, are "improperly motivated" by malice and will "seriously jeopardize" Pizza Pizza's financial health.
>
> Chicken Chicken has already asked the Supreme Court of Ontario for summary judgment dismissing the original Pizza Pizza lawsuit. A decision on that motion is expected shortly.

Source: Kenneth Kidd, The Globe and Mail, *Friday, August 10, 1990, p. B5.*

of a condition. However, by accepting the painting, Singh then has to live up to the obligation to pay but retains the right to sue for any damages suffered. A breach of condition in a contract that has been accepted by the other party is treated as a breach of warranty.

Terms that might normally be considered insubstantial or unimportant can be upgraded to the stature of conditions by the parties so declaring in their agreement. For example, suppose someone orders a new automobile and stipulates that it come with a digital quartz clock. Such a term would normally be a warranty and the purchaser must accept delivery of the automobile and make payment even if the car is delivered without the clock. But the purchaser can write into the purchase contract that the clock be a condition of the contract. Failure to include it would be a breach of a condition and the purchaser would be able to refuse delivery of the automobile. Similarly, a term that would normally be a condition can be relegated to the position of a warranty by the parties so specifying in the agreement.

Warranties can become conditions and vice versa

Exemption Clauses

A warranty card included with a purchase document summarizes the seller's obligations under the contract and states that these obligations are merely warranties. Even when these limited obligations are not honoured, victims cannot return the goods or withhold payment for them if there has been a breach. The *Sale of Goods Act* states that in transactions governed by the Act, the court has the option of treating a term specified as a warranty as a condition.

The term warranty used in this way is often referred to as either an **exemption**, an **exclusion** or an **exculpatory clause**. It is an attempt by the sellers of goods or services to significantly limit or eliminate their liability under an agreement. The courts will generally enforce exemption clauses because the object of contract law is to carry out whatever the parties have freely bargained to do. But they do so reluctantly. If there is any ambiguity in the terms of the exemption clause, the narrow or restrictive meaning will be used. For example, if a restaurant has a sign above the cloakroom stating, "Not responsible for lost or stolen clothing," bringing this term to the customer's attention would make it part of the contract of **bailment** in which goods are being cared for by someone else. If clothes left there are damaged by

Exemption clauses attempt to limit liability
Exemption clauses strictly interpreted

fire or water instead of being stolen or lost, the proprietor would not be able to rely on the sign to avoid liability because of the narrow interpretation the courts would apply. Similarly, if a briefcase left with the proprietor was stolen, the proprietor would not be able to rely on the exemption clause because it was not clothing that was stolen. Exemption clauses are intricate and involved because the people who draft them try to cover all possible eventualities knowing that the courts will take a restrictive approach in their interpretation. Consumer protection legislation that significantly limits the scope of exemption clauses is becoming much more common.

Must be brought to the attention of party at time of contract

Exemption clauses usually form a part of the written document but the term could be included in a sign or notice. In any case, the terms must be brought to the attention of the customer. If the clause is on the back of the ticket or receipt, there must be a reference on the front directing the holder to read the back. The key point to remember when dealing with exemption clauses is that one party cannot unilaterally impose a restriction of liability on the other. Both parties must agree to it as part of the contract. An exemption of liability sign at a car park, train station or dry cleaners must be in clear view so that a reasonable person would notice it when entering the premises or undertaking a contractual obligation. It is only then that the term will form part of the agreement, and even then the words will be interpreted narrowly.

Fundamental Breach

Exemption clauses will not completely eliminate liability

Suppliers of goods or services try to limit their liability as much as possible. But the courts have shown a considerable reluctance to allow suppliers to eliminate their liability entirely. It is in these circumstances that the concept of **fundamental breach** has developed. Fundamental breach means that some types of failure to perform are so basic to the contract that they destroy any semblance of performance of the contract, leaving one party bereft of any benefit from it at all. In the face of such a breach, an exemption clause will not protect the breacher from liability for damages. Thus, if a new car is plagued with problems to the point that it is not capable of being driven, the purchaser will be entitled to return it and get a refund. The breach has been fundamental; what was received was something essentially different from what was bargained for. "A car is not a car if it has to be towed."[3]

Exemption clauses ineffective in cases of fundamental breach

The courts have refused to give effect to exemption clauses in cases of fundamental breach. They have allowed the victim of the breach to return the goods and demand compensation. The justification for this policy is based on two different lines of reasoning and there was, until recently, considerable debate over this apparent interference with the freedom of contracting parties to agree to whatever they want. When the doctrine was developed, it was thought to be a rule of contract law that the parties could not contract out of all liability. If the breach was so basic that it changed the nature of the agreement, the exemption clause would simply be overruled. This approach has been rejected and the accepted view today is that the judge will examine the entire contract as well as the exemption clause and imply from the terms whether the parties intended the ex-

---

[3] *Burkitt, L.J., Yeoman Credit, Ltd. v. Apps* [1961] 2 All E.R. 281 at p.288 (Court of Appeal).

emption clause to cover this fundamental breach. As a result, it is now feasible to draft an exemption clause that excludes all liability, but the courts will still, if they can, interpret it in such a way as to give it less effect when a fundamental or basic obligation of the contract is breached. This is referred to as the construction approach and has been firmly adopted by the Supreme Court of Canada.[4]

Repudiation

Repudiation occurs when one of the parties to a contract indicates to the other "an intimation or an intention to abandon and altogether to refuse performance of the contract."[5] If this refusal occurs before performance is due, it is called **anticipatory breach**. In such circumstances, it makes little sense to insist that innocent parties continue to perform their part of the agreement. The courts, therefore, allow the victim to treat the contract as breached, sue and refuse to go through with any further performance. Alternatively, the victim of the repudiation can insist that the contract be fulfilled by performing his or her side of the agreement and waiting until the performance date to see if the other party carries through with the threat of nonperformance. If the repudiating party fails to perform, the innocent party can then sue for breach of contract and the party repudiating will be held responsible for damages incurred after the repudiation. Once the choice is made either to ignore the repudiation and insist on performance or to accept it and treat the contractual obligations as ended, that choice is binding. This can have serious consequences on the victim's legal position. If the innocent party insists on performance of the repudiated contract and is then unable to perform for any reason, the victim will be subject to a breach of contract action.

The innocent party to a repudiated contract also runs the risk of being affected by changing circumstances. In the case of *Avery v. Bowden*,[6] the defendant chartered the plaintiff's ship and agreed to supply it with a cargo at the Russian port of Odessa. However, when the ship arrived, the defendant refused to supply a cargo and insisted that the boat leave. The captain stayed in port hoping that the supplier would change his mind. The Crimean War then broke out, before the expiration of the specified time in which the cargo had to be supplied, which would have made it impossible to go through with the original contract even if the defendant had not repudiated. The owner of the ship sued for breach of contract. Although the court agreed that the plaintiff would have had the right to treat the contract as discharged by breach once the defendant had clearly indicated that he was not going to go through with the agreement, the defendant had chosen not to acknowledge the repudiation. Therefore, the contract had not been breached since the time specified for performance had not yet expired when the war broke out. The contract was discharged by frustration, not by breach. Frustration will be discussed later in the chapter.

Victim is discharged and can sue if repudiation occurs before due date —or demand performance and wait

Victim is bound by choice

Changing circumstances may affect repudiation

---

[4] *Beaufort Realties v. Chomedey Aluminum Co.* (1981) 116 D.L.R. (3d) 193 (S.C.C.).
[5] Comment of Lord Coleridge, C.J. in *Freeth v. Burr* (1874) L.R. 9 C.P. p. 208, at p. 213 (Court of Common Pleas).
[6] *Avery v. Bowden* (1855) 5 E. & B. 714; Aff'd. (1856) 6 E. & B. 953 (Court of Exchequer).

Repudiation can also be implied from the conduct of the parties. Repudiation is implied if the subject matter of an agreement is sold to a third party before the date of delivery or if an effort has been made to sell the goods. It is clear that the owner does not intend to honour the original agreement. Repudiation may also be implied by an actual breach of the terms of the agreement. Failure to perform one part of an ongoing contract, such as an important instalment, may be taken as repudiation of the rest of the contract. The failure to perform must be of a condition and serious enough for the victim to assume that the rest of the agreement will not be performed.

Repudiation may be implied by conduct

DISCHARGE BY AGREEMENT

Contracts can be modified or ended by agreement

There is no difficulty in entering into an agreement to end or modify a previous contract. This is referred to as discharge by agreement. As in creating any contractual relationship, all of the ingredients necessary to form a contract must be present. It may be important to determine whether the old agreement has been ended and a new one substituted or whether the old agreement has been merely modified. Generally, if it is only a minor term that is altered, the old agreement continues, but the change of a major term will result in a new contract, depending, of course, on what the court determines is the intention of the parties. Terms in the original agreement that are not referred to in the new one will still be in place if the agreement has been modified, but they will no longer apply if a new agreement has been created. If the *Statute of Frauds* required the original agreement to be in writing, then any modifications to it must also be in writing. A verbal agreement to discharge such a written contract would be valid, but the new contract must be in writing.

Must have consensus

The requirements of consensus and consideration are most frequently called into question by the courts when a contract to discharge or modify an agreement is challenged. One party to a contract cannot unilaterally impose modification or termination on the other. A merchant might be tempted to charge an exorbitant amount of interest to a customer who does not pay a bill on time. There is no problem if this had been agreed to in the original contract, but if the merchant imposes such a term only upon default of payment, it will not be binding on the customer. This does not excuse the customer from the debt, but the courts will protect customers from excessive interest rates imposed unilaterally after the fact.

Must have consideration

Consideration is necessary to support a new agreement to discharge or modify the first contract. If both parties have something left to do under the original contract which the agreement to modify relieves them of, there is valid consideration on both sides to support the change. This is called **bilateral discharge** or mutual release. When both parties agree not to hold each other to the performance of their remaining obligations under the contract, this is often referred to as a waiver. But if only one party is relieved of obligations under the contract, such a one-sided waiver or unilateral discharge will not relieve the other party of the original contractual obligations since it is not supported by consideration. If the person being unilaterally discharged in such circumstances relies on the other party's promise not to insist on performance, that person may be able to raise the defence of promissory estoppel if there is a change of heart and the other party later insists on performance. Promissory estoppel was discussed in Chapter 3.

The most serious problem with consideration in a contract discharged by agreement occurs when both parties agree to relieve the party who has not yet performed under the contract after the other party has completely performed his or her side of the agreement or when the discharge is otherwise entirely one-sided. Such a release would not be binding except in cases in which the unilateral discharge was supported by some further consideration or where promissory estoppel is available as a defence.

Unilateral discharge requires accord and satisfaction

When the parties discharge the contract on the payment of some substituted consideration, they have reached an **accord and satisfaction**. "Satisfaction" refers to the additional consideration given to support the discharge. To illustrate this point, consider the situation in which Aiello agrees to paint Newcombe's house for $500 to be paid in advance. After payment Aiello tells Newcombe that she is no longer able to paint the house. If Newcombe were to tell Aiello that there was no need to worry about it, would he be bound by those words? The release would not be binding because there is no consideration. But if Aiello were to agree to paint Newcombe's fence instead, there would be an accord and Newcombe would obtain satisfaction. The agreement is supported by new consideration and this arrangement would be binding on both parties.

The classic example of a one-sided attempt to change a contractual obligation is when a debtor approaches a creditor and offers to pay less than the full amount of debt owed. The creditor might be tempted to take part payment rather than risk getting nothing at all or having to sue for full payment. If the creditor accepts the part payment and leads the debtor to believe that the debt is discharged, can the creditor still sue for the unpaid balance? The case of *Foakes v. Beer*[7] established that, when part payment is accepted, the full debt is not abolished unless there is additional consideration. The creditor would be able to sue for the unpaid amount. However, if the debtor agreed to pay the lesser amount before the due date, this early payment would be sufficient consideration to support the discharge. Knowing that they will still be liable for the full debt if they make partial payments discourages debtors from taking such a step. This has caused some difficulty in the business world because many creditors might prefer partial payment over no payment at all. As a result, all of the common law provinces have adopted legislation which largely overrules the precedent

Partial payment of debt acceptable if taken

set in *Foakes v. Beer*. If partial payment is offered and taken as full payment of a debt, the creditor cannot sue for any deficit. Nothing forces the creditor to accept the lesser amount, but if it is accepted the creditor must be satisfied with it.

Contractual Terms

Contracts that involve ongoing relationships between parties may not provide for the termination of those relationships. In these cases, the courts will imply a provision

---

[7] *Foakes v. Beer* (1884) 9 App. Cas. 605 (House of Lords).

requiring each party to give the other reasonable notice of the termination of the agreement. Reasonable notice will vary depending on the nature and subject matter of the contract, such as the payment period in the lease or the length of the term of employment. The contract can also provide that either party has the right to end their obligations, usually by simply giving the other notice. When the contract does specify the circumstances under which it will end, the provision will be binding.

Contract may provide for its own discharge

Conditions precedent

The contract itself can specify conditions under which the obligations of the parties may begin or end. These are generally called **conditions precedent** and **conditions subsequent**. Conditions precedent exist when the parties specify in their agreement some event or requirement that must be satisfied before either party to the contract is obligated to do anything. The agreement will not be binding on either party if that event fails to take place. For example, if Nishi were to agree to buy Fafard's house, subject to the sale of her own house, the contract is conditional on that event. Thus, if Nishi fails to sell her house, she is not obligated to go through with any agreement for the purchase of Fafard's house. When a condition precedent is not satisfied, there is no contractual obligation on either party. For this reason subject to clauses in contracts can be extremely important.

Conditions subsequent

Sometimes terms are included in a contract that bring the obligations of the parties to an end upon some event or condition taking place. They are called conditions subsequent and differ from conditions precedent which prevent the obligations set out in the agreement from resting on the parties. Conditions subsequent bring those obligations to an end once they have rested on the parties. For example, if Agar agreed to pay Nguyen $400 per month for janitorial services "until Nguyen ceases to be a full-time student," this term is a condition subsequent. Agar will be obligated to pay until Nguyen finishes school. In this way, a contract can provide for its own end. But the parties can also agree to end, modify or substitute obligations with a new agreement. Some statutes, such as the *Bankruptcy Act*, also end contractual obligations by operation of law. Bankruptcy will be discussed in Chapter 8.

FRUSTRATION

A founding tenet of contract law was strict liability for contractual obligations. Historically, only performance would satisfy the terms of a contract and any failure to perform, even if it was through no fault of the parties, would result in the victim of that failure having the right to sue for breach. This is a harsh doctrine and the principle of frustration has been developed over the last century to alleviate some of the hardships. When, after the creation of the contract, some unforeseen outside event interferes with the performance of the contract, making the basic object of the agreement unobtainable, the contract is said to be discharged through frustration. This interference can make the performance of the agreement impossible or it might result in the performance being something essentially different from what the parties had anticipated when they entered into the agreement. It is easy to understand frustration when performance of the contract is made impossible, such as

Frustrating event may end a contract

when a person agrees to paint a house which is subsequently destroyed in a fire. The difficulty arises when performance is still possible but the difference in the effect of performance is significant enough to amount to frustration. In the case of *Krell v. Henry*,[8] the parties agreed to the rental of an apartment to view the coronation parade of Edward VII. A small deposit was paid at the time the contract was entered into, but the coronation parade was cancelled before the balance was paid because of the king's sudden illness. It was still possible for the parties to go through with the performance of the contract and for the tenant to occupy the flat, but to do so with no coronation parade to watch would be something essentially different from what the parties had in mind when they entered into the contract. Although performance of the contract was possible in a literal sense, it was no longer possible to obtain the purpose or object of the contract itself. Thus, the contract was said to be frustrated. It must be noted, however, that frustration requires the essential nature of the contract to have changed; it is not enough that performance is just more difficult.

Common mistake not the same as frustration

Care should be taken not to confuse frustration with shared or common mistake. There is no contract if the parties make a mistake about the existence of the subject matter at the time they enter into the agreement. There is no contract at all if a ship is destroyed, unknown to the parties, before they enter into an agreement involving that ship or its cargo. With frustration, however, the interference takes place after the parties have entered into the agreement. In addition, the *Sale of Goods Act* provides that, when goods are being sold and through no fault of the parties perish before the risk passes to the purchaser, the contract is not binding on that purchaser. Frustration commonly arises in the following circumstances:

Circumstances constituting frustration

1. *Performance of a contract becomes impossible because the subject matter of the agreement is destroyed or is otherwise unusable.* In the case of *Taylor v. Caldwell*,[9] there was an agreement between the parties to rent out a music hall. The music hall burned down six days before the performance was to take place. The court held that the contract was discharged through frustration. Contracts may be frustrated when a person who has agreed to supply personal services becomes ill or dies and when the specific article that formed the object of the contract is destroyed before the agreement can be performed.

2. *An event that forms the basis of a contract fails to take place.* An example of this is *Krell v. Henry* cited earlier.

3. *Acts of the government can affect performance.* Government policy can interfere with the performance of a contract in several different ways. A perfectly appropriate commercial contract with someone in another country may become unlawful through a declaration of war between the two countries. Contracts involving the manufacture and production of particular drugs or foodstuffs may become illegal by statute. A contract may anticipate the acquisition of a

[8] *Krell v. Henry* [1903] 2 K.B. 740 (Court of Appeal).
[9] *Taylor v. Caldwell* (1863) 3 B.&S. 826 (Court of Queen's Bench).

licence or permit which the government does not grant. Also, all levels of government have the power in certain circumstances to expropriate the property which may form the basis of a contract.

Circumstances Constituting Frustration

Self-induced frustration is caused by one of the parties to the contract and, although it may appear to be frustration, it is treated as a breach. For example, if Moser has a contract to build an apartment building for Wu but the city refuses to grant Moser a building permit, we would expect the contract to be frustrated. However, if the building permit is refused because Moser failed to submit the appropriate plans as required by city bylaw, the frustration is self-induced. Moser is responsible for the misfortune; the refusal of the city to grant a permit will not prove an excuse for Moser's failure to perform the contract.

Similarly, if the parties have anticipated the frustrating event or have provided for one of the parties to bear the risk of such an eventuality, these contractual terms will prevail and the parties will not be able to claim that their agreement has been frustrated. It is only when the event is an unforeseen interference not caused by either party that the courts are willing to find frustration.

Finally, the contract is not frustrated if the unforeseen outside event only makes the performance of the contract more costly or more difficult. In the case of the *Tsakiroglou and Co. Ltd. v. Noblee and Thorl G.m.b.H.*,[10] the defendant agreed to sell and deliver a cargo of Sudanese groundnuts from a port in the Sudan to Hamburg. Then the Suez War broke out which prevented the defendant from using the Suez Canal to deliver the cargo. It was not shipped; the purchaser sued for breach of contract and the seller claimed frustration. The court held that, although it was more difficult and costly to ship the cargo around Africa, the essential nature of the contract remained intact and frustration did not apply. The seller was held liable for breach of contract. The contract would probably have been frustrated if the parties had specifically referred to the Suez Canal in the contract.

Effect of Frustration

Let loss lie where
it falls under
common law

When a contract was frustrated under common law, the general principle was, "Let the loss lie where it falls." In other words, the party who had done work or provided services before the frustrating event would bear the loss and could not seek compensation from the other party. Similarly, money already paid as a deposit was lost. This approach was considered unsatisfactory and the House of Lords modified this position in the *Fibrosa* case.[11] An English company had agreed to supply a Polish company with machinery to be delivered four months later. A prepayment of

---

[10] *Tsakiroglou and Co. Ltd. v. Noblee and Thorl G.m.b.H.* [1962] A.C. 93 (House of Lords).
[11] *Fibrosa Spolka Akeyjna v. Fairbairn, Lawson, Combe, Barbouk Ltd.* [1943] A.C. 32 (House of Lords).

£1000 was made by the Polish company but, before the contract could be performed, the Second World War broke out and the contract was frustrated. The Polish company sued for the return of the prepayment. The court declared that when there has been a complete failure of consideration resulting in one of the parties receiving nothing, any prepayment or deposit must be returned. This modification is the present common law position, but is only a partial solution. It is still an all-or-nothing situation with no option to apportion the loss between the parties whenever that might be the more appropriate course of action. Most common law jurisdictions have passed legislation to overcome these inadequacies.

Legislation

Legislation allows deposits to be split

The English *Law Reform Act*[12] states that a prepayment made before the frustrating event discharging the contract took place must be returned. The court, however, is given the right to allow the other party to retain a portion of that prepayment to compensate for expenses incurred. This provision of the Act eliminates the all-or-nothing consequences of the *Fibrosa* decision. However, the performing party is out of luck if it incurred expenses and there was no prepayment unless performance or part performance resulted in a substantial benefit to the other party. The provisions of this legislation were adopted by Alberta, Manitoba, New Brunswick, Newfoundland, Ontario, Prince Edward Island and the Northwest Territories in their *Frustrated Contracts Act*. British Columbia and the Yukon have also adopted a *Frustrated Contracts Act*, but their legislation allows the courts to go further. The British Columbia and Yukon courts can split the costs incurred between the parties whether or not a prepayment or deposit has been paid and even when no significant benefit has been bestowed. The various frustrated contracts acts in place also provide that, when one party has received a benefit from the other before the frustrating event takes place, the court has the power to order the benefiting party to pay the party creating that benefit an amount equal to its value.

REMEDIES FOR BREACH OF CONTRACT

Rescission and Rectification

A breach of a condition in a contract does not automatically end all obligations of both parties to that contract. The victim of the breach has the right to ignore the breach and continue to treat the contract as if it were in force. If Mouzakis agreed to sell Smith a car and delivered a boat, Smith can choose to take the boat. It takes both parties to discharge a contract by breach of condition. Even if the victim of the

---

[12] *Law Reform Act* [1943] 6 and 7 Geo. 6, c.40.

breach elects to treat the contract as discharged, this does not end the obligations of the breaching party. The nature of those obligations is changed; the breaching party becomes liable for the remedies that are discussed below.

The remedies of rescission and rectification available to victims in contractual relationships are discussed in Chapter 5. These remedies usually come into play when problems with the formation of a contract affect its validity. A contract lacking consideration, legality or capacity can be rescinded and the parties can ask the courts to return them to the position they would have been in had they never entered into the contract. Similarly, if duress, undue influence, misrepresentation or mistake has led to a lack of consensus, rescission may be available. Rescission is also available when there has been a repudiation in the form of an anticipatory breach or when goods have been returned because they are defective. Rescission is only possible if the breach of the agreement is significant and the parties can be returned to their original positions. Unlike other remedies available in contract law, rescission involves returning the parties as near as possible to the position they would have been in had the contract not been made as opposed to putting the victim in the position he or she would have been in had the contract been properly performed. Rescission looks backward. Rectification is another remedy available to correct defects in the formation of contracts but it is not available as a remedy for defective performance. As was discussed in Chapter 5, rectification is the process by which the court corrects the wording of a written document that has incorrectly recorded the terms of the agreement. Rescission and rectification are equitable remedies developed in the Courts of Chancery.

Remedies available where formation of contract was defective

Remedies Provided in Contract

LIQUIDATED DAMAGES. It is possible for a contract to provide a consequence if one of the parties fails to honour its terms. These consequences may be quite varied. For example, the contract may include a term stating that arbitration will determine compensation to be paid in the event of disputes. The contract might also delineate the maximum amount of compensation to be paid by the breaching party, such as when establishments post signs indicating they are not responsible for losses over a specified amount. Failure to make an instalment payment will often trigger a term of the contract called an **acceleration clause**. Upon default of payment, this clause makes all the entire outstanding debt due and payable immediately.

Deposits to be forfeited upon breach

The most common alternative remedy specified in a contract is a **liquidated damages** clause. A liquidated damages term states that the responsible party will pay a certain amount of money if a breach occurs. This amount is called a **deposit** when the money is advanced at the outset of the agreement. Suppliers of goods or services will often insist that purchasers make prepayments with the understanding that the supplier will be able to retain the deposit if the purchaser fails to perform the contract. It must be clear that the deposit is intended to be liquidated damages and that it is to be forfeited upon failure to perform. For example, the vendor of an automobile will usually require the buyer to pay a substantial deposit when ordering to secure the purchase. If the purchaser fails to go through with the deal when the car arrives, one of the remedies available to the vendor is to retain the deposit.

Temptation to take a large deposit entails significant risk. To qualify as liquidated damages, a deposit must be an honest attempt by the parties to estimate the damages that would be suffered if the contract were breached. If the amount involved crosses the line from being an honest attempt to estimate the possible injury or damages that would be suffered to an attempt to punish or impose a penalty for failure to perform, the provision may be void. A $1000 deposit on a new car might be fair in view of the cost of advertising, the time lost, the extra interest payments and so on. A $10 000 deposit on a $15 000 car is no longer an attempt to compensate for possible loss or injury but becomes an attempt to punish the breaching party for failure to go through with the contract. Such a penalty clause, when it is excessive, is unconscionable and void. The $10 000 would not be a deposit at all and the prepayment would be returned subject to an action for damages for the injury actually suffered. Even when no prepayment is involved, a liquidated damages clause may be brought into question if the object is to punish rather than to compensate and the amount involved is exorbitant.

Deposit must not be penalty

DOWN PAYMENTS. Another difficulty the courts must face is to distinguish between a **deposit** and a **down payment**. When a prepayment is meant to be forfeited in the event of a breach of contract, this sum is usually called a deposit. But when there is no intention that the amount be forfeited, the prepayment becomes a first instalment or a down payment. A down payment must be returned to the purchaser even if it is the purchaser who breaches the contract. The vendor then retains the right to sue for compensation for the injuries suffered. Of course, possession of the down payment will often give the vendor a lever to force the other party into settling the dispute. The term applied to a particular prepayment does not always determine its nature. Even when the parties have consistently referred to a particular payment as a deposit, the courts will not treat it as such unless they can find a clear intention by both parties that the amount was to be forfeited in the event of a breach. And if the courts do determine that the intention was for the amount to be forfeited, the amount of the deposit must reflect an honest attempt by the parties to estimate their damages rather than to impose a penalty.

Deposit is forfeited—down payment is not

Damages

The remedy of damages or monetary compensation was developed by the common law courts, but it is not always appropriate when a contract is breached. Although the Courts of Chancery developed other remedies, the significance of damages as a remedy for breach of contract must be emphasized since it is still the most important remedy available to the courts. Courts assess what loss the victim of the breach has suffered and order the breaching party to pay an amount that will compensate for that loss to try to put the victim of the breach in the position he or she would have been in **if the contract had been properly performed**. For example, if a person

Damages in contract law designed to compensate

Victim of breach
compensated as
if contract had
been properly
performed

bought defective paint from a supplier which blistered when put on the house, necessitating repainting, the court would not only award the cost of the paint as damage but would also take into consideration the amount it would cost for a painter to scrape the blistered paint off and repaint the house. The courts will then order the vendor to pay a sum sufficient to put the purchaser in the position he or she would have been in if the paint had not been defective. In the case highlighted at the beginning of the chapter, the only appropriate remedy was to have Bell Canada pay damages to the Wrights for having charged them for their long distance calls when no charge should have been imposed.

Limitations on Recoverable Damages

Although damages are designed to compensate a person for losses suffered, not all injuries suffered are recoverable. Remoteness and mitigation are two limitations on the recoverability of damages.

REMOTENESS. In the important case of *Hadley v. Baxendale*,[13] the plaintiff asked the defendant, a shipper, to send the crank shaft of a steam engine to the manufacturer to be used as a sample for a new one. The shipper was asked to send it quickly but failed to do so. Unknown to the shipper, the plaintiff's entire plant was shut down while waiting for the crank shaft. This caused great expense to the plaintiff who sued the shipper. The defendant claimed that he could not be responsible for the unusual damage because he had no knowledge of it. The court used the reasonable person test to determine the extent of the shipper's responsibility for damages and held that the shipper was only responsible for the usual damages that could be expected if the contract was breached.

Must pay
reasonably
anticipated losses

The principle that has developed from this and other cases is essentially that a breaching party is only responsible for those damages which, at the time the contract was entered into, seem a not unlikely outcome if the contract were breached. Thus, the breaching party is also responsible for any unusual damages for special circumstances when communicated to him or her at the time the contract is entered into. In short, the breaching party is responsible in contract law for any damages that can be reasonably foreseen at the time the contract is entered into.

Unique
circumstances
must be
communicated

One area in which the problem of remoteness often arises is in a claim for damages to compensate for lost profits. The breaching party must be aware of the details of the other person's business at the time the contract is entered into for a claim of lost profits to be considered. Goods purchased for some unusual or specialized purpose may have a greater than normal potential to cause injury, but it is only when that unusual or specialized purpose is communicated to the vendor that the vendor can be held responsible for all of the damages suffered. If Seto bought glue from Mishra to waterproof the foundation of his house, Mishra would not be liable if it failed to do the job unless he knew what the glue was to be used for at the time it was purchased.

---

[13] *Hadley v. Baxendale* (1854) 156 E.R. 145 (Court of Exchequer).

MITIGATION. Victims of breach have an obligation to mitigate their losses, that is, to keep them as low as is reasonably possible. If a vendor has an obligation to deliver and instal goods at a person's house but leaves them on the front lawn instead, the purchaser must mitigate the loss by bringing the goods in and having them installed. The purchaser will not be able to claim for all of the injury suffered if he leaves the goods out on the lawn to be destroyed by the weather. The purchaser can sue the vendor for the cost of installing the goods but he is limited to the amount of loss that would have been suffered if he had acted reasonably in the circumstances.

Another situation in which losses must be mitigated is in the case of wrongful dismissal. A person who is dismissed from employment without just cause and without proper notice has a right to sue for wrongful dismissal. The amount of damages that may be recovered will be equal to the amount of notice that should have been given or the pay that should have been received in lieu of notice. The dismissed employee does have an obligation to go out and try to find another job, and, if one is found, the damages that can be claimed from the employer will be reduced by the amount earned during the time of required notice. If the fired employee does not attempt to find another job and the court determines that one could have been found, it will reduce the amount of compensation for wrongful dismissal by the amount that would have been earned if the person had found another job. However, the onus is on the breaching party to show that the fired employee failed to mitigate, which may not be easy to do. It is also important to note that the person who is required to mitigate is not obligated to take personal risks. The obligation to mitigate means simply that the victim of the breach must take all reasonable steps to minimize losses suffered.

Victims must mitigate their losses

Equitable Remedies

The following are examples of remedies that have been developed by the Courts of Chancery to deal with special situations in which the ordinary remedy of damages would not be adequate for the injuries suffered in a breach of contract situation.

SPECIFIC PERFORMANCE. **Specific performance** occurs when the court orders the defaulting party to live up to the terms of the contract. A person who buys a house and then finds that the vendor refuses to go through with the deal could sue the vendor for the expenses incurred and the cost of finding another house. If the purchaser has to pay more for a comparable house, the purchaser will be able to claim the difference as part of the damages. If the purchaser particularly liked the original house because of its unique design or location, monetary compensation may not be an adequate remedy. In such circumstances, the courts may grant specific performance and order the vendor to convey the house to the purchaser for the agreed-upon price.

Court can order performance of contract

—but only where damages would be inappropriate

If a vendor reneges on an agreement to sell a new Ford automobile to a purchaser, it is usually possible for the customer to acquire an identical vehicle from a different dealer; the difference in price can be charged to the breaching vendor. Specific performance will not be available to the victim of the breach because the automobile is not unique and because monetary compensation is sufficient. But if the item being sold is an antique or one of a kind, money would not compensate the purchaser and specific performance would be available.

The courts will not order the defaulting party to perform the requirements of a contract that requires personal service. If a famous painter has a contractual obligation to paint a portrait and then refuses to do so, the courts will not order specific performance. Similarly, the courts will not award specific performance as a remedy in any situation that would require close supervision to ensure that the contract is properly performed.

Courts will not force performance of contracts for personal services

INJUNCTION. If a person agrees specifically not to do something and then goes ahead and does it anyway, the appropriate remedy is an **injunction**. In an injunction, the court orders the defaulting party to stop the offending action. The injunction is available in any situation in which wrongful conduct is involved.

Courts may order breaching conduct to stop

In rare circumstances, the courts may issue a **mandatory injunction** when a person does something to violate a contractual term and thereby creates an ongoing problem. For example, if neighbours have a contract between them promising not to build over 50 metres high and one of them builds a structure 75 metres high, the courts may issue an injunction requiring removal of the structure. Such mandatory injunctions are not common.

As with specific performance, there are many instances in which the courts will refuse to issue an injunction. The courts will not order an injunction that would make it impossible for the person defaulting on the contractual agreement to earn a living any other way. A football team might be able to require one of its players to agree not to play for any other football team, but it would not be able to enforce a requirement that the football player not be employed by any other person at all. Similarly, the courts will not issue an injunction when damages provide a sufficient remedy. An injunction is not designed to punish someone for breaching a contract but rather to prevent further injury.

But not where damages more appropriate

ACCOUNTING. It is often difficult for the victim of the breach to determine just what kind of injuries he or she has suffered. This is especially true when there is a fiduciary relationship between the contracting parties, that is, a relationship in which the person dishonouring the contract has a duty under the terms of the agreement to act in the best interests of the other party. In these circumstances, the court can order that the defaulting party disclose all financial dealings and records so that the injured party can determine what he or she is entitled to claim. The court will then order the offending party to pay over any profits made from the wrongful conduct to the injured party.

Court may order accounting

QUANTUM MERUIT. In some situations, the contract is breached before the amount agreed to in the contract is due and payable to the injured party. The courts have the power to award compensation for the value of work performed on

Court may order payment for part performance

the basis of *quantum meruit* if the injured party has done a considerable amount of work towards earning that payment. Care must be exercised because the same does not apply if the breaching party has done some work but payment for this work is not due at the time the breach takes place. The courts are extremely reluctant to grant any compensation for the breaching party's partial performance of the agreement.

It is important to note that whether or not any partial payment was due and owing before the default takes place depends on how the contract is worded. The courts will often find that, under the terms of the agreement, the victim of the breach was entitled to some payment for what was performed before the breach. The courts are also willing to find that the victim of the breach can rescind the contract if its terms do not contain an implied promise to pay for partial performance. Once rescinded, the contract no longer exists and the courts are then free to imply a promise to pay the victim of the breach for the partial work done. Suppose Scholz agrees to build a house for Banerjee according to Banerjee's specifications and the contract makes clear that no money is due until the job is complete. If Scholz refuses to complete the second half of the job, Banerjee would simply get someone else to finish it. If Scholz sues for compensation for the amount of work done, Banerjee can defend by saying no amount of money was due or payable until the job was completed and, since it was not completed, no money is owed. In these circumstances, the court is unlikely to find a provision in the contract allowing for partial payment and Scholz will be out of luck. But if Banerjee had refused to allow Scholz to finish the house, the court would have no hesitation in awarding compensation to Scholz for the work done.

Undue delay

Some general requirements must be met before the courts will grant an equitable remedy. If there has been laches, an undue delay on the part of the person seeking the equitable remedy, the courts can refuse to grant the remedy. The plaintiff will still be able to pursue any common law remedy such as damages without penalty for delay, provided the action is brought within the limitation period in place, as discussed in Chapter 1. The courts can refuse to award an equitable remedy in any situation in which it would cause hardship to the parties or to some other person, or would be inappropriate for any other reason. A person seeking equity must come to the court with clean hands. The remedy will be denied when the person seeking the equitable remedy is guilty of some wrongdoing. These requirements apply to all equitable remedies.

Hardship

Clean hands

Another factor that may affect the right of the victim of a breach of contract to bring an action in court is the *Statute of Limitations* discussed in Chapter 1. The limitation periods outlined in such statutes also apply to the field of contracts, thus limiting the availability of the remedies discussed after the passage of specified time periods.

Contempt

Finally, it should be noted that when a judgment or an equitable remedy has been awarded and a defendant refuses to comply, the defendant may be held in contempt of court and can be jailed. The remedies to enforce a judgment outlined in Chapter 1 are available to the victim of a breach of contract as well.

SUMMARY

Performance, including substantial performance, will bring a contract to an end. When one party properly tenders performance and is refused, the contract is normally discharged. When money is involved, however, it is still owed, but the creditor must bear the cost of its collection. When a condition is breached, the victim may treat the contract as discharged and sue. A breach of warranty, however, means the contract is still binding but the victim can sue for damages. When a party repudiates an agreement before performance is due, it is an anticipatory breach and the victim has the option of either treating the contract as discharged immediately or waiting to see if the contract is performed.

A contract is ended by agreement when all of the requirements of a contract including consideration and consensus are present. If one of the parties has already performed and promises not to insist on performance by the other, that promise is not enforceable. It may, however, be raised as a defence under the principle of promissory or equitable estoppel. The contract may provide for its own end with conditions precedent or conditions subsequent. An unexpected intervening event that makes the contract impossible to perform or something essentially different from what the parties expected may discharge the contract by frustration. In most jurisdictions, when there is frustration, the normal result of "let the loss lie where it falls" has been modified by statute to allow the courts to apportion any monies advanced to compensate for expenses or losses incurred. Self-induced frustration is merely breach of contract.

The victim of a breach of contract is entitled only to the damages that were reasonably within the contemplation of the parties when they entered into the agreement and then only after all has been done to mitigate the loss. When the contract itself sets out the damages to be paid, it must be an honest attempt to pre-estimate the loss to be enforceable. Similarly, a prepayment in the form of a deposit cannot be a penalty. The equitable remedy of specific performance requires the breaching party to carry out the terms of the agreement. An injunction is a court order that the breaching party stop doing something inconsistent with the terms of the contract.

QUESTIONS

1. Describe the various ways in which a contractual relationship can come to an end.
2. Under what circumstances would a breaching party who had partially performed the terms of the contract be entitled to receive part payment?
3. Describe the differences between a condition and warranty. What is the significance of the distinction?

4. How may the victim of the breach of a condition lose the right to rescind the contract?

5. What constitutes adequate tender of performance?

6. What recourse is available to one party to a contract when performance is made impossible by the other party's conduct?

7. What options are available to the victim of an anticipatory breach? Explain the advantages, disadvantages and risks associated with these options.

8. How do the courts approach an exclusionary or exculpatory clause in a contract?

9. What is meant by fundamental breach and what are the two different philosophies developed by the courts in applying this principle?

10. What two factors are most likely to be absent when a claim that a contract was discharged or modified by agreement is challenged in court?

11. Explain what rule the case of *Foakes v. Beer* established. How has it been modified by statute since then?

12. Distinguish between contractual terms that are conditions precedent and conditions subsequent.

13. Define frustration. List three ways frustration can take place.

14. What is the significance of a court's determination that a contract was frustrated through the fault of one of the parties?

15. Explain how the House of Lords decision in the *Fibrosa* case modified the previously accepted common law rule on the obligations of the parties in the face of a frustrating event. Explain how this decision was further modified by statute.

16. Distinguish between a deposit and a down payment. What is the significance of this distinction?

17. What must be the demonstrated intention of the parties for money paid under a term of a contract to be categorized as a deposit?

18. Explain what limitations on the recovery of damages were developed from the case of *Hadley v. Baxendale.*

19. Describe what is meant by mitigation. Explain how the obligation to mitigate damages limits the ability of the victim of a breach to obtain damages.

20. Distinguish between specific performance and injunction. Explain the restrictions on their availability.

CASES

1. *Sumpter v. Hedges.*
    The plaintiff agreed to erect certain buildings for the defendant for a lump sum payment to be paid upon completion. The plaintiff failed to finish the work and asked for reimbursement for the amount he had done. The defendant refused. The plaintiff then sued for payment for the work he had

done. What factors would the court need to determine before they decided the case? Explain the likely outcome.

2. *Stevenson v. Colonial Homes Ltd.*

   The plaintiff contracted with the defendant to buy a prefabricated cottage and paid $1000 as a down payment. The plaintiff refused delivery of the cottage and the defendant refused to return the down payment. The total purchase price of the cottage was $2206 and the $1000 paid was referred to as a down payment. However, another portion of the document, which was filled in after the plaintiff received his copy, was marked "for head office use only" and referred to the money paid as a "deposit received." The document did not mention that the $1000 would be forfeited if the contract were not performed. What questions would the court have to determine before they could decide whether the plaintiff's suit for the return of the $1000 was valid? Explain the probable outcome.

3. *Gilbert Steel, Ltd. v. University Construction, Ltd.*

   The plaintiff, a steel manufacturing company, entered into a contract with the defendant, a construction company, in which the plaintiff agreed to deliver a considerable amount of fabricated steel at a specific price. Before the building was complete, the plaintiff's suppliers of unfabricated steel increased their price so much that the venture became unprofitable for the plaintiff. The plaintiff approached the defendant, explained the problem and the defendant agreed to pay more for the fabricated steel. The plaintiff continued to supply steel to the defendant and the defendant continued to pay its accounts regularly, although not enough to cover the higher amount. This action was brought by Gilbert Steel when University Construction, Ltd., refused to cover the higher amount agreed to for the steel. Identify the major hurdle to be overcome by the plaintiff in order to be successful in this action and suggest several arguments which it could raise. Explain the likely outcome.

4. *Capital Quality Homes, Ltd. v. Colwym Construction Ltd.*

   The defendant paid a $13 980 deposit to the plaintiff for some undeveloped land in Windsor, Ontario. The agreement involved the conveyance of 26 separate building lots and the plaintiff was required to deliver 26 individual deeds of conveyance, one for each building lot. After the contract was entered into by the parties but before it was executed, legislation was passed bringing planning consent for the land in question under the control of a designated committee. The parties disagreed about who bore the obligation to acquire the required consents. At the closing date, the defendant was unable to deliver the individual deeds required even though the plaintiff was ready to pay the required funds. It should be noted that this change of law took place only 33 days before the closing date for the transfer of the property and it is questionable whether it was possible to obtain the required consent in time. The plaintiff sued for the return of the $13 980 deposit paid. Explain the likely outcome. Would your answer be affected if the reason consent was not obtained was that the defendant had made no effort to obtain the required consents?

5. *Groves v. John Wunder.*
   The plaintiff owned 24 acres of undeveloped suburban real estate in Minneapolis that contained a deposit of sand and gravel which the plaintiff's company was in the process of excavating and selling. In August, 1927, the plaintiff agreed to lease this land to the defendant for seven years. In addition to a substantial payment, the defendant agreed to remove the sand and gravel and leave the property at a uniform grade substantially the same as the grade now existing at the roadway on said premises and that in stripping the overburden it would use said overburden for the purpose of maintaining and establishing said grade. The defendant removed the best and richest part of the gravel and intentionally left the grounds in a very uneven manner, thus deliberately refusing to comply with the terms of the contract. The plaintiff sued, demanding about $60 000 as damages to cover the cost of putting the property in the shape it was required to be in under the contract. Evidence was given that made it clear that the property would be worth only $12 160 even if it was brought up to the shape required in the contract. What arguments can be raised to support the plaintiff's claim for $60 000 and what arguments could the defence raise? Explain the probable outcome.

6. *Kerr S.S. Co. v. R.C.A.*
   The defendant agreed to transmit a certain message by radio in return for a fee from the plaintiff. The defendant was unaware of the message's nature because it was in code. Because this message had to be sent from New York to the Philippines, it had to pass through several different hands. There was a mix-up in this process and the message, which involved instructions from the plaintiff to his agent to load freight on a ship, was lost; the message was never received and the ship was never loaded. The plaintiff sought damages from the defendant for breach of the agreement. The damages were calculated as equalling the profits that would have been received from shipping the freight if the message had been received. The cost charged for sending the message was $26.78. What arguments are available to the defendants to resist this claim? Explain the probable outcome.

7. *Computer Workshops v. Banner Capital Market Brokers.*
   Banner, the defendant in this action, was in the brokerage business and was developing a computer software network to handle his business. The plaintiff, Computer Workshop Ltd., entered into an agreement with Banner to provide him with the necessary hardware and software equipment to do the job. After 25 of the 100 computers agreed to were delivered, Banner discovered that Computer Workshops was negotiating with Banner's competition to provide

them with a similar system with similar capabilities. Banner learned that in those discussions certain confidential information that he had given to Computer Workshops had been disclosed to their competitor. Banner refused to take the rest of the computers. Computer Workshops sued for breach. Explain the arguments on both sides and any defence that might be available to Banner in these circumstances.

ISSUES

1. When a contract is repudiated by anticipatory breach, the victim has the option of treating the contract as discharged at the point of repudiation and suing, or waiting until the day of performance, insisting on performance and suing then, if the contract is breached. Is it fair or consistent with the enforcement of the reasonable expectations of the parties to an agreement for the victim of a repudiation to have this kind of option? The case of *White and Carter (Council) Ltd. v. McGregor* [1961] 3 All. E.R. p. 1178 (House of Lords) illustrates the dilemma this option can cause. In that case, the defendants agreed to purchase advertising which was to be placed on various litter bins throughout Great Britain. The defendants cancelled the contract the same day the order was placed. Even though no costs had been incurred, the plaintiffs refused to accept this repudiation. They elected instead to perform their side of the contract and insist on payment. They proceeded to produce the advertising posters and placed them on the litter bins. When payment was not forthcoming, they sued. The court held that they were in a position to have minimized their losses at the time of repudiation, yet they chose to defy the repudiation and continue to insist on performance, thereby incurring tremendous unnecessary expenses. The House of Lords decided that, since they had the option to insist on performance and no obligation to mitigate until the contract was actually breached, they were merely doing what they had the contractual right to do and awarded them compensation. In your discussion of this problem, consider the obligation to mitigate and the way this principle was applied to the facts discussed.

2. The principle of fundamental breach was treated as a basic tenet of contract law when it was first developed, overriding exculpatory clauses included in the contract. The present approach seems to treat this principle as a rule of construction only. It is, at least in theory, possible to draw up contractual terms that will completely eliminate all obligations for the breaching party. Today it is almost a game in which experts draw up very intricate exculpatory clauses and the courts go through involved mental gymnastics to find that the breaching conduct was outside the purview of the exculpatory clause. It has also been argued that such a doctrine of fundamental breach is inconsistent with the concept of freedom of contract and

that the parties to a contract ought to be able to enter into any kind of contract they want. Does the principle of fundamental breach have any role to play in contemporary business practice? Should it be treated as a rule of law or a rule of construction? Would it not be more appropriate for the courts to simply discard such blanket exculpatory clauses as unreasonable? In your answer, consider the power of large corporations and the use of standard form contracts and whether the assumption of freedom of contract has any place in our modern complex society.

3. There are many situations in which performance of a contract in the face of frustration is still possible, but in which the parties are relieved of any obligation because some outside, unforeseen event has significantly affected the value of such performance to the party. The case of *Krell v. Henry* discussed earlier is a good example of how performance of the contract was still possible but the contract was considered frustrated nonetheless. Similarly, there is a growing trend for the courts to find frustration when a contract becomes unprofitable for one of the parties because of some unforeseen outside event. Should anything short of impossibility of performance ever be permitted to discharge a contract through frustration? In your answer, evaluate the alternatives from the point of view of each of the parties. You should also consider the fact that economic realities are more significant when business ventures are involved than with physical events such as the closure of a canal, the sinking of a ship or the denial of a licence.

4. Originally, the common law provided that anything short of complete performance of the contractual obligation would constitute a breach and entitle the victim to sue for compensation. The doctrine of frustration must be viewed as an exception to the original common law requirement because it discharged both parties from any further obligation to perform the contract after the frustrating event. This tenet has been considerably modified by the *Fibrosa* case and subsequent legislation. Have these modifications defeated the very purpose of discharge by frustration or is the present approach a fairer and more responsible one? Contrast the British Columbia statute with the other Canadian legislation.

5. The principle of law developed in *Hadley v. Baxendale* and subsequent cases established that a contracting party was responsible for damages if they were a reasonably foreseeable consequence of a breach at the time of the agreement. As a result, there are many situations in which contracting parties cannot expect full compensation for their losses through breach of contract. Should this limitation on the availability of damages set out in *Hadley v. Baxendale* be in effect in modern contract law? Why should a person who chooses to breach contractual obligations not be responsible for all the damage such a breach causes? Why should lack of knowledge of the injuries which could be suffered relieve the breacher of responsibility for wrongful conduct?

6. The law of contract requires that the deposit be forfeited when the person giving the deposit has failed to perform contractual obligations. The money

constituting a deposit must be returned when a deposit is a penalty rather than an honest attempt to estimate what the damages would be in the event of a breach. The question for discussion is: Should the forfeiture of a deposit in the face of a breach be limited in this way? Would it not be more appropriate to hold the party to his or her agreement? A related question also arises: Should liquidated damages be permitted at all? You will recall that liquidated damages include any situation in which the parties have set out the money compensation to be paid in the event of a breach. A deposit is an example of liquidated damages and it is argued that such liquidated damages limit the freedom of the court to determine what is appropriate compensation.

LEGISLATION

Alberta
Frustrated Contracts Act, R.S.A. (1980) c.F-20

British Columbia
Frustrated Contracts Act, R.S.B.C. (1979) c.144
Law and Equity Act, R.S.B.C. (1979) c.224

Manitoba
Frustrated Contracts Act, R.S.M. (1987) c.F-190

New Brunswick
Frustrated Contracts Act, R.S.N.B. (1973) c.F-24

Newfoundland
Frustrated Contracts Act, R.S.N. (1970) c.144

Ontario
Frustrated Contracts Act, R.S.O. (1980) c.179

Prince Edward Island
Frustrated Contracts Act, R.S.P.E.I. (1988) c.F-16

Northwest Territories
Frustrated Contracts Act, R.S.N.W.T. (1974) c.F-10

Yukon
Frustrated Contracts Act, R.S.Y. (1986) c.73

Federal
Currency Act, R.S.C. (1985) c.C-52

CHAPTER

7

LEGISLATIVE INTERFERENCE IN THE CONTRACTUAL RELATIONSHIP

Objectives of the Chapter

◼ to review the main features of Sale of Goods Acts

◼ to outline the legislation designed to protect consumers

Mrs. Knuude was an eighty-year-old homeowner who was approached by a door-to-door sales representative for a home improvements company. The sales representative told Mrs. Knuude she had a problem with her windows that needed fixing. After four hours of extremely high-pressure selling which included a refusal to leave unless the contract was signed, the sales representative left with a contract signed by her for repair and installation of an aluminum soffit, eavestroughs, flashing, repairing a damp wall and weather-stripping all the doors and windows in the house. Mrs. Knuude signed a $300 cheque as a deposit but stopped payment on it immediately after the salesman left. The next day, workers from the firm came to do the work and she insisted they leave. This brought the sales representative back, who, by devious means, persuaded her to reinstate the contract. The work was done. She again refused to pay and the company sued for the money owed under the contract. The judge determined that this was a clear case of fraud; that the contract was not binding on her as it was unconscionable; and that it did not conform to the requirements set out in the provincial consumer protection act.[1] This

[1]*Dominion Home Improvements Ltd. v. Knuude* 605-029, *The Lawyers Weekly*, May 30, 1986.

is an example of the unscrupulous business practices engaged in by some people that have led to the increase in legislation designed to protect consumers, the subject matter of this chapter.

The preceding four chapters have been devoted to a general examination of the law of contracts. It should be apparent that this body of law has been developed by the courts rather than enacted through legislation. Although some incidental statutes modify particular aspects of contract law, it is still accurate to say that the law of contracts is based primarily on case law. There are, however, two particular areas where legislation has been enacted that profoundly affects the contractual relationship. The first part of this chapter is devoted to legislative statutes relating to the sale of goods. The second part of the chapter deals with consumer protection legislation.

THE SALE OF GOODS

The Sale of Goods Act

A large body of case law has developed in the area of contractual disputes involving the purchase and sale of goods. This body of case law was codified and enacted by parliament in 1893 as the *Sale of Goods Act*, part of the general reforms in nineteenth century Britain. This statute was adopted with only minor variations by every common law province in Canada.

People seldom think about the technicalities of contract law when they buy and sell items in the marketplace. They quite often neglect to set out all the terms necessary to cover the various eventualities that may arise in their transactions. Major terms of the agreement may be specified but small details are often taken for granted by the parties. The courts may imply missing terms when disputes arise that involve unstated details. For example, the parties may not specify a date for payment when one person sells a car to another because each would assume that payment would be made on delivery of the car. These omissions put quite a burden on the courts and a great body of precedent law has been developed to fill in the gaps left by parties to contractual relationships. A

Act implies terms into contract

major purpose of the *Sale of Goods Act* is to provide a standardized approach for the courts to use as they imply omitted terms in disputed contracts. It must be emphasized that the *Act* is only intended to fill the vacuum left by parties who neglect to specify all the terms of their agreement. It is not the courts' responsibility to impose new terms or conditions on the parties. It must be emphasized as well that the *Sale of Goods Act* is not limited to retail or consumer transactions, but applies to all situations where goods are bought and sold.

A major feature of the *Sale of Goods Act* is that terms specified in the contract will generally prevail over the provisions set out in the legislation. Generally, the

Parties can contract out of provisions of Act

parties can contract out of the operation of the *Sale of Goods Act* and thus override its provisions. A second point to note about the *Sale of Goods Act* is that it is merely a summation of the common law and complements the normal rules of contract law described in the four previous chapters. These apply to sale of goods contracts as well. To be bound by the contract for the sale of goods, the parties must show that a consensus was reached through offer and acceptance, that consideration was exchanged, that neither party was incapacitated, that the terms of the contract were legal and not against public policy, and that the parties intended legal consequences to flow from their transaction. The presence of mistake, misrepresentation, undue influence or duress can affect the obligations of the parties. The rules of breach and privity also apply.

Consensus and reasonable price often assumed by court

The requirement of consensus is somewhat modified by the *Sale of Goods Act*. Under normal circumstances, the parties must agree on a price; failure to state a price would result in a non-binding agreement. The *Sale of Goods Act* permits the parties to omit reference to a price or a method of calculating it and requires that a reasonable price will be paid for the goods in question.

GOODS AND SERVICES.

Because the types of transactions affected by the *Sale of Goods Act* are quite restricted, it must be determined to which contractual relationships the *Act* applies. It must first be established that goods are the subject of the contract. **Goods** are tangible items such as watches, televisions, books and so on. The term *goods* does not include real estate but does include crops still growing on land. The *Act* does not apply to such non-tangible items as the sale of a **chose in action** (the right to sue another) or to the exchange of pieces of paper representing negotiable instruments, stocks, bonds and so forth.

Act applies only to sale of goods —not services

Contracts for services or the exchange of negotiable instruments, stocks, bonds and other documents representing rights or claims are excluded from the jurisdiction of the *Act*. Therefore, transactions involving both goods and services can pose a problem. Although a will is a physical item that becomes the client's property, a major portion of the lawyer's fee is for the service rendered in drawing it up. When an artist is commissioned to paint a portrait, the primary component of the transaction is the service provided by the artist even though the consumer receives a tangible item. In such circumstances, the *Sale of Goods Act* will not apply. If the customer were to resell the portrait to a third party, that transaction would be covered by the *Sale of Goods Act* since the entire amount paid is for the physical item transferred. There is no service component in this resale. When the service rendered involves the installation of goods, however, as in the repair of an automobile, the *Sale of Goods Act* applies to the goods portion of that contract.

Goods must be transferred

TRANSFER OF GOODS. The *Sale of Goods Act* applies when it can be demonstrated that the parties intended that the actual possession and property of the goods would transfer to the purchaser. The *Act* does not apply when the goods are used merely as security for a loan. If the person borrowing the money retains possession of such goods and will regain title to those goods upon payment of the money borrowed, the *Act* does not apply because it is not a sales transaction.

This point may seem obvious, but the tool used to accomplish the granting of security for a loan is often a bill of sale which purports to sell the goods in question to the creditor loaning the money. These transactions are covered by the personal property security legislation in place in each province. This type of transaction is called a chattel mortgage and will be discussed in the following chapter.

The *Sale of Goods Act* does apply at least partially when the seller of the goods is also providing credit. This type of sale is referred to as a **conditional sale** in which the eventual transfer of the property is anticipated in the agreement. The purchaser obtains possession of the goods but the title or property of those goods remains with the seller until the final payment is made. At that time, the title is transferred to the purchaser as well. Since this type of contract envisions a sale of the goods involved, albeit delayed, the *Sale of Goods Act* does apply. The financing aspect of the transaction, however, is covered by a *Conditional Sales Act* or its equivalent in the various jurisdictions.

MONETARY CONSIDERATION. It is also necessary that monetary consideration be given for the goods for the *Sale of Goods Act* to apply. Money must change hands. The *Act* does not cover barter transactions. Often goods are traded in when new ones are purchased, but as long as some money is exchanged in addition to the trade-in, the *Sale of Goods Act* applies.

Act does not apply to barter

REQUIREMENT OF WRITING. Some formal requirements must be met for the sale of goods to be binding on the parties. Originally, the *Statute of Frauds* contained provisions which affected the sale of goods. These provisions are now covered in *Sale of Goods Acts* in the various provinces. The sale of goods above a specified value, varying from $30 to $50 depending on the jurisdiction, must be evidenced in writing for the transaction to be legally enforceable. When the total value of goods purchased at any one time exceeds the prescribed limit, this section of the *Sale of Goods Act* will apply. As is the case with the *Statute of Frauds*, failure to comply with this portion of the *Act* does not make the contract invalid but the courts will not enforce it. This distinction can be significant when the parties have the right to self-help or set-off. If the value of the purchase exceeds the specified amount and there is no evidence in writing, the contract will be enforceable if something has been given in earnest. This means that the purchaser has given something of value to bind the contract. Similarly, the contract will be enforceable in court when there has been part payment or part performance, which means that some of the goods have been taken by the purchaser. Some provinces, British Columbia and Manitoba, for example, have eliminated this requirement.

Requirement of writing

Title and Risk

Distinction between sale and agreement to sell

There is a distinction between a **sale and an agreement to sell**, although both are covered by the *Sale of Goods Act*. Sale refers to a situation in which the title and goods are transferred immediately. When the goods or title will be transferred at some future time, either because the goods have not yet been manufactured or because something remains to be done to them, the transaction is referred to as an agreement to sell.

The sale of goods involves the transfer of both possession and property rights of the goods from the seller to the purchaser. Disputes between parties are often concerned with determining at what stage the property or title transferred from the seller to the purchaser. Determining the precise time of exchange is important because the *Sale of Goods Act* provides that risk follows title. **Risk** refers to any potential loss due to the destruction or damage of the goods. As with other sections of the Act, the parties can change who bears the risk by agreement.

Normally risk follows title

SPECIFIED RISK. There are three common methods of specifying who will bear the risk if it is to be anyone other than the title-holder.

Exceptions to assumption of risk

1. *C.I.F. Contracts (Cost, Insurance and Freight)*. In this type of contract, the purchaser may obtain title at an early stage in the transaction but the seller has assumed responsibility to pay for the costs involved in the shipping of those goods as well as arranging insurance to a specific point in the process, such as to the transport service or the destination
2. *F.O.B. Contracts (Free on Board)*. With F.O.B. contracts, the parties have specified that the seller will bear the risk until the goods are placed on board the carrier chosen to transport them to the purchaser. At that point the purchaser assumes the risk.
3. *C.O.D. Contracts (Cash on Delivery)*. This type of contract entitles the seller to maintain both the proprietary rights or title as well as control over the possession of those goods until they are delivered to the purchaser's premises and paid for. The risk then stays with the seller.

Bills of lading may determine title

Another method by which the seller may maintain control of the goods during shipment is through a bill of lading. A **bill of lading** is a document given by the transporter or shipper of the goods to the sender as a form of receipt. The person designated as the consignee on a bill of lading has the right to take delivery of the goods at their destination. A straight bill of lading usually names the purchaser as the consignee on the document; the seller no longer has control and the risk shifts to the purchaser during shipping. When **order bills of lading** are used, senders name themselves as consignees and retain the right to receive the goods at their destination or to designate that right to someone else. Sellers who have maintained control in this way bear responsibility for the goods until they have reached their destination. It should be noted that the use of order bills of lading provides sellers with maximum flexibility and facilitates arrangements such as financing in which the goods are used as security.

Remedy may depend on who has title

TRANSFER OF TITLE. The timing of the transfer of the property or title of the goods can control more than risk. Whoever has the proprietary interest will determine whether the seller can sue for the entire price of the goods or merely for damages upon default by the purchaser. The time of the transfer of title and the risk will be implied according to the following rules when no contrary intention is indicated by the parties.[2]

Rules for
determining title

Rule 1

Where there is an unconditional contract for the sale of specific goods in a deliverable state, the property in the goods passes to the buyer when the contract is made and it is immaterial whether the time of payment or the time of delivery or both is postponed.

This rule states that when the contract involves the sale of a specifically identified and finished item, the proprietary interest transfers to the purchaser at the time the contract is made. For example, if Lynch walked into Amann's T.V. Store on Thursday night, pointed to a television set and said, "I want to buy that one," the property in that television would transfer to Lynch as soon as that contractual arrangement was made. If Lynch decided to pick up the set the following night, Lynch would still have the proprietary interest and the risk in the set during the interim. Lynch would bear the loss if the set were destroyed by fire early Friday morning and it was not Amann's fault.

Title transfers
immediately

Rule 2

Where there is a contract for the sale of specific goods and the seller is bound to do something to the goods for the purpose of putting them into a deliverable state, the property does not pass until such thing is done and the buyer has notice thereof.

Contracts will often require that the seller make some modification, such as repair or service, before the purchaser takes possession of the goods. The title to these goods is transferred only after the work has been performed and the purchaser has been given notice of the completion of the work. This notice usually comes in the form of delivery of the goods, but it would probably be sufficient notice for the seller to telephone the purchaser and say, "Your goods are ready." In the example used earlier, if Lynch required that Amann repair a scratch on the television set before taking delivery, the title and risk would still be with Amann at the time of the fire on Friday morning and Amann would bear the loss. This would be true even if Amann had finished repairing the components or the scratch the night before if Lynch had not yet received notice.

Notice required if
something
needed to put
goods into
deliverable state

Rule 3

Where there is a contract for the sale of specific goods in a deliverable state, but the seller is bound to weigh, measure, test, or do some other act or thing with reference to the goods for the purpose of ascertaining the price, the property does not pass until such act is done and the buyer has notice thereof.

---

[2] These provisions are taken from Section 19 of the Ontario *Sale of Goods Act*. References to the *Act* throughout this chapter refer to the *Sale of Goods Act*, R.S.O. (1980) c.462. Every province has a similar act although the wording of the provisions may vary.

The provisions of this rule are similar to those set out in Rule 2. However in this instance some evaluative process must be completed and notice given before property in the goods and thus risk can pass. For example, if Schmidt agreed to purchase a particular truckload of potatoes from Naslund, it would probably be necessary to weigh the load to determine the exact price. Title to the potatoes would only transfer to Schmidt after the weighing was completed and notice given.

Notice required if testing needed

Rule 4
When goods are delivered to the buyer on approval or on 'sale or return' or other similar terms, the property therein passes to the buyer:
(i) when he signifies his approval or acceptance to the seller or does any other act adopting the transaction;
(ii) if he does not signify his approval or acceptance to the seller but retains the goods without giving notice of rejection, then if a time has been fixed for the return of the goods on the expiration of such time, and if no time has been fixed on the expiration of a reasonable time and what is reasonable time is the question of fact.

When approval or acceptance is signified or a reasonable time has passed

This rule covers situations in which goods are taken by the purchaser to test for a trial period before deciding to keep them. It becomes difficult to determine when the proprietary interest transfers in these circumstances. It is straightforward when the purchaser contacts the seller to say the goods are acceptable, but, if the purchaser fails to do so, the proprietary interest can still transfer to the purchaser. If the purchaser tries to resell, modify or install the goods, these acts are inconsistent with the seller maintaining title to the goods. In other words, if the purchaser acts as if he or she owns the goods, the purchaser does own them, and title transfers. Otherwise, the title transfers when the trial period agreed on is over. If no period was agreed on, a reasonable time must pass before title transfers. In our earlier example, if Amann had allowed Lynch to take the television home and try it for four days, title would not transfer to Lynch until the expiration of those four days, unless Lynch notified Amann before that time that he was happy with the goods. However, if Lynch built the television set into the wall of his den, that action would be inconsistent with Amann still having title to the goods. Title would pass to Lynch. If the title had not passed during those four days and the goods were damaged or destroyed, the risk would remain with the seller unless the parties had agreed otherwise.

Rule 5
(i) Where there is a contract for the sale of unascertained or future goods by description, and goods of that description and in a deliverable state are unconditionally appropriated to the contract, either by the seller with the assent of the buyer, or by the buyer with the assent of the seller, the property in the goods thereupon passes to the buyer and such assent may be express or implied and may be given either before or after the appropriation is made.
(ii) Where in pursuance of the contract the seller delivers the goods to the buyer or to a carrier or other bailee (whether named by the buyer or not) for the purpose of transmission to the buyer and does not reserve the right of disposal, the buyer shall be deemed to have unconditionally appropriated the goods to the contract.

The goods covered by Rule 5 are those that have not been manufactured at the time the contract was entered into or that exist but have not yet been separated out and identified as the particular goods to be used in a given transaction. Suppose that, in the example used earlier, Lynch had walked into Amann's television store, pointed toward a particular television and said, "I want a set like that one," and Amann had agreed to supply Lynch with a television from a stock of new sets in the back of the store. This situation would be covered by Rule 5 because no particular television set had yet been appropriated to the contract. Rule 5 also applies when a person orders a new car from the factory to be manufactured to particular specifications because the goods are not in existence at the time the contract is entered into.

Only when the goods have been manufactured or separated out and unconditionally committed to the purchaser with the purchaser's assent does title pass. While notice to the purchaser that the goods are ready may be the most common method of satisfying the assent or approval provision, assent is often implied from the circumstances. Thus, if a person were to leave her car with a dealer for the installation of a new stereo cassette player, she will be taken to have assented to the selection of the stereo when it is installed since she left her car there for that purpose.

The parties can specify an intent contrary to that set out in the *Act* in relationship to who bears the risk. In addition to the traditional methods (C.O.D., F.O.B. and C.I.F. contracts discussed above), care must also be taken to examine other contractual terms to determine whether the parties have contracted out of the provisions of the *Sale of Goods Act* dealing with risk. For example, if the parties clearly state in their contract that the goods are to remain at the risk of the seller until they are delivered to the purchaser's place of business, that stated intention will prevail over the implied provisions of the *Sale of Goods Act*.

Rights and Obligations of the Parties

The *Sale of Goods Act* has provisions intended to supply terms that affect the very substance of the contractual relationship between the parties. These terms are referred to in the *Act* as conditions or warranties. As was discussed previously, conditions are important terms of the contract, the breach of any of which entitles the victims to consider themselves no longer bound. Breaches of warranties do not release victims from their obligations under the contract. Parties are free to agree that a term that would normally be considered a warranty become a condition. The opposite is possible as well. But under the *Sale of Goods Act* the courts retain the power to treat a term designated as a condition as a warranty and one designated as a warranty as a condition.

Conditions and warranties under Sale of Goods Act

Acceptance causes victims of breach to lose right of discharge

The victim of a breach of a condition has the option to ignore it or to treat it as a breach of warranty. The victim of a breach may lose the right to have a contract discharged by a breach of condition by accepting the goods. In our example of the television set purchased from Amann's television store, Lynch would be entitled to return the set and demand a refund if he had specified as a condition of the contract that the television have a remote control device and he did not discover until he got it home that his set did not have one. Although Lynch had taken delivery of the goods and brought them home, he was unaware of the breach of condition and therefore cannot be said to have accepted the goods. But once Lynch became aware that the set had no remote control, plugging it in and using it over the weekend is inconsistent with Amann still owning the set. Lynch would then have accepted the goods with full knowledge of the breach of condition. It is likely that he would only be able to sue for damages and would be required to perform his part of the contractual obligation.

Title

Seller must convey good title

The *Sale of Goods Act* implies several terms into sales agreements which cover a seller's right to sell goods to a purchaser. Section 13a. of the Ontario *Sale of Goods Act*[3] states that it shall be a condition of a contract for sale that the seller has the right to sell the goods or, when dealing with an agreement to sell, that the seller will have that right at the time the property is transferred. Thus, Amann breaches a condition of the contract if he does not own the television set he tries to sell to Lynch and has no right to acquire it. Lynch would be free from any further obligation under the contract.

—and quiet possession

Section 13b. requires that the seller provide **quiet possession of the goods** as a warranty of the contract. This means that the goods must be delivered in such a condition that they can be used and enjoyed by the purchaser in the way they were intended, free from any interference. If the seller does not have the right to sell the goods because they belong to somebody else and the rightful owner seizes the goods from the purchaser, this would contravene both Part a. and Part b. of Section 13. Some overlap exists between the two provisions. However, Section 13b. is somewhat broader than Section 13a. because quiet possession may be interfered with for reasons other than mere title. For example, it is quite possible that the purchaser could be restrained from using a product which violates a copyright, patent or trademark. This is not a problem of title because the seller did own the goods and did have the right to convey good title, but the patent infringement interfered with the purchaser's quiet possession of the goods and therefore violated an implied warranty in the contract.

—and goods free from charge or incumbrance

Section 13c. of the *Act* specifies that it shall be an implied warranty of the contract that the goods shall be free from any charge or incumbrance which has not been disclosed to the purchaser. When personal goods are used as security in loan transactions, the creditor obtains the right to seize the goods and sell them if the debt is not honoured. This is a charge or incumbrance, often called a **lien**. The lien or charge gives the creditor the right of seizure even when the goods are passed on to innocent third parties. Transactions in which personal property is taken as security

---

[3] *Ibid*. s.13a. The numbering will vary in different provinces but the provisions are essentially the same.

must usually be registered. Creditors obtain rights of priority only when these formal requirements are met. For this reason, it is always prudent to search the title of a motor vehicle before purchasing it. A purchaser who later discovers a charge or incumbrance against goods purchased has the right to sue the seller for breach of this implied warranty. If it is not possible to obtain a remedy against the seller because the seller is insolvent or unavailable, the priority of the creditor will prevail and the purchaser will be required either to pay off the lien against the goods or to surrender the goods to the creditor.

Description

Goods are often sold by catalogue, mail order or other forms of distance shopping. In such circumstances, the goods have to be sold by description. The written text is often accompanied by a picture or illustration. Section 14 of the Ontario *Sale of Goods Act* provides that, when the sale is accomplished by description, there shall be an implied condition in contracts that the goods delivered must match the description or illustration provided. If Afsari based her order for a new camera from a catalogue on an illustration showing a Nikon camera and the camera that Afsari eventually received was a Pentax, there has been a breach of the implied condition that the goods match the description. Although there is some dispute over just what sale by description means, there is little doubt that the term is broad enough to cover the sale of virtually all manufactured goods, even when the customer makes the selection. The manufacturer has produced many identical, essentially indistinguishable items, so the purchaser relies on the general description given by the manufacturer as to what those goods can do. The fact that she chooses one over another does not lessen that reliance. Even when the purchaser inspects a sample of the goods in addition to relying on the description contained in the brochure or catalogue, the purchaser would be entitled to claim that a condition had been breached if the goods matched the sample but failed to live up to the description in the brochure or catalogue.

Goods must match description

Most sales of manufactured goods are by description

Fitness and Quality

Another condition the *Sale of Goods Act* implies into a sale by description is that the goods provided must be of a **merchantable quality**. This means that the goods must be free of any defect that would have persuaded the purchaser not to buy them at the agreed-upon price if the purchaser had known of the defect at the outset. If a sample has been inspected, the defect must not have been readily apparent upon examination. Note that with the broader approach taken by the courts as to what qualifies as sale by description, this provision will apply to virtually all sales of manufactured goods.

Goods must be of merchantable quality

A similar provision requires that, if the purchaser has relied on the skill and ability of the salesperson to advise on the suitability of a particular product for an intended

Goods must be
suitable for
purpose of
purchase when
salesperson
relied upon

purpose, there is an implied condition that the product will be reasonably fit for that purpose. For example, if Florio bought a particular kind of paint from McGregor's Paint Company after asking if it was suitable for concrete and later found that the paint peeled, Florio would be able to sue McGregor for compensation because of the breach of the implied condition that the goods would be reasonably suitable for their intended purpose.

There are, however, two situations in which this provision of the *Act* does not apply. If it is not in the course of the seller's usual business to supply this type of product or if the purchaser requests the product by trade name, the seller is not responsible. The courts, however, have adopted a broad interpretation of this latter provision. In the case of *Baldry v. Marshall*,[4] the courts suggested that, to avoid liability, the request for an article by its trade name must be made in such a way that it is clear that the skill of the seller is not being relied on. Similarly, the courts have moved in the direction of finding that there is sufficient reliance on the skill and ability of the seller whenever the customer goes to a specific store to purchase the goods. It should also be noted that this section is broad enough to cover not only goods sold for special purposes but also goods to be used under normal conditions. The courts' liberal approach means that the provisions related to fitness and quality apply in most sale of goods situations. The principle of *caveat emptor* discussed in Chapter 4 applies to transactions that come under the *Sale of Goods Act*. It must be remembered, however, that *caveat emptor* only means that the buyer is required to be careful in these transactions; he or she still has the right to expect a certain level of quality and protection when such care has been shown.

Sample

Goods must
match sample
and be free of
significant hidden
defects

The *Act* uses a similar approach for the purchase of goods after examining a sample. When a purchaser places an order after being given an opportunity to inspect a sample of the goods, the bulk of the goods must correspond to the sample inspected and the purchaser must be given an opportunity to compare the original sample to the goods delivered. The goods must also be "free from any defect that would render them unmerchantable." That is, the goods must be free from any hidden defects which would have persuaded the purchaser not to buy them at that price if he or she had been aware of the defects when inspecting the sample. For example, if the load of bricks Tsang bought from Cashin after first inspecting a sample brick looked fine but, in fact, had not been baked properly and disintegrated after being used in Tsang's building, the bricks would be of unmerchantable quality. In these circumstances, Tsang would be able to sue Cashin for the breach of the implied condition that the goods be free from any hidden defect that would render them unmerchantable.

Parties free to
contract out

It must be re-emphasized that, under the terms of the *Sale of Goods Act*, the parties are generally free to include clauses which override the provisions set out in the *Act*. Most sales contracts dealing with manufactured goods contain warranty

---

[4] *Baldry v. Marshall* [1925] 1 K.B. 260 (Court of Appeal).

provisions which include exculpatory clauses that limit or eliminate any responsibility on the part of the seller for defects in the product. When parties to a contract include such exculpatory or exemption clauses, they too will override the provisions of the *Sale of Goods Act* unless prohibited by provincial legislation.[5]

Other Implied Terms

Where price omitted— reasonable price

The *Sale of Goods Act* implies a term in the contract that the purchaser shall pay a reasonable price for the goods delivered if the parties fail to stipulate a price. When parties have not agreed otherwise, there is also an implied term in the contract that payment is due and payable when the goods are delivered. Delivery and payment are regarded as concurrent obligations. Time provisions relating to payment that appear in a contract will be treated as warranties unless the parties have shown a contrary intention. But whether other terms, such as the time of delivery, will be treated

Time, payment and place for delivery implied terms

as conditions or warranties will be implied from the conduct of the parties. When the contract contains no provision for when the seller is to deliver the product to the purchaser, it will be implied that the delivery be made when the purchaser demands it. However, this must be at a reasonable time, such as during business hours. The place for delivery will be at the seller's place of business unless otherwise stated.

When a considerably incorrect quantity of goods is delivered, the purchaser is free either to reject them, if there are not enough or to keep and pay for them at the contracted rate. If significantly too many of the goods are delivered, the purchaser can

When quantity delivered is wrong purchaser has choice

take out the contracted portion and return the remainder or reject them all. The provisions affecting delivery, place, time and quantity of the goods are usually made conditions by the parties.

Remedies of Default

Unpaid seller's lien and stoppage in transit

The seller has several options when the purchaser has defaulted or breached. The seller holds an unpaid **seller's lien** against the goods if they have not been paid for and are still in the seller's possession. This means that, even though the proprietary interest in the goods has transferred to the purchaser who is, therefore, entitled to possession by the terms of the agreement, the seller has the right to retain the goods until payment is received. If credit arrangements for payment have been made, the seller is only entitled to a lien against the goods when the purchaser has defaulted on the credit terms. Similarly, if the seller has delivered the goods to a transporter or shipper and they are en route to the purchaser, the seller retains the right of **stoppage *in transitu***. This means that the seller can stop the delivery of the goods to the purchaser and retake possession of them as long as they have not yet reached the purchaser. Unless the contract has a provision authorizing the resale of the goods in such circumstances, the seller must notify the purchaser of an intention to resell the goods.

[5] *Sale of Goods Act*, R.S.B.C. (1979) c.370 s.20 ss.2.

If payment is not made within a reasonable period of time, the seller can then resell the goods. There is no requirement that notice of resale be given when the goods are perishable. This right of lien and the right to stop the goods in transit can be very important to the seller because, once the goods get into the possession of the purchaser, they become part of the purchaser's estate. Under the new Canadian *Bankruptcy and Insolvency Act*, however, a supplier of such goods has the right to retake those goods if, within thirty days of delivery, the debtor has become bankrupt or a receiver has been appointed and, of course, providing the debtor or trustee still has them.

> Seller protected
> in case of
> bankruptcy

Sellers can sue for breach of contract whenever the purchaser defaults on the contract of purchase, whether or not the purchaser is insolvent. Sellers have at their disposal all of the contractual remedies described in Chapter 6. The seller has the right to sue for the whole purchase price when the proprietary interest has passed to the purchaser. It must be remembered that the proprietary interest or title in the goods may transfer in advance of the actual possession. When the title has passed but the purchaser refuses to accept delivery of the goods, the purchaser is rejecting his or her own goods and may still be required to pay the entire purchase price. If the time specified in the contract for full payment passes, the seller can sue for the full purchase price of the goods sold even when the title has not yet passed. Purchasers are only entitled to refuse delivery when they can show the following:

> Seller can sue for
> price in cases of
> default or refusal
> of delivery once
> title has passed

1. The property or title of the goods has not yet passed.
2. Payment is not yet due.
3. The seller has breached some condition of the contract.

By refusing delivery in the absence of one of these conditions, the purchaser takes the risk of not getting the goods but still being required to pay full price for them.

The seller may be able to claim for damages for breach of contract to compensate for loss even in situations in which it is not possible to claim the full purchase price. But it is often difficult for the seller to claim lost profits on the sale as damages. To do so, the seller may be required to show that the product could not have been sold to anyone else. If this cannot be proven, the damages will be limited to the costs incurred in the process of resale. In many cases, it may not be worthwhile to sue for damages if suing for the full purchase price is not permitted. The seller also has an obligation to mitigate losses or keep damages as low as possible. This usually means that the seller must take steps to resell the goods immediately. Delay might lead to a claim that there was a failure to mitigate. The obligation to mitigate damages generally does not require that the seller spend any further money to sell the goods.

> Seller still entitled
> to sue for
> damages for
> breach

The remedies available to the purchaser if the seller defaults are those of general contract law. The purchaser can have the contract rescinded in cases of misrepresentation. Damages may also be available if the misrepresentation is fraudulent or negligent. When the misrepresentation becomes a term of the agreement, it is treated as any other condition or warranty under the *Act*. If the seller has breached a condition of the sales contract, the purchaser can repudiate. When the purchase price has not yet been paid, the purchaser can refuse to pay it. When the purchase price has been

> Purchaser's
> remedies those
> of contract law

paid, the purchaser can demand its return. When the term breached is a warranty, the purchaser must fulfil his or her side of the contract but can withhold sufficient payment to compensate for losses incurred. The purchaser can commence an action for damages if he or she has already paid. When the seller fails to deliver the goods to the purchaser, the damages will usually be based on the difference between what the purchaser had agreed to pay for the goods and the cost of obtaining those goods from another source. But when there are additional injuries suffered because of the delay in obtaining the goods, the purchaser will be able to claim them as well.

Extent of
damages
depends on
circumstances

Goods supplied by the seller that fail to meet the standard of quality required in the contract or as set out in the *Act* can cause substantially different sorts of injuries. These injuries can be claimed as damages for breach of contract as long as they were reasonably within the contemplation of the parties at the time the contract was entered into.[6] Thus, someone who suffers food poisoning because of poor quality food at a restaurant can seek compensation for their injuries under the *Sale of Goods Act* provisions. When the goods being sold are unique in their nature, the purchaser may also be able to claim a remedy of specific performance and force the seller to go through with the sale rather than pay damages in compensation.

Finally, it should be mentioned that most provinces have recently enacted an *International Sale of Goods Act*. The federal government is a signatory to a United Nations convention along with other nations in this area, and the provincial legislation is intended to implement that international treaty. A great deal of trading today is done in the international arena and these statutes bring the same kind of structure and certainty to import and export dealings as the *Sale of Goods Act* provides domestically.

CONSUMER PROTECTION LEGISLATION

Consumer
transaction made
by ultimate
consumer

The second major area in which legislation has interfered with contractual relationships and modified the case law developed by the courts is when **consumer transactions** are involved. Consumer transactions involve goods or services that are not being obtained for resale or other business activity. The products or services are being acquired by the ultimate consumer for personal use. Although consumer protection statutes vary greatly, they do have common objectives. Consumer protection statutes impose standards and responsibilities on manufacturers and suppliers of goods, and control unethical or otherwise unacceptable business practices. The rest of this chapter will examine these areas and consider the various regulatory bodies created by these statutes. Although provincial statutes predominate, there is also considerable federal legislation in the field.

The main purpose of the *Sale of Goods Act* is to imply terms into a contract which the parties have omitted. Consumer protection legislation, on the other hand,

---

[6] *Hadley v. Baxendale* (1854) 156 E.R. 145 (Court of Exchequer).

Consumer
protection
legislation
imposes
contracts

is designed to impose restrictions on the conduct of the parties by enforcing, controlling, modifying, limiting or otherwise altering the effects of contractual relationships entered into between merchants and consumers. A form of consumer protection legislation has been present in our legal system for centuries but, in the last twenty years, statutes have been passed which have expanded this area to its modern dimensions. These statutes and recent court decisions have significantly modified the law relating to consumer transactions. Until recently, the common contractual themes of *caveat emptor* and freedom of contract dominated consumer transactions. Consumers today are vulnerable to unscrupulous or careless merchandising and manufacturing practices. This growing abuse and an increase in the inequalities of the bargaining positions of individual consumers in relation to large corporate manufacturers and merchandisers led legislators to place limits on these previously accepted principles. Although some still retain separate acts, most provinces have concentrated their consumer protection legislation into a single statute, the *Consumer Protection Act*. Some provinces have added a second act referred to as the *Trade Practices* or *Business Practices Act*.

Responsibility for Goods Sold

Consumer protection provisions have been incorporated into the *Sale of Goods Act* of the provinces. The requirements that the seller have good title, and that goods correspond to their description and are fit and of merchantable quality are of great value to the consumer. In Ontario and British Columbia, the right to contract out of

Effect of
exemption
clauses limited by
statute

these provisions in consumer transactions by exculpatory clauses has been eliminated.[7] New Brunswick and Saskatchewan have imposed conditions requiring goods to be durable.[8] Pre-contractual statements made by salespeople also become terms of the contract. The result of these provisions is that merchants cannot rely on exemption clauses to relieve themselves of the obligation to deliver quality goods to the purchaser. Purchasers can usually sue for breach of contract and receive compensation for the damage done when products are unfit. Damages are usually simply a refund of the purchase price. Other expenses incurred while using the defective product may be recoverable as well, if they were reasonably foreseeable when the contract was made.

Victims of unsafe products are entitled to sue the manufacturer in tort for negligence. If the victim was also the purchaser of the product that led to the injury, a breach of contract has taken place and the seller is liable under contract law. There is a considerable advantage in establishing the right to sue in contract rather than tort.

Tort liability
requires fault

A tort action requires that the person bringing the action establish that the defendant was at fault in some way, which is often difficult to do. A breach of contract, on the other hand, requires only that the plaintiff establish that a term of the contract was breached. The merchant is required to perform the terms of the contract and failure

---

[7] *Sale of Goods Act*, R.S.B.C. (1979) c.370 s.20 ss.2

[8] *Consumer Product Warranty and Liability Act*, S.N.B. (1978) c.C-18 s.12(1), (2) and *Consumer Product and Warranties Act*, R.S.S. (1978) c.C-30 s.11 (7).

to do so causes liability for damages. It is no defence for the merchant to show there was no negligence. Where personal injury has resulted, the damages payable under such a breach of contract action can be substantial

Contractual
liability limited to
immediate
parties

A difficulty arises when the injured user of the product did not buy it but received it secondhand. Because of the principle of privity of contract, only those who are party to the contract are permitted to claim breach of contract and sue for damages. The case of *Donoghue v. Stevenson* discussed in Chapter 2 has had a great impact on the development of the law of negligence in general and of product liability specifically. Recall that Mrs. Donoghue consumed a contaminated bottle of ginger beer given to her by a friend but could not sue the seller because she was not privy to the contract of purchase. Even though it was clearly established that the seller had no idea that the ginger beer was defective and that there was no way he could have known it, he would have been liable for breach of contract if Mrs. Donoghue had purchased the product from him. Since this was not the case, the victim turned to the manufacturer of the ginger beer and successfully sued in tort for negligence. This case is important because it establishes the users' ultimate right to sue manufacturers in tort for damages caused by the products they produce even though there is no contractual relationship between them. It is important to note that in Canada the user must still prove that the manufacturer or manufacturer's servant was actually negligent in the manufacture of the product. Fault must be demonstrated.

Contractual
liability does not
require fault

It is much easier to sue for breach of contract than to sue for tort in product liability cases because a breach of contract does not require a demonstration of fault. There are many situations in which the ultimate consumer of the product is not the person who purchased it and because of the principle of privity of contract cannot sue for breach. New Brunswick and Saskatchewan have extended their consumer protection legislation beyond the immediate parties to the contract.[9] In these provinces, the requirements of fitness and quality extend to anyone the seller could reasonably foresee might use the product. The impediment of privity of contract in product liability cases is overcome, allowing injured consumers to sue for breach of contract even when they were not one of the immediate parties to the contract. It is possible in these provinces for an injured consumer, although not a party to the contract of purchase, to sue the seller for breach of contract rather than for negligence. That seller will then be liable for the injuries of the consumer even if it can be demonstrated that the seller had no way of knowing about the defects in the product.

Collateral
contracts can
protect ultimate
purchasers

Another significant development in Canadian law in this area is exemplified by the Ontario case of *Murray v. Sperry Rand Corp.*[10] In this case, the purchaser of a harvester was able to sue the manufacturer as well as the vendor for breach of contract even though the machine was purchased from a retailer. The court found that, because of false claims made in the advertising brochures, there was a breach of a **collateral contract** existing between the purchaser and the manufacturer. A collateral contract is one which exists between the ultimate purchaser and manufacturer in addition to the primary contract between the retailer and the purchaser. Normally,

[9] *Consumer Product Warranty and Liability Act*, S.N.B. (1978) c.C-18 s.23 and *Consumer Product and Warranties Act*, R.S.S. (1978) c.C-30 s.14(1).
[10] *Murray v. Sperry Rand Corp.* (1979) 23 O.R. (2d) 456 (Ontario High Court of Justice).

the principle of privity of contract prevents consumers from suing anyone for breach of contract but the person who sold the goods to them. The contract is between the purchaser and the retailer, not between the purchaser and the wholesaler or manufacturer. The significance of the Murray case is that privity of contract was circumvented through the application of collateral contracts. Since the manufacturer had advertised directly and the consumer had been influenced to buy by the advertisement, a direct relationship had been created between the manufacturer and the purchaser. This relationship took the form of a separate or collateral contract imposing obligations on the manufacturer to deliver a product that lived up to the claims stated in the advertisement. This willingness to find collateral contracts based on the advertising and promotional claims of the manufacturer may help to overcome the obstacle of privity of contract in product liability cases if it is followed in other jurisdictions. The Supreme Court of Canada has recently shown a willingness to abandon the privity principle in other situations.[11]

Duty to warn when product hazardous

Some useful products, by their very nature, are hazardous. The obligation of the manufacturer and seller of such products is to make them as safe as possible, warn the potential user of the dangers and provide information on their proper use. An injured consumer can sue the manufacturer for negligence when these steps are not followed. A warning incorporated into the product label must alert the consumer to the hazards associated with the product. If the warning is inadequate, the manufacturer and seller are liable for the injuries that result.[12] Federal legislation dealing with the merchandising of dangerous products will be covered later in this chapter. Several jurisdictions have now modified their consumer protection legislation to extend this kind of protection to long-term lease arrangements as well.[13]

Unacceptable Business Practices

Another major thrust of consumer protection legislation is to prohibit or control certain unacceptable practices sometimes engaged in by merchants selling products and services. One such practice is the use of misleading or false statements to persuade people to buy a product. Unless the misleading statement actually becomes a term of the contract, the consumer's only course of action in common law is to rely on the remedies available for misrepresentation. Rescission is the only remedy available when the misrepresentation is innocent and that remedy may be lost due to the circumstances of the sale. To obtain damages as a remedy, the misrepresentation must be either fraudulent or negligent. To make the remedy of damages more accessible, most provinces have passed legislation making merchants and their agents more responsible for their statements by incorporating these statements as terms of the contract. Once these statements become part of the contract, it is no longer necessary to rely on the principles of misrepresentation. The consumer can sue for breach of contract seeking all the remedies normally available. Thus, any statements made by

Legislation incorporates misleading statements into contract

[11] *London Drugs Ltd. v. Kuehne & Nagel International Ltd.* [1993] 1 W.W.R. 1 (S.C.C.)
[12] *Lambert v. Lastoplex Chemicals Ltd.* (1972) 25 D.L.R. (3d) 121 (Supreme Court of Canada).
[13] British Columbia's Bill 21 enacted in 1993.

salespeople or contained in advertisements become terms of the contract and are actionable as breaches if they prove incorrect or are not honoured.

Holberg, the purchaser of a used car from Affleck's Fine Car Co., was informed by the salesperson that the car had only been driven to church on Sunday. That statement would, under these provisions, be incorporated into the contract even if it was not contained in the written document. Holberg could sue for breach of contract if she later found that the statement was false. This type of provision is included in the New Brunswick and Saskatchewan legislation dealing with consumer product warranties.[14] Several other provinces have incorporated similar provisions into unfair business practices legislation, variously referred to as *Trade Practices Act*, *Unfair Trade Practices Act* and *Business Practices Act*.

Typically, this type of statute lists several different kinds of misleading and deceptive statements deemed to be unfair practices. The consumer is then given the right to have the contract rescinded or to sue for damages. The government department involved is also given considerable power to investigate complaints and to deal with complaints against offending merchandisers. Ontario, Newfoundland, British Columbia, Prince Edward Island and, to a lesser extent, Manitoba have versions of business practices legislation. There are also many other federal and provincial statutes which contain provisions prohibiting deceptive and misleading statements. The common law provisions concerning false and misleading claims in consumer transactions have been considerably strengthened by the expansion of the areas covered by statutory provisions and by the remedies available.

Government bodies have been given significant powers

UNCONSCIONABLE TRANSACTIONS. One of the facts of modern society is that the merchants selling goods and services are increasingly large corporate bodies. This change further emphasizes the considerable inequality in the bargaining positions of the two parties in consumer transactions. When this inequality becomes so great that the consumer is taken advantage of because of desperation, poverty or mental weakness, the courts are now able to interfere with the resulting contract by setting it aside, modifying its terms or ordering the refund of money. The legislation permitting the courts to do this exists in every province and is known as the *Unconscionable Transactions Relief Act* or, in some provinces, as the *Unconscionable Transactions Act*. It is important to note that this legislation, as a general rule, applies only to the lending of money. To be able to rely on the provisions of these acts, it is necessary to demonstrate that the cost of borrowing charged to the consumer was excessive in the circumstances.

Unconscionable transactions or unfair bargains controlled

Creditor's risk considered

One of the factors the courts must take into consideration is the risk borne by the creditor. Even when it can be demonstrated that the borrower was of weak intellect or in desperate straits and that an unreasonably high rate of interest was charged, the court must also be satisfied that the rate of interest was excessive considering the risk faced by the creditor. If somebody is desperate because no one else will lend him money, the transaction will probably not be considered unconscionable because even a high rate of interest would not be considered excessive in such a risky situation.

---

[14] *Consumer Product Warranty and Liability Act*, S.N.B. (1978) c.C-18.1 s.4 and *Consumer Product and Warranties Act*, R.S.S. (1978) c.C-30 s.8,9.

This position has been taken further in the consumer protection legislation of Ontario, Prince Edward Island and British Columbia where it is possible to declare that some types of business practices are unconscionable representations. To determine whether or not a practice is unconscionable, the legislation specifies that several factors be taken into consideration including physical infirmity, ignorance, illiteracy, inability to understand the language of an agreement, undue influence, a price that grossly exceeds the value of the goods and the lack of a reasonable benefit to the consumer. A consumer who has been taken advantage of can claim the same remedies that are available for misrepresentation. These include rescission of the contract, damages, exemplary damages and the services of a government body to assist in the process. British Columbia and Newfoundland legislation permit the government body to initiate and carry through an action against the merchant on behalf of the consumer. The concept of unconscionable transactions has been extended in these provinces to cover consumer transactions involving the purchase of goods and services as well as money lending transactions. In addition to these legislative provisions, the common law doctrine of unconscionability in contract law has recently become much more accepted and, thus, as discussed in Chapter 5, important in these situations.

In some provinces government can initiate action

In the case introducing this chapter, Mrs. Knuude was able to escape her contractual obligations because she was taken advantage of and unreasonably pressured by the sales representative. This made the contract unconscionable.

Door-to-door sales controlled

DOOR-TO-DOOR SALES. Another type of activity which all provinces vigorously control is door-to-door sales. Some provinces, including Ontario and British Columbia, embody these provisions in their *Consumer Protection Acts* and others use special legislation, usually referred to as *Direct Sellers Acts*. Because door-to-door selling often involves a great deal of pressure, one of the main provisions of this legislation is for a cooling-off period. This provision gives the consumer a specified time after the contract has been entered into, in some provinces, as much as ten days, within which to rescind the contract and insist upon the return of any monies paid. The cooling-off period allows the purchaser to rethink the transaction in the absence of pressure and then to rescind the contract without any disadvantage if dissatisfied. In some jurisdictions, contracts over a certain value are required to be in writing and a copy must be given to the customer for the contract to be enforceable. The statutes also require the registration of direct sellers. By retaining the right to suspend registration for specific offences, the government body involved can exercise considerable control over door-to-door sellers. The Ontario *Consumer Protection Act* provides a two day cooling-off period for all executory consumer contracts (ones in which the transaction is to be completed at some future time.)

Referral selling controlled

REFERRAL SELLING. Another activity often prohibited or controlled by legislation is referral selling. With this practice, the seller has the purchaser make a list of friends and acquaintances that the salesperson then uses, often accompanied by introductory letters, to put pressure on those people. The purchaser is usually persuaded to provide this list of referrals by a promise of a discount for each referral that bears fruit. Several provinces, including Ontario and British Columbia, have controlled or completely prohibited this type of activity because it is susceptible to so much abuse.

Control of Specific Businesses

There are many other kinds of consumer protection legislation designed to guard against abuses in particular industries. *The Consumer Protection Act*[15] of British Columbia has provisions controlling mortgage transactions, food plan transactions, the practice of discounting income tax returns, solicited and unsolicited credit card transactions and door-to-door transactions dealing with the sale of goods and services. Nova Scotia has similar legislation for income tax refund discounting and credit cards. Saskatchewan has legislation controlling the sale of training courses and other provisions dealing with unsolicited goods and credit cards. Manitoba's legislation controls prearranged funeral services, credit cards and unsolicited goods. Ontario's *Consumer Protection Act* requires the cost of consumer borrowing to be clearly set out, not only in the actual contract but in all advertising as well. It also removes any obligations on the consumer who uses unsolicited goods or credit cards sent to him or her and has provisions which prohibit misleading advertising. In Ontario the fines for offences are $25 000 for an individual and $100 000 for a corporation. All jurisdictions have legislation designed to curtail and control abusive practices used in areas such as debt collection.

New methods
used to control
abusive activity

METHODS OF CONTROL. Controlling these unacceptable activities through legislation is accomplished by several methods. Businesses are required to register with a government body which is given the power to withdraw registration for misbehaviour. The government department that has the job of overseeing the legislation usually also has the power to enforce it through levying fines for the commission of offences. To facilitate this process, the government body also has the power to investigate and seize records. It can also have the right to enforce legislation by initiating actions on behalf of consumers or to help them start their own actions. Another method of enforcement is to create new rights and obligations between the parties under the *Act* and to give consumers the right to enforce those obligations by suing the other party.

Loan Transactions

Every province has unconscionable transactions legislation prohibiting excessive rates of interest and costs in loan transactions such as mortgages. The provinces have also enacted legislation either in their consumer protection acts or in separate legislation which is usually called *Cost of Credit Disclosure Act* (in Alberta, it is called the *Consumer Credit Transactions Act*). This legislation requires that the true cost

[15] *Consumer Protection Act*, R.S.B.C. (1979), c.65, part 2, 3 and 4.

of borrowing be disclosed to the consumer. Loan transactions often involve the payment of bonuses that are added to the money to be repaid. Debtors are often surprised to discover that the rate of interest they were quoted is payable on the amount of the loan plus the bonus. For example, Abrams borrowed money at a rate of 10 percent on a $10 000 loan but also agreed to pay a $5000 bonus. Abrams walked out of the office with $10 000 but, when the time came to repay the money, discovered that the 10 percent interest quoted was on the $15 000 now owing, not the $10 000 that was borrowed. These statutes are designed to have all this information fully disclosed to the borrower at the outset. They usually prohibit misleading information in advertisements about the cost of borrowing and require moneylenders to be registered, which makes them subject to suspension by the government body for misbehaviour or incompetence.

A related issue is businesses that supply information on the creditworthiness of customers. They provide a very useful function from the merchant's point of view, but the harm that could be done to the customer through carelessness or abuse is great. Most provinces have introduced legislation controlling credit-reporting bodies. This legislation varies from province to province, but typically the reporting agency must be registered, giving the government agency some direct power over them. The acts usually set out what types of information reports can include and make it an offence to include any information known to be incorrect. The consumer is usually given the right to inspect the file and the right to remove or correct any incorrect information. In some jurisdictions, the credit-reporting body can only give a report to a merchant when the consumer has requested it in writing. This gives the consumer complete control over the dissemination of information regarding creditworthiness.

Debt Collection Processes

Creditors will often turn to methods other than court action to pressure debtors to pay their obligations. These collection practices range from the simple sending of a bill marked "overdue" to harassment. Creditors can undertake collection, but they often turn to debt collection agencies. Since there are many situations in which collection practices can become abusive, methods of controlling them have been developed. Most common law remedies available to the victims of excessive debt collection practices are based on tort actions for such offences as defamation, assault and battery, trespass and even false imprisonment. British Columbia and Manitoba have passed privacy legislation that may also have an impact on this area. As a general rule, common law remedies for abusive debt collection processes are ineffectual. As a result, provincial legislation requires that debt collection agencies be registered and licensed. Agencies which consistently use unacceptable practices can have their licences revoked. This legislation usually lists the types of unacceptable collection practices and varies from province to province. Most statutes list specific types of prohibited conduct, such as the use of excessive phone calls, calls at unreasonable hours, collect calls, threats of legal action with no foundation, issuing letters of collection that resemble official court documents, deceptive or misleading statements, communicating

True cost of borrowing must be disclosed

Credit reporting practices controlled

Abusive debt collection practices controlled

with employers, friends or relatives, and putting pressure on innocent relatives to pay the debt. Some provinces require that debt collection agencies use only previously approved form letters in their demands for payment. In British Columbia, any practice which involves the use of "undue, excessive, or unreasonable pressures on debtors or any member of his family or household or his employer" is prohibited.[16] The punishment for parties engaged in such activities may range from the loss of their licence to prosecution and a fine. Manitoba and British Columbia have also given debtors the right to sue civilly for any damages suffered because of the abusive practices. The threat of criminal prosecution to pressure a debtor to pay is a violation of the Criminal Code and can result in prosecution against the person making the threat.

Consumer Service Bodies

Role of
government
agencies

Most of the consumer protection statutes referred to in this chapter empower a government body or agency to implement the legislation. The authority given to such departments usually includes the right to hear and investigate complaints, seize records, search premises, suspend licences, impose fines or some other corrective action and initiate civil actions on behalf of the consumer. In some jurisdictions, these bodies have become clearing houses of consumer information with a mandate to collect and disseminate that information to the public. Consumer bureaus can collect information on dangerous products, consumer business scams or unacceptable practices. They may get involved in advertising to educate the consumer. Private organizations such as the Better Business Bureau are also designed to be clearing

Also private
agencies

houses for this information. It must be remembered, however, that the Better Business Bureau is supported and sustained by the business community and thus has a vested interest in serving that community. The theory is that it is in the best interests of the business community to maintain high standards by weeding out disreputable businesses. The Better Business Bureau and similar organizations serve that function for members of the business community who join them.

Federal Legislation

Although the most dramatic developments in consumer protection legislation have taken place provincially in recent years, there are some significant and effective statutes federally as well. The Department of Consumer and Corporate Affairs was established by the *Department of Consumer and Corporate Affairs Act*[17] with a mandate to enforce legislation and provide service to consumers. The *Act* establishes that the department is to be concerned with consumer affairs, restraint of trade and bankruptcy as well as providing systems to educate and protect consumers. The Department of Consumer and Corporate Affairs has established ex-

[16] *Debt Collection Act*, R.S.B.C. (1979) c.88 s.14(1).
[17] *Department of Consumer and Corporate Affairs Act*, R.S.C. (1985) c.C-37.

tensive research facilities to identify unsafe products. It has also become active in consumer matters at the provincial level, hearing and investigating complaints and communicating with consumers and merchants.

Competition Act controls government abuses

COMPETITION ACT. One of the most important federal acts related to the protection of consumers is the *Competition Act*[18] (formerly the *Combines Investigation Act*). The *Act* is primarily intended to prevent activities that interfere with the operation of the free market system and thus protect the public from unfair pricing. To enforce the provisions of the new *Competition Act*, the *Competition Tribunal Act* sets up a competition tribunal which functions like and has the power of a court. Violations are treated as prosecutions with the potential imposition of significant penalties. These penalties include fines or imprisonment for periods of up to five years.

Mergers controlled

One of the main purposes of the *Act* is to control mergers that may have the effect of limiting or restricting competition. Such mergers are no longer treated as inherently bad and the tribunal has the power to review them to determine whether they will have the effect of substantially limiting or lessening competition. Such mergers can take three forms. Horizontal mergers take place when firms that would normally compete directly with each other join together into one operation, for example, when one department chain buys out another. In this case, the competition tribunal would look not only at the anti-competitive effect of such a merger but also at any efficiency that might be gained and balance these factors in terms of public benefit. Vertical mergers take place when a supplier and retailer are merged, for example, when a supplier of foodstuffs purchases a chain of retail grocers. There is a temptation on the part of such a merged operation to "squeeze" competitors that buy foodstuffs from the same supplier by charging higher prices, giving poorer service or otherwise favouring its own retail operation. The tribunal has the power to review such effects. Conglomerate mergers are mergers of companies that are not in direct competition; the main concern here is whether such a merger eliminates or limits potential competition.

Abusive trade practices prohibited

The *Competition Act* has specific provisions prohibiting certain anti-competitive, abusive trade practices. This *Act* seeks to prevent one company that is dominant in a particular market from using its position to impose anti-competitive forces in that market. For example, suppose a dominant company in a market has a sale or uses loss leaders in such a way as to drive its competitors out of business. This is known as predatory pricing and is prohibited. Other more indirect activities that have a similar effect are also prohibited. For example, the vertical price squeeze involves a vertically integrated supplier raising prices so that other retailers have to sell the goods at the supplier's costs. This price increase affects the supplier's own retail operation as well; however, its profit is made at the wholesale level at the expense of the retail level. A similar prohibited practice involves a newly vertically integrated company that refuses to supply other retailers as it has in the past in order to enhance the competitive position of its own retail operation. A third variation involves manipulating freight prices to give an advantage to its own retail operation at the expense of the competition.

[18] *Competition Act*, S.C. (1984-85-86) c.91.

Other examples of prohibited activities are bid rigging (a group of bidders gets together and agrees ahead of time who will be the low bidder); blacklisting someone in professional sports; agreements between banks controlling interest rates; and suppliers discriminating between customers with rebates and special discounts for only some.

The *Act* also prohibits such direct offensive practices as misleading advertising in any form, double ticketing, which means that more than one price ticket is displayed on an item (goods must be sold at the lowest price), and bait and switch advertising by which customers are enticed into a store by unreasonably low advertised prices. When the goods are not available, the customers are switched to higher priced items. The *Act* also controls referral selling schemes, pyramid selling schemes and selling for higher prices than advertised, and requires that, when promotional contests are involved, the chances of winning be clearly stated.

Previously, one of the most common complaints about both federal and provincial consumer legislation was that it was toothless. Ineffectual enforcement provisions often made it more profitable to break the law than to follow it. Many provincial consumer protection statutes have recently been significantly strengthened through increased maximum fines and the introduction of other methods of enforcement, such as allowing consumers to sue in their own right for violation of the legislation. Jail sentences for violation (up to five years) go a long way towards making the *Competition Act* effective. The *Competition Act* also contains provisions allowing consumers the right to sue offending parties for damages suffered due to misleading or deceptive sales practices described in the *Act*, and provides for significant fines (up to $10 million) for the commission of offences .

Effective penalties available

OTHER FEDERAL LEGISLATION. Several other pieces of federal legislation have the effect of protecting the consumer. *The Food and Drug Act*[19] is intended primarily to control the sale of food, drugs and cosmetics unfit for consumption or use. The legislation also prohibits misleading or deceptive claims associated with the sale, labelling, advertising and so on of these products. The *Food and Drug Act* also creates several categories of drugs which are controlled in various ways. For example, unsafe drugs, such as thalidomide, cannot be sold in this country. The *Act* also makes it an offence to traffic in or possess controlled drugs such as amphetamines. As with the *Competition Act*, the presence of strict enforcement provisions makes legislation very effective.

Food and Drug Act carries strict penalties

The *Hazardous Products Act*[20] similarly controls the manufacture, importation and sale of products inherently dangerous. The *Act* creates two categories of substances: those which are restricted and those which are merely controlled. The products restricted by Part 1 of the *Act* cannot be imported, advertised or sold in Canada. Children's toys, clothing and furniture that are excessively flammable, toxic or otherwise dangerous are prohibited under this section. Some other items controlled by Part 1 are products containing carbontetrachloride meant for consumer use and glass soft drink containers over 1.5 litres that do not meet certain specifications.

Effective control over hazardous products

[19] *Food and Drug Act*, R.S.C. (1985) c.F-27.
[20] *Hazardous Products Act*, R.S.C. (1985) c.H-3 (and amendments R.S.C. (1985) 3 supp. c.24).

Part 2 of the *Act* lists goods that can be imported, marketed and sold in Canada as long as the regulations set down are followed. Products such as cradles, cribs, carpets, kettles, toys and pacifiers are controlled under this section, as well as many other products. This *Act* also provides for analyses of products and authorizes inspection processes to uncover violations. Enforcement provisions allow for search and seizure and prosecution for violations. Some hazardous products are covered by their own legislation such as the *Explosives Act*,[21] *Pest Control Products Act*[22] and the *Motor Vehicle Safety Act*.[23]

The *Weights and Measures Act*,[24] the *Consumer Packaging and Labelling Act*[25] and the *Textile Labelling Act*[26] are intended to force proper disclosure of information and thus help consumers make comparisons between products. There are also examples of federal and provincial legislation designed primarily for a purpose other than consumer protection which do have consumer protection aspects to them. For example, the *Bills of Exchange Act*[27] was designed to regulate the use of negotiable instruments such as cheques and promissory notes. But, in response to a particular abuse of negotiable instruments in consumer transactions, the *Act* has been amended to create a consumer note. This amendment significantly lessens the advantage to the creditor or merchant when negotiable instruments are used in consumer transactions. This *Act* will be discussed in considerable detail in Chapter 12.

SUMMARY

When the contract involves the sale of goods, a number of terms are implied into that contract by the *Sale of Goods Act*, unless the parties have agreed otherwise. The *Act* only applies when goods are being sold. The *Act* provides that risk follows title and supplies five rules to determine when title is transferred. Other provisions specify that the seller must convey good title and quiet possession, and that the goods must be free of any lien or charge and be of merchantable quality. When a sample has been shown or where goods are sold by description, the goods must match the sample or description. In the event of a default and that the goods are not yet in the hands of the purchaser, the seller has an unpaid seller's lien and has the right of stoppage *in transitu*.

When consumer transactions are involved, a number of statutes are in place to protect consumers. Consumer protection acts, trade practices acts, unconscionable transactions acts and direct sellers acts are examples of such legislation. These statutes control unacceptable business practices such as misrepresentation and other forms of misleading advertising, and prohibit unconscionable transactions, that is,

---

[21] *Explosives Act*, R.S.C. (1985) c.E-17.
[22] *Pest Control Products Act*, R.S.C. (1985) c.P-9.
[23] *Motor Vehicle Safety Act*, R.S.C. (1985) c.B-10.
[24] *Weights and Measures Act*, R.S.C. (1985) c.W-6.
[25] *Consumer Packaging and Labelling Act*, R.S.C. (1985) c.C-38.
[26] *Textile Labelling Act*, R.S.C. (1985) c.T-10.
[27] *Bills of Exchange Act*, R.S.C. (1985) c.B-4.

when a merchant takes advantage of a weak-willed or otherwise unequal customer. Specific activities are also controlled. Door-to-door selling is controlled by imposing a cooling-off period, money lenders are required to disclose the true cost of borrowing to their customers and abusive debt collection practices are restricted. The federal government has passed legislation controlling inappropriate practices with the *Competition Act* and controlling and restricting dangerous products in acts such as the *Hazardous Products Marketing Act*.

QUESTIONS

1. Explain the purpose of the *Sale of Goods Act* in relation to the obligations of the parties to a sale of goods transaction.
2. What three qualifications must be met before the *Sale of Goods Act* applies to a transaction?
3. What is the distinction between a sale and an agreement to sell? What is the significance of that distinction?
4. When does the risk transfer to the purchaser in a sale of goods transaction? Explain the exceptions to this general rule.
5. What is a bill of lading? How can it affect who bears the risk in a sale of goods transaction?
6. Indicate when title transfers in the following situations:
   a. When the contract for sale is unconditional and the goods involved are in a deliverable state at the time the purchase is made.
   b. When the subject of the contract involves specific goods to which the seller is obligated to do something, such as repair, clean or modify, to get them into a deliverable state.
   c. When the contract for sale involves specific, identified goods which must be weighed or measured before being given to the purchaser.
   d. When the goods are delivered to the purchaser on approval.
   e. When goods purchased by description have not been selected, separated out or manufactured at the time the sales contract is entered into.
7. The *Sale of Goods Act* imposes terms relating to goods matching samples or descriptions, and meeting standards of fitness, quality and title. Explain the nature of these implied terms and their effect on the parties. Indicate which terms are conditions and which are warranties. Explain the significance of the distinction.
8. Explain what merchantable quality means.
9. Explain the effect of an exculpatory clause included in a contract which is inconsistent with the terms set out in the *Sale of Goods Act*.
10. Explain the rights of the seller when the purchaser of goods
   a. becomes insolvent;

    b. defaults on the contract of sale while the goods are still in the hands of the seller;

    c. defaults after the goods have been given to a third party to deliver but before they are received by the purchaser;

11. Explain why it might be more difficult for a seller of goods to sue for damages than for price.

12. Under what circumstances may a purchaser refuse delivery of goods?

13. The *Sale of Goods Act* in each province implies certain terms into contracts of sale relating to the fitness and quality of the product. What are the approaches used in various Canadian jurisdictions to make these provisions mandatory in consumer transactions?

14. How does the concept of privity of contract limit the effectiveness of many consumer protection provisions? How have some jurisdictions overcome this problem?

15. What common law provisions are available to protect consumers from unscrupulous business practices? Describe the limitations inherent in these provisions and the steps that have been taken to overcome these limitations.

16. Explain the object of the *Unconscionable Transactions Relief Act* and the limitations to its application. In your answer, discuss significant variations between provinces.

17. What statutory provisions have been introduced throughout Canada to control door-to-door selling, referral selling and the practice of purchasing tax refunds?

18. Describe the methods outlined in federal and provincial consumer protection statutes to control businesses prone to abuse. Discuss the effectiveness of these tactics.

19. What services are provided to consumers through organizations set up by the federal and provincial governments? Discuss whether these services are adequate.

20. Describe the practices controlled by the *Competition Act* and explain how that control is accomplished.

CASES

1. *Kelly v. Mack Canada Inc. et al.*

    David Kelly bought a used truck from Mack Sales, a dealership. The truck proved incapable of the job for which it was required. Kelly had been told that the truck had a rebuilt engine; this was not the case. After significant repairs, Mack Sales agreed to take it back as a trade-in on a new Mack truck with a new vehicle warranty from the manufacturer, Mack Canada Inc. Again the truck was not up to the task. It was in need of constant repair with a considerable amount of downtime. Mack Canada had warranted the truck to be free from defects with the obligation that they would repair or replace any defective parts. Kelly sued both the dealer, Mack Sales, under the *Sale of Goods Act* and the manufacturer, Mack Canada, under the manufacturer's warranty. He claimed return of the purchase price and costs incurred. Explain the arguments that both the dealer and the manufacturer will use in these circumstances and Kelly's likelihood of success.

2. *Holm v. Morgan.*

The purchaser of an automobile agreed in a contract that the ownership of the goods was to remain with the seller until payment was made but that the risk would rest with the purchaser. He said, "The ownership of the goods for which this note is given shall remain at my risk in the owner, and shall not pass from the owner to me until this note and any renewal or renewals thereof, and all judgments recovered in respect of this note or any such renewals are paid with interest." The car was repossessed for non-payment of the instalments owing and was destroyed by fire while at the seller's place of business. The purchaser refused to pay. What arguments could be raised in his defence? Predict the outcome of this case.

3. *Yelland v. The National Cafe.*

The plaintiff in this action bought a bottle of Coca-Cola from a restaurant. It exploded and a splinter of glass hit her in the eye. She sued the restaurant, the Coca-Cola Company that supplied the syrup and the bottling company. There was no evidence that there was any problem with the bottle at the time it was filled. Discuss the basis for her action against each of the parties and indicate the defences available to them.

4. *Harry v. Kreutziger.*

Harry was a Native Indian with a grade five education, a hearing defect and a retiring manner. He owned a fishing boat worth very little except for the fishing licence that went with it. With the licence, the boat was worth about $16 000. Kreutziger persuaded Harry to sell the boat and licence to him for $4500 saying that, as a Native Indian, Harry would have little trouble getting another licence. Harry sued to have the contract set aside. What would be the nature of Harry's complaint against Kreutziger? What defences would be available to Kreutziger in response to Harry's action? Predict the outcome.

5. *W.W. Distributors & Co. v. Thorsteinson.*

A salesman and his manager approached a young engaged girl and her mother at their home one evening and, after using some very high pressure sales tactics, sold them some cooking utensils. The mother was persuaded to sign the contract after being told that it was not really important. By so doing, the mother became a party to the agreement, even though it had been made clear to the salesman that her only involvement was to lend her daughter $50 towards the purchase. The daughter was led to believe that she was getting very good value for her money but experts clearly established the price was over 75 percent more than the maximum value of the goods involved. The following day, unable to contact the plaintiff, the mother stopped payment on the cheque. When this was discovered, the salesman went by the home and was informed that the mother and daughter were repudiating the agreement. The company immediately commenced an action to recover the purchase price and the various penalties and service charges built into the agreement. Explain the arguments which could be raised on both sides and the likely outcome. What effect would it have on your answer to learn that the engaged girl was under the age of majority? What legislation provisions have been put into place in most jurisdictions to curb this type of abuse?

6. *Gee v. White Spot Ltd.*
Mr. Gee went to the White Spot restaurant and ordered a meal. Unfortunately, the food was contaminated and Mr. Gee suffered botulism poisoning. He sued the White Spot restaurant claiming compensation for the serious damages he suffered. What arguments might Mr. Gee raise to establish liability on the part of White Spot under the Sale of Goods Act? What arguments might White Spot raise to refute such liability?

ISSUES

1. A fundamental precept of contract law is the principle of freedom of contract. Parties to a contract are assumed to be in equal bargaining positions and free to enter into whatever agreement they wish as long as it is not immoral or illegal. There are always many aspects to an agreement that parties neglect to cover in the contract. One of the main purposes of the *Sale of Goods Act* is to supply by implication many of the terms that have been inadvertently left out of contracts involving the purchase of goods. Many of the imposed terms favour one party over the other instead of being neutral and only facilitating the agreement. For example, the terms applying to fitness and quality put significant obligations on the seller. Although these provisions can be avoided by so stating in the agreement, some provinces prohibit the parties from altogether contracting out of some of the provisions of the *Act*. The question for discussion is: Do the terms of the *Sale of Goods Act* excessively interfere with the principles of *freedom of contract* and *caveat emptor*? Distinguish between commercial and consumer sales and discuss the value of the right of the parties to contract out of the terms of the *Act*. Consider the abuses associated with the use of exculpatory clauses in consumer transactions and the

steps taken in some jurisdictions to limit their use. Discuss consumer protection legislation in relation to these concerns. Is such legislation appropriate? Is it the place of the courts to protect fools from the folly of their bargains?

2.   Several complicated rules are set out in the *Sale of Goods Act* to determine when title transfers from the seller to the purchaser. The determination of who has title can affect several things, including who bears the risk of loss or damage. It is possible for the purchaser to bear the risk even though the goods are still in the hands of the seller. The question for discussion is: Should the purchaser ever have to bear the risk of loss or damage to the goods before receiving possession? Should the parties be free to make their own arrangements as to who bears the risk by using C.I.F., F.O.B. or C.O.D. contracts?

3.   Should there be a general requirement in law, independent of contract or tort law, that products be safe and capable of living up to the claims made for them? Discuss the approaches adopted by different jurisdictions in Canada and the United States to address this problem. Describe the disadvantages associated with actions grounded in contract law or tort that would be overcome by these approaches. Should strict liability for products be restricted to the manufacturer or extended to the supplier of the product as well?

4.   Consumer protection legislation controls the quality of goods and services supplied and the actual sales practices used by businesses to encourage customers to purchase their wares. In addition to prohibiting misleading statements, the statutes impose other restrictions as well, such as preventing the exploitation of people in desperate circumstances, holding sellers responsible for salespeople's statements and allowing the rescission of contracts made at the door within a certain period of time. The question for discussion is: Does this kind of legislation interfere with commercial activities to the extent that many businesses are overregulated and unable to function efficiently in the marketplace?

5.   Consumer protection legislation attempts to find acceptable ways to control abusive and unacceptable practices in consumer transactions. Steps have been taken to provide the consumer with greater access to the courts, both by creating new causes of action and by making the use of the courts more available through financial assistance. In some cases, government bodies actually bring the action on behalf of the customer. The legislation also provides for government persecution which can result in fines and imprisonment for the offending party. Requiring registration of abuse-prone businesses is also a method of control used. Discuss the effectiveness of these enforcement provisions and make recommendations for improvement.

6.   Every province in Canada has unconscionable transactions legislation designed to provide relief in those situations in which, although there has been

no undue influence or duress, the court is satisfied that a person has been taken advantage of. In most provinces, these provisions are restricted to contracts involving the loan of money but some provinces have extended this protection to other consumer transactions as well. Discuss the development of the principle of unconscionable transactions and consider whether this principle can play a more effective role in protecting vulnerable people. Some have argued that, if the principle of unconscionable transactions was fully developed, many of the common law and statutory provisions intended to protect vulnerable people, such as duress and undue influence, incapacity due to infancy, insanity or drunkenness, and so on, could be eliminated. Discuss the validity of this position.

LEGISLATION

Alberta
Consumer Credit Transactions Act, S.A. (1985) c.22.5
Direct Sales Cancellation Act, S.A. (1980) p.35
Financial Consumers Act, S.A. (1990) c.F-9.5
Sale of Goods Act, S.A. (1980) c.S-2
Unconscionable Transactions Act, S.A. (1980) c.U-2
Unfair Trade Practices Act, S.A. (1980) c.U-3

British Columbia
Business License Act, S.B.C. (1980) c.3
Consumer Protection Act, R.S.B.C. (1979) c.65
Credit Reporting Act, R.S.B.C. (1979) c.78
International Sale of Goods Act, S.B.C. (1990) c.20
Multilevel Marketing Regulation Act, R.S.B.C. (1979) c.351
Sale of Goods Act, R.S.B.C. (1979) c.370
Trade Practices Act, R.S.B.C. (1979) c.406

Manitoba
Business Practices Act, passed C.C.S.M. B-120
Consumer Protection Act, C.C.S.M. C200, as amended by S.M. (1989)
Dangerous Goods Handling and Transportation Act, R.S.M. (1989) c.37
International Sale of Goods Act, R.S.M. (1989) c.18
Sale of Goods Act, R.S.M. (1981) c.S-10
Unconscionable Transactions Relief Act, R.S.M. (1989) c.U-20

New Brunswick
Collection Agencies Act, R.S.N.B. (1973) c.C-8
Consumer Product and Warranty Act, R.S.N.B. (1978) c.C-18.1
Cost of Credit Disclosure Act, R.S.N.B. (1973) c.C-28

Direct Sellers Act, R.S.N.B. (1973) c.D-10
Sale of Goods Act, R.S.N.B. (1973) c.S-1
Unconscionable Transactions Relief Act, R.S.N.B. (1973) c.U-1

Newfoundland
Consumer Reporting Agencies Act, R.S.N. (1990) c.C-32
Direct Sellers Act, R.S.N. (1990) c.D-24
Consumer Protection Act, R.S.N. (1990) c.I-22
Sale of Goods Act, R.S.N. (1990) c.S-6
Trade Practices Act, R.S.N. (1990) c.T-7
Unconscionable Transaction Act, R.S.N. (1990) c.U-1
Unsolicited Goods and Credit Cards Act, R.S.N. (1990) c.U-6

Nova Scotia
Bills of Lading Act, R.S.N.S. (1989) c.38
Collection Agencies Act, R.S.N.S. (1989) c.77
Consumer Creditor's Conduct Act, R.S.N.S. (1989) c.91
Consumer Protection Act, R.S.N.S. (1989) c.92
Consumer Reporting Act, R.S.N.S. (1989) c.93
Direct Sellers Licensing and Regulation Act, R.S.N.S. (1989) c.129
Money-Lenders Act, R.S.N.S. (1989) c.289
Mortgage Brokers and Lenders Registration Act, R.S.N.S. (1989) c.291
Sale of Goods Act, R.S.N.S. (1989) c.408

Ontario
Business Practices Act, R.S.O. (1990) c.B.18
Consumer Protection Act, R.S.O. (1990) c.C.31
Consumer Reporting Act, R.S.O. (1990) c.C.33
Discriminatory Business Practices Act, R.S.O. (1990) c.D.12
Sale of Goods Act, R.S.O. (1990) c.S.1
Unconscionable Transactions Relief Act, R.S.O. (1990) c.U.2

Prince Edward Island
Business Practices Act, R.S.P.E.I. (1988) c.B-7
Collection Agencies Act, R.S.P.E.I. (1988) c.C-11
Consumer Protection Act, R.S.P.E.I. (1988) c.C-19
Consumer Reporting Act, R.S.P.E.I. (1988) c.C-10
Direct Sellers Act, R.S.P.E.I. (1988) c.D-11
Sale of Goods Act, R.S.P.E.I. (1988) c.S-1
Unconscionable Transactions Relief Act, R.S.P.E.I. (1988) c.U-2

Québec

Bills of Lading Act, R.S.Q (1977) c.C-53

Consumer Protection Act amended, S.Q. (1991) c.23

International Sale of Goods Act, R.S.Q (1991) c.68

Saskatchewan

Agreements of Sale Cancellation Act, R.S.S. (1978) c.A-7

Consumer Products Warranties Act, R.S.S. (1978) c.C-30

Cost of Credit Disclosure Act, R.S.S. (1978) c.C-41

Credit Reporting Agencies Act, R.S.S. (1978) c.C-44

Direct Sellers' Act, R.S.S. (1978) c.D-28

International Sale of Goods Act, R.S.S. (1978) c.I-10.3

Sale of Goods Act, R.S.S. (1978) c.S-1

Sale of Training Courses Act, R.S.S. (1978) c.S-3

Unconscionable Transactions Relief Act, R.S.S. (1978) c.U-1

Northwest Territories

Consumer Protection Act, R.S.N.W.T. (1988) c.C-17

Fair Practices Act, R.S.N.W.T. (1988) c.F-2

Sale of Goods Act, R.S.N.W.T. (1988) c.S-2

Yukon

Consumer Protection Act, R.S.Y. (1986) c.31

Sale of Goods Act, R.S.Y. (1986) c.154

Federal

Bills of Lading Act, R.S.C. (1985) c.B-5

Competition Act, R.S.C. (1985) c.C-34 (and amendment 2nd Supp. 610)

Competition Tribunal Act, R.S.C. (1985) c.19 (2nd Supp.) Part 1

Consumer Packaging and Labelling Act, R.S.C. (1985) c.C-38

Food and Drugs Act, R.S.C. (1985) c.F-27

Hazardous Products Act, R.S.C. (1985) c.H-3 (and amendments 3rd Supp. c.24)

International Sale of Goods Contracts Convention Act, R.S.C. (1991) c.13

Weights and Measures Act, R.S.C. (1985) c.W-6

8

PRIORITY OF CREDITORS

Objectives of the Chapter

- to describe the methods and process of securing debt
- to outline the rights and obligations of the parties to a security transaction
- to consider the effect of builders' liens and bankruptcy

Calderbank was the driving force in Skyhook Operations Ltd., a company incorporated to carry out helicopter logging. Calderbank held 50 percent of the shares and two investors, Rodenbush and Rooke, held the other 50 percent. The bank had granted Skyhook Operations a $25 000 line of credit as well as a fixed loan of $112 000; the investors had signed a personal guarantee for this debt. At the end of a year's operation, the line of credit was at its limit and Skyhook had defaulted on its fixed loan payments. Calderbank met with the bank manager to request an increase in the line of credit. He assured the bank manager that the investors would be putting another $20 000 into the business. Calderbank also confided to the bank manager that he was planning to start up another company to compete with Skyhook. When asked why, he stated that he wanted to run the business his way and get 100 percent of the profits. The bank manager sought and obtained a promise from Calderbank that any funds from the extended line of credit and the additional funds injected by Rooke and Rodenbush would be used only for the operation of Skyhook and not for the new company. When he received this assurance, he extended the line of credit to $40 000. When the bank manager received the investors/guarantors' approval for the change in the line of credit, he did not tell them about the new company that Mr. Calderbank intended to start, believing that the information was given to him in confidence. Rooke and Rodenbush invested a further $20 000 into Skyhook. Shortly afterwards, Calderbank exhausted the line of credit, and took these funds and the extra funds invested by Rooke and Rodenbush and diverted them to his new company. When the investors learned of this action, they informed the bank that they would not be responsible for any further debts of Skyhook. Skyhook failed and shortly thereafter Rooke and Rodenbush learned that the bank manager had known all along of Calderbank's intention to form the competing company and had not told them. They refused any responsibility for the guarantee and the bank brought an action to enforce it.[1]

Personal guaranties are common and a vital aspect of doing business in Canada today. Since corporations are separate legal entities and responsible for their own debts, creditors usually insist on having personal guaranties from real individuals with substantial assets before they will loan money to such entities. The creditors want to ensure that people will be responsible for the debt in the likely event that the new company does not succeed. It is vitally important that people understand that when they sign such a personal guarantee there is a real possibility that they will be called on to pay back the debt. In this case, however, the court found that the investors were not bound by the guarantee they had signed. Because a guarantor's position is so vulnerable, the law has imposed an obligation on the creditor not to make new arrangements with the debtor that will put the guarantor at greater risk without first obtaining the guarantor's permission for the change. Part of the creditor's obligation is to disclose any unusual factors that the creditor is aware of which might persuade the guarantor not to agree to the change. The bank manager's failure to disclose that Calderbank was about to start another company in competition with Skyhook amounted to misrepresentation and therefore Rooke and Rodenbush were not required to pay the guarantee. The personal guarantee is one of the important topics discussed in this chapter.

A considerable industry has developed around the practices of lending money and granting credit. This chapter will examine the various methods that have been developed to ensure that money owed is properly repaid and the legislation that has been created to control such transactions. Although there is some overlap, this area is primarily under the jurisdiction of the provinces. Provincial legislation varies considerably from province to province, but there are many common principles which, along with significant variations, will be examined in this chapter.

[1] *Toronto Dominion Bank v. Rooke et al.* (1984) 3 D.L.R. (4th), 716 (B.C.C.A.)

METHODS OF SECURING DEBT

Security helps assure creditor of repayment

Certain steps must be taken to protect a moneylender's interests because a simple contractual arrangement cannot guarantee that the lender will be repaid. Because a debtor who becomes insolvent and unable to honour a debt is unlikely to hold enough assets to cover all the outstanding creditor claims, a lender stands to lose part or all of the loan. To persuade a creditor to lend money, a debtor must ensure that the creditor will be paid before other debts are cleared, even in the event of insolvency. Several methods have been developed to satisfy this requirement. When the parties are successful in creating a priority system of one creditor over the others, the party with priority is said to be a secured creditor.

Personal Property

Real property includes land and buildings

Personal property can be used as security

Both real and personal property have been used to create security. **Real property** includes land and any buildings or items attached to the land, called fixtures. Non-real property is called personalty or **personal property**; similar methods have been developed to allow personal property to secure the payment of money owed. Personal property can be divided into tangible chattels and intangible rights. The creditor of a dishonoured debt has the right to initiate an action to recover the money. This right or claim is called a **chose in action**. A cheque or a promissory note is actually a chose in action because the paper merely represents an obligation to pay and a right to sue for failure to do so. Both a chattel and a chose in action can be used to secure a debt. The most common method in consumer transactions is to take tangible real property or chattels as security.

The oldest system for using personal property as security is a pledge or a pawn in which a creditor (pawnbroker) takes possession of a particular item as security and holds it until repayment. The creditor has possession of the goods but the debtor still has title and remains the owner. Only when there is no repayment does the pawnbroker acquire the right to sell the goods to recover the amount lost.

Personal property security involves right to take possession upon default

In most circumstances, it is inconvenient and contrary to the intention of the parties for the creditor to take possession of the goods to be used as security. It is now customary for personal property to be used as security in the same way as real property is used. The creditor in such circumstances has the right to seize the goods upon default while the debtor continues to enjoy the possession and use of those goods. Only when the debtor fails to repay the loan can the creditor take possession of the personal property. It must be emphasized that, even in those contracts which state that the title to the goods transfers to the creditor, the primary nature of the transaction is the loan of money, not the conveyance of any interest in the goods used as collateral.

RECENT DEVELOPMENTS. Over the years, business people have developed several different methods of using personal property as security by using the tenets of common law. Some of the most significant of these methods are conditional sales, chattel mortgages and the assignment of book accounts. Because these methods developed gradually and independently of each other, the principles which apply are usually unique to the form of security taken. Similarly, legislation passed to control each form of security has contained significant variations. In the recent past, most jurisdictions had separate conditional sales acts, bills of sale acts for chattel mortgages and assignment of book accounts acts. The result was considerable confusion and sometimes injustice. Many of these statutes had different conditions under which registration must take place, different time limits, different places for registration, different remedies and no unified system of enforcement.

In reaction to this situation, Ontario, Saskatchewan, Manitoba and, most recently, British Columbia, Alberta and the Yukon have made considerable advancement by passing personal property security acts. Prince Edward Island has enacted a similar act but it had not yet been proclaimed into law at the time of writing. The significance of these acts is that one set of provisions controls all types of personal property used as security, which eliminates much of the confusion. There can still be contractual differences between conditional sales, chattel mortgages and the other types of secured transactions covered by this legislation, but the formal requirements and procedures for all of these types of securities are the same. As well, the *Personal Property Security Act* allows other, less traditional, forms of personal property such as negotiable instruments, shares and bonds to be used as security and treated in a uniform way. While several provinces still retain the old system, it is likely that they will soon adopt similar property security legislation.

Before looking at the personal property security acts, we will first examine conditional sales, chattel mortgages and the assignment of book accounts. In those provinces where there is no personal property security act, there is a separate statute for each of these types of security. In the other provinces and territories, conditional sales, chattel mortgages and assignment of book accounts are still important because they usually form the contractual basis of the security arrangement; the various personal property security acts in place only create a unified approach to enforcing the rights and obligations set out in those contracts.

Personal property security acts rationalize the area

CONDITIONAL SALES. Some contracts involving the sale of goods include special provisions whereby the seller retains title as a form of security until the last payment is made. Upon receipt of the last payment, title then follows possession into the hands of the purchaser. This type of arrangement is referred to as a conditional sales agreement and is, in effect, a sale that takes place in two stages. The first stage occurs when the agreement is entered into and the purchaser is given possession of the goods. Only when the last payment is made, including any costs or interest charges, does the second stage of the sale take place. At this point, the title or property of those goods follows the possession into the hands of the purchaser. The conditional aspect of the sale is now satisfied. A conditional sales agreement is used when the seller is providing the financing for the goods being sold. The seller retains title to the goods until the final payment is made. In England and in some

Conditional seller retains title until payment is completed

provinces of Canada, **hire-purchase agreements** are used to accomplish similar results. In this type of arrangement, the customer agrees to rent or lease goods at a set rate and then has the option to purchase the goods outright at a prearranged price at the end of the rental period.

If the purchaser defaults, the seller has available all of the remedies normally available for breach of contract, including judgment and damages. The security obtained through the conditional sales agreement allows the seller, in the event of default, the additional remedy of retaking the goods and reselling them to recoup the loss. This right of repossession and resale gives rise to certain problems. When the purchaser of those goods possesses them, it appears to an outsider that the possessor is the owner and able to resell them. If an innocent third party buys the goods from an apparent owner who has failed to make proper payment, there are two competing claims on the goods, each of which appears to have fairness and justice on its side. If Palmer buys a car from Lee on time, using the car as security, and then sells that car to Busch, both Busch and the unpaid Lee have legitimate claims against the car. Provincial conditional sales acts or personal property security acts now require registration of the security to alleviate this difficulty. Repossession, resale and the statutory process of registration will be discussed below as the general principles common to most secured transactions.

Conditional sales are not restricted to consumer transactions; it is quite common for the suppliers of goods on credit to a retail business to use a conditional sales agreement as a method of acquiring security. But if such a secured title were to prevail against the ordinary customers of the retail business, it would significantly interfere with the normal course of merchandising operations. In response to this problem, legislation in many provinces provides that, when goods are put into the hands of a retailer to be resold, the supplier of those goods loses any right to retake possession of them from the ultimate purchaser. Thus, if Lee bought a new car from Palmer's Fine Cars Ltd., he would be unaffected by any conditional sales agreement between Palmer and his supplier. If Palmer's Fine Cars Ltd. became insolvent, the supplier could not take possession of Lee's new car even though it was the subject of a conditional sales agreement between Palmer and the supplier.

The effect of conditional sales legislation and other forms of secured transaction statutes is to force the parties to use the registries and to put the risk of loss on a party who fails to do so. Some jurisdictions exempt certain types of goods from the requirement of registration when taken as security.

A common practice among creditors who are involved in conditional sales agreements is to assign them to third parties. Conditional sellers are not usually in the business of lending money; they want to sell products. A retailer sells or assigns the conditional sales agreement to a company in the business of lending money and gets cash from the finance company for the goods sold. The terms of the conditional sales agreement reflect the requirements of the finance company, the ultimate creditor, because the arrangement with the finance company is usually made before the sales transaction. Purchaser are sometimes surprised to discover that, having purchased goods on time from one retailer, they get a bill from another party entirely. This is perfectly within the rights of the parties. The debtor is well advised to heed the notice and make subsequent payments to the assignee.

It must be clearly understood, however, that the seller does not escape his or her obligations under the agreement by assigning the contract to someone else. As discussed in Chapter 5, when a contract is assigned, the assignee acquires only the benefits of that contract. The conditional seller remains obligated to the purchaser for the performance of the contract. The purchaser can still sue the conditional seller if there is a breach or if the goods are defective. A purchaser who is still paying off a debt can withhold payment from the assignee if there is a breach because the assignee has assumed the contract subject to the equities between the original parties. A vendor will often require that a promissory note be included as part of the transaction. The inclusion of negotiable instruments can have a significant impact on the rights and obligations of the parties. Negotiable instruments are discussed in Chapter 13.

Assignee of conditional sales agreement only acquires benefits

MORTGAGES ON PERSONAL PROPERTY. A common method of providing security for the lender when land and buildings are involved is for borrowers to grant mortgages on their real property. The mortgage transaction means the borrower temporarily transfers title to the land to the lender while retaining possession of the property. Title is returned when the debtor repays the loan. Failure to repay results in the title remaining with the creditor who then has first claim against the land. In some provinces where a special land titles system has been introduced, the mortgagee is not registered as the new owner when a mortgage is involved. Rather, the mortgage becomes a charge registered against the debtor's title. In either case, the creditor's interests will prevail against any other creditors. Mortgages of real property will be discussed more extensively in Chapter 14.

Chattel mortgage —title to goods transferred to secure loan

A **chattel** is any form of tangible, personal property other than land or buildings. When people put up chattels as security for debts, they grant a **chattel mortgage** to the lender. Both the chattel mortgage and conditional sale provide security to the creditor while the debtor maintains possession of the goods. The chattel mortgage is much more flexible than a conditional sales agreement because it can be used when the party providing the financing is not the seller but a third party such as a bank or finance company. A chattel mortgage can also be used even when the goods used as security are not newly purchased. In provinces where there is no personal property security act, the legislation governing chattel mortgages is the Bills of Sale Act. A bill of sale is a document containing a contract of sale and giving the purchaser proof of ownership. In a simple sale contract, title transfers to the purchaser through the completion and transfer of this document. The purchaser is given proof of title even when possession of the goods remains with the seller for some period. In a chattel mortgage, the bill of sale is used to give the creditor title to the goods until the amount of the loan is repaid. In the event of default, the creditor has proof of title and thus security in the goods. In fact, this is not a true sale since there is no intention that the creditor will actually gain possession of the goods. Instead it creates a secured interest by this temporary transfer of the title. In addition to the normal contractual remedies for breach, the creditor can retake

Repossession available upon default

and resell the goods and has this right in preference to other unsecured creditors. In provinces with a personal property security act, the title in the goods does not actually transfer to the creditor but the effect is the same: the creditor gets security in the goods in preference to other unsecured creditors.

ASSIGNMENT OF BOOK ACCOUNTS. Intangible property or a chose in action can also be used as security. A typical method of creating security for businesses is through the general assignment of book accounts or debts. The creditor takes an assignment of the accounts receivable from the debtor to secure a loan. The debtor has thus transferred rights to collect on the accounts owed to the business by customers. As long as the merchant debtor makes payment to the creditor, the merchant will be able to collect on the accounts receivable in the normal way. But when the merchant debtor defaults, the right to collect on those outstanding accounts falls to the creditor. This right is the creditor's security. Legislation to cover this practice in provinces that have no *Personal Property Security Act* is called the *Assignment of Book Accounts Act*. In provinces with *Personal Property Security Act*s, such general assignment of book debts is included in these statutes. The main thrust of this legislation is that the assignment of book accounts as security must be registered to ensure priority and protect subsequent creditors.

Accounts receivable can be used as security for a loan

Registration required for assignment of book accounts

BANKS. A disadvantage of chattel mortgages and conditional sales is that they must be attached to specific goods or claims and these goods or claims usually cannot be resold without violating the terms of the mortgage and defeating its objectives. Another difficulty is that only tangible items can be used as security. These problems are now largely overcome in provinces with personal property security acts

The federal *Bank Act*[2] has been enacted to solve these problems and to give the banks more flexibility in their financing operations. This legislation allows banks to use items such as crops that are still being grown and goods that are still being manufactured as security. This kind of financing arrangement requires that the goods be sold to repay the loan. Normally, not all of the products from the farming or manufacturing process are sold at the same time, but Sections 426 and 427 allow goods to be sold and new goods to be produced as part of an ongoing process without altering the nature of the security. This would be much more difficult, if not impossible, to arrange with the more conventional forms of security already discussed. Because the *Personal Property Security Acts* are much more flexible, there is more overlap and, as a result, more potential conflicts between those statutes and these provisions of the federal *Bank Act*. One important feature of the *Act* is that the loan is registered with the local branch of the Bank of Canada. This banking legislation also permits banks to continue to use the normal types of secured transactions available to everyone such as chattel mortgages, guarantees, real estate mortgages, assignment of debts and so on.

Anticipated crops can be used as security

---

[2] *Bank Act*, R.S.C. (1985) c.B-1.

Registration

Registration
establishes
priority

The objective of a secured transaction is to give first claim on the assets to the secured creditor in the event of default. There are some difficulties with this process because the principle involves giving one creditor priority over another. A creditor who has followed the appropriate procedures is able to prevent other, perfectly innocent, parties from receiving what they would normally be entitled to. Security is an understandable objective from the point of view of the secured creditor but may seem completely unjust when viewed from the position of unsecured creditors. A further difficulty with the practice is that, because possession of the goods stays with the debtor, outsiders can easily be led to believe that the debtor owns the goods and has the legal right to sell them. It would defeat the whole purpose of security if an innocent outsider could purchase those goods from the debtor and obtain good title. However, it would be equally unjust if a secured creditor were able to take the goods back from an innocent third party who had purchased them from a fraudulent debtor.

Every province has legislated solutions to these difficulties. The statutes dealing with such secured transactions, *Bills of Sale Acts*, *Assignment of Book Accounts Acts*, *Conditional Sale Acts* and *Personal Property Security Acts*, put the obligation on the secured creditor to register the security at a central registry. The registry serves as a centre of information and potential third parties should search the registry before purchasing or taking goods as security for a loan. Creditors who fail to register the security lose their priority over anyone who subsequently deals with that property. When the security is properly registered, the onus shifts to the third

Onus on third
party to search
registry

party to search the records to determine whether or not a security has been taken against the goods. When a security has been registered by the creditor, third parties are well advised to avoid the transaction. If they ignore the registered security or neglect to search the registry, they must suffer the consequences. In the event of a default by the debtor, such security, properly registered by the creditor, will give the creditor the right to retake the goods even from the innocent third party or from anyone else who subsequently acquired the goods or an interest in them. Although the process of registration and search is an artificial step, it does introduce the element of fairness into the process.

Provincial registration legislation imposes various obligations. Potential third parties may have to check several different registries to determine the existence of a security against the goods. There may be significant differences between provinces and even within a province because of the various statutes involved. The procedure has been standardized in provinces with a *Personal Property Security Act*. Most statutes impose a time limit within which registration must take place after the initial creation of the security to ensure priority.

Remedies

A purchaser who honours the terms of the agreement and makes the appropriate payments can require the creditor to transfer or return the title in the property.

When the security is in the form of a pledge or a pawn and the possession of the goods is in the hands of the creditor, the creditor is required to return the goods when the debt is paid. The true significance of the secured transactions comes into play in the case of default. All of the contractual remedies for breach of contract are available against the defaulting parties. Because security has been taken, foremost among the options available to the creditor is to take possession of the goods used as security. Because the terms of the contract give the creditor the right to retake those goods upon default, it is generally not necessary to obtain a court order to repossess.

The creditor or an agent, usually a bailiff, can take possession of the goods by going to the debtor's place of business or residence and seizing the goods. The bailiff is not permitted to break down doors, force open windows or use any threat of violence. Suppose Wizinsky has loaned money to Barbosa and has taken security in the form of a chattel mortgage against Barbosa's car and Barbosa defaults. Wizinsky would be able to tow the car away from Barbosa's open carport. If the car were in a locked garage, Wizinsky could not seize the vehicle without the court's assistance because it would be necessary to force open the garage to do so. The creditor or bailiff would not be permitted to remove Barbosa forcibly from the vehicle to take possession of it. In such circumstances, the appropriate procedure is to get a court order and then get the local judicial officer, usually a sheriff, to enforce the order. Such officers can use whatever force is necessary to fulfil their duties and enforce court orders. The *Personal Property Security Act*[3] of Ontario prohibits the use of any unlawful methods in retaking the goods. The remedy of repossession may be limited in some jurisdictions. For example, in British Columbia, the new *Personal Property Security Act*[4] requires that, when two-thirds of the debt has been paid, consumer goods cannot be retaken unless there is a court order. The *Consumer Protection Act*[5] of Ontario has a similar provision.

After the goods have been repossessed, they can be sold to recover the money owed. Although it is possible for the secured creditor to obtain possession and hold the goods as in foreclosure, this remedy is rarely used because the process does not facilitate the creditor's business interests. When the procedures for repossession and resale are set out in legislation, the goods must be retained by the creditor for a specified period of time, usually from fifteen days to one month, to enable the debtor to make arrangements to pay for and recover the goods. In most jurisdictions, the entire amount owing, costs arising out of the repossession process and any accrued interest must be paid to redeem the goods. In jurisdictions such as Saskatchewan, the contract can be reinstated by paying only the arrears owing. At the expiration of the period of time set out in the statute, the goods can be sold. Some jurisdictions require that such goods be sold at public auction while others permit private sales for a fair price. These provisions protect the debtor's interest in the goods because he or she has a right to any surplus over and above the amount owed plus costs and interest.

[3] *The Personal Property Security Act*, R.S.O. (1990) c.P.10 s.59(2).
[4] *Personal Property Security Act*, S.B.C. (1989) c.36.
[5] *Consumer Protection Act*, R.S.O. (1990) c.C-31.

Any deficit must
be repaid by
debtor

In most jurisdictions, if the creditor resells the goods, the debtor is still responsible for any deficit left after the resale. That is, if the amount still owing is greater than the amount realized by the creditor on the resale of the goods, the debtor can be required to make up that difference unless the contract says otherwise. If there are provisions in the legislation governing resale, those provisions must be followed to be able to claim an unpaid deficit. In jurisdictions where the *Personal Property Security Act* is in force, the creditor has a choice between the right of retention (to take possession of the goods with possession being the end of the remedy) and the right of disposition or sale (this remedy allows the creditor to sue for a deficiency) but, in disposing of the goods, the creditor must carefully adhere to the procedures set out in the *Act*.

THE PERSONAL PROPERTY SECURITY ACT. Ontario, Manitoba, Saskatchewan, Alberta, British Columbia and the Yukon have each replaced their *Conditional Sales Act*, *Bills of Sale Act* and *Assignment of Book Accounts Act* with one statute called the *Personal Property Security Act*.[6] Prince Edward Island has passed such legislation but it had not been proclaimed at the time of writing. The agreement between the parties may be a chattel mortgage, conditional sales agreement or a general assignment of book accounts, but, regardless of the form the personal security takes, the parties need only follow the provision of this one act. The *Act* is

Act creates one
cohesive process

designed to cover any situation in which a creditor is given a secured interest against the assets of a debtor to ensure repayment of a loan or obligation. It should be noted that this combined legislation results in a much broader application than is found in more specific legislation such as the *Conditional Sales Act* or *Bills of Sale Act*. Here, title in the property (called the collateral) need not change hands to create a security. The security is any situation in which the creditor (called the secured party) receives priority or an assurance of payment before other creditors of the debtor. These rights and obligations are not affected in any way by who has title to the goods. The *Act* permits a security interest to be created in all types of tangible and intangible assets of the debtor. In addition to the traditional chattel mortgages and conditional sales, the *Act* covers assignment of contracts and debts and leasing arrangements intended to create a security. It should be noted that in some situations the *Act* does not apply, for example, when possessory liens such as unpaid seller's liens are used or when automobiles are retained by mechanics who have done work on them for which they have not been paid. As well, the legislation does not cover interests in insurance policies and negotiable instruments. The *Personal Property Security Act*, then, is intended to replace a number of confusing and complex statutes governing secured transactions by one all-encompassing and standardized *Act*.

Contract prevails

One of the primary objectives of the *Act* is to give effect to the contractual obligations entered into by the parties. Throughout this examination of the *Personal Property Security Act*, it is important to keep in mind that the rights and obligations set out in the original contractual agreement between the parties have priority. The method of creating a secured relationship under this statute is unique. The

---

[6] *Personal Property Security Act*, R.S.M. (1987) c.P-35; *Personal Property Security Act*, R.S.O. (1990) c.P.10; *Personal Property Security Act*, S.S. (1979-80) c.P-6.1.

security is created in three stages. First, the parties enter into the contractual agreement; second, the secured interest must **attach** to the collateral which has been identified to provide the security; and, third, the secured interest must be **perfected**. For attachment to take place, the parties must have performed or partially performed the contract. That is, if a person requiring a business loan makes an agreement with a bank to that effect and uses a car as collateral for the loan, that security does not attach until the debtor has actually received the money from the bank. The contractual agreement must state that a security arrangement has been created that gives the creditor a preferred position in relation to the collateral. These contracts usually take the form of the more traditional conditional sales, chattel mortgages or assignment of book accounts discussed above, but they need not be restricted in this way. The attachment process will give the secured party (the creditor, in this instance, the bank) certain rights and remedies in relationship to the car which has been used as security. But those rights and obligations apply only in the relationship between those two parties (creditors and debtor).

For the creditor to obtain priority or the assurance that he or she will be able to enforce that security against others, the secured transaction must be perfected. This perfection can be accomplished in one of two ways. The first is by registering the initial contractual agreement. The form of this agreement has been simplified into a standardized financing statement which sets out the terms of the agreement that created the security. In Ontario, when consumer goods are involved, the financing statement must give the amount owed, the date of maturity of the agreement and, when a motor vehicle is used as collateral, the make and the last two digits of the model year.

The second way the transaction can be perfected is by the creditor obtaining possession of the collateral used. The whole purpose of requiring registration is to provide a method whereby a third party will not be misled by the debtor when he or she is in possession of the collateral property. This, of course, is not a problem if the property used as collateral is in the possession of the creditor. Therefore registration is not required for perfection or to protect the rights of innocent third parties. In these circumstances, if more than one secured interest is perfected by registering different financing agreements against the same collateral, the priority between those secured parties is generally determined by the date registration takes place.

RIGHTS AND REMEDIES UPON DEFAULT. It must always be remembered that, when a default takes place, the normal common law remedies set out in the original contract are available. Only when the secured party enforces his or her rights in relationship to the collateral property do the provisions of the legislation come into play. Under the personal property security legislation, the creditor, in the event of default, has the right to take possession of those goods and have them disposed of (sold) for the amount owing. But, of course, these rights have to be set out in the original contract between the parties. As a general rule, once there has been a default, the secured party or creditor can take possession of those goods in any way that does not violate the law. When a conditional sales agreement is involved, the creditor can come onto the property of the debtor and seize possession of the chattels used as security, providing that no force is used. There are some restrictions, however, when consumer goods are involved. While the goods are in the possession of the creditor, "commercially reasonable" care must taken to protect the goods and keep them in good repair. If the goods require repair to sell them, such "commercially reasonable" expenses will be added to the amount the debtor owes. In British Columbia, the creditor cannot take possession of the goods without a court order if two-thirds of the debt has been paid off.

Retain the collateral

Once the creditor has taken possession of the goods, he or she can choose to retain the goods as satisfaction of the amount owed by the debtor, and end the debtor's obligation to the creditor and the relationship between them. The creditor makes this choice by serving notice on the debtor (and any other party with a registered interest) that the creditor intends to retain the goods. Once this notice is served, the debtor or any other interested party has fifteen days in which to respond, if any of those parties sends a notice of objection within that fifteen-day period, the creditor must dispose of the goods in the normal way within ninety days. If there is no such objection, the creditor can keep the property.

Where the creditor either does not or cannot elect to retain the goods, the creditor must dispose of (sell) the goods by private sale, public auction or in any other way. The only qualification is that the method used must be commercially reasonable. The secured party must follow certain requirements, the most significant of which is that fifteen days notice must be given to the debtor and other interested parties about the sale. The notice must describe the property, the amount owed, including any interest and reasonable expenses, and a statement that the debtor can redeem those goods by paying the amount due and that failure to do so will result in the property being sold and the debtor being responsible for any deficiency.

Creditor must take care of collateral in his or her possession

Obviously, the creditor must adhere to some stringent requirements after taking possession of the goods. He or she must take care of them and in the process of disposing of them must give proper notice. If he or she fails to do so and the goods are sold, the debtor will be able to turn to the secured creditor and sue for any losses the debtor has suffered. If the purchaser is an innocent third party who has given good value for the goods, that third party will still get good title to the goods. If the creditor has disposed of the goods properly and there is any surplus after repayment of the debt owing, expenses, legal fees, etc., that surplus must be paid over to the debtor. On the other hand, if there is a deficiency, that is, if the entire amount recovered is not enough to cover the amount due and owing, the creditor will be able to turn to the debtor for the recovery of that deficiency. Similarly, if the creditor does not properly look after the goods and fails to dispose of them in the prescribed manner, causing losses to the debtor, the debtor can recover those losses by suing the creditor for the damages suffered. It should be noted that, where consumer goods are involved, if the procedures are not properly followed, quite a penalty is imposed on the secured party (creditor). Not only can the debtor recover all of the service charges or cost of borrowing but also a portion of the principal paid (cash price paid for the goods). This is true even when the debtor has not suffered any damages. In British Columbia, when consumer goods are involved, the debtor has no obligation to pay for such a deficiency in any case.

Where personal property security legislation is in place and a person goes to a bank or credit union using a car as security, the security becomes attached to the car once the contract has been entered into and the monies advanced. The credit union then perfects the security by registering the contract (the financing statement) with a central registry. Thereafter, if the debtor tries to sell that car, the buyer may search the registry and should find the registered security against the vehicle. If the third party buys the car anyway, and there is a default, the creditor will be able to recover the vehicle even from an innocent third party. This is the essence of the creditor's security. Once there is a default, the credit union has the option of either pursuing its normal breach of contract remedies or taking possession of the vehicle. If it chooses the latter, it must keep the vehicle in good repair and thereafter can choose to dispose of the car (sell it) to recover the amount of money owing. But first notice of such disposition must be given to the debtor and any other interested parties so they have a chance to redeem it by paying off any money owing. Any surplus from the sale after paying off the principal, interest, legal fees, repair expenses, etc., will go to the debtor and in most cases any deficiency (shortfall) can be recovered from the debtor. Alternatively, the credit union can choose to retain the car by serving notice of its intention of so doing. If the credit union chooses this route, it can do whatever it wants with the car but the debtor's obligation ends. If there is a deficiency, the creditor will not be able to claim it against the debtor.

Floating Charges

Although a corporation is an artificial creation, it has the same rights and obligations as a person. A corporation can be either a creditor or a debtor in a secured transaction. As with an individual, the corporation can grant security to a creditor in all of the standard ways, such as a real estate mortgage, a guarantee, a lease, consignment, chattel mortgage, conditional sale, assignment of book accounts and so on. A

A debenture acknowledges debt

debenture is one form of security unique to corporations. A **debenture** is a document acknowledging debt that corporations often use to assume a debt obligation involving more than one creditor. Since the debenture is merely an acknowledgment of debt, it can take several forms and can be either secured or unsecured. A common practice is for corporations to secure a debenture through a **floating charge**. Typically, there will be a mortgage against the specific property and a floating charge as well. A floating charge is not fixed against any specific item or goods; rather the property of the corporation generally, such as inventory, is taken as security in such a way that the corporation can continue to deal with it. The company is free to purchase new goods and sell its inventory in the normal course of business as long as it is not in default of its agreement. The customers of such a firm take the goods they purchase free and clear of any incumbrance. It is only upon default or some other

Floating charge not fixed on goods until default

crystallizing event that the floating charge descends and attaches to the specific goods described in the debenture. The debenture document sets out the nature of the security and under what condition the floating charge becomes fixed. Such crystallizing events may include the making of an unauthorized payment, such as a dividend to the shareholders, or the sale of a valuable asset used as security, such as a factory, offices or other building owned by the debtor. If any other creditor manages to obtain a security fixed to the specific goods before the floating charge becomes fixed, the fixed charge will have priority. The real advantage of a floating charge is to give the creditor priority over general creditors. The advantage of the floating charge to corporations involved in manufacturing is that it allows them to use their work in process, inventory and other assets as security but does not interfere with their business. The requirement of registration is present with floating charges as well. Since the *Personal Property Security Act*s in place in various jurisdictions allow inventory and other changing assets to be used as security, in those jurisdictions the floating charge is of diminishing importance.

Bulk Sales

Creditors protected when merchant sells the bulk of business

Certain similarities exist between the protection given to secured creditors and the protection given to general or unsecured creditors in bulk sales transactions. A **bulk sale** involves a merchant selling all or almost all of a business's inventory, equipment or other assets in other than the ordinary course of business. For example, it is a bulk sale if Alberti owns a hardware store and sells not only all of its merchandise to Nystrom but some of the display tables as well. Such an action by a debtor is obviously inconsistent with continuing in business and means that assets that would have been available to satisfy the claims of creditors may have been taken beyond their reach. If Alberti has an unsecured creditor named Jamal, Jamal would expect to have a claim against the store's merchandise and fittings to satisfy the debt. But if they are sold to Nystrom there is nothing left for Jamal when Alberti defaults. Under common law, in these situations unsecured creditors might be left in the position of getting nothing.

Bulk Sales Acts regulate bulk sales activities

The western provinces have repealed their *Bulk Sales Acts* but all of the other common law provinces and the territories have in force bulk sales acts to protect general creditors. Although these statutes vary somewhat from province to province, they share a common objective. The *Bulk Sales Act* puts an obligation on the purchaser in a bulk sales transaction to ensure that the general creditors have first claim on the proceeds of the sale. The legislation also gives the creditors a say in the price paid for the goods to prevent the bulk seller from selling them at an unreasonably low price. The legislation requires that the purchaser demand from the bulk seller a list of all creditors who must be notified of the impending sale. The sale can take place if the creditors waive their rights under the legislation; the proceeds can then go directly to the bulk seller. If the creditors do not waive their rights but merely consent to the sale, the purchaser is obligated to give the proceeds of the sale to a trustee appointed by the creditors. The trustee will distribute the funds and any excess will go the bulk seller. It is not usually necessary for the consent to be unanimous. For instance, the *Ontario Act* requires the consent of only 60 percent of the creditors (calculated on the total amount owed and on the basis of the total number of creditors owed more than $50). Some jurisdictions also require that the purchaser register the bulk sale transaction. If the claims of the creditors are less than a certain amount, for example, $2500 in Ontario, the sale is exempted from the legislation. The exemption amount is greater if any creditor is secured.

When a purchaser fails to comply with the requirements set out in the bulk sales legislation of a particular province, the sale is void against the creditors. The creditors will be able to require from the purchaser the return of the goods or their value if they have been resold. Bulk sales legislation protects general creditors from merchants' abusive practices by putting the responsibility on the shoulders of the would-be purchaser. Their failure to comply with the requirements of the legislation puts the purchaser in the dangerous position of being required to account to the creditors for the value of the goods.

Other Legislation

Fraudulent
conveyance void

Other legislation has been enacted to protect creditors against frauds committed by debtors. Debtors are often tempted to hide property or otherwise protect it from the claims of creditors. Giving or selling property to a friend or relative to avoid the debt becomes a void transaction. The creditor can seek out the fraudulently transferred property and get it back from the purchaser. If the transfer is a proper sale from the point of view of the purchaser, that is, an arm's-length transaction in which the purchaser is unaware of any debts owing to the creditors and a fair price was paid, it is exempted from the legislation. In these circumstances, the third party is called a *bona fide* purchaser for value.

Fraudulent
preference void

Another way in which a debtor might attempt to cheat a creditor is by paying one creditor in preference over another. The unpaid creditor can challenge this type of fraudulent preference. Legislation embodying these provisions varies from province to province and there is some overlap with the federal bankruptcy legislation. The statutes embodying these provisions are called variously the *Fraudulent Conveyances Act*, *Fraudulent Preferences Act*, *Assignment and Preferences Act* and *Fraudulent Creditors Act*. This legislation is designed primarily to prevent debtors from unfairly making payments or transferring property in such a way as to keep it from the just claims of creditors.

GUARANTEES

Guarantor must
pay when debtor
defaults

Another method creditors use to ensure the repayment of a debt is the **guarantee**. The essential nature of a guarantee is that some third party assumes an obligation to ensure the debt is repaid. The borrower produces a relative, friend or business associate who is willing to take responsibility for the debt if the borrower defaults in the performance of the contractual obligation. When the third party agrees to be directly responsible for paying the debt or to indemnify the creditor for any loss, the liability is not a guarantee but a direct obligation, generally referred to as co-signing for a loan but more correctly as an **indemnity**.

Evidence in writing of guarantee required

The distinction, although subtle, can be important. As we discussed in Chapter 4, the *Statute of Frauds* requires that certain types of contracts be evidenced in writing to be enforceable in the courts. In most provinces, only the guarantee must be evidenced in writing. British Columbia requires that both indemnities and guarantees be evidenced in writing to be enforceable. Alberta requires that all guarantees be entered into in the presence of a notary public and a certificate to that effect must be produced.

Contractual requirements must be met for guarantor to be bound

Since a guarantee is a separate contract, all of the elements of a contract must be present. Sometimes the question arises as to whether the creditor has in fact accepted the guarantee. The creditor's performance of whatever act the guarantee was required for is usually sufficient indication of acceptance.

A related but often more contentious problem is the requirement that consideration be present. The consideration requirement is satisfied when it can be shown that the creditor has either done or refrained from doing something, such as advancing goods or money, or forbearing to take the remedies available to enforce an existing debt, in exchange for the guarantor's promise. There is little difficulty in identifying consideration if a merchant refrains from advancing the goods involved until the guarantee has been received. It is when the creditor extracts the guarantee after the subject matter of the contract has been delivered or the creditor's obligations under the contract have been performed that the question of consideration arises. If Kotsalis borrows money from the Business Bank and the manager of the bank asks for a guarantee after giving the money to Kotsalis, the requirement of consideration will probably not be satisfied. When a guarantor adds a seal to the document, this prevents any future claim by the guarantor that he or she is not bound because there was no consideration. As we discussed in Chapter 3, when a seal is present, consideration is conclusively presumed. Similarly, if the debtor is in default and a guarantee is obtained which persuades the creditor not to sue, there has been an appropriate exchange of consideration. That is, the creditor has refrained from suing.

Rights and Obligations of the Parties

Creditor must not weaken the position of the guarantor

Significant changes may release guarantor

Creditor can reserve rights against guarantor

The creditor has significant duties with a guarantee situation. The creditor is obligated to do nothing to weaken the position of the guarantor; therefore, the agreement must be strictly adhered to. Subsequent dealings between the creditor and debtor are the most common grounds for ending a guarantor's obligation. The principle is that any substantial change in the nature of the contract between the creditor and debtor without the guarantor's consent will relieve the guarantor of any obligation. If the creditor simply delays bringing an action to give a defaulting debtor a chance to pay, this will not be considered a substantial change in the relationship. But if, rather than simply being a gratuitous forbearance by the creditor, the change was entered into by agreement, the change in the agreement would be significant enough to relieve the obligations of the guarantor. However, when the creditor makes a specific statement reserving rights against the guarantor at the time of extending the repayment period, the guarantor will continue to be bound by the original agreement. When there has been no default but the creditor agrees to a different method of payment, imposes a higher rate of interest or changes the size of instalments, such changes can release the guarantor from obligation.

The guarantor is also released from obligation when other forms of security, such as chattel mortgages, are released. For example, if Kotsalis were to go to the Business Bank requesting a loan and the bank required that Bruno guarantee the loan in addition to taking a chattel mortgage against Kotsalis's car as security, such an arrangement would cease to be binding on Bruno if the bank subsequently allowed Kotsalis to sell the car. Similarly, Bruno would be released if the bank advanced Kotsalis more money or agreed to a change in the nature of the repayment terms without Bruno's consent. However, the guarantor is still bound if the agreement between the guarantor and the creditor permits such modification. Thus, a contract that allows the debtor to borrow more money continues to be binding on the guarantor even though the nature of the debt continually changes. This is called a continuing guarantee and will not release the guarantor unless the pre-arranged limit of funds is exceeded. Even when the guarantor does consent to such a change, he or she may not be bound. If the creditor is aware of special circumstances which, if known to the guarantor, would cause him or her to withhold consent to the change and the creditor fails to disclose this information to the guarantor, it can constitute misrepresentation and void the guarantee. This is what happened in the Skyhook case discussed at the beginning of the chapter. To be considered misrepresentation, the withheld information must be of some substantial and unusual nature and not simply the normal kind of information that would pass between business associates. In the Skyhook case, the information that the driving force behind the company, Calderbank, intended to start another company in competition was of such a significant and unusual nature as to void the guarantee.

When a default occurs, the creditor can turn to the guarantor for payment but the creditor usually first informs all the parties involved, giving them the opportunity to satisfy the obligations. When the debtor has put up some other form of security, such as a chattel mortgage on a car, the creditor is not normally obligated to seize the chattel before looking to the guarantor for payment, unless it has been

Guarantor assumes rights of creditor upon payment

otherwise agreed to in the contract. A guarantor who pays the debt is subrogated to the rights of the creditor which means, in effect, the guarantor steps into the creditor's shoes. Any remedy or right available to the creditor is thus available to the guarantor, including the right to seize a chattel used as security for the debt and to sue the debtor and take advantage of the proceedings available to assist in collecting the debt.

Defences of debtor are available to guarantor

Since the obligation of the guarantor is contingent upon default by the debtor, any defence available to the debtor is also available to the guarantor. If breach of contract, fraud or misrepresentation on the part of the creditor has barred an action by the creditor against the debtor, the creditor cannot then look to the guarantor for payment because the guarantor is entitled to the same defences as are available to the debtor.

BUILDERS' LIENS

A person who supplies goods or services that will be incorporated into another person's property faces two potentially significant problems in common law. First, if the contract is with the owner of the property who defaults on the agreement, the only course of action available to the supplier under common law is to sue. Even though the supplier's goods or services are incorporated into the property of the person with whom the contract was established, the supplier has no prior claim to recover the amount owed over the claim of any other general creditor. A second problem often facing the supplier of the goods or services is that there may not be a contract with the owner of the property at all. In the construction industry, for example, the owner of a property will often hire the services of a general contractor who will then enter into independent contracts with tradespeople and suppliers to complete the project. As discussed in Chapter 5, the principle of privity of contract establishes that, without such a direct contractual relationship, these suppliers have no claim against the owner of the property who benefits from their work. The subcontractors and wage earners must look to the general contractor for satisfaction.

Lien against property available to supplier of goods and services

To alleviate these difficulties the *Mechanics' Lien Acts*, the *Builders' Lien Acts* and, in Ontario, the *Construction Liens Act* were passed. The resulting liens are variously called mechanics' liens, builders' liens or construction liens. This text will use "builders' liens." The principle and object of the legislation is to create a lien in favour of the supplier of goods and services and against the property to which those goods and services have been supplied. This lien or charge is entirely a creation of the legislation and provides direct access to the property even when there is an intervening general contractor. It gives suppliers of goods and services priority in the event of insolvency or default on the part of the owner or contractor. It should be further noted that the people who can file liens and thus obtain security and priority against the property of the landowner are typically contractors, subcontractors, wage earners, suppliers of materials and, in some provinces, a lessor of equipment used on the project.

Lien must be registered within time specified

REGISTRATION. Failure to register a builder's lien within the time specified in the legislation is fatal to that lien. The time limits required for the registration vary from thirty days in New Brunswick and Newfoundland to sixty days in Prince Edward Island. Registration of the lien must take place within that time period after the goods have been supplied or the work has been substantially completed. In British Columbia, a subcontractor has an additional thirty-one days in which to register a builder's lien from the time the obligations of the general contractor are substantially performed or the whole project is completed. Thus, if a subcontractor does the foundation work on a building which takes a year to complete, he or she has thirty-one days after the whole project is finished in which to register a lien. Others, such as wage earners and suppliers of goods, must register within the specified time period from the date they supplied the service or goods. Although failure to register the lien within the appropriate time ends any claim the supplier of goods or services may have, the supplier of those goods or services still has access to general contract remedies.

Many provinces have created trust provisions in their legislation and some, such as Ontario, allow the lien to attach against either the property or the trust so created. In Ontario, the *Construction Liens Act* takes the same approach as the personal property security legislation. It provides that, when a contractor, subcontractor or supplier has supplied goods or services, that person has a lien against the property involved.[7] But, to take advantage of that lien, it must first be preserved and then perfected. The lien is preserved either by registering it at the local land registry office or by serving notice on the owner of the property, depending on whether the lien attaches to premises or not. Preservation must take place within forty-five days of the substantial completion of the job. Only when these procedures are followed does the lien claimant have a claim against the holdback discussed below. After the lien has been preserved, the claimant must take steps to have the lien perfected. In effect, the claimant must begin an action to enforce the lien. Although the terminology used is different in Ontario's *Construction Liens Act*, the results are essentially the same as in other provinces.

HOLDBACKS. It would cause significant hardship on property owners if suppliers of goods and services could use builders' liens to force them to pay whenever the suppliers did not receive proper payment from the general contractor. To eliminate the possibility of having to pay twice, the legislation requires that the owner of the land retain a certain percentage of the contract price in reserve to satisfy any builders'

Owner must hold back part of contract price

liens that may eventually be registered. This retained amount is called a **holdback** and the percentage that must be retained varies from a low of 10 percent to a high of 20 percent, depending on the province. This holdback must be retained for a specified period of time, from thirty days to sixty days in the various jurisdictions. The amount that must be retained in Ontario is 10 percent for forty-five days. The time the holdback must be retained equals or exceeds the period in which the builder's lien must be filed, which eliminates the possibility of a valid builder's lien being filed after the expiration of the holdback period. The owner is thus able to pay out the holdback amount at the end of the holdback period without incurring any risk. Although the total amount of claims in the form of builders' liens may exceed the total amount re-

Owner's liability limited to holdback

tained in a holdback, the owner cannot be required to pay more than has been held back as long as all of the provisions set out in the legislation have been followed and he or she has had no notice of disputes before making payments. The holdback provision in the legislation gives some protection to the builder's lien claimant and ensures that the owner of the property does not have to pay twice for the work done.

Many provinces have amended their legislation to require that a certificate of substantial completion be made when the job is finished; the times discussed here will run from the creation of that certificate. In Ontario, before the owner can pay out the holdback to the contractor, the lien must come to an end. This happens automatically if the lien has not been preserved or perfected within the specified periods. It can also come to an end when the claimant's action is dismissed, by payment into court of the monies claimed or when the claimant is paid what is owed.

[7] *Construction Liens Act*, S.O. (1983) c.6.

RIGHTS OF THE PARTIES. A person who has filed a properly registered builder's lien has the right to enforce it against the owner of the property in the event of default. The property owner's obligations are satisfied by the amount retained in the holdback for the time required by the legislation. In many provinces, if the owner receives notice of a registered builder's lien before making payments to the general contractor, the owner is required not to pay out further funds to the general contractor until the matter is settled, even if this amount exceeds the holdback percentage. In the event of a dispute, the owner of the property who has paid all of the funds owing to the general contractor except the holdback percentage or who has withheld an amount greater than the holdback percentage because there has been specific notice of a registered builder's lien should then pay that money into court so that the court can resolve the dispute. The owner of a property who ignores this obligation and pays directly to the general contractor assumes a considerable risk because he or she may also be required to pay the builders' lien claimants.

Liability may exceed holdback with notice of lien

If no builders' liens are registered within the statutory time specified, the owner of the property is free to pay the retained amount to the general contractor. If the owner of the property fails to make proper payments to the builders' lien claimants, the registration of the lien gives the claimant priority against the property. A person who holds a mortgage at the time of the creation of the builder's lien will retain a prior claim. But, if the registered mortgage is for funds, not all of which have been dispersed, the priority will only be for those funds already given to the owner before the registration of the builder's lien. Subsequent mortgagees or purchasers of the property will be subject to the builder's lien. As with other forms of registered security, the builder's lien gives the holder the right to have the property sold to satisfy the debt.

Lien creates priority over subsequent creditors

Because a builder's lien holder has priority over subsequent parties obtaining interest in the property, the filing of such a lien puts tremendous pressure on the owner of the property to have the lien removed by satisfying the lien claimant. Subsequent purchasers or mortgagees will be reluctant to deal with the property as long as the builder's lien is registered against it. However, the owner may not be able to pay disputed claims without incurring liability to the other claimants. Under these circumstances, the owner can pay the amount of the claim or holdback into court and ask the court to remove the lien. The court will do this because the lien has accomplished its purpose; the payment of valid claims is now assured because the funds are in the possession of the court. Using the court also prevents the frivolous or abusive use of builders' liens to tie up property and bring pressure to pay when it is not justified because the owner needs to pay only the disputed amount into court and ask that the property be freed from the lien. The owner is still free to dispute the claim of the builder's lien when the holder applies to the court for the money.

When claim is disputed, owner may make payment to court

The existence of the lien itself does not determine liability. The lien is merely a tool designed to help suppliers of goods and services enforce their rights when there has been a default. The lien holder must demonstrate through a civil action that the claim is justified. This prevents builders' liens from being used as a means of harassment or bluff. Most jurisdictions set a time limit in which an action must be brought, for example, 180 days in Alberta and ninety days in Ontario. The onus is on the builder's lien claimant to follow through with the claim and sue for payment.

Judgment must be obtained to execute lien

In British Columbia, the owner of the property has the right to send a letter to the builder's lien holder demanding that action be commenced within twenty-one days. Failure to do so means the claimant loses the protection of the lien. The owner is permitted to say to the lien holder in effect, "Put up or shut up."

Generally speaking, all lien holders or claimants are treated the same. When the amount available is less than the total amount of the claims, they share the loss equally, each being paid the same percentage of the amount of claim. In all common law provinces, wage earners have been given a priority over other builder's lien claimants, but this priority is limited to the wages earned in a specific time period. This period varies from thirty days to six weeks depending on the jurisdiction

Some claims may have priority

A supplier of goods and services who has not complied with the legislation loses the right to a builder's lien and reverts to the position of any other creditor. The supplier must sue the defaulting party for breach of contract. Several provinces, including British Columbia and Ontario, have declared that any funds paid to the general contractor by the owner constitute a trust fund with the suppliers of goods and services as beneficiaries of that trust. This decision is significant because it provides both civil and criminal remedies when the general contractor breaches that trust. It also protects these funds from any claims levied against the general contractor by other creditors who had nothing to do with the project for which funds were paid. Such outside creditors have no claim against the funds in the hands of the general contractor; because of this trust provision, they must be kept for the lien claimant. Only after the payment of all wage earners, subcontractors and suppliers will outside creditors receive payment from these funds.

Legislation prevents unjust enrichment

Some provinces (for example, Ontario) have taken this idea further and declared that "not yet paid" funds in the hands of the owner are a trust for the benefit of the lien claimants as well. The effect of the legislation is to prevent the owner of the property from unjustly benefiting from the goods and services which enhance the value of the property without paying for them. It should also be noted that similar legislation creates liens to the benefit of garage mechanics, appliance repairers, warehouse owners and so on.

BANKRUPTCY

While the bulk of this chapter is devoted to the position of a secured creditor, consideration must also be given to the position of an unsecured creditor. When the value of the security is not great enough to cover the debt, a secured creditor is an unsecured creditor for that outstanding amount. In these circumstances, the creditor is usually just one of many and must rely on the normal debt collection methods discussed in Chapter 1. The creditor may have the right, before judgment is obtained, to get an order to garnishee bank accounts and otherwise prevent the debtor from dissipating assets, but, in general, the creditor must proceed to judgment to recover the money owed by the debtor. After judgment, the creditor has many remedies available to enforce the judgment, including garnisheeing wages and having property of the debtor seized to satisfy the judgment, as discussed in Chapter 1. It must be emphasized, however, that there is considerable truth in the old adage that you can't get blood from a stone. If the debtor has no money, such procedures may only consume more of the creditor's resources without any substantial return. If the debtor owes more money than there are assets to recover, a real alternative is the process of bankruptcy.

Legislation has been created to provide a way in which debtors who are unable to pay off their debts can be forgiven of their obligations. The legislation saves a productive member of society from facing a lifelong burden of insurmountable debt. It also protects the interest of creditors and provides for the punishment of fraudulent debtors. The *Bankruptcy and Insolvency Act*[8] is a federal statute uniformly applicable throughout Canada. In 1992, it was the subject of significant amendment. It should be noted that some people and bodies are exempt from this legislation; banks, trust companies and railways, for example, are not covered by the *Bankruptcy Act*.

Bankruptcy must be distinguished from **insolvency**, which simply means that a person is unable to pay his or her debts. **Bankruptcy** is the process by which debtors convey their assets to a trustee in bankruptcy who then deals with them for the benefit of the creditors. When a debtor voluntarily assigns property to a trustee in bankruptcy, it is referred to as an **assignment**. Bankruptcy can also take place against the debtor's wishes. A creditor who is owed more than $1000 can petition the court to force the debtor into bankruptcy. The court grants a **receiving order** which results in the forceful transfer of the assets of the debtor to the trustee. This is a statutory assignment of the debtor's assets and includes any real property. This transfer ensures that the creditors will get paid at least some of what they are owed. It also ensures that any assets that do exist are preserved and distributed fairly among the creditors.

To obtain a receiving order, the creditor must show that the debtor has committed an act of bankruptcy. Significant acts of bankruptcy include the voluntary assignment of assets to a trustee in bankruptcy, fraudulent transfers of money or assets to keep them out of the hands of the trustee, a fraudulent preference given to one of the creditors, trying to leave the jurisdiction without paying debts and general insolvency.

The new *Bankruptcy Act* provides an alternative to bankruptcy. It allows the debtor to propose to the creditors another method for satisfying their claims. Two separate procedures are involved, depending on whether the insolvent debtor is a commercial or a consumer debtor. Commercial debtors, including under the new legislation corporations, are permitted to make a reorganization proposal to their creditors. This process has three stages. First the debtor files a notice of intention to file a reorganization proposal. Within ten days, the debtor must file a statement of projected cash flow and then, within thirty days, the reorganization proposal itself. This filing is followed by a meeting of the creditors who accept or reject the proposal. Two-thirds of the creditors by value and a majority by number must approve the proposal. If they do, all are bound by it, including secured creditors who have approved the proposal. If the creditors reject the proposal, the insolvent debtor is deemed to have made an assignment in bankruptcy from the day the notice of intention was filed and the normal bankruptcy procedures follow. The effect of filing the notice is to stop

Bankruptcy—to pay creditors and rehabilitate debtor

Assignment— voluntary transfer of assets to trustee

Receiving order— forceable transfer of assets to trustee

Commercial and consumer proposals— alternative to bankruptcy

[8] *Bankruptcy and Insolvency Act*, R.S.C. (1985) c.B-3, as amended by S.C. (1992) c.27

any creditors, including secured creditors who have not yet acted upon the security, from taking any action against the debtor at least until the date of the vote, about two months later. The time may be extended in some circumstances. In effect, for this two month period, the insolvent debtor is protected from the creditors. If the proposal is accepted by an appropriate number of them, that protection continues.

Consumer debtors are similarly protected when they make a consumer proposal. The insolvent debtor goes to a professional administrator who examines the debtor's finances, prepares the proposal and any reports required, and provides counselling for the debtor. With the administrator's help, the insolvent debtor files a consumer proposal which provides protection against unsecured creditors. With consumer proposals, an actual meeting of the creditors is not necessary. Creditors are given notice of the proposal and, if they do not demand a meeting, the proposal is deemed to be accepted by them. It is then up to the consumer to live up to the terms set out in the proposal. These terms must include a payment to the administrator at least once every three months; the administrator in turn must make payments to the creditors. As long as the debtor lives up to the terms of the proposal, action cannot be taken against him or her by unsecured creditors, public utilities, landlords, etc. But if the debtor defaults, the proposal is annulled and the debtor will then face the normal bankruptcy procedures.

Trustee distributes assets or proceeds of sales to creditors

Once the trustee has been given the assets of a bankrupt debtor, it is the trustee's responsibility to divide them so that all the creditors get a fair share. This task may not be easy because some of the creditors may be secured and others may be general creditors. Even in the case of bankruptcy, a secured creditor remains in a better position than the other creditors. Normally the trustee will sell the asset used as security and pay off the secured creditor. When there is a shortfall, the secured creditor becomes a general creditor for any outstanding amount. When the goods are sold for more than is owing, the excess will be paid out to the other creditors. When the trustee and the creditor agree on a value, the creditor may be permitted to take the item used as security for that value and become a general creditor for any shortfall.

Supplier of goods can reclaim

A significant change under the new *Act* is the position of a supplier of goods to a bankrupt. Previously, once such goods became part of the estate of the bankrupt, the seller simply became a general creditor for the purchase price and could not seek the return of the goods unless there was some added security arrangement. Under the new *Act*, such a supplier has the right to demand the return of the goods upon learning of the bankruptcy or receivership, provided this is within thirty days of delivery of those goods and the debtor or trustee still has them. The position of farmers, fishermen and aquaculturists is somewhat different because of the nature of the goods they supply. Crops and fish become commingled with those supplied by others and are no longer identifiable. In this case, the supplier becomes a secured creditor for the unpaid amount and has priority over all claims of other creditors, except the supplier of specific goods as discussed above, provided the products were delivered within fifteen days and the claim filed within thirty days of the bankruptcy.

The trustee must also evaluate the worth of each claim of the various creditors. If the trustee feels that a claim has no substance, the creditor will not share in the proceeds unless the creditor successfully challenges that decision in court. After the secured creditors have received what they are entitled to, the trustee distributes the remaining assets, or the proceeds from the sales of those assets, to the other creditors. There is a system of priority amongst these creditors, some claims being preferred over others. The following claims are paid in the order listed to the preferred creditors: funeral expenses, costs associated with the bankruptcy process, claims for arrears in wages for a limited amount and time period, municipal taxes, arrears in rent for a limited period, some direct costs incurred by creditors in the execution process, amounts owed to Workers' Compensation, Unemployment Insurance and Income Tax which should have been deducted from salaries, and other claims of the Crown. General creditors are paid only after these obligations have been met.

Priority Amongst Creditors

Fraudulent transfers and preferences prohibited

People going through bankruptcy often try to keep some of their property out of the hands of creditors by transferring it to friends or family as a gift or for a nominal amount. The trustee in bankruptcy can reverse these **fraudulent transfers** (or settlements as they are called in the *Act*). For example, if Kincaid transfers his house or his car to his wife's name to avoid creditors, this action will not prevent the trustee in bankruptcy from including the house or car in the assets available to the creditors. This transfer is classed as a settlement and is, therefore, void. People who become insolvent may choose to pay only one or two of their creditors because they expect to deal with them later or because they think that failure to pay those creditors will do them more harm. Showing preference to one creditor over another is unfair to the unpaid creditors and is classed as a **fraudulent preference**. Such a transaction would be void and the preferred creditor can be forced to return the goods or funds so that they are equally available to all the creditors. As part of the bankruptcy process, the debtor must file an affidavit setting out all debt, creditors and assets.

Limitations on undischarged bankrupts

The debtor is classified as an **undischarged bankrupt** once the assignment in bankruptcy has been made or a receiving order obtained. This status prohibits the bankrupt from borrowing over $500, and that amount only for necessaries, without disclosing the fact of the bankruptcy. A bankrupt is also not permitted to sit on the board of directors of any corporation. Failure to comply with these provisions can lead to imprisonment. Once the bankrupt has gone through the entire process and the creditors have received all they can from the assets, the bankrupt is in a position to be discharged from the bankruptcy. The court may issue an order discharging the bankrupt if it is satisfied that the request is appropriate. When an individual is involved, the bankruptcy procedure contains an automatic application for discharge. When it is the first bankruptcy, that discharge is generally automatic.

Eventually a bankrupt may be discharged

Upon discharge, the debtor is freed from all previous claims by creditors and is in a position to start over. Any assets subsequently obtained by the discharged bankrupts are theirs to do with as they wish and unpaid creditors cannot claim against them. Some obligations survive the discharge. For example, debtors who have been ordered to pay maintenance for dependants will continue to bear that obligation even after being discharged from bankruptcy. Similarly, any fines resulting from the conviction of an offence are still owing.

Discharge not granted if bankruptcy offence committed

Debtors who commit bankruptcy offences are liable to be imprisoned. The court will not discharge a bankrupt who has committed such an offence. In addition to settlements such as fraudulent preferences and fraudulent transfers, the *Bankruptcy Act* sets out several other bankruptcy offences: lying while under examination by the trustee in bankruptcy, hiding or concealing property, misleading or falsifying records, or otherwise trying to cheat the creditor. The court will also be reluctant to discharge bankrupts who have paid creditors less than 50 cents on the dollar. Under such circumstances, the court can put conditions or restrictions on the bankrupt, granting only a conditional discharge.

Bankrupt corporations are dissolved

Bankruptcy proceedings also apply to corporations but, unless the corporation can pay back the full amount owed or has completed the "proposal" process outlined above, it cannot receive a discharge for the bankruptcy. Instead, it faces dissolution. It should be noted that other statutes, both federal and provincial, such as the *Winding Up Act*, *Company Creditor's Arrangement Act*, *Bulk Sale Act* and *Mechanics' Lien Act*, are available to disgruntled shareholders and creditors of corporations.

Receivership may be based on contract

Corporations that go into **receivership** are often not involved in bankruptcy at all. When a corporation borrows significant funds from a lender, the creditor will usually set out certain terms in the agreement which will trigger a provision that allows the creditor to appoint a receiver to take over the business without going through the bankruptcy procedure if the provisions of the agreement are not met. Such an assignment of assets to a receiver is not actually a bankruptcy, but the effect can be every bit as devastating to the business. The rights of creditors to appoint such receivers have been limited to some extent by the recent revisions to the *Bankruptcy and Insolvency Act* discussed above.

Orderly payment of debt set out in legislation

Legislation also exists to assist in the orderly payment of debt. If the account owed is less than $1000 or if the debtor obtains the consent of the creditors, the debtor can make arrangements to consolidate all of the debts and pay all of the creditors back at one rate with one payment. Government agencies available to assist in this process can be helpful for both the debtor and the creditor. It must be remembered that the creditor is in the business of making money, not destroying the debtor. If the debtor cannot pay, the creditor gains nothing by harassment. The two main purposes of the *Bankruptcy and Insolvency Act* and the other legislation discussed in this chapter are to ensure that the creditor realizes as much of the amount owed as possible and to rehabilitate the debtor. The legislation also provides punishment for fraudulent activities by the debtor and provides a uniform system of laws throughout Canada. The idea is to restore the debtor as a productive working member of the community as soon as possible.

SUMMARY

Security involves giving the creditor some assurance that he or she will be paid even when other creditors are not. With a conditional sales agreement, the creditor retains title while giving the debtor possession of the goods. With a chattel mortgage, the debtor gives up title to the creditor while keeping possession. In both cases, in the event of default, the creditor may retake the goods. Assignment of book accounts can also be used as security. In many provinces, the statutes controlling these traditional approaches have been replaced by the *Personal Property Security Act* which allows both chattels and intangible forms of personal property to be used as security. The security must first attach but the priority is usually established by perfection (involving registration or taking possession of the property). In the event of default, the creditor can retake the goods and resell them and/or sue for the debt. In some situations, the creditor must choose one or the other but cannot do both. A floating charge allows a debtor to bring new goods into the security group and dispose of others out of it. It is only with default that the charge attaches and prevents further dealing with the goods.

A guarantee is a contingent liability in which someone agrees to be responsible when a debtor fails to pay. An indemnity involves a co-responsibility for the debt. If a guarantor pays the creditor, he or she steps into the shoes of the creditor and can seek redress from the debtor.

A builders' lien gives the supplier of services or materials (when not paid) the right to register a lien against the building in which the materials or services were used. The owner of the property, when paying the general contractor, must hold back a certain amount to make sure all debts are paid.

Bankruptcy can take place voluntarily through assignment or involuntarily through a receiving order. It involves the transfer of the debtor's assets to a trustee in bankruptcy who sells the assets and distributes the proceeds to the creditors. The debtor, after meeting certain qualifications, can apply to be discharged. Discharge relieves responsibility for these prior debts.

QUESTIONS

1. Distinguish between the following:
   a) a chattel mortgage and a mortgage on real estate;
   b) a chattel mortgage and a conditional sale;
   c) real property and personal property;
   d) a chose in action and a chattel;
   e) a conditional sale agreement and a hire purchase agreement.
2. What significant problem associated with the practice of taking goods as security is alleviated by the registration requirements introduced by legislation? Describe the resulting obligations on all parties.
3. What obligations are imposed on the secured creditor who retakes goods used as security when a debtor defaults?
4. Explain the rights and obligations of all parties when a secured transaction agreement is assigned to a third party.

5. Why is the security allowed banks under the *Bank Act* significantly different from other forms of secured transactions? How are the registration requirements different?

6. In what ways was the passage of the *Personal Property Security Act* in several provinces such a significant departure from the traditional treatment of secured transactions?

7. Distinguish between the security contract, the attachment and the perfection, and explain the significance of each step.

8. Where personal property security legislation is in place, how is a security perfected and what is the significance of such a perfection?

9. In the event of a default, explain what the rights of a secured party are and what limitations there are on those rights.

10. Explain the difference between retention and disposal on the part of the secured party in the event of default and explain the procedure and limitations associated with each alternative.

11. What kinds of property can be used as collateral under personal property security legislation?

12. Explain the rights of debtors after they have defaulted and the secured party has taken possession of the collateral.

13. What happens upon default when a floating charge has been used to secure a debt? How does this form of security affect the priorities between types of creditors?

14. Explain how the *Bulk Sales Act* protects a merchant's unsecured creditors. Summarize the obligations of all the parties.

15. Explain the position of the secured creditor in relation to the debtor and other creditors in the following situations in which assets have been used as security. Indicate provincial variations in your response.
    a) The amount still owing to the secured creditor is less than the value of the asset used as security.
    b) The amount still owing to the secured creditor is greater than the value used as security.

16. What obligations does the guarantor of another person's debt incur? What protection is available to guarantors in subsequent dealings between the creditor and debtor?

17. When a debtor defaults on a loan and the guarantor is required to pay, what rights does the guarantor have in relation to the debtor?

18. What significant difficulty facing the supplier of goods and services in the construction industry is overcome by the creation of the mechanic's or builder's lien? Include an explanation of the significance of the declaration that any money paid by the owner to the contractor is held in trust.

19. What remedies are available to a supplier of goods and services who has filed a builder's lien?

20. How is the claimant's position affected when the lien has not been properly registered?

21. Define the objectives of bankruptcy legislation and explain how these objectives are accomplished. Explain what role the process of discharge and the function of the trustee in bankruptcy have in the realization of these goals.

CASES

1. *Royal Bank of Canada v. J. Segreto. Construction Ltd. et al.*
   The debtors were two corporations that had executed promissory notes with the assets of the corporations used as collateral security for the loan. When they defaulted, the Royal Bank seized the security and resold it without notifying the debtors that they were doing so. The Royal Bank is suing for the deficit, the shortfall between what was owed and what was realized from the sale of the assets. Explain the arguments that the bank and the debtors would present to support their relative positions. Would your answer be affected by the knowledge that nothing in the original security agreement (the promissory notes) indicated a right to sue for a deficit? Or that the relevant section in the *Personal Property Security Act* was not complied with? This section requires that notice be given to the debtor before resale stating that, unless the amounts due are repaid, the collateral will be disposed of and the debtor may be liable for any deficiency.

2. *Boehmers v. 794561 Ontario Inc.*
   The numbered company, 794561, was a general contractor building a series of townhouses for the property owner. This contractor defaulted in its payments to subcontractors, and several liens were registered against the property. Royal Life was a creditor with a secured mortgage against the property for $3 895 000. Of this money, $1 606 586 had been advanced before the first liens were registered. Subsequent to the registration and perfection of those liens, Royal Life made a further series of advances, bringing the amount up to the $3 895 000 total. In these circumstances, explain the priority of creditors (the secured mortgagee or the lien claimants) in relationship to the property and any funds available.

3. *First City Capital Ltd. v. Hall et al.*
   Karsha Holdings Ltd. was a company whose sole shareholders and officers were Hall and deHaan. When the company needed word processing equipment, it went to First City Capital where it borrowed a considerable amount of money to buy the equipment. First City Capital required a personal guarantee for the funds to secure this equipment. The equipment was purchased through seven lease arrangements. A few years later, Hall sold her interest in Karsha

Holdings to deHaan. Shortly after that, Karsha Holdings defaulted on its payments to First City Capital for the seven leases as well as on a separate indebtedness to the Royal Bank of Canada. This indebtedness was also secured against the assets of the corporation. First City Capital had failed to perfect the security arrangements with Karsha Holdings (the seven leases), which it should have done by registration, and the Royal Bank had perfected its interest. The Royal Bank, therefore, seized the word processing equipment and First City Capital turned to Hall on the personal guarantee for payment. Explain the legal position of Hall in these circumstances and what arguments she could raise in her defence. How would your answer be affected by the knowledge that a term in the personal guarantee with First City stated that Hall would be required to pay "notwithstanding that the lease or any other arrangements shall be void or voidable against the lessee...including...by reason...of...failure by any person to file any document or take any other action to make the lease...enforceable"?

4. *Red Deer College v. W.W. Construction, Lethbridge, Ltd.*
   Red Deer College owned property and hired W.W. Construction as the general contractor to complete certain buildings on that property. W.W. Construction then hired several subtrades to continue with the work. A number of liens were registered against the project and Red Deer College held back not only the 15 percent required by law but also refused to pay out any further money to the defendant. The defendant then failed to complete the project and abandoned it. Red Deer College had to get other people to finish the job. In this action, W.W. Construction claimed for money owed less the 15 percent holdback. Explain the legal obligations of Red Deer College.

5. *Jaron Construction Ltd. v. McNeil et al.*
   The owner of a construction project properly held back the appropriate amount from a general contractor who subsequently abandoned the project. The owner then completed the project himself but at considerably increased cost which he deducted from the amount of holdback he had retained. When the subcontractors hired by the general contractor who had abandoned the project registered their mechanics' liens, only this reduced amount of the holdback was made available to them. They sued the owner, claiming the entire amount of holdback. Explain the rights of the parties involved. If the owner had neglected to hold back any funds, how would this have affected your answer?

6. *Finning Tractor and Equipment Company Limited v. Mee.*
   In April, 1976, Morrill and Sturgeon Lumber Company signed a conditional sales agreement with Finning Tractor to purchase a new caterpillar wheel loader. The agreement was guaranteed by Mee. The purchaser defaulted after some payments were made. Finning chose to seek payment from the guarantor instead of seizing the tractor under the conditional sales agreement.

Explain the liability of the guarantor in these circumstances. Would your answer be any different if you learned that Finning had neglected to register the conditional sales agreement and therefore had lost its priority against other secured creditors?

7. Re *Bank of Montreal and International Polyeurothane Company Ltd.*
International Polyeurothane entered into a thirty-month lease with a landlord. Subsequently, they acquired goods to be used at the premises and granted the Bank of Montreal a chattel mortgage covering the items. The company became insolvent and the landlord had the sheriff seize these goods for unpaid rent. The municipality issued a similar order for unpaid taxes as did the Workers' Compensation Board for an overdue assessment. Explain how these claims would affect the right of the Bank of Montreal to repossess the goods under their chattel mortgage security. Set out the priorities between the parties.

ISSUES

1. The practice of taking a property as security accomplishes two goals for the creditor: it ensures that there is something of sufficient value to cover the debt and that the creditor will have priority over any other creditors, at least to the value of the asset used as security. This arrangement can appear quite unjust to the other creditors who have to share what is left. Although the requirement of registration goes some way towards correcting this problem, it can be argued that the practice of taking security is just an assurance that one group of creditors will have an unfair advantage over another. Should one creditor be able to gain ascendancy over the others in this way? In your answer, consider whether the registration requirements introduced by legislation provide adequate protection to unsecured creditors.

2. In most instances, the practice of taking various forms of property as security for debt depends on being able to separate the possession of property from the title to that property. This separation of title and possession, however, makes it possible for the debtor to mislead an innocent third party into thinking that the possessor of the goods is legally able to sell them. In effect, the creditor has provided the opportunity to cheat this innocent third party. Considerable benefits are gained by the process of separation of title and possession but in your discussion consider whether the disadvantages outweigh any benefits.

3. A builder's lien is an artificial device created by statute. It allows the suppliers of goods and services to impose considerable obligations and risk on

a property owner with whom they may have had no direct dealings because their contracts were with the general contractor. The process of filing the lien can also result in the filer of the lien acquiring a prior claim over the other creditors which can tie up the title to the property and hamper any possible sale. The question for discussion is: Is it fair for the owner of the property to be subject to such an intrusion into traditional property rights? Would it not be more appropriate for the suppliers of goods and services to look only to the general contractor they dealt with for satisfaction of their claims? Are holdbacks and other registration provisions enough to overcome these objections?

4. Generally, creditors must proceed to judgment to collect the amount due from debtors who refuse to pay. This process can be quite expensive and the cost will often persuade a person with a legitimate claim not to sue. From this dilemma arises the allegation that our system of civil justice favours the wealthy and is inequitable and prejudicial. Discuss the validity of this allegation. Consider not only the factors that make the process expensive and risky but also any steps that have been taken to overcome the problem.

5. Discuss the development of the principle of unconscionable transactions and whether or not this principle should be expanded to more effectively protect people who are liable to be taken advantage of. Some have argued that, through the principle of unconscionable transactions, the common law and statutory provisions designed to protect people at a disadvantage in a contractual bargaining situation could be eliminated. Discuss the viability of this concept. Consider the role of this principle in consumer transactions.

LEGISLATION

Alberta
Builders' Lien Act, R.S.A. (1980) c.B-12 (as amended S.A. (1985) c.14)
Civil Service Garnishee Act, R.S.A. (1980) c.C-11
Collection Practices Act, R.S.A. (1980) c.C-17
Debtors' Assistance Act, R.S.A. (1980) c.D-5
Department of Consumer and Corporate Affairs Act, R.S.A. (1980) c.D-14
Execution Creditors Act, R.S.A. (1980) c.E-14
Fraudulent Preferences Act, R.S.A. (1980) c.F-18
Garagemen's Lien Act, R.S.A. (1980) c.G-1
Guarantees Acknowledgement Act, R.S.A. (1980) c.G-12
Personal Property Security Act, R.S.A. (1988) c.P-4.05
Possessory Liens Act, R.S.A. (1980) c.P-13
Seizures Act, R.S.A. (1980) c.S-11
Threshers' Lien Act, R.S.A. (1980) c.T-4

Wage Assignments Act, R.S.A. (1980) c.W-1
Warehousemen's Lien Act, R.S.A. (1980) c.W-3
Woodmen's Lien Act, R.S.A. (1980) c.W-14

British Columbia
Builders' Lien Act, R.S,B.C. (1979) c.40
Court Order Enforcement Act, R.S.B.C. (1979) c.75
Court Order Interest Act, R.S.B.C. (1979) c.76
Creditor Assistance Act, R.S.B.C. (1979) c.80
Debt Collection Act, R.S.B.C. (1979) c.88
Debtor Assistance Act, R.S.B.C. (1979) c.89
Fraudulent Conveyance Act, R.S.B.C. (1979) c.142
Fraudulent Preference Act, R.S.B.C. (1979) c.143
Repairers' Lien Act, R.S.B.C. (1979) c.363
Warehouse Lien Act, R.S.B.C. (1979) c.427
Woodworkers' Lien Act, R.S.B.C. (1979) c.436

Manitoba
Builders' Lien Act, R.S.M. (1987) c.B-91
Distress Act, R.S.M. (1987) c.D-90
Executions Act, R.S.M. (1987) c.E-160
Fraudulent Conveyances Act, R.S.M. (1987) c.F-160
Garnishment Act, R.S.M. (1987) c.G-20
Guarantors' Liability Act, R.S.M. (1987) c.G-120
Judgments Act, R.S.M. (1987) c.J-10
Personal Property Security Act, R.S.M. (1987) c.P-35
Sheriffs' Act, R.S.M. (1987) c.S-100
Threshers' Lien Act, R.S.M. (1987) c.T-60
Warehousemen's Lien Act, R.S.M. (1987) c.W-20
Woodmen's Lien Act, R.S.M. (1987) c.W-190

New Brunswick
Absconding Debtors Act, R.S.N.B. (1973) c.A-2
Assignment of Book Debts Act, R.S.N.B. (1973) c.A-14
Assignments and Preferences Act, R.S.N.B. (1973) c.A-16
Bills of Sale Act, R.S.N.B. (1973) c.B-3
Bulk Sales Act, R.S.N.B. (1973) c.B-9
Conditional Sales Act, R.S.N.B. (1973) c.C-15
Creditors Relief Act, R.S.N.B. (1973) c.C-33
Liens on Goods and Chattels Act, R.S.N.B. (1973) c.L-6
Mechanics' Lien Act, R.S.N.B. (1973) c.M-6
Wage Earners' Protection Act, R.S.N.B. (1973) c.W-1

Warehousemen's Lien Act, R.S.N.B. (1973) c.W-4
Woodmen's Lien Act, R.S.N.B. (1973) c.W-12

Newfoundland
Assignment of Book Debts Act, R.S.N. (1990) c.15
Assignment of Wages Act, R.S.N. (1990) c.16
Bulk Sales Act, R.S.N. (1990) c.B-11
Conditional Sales Act, R.S.N. (1990) c.C-28
Fraudulent Conveyances Act, R.S.N. (1990) c.F-24
Limitation of Personal Actions Act, R.S.N. (1990) c.L-15
Mechanics' Lien Act, R.S.N. (1990) c.M-3
Mortgage Brokers' Act, R.S.N. (1990) c.M-18
Public Officials' Garnishee Act, R.S.N. (1990) c.P-41
Warehousers' Lien Act, R.S.N. (1990) c.W-2

Nova Scotia
Assignment of Book Debts Act, R.S.N.S. (1989) c.24
Assignment of Preferences Act, R.S.N.S. (1989) c.25
Bills of Sale Act, R.S.N.S. (1989) c.39
Bulk Sales Act, R.S.N.S. (1989) c.48
Collection Act, R.S.N.S. (1989) c.76
Conditional Sales Act, R.S.N.S. (1989) c.84
Creditors' Relief Act, R.S.N.S. (1989) c.112
Indigent Debtor Act, R.S.N.S. (1989) c.220
Mechanics' Lien Act, R.S.N.S. (1989) c.277
Sheriffs' Act, R.S.N.S. (1989) c.426
Warehousemen's Lien Act, R.S.N.S. (1989) c.499

Ontario
Absconding Debtor Act, R.S.O. (1990) c.A.2
Assignments and Preferences Act, R.S.O. (1990) c.A.33
Bailiffs' Act, R.S.O. (1990) c.B.2
Bulk Sales Act, R.S.O. (1990) c.B.14
Construction Lien Act, R.S.O. (1990) c.C.30
Costs of Distress Act, R.S.O. (1990) c.C.41
Creditors' Relief Act, R.S.O. (1990) c.C.45
Debt Collectors' Act, R.S.O. (1990) c.D.4
Execution Act, R.S.O. (1990) c.E.24
Fraudulent Conveyances Act, R.S.O. (1990) c.F.29
Fraudulent Debtors Arrest Act, R.S.O. (1990) c.F.30
Guarantee Companies Securities Act, R.S.O. (1990) c.G.11
Pawnbrokers' Act, R.S.O. (1990) c.P.6

Personal Property Security Act, R.S.O. (1990) c.P.10
Wages Act, R.S.O. (1990) c.W.1

Prince Edward Island
Assignment of Book Debts Act, R.S.P.E.I. (1988) c.A-22
Bills of Sale Act, R.S.P.E.I. (1988) c.B-3
Bulk Sales Act, R.S.P.E.I. (1988) c.B-6
Conditional Sales Act, R.S.P.E.I. (1988) c.C-15
Frauds on Creditors Act, R.S.P.E.I. (1988) c.F-15
Garage Keepers' Lien Act, R.S.P.E.I. (1988) c.G-1
Garnishee Act, R.S.P.E.I. (1988) c.G-2
Judgment and Execution Act, R.S.P.E.I. (1988) c.J-2
Mechanics' Lien Act, R.S.P.E.I. (1988) c.M-4
Personal Property Security Act, S.P.E.I. (1990) c.42 (Not proclaimed as of Jan. 1, 1994)
Sheriffs' Act, S.P.E.I. (1990) c.60
Warehousemen's Lien Act, R.S.P.E.I. (1988) c.W-1

Québec
Bailiffs Act, R.S.Q. (1977) c.H-4

Saskatchewan
Absconding Debtor Act, R.S.S. (1978) c.A-2
Assignment of Wages Act, R.S.S. (1978) c.A-30
Attachments of Debts Act, R.S.S. (1978) c.A-32
Builders' Lien Act, S.S. (1984-85-86) c.B-7.1
Building Trades Protection Act, R.S.S. (1978) c.B-8
Choses in Action Act, R.S.S. (1978) c.C-11
Close Out Sales Act, R.S.S. (1978) c.C-13
Collection Agents Act, R.S.S. (1978) c.C-15
Creditors' Relief Act, R.S.S. (1978) c.C-46
Distress Act, R.S.S. (1978) c.D-31
Executions Act, R.S.S. (1978) c.E.12
Fraudulent Preferences Act, R.S.S. (1978) c.F-21
Judges' Order Enforcement Act, R.S.S. (1978) c.J-12
Personal Property Security Act, S.S. (1979-80) c.P-6.1
Sale on Consignment Act, R.S.S. (1978) c.S-4
Threshers' Lien Act, R.S.S. (1978) c.T-13
Warehousemen's Lien Act, R.S.S. (1978) c.W-3
Woodmen's Lien Act, R.S.S. (1978) c.W-16

Northwest Territories
Assignment of Book Debts Act, R.S.N.W.T. (1988) c.A-T

Bills of Sale Act, R.S.N.W.T. (1988) c. B-1
Choses in Action Act, R.S.N.W.T. (1988) c.C-7
Conditional Sales Act, R.S.N.W.T. (1988) c. C-14
Creditors' Relief Act, R.S.N.W.T. (1988) c. C-24
Garagekeepers' Lien Act, R.S.N.W.T. (1988) c. G-1
Miners' Lien Act, R.S.N.W.T. (1988) c. M-12
Warehousekeepers' Lien Act, R.S.N.W.T. (1988) c. W-2

Yukon
Bulk Sales Act, R.S.Y (1986) c.14
Collections Act, R.S.Y (1986) c.26
Creditors' Relief Act, R.S.Y (1986) c.38
Fraudulent Preferences and Conveyances Act, R.S.Y (1986) c.72
Garnishee Act, R.S.Y (1986) c.78
Mechanics' Lien Act, R.S.Y (1986) c.176
Personal Property Security Act, R.S.Y (1986) c.130
Warehouse Keepers' Lien Act, R.S.Y (1986) c.176

Federal
Bankruptcy and Insolvency Act, R.S.C. (1985) (See Amendment S.C. (1992) c.27)
Companies' Creditors Arrangements Act, R.S.C. (1985) c.C-36
Garnishment, Attachment and Pension Diversion Act, R.S.C. (1985) c.G-2
Wages Liability Act, R.S.C. (1985) c.W-1

9 EMPLOYMENT

Objectives of the Chapter

▪ to distinguish between employees and contractors

▪ to review the laws concerning employment relationships

▪ to describe the requirements for collective bargaining and trade union action

Jack Gibson was 67 when he was hired by a food distribution company on a two-year contract which included $3000 a month, car expenses and a membership at an exclusive golf and country club. As the sales manager, he was required to supervise other sales staff, and telephone and visit various supermarkets in the area to see that they were properly stocked with the company's products. His employer went away for two months and, when he returned, he discovered that certain stores were not properly stocked and that the company had lost the account of a major customer. When asked about this, Gibson told his employer that stores were being regularly called, visited and serviced. The employer doubted this and hired a private detective to follow Gibson. From the reports of the detective, the employer learned that Gibson regularly visited the golf club. He called the sales manager back into his office and asked specifically how many calls had been made during the surveillance period. When Gibson responded with "fifty," the employer presented him with the detective's report and challenged him on the information. Gibson then admitted that he had not made the calls because of health problems. Gibson went on vacation for a while and on his return was

> fired. He sued for wrongful dismissal. The court said that, while Gibson's failure to perform his duties may have supported his dismissal, it was his dishonesty that caused a fundamental breach of the employment contract.[1]

A contract for employment is one of the most important in which a person will become involved. The following chapter is devoted to exploring the different legal ramifications of the employment relationship.

Not all work is employment

Employment law deals with business relationships in which one person works for another. But not all work done by one person for another is classed as employment. When someone acquires the services of a plumber to fix a faucet, a doctor to diagnose and treat an illness or a lawyer to draw up a will, the plumber, doctor and lawyer are performing services on behalf of the person paying them but they are not normally employees. The relationship is based on contract, not on an employment contract, and the person doing the job or providing the service is called an independent contractor. Usually it is when someone works for another regularly that an employment arrangement results. Even then, if the person is paid by the job or by commission, it is sometimes difficult to determine where the independent contractor relationship ends and employment begins. The third category in business relationships is called agency and will be discussed in detail in the following chapter. Each of these relationships imposes different legal rights and obligations on the parties; understanding which body of rights governs a particular relationship can be of vital importance.

WHAT IS EMPLOYMENT?

THE CONTROL TEST. The traditional method of determining whether or not an employment relationship exists is to assess the degree of control exercised by the person paying for the service. A person who is told not only what to do but how to do it is classed as an employee. But if the person doing the work is free to decide how the job should be done, the position is that of an independent contractor. For example, if Fong hires Kirk to paint a house, Kirk could be either an independent contractor or an employee. If Fong tells Kirk what tools to use, when to work and how to perform the job, then Kirk is an employee. If Kirk supplies the tools, and determines what time to start work and the best way to perform the job, then Kirk is probably an independent contractor. Whether the person is paid a wage or salary or is paid by the job is also taken into consideration in determining employment. The employment relationship involves a contract in which the person being hired agrees generally to

Employee controlled by employer

---

[1] *The Lawyers Weekly*, Nov. 6, 1987, p.6

Independent
contractor works
independently

Organization test
substituted for
control test

Definition of
employment
broadened

An employee can
be an agent

An agent can be
independent

serve the employer. That is, the person acquiring that service has the right to supervise and direct. On the other hand, an independent contractor is entering into a contract to do a particular job and does not contract to serve the other person. In other words, employees work for their employer whereas independent contractors work for themselves.

THE ORGANIZATION TEST. In recent years, the courts have supplemented the control test with the organization test. This test involves deciding whether the person to be designated an employee can be said to be part of the employer's organization. If the person is part of the employer's organization and subject to group control, then that person is considered an employee.[2] Mr. Justice Spence, when voicing a majority decision for the Supreme Court of Canada in *Cooperators Insurance Association v. Kearney*,[3] adopted the organizational test as put forward by Fleming. He indicated that there are many situations in which a person might be an independent contractor for most purposes but could still be a servant in some specific instances.[4] This ruling has prompted the courts to find employment relationships in areas which were traditionally considered purely independent. A person can now be determined to be a servant when engaging in one activity although the general relationship remains that of an independent contractor. Many statutes contain a definition of employment but it is important to note that the definition is valid only for the purposes of the legislation. There is no general legislated definition of an employee.

There is a great temptation to think of the three categories of business relationships as mutually exclusive. People often make the mistake of assuming that a person who is an employee cannot also be an agent. It may be generally true that a person cannot be an employee and an independent contractor at the same time for the same employer, but that is not so with an agent. An **agent** is someone who enters into legal relationships with others on behalf of a principal. It is important to realize that nothing prevents a person from being both an agent and an employee at the same time. A common example of an employee acting as an agent is a clerk in a store. Although the customer deals with the clerk, the sales contract that results is between the clerk's employer and the customer; the clerk merely functions as an agent for the principal. It is also possible for an independent contractor to act as an agent for the principal. Even though the employer/employee relationship is distinctly different from the relationship between an independent contractor and the other party to the contract, an agent can fall into either category. It does not necessarily follow that all employees are agents, just those who enter into contractual relationships on behalf of their principals. A checkout clerk at a grocery store is both an employee and an agent but the person packing the groceries is generally only an employee. These distinctions are important because the liability of the parties is determined by which of these relationships exists. If an individual qualifies as an employee, not only will the employer's liability for the employee's wrongful conduct

[2] Fleming, John G., *The Law of Torts*, (8th ed.), The Law Book Co. Ltd., Australia (1992), p.372.
[3] *Cooperators Insurance Association v. Kearney*, (1965) 48 D.L.R. (2d).l.
[4] *Ibid.*, p. 21.

be greater than for an independent contractor but the legislation providing protection, rights and benefits to employees will also apply. If an agency relationship exists, the agent's actions in creating new legal relationships will probably be binding on the principal.

The legal principles governing the independent contractor are embodied in the general rules of contract law already covered in Chapters 3 to 6. This chapter will examine the law of master and servant, the federal and provincial legislation, the trade union movement and collective bargaining. The law of agency will be discussed in the following chapter.

THE LAW OF MASTER AND SERVANT

The employment or master/servant relationship is governed by the general provisions of contract law. The common law courts have developed special rules to deal with employment problems and have outlined the responsibilities and obligations the parties have towards one another. The main responsibility of the employer is to provide a safe workplace and good working conditions for the employee. The employee is entitled to leave the job when conditions are dangerous, such as open or unprotected shafts. It is not enough that the employee dislikes the conditions; the danger must be real in the eyes of a reasonable person. Some types of jobs, such as construction, involve a certain amount of inherent danger and the employer's obligation in these circumstances is to take reasonable steps to minimize that danger. This duty requires not only the erection of protective fences and the supplying of appropriate safety equipment but also extends to hiring competent people. If the employer knowingly hires a careless or improperly trained person who causes an accident which injures another employee or some other person, that employer could be held responsible for the injury suffered. The workers' compensation rules discussed below now significantly modify these responsibilities towards other employees.

The employer is also obligated to compensate the employee for any reasonable expenses incurred in the course of employment, such as gasoline for a car, parts for repair work and so on. The employer must also provide work, direction and the agreed-upon wages for the employee. The employee must be informed of any special terms in the contractual relationship such as bonus arrangements and employee benefit packages.

The employee also has obligations to fulfil. The employee must possess the skills claimed and exercise them in a reasonably competent and careful manner. The employee has an obligation to follow any reasonable order pertaining to the employment and must treat the property of the employer carefully. The employee must be honest, loyal and courteous; an employee who does the work required but acts in an insubordinate or disloyal way can be fired. Similarly, an employee must be punctual and work for the time specified in the contract. There may also be an obligation to act in the best interests

Employer must provide safe working conditions

Other obligations of employer

Obligations of
employee

General contract
law applies to
employment

Restrictive
covenants must
be reasonable

Reasonable
notice of
termination
required of both
employer and
employee

of the employer; an employee who becomes aware of financial opportunities in such circumstances must offer them first to the employer. In the same way, if the employee uses company time or facilities without permission to do something which earns a profit, the employee is obligated to pay that profit to the employer.

Some examples of the more general contract provisions that may also apply to the employment contract are as follows. In some provinces, if the term of a contract of employment is for a definite period of time and will not be completed in one year, the contract must be in writing to satisfy the requirements of the *Statute of Frauds*.[5] Similarly, a contract that includes a restrictive covenant committing the employee not to work in a particular geographic area or in a particular industry after leaving the position has to be for a reasonable time and area, the most appropriate way of protecting the employer's interests and not against the public interest. For example, if an employer invents a special production method, the secrecy of which could only be maintained by requiring that the employees commit themselves not to work in a similar industry for a period of time, a restrictive covenant in the contract of employment to that effect would likely be valid.

Termination

An employment contract may provide for its own discharge or parties can mutually agree to bring it to an end. However, most contracts of employment are for an indefinite period of time and rules have been established by which contracts can be terminated at the instigation of either party. An employee can be terminated with reasonable notice when there is no legislation or agreement, such as a special employment contract or collective agreement, to the contrary. Alternatively, the employee can be given pay comparable to what would have been earned if proper notice had been given. Such monies are called **pay in lieu of notice**. Most people have little difficulty appreciating an employee's right to leave a job, but they may forget that an employer has the right to dismiss an employee for any reason, providing appropriate notice is given. An employee can leave a job for any reason just as an employer can terminate the relationship for any reason as long as sufficient notice is given. It should be noted that provincial and federal human rights legislation including the *Charter of Rights and Freedoms* restricts this power to some extent.[6] When the dismissal amounts to a violation of one of these human rights provisions, such as discrimination on the basis of sex, religion, colour or age, the employer is liable to the enforcement provisions of that legislation.[7]

The difficulty in employment relations is determining what constitutes proper notice. The employment contract itself may have a provision setting out what is proper notice for termination of that agreement. In the event that no such term is included, common law has provided that **reasonable notice** must be given. The amount of time

[5] The general requirement that contracts to be performed beyond one year be in writing does not apply in British Columbia or Manitoba.
[6] *Constitution Act (1982)* Part 1 *Canadian Charter of Rights and Freedoms*, Sections 15, 16 and 28.
[7] For example, *Human Rights Code*, R.S.O. (1990) c.H.19 s.5.

What constitutes
reasonable notice
varies with
circumstances

constituting reasonable notice varies with the circumstances. It used to be that if a person were hired on a weekly basis, one week's notice was appropriate. And a person who was hired on a monthly basis would require one month's notice of dismissal. However, this is no longer always the case; the courts will take other factors, such as length of service, the type of job, the employee's qualifications and the nature of the job market, into consideration to determine what constitutes reasonable notice. In addition to these common law provisions, most provinces have included provisions for minimum notice of dismissal in their employment standards regulations. Trade unions usually insist that provisions relating to the circumstances under which employees can be dismissed and to the nature of notice or pay in lieu of that notice be included in the collective agreements they negotiate with the employer.

Notice not
required when
there is
just cause

An employer who can demonstrate that an employee is being fired for **just cause** is not required to give notice. An employee can be dismissed without notice for serious absenteeism, consistent tardiness, open disobedience, habitual negligence, incompetence, or immoral conduct on or off the job. In the example used to introduce this chapter, it was the employee's dishonesty in lying to his employer about how many calls he had made that justified the dismissal. Such dishonesty need not be tolerated by the employer no matter how sympathetic the plight of the employee.

An employee who becomes seriously ill can be discharged without notice for failure to perform his or her job. Although an employee is entitled to refuse to work because of dangerous working conditions, failure to perform a reasonable order is also grounds for dismissal without notice. Employers are well advised to let employees know when the level of performance is unacceptable as soon as it becomes apparent. It may appear to be easier to let the matter go, but the employer may then be faced with the argument that there was no incompetence when he or she finally makes the decision to discharge the employee. Because the employer has tolerated the incompetent conduct, he or she has led the employee to believe that level of performance was acceptable. This argument will be especially difficult to overcome if bonuses or wage increases had been given to the employee in the past despite the poor performance.

Dismissal without notice must be based on the wrongdoing of the employee or his or her failure to perform the job. Running out of work for the employee to do does not justify discharge. Provisions in collective agreements often cover layoffs and recalls, and several provinces have included provisions covering temporary layoffs in their employment standards legislation.[8] An employee who has been discharged without adequate notice can sue for **wrongful dismissal**. (Also see Box 9.1, "Top court orders compensation for wrongful hiring".) It should be noted that, if an employer fires a person without just cause, the employee could not successfully claim wrongful dismissal if it later comes to light that there had been just cause even though the employer was not aware of it.

Wrongful
dismissal can be
grounds for court
action

It is just as wrong for an employee to leave without proper notice as it is for the employer to terminate without proper notice. Although an employer has the right to sue

---

[8] For example, *Employment Standards Act*, R.S.O. (1990) c.E.14, s.57 ss.17.

Box 9.1

Top court orders compensation for wrongful hiring

First there was wrongful dismissal, now there is wrongful hiring.

The Supreme Court of Canada ruled yesterday that workers can sue their employers if they are hired based on misleading and inaccurate information during a job interview.

In a 6-0 ruling, the top court ordered Ottawa computer software giant Cognos Inc. to pay $67,224 plus interest to accountant Douglas Queen for making false representations when they hired him in 1983 from a secure, well-paying job in Calgary.

Queen was hired to help develop an accounting software package, but two weeks later, the company decided to shift research funds into a more successful product.

Justice Frank Iacobucci ruled the company should have told Queen, who was let go about 18 months later after a number of fill-in jobs, that the project was not yet a reality because senior management had not approved financing or conducted a feasibility study.

"(Queen) had a relatively secure and well-paying job in Calgary and he would not have chosen to move across the country if there was a substantial risk that the employment opportunity described to him would no longer exist after his arrival in Ottawa," wrote Iacobucci.

The court said employers must tell job applicants all "highly relevant information" about the nature and existence of the job and must ensure their statements are accurate.

Queen's lawyer Peter Bishop said employees now have a legal right to accurate information when they consider taking a new job.

"An employer can't just paint a bright rosy picture and give you the sun and the moon and then you take the job on and find that it's a totally different situation."

Source: Stephen Bindman, "Top court orders compensation for wrongful hiring," Southam News, 1993.

When employees can leave without notice

an employee who leaves without proper notice, it is generally not worth the effort. In some situations, however, employees are entitled to leave without notice. An employee has the right to quit immediately if the employer gives an unreasonable or dangerous order, if the working conditions are dangerous and the employer refuses to correct them, or if the employer involves the employee in illegal or immoral activities.

Constructive dismissal— employer breaches contract when nature of job is changed without consent

Although there are conflicting cases in this area, it appears that an employer can breach a contract of employment without realizing it. When an employer unilaterally changes the nature of a job and requires an employee to do something entirely different or demotes that employee, the contract of employment may have been breached as much as if the person had been fired. Such breach of the employment contract on the part of the employer is known as **constructive dismissal**. In these circumstances, the employee may be entitled to treat the contract of employment as ended and sue for wrongful dismissal. On the other hand, if the employee accepts the change and the employment relationship continues, the parties have by mutual agreement simply changed the terms of the contract. This is not actionable.

Compensation based on notice that should have been given

The compensation awarded by the court for wrongful dismissal is usually calculated based on the difference between the notice the person was given and the notice that should have been given. If a person who would normally have been entitled to three months' notice is fired without cause, he or she would be entitled to an amount equal to what would have been earned in those three months if the appropriate notice had been given. The court will reduce the amount of the award if the person obtains other employment within that period of time. There is an obligation to try to do since the employee must try to mitigate his or her losses. The court will sometimes take into consideration damage done to the person's reputation because of the dismissal and claims made by the employer. A person who is dismissed from a corporation will sue the corporation itself for damages. But, if the individual implementing the decision to discharge the employee has committed a tort, such as defamation, that conduct is also actionable against both the corporation and the manager who made the defamatory statement.

Claims for damages in wrongful dismissal actions will often include lost fringe benefits and pension rights if they were part of the employment contract. Damages are the appropriate remedy for wrongful dismissal and it is rare for the court to order that an employee be given back the job. Reinstatement is more common when collective agreements are involved since disputes are usually settled by an arbitrator and are not under the jurisdiction of the courts. Some jurisdictions have provided for reinstatement in non-union situations by statute. The *Canada Labour Code* is one example but such reinstatement is still rare.

Liability of Employer

An employer can be held liable for the tort committed by an employee during the course of employment. This is the principle of vicarious liability discussed in Chapter 2. Even though the employer has done nothing wrong, the employer is responsible for the wrongful conduct of the employee under the theory that, since the employer has benefited from the work of the employee, the employer should be responsible when that work causes injury. But the employer's liability does not forgive the employee for the action that forms the basis of the tort. In fact, the employee, the employer or both can be required to compensate the victim. The employer may have done nothing wrong under these circumstances but the employer does bear responsibility to compensate anyone injured by an employee in the process of work. It must be emphasized, however, that vicarious liability imposed on an employer is limited to torts committed during the course of employment. An employer is not liable for conduct not connected to the employment, for acts not connected to the employment or for when the employee was on a "frolic of his own." The problem of whether the tort was committed during the course of employment is determined not only on the basis of whether the incident occurred during working hours. The real question is whether the act complained of was part of the employment activity. If Pawluk is asked by his employer to deliver a letter to Caron on his way home from work and, rushing to do so, he carelessly knocks over and injures a fellow pedestrian, the pedestrian could sue not only Pawluk but his employer as well. The negligent act occurred during the course of employment even though it did not happen during working hours. But if the same employee decides to go across the street to do his personal banking during working hours and carelessly injures someone in the process, the injured person could sue only Pawluk and not his employer. In this case, Pawluk is on a "frolic of his own." He is not involved in employment activities, even though the accident occurs during working hours, so there is no vicarious liability.

An even more fundamental question than whether the tort was committed during the course of employment is whether there was an employment relationship at all. In general, if there is no employment relationship, there is no vicarious liability. This is why the tests for determining if an employment relationship exists are so important. Vicarious liability is generally restricted to situations in which an employment relationship exists. An exception to this limitation on the application of vicarious liability is when there has been fraudulent misrepresentation in an agency relationship. This subject is discussed in the following chapter.

Some jurisdictions have legislated vicarious liability in special situations. For example, in British Columbia and some other provinces, the owner of a motor vehicle is vicariously liable for any torts committed by someone to whom the vehicle has been loaned.[9]

When an employer is held vicariously liable for the torts committed by an employee, that employer will generally have the right to turn to the employee to compensate for the losses suffered. This remedy is often hollow, however, since the employee is usually in no financial position to pay such compensation.

Legislation

As a consequence of the relatively weak position of individual employees in the employment relationship, employees have tended to band together to exert greater pressure on the employer. Such collective action is now governed by legislation and will be discussed under the heading of Collective Bargaining. A considerable amount of legislation has also been passed which is designed to protect employees, whether unionized or not, by setting minimum standards of safety, remuneration, hours of work and other benefits. Conditions of employment normally fall under the provincial jurisdiction, but there are a number of activities such as banking, the military, activities on Indian reserves, the post office, telephone and broadcast companies, airlines, railroads and steamships that fall under federal jurisdiction. Most provinces have concentrated their employee welfare legislation into one statute, generally called the *Employment Standards Act* or *Labour Standards Act*. Ontario's act is typical of such legislation and will be used as an illustration.[10]

EMPLOYMENT STANDARDS. It should be noted at the outset that statutory provisions set a minimum standard only. Where the parties have agreed to a higher standard or where a higher standard is imposed by the common law, that higher standard will normally prevail (as set out in Section 4.1 of the Ontario Act).

---

[9] *Motor Vehicle Act*, R.S.B.C. (1979) c.288 s.79.
[10] *Employment Standards Act*, R.S.O. (1990) c.E.14.

Minimum wage is
legislated

WAGES. Every province has passed legislation setting minimum wages within its jurisdiction. Under Section 23 of the Ontario *Employment Standards Act*, the minimum wage is to be set by regulation, giving the government more flexibility to make adjustments. In many jurisdictions, such legislation also contains provisions that set standards of payment for piece work, tips or gratuities, and that restrict the amounts that can be deducted from wages to pay for meals, accommodation and other expenses. In many provinces, the minimum wage will vary among industries and, in most provinces, some categories of employment are exempted from minimum wage requirements altogether. Domestic workers and farm workers are often excluded from the operation of the minimum wage statute although this seems to be changing. Ontario now requires that an employer obtain a permit before a homeworker can be hired. Legislation also requires that proper records be kept by the employer and that a statement of wages earned be supplied to the wage earner. This requirement is contained in Part II of the Ontario *Act*, which also specifies that an employer cannot fire an employee simply because the employee has had his wages garnisheed.

Another important amendment to the Ontario *Employment Standards Act* provides for a wage protection program for employees. When companies fail, they are often unable to pay severance and fulfil other obligations to the workers. This program is intended to provide compensation to workers when this happens, but it also places a personal obligation on the directors of the corporation to ensure that a company in such a position does honour its obligations.[11]

Hours of work
legislated

HOURS OF WORK. The Ontario *Employment Standards Act* and similar statutes in other jurisdictions provide that employees do not work excessive hours without appropriate compensation. In Ontario, the maximum amount to be worked in one day is eight hours and in a week no more than 48 hours (Part IV). The employer is obligated to pay a premium for overtime (usually one and a half times the normal rate of pay) (Part VI). These provisions also typically set out minimum break periods such as lunch and coffee breaks and a minimum period free from work, such as one day off in seven. Part VIII of the Ontario *Employment Standards Act* states that a vacation of at least two weeks must be given after a year of employment and that the pay for that vacation period must equal at least 4 percent of the wages earned. This requirement is typical of other jurisdictions as well. In some provinces, the amount of vacation entitlement increases with the length of employment, as with British Columbia's *Employment Standards Act*.[12] Most jurisdictions have provisions for paid statutory holidays, such as New Year's Day and Christmas, although the specific holidays vary from province to province. Overtime must be paid to a person who works on a statutory holiday.

TERMINATION. Because the common law dealing with termination was considered inadequate in many situations, legislation was passed to supplement it. In Ontario, after one year of employment the employee must be given at least one week's notice upon termination. This period increases each year by one week up to a maximum of eight weeks (Part XIV of the Ontario *Act*). Most jurisdictions have

[11] *Employment Standards Act*, (Wage Protection Program), S.O. (1991) c.16.
[12] *Employment Standards Act*, S.B.C. (1980) c.10 s.42.

passed similar legislation, but the provisions vary substantially from province to province. Ontario also provides that, when a person has been temporarily laid off for a period longer than 32 weeks of the year, he or she can treat this layoff as a termination. Note that these statutes set minimum standards which do not override the common law requirements of reasonable notice. As well, collective agreements can usually override these minimum standards.

DISCRIMINATION. Every province and the federal government has legislation ensuring that a woman can get time off without pay for maternity purposes and be guaranteed that she will have a job to come back to without losing seniority. An example of this legislation is found in the *Ontario Employment Standards Act*.[13] Several provinces, including Ontario, also provide for paternity leave for fathers and leave when children are adopted, but the time allocated is considerably less. Whether the leave involved is maternity, paternity or adoption, most statutes require a minimum time of employment before becoming eligible, usually one year. The Ontario *Act* also prohibits discrimination in benefits based on age, marital status or gender (Part X).

Federal and provincial legislation prohibit most forms of discrimination

In addition to these employment standards provisions, both the provincial and federal human rights legislation, as well as the *Charter of Rights and Freedoms*, prohibit discrimination on the basis of sex, race, religion, cultural background and sometimes age. Several provinces, including most recently Ontario, now have statutes that ensure men and women and in some cases minority groups receive equal pay for equal work of equal value.[14] Most provinces have such requirements for public sector employees but some provinces, including Ontario, have recently extended these requirements to large sections of the private sector as well. Many of the cases of discrimination and harassment that are brought before various commissions and courts involve violations in the workplace of the *Charter of Rights and Freedoms* or provincial human rights statutes.

Use of children in workforce tightly regulated

CHILD LABOUR REGULATIONS. Some of the most significant labour legislation deals with child labour. Every jurisdiction in Canada has legislation designed to control the use of children in the workforce although not every jurisdiction sets a minimum age for work. These provisions vary not only between provinces but also within a province and with the nature of the work involved. For instance, in Ontario, a person under the age of eighteen cannot work underground in the mining industry and a person needs to be sixteen to work in the construction industry. In hotels, restaurants and shops, the minimum age is fourteen, provided the work does not interfere with school hours. Most of the other provinces set blanket minimum age requirements but these can vary from industry to industry. Related legislation deals with the statutory requirement that children stay in school until reaching a certain age. All provinces have such statutes, with the age varying from fifteen to sixteen years old,

---

[13] *Employment Standards Act*, R.S.O. (1990) c.E.14 Part XI. The maternity leave period varies with the jurisdiction, and typically there is a prenatal period varying from six to twelve weeks and a post-natal period of six weeks.

[14] *Employment Standards Act*, S.N.B. (1982) c.E-7.2, as amended by S.N.B. (1986) c.32 s.4.

but most provinces also provide for some exceptions to this rule. The federal government does not set a minimum age of employment but does set guidelines designed to control abuses, such as restricting the hours in which a child can work and requiring that a certain wage level be maintained.[15]

Workers'
compensation—
compulsory
insurance
coverage

WORKERS' COMPENSATION. The common law was often unable to provide an appropriate remedy for an employee injured on the job. This was especially true when the accident resulted from the employee's own carelessness. All provinces have now passed workers' compensation legislation which provides a compulsory insurance program covering accidents that take place on the job. The legislation sets rates of compensation to be paid for different types of injuries and establishes a board that hears and adjudicates the claims of injured employees. Careless conduct will not in itself disqualify an injured employee from receiving compensation. The program is financed by assessments levied by the various workers' compensation boards in each province against the employers. The amount levied can vary with the risks associated with the industry involved. Some types of employees are excluded from workers' compensation coverage, such as small businesses, casual employees and farmers. British Columbia has recently extended workers' compensation coverage to almost all workers in the province.

Worker gives up right to any other compensation and cannot sue

A significant aspect of workers' compensation legislation in most jurisdictions is that the worker gives up the right to any other compensation which would normally be available under common law in the absence of such legislation. Thus, even if it can be established that another worker or the employer was negligent, the employee is limited to the benefits bestowed by the workers' compensation legislation even though the injured employee would have the right to sue for damages under common law. The workers' compensation benefit might be considerably less than what the employee would have received through normal litigation. A significant limitation on the availability of workers' compensation is that the injury complained of must have arisen in the course of the employment. While this restriction is not normally a problem, in cases of disease, it is often difficult to determine that the disease was caused by the work of the employee.

Safety boards ensure regulations are adhered to

HEALTH AND SAFETY. In conjunction with workers' compensation legislation, the federal government and the provinces have passed legislation controlling health and safety conditions in the workplace. The objective of this legislation is not only to help the worker by providing a safer working environment but also to keep the premiums paid by employers into the workers' compensation fund at a manageable level by reducing the number of claims. In some jurisdictions, health and safety requirements are embodied in general labour statutes, as in the *Canada Labour Code*. In other jurisdictions, separate statutes are in place dealing with employment, health and safety as in Ontario's *Occupational Health and Safety Act*.[16] The main thrust of these statutes is:

---

[15] For example, under the *Canada Shipping Act*, R.S.C. (1985) c.S.9 s.273, the minimum age in that industry is 15.

[16] *Occupational Health and Safety Act*, R.S.O. (1990) c.O.1.

1. To provide safer working conditions. This is done by requiring fencing of hazardous areas, safety netting, proper shielding of equipment, environmental control and so on.
2. To ensure safe employment practices, such as the use of hard hats, goggles and protective clothing.
3. To establish programs to educate both the employer and employee on how to create a safer working environment for all concerned.

These objectives are facilitated through the establishment of a board which has the power to hear complaints and enforce correction. These statutes also provide for inspectors who have the power to inspect and investigate working conditions in any place of employment without a warrant. When these inspectors encounter dangerous conditions, they have the right to order the problem corrected or, if serious enough, to require that the activity stop altogether. When serious injury or death results from violation of these provisions, provinces are more willing to initiate prosecution. One of the most effective aspects of recent changes to Ontario's legislation is the power to hold directors of corporations personally responsible for harmful and dangerous practices. The result is that an increasing number of offending companies and their directors are facing substantial fines and even imprisonment.

Unemployment insurance is federal jurisdiction

UNEMPLOYMENT INSURANCE. The provision of insurance coverage for unemployed workers would normally fall under the jurisdiction of the provinces under the *Constitution Act 1867*. But an amendment to that *Act*, made with the consent of all the provinces, gives the federal government that responsibility. The *Unemployment Insurance Act* sets up a scheme whereby both employers and employees pay into a government-supplemented fund.[17] Upon being laid off, an employee applies to and is paid out of this fund for a specific period of time, called the entitlement period. The payments made are insurance premiums. This means that a claimant is only entitled to receive payments when the required qualifications are met and then only such benefits as are permitted under the legislation. The benefits received may bear little or no relation to the amount paid in, although the total benefits the employee is entitled to will be based on the number of weeks worked before the claim and the amount of wages he or she had been receiving. Recent changes make it very difficult for a person who voluntarily leaves employment to receive unemployment insurance benefits. As with other federal programs, the worker may appeal any decisions made to an administrative body set up under the legislation. The rights of individuals before such administrative tribunal will be discussed in the Chapter 16.

Employee must meet qualifications to receive benefits

Other Legislation

Many other statutes affect the employment relationship. Most jurisdictions have legislation controlling the apprenticeship process and trade schools. Pension benefits are established in some cases and in all cases are controlled by legislation. Some

---

[17] *Unemployment Insurance Act,* R.S.C. (1985) c.U-1.

jurisdictions have legislation controlling the licensing of private employment agencies and restricting the types of payments they can receive from their clients. And, as has been discussed in other chapters, legislation such as the *Bankruptcy Act* and the *Mechanics'* or *Builders' Liens Acts* provide security to the worker in the payment of wages. All jurisdictions have legislation dealing with special categories of employees, such as teachers and public servants.

COLLECTIVE BARGAINING

The most significant impact on labour legislation in Canada has come from the process of collective action brought about by unionized workers. Although a significant part of the Canadian workforce is unionized, this percentage has been declining in recent years. The trade union movement today finds itself in the position of fighting to hold onto what it has gained and to resist the trend of changes in various statutes that are detrimental to its interests.

The modern trade union movement can trace its roots back to the industrial revolution in Britain and the resulting shift in population from rural to urban areas. The conditions under which people lived and worked were appalling; both adults and children were required to work long hours in unsafe conditions for small returns. These circumstances gave rise to a significant movement to organize workers to pressure employers to provide safer conditions and better wages. The government's initial reaction was repression. The courts treated attempts to organize workers as criminal conspiracies and participants were severely punished. The subsequent history of organized labour is a chronicle of the gradual acceptance of the trade union movement as a legitimate economic force that had to be given a respectable place in the economic and social structure. These changes were accompanied by significant legislative advances both in Britain and Canada. The establishment of organized labour in the United States followed a roughly parallel course but, although the resistance of employers was as great, the governing legislation was not as repressive.

The resistance of employers to trade unions and the corresponding demands of employees for their "rights," which were often based more on emotion than economic reality, resulted in confrontation. This spirit of conflict and confrontation is most evident when an employer is asked to recognize a trade union and a considerable amount of violence is often associated with the organization process.

Because of growing public intolerance of this violence, the U.S. Congress passed the 1935 *National Labour Relations Act* also known as the *Wagner Act*.[18] The main thrust of this *Act* was to eliminate conflict between management and labour at the main point of contention, the process of recognition. The *Wagner Act* required that the employer not interfere in any way with the organization process. A trade union successful in persuading over 50 percent of the employees to join was recognized as the official bargaining agent for all of the employees in that workforce by the government agency created by the legislation. The employer was then required to negotiate with

Legislation designed to reduce conflict

---

[18] *National Labour Relations Act* is also known as the *Wagner Act* (1935) 49 Stat. 449.

the trade union in good faith. The primary objectives of the *Wagner Act* were to promote labour peace and to give some stability and structure to the field of labour relations in the United States.

A major problem in Canada was that each province and the federal government had the power to pass labour relations legislation for its own jurisdiction. Different rules and regulations proliferated before the Second World War. In 1944, after a considerable amount of labour strife, the federal government passed the *Wartime Labour Relations Regulations* by an order-in-council.[19] This order incorporated most of the provisions set out in the *Wagner Act*, and most Canadian provinces added the provisions of this federal legislation to their provincial statutes after the war. It should be noted that the Canadian legislation, in addition to following the lead of the *Wagner Act* in controlling **recognition disputes** (disputes arising between unions and employers during the organization process), included provisions that reduced conflict in interest disputes and rights disputes as well. An **interest dispute** is a disagreement between the union and employer about what should be the terms of their collective agreement. A **rights dispute** is a disagreement over the meaning or interpretation of a provision included in a collective agreement. Another type of dispute that can arise is a **jurisdictional dispute** which is a dispute between two unions over which one should represent a particular group of employees or over which union members ought to do a particular job. For example, should carpenters or steel workers put up metal stud walls in an office building? The employer is usually caught in the middle in jurisdictional disputes and has little power to affect the situation.

The federal collective bargaining legislation is embodied in the *Canada Labour Code*.[20] This legislation covers those areas over which the federal government has jurisdiction, such as railroads, shipping and dock work. Each provincial government has passed collective bargaining legislation covering areas in which it has jurisdiction. These acts are variously called *Labour Codes*, *Trade Union Acts*, *Labour Relations Acts*, *Industrial Relations Acts* and *Labour Acts*. These statutes cover most labour relations situations arising within the jurisdictions of the provinces as set out in Section 92 of the *Constitution Act 1867*. Some types of activities such as public services, schools and hospitals have unique federal or provincial legislation specifically designed to cover labour relations within that industry. Because Canadian labour legislation is divided among so many different government bodies, it is impossible to examine them in detail. However, it is possible to make some general observations that apply to most jurisdictions.

Marginal notes:
Canada followed example of U.S. legislation

Types of disputes— recognition, interest, rights, jurisdiction

Both federal and provincial legislation cover collective bargaining

Organization of Employees

CERTIFICATION. While in some Canadian jurisdictions, it is possible for employers to voluntarily recognize a trade union as the bargaining unit for their employees, the most common method of union recognition in Canada results from the

---

[19] *Wartime Labour Relations Regulations of 1944*, P.C. 1003. Because of the war emergency the federal government had the power to pass general legislation for Canada.
[20] *The Canada Labour Code*, R.S.C. (1985) c.L-2.

Certification of
bargaining unit
set out in
Wagner Act

Majority of
workers must be
members of
union

certification process adopted from the *Wagner Act* of 1935. For a union to obtain certification as the bargaining agent for a group of employees, it must apply to the labour relations board for certification and satisfy the board that a certain percentage of the workforce are members of the union. In most provinces, a majority vote supporting the union is necessary for it to obtain certification. In some provinces, the labour relations boards have the power to certify without such a vote but the union must show that it has the support of a greater portion of the workforce. For example, in Ontario and British Columbia, a union can apply for certification when only 45 percent of the workforce have joined the union, and certification without a vote can take place automatically when over 55 percent of the workforce are members.

BARGAINING AGENT. An essential feature of the legislation in all jurisdictions is the requirement that there be only one bargaining agent for a given unit of employees. The trade union that obtains certification has exclusive bargaining authority for the employees it represents and a unionized employee has no opportunity to negotiate personally with an employer as would be the case under the common law. As a result, a trade union must meet several other qualifications to obtain certification. It must be established that the workforce the trade union intends to represent is an appropriate bargaining unit. Labour relations boards discourage bargaining units that are either too small or too large, or that contain groups of employees with conflicting interests. In several provinces, the trade union cannot be guilty of any discriminatory practices and in all jurisdictions the union must not be employer-dominated. A union that has applied for certification and failed must wait a specified period before trying again.

In some
provinces, unfair
labour practices
can result in
certification
without a vote

UNFAIR LABOUR PRACTICES. The primary objective of labour legislation is to create an orderly process for the organization and recognition of trade unions. Specific rules of conduct are laid down for both labour and management in an effort to reduce or eliminate the conflict which often takes place in such circumstances. Prohibited conduct, called unfair labour practices, can include threats or coercion of employees by either the union or management, the threat of dismissal for joining a trade union and the requirement that an employee refrain from joining a trade union as a condition of employment. Once the organization process has begun in most provinces, the employer has an obligation not to change conditions or terms of employment in order to influence the bargaining process. In some jurisdictions, if the labour relations board concludes that a vote would not reflect the true feelings of the employees because the employer has indulged in unfair labour practices, it is empowered to grant certification without a vote.

However, a labour relations board will not usually take this step unless the union can demonstrate that it has the support of a majority of the employees. For example, if an employer named Schneider learned that Takeda was trying to get a union certified and fired Takeda as a lesson to all the other employees, this would be an unfair labour practice. It is likely that a certification vote would not reflect the true feelings of the employees because of this intimidation, so the board may grant certification without a vote. Requiring that an employer not coerce or intimidate employees does not eliminate the employer's right to state his or her views during the electioneering process that precedes a certification vote. Freedom of expression as set out in the *Charter of Rights and Freedoms* requires that, as long as such statements are merely statements of opinion or fact and do not amount to threat or coercion, they are permitted.

Although the legislation provides for a process whereby an employer can eventually be forced to recognize and bargain with a certified trade union, the provisions do not give the union representatives the right to trespass on the employer's property to carry out union activities, nor do they have the right to carry out those activities while on the job. However, employers will often permit their premises to be used for such purposes because then at least they know what is going on. Once the trade union has successfully completed the certification process, it becomes the certified bargaining agent for all the employees in the bargaining unit. As such, the employer is forced to recognize the trade union and bargain with it. The trade union has the right to serve notice on the employer requiring that the employer begin collective bargaining.

Employer organizations help employers bargain with unions

In some jurisdictions, the legislation provides for the certification of **employer organizations** to be exclusive bargaining agents for their membership. This organization is a stronger unit able to more successfully resist the economic pressures of unions. Employer organizations are most frequently found in areas such as construction which have a number of small employers. Local trade union organizations are often affiliated with much larger, parent unions which generally bring considerable benefits to the local bargaining units, such as providing funds in a prolonged strike and making available a pool of expertise to assist in negotiations.

Bargaining

COLLECTIVE AGREEMENTS. Once a union is certified as a bargaining agent for a group of employees, the next step is for the union and employer to get together and bargain towards a collective agreement. If they have never had a collective agreement before, either party can give notice to commence bargaining within a specific period of time, usually ten to twenty days, depending on the jurisdiction. In most jurisdictions, this notice can be given any time after certification is granted. If the union has been certified for some time and a collective agreement is already in force, the parties are still free to give the other notice to commence bargaining, but this notice can only be given within a relatively short period of time before the end of the previous agreement, usually three to four months. Once this notice has been given, the parties must begin to bargain or negotiate with each other. Most provinces require that the parties negotiate in good faith. There is some question as to what this term means, but if the parties meet together with a willingness to explore compromises and try to find an area of agreement, they are bargaining in good faith. It does not mean that either party has to agree to the other's terms. Some provinces have adopted the wording used in the federal legislation requiring the parties to make "every reasonable effort" to reach an agreement.

Either party can give notice to commence collective bargaining

Parties must bargain in good faith

Agreement must be ratified by both employer and employees

RATIFICATION. A bargain is the result of a successful negotiation process. The agreement is put into writing, approved by the employer and presented to the union membership for ratification. If a majority of the union membership ratifies the agreement, it becomes a collective agreement which is binding on both parties. The agreement is a contract but because of the modifying legislation, it must be viewed as a special form of contract with unique features, such as the method of enforcement. In most jurisdictions, while bargaining is proceeding, the employer is not permitted to change the terms and conditions of the employment, such as wages, benefits or hours of work. When it is clear that the parties cannot reach an agreement, it is possible in some jurisdictions for the *Labour Relations Board* to impose a first contract although this option is seldom used.[21]

CONCILIATION. A very important aspect of the Canadian labour relations system is third party intervention in the negotiation process. This is called conciliation or, in some jurisdictions, mediation. Most provinces and the federal government have provisions for conciliation or mediation to take place to assist the parties in reaching an agreement. Either party has the right to make application to the appropriate government agency for the appointment of a conciliator, sometimes called a mediator, when negotiations begin to break down. This person then meets with the two parties and assists them in their negotiations. The hope is that communications between the two parties will be greatly facilitated by this third person go-between. The conciliator usually has the right to publish unreasonable positions taken by either party which often makes the parties more reasonable in their negotiations. The parties are prohibited from taking more drastic forms of action such as strike or lockout as long as a conciliator is involved in the negotiations. Some provinces provide for a two-tiered process of conciliation with first a single officer and subsequently a conciliation board consisting of three mediators, but the function is essentially the same. It is only after the conciliator or conciliators have removed themselves from the process, by booking out of the dispute and by filing a report, that the parties are allowed to proceed to strike or lockout. In some jurisdictions, conciliation is a prerequisite to strike or lockout. Although conciliators have no authority to bind the parties, they do have the power to make recommendations which will be embarrassing to an unreasonable party. Outside intervention also forces the parties to continue to negotiate for the period of time the conciliator feels is appropriate. Note that in many jurisdictions, a conciliator can be imposed by the labour relations board on the parties, even when neither party has requested one.

In Ontario, arbitration can be requested when agreement cannot be reached on a first contract.[22] In other provinces, such as British Columbia and Newfoundland, the boards have the power to impose a first contract in such situations.

Contract Terms

Conciliation assists negotiation process

Contract must be for at least one year

When the negotiations between the parties have been successful, certain requirements must be contained in the collective agreement. The agreement must be for at least one year; if the parties have placed no time limit on the agreement, it will be deemed to be for one year. The parties will often find themselves bargaining well

---

[21] *Labour Relations Code*, S.B.C. (1992) c.82 s.55.
[22] *Labour Relations Amendment Act*, R.S.O. (1990) c.L.2 s.16.

after the new contract should have come into force and so, in effect, the contract will last only a few months. For example, if Sami is involved in collective bargaining with her employees whose agreement expires on December 31, it is possible that the parties would still be bargaining in the following April. If Sami and her employees finally reach an agreement in June, to run for one year, the agreement would probably be retroactive to the prior January 1 and expire on the following December 31. The agreement would only be in effect for a further six months after the date the agreement was reached. It can be readily seen why every province has taken the approach that any agreement for a period shorter than one year is unworkable.

ARBITRATION. All collective agreements must contain provisions which set out a method for the settlement of disputes arising under the agreement. This is usually accomplished through the process of **arbitration** whereby the parties agree upon a third person or group of people to sit as a court and decide the matter in dispute. If either of the parties under the contract feels that its terms are not being lived up to, they can initiate the process as outlined under the agreement. While both arbitration and conciliation involve the intervention of an outside third party, the distinction is that the parties are not required to follow the recommendations of a conciliator but the decision of the arbitrator is binding on both parties. Arbitration, therefore, is a substitute for court action. Each party in an arbitration hearing is given an opportunity to put forth its side of the argument and present evidence before the arbitrator makes a decision. Arbitrators are not required to follow the same stringent rules of procedure that normally surround judicial proceedings and their decisions can usually be appealed to the labour relations board and, in some jurisdictions, the courts. The collective agreement replaces any individual contract that may have existed previously between the employer and employee, so all disputes between the parties must be handled by the grievance procedure and arbitration. This method of dispute resolution is compulsory. It is not permissible for the parties to indulge in strikes or lockouts to resolve a dispute over the terms of the contract once it is in force.

OTHER TERMS. There are various other terms which often appear in collective agreements. The federal government and some provinces have passed legislation which requires the contract to cover how technological changes in the industry will be handled. British Columbia now requires that union/management committees be set up to handle such conflicts. Throughout Canada the parties can agree to terms that provide for union security, such as the union shop clause. This clause simply requires that new employees must join the union within a specified period of time. In some jurisdictions, particularly in industries such as construction or longshoring, the agreement may require that the employee be a member of the union before getting the job. This requirement is called a **closed shop** clause. Similarly, the statutes permit the collective agreement to contain a **checkoff** provision. This means that the parties can agree that the employer will deduct union dues from the payroll.

Interpretation of contract disputes to be arbitrated

Decision of arbitrator binding on both parties

No strike when contract in force

Statutes cover other terms

Strikes and Lockouts

Job action may involve strike, lockout, work to rule

Some sort of job action will probably result if the parties cannot agree on what terms to include in the agreement. A **lockout** is action taken by the employer to prevent employees from working and earning wages. A **strike** is the withdrawal of services by employees. Although a strike usually consists of refusing to come to work or intentional slowdowns, other forms of interference with production may also be classified as strikes. For example, post office employees announced just before Christmas 1983 that they would process Christmas cards with ten cent stamps on them despite the fact that the appropriate rate was thirty-two cents per letter. This action was taken to draw attention to the fact that certain commercial users of the postal system got a preferential bulk rate which was not available to the public. The courts declared that the action was a strike and since a strike would have been illegal under the circumstances the union reversed its position. Employees can pressure an employer by strictly adhering to the terms of their agreement or by doing no more than is minimally required. This behaviour is called **working to rule** and will often prompt a lockout. Strikes and lockouts are both work stoppages, but they are initiated by different parties.

Because the object of the *Wagner Act* and subsequent legislation was to eliminate conflict and stabilize the labour relations climate as much as possible, the right to strike and the right to lockout have been severely limited by current legislation. It is unlawful for a strike or lockout to occur while an agreement is in force. Strikes and lockouts can only take place after the last agreement has expired and before the next one comes into effect. Any strike or lockout associated with the recognition process is illegal. Similarly, any strike that results from a conflict between two unions about which one should be the bargaining agent for a particular employee (jurisdictional dispute) is also illegal. Only when the dispute is part of the negotiation or bargaining process and concerns the terms to be included in the collective agreement (interest dispute) is a strike or lockout legal.

Strike or lockout can only occur between contracts

Strike and lockout only legal in an interest dispute

If a dispute concerning the interpretation of a term of an agreement between the parties (rights dispute) arises after the contract is in force, it must be settled by arbitration. Any strike associated with such a dispute is illegal. Even when the dispute between the parties is an interest dispute, there are still some limitations on strike action. Typically, no strike can take place until after the parties have attempted to bargain in good faith. A vote authorizing strike action must be taken and a specified period of notice must be given, for example, seventy-two hours in Alberta and British Columbia. The employer must give the same notice to the employees when a lockout is about to take place. No strike or lockout can take place until a specified period of time has passed after a conciliator has made a report to the Minister of Labour. In some jurisdictions, notably Ontario and British Columbia, the employer is now prohibited from hiring replacement workers during a strike. This restriction puts considerably greater pressure on the employer to settle the dispute and goes some way in reducing the violence associated with such labour-management confrontation. Québec has had a similar provision for years.

Must bargain in good faith first and vote before strike

Picketing

Once a strike or lockout has taken place, one of the most effective techniques available to trade unions is picketing. But as with striking, the use of picketing is severely limited and controlled. Picketing involves strikers standing near or marching around a place of business trying to dissuade people from doing business there. When the information communicated does not try to discourage people from crossing the picket line, the action may not qualify as picketing. For example, postal employees handing out pamphlets to customers in front of post offices stating the preferred rates charged to bulk users may not be classed as picketing even though it is embarrassing to the employer. Picketing is permissible only when a lawful strike or lockout is in progress. Employees who picket before proper notice has been given or somewhere not permitted under the labour legislation of the province are in violation of the law. A picketer responsible for communicating false information can be sued for defamation.

Picketing must be peaceful and merely communicate information. Violence will not be tolerated. A tort action for trespass may follow the violation of private property and, if violence erupts, the assaulting party may face criminal and civil court action. When picketing goes beyond the narrow bounds permitted in common law and legislation, the employer can resort to the courts or labour relations boards to get an injunction to limit or prohibit the picketing. Under some circumstances, the number of picketers used may be excessive. When mass picketing goes beyond simple information communication and becomes intimidation, at the request of the employer, the courts or labour relations boards will restrict the number of picketers. Employees face considerable risk of personal liability for damages caused when they involve themselves in illegal picketing.

Picketing may seem to be an ineffectual weapon, limited as it is to those types of activities specifically prescribed under the statutes or permitted by the common law. It must be remembered, however, that there is an extremely strong tradition among union members and many others never to cross a picket line. Others simply wish to avoid the unpleasantness of a confrontation. This observance is perhaps the most effective tool available to a union. Employers must deal with other businesses who employ union members such as suppliers, truck drivers, electricians, plumbers and telephone service people. Because most collective agreements have terms which protect union members from punishment for refusing to cross a valid picket line, it is unusual for a member of one union to cross the picket line of another. It eventually becomes very difficult for an employer to continue in business surrounded by a picket line.

One of the more difficult problems associated with picketing is determining which locations can be legally picketed. Employees in every jurisdiction can picket the plant or factory where they work. In some jurisdictions, such as New Brunswick, secondary picketing can be extended to any place at which the employer carries out business.[23] These provisions are significant because the striking employees are

---

[23] *Industrial Relations Act*, R.S.N.B. (1973) c.I-4, s.104.

able to picket other locations where the employer carries on business. In any case, unrelated businesses cannot be legally picketed even if they are located on the same premises as the one struck. Of course, whether the picketing is directed towards such an unrelated business in a given dispute is a question for the court or board to decide in each case. But the more extensive the picketing, the more effective the economic pressure placed on the employer.

Anyone has the legal right to cross a picket line. Customers are free to continue doing business with an employer involved in a strike or lockout; suppliers are free to continue supplying goods and services to the employer if they can persuade their employees to cross the picket line; and the employer has the right to continue on with normal business activities. Unfortunately, picketers can lose sight of these basic rights when they think their picket line is not being effective. As a result, a considerable amount of intimidation, coercion, violence and injury still takes place despite all the precautions introduced into the labour relations system in Canada.

Public Sector and Essential Services

The provisions discussed under the heading of Collective Bargaining relate to people employed in private industry. However, many people are employed either as part of the public sector or in service industries which are considered essential to society, such as power companies, hospitals, police and fire departments. Employees falling into these categories are treated differently from those employed in private industry, and special legislation governs their activities. Although labour issues and disputes in these occupations are virtually the same as those in the private sector, the government and the public regard the position of public service employees as quite different. Normal collective bargaining with its attendant pressures in the form of strikes, lockouts and picketing can be viewed as interference with the government's right to govern because the government itself is either directly or indirectly the employer.

Strikes by police, firefighters, hospital workers, school teachers and other public servants are usually considered inappropriate by members of the public. Every province has special legislation to deal with these groups. Most provinces permit collective bargaining to some extent but only a few allow public sector employees to participate in strikes and picketing. Of course, in all labour disputes the government retains the right, either by existing statute or by the passage of a specific bill, to impose a settlement or an alternative method of resolving the dispute such as compulsory arbitration. In recent recessionary times there has been great pressure to reduce costs. Governments have sometimes responded by unilaterally reducing the salaries, benefits and work of their employees whether or not they have a collective agreement. The governments of Ontario and Alberta have both recently exercised their legislative power to impose such changes. The Ontario government attempted to do so with the cooperation of their trade union constituency by negotiating a new "social contract" reflecting these new realities. In fact, the resulting cutbacks and reductions have been received with bitterness by many in the trade union movement who expected "better" from a government they helped to elect.

Union Organization

Trade unions must be democratic organizations in which policy is established by vote and executives and officers are elected. Members can be expelled or disciplined for misbehaviour such as crossing picket lines after being instructed not to by the union executive. Expulsion can be devastating for a worker since many collective agreements provide for a **union shop** in which all employees must be members of the union. Some jurisdictions have passed legislation stipulating that a person who loses his or her union membership for reasons other than failure to pay dues will be able to retain employment.[24] There are some employees whose religious beliefs prevent them from joining or contributing to organizations such as trade unions, which presents a real dilemma in a union shop situation. Some provinces have passed legislation exempting such individuals from the operation of this provision of the collective agreement although the other terms of the collective agreement still apply.

Trade unions are subject to the human rights legislation in place in their jurisdiction. In some jurisdictions, the labour legislation provides that they can lose their status as a trade union if they discriminate. Unions have an obligation to represent all their members fairly. Employees who feel unfairly treated by the union or who feel that the union is not properly representing them in disputes with employers can lodge complaints before the provincial labour relations board.

From this discussion, it seems that labour relations boards have considerable power. In fact, this power varies from province to province and in some jurisdictions the courts still have a significant role to play. In others, such as British Columbia, the power to resolve disputes in labour relations matters has been given entirely to the provincial industrial relations council. Labour relations boards in most provinces take on the trappings of courts; they are, however, administrative tribunals and the parties before them have certain protected rights that will be discussed in Chapter 16.

Trade unions were once considered illegal organizations with no status separate from their membership and therefore no corporate identity. Most provinces have passed legislation giving a recognized trade union the right to sue or be sued on its own behalf, at least for the purposes outlined in the labour legislation.

SUMMARY

The employee provides service to the employer generally whereas the independent contractor contracts to do a specific job. The employer is vicariously liable for the acts of the employee done during the course of employment. The employer must also provide a safe working place, direction and wages. The employee must follow these directions, and honestly, carefully, and loyally carry them out. In the event of termination, both parties are obligated to give the other reasonable notice. After a long period of employment this notice period can be quite lengthy. No notice is required where there is just cause for dismissal such as dishonesty or incompetence. In the event of

---

[24] *Canada Labour Code*, R.S.C. (1985) c.L-2 s.95e.

wrongful dismissal, the employee is required to mitigate losses by trying to find other employment.

There are a number of federal and provincial statutes controlling such things as minimum wage, hours of work, termination, child labour, discrimination, employment standards, health and safety standards, unemployment insurance and workers' compensation.

A major category of legislated intervention in the field of employment is in the area of collective bargaining. The organization of the employees by unions into bargaining units is controlled by the certification process. After a majority vote of the employees, the government certifies the union as the official bargaining agent for those employees and the employer is required to bargain fairly with them. Only when that bargaining process breaks down, usually after an attempt at conciliation, is a strike or lockout permitted and then only after a majority vote and proper notice. During the strike, persuasive picketing is allowed but no physical confrontation. Once the contract is in place, any disputes arising under it must be dealt with through an arbitration process provided for in the agreement.

QUESTIONS

1. Distinguish between an employee, an independent contractor and an agent.
2. Explain how a court will determine whether a person is an employee rather than an independent contractor.
3. Summarize the employer's obligations to the employee and the employee's obligations to the employer under common law in a master/servant relationship.
4. Explain what is meant by a restrictive covenant and what factors determine whether it is enforceable or not.
5. What is the proper way to terminate an employment contract that is for an indefinite period of time?
6. How is the appropriate notice period to terminate a master/servant relationship determined?
7. Under what circumstances can an employee be dismissed without being given notice? When can an employee leave employment without giving notice?
8. What risk does an employer face who ignores an employee's incompetence over a period of time?
9. What factors will a court take into consideration when determining compensation in a wrongful dismissal action? Indicate any other types of remedies which may be available to the victim.
10. Explain what is meant by vicarious liability. Describe the limitations on its application and how vicarious liability will affect the liability of the employee.
11. Explain the object and purpose of workers' compensation legislation. How does the legislation attempt to accomplish these objectives? Explain what the position of the parties would be if only the original common law applied.

12. What is the significance of the American *National Labor Relations Act* (*Wagner Act*) in Canada?

13. Distinguish between recognition disputes, jurisdiction disputes, interest disputes and rights disputes.

14. Explain the difference between conciliation and arbitration. Describe how these tools are used in Canadian labour disputes.

15. Once a collective agreement is in place, what effect will it have on the individual rights of employees? How will it affect employers?

16. Strikes and lockouts are limited to what kind of disputes? How are the other types of disputes between union and employer dealt with?

17. Distinguish between a strike and a lockout. Describe the type of job action that can constitute a strike.

18. Explain what steps must take place before a strike or lockout is legal.

19. Explain what is meant by picketing. Under what circumstances is this type of job action available? What limitations have been placed on picketing in different jurisdictions?

20. What is the legal position of a person who wishes to cross a picket line?

CASES

1. *Wallace v. Toronto Dominion Bank.*
   The plaintiff started working for the defendant in 1970. In 1975 he moved to the bank's inspection department. At that time he signed a contract which included a clause requiring only four weeks' notice in the event of termination. In 1978, the bank decided to put him on probation and reduced his salary by $6100 per year because of dissatisfaction with his service. In November 1978, when the bank refused to restore his salary and refused to remove the probation designation on his file, the plaintiff quit. He then sued the bank for wrongful dismissal. Explain the arguments of both sides and the amount of damages the plaintiff would be entitled to if successful.

2. *Clare v. Canada (Attorney-General).*
   Clare was an employee of the federal government who was fired from his job for incompetence after 23 years of service. After a number of years of satisfactory service in various capacities with the federal public service, the plaintiff received an unsatisfactory evaluation in his performance appraisals for three consecutive reviews. On the basis of this performance, the plaintiff was fired from his position. During that time, his wife had suffered from a series of major illnesses and nearly died. He was also having serious problems with his son including physical confrontation. As a result, Clare was experiencing an extreme amount of stress in his life. In addition to his personal

troubles, he had a personality conflict with his immediate supervisor which introduced work-related stress. During this period, Clare was receiving counselling and had asked to participate in a federally sponsored program designed to help employees experiencing these kind of difficulties. The plaintiff sought reassignment which was refused and he was fired from his position. Explain the legal position of the parties and whether the dismissal was justified in the circumstances. Would your answer be different if it were established that he had experienced family problems over his entire work history with the department, and that several of his transfers from one department to another had been to accommodate a "problem or troubled employee and that his performance had never been fully satisfactory."

3. *DiCarlo v. DiSimone et al.*
The plaintiff was in a car owned by his employer and driven by a fellow employee when they were in an accident while in the process of work. They collided with a car driven by Lilian Watson and owned by her husband Alfred. Both drivers were found to be negligent and partially the cause of the accident. The plaintiff sued for damages from both drivers, his employer and Mr. Watson, the owner of the other vehicle. Describe the arguments that can be used by the employee and employer and any limitations on the amount that can be collected from the Watsons.

4. *Reilly v. Steelcase Canada Ltd.*
The plaintiff had worked for the defendant for two and a half years as a successful and competent district sales manager. He then began an adulterous relationship at a sales convention with a colleague's wife. The company subsequently dismissed him; no reasons were given at the time although later the adulterous relationship was relied on as the basis of the dismissal. The plaintiff then sued for wrongful dismissal. Explain the arguments on both sides and indicate the likely outcome. How much notice or payment in lieu of notice would be appropriate compensation if the plaintiff were successful? Would your answer be affected if it was revealed that the plaintiff had disclosed the relationship and discussed it with his immediate superior five months before the dismissal and felt the matter was considered closed?

5. *Dixon v. The Bank of Nova Scotia and Collins.*
Collins was a bank manager for the Bank of Nova Scotia where the plaintiff Dixon was a customer. One day Collins told Dixon that he should consider buying shares in Nicola Copper Mine Ltd. He indicated that he had purchased such shares, that it was a good investment, that it had been investigated by the bank and that the bank was "endorsing" Nicola financially. Dixon later sold the shares he had purchased, losing about $1000. Subsequently he accidentally learned through speaking to another employee of the bank that the bank had no involvement with Nicola. Dixon brought the action against Collins and the bank. Explain the legal position of each of the parties, the arguments each will raise and the likely outcome.

6. *United Association of Journeymen Apprentices, Local 264 v. Metal Fabricating and Construction Ltd.*

    The union and the employer entered into an agreement which was to remain in force until April 1984. In March 1984 the employer served notice on the employee that the agreement was to be considered terminated at the end of April. The parties then began to bargain for a new collective agreement. This bargaining went on for three years; during that time, the terms of the old agreement were adhered to. At the end of the three years (in 1987), the employer made certain changes to working conditions without the consent of the union. Does the employer have the right to do so? Explain the arguments available to both parties as to whether the terms of the old collective agreement were in place and binding on the parties in spring, 1987.

7. *United Steel Workers of American L. 7917 v. Gibraltar Mines Ltd.*

    In this case, a number of truck drivers were suspended because they refused to drive their trucks. One of the truck drivers was a union official. The truck drivers claimed that the conditions were unsafe. They had to drive up a ramp beside an open pit. The weather conditions made the ramp slippery. A protective device, called a berm, which was designed to keep the trucks from falling into the pit was missing for a stretch of four or five hundred feet. The company claimed that it was an illegal strike and suspended the truck drivers. The drivers brought an application to be reinstated. Explain the arguments on both sides and the probable outcome. Would your answer differ with the added information that, upon learning that the mining operation was still functioning, a union official set up a picket line and encouraged the entire crew to stay off the job?

8. *Amalgamated Clothing and Textile Workers Union (Toronto Joint Board) v. Straton Knitting Mills Ltd. et al.*

    When the union in question tried to organize the workers at the respondent's premises, the co-owner held three meetings with the employees in an attempt to dissuade them from joining the union. He told them it was not necessary for them to have a union, that it would be divisive, that they would have to pay union dues, that there was the possibility of a strike and that it might result in the loss of contracts for the company which would mean less work for the employees. The company also changed the pay scale which resulted in higher wages. A petition was circulated to oppose the union, but there was some suggestion that management was behind it. Part of the message that got through to the employees was that the employer did not want a union, that if it came there would be layoffs, short weeks and perhaps closure of the business. What course of action would you recommend to the union in these circumstances?

ISSUES

1. In Canada, it is necessary for reasonable notice or pay in lieu of notice to be given whenever employment is terminated in the absence of just cause. The amount of notice involved may be considerable and in some cases may exceed two years. In the United States, however, the courts are less willing to impose lengthy notice periods even when the employment has been for a long time. Is the Canadian approach an unjust intrusion into the employers' rights to manage their own businesses and respond to changing economic requirements? Would it be more appropriate to leave the provision of notice of termination to the parties to agree between themselves as part of the contract of employment? If the Canadian approach is to be retained, why should this considerable notice period be eliminated when there is just cause? Would it not be more appropriate to require the employer to give notice, or pay in lieu of notice, even when there has been some misbehaviour on the part of the employee? Consider whether the period of employment should give the employee a right to an entitlement or a fund the employer is required to pay regardless of the circumstances of the dismissal.

2. An employer can be held vicariously liable for the tortious acts of employees committed during the course of their employment. The substantial justification for this is that, because the employer is benefiting from the employee's conduct, the employer ought to bear the responsibility. This is a policy decision. Do you agree with the policy? Consider the arguments, both pro and con. Consider the extent to which the principle ought to be applied and that there are a variety of relationships which fall between employment and independent contracts. In the past, a master/servant relationship had to be demonstrated for vicarious liability to apply; today the availability of vicarious liability has been expanded by broadening the definition of employment. Where would you draw the line as to the availability of vicarious liability? Should the employee be held liable as well as the employer?

3. A considerable amount of legislation in the field of employment affects the responsibilities of the parties. This legislation takes the form of minimum standards of pay, hours of work, wages, vacations, health and safety, child labour, workers' compensation, unemployment insurance and collective bargaining legislation. The question that must be asked is: Is this legislative intervention detrimental to our economic system? Consider whether there is any non-economic justification for this legislative interference. Consider whether, as a result of the restrictions imposed by the workers' compensation process, it is appropriate for an employee who is injured in the process of employment to be

denied the right to seek compensation from the person who caused that injury through the normal litigation process for tort.

4. The right to strike is fundamental to the trade union movement and has been incorporated into most of the collective bargaining legislation in place in Canada. However, the right to strike has been limited to interest disputes and eliminated completely in many jurisdictions if public sector employees are involved. Many jurisdictions require that an involved process of conciliation and mediation take place before the right to strike can be exercised. Should a union ever be permitted to withdraw its services in a strike? Should an employer be permitted to lock out its employees? In your answer, consider the arguments on both sides. Is it fair that public sector employees should be denied the right to strike when others have it? In your response, consider any alternative to the strike and lockout process.

5. One of the most effective tools available to unions during a strike is the process of picketing. In most jurisdictions, the right to picket is restricted to the actual job site being struck. In some provinces, however, secondary picketing is permitted. Should picketing ever be permitted and, if so, what locations should be picketed? This question illustrates a major problem that results from collective bargaining legislation, that is, the necessity of keeping a fine balance between the power of the employer and the power of the union. Does current legislation create an imbalance in favour of the trade unions? Consider the arguments that can be raised on both sides of this issue.

LEGISLATION

Alberta
Blind Workers' Compensation Act, R.S.A. (1980) c.B-7
Employment Standards Code, S.A. (1988) c.E-10.2
Industrial Wage Security Act, R.S.A. (1980) c.I-3
Labour Relations Act, R.S.A. (1980) c.L-1.2
Master and Servants Act, R.S.A. (1980) c.M-8
Occupational Health and Safety Act, R.S.A. (1980) c.O.2
Public Service Act, R.S.A. (1980) c.P-13
Public Service Employee Relations Act, R.S.A. (1980) c.P-33
Workers' Compensation Act, R.S.A. (1980) c.W-16

British Columbia
Apprenticeship Act, R.S.B.C. (1979) c.17
Employment Standards Act, S.B.C. (1980) c.10
Labour Relations Code, S.B.C. (1992) c.82

Labour Regulations Act, R.S.B.C. (1979) c.213
Public Sector Employers Act (Bill 78—1993)
Public Service Act, R.S.B.C. (1979) c.15 (Bill 66—1993)
Public Service Labour Relations Act, R.S.B.C. (1979) c.346
Workers' Compensation Act, R.S.B.C. (1979) c.437
Workplace Act, R.S.B.C. (1979) c.34

Manitoba
Apprenticeship and Tradesmen's Qualifications Act, R.S.M. (1987) c.A-110
Civil Service Act, R.S.M. (1987) c.C-110
Construction Industry Wages Act, R.S.M. (1987) c.C-190
Employment Services Act, R.S.M. (1987) c.E-100
Employment Standards Act, R.S.M. (1987) c.E.110
Labour Relations Act, R.S.M. (1987) c.L-10
Payment of Wages Act, R.S.M. (1987) c.P-31
Public Sector Compensation Management Act, S.M. (1991-92) c.43
Trade Practices Inquiry Act, R.S.M. (1987) c.T-110
Vacations with Pay Act, R.S.M. (1987) c.V-20
Workers' Compensation Act, R.S.M. (1987) c.W-200
Workplace Safety and Health Act, R.S.M. (1987) c.W-210

New Brunswick
Apprentice and Occupational Certification Act, S.N.B. (1981) c.34
Blind Workmen's Compensation Act, R.S.N.B. (1973) c.B-6
Civil Service Act, R.S.N.B. (1973) c.C-5.1
Employment Standards Act, S.N.B. (1982) c.E-7.2
Industrial Relations Act, S.N.B. (1989) c.14
Occupational Health and Safety Act, S.N.B. (1983) c.O-0.2
Pay Equity Act, R.S.N.B. (1989) c.P-5.01
Public Service Labour Relations Act, R.S.N.B. (1973) c.P-25
Workers' Compensation Act, R.S.N.B. (1973) c.W-13

Newfoundland
Apprenticeship Act, R.S.N. (1990) c.A-12
Industrial Standards Act, R.S.N. (1990) c.I-4
Labour Relations Act, R.S.N. (1990) c.L-1
Labour Standards Act, R.S.N. (1990) c.L-2
Occupational Health and Safety Act, R.S.N. (1990) c.O-3
Public Service Collective Bargaining Act, R.S.N. (1990) c.P.42
Teachers' Collective Bargaining Act, R.S.N. (1990) c.T-3
Workers' Compensation Act, R.S.N. (1990) c.W-1

Nova Scotia
Apprenticeship and Tradesmen's Qualifications Act, R.S.N.S. (1989) c.17
Blind Workmen's Compensation Act, R.S.N.S. (1989) c.41
Civil Service Collective Bargaining Act, R.S.N.S. (1989) c.71
Construction Projects Labour-Management Relations Act, R.S.N.S. (1989) c.90
Employment Agencies Act, R.S.N.S. (1989) c.146
Labour Standards Code, R.S.N.S. (1989) c.246
Labour Standards Code, S.N.S. (1991) c.14
Occupational Health and Safety Act, R.S.N.S. (1989) c.320
Pay Equity Act, R.S.N.S. (1989) c.337
Public Service Act, R.S.N.S. (1989) c.376
Teachers' Collective Bargaining Act, R.S.N.S. (1989) c.460
Trade Union Act, R.S.N.S. (1989) c.475
Workers' Compensation Act, R.S.N.S. (1989) c.508

Ontario
Arbitration Act, S.O. (1991) c.17
Blind Workmen's Compensation Act, R.S.O. (1990) c.B.8
Crown Employees Collective Bargaining Act, R.S.O. (1990) c.C.50
Employers and Employees Act, R.S.O. (1990) c.E.12
Employment Agencies Act, R.S.O. (1990) c.E.13
Employment Standards Act, R.S.O. (1990) c.E.14
Employment Standards Amendment Act, S.O. (1991) c.16
Forestry Workers' Employment Act, R.S.O. (1990) c.F.27
Labour Relations Act, R.S.O. (1990) c.L.2
Occupational Health and Safety Act, R.S.O. (1990) c.O.1
Public Service Act, R.S.O. (1990) c.P.47
Rights of Labour Act, R.S.O. (1990) c.R.33
Trades Qualification Act, R.S.O. (1990) c.T.17
Workers' Compensation Act, R.S.O. (1990) c.W.11
Workmen's Compensation Insurance Act, R.S.O. (1990) c.W.12

Prince Edward Island
Apprenticeship and Tradesmen's Qualification Act, R.S.P.E.I. (1988) c. A-15
Blind Workmen's Compensation Act, R.S.P.E.I. (1988) c. B-4
Civil Service Act, R.S.P.E.I. (1988) c. C-8
Labour Act, R.S.P.E.I. (1988) c. L-1
Employment Standards Act, S.P.E.I. (1992) c.18
Occupational Health and Safety Council Act, R.S.P.E.I. (1988) c.O-1
Pay Equity Act, R.S.P.E.I. (1988) c. P-2
Workers' Compensation Act, R.S.P.E.I. (1988) c. W-7
Youth Employment Act, R.S.P.E.I. (1990) c.Y-66

Québec
An Act Respecting Collective Agreement Decrees, R.S.Q. (1977) c.D-2
An Act Respecting Labour Relations in the Construction Industry, R.S.Q. (1977) c.R-20
An Act Respecting Labour Standards, R.S.Q. (1977) c.N-1.1
An Act Respecting Occupational Health and Safety, R.S.Q. (1977) c.S-2.1
Industrial Accidents and Occupational Diseases Act, R.S.Q. (1977) c.A-3.001
Public Service Act, R.S.Q. (1977) c.F-3.1.1

Saskatchewan
Apprenticeship and Trade Certification Act, S.S. (1984-85-86) c.A-22.1
Education Act, R.S.S. (1978) Supp.c.E-O.1
Employment Agencies Act, R.S.S. (1978) c.E-9
Labour Standards Act, R.S.S. (1978) c.L-1
Occupational Health and Safety Act, R.S.S. (1978) c.O-1
Provincial Mediation Board Act, R.S.S. (1978) c.P-33
Public Service Act, R.S.S. (1978) c.P-42
Securities Act, R.S.S. (1988-89) c.S-42.2
Thresher Employees Act, R.S.S. (1978) c.T-12
Trade Union Act, R.S.S. (1978) c.T-17
Wage Recovery Act, R.S.S. (1978) c.W-1
Workers' Compensation Act, S.S. (1979) c.W-17.1

Northwest Territories
Arbitration Act, R.S.N.W.T. (1988) c.A-5
Labour Standards Act, R.S.N.W.T. (1988) c.L-1
Wage Recovery Act, R.S.N.W.T. (1988) c.W-1
Workers' Compensation Act, R.S.N.W.T. (1988) c.W-6

Yukon
Employment Standards Act, R.S.Y (1986) c.54
Mediation Board Act, R.S.Y (1986) c.113
Workers' Compensation Act, R.S.Y (1986) c.180

Federal
Canada Labour Code, R.S.C. (1985) c.L-2
Fair Wages and Hours of Labour Act, R.S.C. (1985) c.L-4
Old Age Security Act, R.S.C. (1985) c.O-9
Public Sector Compensation Act, S.C. (1991) c.30
Public Service Employment Act, R.S.C. (1985) c.P-33
Public Service Staff Relations Act, R.S.C. (1985) c.P-35
Unemployment Insurance Act, R.S.C. (1985) c.U-1
Wage Liability Act, R.S.C. (1985) c.W-1

10 AGENCY

Objectives of the Chapter

- to identify the agency relationship
- to discuss the rights and responsibilities of an agent and a principal
- to explain the implications of a fiduciary relationship

Mr. Snarey was a "well-respected agent" working for the Mutual Life Assurance Company of Canada when he was approached by a customer who wanted to take advantage of one of the investment opportunities offered by the company. Mr. Snarey persuaded the customer to part with $16 000 by way of a cheque made out to Mr. Snarey. The customer was told that his money was going into an "investment vehicle offered to the public by Mutual Life." Actually, the company did not offer this kind of investment plan and never had. This was simply a scheme used by Mr. Snarey to cheat a trusting customer out of a considerable amount of money. When the customer discovered the fraud, he turned to the Mutual Life Assurance Company for compensation. In the resulting action, it was determined that Mr. Snarey had devised and conducted a fraudulent scheme. Because he was an agent of Mutual Life with the actual authority to enter into this general type of transaction with the company's customer, the company was vicariously liable for his conduct and had to pay compensation to the client.[1]

Fraudulent misrepresentation is one of the few circumstances in which a principal will be held vicariously liable for the acts of an agent even in the absence of an employment contract between them, providing that agent is acting within the authority he has been given by the principal. This case illustrates that such an agency relationship can have a tremendous impact on the principal. A discussion of how agency relationships are created and the obligations which arise between the parties is the topic of this chapter.

The subject of agency is a vital component in any discussion of business law. The legal consequences that stem from an agency relationship are of utmost concern to business people because at least one of the parties in most commercial transactions is an agent. Agency law is the basis of the law of partnership and an understanding of it is essential for coming to terms with corporate law. These subjects will be dealt with in the next two chapters.

Agent represents and acts for principal

An agent's function is to represent and act on behalf of a principal in dealings with third parties. Although by far the most common type of legal relationship in which agents represent principals is in the creation of contracts, agents also find themselves involved in other types of legal relationships. Real estate agents do not usually have the authority to enter into contracts on behalf of vendors but they function as agents nonetheless because they participate in the negotiations and act as go-betweens. Other professionals, such as lawyers and accountants, also create special legal relationships on behalf of their clients or principals which are not necessarily contractual in nature. The term **agency** refers to the service an agent performs on behalf of the principal. This service may be performed within the scope of employment, as an independent agent or contractor, or gratuitously. When an independent contractor is performing this agent function, the business performing the service is often called an agency, such as a travel agency, employment agency or real estate agency. This use of the term is unfortunate because it leads people to believe that the agency relationship is restricted to these service situations when, in fact, the agency function is much more common in employment relationships. A customer who deals with someone other than the owner when purchasing a product from a store has created a contract through the services of an agent, the sales clerk. To distinguish between the two kinds of agents, we will refer to those who are not employees as independent agents.

Agency refers to service performed by an agent

THE AGENCY RELATIONSHIP

The agency relationship can be created by an express or implied contract, by estoppel, by ratification or gratuitously.

Agency relationship usually created through contract

FORMATION BY CONTRACT. Usually an agency relationship is created through a contract, called an **agency agreement**, between the agent and the principal. It is important not to confuse this contract with the contract created by the agent between the principal and the third party, which is the object of the agency relationship. Because the agency agreement is a special application of contract law, the principles outlined in Chapters 3 through 6 apply. The authority of the agent to act on behalf of the principal is defined in the agency agreement. Similarly, the payment the agent is to receive for services rendered is set out in the contract. There are no formal requirements for the creation of such a contract, which can be either verbal or in writing. An agency contract that is to last over one year must be evidenced in writing to satisfy the requirements of the *Statute of Frauds* except in jurisdictions such as British Columbia and Manitoba where this requirement has been abolished. (See the discussion of the *Statute of Frauds* in Chapter 4.) It is always best to put an agency contract in writing to assist in resolving potential disputes between the parties later. There is no requirement that agency agreements be under seal unless the agent will be sealing documents with third parties on behalf of the principal or when required by statute, such as in some provinces when an agent actually sells land for a principal. An agency agreement in writing and under seal is called a **power of attorney**.

Basic rules of contract apply to agency contracts

All the elements of a contract, such as consensus, consideration, legality, intention to be bound and capacity on the part of both parties, must be present for an agency agreement to be binding. The lack of any one of these elements may have serious ramifications for the agreement between the agent and the principal. But problems with the agency agreement may not have any effect on the binding nature of any agreement the agent enters into on behalf of the principal. Thus, if Clarke is underage and acts as Jiwan's agent in the sale of Jiwan's car to Skoda, the agency contract between Clarke and Jiwan is voidable because of the incapacity of Clarke. But the contract between Jiwan and Skoda for the purchase of the car is still binding. Only when agents are so young, drunk or otherwise incapacitated that they do not understand what they are doing does the contract between the principal and third party becomes doubtful. An agency agreement may take the form of an employment contract or an independent contractual relationship between the principal and agent. In either case, defects in the agency agreement will not usually have a negative effect on the binding nature of the contract between the principal and the third party.

Consent the only essential requirement for agency

FORMATION WITHOUT A CONTRACT. Unlike many other areas of the law, the essential requirement for the formation of an agency relationship is merely the consent of both parties. It is quite possible for a principal to be bound by an agent's actions even when no contract exists between them. This point explains why the contract for the purchase of the car is binding between Jiwan and Skoda despite the incapacity of the agent, Clarke. The resulting contract between a principal and third party is binding even when a person serves as an agent gratuitously. It must be emphasized that most agency relationships are created by binding contracts which have been expressly entered into by the parties or implied from their conduct. Often these are simply employment contracts.

Authority of Agents

The most significant part of any agreement between a principal and agent, and the source of most disputes, is the extent of the authority given to the agent by the principal to create a binding relationship with a third party. An agent's authority can be derived from the principal in several ways.

ACTUAL AUTHORITY. The agency relationship is established when a principal grants authority to an agent to act on his or her behalf. This power is limited and is called the agent's **actual authority**. When the agency agreement is in writing, the written document will set out the limitations on the agent's authority. When the principal sets out the specific nature of the agent's authority, it is called **express authority**. But the actual authority of the agent is not limited to that expressed by the principal; it will also include an **implied authority** conveyed by the principal. As in other forms of contracts, certain provisions in the agency agreement are implied from the circumstances and form part of the contract. A person who is appointed as an agent to perform a specific function for a principal also has the authority to enter into contracts necessarily incidental to the main activity he or she has been engaged to perform. A person who is hired as a purchasing agent has the authority to carry out the customary and traditional responsibilities of purchasing agents. This actual authority is granted through implication. Of course, normally no such authority is implied if the principal has specifically stated that the agent does not have it.

In the example used to introduce this chapter, the contract entered into by Mr. Snarey was just the kind of contract he was authorized to conclude with his clients. Because of this actual authority, the principal was liable for his fraud.

The agreement between principal and agent should set out specifically the express authority the agent has to bind the principal and should avoid the need to imply authority where possible. An agent who exceeds this actual authority may be liable for any injury his or her conduct causes the principal. It would be incorrect, however, for principals to assume that they cannot be bound by actions of their agent which exceed the actual authority the agent has been given.

APPARENT AUTHORITY. A principal who behaves in a way that makes it appear to a third party that an agent has the authority to act on the principal's behalf is bound by any legal relationship entered into based on that apparent authority. The agent's actions may exceed the authority given, or may even have been specifically prohibited, but when the principal's conduct has led a third party to believe the agent has authority to so act, this apparent authority will bind the principal.

The existence of apparent authority based on the conduct or statements of the principal is an application of the principle of **estoppel**. When a person claims that a certain condition exists, such as, "George is my agent and has my authority," estoppel comes into effect. Such a statement may be wrong, but the person making the statement cannot later claim that what was said was incorrect to escape responsibility. Estoppel applies when a principal has done something to lead the third party to believe that an agent has authority to act on his or her behalf. When a principal leads a third party to believe the agent has authority in this way, that principal is said to have "held out" that the agent has authority to act on his or her behalf. If a third party has relied on this representation, the principal cannot then claim that the agent

Actual authority expressed or implied

Apparent authority presumed from actions of principal

Estoppel applies when principal indicates that agent has authority

had no authority. The most important example of the application of estoppel is in the field of agency. It is important not to confuse this principle of estoppel with equitable or promissory estoppel as described in Chapter 3. Equitable estoppel involves a promise or commitment to do something in the future. Here we are dealing not with a promise but with a claim or a statement of fact made by the principal.

When an agent acts with apparent authority, the principal must look to the agent, not the third party, for compensation for any injuries. Only when the agent has acted beyond both actual and apparent authority is the principal not bound by the agent's actions. If Pedersen operates a used car dealership and employs Mohammed as sales manager, customers could presume that Mohammed has the authority to sell cars and to take trade-ins because these are the responsibilities that sales managers of car lots normally assume. If Pedersen instructs Mohammed not to accept any trade-in over $500 without first getting Pedersen's express approval, Mohammed's actual authority has been limited. Suppose Kim wants to trade in a 1985 Mercedes on a 1983 Cadillac and Mohammed, in a burst of enthusiasm, gives a $5000 trade-in on the deal. Could Pedersen later claim that the contract was not binding because he did not give permission for the trade-in? No. Pedersen behaves as if Mohammed is his sales manager, leading Kim to believe that Mohammed has the ordinary authority and power of a sales manager. The agent acted within his apparent authority and the contract was binding on the principal. If, however, the agent had sold Kim the entire car lot, this would be beyond both his actual and apparent authority and would not be binding on Pedersen.

A principal can also be bound by the actions of an agent that would normally be beyond the agent's authority if the principal has sanctioned similar actions in the past. Kim's chauffeur, Green, would not normally be expected to have the authority to purchase automobiles on behalf of his principal. For several years, however, Green has purchased cars from Pedersen's Used Cars on behalf of Kim. The deals have always gone through without any problems leading Pedersen to believe that Green had authority to make this kind of purchase. Even if Kim specifically told Green not to buy any more cars, if Green returned to Pedersen's car lot and purchased another car, the contract would be binding on Kim because of the apparent authority possessed by the chauffeur. The existence of this apparent authority is based on the statements and conduct of the principal, not the agent. When the misleading indication of authority comes from the agent rather than the principal and the action is otherwise unauthorized, the third party will have no claim against the principal. Only when the agent has no actual and no apparent authority is the principal not bound and then the third party must turn to the agent for compensation.

The reasonable person test has a significant role to play in determining the existence of apparent authority. The usual authority associated with the position in which an agent has been placed is based on this test. The reasonable person test is also used to determine whether the third party should have been misled into believing that the agent had authority by the statements and conduct of the principal.

To determine whether a principal is bound in contract with a third party by the actions of an agent, a person must first ask, "Was the agent acting within the actual authority given by the principal?" If the answer is yes, then there is a contract,

Agent acting on apparent authority will bind principal

Previous acceptance of agent's actions

Reasonable person test used to determine existence of authority

providing all the other elements are present. If the answer is no, then the question to ask is, "Did the principal do anything to lead the third party to believe that the agent had the authority to act?" In other words, was the agent acting with apparent authority? If the answer is yes and the third party relied on that apparent authority, then there is a contract between the principal and the third party. It is only when the answer to both of these questions is no that there is no contract and the third party must look to the agent for redress.

Ratification

If principal ratifies unauthorized agreement it is binding

A principal can still **ratify** a contract even if the agent has acted beyond both actual and apparent authority. If a mechanic working at Pedersen's Used Cars were to sell one of the cars on behalf of Pedersen, it is quite likely that the contract would not be binding since a reasonable third party would not expect a mechanic to have the authority to sell cars. However, if Pedersen liked the deal and wanted the sale to proceed, he could force the third party to honour the contract through ratification even though the agent had exceeded both actual and apparent authority. The effect of such ratification is to give authority to the mechanic to act on behalf of the principal retroactive to the time he entered into the sale. The result can seem unfair because the principal is not bound when an agent goes beyond the authority given and the third party can do nothing to change that. The third party, however, is bound if the principal ratifies the deal. In fact, the rights of the parties have been qualified to a great extent. The

Third party can set time limit for ratification

third party has the right to set a reasonable time limit within which the ratification must take place. In the case of a mechanic selling a car without authority, if the customer, after learning of this lack of authority, approached Pedersen to try to get out of the deal, Pedersen could ratify the agreement at once which would force adherence to the contract. But in the absence of such immediate ratification, the customer is not required to have this possibility dragging on for any length of time. The customer is free to say, "You have until noon tomorrow to decide." In the United States, once the third party revokes, it is too late for the principal to ratify.

Agent must have been acting for a specific principal

Another requirement for ratification is that the agent must have been acting for the specific principal who is now trying to ratify. A person cannot enter into a contract with a third party while purporting to be an agent and then search for a principal to ratify. The customer would be free to repudiate the purchase since the would-be agent did not have a particular principal in mind when entering into the contract. There is, therefore, no one to ratify the agreement.

Principal must be capable of entering contract

The principal has to be fully capable of entering into the contract at the time the agent was claiming to act on his or her behalf. A principal who did not have the capacity to enter into the original deal because of drunkenness or insanity does not have the power to ratify upon becoming sober or sane. The natural extension of

—when it is entered into

this qualification can cause a serious problem for the people who initiate the process of incorporating a company. Often, promoters who are planning an incorporation will enter into contracts, such as the purchase of property on behalf of the proposed company, assuming that once the company is formed it will ratify the agreements.

But there was no company at the time the contract was entered into. For a company to ratify a contract, it must have been in existence and capable of contracting at the time the would-be agents entered into the contract on its behalf. The promoter, because she by implication warrants that she had the authority to act for her principal would be held responsible for any injuries suffered by a third party. Legislation in some jurisdictions has modified this principle to allow a corporation to ratify a contract entered into on its behalf before its incorporation.[2]

—when it is ratified

A further restriction on the ability to ratify is that the principal must be able to enter into the contract at the time of the ratification. If it would be impossible to enter into the contract at the time the principal attempts to ratify, the contract cannot be ratified. For example, if an agent enters into a contract on behalf of a principal to insure a building against fire, the principal cannot ratify the agreement after a fire. There is no building to insure when ratification is attempted, so there can be no contract.

Consensus necessary for contract

The contract the agent enters into must not make any reference to the need for ratification. If the contract includes terms such as "subject to principal's approval" or "subject to ratification," it becomes merely an agreement to enter into an agreement. The contractual requirement of consensus is not satisfied and there is no contract.

Ratification can take place inadvertently

INADVERTENT RATIFICATION. The ratification process can work against the principal in other ways. It is possible for the principal to ratify the contract inadvertently by accepting some sort of benefit under the agreement knowing where it came from. If Kim's chauffeur bought a new Rolls Royce on Kim's behalf without the actual or apparent authority to do so, Kim would normally not be bound by such a contract. However, if Kim were to use that car in some way, such as driving it to work or going for a ride in the country before returning it to the dealer, Kim would have accepted some benefit under the contract. The principal could then argue that the contract of purchase had been ratified and Kim would be bound to go through with the purchase of the automobile provided that, at the time she received the benefit, Kim knew that the purchase was made on her behalf.

Agency by Necessity

Agency by necessity rarely used today

At the heart of agency law is the requirement that the principal and the agent must both consent to the agent's acts on behalf of the principal. It is the application of this requirement that renders an agent's act performed without actual or apparent authority not being binding on the principal without ratification. As a result, the courts are extremely reluctant to impose agency relationships on principals against their will. However, there are a few situations in which the courts are willing to impose an agency relationship on the principal despite the clear lack of consent. This move is called **agency by necessity**. The doctrine had more application in the past than it does today when communication systems are so much more effective. The classic illustration of agency by necessity is the captain of a ship putting into port and selling

[2] For example, the *Ontario Business Corporation Act*, R.S.O. (1990) C.B. 16 s.21

damaged cargo for the best possible price in order to preserve some value for the owners. The owners cannot later attack the sale as being unauthorized and claim the return of the cargo or compensation from the third party. Nor can they claim compensation from the ship's captain on the basis of unauthorized action. In this circumstance, the ship's captain was authorized to act by the principle of agency by necessity. Today, modern communication systems allow the captain to get instructions from the owners about what should be done with the cargo, thus avoiding the need to act unilaterally and rely on agency by necessity. Merely finding another person's property in danger does not, in and of itself, create an agency by necessity relationship. There must be some duty or responsibility placed on the agent to care for those goods before an agency by necessity relationship can arise. Even then the courts will be reluctant to impose such an obligation on the principal.

Spouses often have the implied or apparent authority to act on each other's behalf for the purchase of necessities and other household goods. When dealing with third parties such as merchants who, because of past dealings, are led to believe a person has authority to act for a spouse, there is apparent authority even when the spouse has been specifically prohibited from making such purchases. In some circumstances, authority can be implied by operation of law against the will of the other party. A wife who is deserted by her husband is presumed to have the authority to bind him to contracts with third parties for the purchase of necessities. What is or is not a necessity will vary with the lifestyle and status of the family. Today, this principle must be viewed in light of modern family law legislation which usually provides a more satisfactory remedy. In some jurisdictions, this principle has been abolished altogether.

—except in some family matters

THE RIGHTS AND RESPONSIBILITIES OF THE PARTIES

The Agent's Duties

THE CONTRACT. When an agency agreement has been created by contract, the agent has an obligation to act within the authority given in that agreement. An agent violating the contract can be sued for breach and will have to compensate the principal for any losses suffered. An agent who goes beyond the authority given in the agency agreement and uses apparent authority to create a binding contract between the principal and a third party can be held responsible for compensating any losses suffered. The agent is also obligated to perform any other functions set out in the agency agreement. Failure to do so may be a breach of contract. However, if the performance of the agency function requires the commission of some illegal act or one against public policy, the agent is not required to perform.

Agent must perform as required by principal

An agent owes a duty of care to the principal. If the agent's conduct falls short of claimed skills or below the level of performance expected from a reasonable person, the agent will be liable to the principal for any damages suffered. For example, if Khan hires Gamboa to purchase property on which to build an apartment building, Gamboa must not only stay within the authority given but must exercise the degree of care and skill one would expect from a person claiming to be qualified to do that type of job. If Gamboa buys a property for Khan that is later discovered to be zoned for single family dwellings, then Gamboa would be liable to compensate Khan because the failure to ascertain that vital information would fall below the standard of care expected from somebody in this type of business.

Agents usually have considerable discretion in carrying out agency responsibilities as long as they act to the benefit of the principal. However, an agent cannot go against the specific instructions received, even if it might be in the principal's best interests to do so. If a stockbroker is instructed to sell shares when they reach a specific price, the broker must do so even though waiting would bring the principal a better price.

DELEGATION. Generally, the agent has an obligation to perform the agency agreement personally and is not permitted to delegate responsibility to another party. When there is consent to such delegation, either expressed or implied by the customs and traditions of the industry, the agent can appoint someone else to perform that function. The agent still has the responsibility to see that the terms of the agency agreement are fulfilled. The authority of an agent is commonly delegated to sub-agents when that agent is a corporation or large business organization such as a law firm, bank or trust company.

ACCOUNTING. Because the agent is acting on behalf of the principal, any monies earned pursuant to agency function must be paid over to the principal. If the agent acquires property, goods or money on behalf of the principal, there is no entitlement to retain any of it other than the authorized commission. Even when the agent has some claim against such funds, the agent must convey them to the principal. If the agent, Brose, collects $500 from Witze while acting for Campbell, that money must be paid over to Campbell. Even if Witze owes Brose money from some other deal, Brose must pay over any money collected to the principal. To facilitate this process, the agent also has an obligation to keep accurate records of all agency transactions.

FIDUCIARY DUTY. The relationship between the principal and agent is based on fiduciary duty, or trust. Therefore, the agent has an obligation to act only in the best interests of the principal. The relationship is often referred to as an **utmost good faith** relationship. The agent has an obligation to keep in strict confidence any communications that come through the agency function. The agent cannot take advantage of any personal opportunity that may come to his or her knowledge through the agency relationship. Even if the agent is in a position where some personal benefit will be lost, he or she must act in the principal's best interest. If the agent does stand to benefit personally from the deal, this must be disclosed to the principal. If there is a failure to disclose, the principal can seek an accounting and have any funds gained by the agent in such a way returned to the principal.

Agent owes duty of reasonable care

Agent cannot delegate responsibility

Agent must turn money over to principal

Agent must account for funds

Agent must act in best interests of principal

If any information comes to the agent in the course of duty that could benefit either the principal or the agent, that information must be disclosed to the principal. For this reason, an agent cannot act for both a principal and a third party at the same time. It would be very difficult for an agent to extract the best possible price from a third party on behalf of a principal when the third party was also paying the agent. If the principal discovers the agent accepting payment from the third party, the principal is entitled to an accounting and the receipt of all such funds. This policy holds true unless the agent has fully disclosed the fact that he or she is acting for both parties at the outset and receives consent from both of them. In the same way, the agent can only overcome this fiduciary duty and be allowed to keep any personal gain in any of these situations by fully disclosing the nature of the transaction and his or her involvement as well as gain, and receiving the consent of the principal to proceed. The principal may repudiate the resulting contract if the agent receives money from the third party. An example of such a violation of a fiduciary duty is when an agent is hired to purchase property or goods. In such circumstances, the agent cannot sell his or her own personal property to the principal as if it came from a third party even if that property fully satisfies the principal's requirements. This kind of deal would be enforceable only if the agent fully disclosed the ownership of the property and charged a fair price.

A similar problem can arise in real estate transactions. Suppose the agent hired to sell a house recognizes it as a good deal and purchases it in such a way that it looks as if it has been bought by a third party, for example, by a corporation or a partner. The agent then has the advantage of a good price and the commission as well. The problem is that the agent is not acting in the best interests of the principal by getting the best possible price for the property. In such a situation, the agent would be required to pay back both profits and commission to the vendor of the property. (See Box 10.1, "Agent must hand over house".)

In the same way, the agent must not compete with the principal, especially if a service is being offered or if the agent also represents another principal selling the same product. The agent must give the principal all of the benefit resulting from the performance of the agency agreement. The agent must not collect any profits or commissions that are hidden from the principal. Such wrongful conduct on the part of the agent who is an employee amounts to just cause for dismissal.

Duties of Principal

THE CONTRACT. The principal's primary obligation to the agent is to honour the terms of the contract by which the agent was hired. The principal must adhere to the terms of remuneration that have been agreed to in the contract. If the contract is silent as to payment, an obligation to pay a reasonable amount can be implied. The amount of effort put forth by the agent as well as the customs and traditions of the industry will be taken into consideration to determine what constitutes reasonable payment. If the agreement provides for payment only on completion of the particular job for which the agent has been hired, no payment will be forth-

---

Marginal notes:

Agent cannot act for both principal and third party without consent of both

Agent must not profit at principal's expense

Agent must not compete with principal

Principal must honour terms of contract and pay reasonable amount for services

Box 10.1

Agent must hand over house

$920,000 purchase broke duty to client, judge rules

Toronto—A real estate agent has been given until Oct. 1 to move out of a house in Markham, Ont. that she bought while acting for a would-be purchaser.

In ordering Linda Chow to yield possession of the house she and her husband purchased for $920,000 through a company they owned, an Ontario Supreme Court judge found that Mrs. Chow had breached a fiduciary obligation to her clients.

"While still an agent and fiduciary, she had a conflict of interest with her principal which she failed to disclose," Madam Justice Janet Boland ruled, adding: "She deliberately deceived her principal and used information gleaned through the course of acting as his agent in usurping the opportunity to purchase the property for herself."

The court was told that in the fall of 1987, plaintiff Yin Hang Lee, a retired businessman, sought Mrs. Chow's assistance in finding a new home in the Bayview Avenue area for about $1-million.

Mrs. Chow showed Mr. Lee and his wife the house on Old English Lane in Markham, northeast of Metropolitan Toronto, that became the subject of the court case, and then represented the couple in two weeks of negotiations. At the end of those talks, the parties were only $10 000 apart, with the vendors asking 905 000 and the Lees offering $895 000.

Judge Boland found that the Chows bid $915 000 for the property on Dec. 14, 1987, less than a week after Mrs. Chow presented a $905 000 oral offer on behalf of the Lees. The final $920 000 price was agreed to four days later.

The judge said the first indication the Lees had that Mrs. Chow was no longer acting for them was on the day of the sale, when they found an envelope containing their deposit in their mailbox.

In finding the real estate agent in breach of her fiduciary relationship, the judge said an agent has a duty "to avoid placing herself in potential conflict of interest with her principal unless the principal has full and complete disclosure."

"The value of the agency relationship would be completely destroyed if agents were allowed to occupy a position of trust and then act in direct competition with their principal."

Judge Boland added that the concept of conflict of interest "not only requires disclosure but it also implies that the fiduciary is prohibited from using his position to reap personal gain." In the case at bar, the agent had used confidential information—the price the vendors were willing to accept—that had been obtained in acting for her clients.

In finding the defendants—Mr. and Mrs. Chow and their company—"constructive trustees" for the plaintiff, the judge ordered the house turned over to Mr. Lee "on or before Oct. 1, 1990. upon payment of the sum of $920,000."

A spokesman for the Toronto Real Estate Board said yesterday the median price of Toronto-area homes rose about 40 percent from December, 1987, to April, 1989, and despite a recent market decline is still about 25 percent above late 1987 levels.

Source: Thomas Claridge, The Globe and Mail, *August 8, 1990.*

coming unless that act is performed. Thus, if an agent is to receive a commission upon the sale of a house, even if the agent puts considerable effort into promoting a sale, there is no entitlement to commission if no sale occurs.

Principal must reimburse agent's expenses

The principal also has an obligation to reimburse the agent for any reasonable expenses incurred in the performance of the agency function. If this obligation has not been expressly included in an agency contract, it will be implied. As long as the agent acts as specified in the contract and within the authority given, the agent is entitled to expenses such as phone bills and car expenses that come from the direct performance of the agency function. It should be noted that this point may be modified by specific contractual agreement or by industry traditions. For example, real estate agents do not receive reimbursement of expenses.

A dispute will sometimes arise between the principal and the agent about the interpretation of the contract between them. When agency agreements are vague about the extent of the agent's authority, the courts will usually favour an interpretation that gives the agent the broadest possible power. Thus, if Jones hires Smith to be sales manager for her manufacturing business and gives Smith authority to enter into all sales related to the business, it is probable that a court would use the reasonable person test to find that the sales manager had the authority to sell large blocks of product but that his authority fell short of selling the plant itself. Although the courts tend to interpret vague agency agreements as granting the agent the broadest possible power, it is important to note that they do just the opposite when the power to borrow money is involved. Thus, if Klassen hired Johnson as a purchasing agent with "all the authority necessary to carry out that function" and Johnson found it necessary to borrow money from a third party to make such purchases, the authorization found in the agency agreement would not give Johnson sufficient authority to borrow money without Klassen's approval. It is necessary for an agent to be given specific authority to borrow money on the principal's behalf in order to proceed.

Ambiguous authority will be interpreted broadly

—except when power to borrow money is in question

Undisclosed Principals

The nature of the relationship between the principal and the third party is most often determined by the authority of the agent. As long as an agent acts within the actual or apparent authority, the contract between the principal and the third party will be binding. It is only when both the actual and apparent authority are exceeded that the agent may be found liable to the third party.

Third party can sue agent or principal if principal undisclosed

The only other situation in which the agent will be held directly liable to the third party is when he or she acts for an undisclosed principal. In some instances the principals may want to keep their identities secret in dealings with third parties. The agent can accomplish this wish in several ways. The agent may make it clear that he or she is functioning as an agent but withhold the identity of the principal. The third party can still elect to enter into the agreement in the face of this knowledge, but there will be no recourse against the agent. In the event of a breach, the third party must seek out the identity of the principal and look to that individual for redress. The second situation in which the agent can act for the principal without revealing the principal's identity is when the agent pretends to be the principal. For example, an agent sells property on behalf of a principal but signs the documents as if he or she was the actual owner. In such circumstances, the third party has been misled and can look to the agent for damages in the event of a breach. The third situation in which an agent can act for an undisclosed principal is when the agent deals with a third party in a way consistent with the agent either being an agent or the main contracting party, for example, when the agent signs a purchase order in a way consistent with being an agent for the purchaser or the actual person purchasing the goods. The third party may not be aware that the deal is through an agent with an undisclosed principal but still has not been misled. In these circumstances, the third party has the option of treating the agent as the contracting party and suing the agent in the event of breach or, if the identity of the principal is discovered, suing the principal for compensation in the event of a breach. The injured party cannot sue both; once the choice is made, the third party is bound by it. As a general rule, the third party is bound by contracts entered into by an agent even when the principal is undisclosed, providing the agent is acting within the authority given.

An exception to this doctrine is when the identity of the undisclosed principal is important to the third party. In a contract involving personal services, the third party would be able to repudiate upon discovering that the deal had been made with an agent rather than with the principal. In the case of *Nash v. Dix*,[3] a religious group acquired the services of an agent to purchase a church building from another religious organization. They felt that the church would not be sold to them if they disclosed who they really were. Their fear was justified in that the sale was challenged when the identity of the principal was discovered. The court held that this was not a situation in which the identities of the parties were important and the sale went through. In the case of *Said v. Butt*,[4] a theatre refused to sell a ticket to someone on opening night because he had caused a disturbance in the past. That person arranged for a friend to acquire the ticket on his behalf but was refused admittance even though he had a ticket. He sued for breach but the court held that, in this situation, the identity of the party was obviously important and the court did not enforce the contract.

Undisclosed principal relationships are often used when well-known companies are assembling land for new projects. Property owners in the area are approached by agents to obtain options on their properties. The options are only exercised if a sufficient number of property owners are willing to sell at a reasonable price. The undisclosed principal approach is used to discourage people from holding out for higher prices.

A third party can choose to sue either the agent or the undisclosed principal but the third party is only bound by this choice once the identity of the principal has been determined. The principal can enforce the contract unless the identity of the parties is an important factor in the contractual relationship. Similarly, the agent may sue or be sued under the contract when the principal is undisclosed. The agent only loses the right to enforce the agreement when the principal chooses to act like a principal and takes steps to enforce the agreement. It is usually possible for a principal to ratify an agreement created by an agent who has exceeded both actual and apparent authority and make the agreement binding on the third party. But to do so, the agent must claim to be acting for a specifically identified principal. An undisclosed principal cannot ratify the acts of an agent.

Third party can repudiate when identity of undisclosed principal important

Only identified principals can ratify

[3] *Nash v. Dix*, (1898) 78 L.T. 445.
[4] *Said v. Butt*, (1923) K.B. 497.

The Third Party

An agent owes an obligation to the third party to actually possess the authority he or she claims to have. If she has exceeded both her actual and apparent authority, she has breached that obligation and is subject to action for breach of "warranty of authority." This action is founded on contract law and is one of the few situations in which the agent can be sued directly by the third party. In addition to this remedy, an agent who intentionally misleads the third party into believing that she has authority she does not hold is liable to be sued for damages for the tort of deceit. Furthermore, agents who inadvertently exceed their authority can be sued for negligence. An action for breach of warranty of authority, however, is much more common in these circumstances.

Third party can sue agent for unauthorized acts

It is important to distinguish between the tortious liability of the agent based on fraud or negligence and an action based on breach of warranty of authority. The damages available for breach of warranty of authority are limited to the type of damages available for breach of contract, such as injuries that are reasonably foreseeable to the parties at the time the contract is entered into or injuries which flow naturally from the breach. The types of damages available when fraud or negligence are involved are governed by tort law. The practical result is that an agent who has exceeded authority in dealings with the third party in such a way that the principal is not liable may escape paying full compensation if sued by a third party for breach of warranty of authority. If, for example, the third party, unbeknown to the agent, planned to resell goods purchased from that agent at an unusually high profit but was unable to do so because of the breach of authority, the agent would not be liable for these unusual losses. They would not have been within the reasonable contemplation of the agent at the time the contract was entered into in the first place, and therefore not reasonably foreseeable. However, if the third party could establish the agent's fraud, the lost profits might be recovered from the agent because they are the direct consequence of the fraud.

Remedies in tort available for fraud or negligence

Liability for Agent's Tortious Conduct

As discussed in Chapters 2 and 9, an employer is vicariously liable for the acts an employee commits during the course of employment. When an agent is also an employee of the principal, the principal is vicariously liable for any tortious acts committed by the agent in the course of that employment. The difficulty arises when the agent is not an employee of the principal but instead is an independent contractor. The Supreme Court of Canada has held that the principle of vicarious liability is restricted to those situations in which a master/servant relationship can be demonstrated.[5] Still, it is often argued that a principal can be held vicariously liable for the wrongful conduct of an independent agent. In this text, we have taken the more conservative position that employment must be present for vicarious liability to exist. It must be emphasized, however, that the courts have been expanding the definition of employment. Fleming pointed out that, "The employment of a servant may be limited to a single occasion, or

Vicarious liability limited to employment

---

[5] *T.G. Bright and Company v. Kerr*, (1939) S.C.R. 63.
[6] Fleming, John G., *The Law of Torts* (8th ed.) The Law Book Co. Ltd. Australia (1990) p. 371.

extend over a long period; it may even be gratuitous."[6] Even if the relationship involves a person who is essentially an independent agent, that agent may be functioning as an employee in a given situation and thus impose vicarious liability on the principal. With such a broad definition of employment, judges will have little difficulty imposing vicarious lability on principals when the circumstances warrant. Of course, the principal can then look to the agent for compensation for any losses incurred by having to pay compensation to the person injured by the agent's wrongful conduct.

Vicarious liability where independent agent deceitful

There are some situations in which vicarious liability will apply even if the agent is acting independently. The courts are clearly willing to hold the principal responsible for the fraudulent misrepresentation of an agent even when no employment exists. The vendor can be held responsible for a fraud committed by a real estate agent in the process of selling a house on behalf of the vendor.

Direct liability if principal is origin of fraud

In the example used to introduce the chapter, it made no difference whether Mr. Snarey was an employee or was acting as an independent agent; because fraud was involved, the principal was liable for the agent's wrongful conduct. In addition to being vicariously responsible for the tortious conduct of an agent, the principal may be found directly liable. If the principal has requested the act complained of, told the agent to make a particular statement that turns out to be defamatory or misleading, or is negligent in allowing the agent to make the particular statements complained of, the principal may be directly liable. In the case of *Junkin v. Bedard*,[7] Junkin owned a motel that was sold to a third party through an agent. Junkin provided false information regarding the profitability of the motel to the agent, knowing that the agent would pass it on to the purchaser, Bedard. The agent did so and Bedard bought the property. Bedard later discovered the falsification and sued Junkin for fraud. Because the agent had innocently passed the information on to Bedard, Junkin alone had committed the fraud even though the agent had communicated the information. This is an example of direct liability rather than vicarious liability. If the agent had been the one to fabricate and communicate the misleading information, the principal's responsibility would have been based on vicarious liability. As was the case with employment law, the fact that the principal is found vicariously liable for tortious acts of the agent or employee does not relieve either the agent or employee of direct liability for his or her own tortious conduct. Both can be sued, but the employer can then turn to the employee and demand compensation for any loss suffered by the employer.

Vicarious liability—both parties liable

Termination of Agency

Termination as per agreement

An agency relationship created through agreement is usually terminated in the same way. If the authority to function as an agent is embodied in an employment contract, the principles discussed in Chapter 9 under the heading "Termination of Employment" apply. In situations where the agent functions outside of the employment relationship, either gratuitously or pursuant to some independent contract, different principles apply. The principal needs only to give notice to withdraw

[7] *Junkin v. Bedard*, (1958) 11 D.L.R. (2d) 481.

authority from an agent who is acting gratuitously. If the agency relationship is based on a separate contractual relationship, the terms of the agreement itself may provide for the termination of the agency. If the agency relationship was created for a specific length of time, the authority of the agent automatically terminates at the end of that period. Similarly, if the agency contract created the relationship for the duration of a particular project or event, for example, "for the duration of the 1995 Canadian National Exhibition," the authority ends when the project or event ends.

If one of the parties wishes to terminate an ongoing agency relationship, simple notice to this effect from either party is usually sufficient. Notice to terminate the agent's authority would take effect immediately upon receipt by the agent. There is no requirement that the notice be reasonable, only that it be communicated to the agent. On the other hand, if the activities the agent is engaged to perform become impossible or essentially different from what the parties anticipated, then the contractual doctrine of frustration may apply and terminate the agent's authority. Similarly, an agent's authority to act on behalf of a principal is terminated when the actions the agent is engaged to perform become illegal. If Cantello had agreed to act as Jasper's agent to sell products in a pyramid sales scheme, Cantello's authority to represent Jasper would have been terminated automatically when the Criminal Code provision prohibiting such activities was passed.[8]

An agent's authority to act on behalf of a principal can be terminated in several other ways. The death or insanity of a principal will automatically end the authority of an agent. The dissolution of a corporation will have a similar effect. An agent will lose authority when a principal becomes bankrupt, although other people may assume such authority under the direction of the trustee. The third party will normally not be affected in the same way. Certainly, as far as termination of authority on the basis of agreement is concerned, unless the principal notifies the third party of such termination, the actions of the agent may still be binding on the principal on the basis of apparent authority. Though it is not entirely clear, this may also be the case when the principal becomes insane. In the case of bankruptcy, death or dissolution of the company, the agent's actual and apparent authority ceases.

Specialized Agency Relationships

There are many examples of specialized services offered to the public which are essentially agency in their nature, such as travel agents, real estate agents, stockbrokers and insurance agents. Some of these agents do not enter into contracts on behalf of their clients but negotiate and act on their clients' behalf in other ways. For example, a real estate agent neither offers nor accepts on behalf of a client. In fact, the client is usually the vendor of property and the agent's job is to take care of the preliminary matters and bring the purchaser and vendor together so they can enter into a contract directly. Nonetheless, few would dispute that these real estate agents are carrying out an essentially agency function. The important thing to remember is

Margin notes:

Frustration may terminate agency

Death, insanity or bankruptcy will terminate agency

Requirement of notification for termination

General principles apply to specialized agencies as well

[8] *Criminal Code*, R.S.C. (1985) c.C-46 s.206.

that the general provisions set out above also apply to these special agency relationships, although there may be some exceptions. For example, in most of these specialized service professions, the rule that an agent cannot delegate usually does not apply. The very nature of these businesses requires that employees of the firm, not the firm itself, will act on behalf of the client.

Special statutes
and professional
organizations

It is important to note that most of these specialized agencies are fulfilling a service function and are governed by special statutes and professional organizations. For example, the real estate industry in each province has legislation in place that creates commissions which govern the industry. The commissions require that anyone acting for another in the sale of property be licensed or be in the employ of a licensed real estate agent. These bodies license their members and provide disciplinary action when required. It is beyond the scope of this text to examine these professional bodies in detail; the student is encouraged to examine the controlling legislation as well as to seek information from the governing professional bodies in these areas directly. Most of these bodies are concerned about their public image and are happy to cooperate.

SUMMARY

An agent acts as a go-between when the principal enters into a contract with a third party. The agent's authority is usually defined in a contract but there might be further apparent authority when the principal has done something to lead the third party to believe that the agent has authority even when such authority has been specifically withheld. Even if the agent has exceeded both the actual and apparent authority, the principal may ratify the agreement. Such ratification works retroactively. Only when the agent acts beyond all authority can he or she be sued (breach of warranty of authority).

When the agent does not disclose that he or she is acting for a principal, the third party has a choice to sue the agent or the undisclosed principal to enforce the contract. In the absence of an employment relationship, the principal is not vicariously liable for the acts of the agent except when fraudulent misrepresentation is involved.

A fiduciary relationship exists between the agent and the principal, and the agent, as a result, has the obligation to act in the best interests of the principal. The agency relationship is typically terminated by simple notification or as agreed in the agency contract. Death or insanity of the principal, or dissolution of the corporation will also terminate the agent's authority.

QUESTIONS

1. What is the agent's function? Why is it important to understand the law of agency in business?

2. Distinguish between agents, employees and independent contractors. Describe the relationship between them.

3. What is the significance of the agency agreement for the parties to it?

4. Explain what effect an agent's limited capacity will have on the contractual obligations created between a principal and a third party. What effect would the incapacity of the principal have on this relationship?

5. Distinguish between an agent's actual, implied and apparent authority. Explain why this distinction can be important from the agent's point of view.

6. Distinguish between promissory, or equitable, estoppel and ordinary estoppel. Explain the role estoppel plays in agency law.

7. Explain what is meant by ratification. Why is the principal's right to ratify often considered unfair to the third party?

8. Describe the limitations on a principal's right to ratify the actions of his or her agent. How can the principle of ratification be as dangerous to the principal as it is to the third party?

9. What effect does it have on the relationship between the principal and the third party when an agent writes on an agreement "subject to ratification?"

10. Agents owe a fiduciary duty to their principals. What are the requirements of that duty?

11. What options are open to a third party who has been dealing with an undisclosed principal if the contract is breached?

12. Does an undisclosed principal have the right to ratify an agent's unauthorized act?

13. Explain how the doctrine of vicarious liability applies in a principal/agent relationship.

14. How does the function performed by a real estate agent differ significantly from that normally performed in a principal/agency relationship? What governs the real estate agent's conduct?

CASES

1. *Kisil v. John S. Stevens Ltd.*

   Mr. and Mrs. Kisil bought a house through Buckley, an agent for the John S. Stevens firm. In the process of selling the house, Buckley assured the Kisils that there was no problem with the water in the well. They decided to buy the house, but Buckley kept them out of the house until after the deal's closing date. All this time, Buckley maintained that the condition of the well was good and that the water would clear up as soon as it was used a bit. In fact, the well had been improperly constructed and the water it produced was unfit for use. The Kisils sued Buckley and the real estate company. Describe the arguments which would form the basis of their complaint, their likelihood of success and the remedies available. Explain as well the legal position of the vendor.

2. *Rockland Industries Inc. v. Amerada Minerals Corporation of Canada Limited.*
    Curtz was a salesman in charge of bulk sales and the manager of marketing who reported to Devron, a senior vice president of Amerada. Curtz negotiated and concluded a deal with Powers and Lederman, employees of Rockland Industries Inc., for the sale of 50 000 tons of sulphur. During the process of negotiation, Curtz gave no indication of any qualifications on his authority. However, any sale of this magnitude had to be approved by an executive operating committee of Amerada and signed by the chairman of the board. After the deal was completed, Rockland's representative was informed of the limitations on Curtz's authority, but was also told that the operating committee had given approval and that the chairman of the board's signature was merely a rubber stamp. In fact, Amerada refused to deliver the sulphur and Rockland had to acquire it from other sources. They were able to acquire only 25 000 tons and sued Amerada for damages. Explain the arguments available to both sides and the likely outcome.

3. *Alberta Housing Corporation v. Achten* and *Alberta Housing Corporation v. Orysiuk.*
    The Alberta Housing Corporation was established to secretly create a landbank to stabilize residential prices as the city of Edmonton expanded. Orysiuk was the managing director of the Alberta Housing Corporation who was given the task of making the acquisitions for the landbank. The Housing Corporation acquired the services of Achten, a lawyer, who was given a commission of 5 percent on the acquisition of lands. Other parties were also engaged to assemble the land, including a real estate company that was given a commission of 3 percent. Achten acquired a large amount of land on behalf of the Alberta Housing Corporation and earned over $200 000 in commissions. After a number of properties had already been acquired under the relationship between Achten and the Alberta Housing Corporation, Achten entered into a separate secret agreement with Orysiuk whereby he paid back one-half of his commission. When this deal was eventually discovered, the Alberta Housing Corporation sued both parties for the recovery of the Corporation's money. Explain the arguments available on both sides and the likely outcome. Would it affect your answer if you learned that the Alberta Housing Corporation was not injured by Orysiuk and Achten's actions and had paid a fair price for the property including legal fees and commissions? The Alberta Housing Commission also insisted on the return of over $30 000 they had paid to Achten in legal fees. Explain the likely outcome.

4. *Guertin v. Royal Bank of Canada.*
    Mrs. Guertin worked at a snack bar. The owners of the snack bar owned another restaurant which was located in the same mall as a branch of the Royal

Bank managed by Mr. Arcand. Mr. and Mrs. Guertin were good customers of the Royal Bank and went to talk to the bank manager about the possibilities of buying this snack bar. They told him that the price was $30 000 but they also told him they thought they could get it for $22 000 or $23 000. In fact, the Guertins were waiting to see if the price would come down. In the meantime, Mr. Arcand offered $23 000 for the snack bar which was accepted. The purchase was made through his wife because the bank rules prohibited him from buying it himself. Explain the liability of Mr. Arcand and the bank in these circumstances and any complaints the Guertins might have about his conduct.

5. *Winnipeg Piano Company v. Wawryshun.*
A wife who helped manage her husband's boarding house business bought a player piano from the plaintiff. In the process, she signed a declaration that the purchase was being made with her husband's approval and on behalf of himself and the family. At this time the husband was away and had clearly not authorized the purchase. The piano company sued the husband for payment. Explain the arguments which can be raised on both sides and the likely outcome. How would your answer be affected by the information that the husband indicated his disapproval to his wife upon his return but she said that it was her business and she would pay for it out of her earnings? In fact, the husband signed the cheque for one payment towards the piano. Would the outcome be affected if the husband had not read the contract and did not know that he was the reported purchaser?

6. *McNeel and McNeel v. Lowe, Lowe and Renfrew Realty Limited.*
The vendor appellants had authorized the respondent agent to try to sell a certain property for $78 000. The agent did find a purchaser, Mr. Tangedal, who was willing to pay the $78 000 but only if the vendors took a $16 000 interest in another property as part of the purchase price. The vendors rejected this offer and eventually the exclusive listing agreement with the agent expired. The appellants encouraged him to continue to try to find a purchaser. Later, the agent entered into a partnership arrangement with Mr. Tangedal and together they approached the vendor offering $70 000 for the property, the agent giving up his commission on the sale. Because only $24 000 was to be paid down and a first mortgage given for the rest, the agent had to pay only $13 000 as his part of the purchase price. Unknown to the vendor, immediately after the contract of purchase was executed, the partnership ended and the agent was given a second mortgage against the property of $8000. In addition, Mr. Tangedal, for the $13 000 the agent had invested, gave him the $16 000 interest in the other property he had tried to get the vendors to take in trade. The effect of this arrangement was that, immediately after the completion of the sale and unknown to the vendor, the agent had assets worth $11 000 more than he had invested. When the vendors discovered the result of this agreement, they sued the agent. Explain the nature of the complaint and

the likely outcome of the action. In your answer, consider how much Mr. Tangedal actually paid for the property.

ISSUES

1. A principal who enters into a contract which specifically limits the agent's authority still faces the possibility of being bound by acts the agent performs outside the actual authority because of the agent's apparent authority. Why should the principal bear responsibility to the third party when it was the agent who violated the authority limitation? Would it not be more appropriate for the third party to turn to the agent for compensation for any losses suffered when the agent violates his or her authority? In your discussion of this issue, consider the matter from the position of both the principal and the third party.

2. When a third party enters into a contract with an agent who is dealing on behalf of a principal, the third party must look to the principal if the contract is breached. There are a few exceptions to this, such as undisclosed principal, but in general the third party cannot sue the agent. Would it not be more appropriate to give the third party the right to sue the agent as well as the principal if a contract is breached and thus hold them both responsible for the performance of the contract? If tort liability is imposed and vicarious liability is present, both the person committing the wrong and the person being held vicariously liable can be sued for compensation for the injuries suffered. Would a similar approach be appropriate when contractual liability is being considered? Should there be any exceptions to the rule of the principal being responsible or should the third party always be required to turn to the principal for compensation, even in an undisclosed principal situation?

3. Vicarious liability imposes liability on an employer for the tortious conduct of an employee performed during the course of that employment. Should vicarious liability be extended to agents acting for principals even when no employment relationship can be demonstrated? Consider the expansion of the concept of employment and the exceptions that are in place in your discussion of this issue.

4. Ratification is an option available to the principal when an agent has acted beyond both actual and apparent authority in entering into a contract with a third party. During the period between the unauthorized act of the agent and the ratification, the principal is not bound but has the option to hold the third

party to the contract. However, the third party faces the possibility that the principal will ratify the agreement and is potentially liable under the contract during this period. The reason for this discrepancy is that ratification works retroactively and the act of the agent becomes an authorized act when the principal ratifies. Because of the apparent injustice involved from the point of view of the third party, many limitations have been placed on the power of the principal to ratify. In some cases, repudiation on the part of the third party will prevent effective ratification. Should the principal's power to ratify be abolished altogether or is the third party harmed in any way by ratification? Does the third party have the right to turn to the agent for compensation for breach of warranty of authority if the principal chooses not to ratify? Is the concept of repudiation, which allows the third party to prevent the ratification process, a step in the right direction or a negative development in our law?

5. A person must be a licensed real estate agent or be an employee of such an agent to sell real property on behalf of others. Such a restriction creates a class of people who control and obtain great benefit from a particular type of trade. Does the legislation that gives real estate agents exclusive control over such a lucrative market benefit or harm the general populace? In your answer, consider the arguments for and against regulating this industry.

LEGISLATION

Alberta
Factors Act, R.S.A. (1980) c.F-1
Land Agents Licensing Act, R.S.A. (1980) c.L-2
Power of Attorney Act, S.A. (1991) c.P-13.5
Real Estate Agents' Licensing Act, R.S.A. (1980) c.R-5

British Columbia
Power of Attorney Act, R.S.B.C. (1979) c.334
Real Estate Act, R.S.B.C. (1979) c.356

Manitoba
Factors Act, R.S.M. (1987) c.F-10
Power of Attorney Act, R.S.M. (1987) c.P.-97
Real Estate Brokers Act, R.S.M. (1987) c.R-20

New Brunswick
Factor and Agents Act, R.S.N.B. (1973) c.F-1
Real Estate Agents Licensing Act, R.S.N.B. (1973) c.R-1

Newfoundland
Real Estate Trading Act, R.S.N. (1990) C.R-2

Nova Scotia
Factors Act, R.S.N.S. (1989) c. 157
Real Estate Brokers Licensing Act, R.S.N.S. (1989) c.384

Ontario
Factors Act, R.S. O. (1990) c.F.1
Power of Attorney Act, R.S.O. (1990) c. P.20
Real Estate and Business Brokers Act, R.S.O. (1990) c.R.4

Prince Edward Island
Factors Act, R.S.P.E.I. (1988) c.F-1
Real Estate Trading Act, R.S.P.E.I. (1988) c.R-2

Québec
Travel Agents' Act, R.S.Q. (1977) c.A-10

Saskatchewan
Factors Act, R.S.S. (1978) c.F-1
Real Estate Brokers Act (1987) S.S. (1986-87-88) c.R-2.1

Northwest Territories
Factors Act, R.S.N.W.T. (1988) c.F-1

Yukon
Employment Agencies Act, R.S.Y. (1986) c.53
Factors Act, R.S.Y. (1986) c.61
Real Estate Agents Act, R.S.Y. (1986) c.145

11 BUSINESS ORGANIZATION: SOLE PROPRIETORSHIP AND PARTNERSHIP

Objectives of the Chapter

■ to describe a sole proprietorship and the government regulations that affect it

■ to identify the rights and obligations of partners

■ to outline the advantages of partnership as a form of business

One of the partners in a law firm was helping to administer an estate when he was asked to transfer the amount outstanding in the estate ($60 025) to a bank in California. These funds were on deposit at a local branch of the Royal Bank and a cheque was drawn up, signed by the executrix of the estate and made out to the California bank as payee. The lawyer, however, made another copy of that cheque with himself as payee, forged the signature of the executrix and destroyed the first cheque. He then cashed the cheque at his own bank. When this action was discovered, he was charged and convicted of fraud. The bank on which the cheque was drawn was required to reimburse the estate and they turned to the convicted lawyer's partners to compensate them. There is no question that the partners were honest and innocent of any wrongdoing. Yet in the subsequent court action, they were found liable to compensate the Royal Bank for their $60 000 loss even though that branch had had no direct dealings with the partnership at all.[1] Although this case deals with lawyers,

---

[1] *Victoria & Grey Trust Company v. Crawford et al.*, Ont. Sup. Ct. 636-012.

the principles apply to any situation in which partnership exists. Partners are responsible for the wrongful conduct of each other. The case also illustrates just how careful people going into business with others have to be. The following chapter is devoted to an examination of partnership law, how partnership is created and the obligations of the parties involved.

A commercial enterprise, usually called a business, can be established on the basis of several different methods of ownership. It is vitally important that the parties participating in the commercial activity clearly understand the legal responsibilities and rights which apply to their choice of business organization. This information could be significant to the owners of the business, its employees or representatives and to outsiders involved in commercial transactions with it.

TYPES OF BUSINESS ORGANIZATION

Sole proprietorship is one person

There are essentially three major types of business organization. The first, the **sole proprietorship**, is an individual carrying on business alone. Employees may be hired and business may be carried on through the services of an agent, but the business is the sole responsibility of one person. A second method of carrying on business is called a **partnership**. In a partnership, ownership responsibilities and profits or losses are shared by two or more partners. As was the case with the sole proprietorship, the partnership may also employ others and act through agents. The third type of business organization is the incorporated company. Any type of business organization involving more than one person can be called a company. A **corporation**, however, is a legal entity. By statute it has been given an identity separate from the individual members who make it up. Thus, contracts with a corporation are dealings with the company itself as if it were a person in its own right.

In a partnership owners share responsibilities

Corporation is a separate legal entity

People in a community can carry on business in other ways. For example, it is possible to set up a **society** under the *Societies Act* if the enterprise is not for profit. The result is also a separate legal entity, but the procedure of incorporation and the obligations of those involved are quite different. There are also several ways in which these various types of business organizations can be combined. For example, it is possible for the business of one incorporated company to be holding shares in another company. Or several different incorporated companies can band together to form a special company or partnership to accomplish a major project by participating in what is known as a joint venture. The discussion in this text will be limited to an examination of the three main types of business organizations outlined

Societies are separate legal entities but obligations differ

above. This chapter will examine sole proprietorship and partnership, and Chapter 12 will deal with corporations.

THE SOLE PROPRIETORSHIP

Sole proprietor carries on business in own right

The sole proprietorship is simply an individual carrying on a business activity in his or her own right. The sole proprietor makes all the decisions associated with the business and is the only one entitled to the benefits deriving from the business. A sole proprietor also bears full responsibility for all of the costs, losses and obligations incurred in the business activity. Thus, there is no distinction between the personal assets of the sole proprietor and those of the business. They are all the assets of the proprietor and are available to creditors if things go badly.

Government Regulations

Must adhere to licensing and governing regulations

The sole proprietor, like all other types of business organizations, must satisfy many federal, provincial and municipal requirements in order to carry on business. A sole proprietor is usually required to register the business name, and buy a licence from the municipality and, in some cases, the province. The provinces control certain types of business activity, such as door-to-door sales, credit information services and moneylenders, through this licensing process. The provinces discourage or restrict some types of business activities which are subject to abuse, including massage parlours, video outlets that deal in pornographic material, steam baths, hotels and cabarets. Sole proprietors who undertake business activities that handle food or dangerous commodities are subject to further controlling provincial and federal legislation. Sole proprietors must also satisfy local zoning bylaws which restrict the types of activities that can be carried out in a particular location. Sole proprietors with employees are subject to employment legislation such as workers' compensation, unemployment insurance and income tax regulations. These regulations apply to all types of business organizations, and fees are levied in proportion to the size and extent of the operation. As a general rule, sole proprietors are subject to fewer government regulations than partnerships and corporations. Only minimal records need be kept, and sole proprietors are usually not required to disclose information about the business to others. They must keep sufficient records to satisfy government agencies such as the tax department. In essence, the sole proprietor has complete control and complete responsibility for the business activity.

Sole proprietor relatively free of outside interference

Sole proprietors have no accountability to others in the running of their businesses, but the responsibility for making important business decisions rests entirely on their own shoulders. Sole proprietors can only look to their own resources to finance the business operation; they cannot sell shares and are restricted to their own credit standing when borrowing money to finance the business. The sole proprietor owns all the assets, receives all the profits of the business and is responsible

Sole proprietor
has unlimited
liability

Sole proprietor
vicariously liable
for employees'
actions

Professionals
bound by certain
rules

for all the debts and liabilities. This **unlimited liability** can be the most significant disadvantage of the sole proprietorship. When debts are incurred or the business faces some other sort of liability, the whole burden falls on the sole proprietor. Under the principle of vicarious liability, the sole proprietor is responsible for any tort committed by an employee during the course of employment. Here again the sole proprietor's entire personal fortune is at risk. It is important for people carrying on business by themselves to have sufficient insurance to cover such potentially devastating liability. Any profit derived from a sole proprietorship is subject to personal income tax, and some tax advantages available to partnerships and corporations are not available to sole proprietors. These factors alone are often enough to encourage the sole proprietor to incorporate.

It should be noted that some individuals cannot incorporate or derive no advantage from doing so. Professionals such as doctors, dentists, lawyers and accountants are usually prevented from incorporating or derive little benefit from doing so. They usually carry on business as sole proprietors or band together in a group as partners. A sole proprietor who is a professional is required to join the appropriate professional organization. Typically, these bodies are set up under legislation which gives them extensive power to regulate educational and professional qualifications and standards of behaviour, and to establish methods of disciplining members for wrongful conduct or incompetence.

PARTNERSHIP

Partnership—
carrying on
business
together for
profit

Partnerships
governed by
contract law

From the earliest times, people have found it more efficient to pool their talents and resources by forming partnerships. **Partnerships** are essentially groups of people acting together for a business purpose with a view to making a profit. The primary relationship between the partners is one of contract, and thus basic contract law applies. However, the courts have developed special provisions to deal with this particular kind of legal relationship. It is important to realize that the group so formed does not take on a legal personality separate from the people who make it up as is the case with a corporation. It has become possible over the years, however, to enter into legal relationships with the partnership as such, thus eliminating the need to enter into a separate agreement with each partner individually. This allows the partnership the convenience of functioning in many situations as a single business unit.

Legislation

Although partnership has always been an important method of carrying on business, the dramatic increase in commercial activity in England in the eighteenth and nineteenth centuries resulted in the development of a considerable body of case law. As part of the great effort to update the laws of England in the nineteenth century, the law of partnership was summarized in one well-drafted statute called the

Partnership Act
still used today

Partnership Act (enacted in 1890). This legislation was adopted in all of the common law provinces of Canada where it has remained in place to the present day with few alterations. Although there have been some additions to the *Partnership Act* (which in some provinces are contained in separate statutes), the legislation varies little from province to province; the principles discussed in this chapter need little qualification for provincial variation. For convenience, the Ontario version will be used whenever the *Partnership Act* is referred to and the sections discussed will refer to that statute.[2]

Creation of the Partnership

Essentially, the *Partnership Act* provides that, whenever two or more people **carry on business in common with a view towards profits**, a partnership exists.[3] This does not mean that a profit was made, only that profit was the object of the exercise. The *Act* goes on to set out a number of circumstances which by themselves will not give rise to a partnership. Owning property in common, even though the object is to make a profit, will not be enough to create a partnership. Two friends who purchase a house and rent it out, sharing the profits, will not be considered a partnership based on this relationship alone. The *Act* also points out that the sharing of gross returns from a business activity does not in itself create a partnership. Only when the net receipts from the investment, or profits, are shared is the existence of a partnership presumed. Two real estate agents who split the commission for selling a vendor's house will not be partners but the sharing of any profits from the sale will be evidence of partnership. The *Partnership Act* goes on to set out a number of other circumstances which, by themselves, will not establish a partnership.[4]

Partnership Act
lists exceptions

1. When a debt is repaid by the creditor taking a share of the debtor's profits. For example, Pallas owes Clegg $10 000 and Clegg agrees to let Pallas pay it back by paying 10 percent of the profits of Pallas's furniture store per month until repaid.
2. When the payment of an employee is based on a share of sales or profits, such as commission selling or profit-sharing schemes.
3. When the beneficiary of a deceased partner receives the deceased partner's share of the profits.
4. When a loan is made in relation to a business and payment of interest varies with the profit. For example, Pallas loans Clegg $10 000 to start a furniture business and Clegg repays it by paying 10 percent of the store's profits per month.
5. When a business is sold and the payment of the goodwill portion varies with the profitability of the business. For example, Pallas sells Clegg a furniture business for $10 000 for the assets and 50 percent of the first year's profits for goodwill.

The question remains: What does constitute carrying on business together with a view towards profit? When evidence indicates that there has been a joint

[2] *Partnership Act*, R.S.O. (1990) c. P. 5
[3] *Ibid.*, s.2
[4] *Ibid.*, s.3

Partnership exists when profits shared

contribution of capital to establish a business, an intention to share expenses, profits or losses, or joint participation in the management of a business, then a partnership will be presumed. If two people operate a restaurant together by sharing the work and the expenses and jointly making decisions, they would be carrying on business together for the purpose of making a profit. The relationship is a partnership. It should be further noted that the *Partnership Act* requires that the parties carry on a continuing business together for a partnership to be present;

Partnership must carry on continuing business

a single, joint project would probably not be classed as a partnership. For example, if two university students combine their resources to put on a school dance, this single project would probably not be classed as a partnership. But if they put on several dances, they would be in the "business" of providing this type of entertainment and thus would be in partnership whether they intended to be or not.

Partnership can be created by conduct

CREATION BY INADVERTENCE. It is important to realize that the partnership relationship can be implied from the conduct of the parties and therefore can be created inadvertently. The existence of a partnership relationship is a question of fact to be determined by the court. The establishment of such a relationship can have significant consequences because each partner must bear the responsibility for the misconduct of fellow partners, and any one partner has the authority to bind the other partners in contracts with outsiders. It is vital to consider the possibility that a partnership exists, with its inherent responsibilities and obligations, whenever a person is involved in any kind of business activity with another. Failure to appreciate this possibility can have disastrous financial consequences when one partner incurs liability to a third party.

—or by agreement

CREATION BY AGREEMENT. The partnership relationship is primarily one of contract, usually created by agreement, but this agreement often does not take a written form. In addition to setting out the responsibilities of partners to third parties, the *Partnership Act* also sets out the rights and obligations of the partners to each other. Although a partnership agreement will not modify the relationship between the partners and outsiders, such an agreement can significantly alter the rights and obligations of the partners between themselves. It is important for the partners to enter into a written agreement setting out the exact nature of the relationship between them. A written document means there is less likelihood of disputes arising between the parties about the terms of the agreement.

Partnership contract must contain all elements of contract

All of the elements necessary for a contract must be present for a partnership agreement to exist. The partnership agreement should set out the duties of each partner in the business activity, what type of work or talent each partner is expected to contribute, the amount of time to be committed to the business, how the profits are to be shared and how the capital is to be distributed, as well as any limitations on the powers or authority of each partner. The partners can also set out methods of resolving any disputes between them and under what circumstances the partnership will be dissolved. It must be remembered that the rights of outsiders dealing with the partnership are determined by the provisions of the *Partnership*

Act and partnership law generally. The rights of outsiders are therefore unaffected by any agreement between the partners.

It should also be noted that, even when the provisions of the *Partnership Act* do not impose a partnership relationship on the parties, such a relationship can still exist because of estoppel. If one of the parties represents to a third party either by words or by conduct that another person is a partner and that representation is relied on, the person holding out the other as a partner will not be able to deny it later, even if it can be clearly demonstrated that the two were not carrying on a business together. The principle of estoppel applies to partnership just as much as it does to agency because each partner acts as an agent for the partnership.

Partnership can be imposed by the principle of estoppel

The Partner as an Agent

Laws of agency apply to partnership

At the heart of partnership law lies the relationship of agency. When dealing with third parties, every partner is considered an agent of every other partner, at least for the purposes of the partnership business. Every partner has the power to bind the other partners in contract as long as the contract involves the business of the partnership.[5] To properly understand the law of partnership, this chapter must be read in conjunction with Chapter 10 on agency. Even if the partners have specifically limited the authority of one of their members to make contracts on behalf of the business, if that partner exceeds the specific authority granted and creates a contract relative to the business with a third party who is unaware of the limitation, the contract is binding on all the other partners. This example demonstrates the apparent authority of an agent and is another illustration of the principle of estoppel. For example, a shoe store opened by Akbari and Carlson would qualify as a partnership if no incorporation had taken place. If Akbari were to take a trip to Toronto and visiting his regular supplier come across a great deal on five hundred pairs of yellow, patent leather oxfords he was unable to resist buying, that contract would be binding on Carlson as well because the two are partners. Even if the partnership agreement between Carlson and Akbari specifically set out that neither partner had the authority to enter into any contracts which committed the firm to pay over $100 without the other's approval, the contract would still be binding on both partners, except in the unlikely event that the party selling the shoes was aware of this particular limitation. However, if Akbari bought a new boat during his trip to Toronto, this purchase would not be binding on his partner because the purchase could not be said to be made pursuant to the partnership business of selling shoes.

Vicarious Liability

Partners fully liable for each other's acts

The liability of a partner is not restricted to contractual obligations created on the basis of agency. All partners are also liable in tort for the wrongful conduct of partners as if they had committed the act themselves. This is an application of the principle of vic-

---

[5] *Ibid.*, s.6 and 7.

arious liability and applies to liabilities incurred in all business-related activities, including personal injury. If a partner carelessly makes a mistake and causes harm to a third party in the course of performing duties in the business, the other partners will also be liable for the damages. If Agostino and Paradis are in the business of selling firewood and Agostino negligently drops a load of wood on a passing pedestrian, both Agostino and Paradis would be liable to pay compensation for the injury. Partners are similarly liable when the wrong has been committed intentionally. For this reason, the partners of the lawyer who fraudulently acquired the $60 000 from his client in the example used to open this chapter were required to make good the loss even though they were completely innocent. Similarly, all partners are responsible for the tortious acts of any employee which are committed in the course of their employment. Partners can also be held responsible for the wrongful conduct of other partners that takes the form of breach of trust, such as the misuse of their clients' money. In such situations, all of the partners are responsible for compensating the victim's loss. It should be noted, however, that the *Partnership Act* states that in such circumstances the other partners will only be liable for the breach of trust if they have prior notice of the trust relationship.[6]

Partners liable for wrongful acts of employees

Partners liable for breach of trust

Since a partnership can employ individuals, the principles set out in Chapter 9 on employment law apply. A partnership with employees has an obligation to adhere to government regulations on workers' compensation, unemployment insurance and income tax.

Unlimited Liability

The sole proprietor's liability is unlimited in that his or her entire personal fortune is at risk to satisfy the claims of an injured party. However, the sole proprietor is responsible only for his or her own wrongful conduct. In a partnership, the partners' liability is unlimited and they are responsible for each other's conduct. Thus, if the assets of the partnership are not sufficient to satisfy the claims of the creditors, the partners must pay out of their own personal assets in the same proportion as they share profits. If a partnership agreement creates different classes of partners in which two senior partners are entitled to 30 percent of the profits and the two junior partners 20 percent of the profits, the senior partners will bear 30 percent of the loss each and the junior partners will bear 20 percent of the loss each.

Partners share losses equally or proportionally by agreement

In some cases, the partnership agreement will specify that one of the partners will bear all or a significant portion of the loss because that party is better able to do so. It must be remembered in all of these cases that such provisions will not affect the position of any creditors or third parties. An outsider is not affected by any term in the partnership agreement that limits the liability of one of the partners. He or she is able to sue any partner for full compensation. If one partner is particularly well off and the other partners have few personal assets, the injured party will look to the partner with significant assets for compensation once the assets of the partnership have been exhausted.

Third party can collect from any partner regardless of agreement

[6] *Ibid.*, s.14.

Partners are jointly liable for the debts and obligations of the partnership as opposed to jointly and severally liable.[7] This means that, for someone to seek a remedy against all of the partners, they all must be included in the action. Thus, if only two of the three partners are sued and it later turns out that they do not have enough assets to satisfy the judgment, it is then too late to sue the third. (Manitoba, however, provides for joint and several liability for the partners arising from debts and obligations of the partnership.) It must be emphasized, though, that when liability arises because of wrongful conduct (tort) or because of breach of trust this liability is both joint and several. This means that it is possible for the injured party to sue one partner and still maintain the right to sue the other partners if not satisfied.[8] The result of this vicarious liability is that all the partners are responsible for the injuries incurred to the extent of their entire personal fortunes.

All personal assets at risk

When a partnership is dissolved or one partner retires from the business, the unlimited liability continues to apply to that ex-partner for any wrongs committed or liability incurred during the partnership period. This liability also continues for acts committed after the dissolution of the partnership or the retirement of the partner unless the third party has been given notice that the retiring party has left the firm. A new partner coming into the firm cannot be required to compensate a third party for any liabilities incurred by the firm before entering the partnership unless the new partner has agreed to take over such an obligation in the partnership agreement.

Registration

Registration usually required

Most provinces require that a partnership be registered. Saskatchewan, Manitoba and Prince Edward Island require that a partnership be registered in all circumstances. Ontario, British Columbia, Alberta and New Brunswick require registration only when the partnerships involve mining, trading and manufacturing. Failure to register properly can result in the partnership having to pay a fine and can make any liability that was only joint be expanded to joint and several liability. Many provinces prohibit an unregistered partnership from maintaining any action against third parties, such as customers who have not paid. Because of these factors, there are pressing reasons for obeying the legislation requiring registration of a partnership and no advantage in not doing so.

Rights and Obligations of the Parties

Fiduciary duty exists between partners

Partners must account for any profits or use of property

FIDUCIARY DUTY. The relationship between partners is primarily governed by an obligation on the part of each partner to act in the best interest of the others. This is a fiduciary relationship, imposing on the partner an obligation to account for any profits that have been made or for any partnership funds or property that have been used. A partner who uses partnership property for personal benefit without the consent of the other partners must pay over any profit made to the partnership and reimburse the partnership for any deterioration of the property. Property brought into a

---

[7] *Ibid.*, s.10.
[8] *Ibid.*, s.13.

partnership for the purposes of the partnership business becomes the property of the partnership even though the title documents might not reflect this ownership. The partner holding title is said to hold the property in trust for the other partners.

Partners cannot compete with partnership

A partner is not permitted to operate a similar business without the consent of the other partners. If this occurs, the partner will be required to pay over to the partnership any profits made which will then be distributed normally to all of the partners. If the separate business loses money, the other partners will not be required to reimburse those losses. If a partnership business was set up to operate a restaurant in Toronto and one of the partners, unknown to the others, independently sets up a restaurant in Vancouver, the other partners could require that partner to pay over any profits made from the Vancouver operation to the partnership to be distributed equally amongst them. If the Vancouver operation lost money, the partner who set it up has the primary obligation to pay.

Partners have an obligation to use any information they discover in their position as partners which might be beneficial to the partnership for the benefit of the partnership and not for personal use. If Noorami were in a mining partnership and an outsider offered to sell him some mining claims because of his position in the firm, he would be required to turn over to the firm any profits earned from the claims if they turned out to be valuable. In effect, the information he used was the property of the partnership. But if the claims turn out to be worthless, he could not ask the firm to participate in his loss.

Other rights and duties

Because a partnership is a special type of contract, the rights and obligations between the partners can be modified by agreement. However, if there is no such agreement, the general provisions set out in the *Partnership Act* governing the relationship between partners will apply.[9] Some of these obligations and rights are as follows:

Profits and losses shared equally or as modified by agreement

1. The partners will share profits equally between them. Similarly, any losses incurred are shared equally between the partners. In the absence of an agreement to the contrary, equal sharing holds true even when the partners have made unequal capital contributions. This provision is often modified by a partnership agreement, but an outside third party will not be affected by such provisions even when a partnership agreement exists. Outsiders can pursue any remedy available and collect the whole amount from one of the partners. That partner will then have the right to seek a contribution from the other partners so that they eventually share the loss equally or in the proportion set out in the agreement.

Partners' expenses reimbursed

2. The partners are entitled to be paid for any expenses they incur in the process of the partnership business. They are also entitled to be repaid for any money other than capital they have advanced to the partnership before the other partners can claim a share of the profits. In addition, the partner advancing such funds is entitled to the payment of interest on that money.

Partners participate in management

3. All partners have the right to take part in management and to have a vote in the firm's affairs. This provision is often modified by partnership agreements which create different classes of partners, particularly in firms with a large number of partners.

---

[9] *Ibid.*, s.24.

No salaries paid
to partners

4. A partner has no right to payment for the work done in a partnership business but only to share in the profits. If one partner is to be paid a weekly salary, this must be stated in the partnership agreement. Usually, partners take a monthly draw against the yet-to-be-calculated profits of the partnership.

Unanimous
agreement
needed for major
changes

5. No major changes can be made to the partnership without the unanimous agreement of all the partners. No new partner can be brought into the partnership nor can a partner be excluded from the firm without the unanimous consent of all the partners. However, for the normal operations of the firm, a simple majority vote is sufficient unless stated otherwise in the partnership agreement.

Assignment
requires consent
of other partners

6. Partners do not have the right to assign their partnership status to some other party without the consent of the other partners. They can, however, assign the benefits they receive from the partnership. The assignees do not have the right to participate in the operation of the business or in the decisions relating to it in any way unless there has been unanimous approval by all the partners to this effect.

Partners must
have access to
records

7. The business records of the partnership must be kept at the partnership office and all of the partners have the right to inspect them.

As can be seen from this summary, the general principle governing a partnership relationship is that the partners function as a unit and have a considerable responsibility to look after each other's interests.

Advantages of Partnership

Insurance
coverage
important

At first glance, the problems associated with a partnership may appear overwhelming. These difficulties can be reduced considerably by having appropriate insurance coverage. It should also be noted that many features of a partnership that are often considered disadvantages are advantages from the point of view of some business people. For example, although the requirement of the unanimous consent of all partners for any changes in the nature of the partnership may be viewed as an encumbrance to effective management, such a requirement provides considerable protection to the individual partner. This requirement significantly increases the individual partner's security in the firm and the control he or she has over it as opposed to minority shareholders in corporations who may find themselves completely ineffectual. Similarly, the right of the individual partner to inspect all records of the partnership business confers advantages not shared by minority shareholders in corporations to the same extent.

Unanimous
consent
protection

Partnership less
costly to form

Another advantage to partnerships is that the legal expenses of drawing up a partnership agreement and of registering the partnership may be less than the expenses involved in incorporating a company. Unlike corporations, partnerships have few formal requirements once the business has been established. For example, a corporation must keep certain types of accounting records and file them with the appropriate government agency. A partnership, on the other hand, has only the needs of the partners to satisfy in this regard. But, as with the sole proprietorship, there are other government regulatory bodies that require records, such as the taxation department, workers' compensation and unemployment insurance. Many of the tax advantages available to a corporation are also available to a partnership.

Too many business people assume that incorporation is a better way to carry on business than partnership because of the unlimited liability and unwieldy management structure of partnerships. While it may be true that an incorporated company is the best vehicle for carrying on business in many situations, there are other situations in which a partnership is more appropriate. Some activities, such as the practice of law, medicine and dentistry, are not allowed by statute to be engaged in by corporations. A partnership is the only alternative when more than one of these professionals wishes to join together to carry on business. Before a decision is made to incorporate, consideration should also be given to the pros and cons of using a partnership to carry on the business instead.

Dissolution of a Partnership

One advantage of the partnership is its ease of dissolution. Typically, a partner need only give the other partners notice of intention to dissolve the partnership to bring the partnership relationship to an end. This ease may be an advantage to some but it can be a considerable disadvantage to the other partners, especially if a large partnership is involved. In these circumstances, provisions are built into the partnership agreement controlling the dissolution process. These provisions usually provide for a mechanism whereby one partner can leave without causing the remainder of the partnership to dissolve.

Dissolution—by notice, death, bankruptcy or insolvency

The partnership can be ended by the death, bankruptcy or insolvency of any partner. (This provision varies slightly from province to province.) Dissolution can give rise to significant problems in ongoing, long-term partnerships of professional groups. Therefore, professionals will typically set out in partnership agreements that the death, insolvency or bankruptcy of one partner will not dissolve the partnership; instead, that partner's share will be made available to the heir or creditor of the partners. Insurance coverage is often taken out to cover such a contingency.

British Columbia's partnership legislation is unique because it establishes that, when more than two partners are involved, the partnership will be dissolved only in relation to the partner who has died or becomes insolvent. This provision can be modified by agreement, but its unique feature is that the death or bankruptcy of one partner will not bring to an end the whole partnership relationship in the absence of an agreement between the partners.[10]

Partnership established for specified time will end at expiry

A partnership that has been set up for a fixed term will end at the expiration of that term. Similarly, a partnership which is set up for a particular project or event will end when that project is completed or the event takes place. A partnership is automatically dissolved if the business engaged in by the partnership becomes illegal. Even if none of these factors is present, if one partner feels that the partnership should be dissolved, that partner has the right to apply to court for dissolution. The

[10] *Partnership Act*, R.S.B.C. (1979) c.312 s.36.

court may dissolve the partnership if it is satisfied that any one of a number of factors are present.[11] For example, when the court is satisfied that the partnership business must continually operate at a loss, it can order the partnership dissolved. If one of the partners becomes mentally incompetent or otherwise unable or unwilling to perform partnership responsibilities, the partnership can be ordered dissolved. Similarly, the court can end the relationship when the conduct of one partner is such that it is prejudicial to the partnership relationship or otherwise in breach of the partnership agreement. Finally, there is a catch-all provision empowering the court to dissolve the partnership whenever it considers that there are "just and equitable reasons to do so."[12]

The effect of the dissolution is to end the partnership relationship, oblige the partners to wind up the business, liquidate the assets to pay off any obligations to creditors and then distribute any remaining assets and funds to the former partners. Individual partners should take care to give public notice of dissolution. The law may require that such notice be filed with the partnership registration office or registrar of companies, depending on the jurisdiction. For further protection, such notice should be sent to all regular customers of the business. Failure to do so may render each partner liable for the acts of the other partners even after dissolution. Note that, although dissolution takes place, the partners still have the authority to act as partners and bind the other partners by their actions in doing whatever is necessary to wind up the business.

Distribution of Assets and Liabilities

The affairs of the partnership must be wound up when the partnership is dissolved. The debts of the firm are paid out of profits and, if there are not enough profits to pay all the debts, they are paid out of the partners' original capital investment.[13] If there is still not enough money to pay the debts, the creditors can then turn to the partners themselves who are liable to the extent of their personal fortunes. On the other hand, once all creditors have been paid and the other obligations of the partnership satisfied, any assets still remaining are applied first to pay back the partners for expenses they have incurred in the process of carrying out the partnership business. Once this has been done, any further funds are used to repay money the partners provided to the partnership in addition to their original capital investment. Any remaining funds are used to pay back the capital investment of the partners and, finally, any funds left after that are divided among the partners on the established basis for sharing profits.[14]

The problem with dissolving a partnership is that all of the firm's assets must be sold to accomplish the division of assets, even when some of the partners want to form a new partnership and carry on the business. To avoid this problem, the parties often agree to a different process in the partnership agreement. It should be noted that, if one partner owes a debt to an outside creditor which has nothing to do with the partnership business, that creditor can claim against only the assets of that

Partnership can be dissolved by request to the court

Public notice may avoid liability

Debts paid out of profits first, then capital, then personal assets of partners

[11] *Partnership Act*, R.S.O. (1990) c.P.5 s.35
[12] *Ibid.*, s.35(f)
[13] *Ibid.*, s.44(1)
[14] *Ibid.*, s.44(2)

partner, including his or her share of the partnership assets left after all other claims against the partnership are settled.

Limited Partnerships

Additions to the legislation governing partnership in every province provide for the creation of limited partnerships. This measure gives some of the advantages of incorporation to partnerships. To qualify as a limited partner, the partnership must closely adhere to all of the requirements of the governing legislation. If a limited partner fails in any way to follow the provisions set out in the statute, the usual outcome is that the limited partner is then deemed to be a general partner with all of the consequences inherent in that designation. The sole advantage of a limited partnership is that it allows the partners so designated to invest money in a partnership but to avoid the general unlimited liability that goes with being a partner. The only loss a limited partner can incur is the original investment.[15] For example, if Pak is a limited partner who has invested $25 000 in a firm with two general partners, Kimmel and Ingram, Pak might conceivably lose the $25 000 but no more. If one of the partners caused injury to a customer through negligence and that customer suffered $250 000 in damage, the customer could sue the other partners for the loss and Kimmel and Ingram would be required to compensate the victim, even if it meant sacrificing their own personal fortunes. Pak, on the other hand, would stand only to lose the initial investment of $25 000. Even if the combined assets of Kimmel and Ingram were insufficient to cover the claim of the injured customer and Pak did have sufficient assets to cover the $250 000 claim, Pak would not be required to pay because a limited partner's liability is limited to the amount invested. The problem with limited liability in a partnership is that it is relatively easy for the limited partner to lose that status, and when that happens the limited partner becomes a general partner with unlimited liability. In the preceding example, if Pak had done something to become a general partner, such as allowing his name to be used in the name of the business or actively participating in the management of the partnership business, the injured customer could have sued Pak along with Kimmel and Ingram and all would have been required to pay with no limitation on liability.

To be a limited partner, the first thing that must be done is to register at the appropriate government registry by filing a certificate. Typically, this certificate must contain information such as the terms of the agreement, the amount of cash contributed and the way the profits are to be shared. The name used by the partnership can contain the name of the general partners but the name of a limited partner cannot be included in the firm name. Limited partners will be deemed to be general partners if these requirements are not satisfied.

A limited partner can contribute money or property to the business but cannot contribute services or participate in the management of the firm without becoming

> **Limited partners liable only to the extent of their investment**

> **Registration required to become a limited partner**

---

[15] *Limited Partnership Act*, R.S.O. (1990) c.L.16 s.9

Limited partners cannot participate in management

a general partner. The limited partner is not prohibited from giving the other partners advice but, since there is no hard and fast rule defining where advice stops and participation in management starts, there is a considerable risk in doing so. This restriction can create problems if the business begins to experience financial difficulty because the natural inclination of the limited partner is to get involved to protect his or her investment. If he or she does so, the partner will probably become a general partner and become subject to a much greater potential loss. It is not possible to form a partnership with only limited partners. The legislation requires that there be at least one general partner in the firm.

SUMMARY

Business is usually carried on as a sole proprietorship, a partnership or a corporation. The partnership involves two or more partners carrying on business together with a view towards profits. This is controlled by the *Partnership Act* and by the specific agreement of the partners. The partnership can be created by agreement but often comes into existence by inadvertence when people work together in concert in a business activity. Each partner is an agent for the partnership and all partners are liable for the contracts and torts of the other partners and employees. That liability is unlimited and all of the assets of the partner, including personal assets, are at risk to satisfy such debts and obligations.

The partners have a fiduciary obligation to each other and must act in the best interests of the partnership. To make significant changes in the partnership, all partners must unanimously agree. The usual method of dissolving a partnership is for the partners to give notice to that effect. Death or bankruptcy of one of the partners will also usually dissolve the partnership unless the partners have agreed otherwise in their partnership agreement. A limited partner is liable only to the extent of the investment made in the business but, to protect that limited liability status, he or she must be registered as such and not participate in the management of the partnership business.

QUESTIONS

1. Distinguish between a sole proprietorship, a partnership and a corporation.
2. What risk does a business person face in a sole proprietorship or partnership that is avoided in a corporation?
3. What advantages and disadvantages are associated with carrying on business as a sole proprietorship?
4. What advantages and disadvantages are associated with carrying on business as a partnership?

5. What distinguishes a partnership from other types of joint activities?
6. Distinguish between sharing profits and sharing fees.
7. If two people enter into a business together with the object of making money but lose it instead, can the business still be a partnership?
8. Why is it impossible to understand the law of partnership without first understanding the law of agency?
9. What danger exists when a third party is led to believe that two people are partners who in fact are not? This situation is an application of what legal principle?
10. What is the significance of the existence of a partnership agreement for outsiders dealing with the partnership? What is the advantage of entering into a formal agreement?
11. Explain the different ways in which a person can become responsible for the acts of his or her partner and describe the limitations on this responsibility.
12. Describe the liability of retiring and new partners.
13. Partners have fiduciary obligations to each other. Explain what this means.
14. What will the consequences be if a partner operates a business similar to the partnership without the partners' consent or uses information acquired through the partnership to his or her own advantage?
15. What events may bring about the end of a partnership prematurely? Under what circumstances might it be necessary to get a court order to end a partnership?
16. What will the normal effect on a partnership be when a partner dies or becomes insolvent? How is the law of British Columbia significantly different?
17. When a partnership is being dissolved and does not have sufficient assets to pay its debts, how is the responsibility for these debts distributed? How are excess assets distributed?
18. Explain the significance of being a limited partner. How are a limited partner's activities registered? What happens when a limited partner violates one of these restrictions?

CASES

1. *Hogar Estates Ltd. (in trust) v. Shebron Holdings Ltd. et al.*
   The defendant and plaintiff companies agreed to go into partnership to develop a certain parcel of land. Because the land was situated on a flood plain, it was difficult to get "permission to build" on it and the land lay dormant for some time. Mr. Klaiman, the principal of Shebron Holdings Ltd., proposed to Hogar Estates Ltd. that Shebron purchase Hogar's interest in the property. Shebron was the active partner dealing with the planning authorities who had blocked the development of property and Shebron was the partner who had informed Hogar of the problems with obtaining "permission to build." After informing Hogar of this difficulty, Klaiman discovered that the planning authority was about to

change its mind and that the prohibition on developing the property would be lifted. He failed to inform Hogar of the change and went through with the agreement to terminate the partnership. When Hogar Estates learned that the property had been built on, it sued Shebron and asked the court to set aside the termination agreement. Explain the nature of the arguments for both sides and the likely outcome. It should be noted that before the change in attitude of the planning authority the principals of Hogar and Shebron had had a disagreement and were barely speaking to each other.

2. *The Bank of Montreal v. Sprackman et al.*
The members of a partnership had a falling out and agreed between them that one of the partners (Sprackman) would retire from the partnership. A handwritten letter was drawn up and signed stating that Sprackman's interest in the partnership and responsibility for liability would be taken over by one of the other partners, Dinardo. Dinardo subsequently sold his interest in the partnership to a third partner, Gotzaminis, who subsequently became bankrupt. When the partnership was active, arrangements had been made for a $3000 loan and an overdraft arrangement with the Bank of Montreal. Sprackman verbally advised Martin, the bank manager, that he was retiring and that his obligation was being taken over by Dinardo. Martin agreed to release Sprackman from the loan if he paid $1500, which he did over some period of time. Unfortunately, neither side said anything about the overdraft which consisted of $2899.66 at the time of Sprackman's retirement. This overdraft increased after Sprackman's retirement to $6029.82 including interest at 18 percent per annum. The bank then insisted on payment of this overdraft from Sprackman. One of the documents Sprackman had signed with the bank required that the overdraft arrangement would stay in force until "terminated by written notice." Explain the arguments available to both sides and the likely outcome of the case.

3. *Fischbach and Moore of Canada Ltd. et al. v. Gulf Oil Canada Ltd. et al.*
Two federally incorporated companies, Fischbach and Canadian International Comstock Company Ltd., entered into an agreement to supply materials to a third company, Gulf Oil Canada Ltd. They made a tender to Gulf Oil which was accepted, and Gulf sent a purchase order for the materials. There were some variations made to the resulting contract and the court concluded that all or part of the contract between Gulf Oil and these partners occurred in Nova Scotia. Subsequently, a dispute arose and this action was brought to enforce a mechanics' lien which had been filed against Gulf Oil. Gulf Oil challenged the right of the partners to bring this action on this basis that they were not registered as required under the Nova Scotia *Partnership Act*. Explain the arguments available to both parties and the likely outcome.

4. *Lambert Plumbing (Danforth) Ltd. v. Agathos et al.*
Magoulas was just starting up as the sole owner of Alpha Omega Construction Company when he signed a contract with Agathos, the owner

of a Toronto radio station, for advertising over a period of time. Magoulas was unable to pay but Agathos continued to give him advertising in hopes that the business would get going to the point that he would be able to pay. Agathos also helped Magoulas out in his business, signed many contracts and performed other acts on behalf of Magoulas, including writing cheques on his personal account. In January, Kreizman, president of the plaintiff corporation, entered into a contract to supply the Alpha Omega Construction Company with certain plumbing and heating equipment. This contract was entered into at the construction company and the person Kreizman dealt with was Agathos. Kreizman thought he was dealing with the owner and Agathos did nothing to dissuade him of this notion. In all of the many subsequent dealings between these two parties, Kreizman continued to think that Agathos was the principal of the construction company and Agathos did nothing to correct it. It is clear that there was no partnership agreement or arrangement between Agathos and Magoulas and that Agathos was helping Magoulas out gratuitously, hoping for eventual payment under the advertising contract. Magoulas only partially paid for the plumbing and heating equipment with $500 outstanding. Lambert Plumbing sued Agathos as a partner for the unpaid funds. Explain the arguments available to both sides and the likely outcome.

5.   *Klutz v. Klutz.*
     The plaintiff and defendant were married for 25 years when Mrs. Klutz left in 1958. During that period of time, two pieces of land had been obtained, both of which were in the husband's name. It was clear that Mrs. Klutz had done considerable work on the land, such as milking cows and feeding livestock, but she had made no financial contribution to the properties. She claimed that the property was held in partnership and demanded an accounting from the husband. Explain the likely outcome and arguments from both sides.

6.   *Barnes v. Consolidated Motors Co. Ltd. et al.*
     Hall was negligently driving a motor vehicle when he struck and injured Mrs. Barnes. Hall was an employee of Distributors Used Car branch which was a business established by Consolidated Motor Car Co. Ltd., Dan MacLean Motor Ltd. and J.M. Brown Motor Company Ltd. for the purpose of disposing of their used cars. The business had its own bank account, management, employees, etc., but the cars remained the property of the company that supplied them. Hall was driving one of the cars owned by Consolidated Motor Car Co. Ltd. to the Distributors Used Car Branch premises when the accident took place. Mrs Barnes sued all three of the car companies claiming that they were a partnership. Explain the arguments for each side. Discuss the likely outcome.

7.   *Castellian v. Horodyski and Lynkowski.*
     Horodyski and Lynkowski were partners in the operation of a hotel which they sold to Castellian in 1953. One of the assets sold in this transaction

was a heater/boiler. Horodyski had made fraudulent misrepresentations about this boiler which induced Castellian to enter into a contract for its purchase. Although Horodyski knew that what he said was false, Lynkowski was not aware of what was said or that there was any problem with the boiler. Shortly after Castellian's purchase, the boiler broke down and had to be rebuilt. Castellian sued both Horodyski and Lynkowski for the cost of rebuilding the boiler. Explain the legal position of the parties and the likelihood of success.

ISSUES

1. It is understandable that people who intend to carry on business together and who enter into a partnership agreement should bring with them the responsibilities that such a partnership organization entails, such as unlimited liability and liability for the conduct of partners. But when people work together, a partnership relationship is often imposed on them when the parties have no intention that such a relationship should be created. Whenever the parties meet certain qualifications under the *Partnership Act*, they not only experience unlimited liability for their own actions but are also liable for the conduct of the people they are working with. Do you feel it is appropriate that people working together should run the risk of having the liabilities associated with a partnership imposed on them? Discuss the arguments to support the imposition of liability in these circumstances, as well as the arguments against it.

2. People who choose to carry on business together are encouraged to put the partnership agreement in writing, setting out the responsibilities of each partner. It is possible for the partners to set out in the agreement the percentage responsibility each partner will bear in the event of the partnership incurring some debt or obligation to a third party. This agreement, however, will have no effect on a third party dealing with that partnership and the third party will be free to seek compensation from any partner who has the ability to pay for the injuries suffered. Why should a third party be able to ignore the contents of a partnership agreement and thus impose a liability on the partner that was never intended by the parties?

3. One of the unique features of a partnership relationship is that no significant changes can take place in it without the unanimous agreement of all partners. Each partner participates equally in the management of the partnership business and therefore each must agree whenever major changes are involved. This pro-

vision is extremely restrictive to the carrying out of the business and allows a minority to impose its will on the majority of partners. Set out the arguments for and against this characteristic of a partnership and contrast it to the position of a shareholder in a corporation. In your response, consider the ability of the partners to modify these rights and responsibilities by agreement and whether this right to modify is inconsistent with the general objectives of the partnership device.

4.   A partnership will end or be dissolved upon the death or bankruptcy of one of the partners. When there are several partners, this requirement can cause severe disruption to the business. British Columbia has passed legislation establishing that, whenever there are more than two partners and one partner dies or becomes bankrupt, the partnership will only dissolve in relationship to that one partner and will remain intact between the remaining partners. Was the passage of this legislation a progressive or regressive step?

5.   In most jurisdictions in Canada, it is possible to create a partnership in which a partner can have limited liability. In all cases, it is necessary that at least one general partner have unlimited liability. Is the availability of such limited liability consistent with the philosophy of partnership law? Explain the arguments which can be made to support the idea of a limited partnership in which a partner's liability is limited to the amount the partner has invested in the firm. Explain how a limited partner can lose his or her limited liability status. In addition, consider the question of whether limited liability ought to be made available to all partners and whether this privilege ought to be extended to sole proprietors as well. At present, this advantage is limited to corporations and limited partnerships. Since the incorporation process is costly and complex, should this ability not be available to the other forms of business organization as well?

LEGISLATION

Alberta
Partnership Act, R.S.A. (1980) c.P-2

British Columbia
Partnership Act, R.S.B.C.. (1979) c.312

Manitoba
Partnership Act, R.S.M. (1987) c.P-30

New Brunswick
Limited Partnership Act, R.S.N.B. (1984) c.L-9.1
Partnership Act, R.S.N.B. (1973) c.P-4

Partnerships and Business Names Registration Act, R.S.N.B. (1973) c.P-5

Nova Scotia
Limited Partnership Act, R.S.N.S. (1989) c.259
Partnership Act, R.S.N.S. (1989) c.334
Partnership and Business Names Registration Act, R.S.N.S. (1989) c.335

Ontario
Limited Partnership Act, R.S.O. (1990) c.L.16
Partnership Act, R.S.0. (1990) c.P.5

Prince Edward Island
Partnership Act, R.S.P.E.I. (1988) c.P-1
Limited Partnership Act, R.S.P.E.I. (1988) c.L-13

Québec
Companies and Partnership Declaration Act, R.S.Q. (1977) c.D-1

Saskatchewan
Partnership Act, R.S.S. (1978) c.P-3

Northwest Territories
Partnership Act, R.S.N.W.T. (1988) c.P-1

Yukon
Partnership Act, R.S.Y. (1986) c.127

12 BUSINESS ORGANIZATION: PART II

Objectives of the Chapter

- to describe the process of incorporation
- to consider how the fact that a corporation is a separate legal entity affects the operation of the business
- to examine the duties of corporate officers
- to consider the advantages and disadvantages of incorporation

Mr. Sinclair was a professional engineer who had worked for Dover Engineering Services Ltd. for a number of years, although he had been paid by Cyril Management Ltd. On January 31, 1985, he was discharged without notice and without cause. He initiated a wrongful dismissal action against Cyril Management Ltd. since Dover Engineering had no assets and was no longer in operation. Dover was owned 50 percent by Mr. Goudal, and he and his wife together owned 100 percent of Cyril Management Ltd. The question the court had to answer was which company had employed Sinclair, Dover Engineering or the management company? The judge decided that the close relationship between the two companies made them both Mr. Sinclair's employers. Sinclair was, therefore, successful in his action against the management company.[1] While there is some question whether the decision will hold on appeal, this case illustrates the significance of the myth that each corporation is a legal entity, separate and apart from

[1] *Sinclair v. Dover Engineering Services Ltd., et al.*, B.C.S.C. (1987) 642-028.

the people who make it up. It also demonstrates the court's willingness in some circumstances to ignore that separate existence by "lifting the corporate veil." The following chapter will discuss the concept of the corporate entity and the legal benefits and responsibilities that result from the creation of a corporation.

The previous chapter dealt with the simpler methods of carrying on business: the sole proprietorship and the partnership. This chapter will examine the third method, the incorporated company. Since incorporation is by far the most common means of setting up a large business organization, exposure to the concepts and forms that regulate this important aspect of the commercial world is a vital part of the study of business law. In this chapter, we will examine the process and effect of incorporation, some features of incorporated bodies and the rights and responsibilities of various parties involved.

THE PROCESS OF INCORPORATION

The concept of an incorporated company developed in response to the need to finance large economic projects without the limitations associated with sole proprietorships and partnerships. The problem with sole proprietorships was that they did not allow for the acquisition of large amounts of capital through the participation of many entrepreneurs, and the difficulty with partnerships was that major decisions had to have the agreement of all the partners, making large partnerships impractical. What was needed was to have a large number of people participate in a venture without playing active roles in it. The incorporated company was the means to accomplish this end. The most significant feature of an incorporated company is that it has a separate legal personality from the people who own shares in it. The shares that represent an individual's interest in the corporation can be bought and sold; thus the shareholders can be continually changing while the company itself remains intact. This structure provides considerably more flexibility in meeting the needs of owners and directors and is a much more effective method of attracting capital.

Corporation is a separate legal entity

The historical practice in England was for the monarch to grant a charter to a city or town making it a separate legal entity capable of contracting in its own right. It was a natural step to extend that practice to commercial ventures. The earliest of English commercial corporations were created by royal charter, including the Hudson's Bay Company. While the crown held exclusive power to create corporations in the early stages, Parliament started to exercise some control

Royal charters created early corporations

Special act companies were corporations

over the incorporation process through "special act companies" in the nineteenth century. Certain ventures were considered important and unique enough to be incorporated by their own special legislation. Ordinary citizens, however, were still precluded from incorporating companies for general business activities. Instead, they created their own unofficial companies through contracts called deeds of settlement. When Parliament decided to permit incorporation on a general scale, a considerable number of these contractual associations had to be accommodated. The resulting legislation gave these companies formal status and the advantages of incorporation by allowing them to simply register at the appropriate government office and pay a fee.

Canada adopted many of the features of the British approach to incorporation. Both the federal and provincial governments have created many corporations through their power to pass special statutes. For example, the Canadian Broadcasting Corporation (CBC) and the Canadian Pacific Railroad (CPR) were created by special acts of Parliament. Some Canadian jurisdictions adopted the British practice of incorporation through registration. Other jurisdictions developed their incorporation process from the royal charter approach which creates incorporated bodies through the granting of letters patent. A third approach has recently been borrowed from the United States based on the filing of articles of incorporation. Although there are technical differences between these three methods of incorporation, it is important to understand that the practical effect of each system is the same. A description of three forms of incorporation follows.

Three general methods of incorporation in Canada

REGISTRATION. The primary basis for incorporation through registration is the contractual relationship between the members. Registration merely entitles a body created by contract to corporate status. In British Columbia and Nova Scotia, the jurisdictions in which the registration system is currently used, incorporation is accomplished by registering a "memorandum of association" and "articles of association" with the appropriate government agency and paying the required fee. The **memorandum of association** serves the same function as a constitution in that it sets out important matters such as the name of the company, the authorized share capital (the total value of shares that can be sold) and, in some provinces, the objects of the incorporation. These objects set out the purposes for which the corporation is created and also set out the limits of the capacity of the corporation to act. In British Columbia, "objects" are no longer permitted but the law does permit the inclusion of "restrictions." The memorandum of association is difficult to alter once it has been registered, so care must be taken in its design.

Registration accomplished by filing memorandum and articles

The internal procedural regulations for governing the ordinary operation of the corporation are contained in the **articles of association** (not to be confused with the articles of incorporation discussed below). These articles deal with such matters as how shares are to be issued and transferred, requirements for meetings of the board of directors and shareholders, voting procedures at those meetings, regulations covering borrowing, powers of directors and other officers, requirements dealing with dividends, regulations concerning company records, and how notice will be given to shareholders. The articles also set out the procedures for altering the articles, so there is considerably less difficulty in changing them than in changing the memorandum.

Because this method of incorporation is accomplished by registration only, the registrar has no discretionary right to refuse incorporation except when the requirements set out in the legislation are not complied with.

LETTERS PATENT.   This method of incorporation derives from the original practice of the monarch granting a royal charter to create a corporation. This process was made available to people generally through legislation. The crown representative (the designated government body) is charged with granting charters of incorporation upon request (called letters patent) when the applicants meet certain qualifications. This method of incorporation was used until recently in the majority of Canadian provinces and by the federal government, but today it is used only in Québec and Prince Edward Island. Incorporation in these jurisdictions is accomplished by an applicant petitioning the appropriate government body for the granting of letters patent. This method is still used in many Canadian provinces to incorporate non-profit associations, often called societies or no-share capital corporations, depending on the jurisdiction. In provinces where registration is used, registration is also the method used to incorporate such societies.

The **letters patent** corresponds to the royal charter and is the document that creates the corporate entity. This document sets out the constitution of the new company and contains information, such as the purpose for which the corporation is formed, the name to be used, the share structure, any restrictions on the transferability of shares, and the rights and obligations of the parties. It corresponds to the memorandum of association used in a registration system. The rules governing the ordinary operation of the corporation are set out in separate bylaws which serve the same purpose as the articles of association in the registration system.

Since the creation of a corporation in a letters patent jurisdiction is based on the exercise of the crown's prerogative power and not on any contractual relationship between the members, there is no intrinsic right to incorporation and applications for letters patent can be freely refused on policy grounds. This discretion to refuse incorporation is made clear in the legislation. Another important characteristic of this method is that corporations in a letters patent system do not have their capacity to contract limited as historically was the case in the registration system. A corporation created by royal charter had all of the powers of a natural person and so does a corporation created by a letters patent. The power or capacity of a corporation in a registration jurisdiction was limited to business dealings associated with the objects or purposes for which the company was created as set out in the memorandum of association. (This restriction has now been modified in British Columbia and Nova Scotia by a statutory declaration. The B.C. act says that an incorporation will have "all the power and capacity of a natural person of full capacity.[2])

Use of letters patent method declining

---

[2] *Company Act*, R.S.B.C. (1979) c.59 s.21.

ARTICLES OF INCORPORATION. In 1970, the Ontario government abandoned the letters patent system of incorporation and adopted a system similar to one used in the United States. It is based on the filing of articles of incorporation and the granting of a certificate of incorporation. This system is sometimes called the certificate of incorporation method. It has features of both the letters patent and the registration methods and was adopted, with considerable modification, by the federal government when it abandoned its letters patent system in 1975. Ontario has since further modified its system to bring it more in line with the federal statute. Of the provinces which previously used the registration system, Alberta, Saskatchewan and Newfoundland have turned to the articles of incorporation method as have the previously letters patent provinces of Manitoba and New Brunswick.

Articles of incorporation method borrows features from each

The **articles of incorporation** method has much in common with the letters patent method of incorporation. Instead of being organizations based on contractual relationship between their members, articles of incorporation companies are primarily the creations of government. The articles that are filed are more similar to a constitution or statute controlling the activities of the parties than a binding agreement between them. A company is granted a certificate of incorporation by filing the articles of incorporation and paying the appropriate fee. The articles of incorporation serve the same function and contain the same types of information as the memorandum of association and the letters patent in the other systems. The day-to-day operation is controlled through bylaws similar to those in a letters patent system, which also correspond to the articles of association used in the registration system. It is not necessary to file these bylaws upon application of incorporation. Another important distinction between the letters patent method and this new approach is that the government body assigned to grant certificates of incorporation has no general discretion to refuse the request.

Incorporation accomplished through granting certificate of incorporation

Other Incorporated Bodies

The concept of incorporation has been used for purposes other than business. Cities, universities and other public institutions are legal entities which can sue or be sued in their own right. A study of these bodies is beyond the scope of this text because their object is not business. However, they owe their existence to legislation and anyone dealing with them should be aware of the statutes which regulate such things as capacity and responsibilities of agents. It should also be noted that in Canada, under both federal and provincial legislation, it is possible for private citizens to establish (incorporate) non-profit bodies, sometimes called "societies" or no-share capital corporations, depending on the jurisdiction. These bodies are primarily cultural, social, charitable and religious organizations such as the Society for the Prevention of Cruelty to Animals (SPCA), the Red Cross and the Canadian National Institute for the Blind (CNIB). The one thing these bodies have in common is the non-profit nature of their activities. The legal obligations and technicalities associated with these bodies are much simpler and more straightforward than corporations generally. Since the subject of this text is business law and these bodies must by definition be non-profit organizations, no attempt will be made to deal with them here.

SEPARATE LEGAL ENTITY

Myth of separate legal entity

When a person goes through the process of incorporating a company with himself or herself as the sole shareholder, the important and difficult concept to grasp is that when the process is complete and the fees are paid, there are now two legal persons, that person and an incorporated company. Although the corporation does not exist in reality and is only a "legal fiction," all of the forces of the law assume that it does exist as a separate entity from the shareholder and that it can function in the commercial world. The company as a separate legal person may be a difficult concept for the "owner" of a newly incorporated business to understand. Advisers may have a problem convincing the business person that he or she does not own the business but that it is owned by the corporation which has been created. The individual may own the shares in the company but not the company itself. Shares held in a company bestow the rights of control and only give the right to share in the liquidation of the assets (right to participate in capital) if the corporation is wound up.

A different problem is encountered when dealing with large corporations such as Sears Ltd. and Imperial Oil Ltd. When most people think of a company such as Sears Ltd., they identify the individual stores and warehouses as the company itself. But they are just assets of the company in the same way that Vandenberg's car is not Vandenberg but an asset owned and used by her. Sears Ltd., the legal personality, owns assets in the same way as Vandenberg owns her car. On the other hand, some people think that the shareholders are the company, the idea being that the legal personality of the company consists of the members that make it up. While this idea describes what happens in a partnership, it does not apply to an incorporated company since it would defeat the whole purpose of incorporation: to create a separate legal personality independent of its shareholders. It must be remembered that this distinct entity is created for the sake of convenience. It does not exist as a real tangible thing; it is a legal fiction or myth that forms the basis of company law.

Unfortunately, business people often act as if the corporation were a real person. Managers often make decisions they find repugnant and which they would not otherwise make because they think that the company they serve is real. They draw a distinction in their minds between the corporate entity and themselves as managers. While it is true that the legal duty of directors and managers is to the company, it must also be remembered that the company itself is merely a fiction.

It is also important to recognize that the status of separate legal entity for a company is a flimsy one. What the law has created, the law can just as easily remove, and it often comes as quite a shock to the business person to see the separate legal entity aspect of a business operation cast aside by the court and government institutions. For example, when one shareholder has set up several companies, the tax department will often deem these companies to be one person for tax purposes.

Courts will sometimes ignore separate legal entity

Similarly, if the object of incorporation is to get around some government regulation or commit a fraud, the courts will usually be willing to "lift the corporate veil" and ignore the separate legal entity aspect of the company in order to gain access to the shareholders or managers who are attempting to commit the fraud or to avoid the operation of the government regulation. The example used to introduce this chapter illustrates a situation where the courts were willing to lift the corporate veil.

The separate legal entity aspect of a corporation is tremendously important for commercial activities. It is this aspect that has permitted the isolation of the shareholders from the business activity. Not only does it allow for the acquisition of capital without involving the shareholders in the operation of the company, it also provides significant flexibility for investors by allowing them to purchase and sell their shares without interfering with the ongoing operation of the system. Because of this separation of the shareholders from the corporation, only the corporation is responsible for its activities, not the shareholders. This is known as **limited liability** since the shareholders are liable to lose only the money they have invested.

The case of *Salomon v. Salomon and Company Ltd.*[3] graphically illustrates the significance of the principle of separate legal entity and limited liability. Salomon ran a successful shoe manufacturing business which he decided to incorporate. He set up a company in which he owned almost all of the shares. He then sold the business to that company. Since the company had no assets to pay for the business, he loaned the company enough money to purchase the business from himself, securing the loan with a debenture similar to a mortgage on the company's assets. In short, Salomon loaned the company which he "owned" enough money to purchase a business from him and had a mortgage on the assets of the business created to secure the loan. Unfortunately, the business suffered financial reverses in the form of strikes and other problems, and the company became insolvent. When the creditors lined up to get what little was left in satisfaction of their debts, they found Mr. Salomon at the front of the line claiming first payment. The creditors were not happy with this state of affairs because they blamed Mr. Salomon for their problems. They had dealt with him; they thought they were doing business with him, and the company was merely a convenience. They claimed in court that not only should Mr. Salomon not get his money first but also that he should be responsible for paying them if the company's assets were not enough. The court decided that, since the company was a separate legal entity, it had a separate legal existence apart from Salomon and so Salomon could indeed sell his assets to the company and could take security back. The end result was that Salomon was a secured creditor who stood in line ahead of the other unsecured creditors and thus had first claim on the remaining assets of the company. For the same reason, the court held that Salomon was a person separate from the company and was in no way responsible for its debts. Creditors have since developed ways of protecting themselves in this type of situation. For example, they can insist that the person incurring the debt on behalf of the company sign a personal guarantee and become a party to the debt. It must be emphasized, however, that the trend today is for the courts to lift the corporate veil as the situation

Limited liability derived from separate legal entity

---

[3] *Salomon v. Salomon and Co. Ltd.*, (1897) A.C. 22 (H. of C.).

warrants. This tendency makes the actuality of limited liability less and less certain for shareholders, directors and other officers of corporations.

Capacity

Once the concept of separate legal entity has been grasped, it is important to identify the extent of the powers or capacity of the separate legal personality. Limitations on the capacity of corporations to enter into business or other transactions were discussed in Chapter 4. To summarize, only companies incorporated in a registration jurisdiction or those bodies incorporated through special statutes may be limited in their capacity to enter into legal relations with others. In these circumstances, a contract with a corporation that is beyond the capacity of that corporation will not be binding on either the corporation or the outsider who entered into the contract. This is more of a nuisance than anything else from the point of view of business people, so British Columbia and Nova Scotia have modified their company legislation. Now, in those provinces, outsiders dealing with a corporation are not affected by any limitations on that company's capacity even if such limitations are set out in the incorporating documents unless they have notice of the limitation.

In jurisdictions that have adopted the articles of incorporation method, the same problems that limited capacity registration jurisdictions face are present. As was the case with British Columbia and Nova Scotia, many of these jurisdictions, notably Ontario[4] and the federal government, have modified their company legislation to declare that such companies now have all the power of a natural person when dealing with outside parties.

The Role of Agents

Since the corporate entity is a legal fiction, it does not have the ability to act for itself. All its activities must be carried out through the services of agents. The principles of agency law set out in Chapter 10 are extremely important when dealing with corporations. When deciding whether a corporation is bound by the actions of an agent, the authority of the agent must be examined and the question of whether the agent was acting within the authority must then be determined. It is important to determine not only what actual authority the agent has been given to enter into the relationship in question, but also whether the agent has apparent authority because of the position occupied in the corporate organization or because of some representation made leading the third party to believe the agent has authority. Not only the directors and managers of a corporation but also the individual employees right down to the clerks may have the capacity of agents to bind that corporation, depending on the nature of their positions and the duties assigned to them. As is the case with other agents, these people undertake special obligations to act in the best interests

---

[4] Ontario *Business Corporations Act*, R.S.O. (1990) c.B.16, s.17

of the corporation as they carry out their agency responsibilities. The specific nature of the responsibilities borne by selected people in the corporate organization will be discussed in detail below.

Historically, a principal's liability for the apparent authority of an agent could be severely limited when the principal was a corporation simply by filing with the incorporation documents a specific limitation on the actual authority of the agent. Since these documents were publicly filed, everyone was deemed to have notice of them. Most provinces have abolished this provision, which is called constructive notice. Today people dealing with corporations can generally rely on the apparent authority of agents.[5]

Filed documents no longer notice of limited authority

FUNDING

One of the main reasons to create a corporate entity is to establish an efficient means of providing capital to an enterprise from a large number of sources. The vehicle for accomplishing this end is the **share**. While the share gives the holder an interest in the corporation, that interest falls short of ownership. The corporation remains an independent personality separate and apart from the shareholders or members who make it up. The share gives the shareholder certain rights in relation to the corporation. These rights are primarily concerned with the control of that corporation and, under certain circumstances, a right to the assets of the corporation upon dissolution. Generally, one of the restrictions placed on a corporation in the constitutional document is the number of shares that can be sold. This authorized share capital sets an upper limit on the number of shares the corporation can sell. If it becomes necessary to go beyond this upper limit, the original incorporating documents must be amended. To avoid this problem, the authorized share capital is usually quite generous. In some jurisdictions, such as Ontario and federally, such a limitation on the authorized share capital is no longer required. This change eliminates a feature with few redeeming benefits, and other jurisdictions are expected to follow this example.

Shareholders do not "own" corporations

Issued shares usually less than authorized share capital

Par Value versus Non Par Value

A share about to be issued can be valued in two different ways. Either the company can place a **par value**, or face value, on those shares, such as one dollar, or the company can issue shares with no face value at all. The idea in this case is that the value of the share will reflect the worth of the business. For example, if Bandura owns one hundred shares of a business with a net worth of $20 000 and only two hundred shares were ever issued, it is not difficult to calculate the total value of Bandura's shares at $10 000, or $100 each. Issuing par value shares can be misleading; if a par

[5] Ontario *Business Corporations Act*, R.S.O. (1990) cB.16, s.18

value share is issued and each share is valued at one dollar, the actual value of the shares would still be $100 each in the above example. The one dollar par value may indicate the price at which those shares were originally issued but, once on the market, such value placed on the share itself would have no significance. The more common practice in Canada and the United States is to put no value on the share

at all, making it a non par value share. With such a share, the only value associated with it is the value determined by the marketplace. Some jurisdictions, such as Ontario and the federal government, have abolished par value shares altogether.[6]

Special Rights and Restrictions

The shares issued by a corporation are normally divided into different classes, usually called common shares and special or preferred shares. Although the rights and restrictions associated with special shares can be designed or moulded to fit the requirements of the corporation issuing them, special shares are usually designed to give the shareholder preference when dividends are declared and are, therefore, called preferred shares. Once dividends are declared, the preferred shareholders will have the right to collect a specified dividend before any dividends can be distributed to the common shareholders. Shares usually carry with them voting rights to control the affairs of the corporation. One of the characteristics usually given to preferred shares is that the right to vote in most matters normally given to common shareholders is denied to preferred shareholders unless the corporation fails to pay a specific dividend in a given year. If Bandura has one hundred preferred, non-voting shares in a corporation which committed to pay a dividend of $10 per share per year, Bandura is entitled to collect $1000 in dividends from that corporation in any given year. Although Bandura has no right to force the corporation to pay this dividend since no creditor/debtor relationship is created between a shareholder and a corporation, Bandura does have the right to payment of such dividends before any dividends are paid to the common shareholder.

Preferred shares usually provide that this right is cumulative. This means that if the company does not pay the appropriate dividend for a number of years, the preferred shareholder will have the right to have the back payments paid before the company can pay dividends to its common shareholders. For example, if Bandura held a special share entitling her to a dividend of $5 per year but did not receive this dividend for five years, she would be able to insist that a back claim of $25 be paid before the common shareholders are paid a dividend. As long as the dividends are properly paid, the preferred shareholder usually has no right to participate in the affairs of the company. If those dividends are not paid, the preferred share normally has a clause incorporated into it which converts it to a voting share. It must be emphasized, however, that whether these features are present or not depends on what has been designed into the preferred share. It should also be noted that there are some situations in which such preferred shareholders have the right to vote re-

---

[6] Canada *Business Corporations Act*, R.S.C. (1985) c.C-44 s.24 (1).

gardless. Typically, when major changes are proposed which would materially affect the position of the preferred shareholder, they retain the right to vote. For example, a proposal to change the rights or nature of the preferred share or to sell the assets of the corporation could not be adopted without allowing the preferred shareholders to vote.

Since a variety of rights and restrictions can be incorporated into preferred shares depending on the interests of the parties, it is important that these matters be negotiated before preferred shares are issued. Commonly included in the shares of a closely-held company is a restriction on the transfer or sale of the shares. For example, the board of directors must approve the sale before it can take place. (Closely-held and broadly-held corporations are discussed below under that heading.)

Special shares can be used to create shares with objectives other than giving creditors preference. For example, often for the purpose of estate planning, two classes of shares will be created: one with a right to vote and some control in the affairs of the company but no right to dividends; another with a right to dividends but no right to vote. In these circumstances, the holder of the voting shares will maintain control of the company and will give the non-voting but dividend bearing shares to his or her heirs. Such a division allows the holder of the voting shares to maintain control of the operations of the company but to surrender the income and the beneficial interests of the corporation to any heirs.

Borrowing

The second major method of acquiring funds for a corporation is to borrow them, much as individuals do. Whether the money is borrowed from a single large investor, such as a bank in the form of a bank loan, or from a number of individuals in the form of secured or unsecured bonds or debentures, the resulting relationship is a creditor/debtor relationship and not a simple investment as is the case with the issuing of shares. Shareholders do not have the right to demand a dividend but creditors do have the right to demand payment of a debt. Failure to repay constitutes a breach of the corporation's legal obligation. Although companies can and often do borrow money in single large loan transactions, they often borrow money from many different sources in much the same way shares are sold. They do so by issuing debentures, usually called bonds in Canada and the United States.

Technically, a bond is an acknowledgement of an obligation or indebtedness in writing and under seal whereas a debenture is simply an acknowledgement of debt. The bond is a particular type of debenture and although business people often use the terms interchangeably the term bond is usually used when some specific asset has been taken as security.

The corporation typically makes a debt commitment to a trustee who then issues shares in the indebtedness to individual bondholders. These individual creditors are entitled to share in the proceeds of the corporation's obligation to pay a certain amount of money on a specific date and at a set rate of interest. This arrangement allows for the free transfer of these instruments from person to person and has resulted in a considerable and viable market for this form of "securities." Such bonds or debentures can be unsecured but are usually secured against specific assets or by a floating charge. If a company becomes insolvent, a secured creditor will have first claim against the assets used as security when that asset is sold. In jurisdictions with a personal property security act, the same effect can be accomplished without the use of a floating charge.

There is a significant difference between shares and bonds. A shareholder is a participant in the corporation, not a creditor. A bondholder, on the other hand, has loaned money to the corporation and thus a creditor/debtor relationship has been established. The company is in debt to the bondholder for the amount of the bond but the company is not in debt to the shareholder for the price paid for the share. It is for this reason that the bondholder has the right to demand repayment of a loan with interest when it comes due and to enforce that right in court. The shareholder has no similar right to demand payment of a dividend. This is true even for a preferred shareholder. Bondholders have no right to participate in the management of the corporation although managerial rights may be acquired, depending on the terms of the agreement, if the company defaults on the loan. In the event of default, this right can extend to the right to appoint a receiver to take over the assets of the company and operate the business much as a trustee does in a bankruptcy.

Bondholder has right to payment

Many business people prefer to use a combination of these methods of acquiring funds. Most large corporations usually maintain a balance between common and preferred shares on the one hand and various types of debt instruments such as large loans and secured and unsecured corporate bonds on the other. To illustrate, suppose Bowman wanted to incorporate a small manufacturing business which he owned. There are several ways to transfer the assets of the business to the incorporated company. Bowman might incorporate a company which would acquire the manufacturing business and any property associated with it in return for all the shares of the company. A better alternative might be to have the corporation purchase the manufacturing business as well as any property associated with it from Bowman, giving him a mortgage on the property as security for the repayment of the debt. Bowman has all the shares in the company in either case. However, there is a significant difference in that, instead of simply having shares in a company with significant assets, Bowman is a creditor of that corporation. Because the debt will be secured, he will be in a better position to get his money back if the corporation eventually runs into financial difficulties. This example is similar to the situation Salomon found himself in the case described above. There may be favourable tax implications to acquiring the property in this way as well.

Closely-Held and Broadly-Held Corporations

Traditionally, company law statutes in the various jurisdictions have recognized a distinction between broadly-held and closely-held corporations which were usually called public and private corporations, and in British Columbia reporting and non-reporting corporations. In recent years, statutory provisions relating to these two classes of corporation have received considerable attention and have been significantly modified. In Ontario, corporations which offer shares to the public are called as "offering corporations,"[7] and such corporations have more stringent auditing and reporting requirements. A **closely-held corporation** is one in which there are relatively few shareholders, some restriction on the sale of shares and the shares are not sold to the general public openly on the stock market. These are usually small corporations, such as a family business, in which the management is performed by the shareholders. In those jurisdictions where the company law statute still distinguishes between closely-held and broadly-held corporations, the closely-held company is much freer of government regulations and control. Some jurisdictions require the **broadly-held corporation** to have more directors than the closely-held company. Some jurisdictions require widely-held companies to have more structured shareholders' meetings, more complete and audited financial statements and more public access to company records and reports. Ontario requires three directors for an "offering corporation," but otherwise just one. The special requirements for broadly-held corporations are not found only in the appropriate federal or provincial corporations acts but also in the securities legislation of that jurisdiction.

Broadly-held corporations more closely regulated

DUTIES OF CORPORATE OFFICERS

Directors (Managers)

While it is true that the shareholders have the ultimate control over a corporation, this control is achieved by the process of electing directors who are responsible for the management of the corporation. Once these directors are elected, the shareholders have little real say in the operation of the business until the next election. It is only when the decision to be made involves a fundamental change in the very nature of the corporation or when the incorporating documents place an obligation on the directors to do so that the directors need to go back to the shareholders to ask for approval before implementing a decision. The knowledge that the directors face reelection theoretically encourages them to act in a way that is consistent with the wishes and interests of the shareholders. To serve as a director, some qualifications have to be met. Generally, a director must not be either a minor, mentally incompetent, or an undischarged bankrupt, or have been convicted of certain crimes, such as fraud. The requirement that directors also be shareholders has been eliminated in most jurisdictions.[8]

Director owes duty not to be negligent

Under common law, a director has always owed a duty to the corporation to be careful, although it was clear that this obligation was restricted. To succeed against a director for negligence under common law, it is necessary to establish some

---

[7] Ontario *Business Corporations Act*, R.S.O. (1990) c.B.16, s.1
[8] *Ibid.*, s.118(2).

blatant or gross carelessness on the part of the director. Some jurisdictions have increased the standard of care required from a director by imposing an obligation to "exercise the care, diligence and skill of a reasonably prudent person."[9] Some other jurisdictions require a director to "exercise the care, diligence and skill that a reasonably prudent person would exercise in comparable circumstances."[10] Directors must show that in carrying out the affairs of the business, they did what a reasonable prudent person would have done.

Director owes fiduciary duty

In addition to this duty to be careful, directors also have a duty based on their fiduciary relationship with the corporation. The duty of a fiduciary is to act in the best interest of the corporation, to be loyal, to avoid conflict and to otherwise act in good faith towards the corporation. In other words, directors are not permitted to take advantage of any opportunities which arise because of their positions as directors. Such opportunities are considered to be the property of the corporation and any gains made by directors must be paid over to the corporation. In these circumstances, directors alone are responsible for any losses they may incur. When a director is personally involved in some transaction that the company then becomes involved in, the director must make a declaration to the board of the personal interest, avoid any involvement in the discussion of the matter and abstain from voting. Similarly, because of a duty of loyalty, the director cannot enter or start any business which is in competition with the corporation.

Director owes duty to corporation, not to shareholders

A significant problem that has always placed limitations on the responsibility of directors to answer for their actions is the question of to whom the director owes the duty. In common law, the answer was clearly established in the case of *Foss v. Harbottle*[11] and has subsequently been incorporated into many statutes. The director owes fiduciary duties to the company, not to the shareholders. Who can sue the director when this duty is violated? The answer is the company, which was the person injured. And since the company is really a myth and all decisions are made on behalf of the company by the director, we have come full circle. Under common law, in other words, it is clear that a decision to sue the directors must be made by the directors and they are not likely to decide to sue themselves. To solve this problem, some jurisdictions have granted shareholders the right to bring action against the directors or others on behalf of the company.[12] This is called a derivative, or in some provinces a representative, action and gives even minority shareholders the right to sue the directors on behalf of the injured company. This change, along with the change in the nature of the imposed duty to be careful, has significantly enhanced the peril associated with being a director.

Representative action

In addition to these general duties, statutes in all jurisdictions set out many specific responsibilities and liabilities the directors are subject to when they make specific prohibited decisions. For example, directors become personally liable if they allow dividends to be paid out to shareholders when the company is insolvent. The

[9] British Columbia *Company Act*, R.S.B.C. (1979) c.59 s.142.
[10] Canada *Business Corporations Act*, R.S.C. (1985) c.C-44 s.122(1) and Ontario *Business Corporations Act*, R.S.O. (1990) c.B.16, s.134 (1.b)
[11] *Foss v. Harbottle*, (1843) 3 HARE 461 (High Crt. of Chancery).
[12] Ontario *Business Corporations Act*, R.S.O. (1990) c.B.16, s.246.

directors may be personally liable when they allow improper manipulation of shares, fail to give proper notice of shareholder meetings, fail to adhere to the restrictions on company power set out in the incorporating documents or otherwise violate the specific responsibilities given in legislation. Directors are prohibited from using "insider knowledge" to their own advantage or to the advantage of their friends or family. That is, directors who are aware that something about to happen will materially affect the value of shares in the company are prohibited from using that knowledge to their own advantage through the purchase or sale of shares.

Statutorily imposed duties on directors are found in many federal and provincial statutes. Perhaps the areas of personal liability of most serious concern for directors fall into three categories. Today, legislation makes it clear that directors can be held personally liable when a company fails while owing workers unpaid wages. In British Columbia, the Westar Mines ran into difficulty and nine members of the board of directors resigned because of the potential personal liability for unpaid wages. The three remaining directors entered into an indemnification agreement with the corporation so that any liability they faced would be reimbursed to them by the company. While indemnification agreements may give the directors some reassurance, if the company fails, such agreements are worthless.

A second area of personal liability for directors is for unpaid taxes. Under federal income tax legislation, the directors are personally responsible if back taxes are left unpaid when a company fails. In many jurisdictions in Canada, if foreign firms wish to operate, they must have local, resident directors, lawyers and accountants. Business people are often approached to fill these positions in a token way but are not actually expected to participate in the decision-making process of the corporation. Whether they actually participate or not, many do not understand their exposure if the company fails, leaving unpaid taxes and other obligations. In some cases, the liability can be ruinous.

The third area is perhaps the most frightening. Under present and contemplated environmental and waste disposal statutes the directors of corporations can be held personally responsible not only for the damages caused to the environment by the activities of the companies but also for substantial fines for violations of the various statutes. In a case involving Bata Industries, two directors were fined $12 000 each for failing to ensure that a waste storage sight was cleaned up. This fine was reduced to $6000 on appeal. They could not even rely on the indemnification agreement they had with the company because the court held that, since they had been convicted of an offence under the statute, such indemnification was prohibited.[13] Under common law, anyone in a corporation can be sued for negligence if he or she has directly caused the loss or injury.

Officers

Other officers are assigned responsibility for the ongoing, everyday management of the corporation. These officers may include a president and a secretary with specific record-keeping responsibilities. In general, the president and secretary of

---

[13] *R. v. Bata Industries Limited (1992)*, 70 C.C.C. (3rd) 394.

the corporation are in the same fiduciary relationship to the corporation as the directors. They have the same types of general responsibilities and duties to the directors but to a much higher standard.

PROMOTERS. A promoter is someone who participates in the initial setting up of the corporation or who assists the corporation in making a public share offering. Promoters may not be officers of the corporation at all but, like directors and the president of the corporation, they are in a fiduciary relationship to that corporation and have similar responsibilities. A person will often acquire property in anticipation of promoting a company and the company will then purchase that property from the promoter. In these circumstances, the promoter has a duty to act in the best interests of the corporation they are going to incorporate. He or she has an obligation not to take advantage of the company by selling the property to the company at an excessive profit. The promoter must divulge the prices paid for the original purchase and not participate in the decision-making process when the company purchases the property from him or her. The promoter has a fiduciary duty to the company and a duty to disclose any personal interest in deals in which the company is involved.

Promoters will often purchase property on behalf of a company before it has been incorporated and then have the company ratify the agreement after incorporation. Such ratification of pre-incorporation contracts is invalid since the company did not exist at the time the promoters were claiming to act on its behalf. Although this approach may be sound legally, it causes some real difficulties from a business point of view and many jurisdictions (notably Ontario and the federal government) have included provisions in their legislation permitting the after-incorporated company to ratify a pre-incorporation contract. The result is that the contract is valid and binding on the company once it is so ratified. Of course, if the company does not ratify or if a pre-incorporation contract is signed in a jurisdiction where the company cannot ratify, the promoter remains solely liable for any losses since there was no authority to act.

Promoters also owe duties

Shareholders

Shareholder has few responsibilities

There are few responsibilities imposed on a shareholder, which is one of the main attractions of incorporation. Unlike the director, the shareholder has no duty to act in the best interests of the company, although in some jurisdictions an obligation can be imposed on shareholders if they hold enough shares to be classified as insiders. The number of shares required to qualify as an insider varies from one jurisdiction to another but shareholders who have been classified as insiders have the same obligation as directors not to use insider information to their own benefit or to the benefit of friends or relatives.

Shareholder has right to see records and reports

However, the shareholders do have significant rights and remedies available to them. The statutes of the various jurisdictions require that specific records be kept at certain designated offices of the company. These records must include the documents of incorporation; lists of all the shareholders; lists of transactions or changes in relationship to the shares; lists of officers, directors and debenture holders; minutes of directors' and shareholders' meetings; audited financial statements; and so forth. Not all of these records are necessarily available to shareholders, but much important information contained in such documents is accessible to anybody who holds a share in the company. Shareholders are also entitled to receive copies of any annual reports and the financial statements that accompany them. Whether the financial statements must be audited or not depends on the jurisdiction and status of the corporation (for example, whether it is broadly-held or closely-held). The audited financial statements are perhaps the most important of these documents to the shareholder. The auditor is an unbiased outsider and part of the auditor's responsibility is to protect the position of the shareholders by providing a correct and impartial financial statement reflecting the true position of the company. The auditor's duty is to the shareholders, not to the directors. In most jurisdictions, shareholders who have some doubts about the accuracy of these audited statements have the right to have an inspector appointed to examine the auditing process.

Shareholders have the right to vote

The shareholders also have some power to affect the decisions made by the company. Shareholders must be given notice of an annual general meeting of shareholders which must include the appropriate financial statements. At that meeting, the shareholders must be given an opportunity to vote for the directors of the corporation. The directors are thus directly answerable to the shareholders for their actions. Any major changes which will affect the nature of the corporation must be placed before the shareholders to vote on before the decisions are implemented. The incorporating documents or bylaws of the corporation may provide for the right of shareholders to vote in other situations as well. Any shareholder entitled to vote at an annual general meeting will also have the right to set out any matter for shareholder decision in the form of a proposal. The corporation need not comply if the proposal is self-serving or is in some way an abuse of the process.

Proxy can be passed to someone else

Shareholders who are not going to be present at the annual general meeting can pass their right to vote on to someone else. This is called a **proxy** and can be quite important when one group of people tries to collect enough proxies to affect the course of the elections at the annual general meeting. The rules for the creation and operation of proxies are quite strict because of the potential for abuse. For example, in some jurisdictions, a management group soliciting proxies is required to state this fact in bold print on the face of the information circulated to the members.[14] The bylaws or articles set out how many votes each shareholder is entitled to but this may vary with the type of shares held. Common shares are usually entitled to one vote per share.

There are several situations in which a shareholder can insist on an extra meeting of the shareholders. A shareholder who holds a significant portion of the shares can usually demand a meeting as a matter of right. A shareholder with fewer shares may be able to convince a court that such a meeting would be appropriate.

A significant risk faced by minority shareholders is the danger of dilution of their shares. A minority shareholder's proportion of the outstanding shares decreases if, when additional shares are sold, none are acquired by that minority

[14] British Columbia *Company Act*, R.S.B.C. (1979) s.59 s.181.

shareholder. For example, if Pantazis holds 500 shares and the total number of shares issued by the company is only 1000, then Pantazis has 50 percent of the shares and 50 percent control. If the directors decided to issue another 500 shares and those shares were sold to anyone else, Pantazis would lose his 50 percent control. Even though he still has 500 shares, they now represent only 33.3 percent voting rights. This problem can be avoided if the shareholder insists in a shareholder agreement or in the incorporating documents that he or she be offered any new shares first and only after a failure to purchase them can they be sold to anybody else. Such a right is called a pre-emptive right. In jurisdictions such as the United States and Britain, pre-emptive rights are in place but in most jurisdictions in Canada pre-emptive rights exist only where actually granted in the incorporating documents.[15] British Columbia does provide such pre-emptive rights for a closely-held corporation in the absence of a stated intention to the contrary set forth in the incorporation documents.[16]

Shareholders who do not like what is happening in a company can usually simply sell their shares; where this is possible, it may be the only remedy the shareholder has. Selling the shares is not always possible, especially with closely-held corporations, since there may be a clause preventing the shareholder from selling them without the approval of the directors. To protect the shareholder from abuse in these circumstances, the statutes have provided several safeguards. The most important safeguard is the shareholder's right to sue the directors on behalf of the company when the directors have done something actionable. The right to derivative or representative action exists in British Columbia, Nova Scotia and in those provinces that use the articles of incorporation method of incorporation. To succeed in these jurisdictions, a shareholder must show that the company was in some way injured by the directors' actions.

A shareholder's complaint might not be that the company was hurt but that the shareholder was being abused in some way. For example, the directors might arrange for the sale of shares just to weaken the voting position of a particular shareholder or, if the shareholder is an employee, the directors might fire the shareholder to force sale of the shares. In some jurisdictions, both shareholders and creditors have the right to go to court and seek an order for relief from oppression if this type of abuse takes place. The court has the power to appoint a receiver to take control of the company or to provide for its dissolution if it feels that the complaint is justified.

When the directors did something that adversely affected the position of a minority shareholder but was beneficial to the company as a whole, historically there was no recourse. In many jurisdictions, however, the injured minority shareholder now has the right to file a dissent.[17] Such dissent procedures are imple-

Pre-emptive rights entitle shareholder to be offered any new shares first

Derivative or representative action

Shareholders have rights to relief from oppression

Dissent provisions provide relief for shareholders

---

[15] Ontario *Business Corporations Act*, R.S.O. (1990) c.B.16 s.2.
[16] British Columbia *Company Act*, R.S.B.C. (1979) c.59 s.41.
[17] *Business Corporations Act*, R.S.O. (1990) c.B.16 s.185. This is a very significant shareholder power but it is only available in limited circumstances, such as when a decision is being made to amend the articles of incorporation in order to restrict the issue or transfer of shares, or to restrict the type of business the corporation can carry on. It is also available when amalgamation with another corporation is involved or when a significant portion of the assets of a corporation are going to be sold or leased. British Columbia, Nova Scotia and the provinces that have adopted the articles of incorporation method of forming a company have similar dissent provisions.

mented when major changes to the company adversely affect the shareholder and require that his or her shares be purchased at a fair price. One of the most useful ways of avoiding the problems associated with the minority position is to draw up an agreement between the shareholders which builds in protections against any of these eventualities. A term will often be included whereby one shareholder must buy out the other if these types of events or other forms of dissatisfaction occur.

Although they may often think otherwise, shareholders do not have the right to claim any dividend or force the directors to declare one. Shareholders only have a right to a dividend if one is declared by the directors. Of course, if the directors fail to declare a dividend when the shareholders expect one, they might have a tendency to vote against them at the next shareholders' meeting, but the shareholders cannot go to court and sue for a dividend. This is true even if they hold preferred shares declaring that they are entitled to a dividend of so much per year. However, in the case of such special shares, the shareholders may have a right to a cumulative dividend which involves the payment of all prior dividends that have been missed. The rights associated with the shareholders' position are rights of control, information and protection, but there is no corresponding right to a specific return on the funds invested. Many provisions are in place to protect the position of shareholders, but it is important to balance these rights against some important drawbacks for shareholders.

PROS AND CONS OF INCORPORATION

Advantages

There are several advantages associated with incorporation, most of which are derived from the concept of the separate legal personality of the corporation.

LIMITED LIABILITY. As illustrated in the *Salomon* case, shareholders are not liable for the debts and other obligations of the corporation because of the separate entity aspect of the corporation. The company, as a separate legal person, is responsible for its own wrongful conduct. The shareholders' liability is limited to the amount they have paid for their shares. If the total assets of the corporation are not sufficient to satisfy the obligation, the creditor demanding payment cannot turn to its shareholders for the difference.

Limited liability is one of the most attractive features of the corporation, and often the primary reason for choosing to incorporate, but such an advantage is often only an illusion. Any institution providing funds to a small, closely-held company will insist that certain principals of the firm, such as the majority shareholder, the president or anyone else the bank feels will have funds, guarantee the indebtedness of the corporation. This effectively eliminates any advantage of limited liability for those asked to sign such a guarantee.

Nevertheless, the principle of limited liability is attractive when unexpected liability is incurred. Thus, if a company's employee negligently causes another injury or if the company fails to honour its contractual obligations, the injured party will not be able to seek compensation from the shareholders for any damages suffered. Similarly, suppliers of materials usually do not obtain any personal commitment from shareholders so suppliers cannot turn to the shareholders for payment if the business becomes insolvent. For example, if a person operating a grocery business incorporates a company and borrows money from the bank for business purposes, that bank will probably insist on a personal guarantee from the shareholder, but a supplier of groceries would normally have no such personal commitment. If the business becomes insolvent, the shareholder will be obligated to pay back the loan to the bank but will not be obligated in any way to the supplier because the contract for the goods supplied was with the corporation rather than with the shareholder. Similarly, if an employee of the grocery business negligently caused an injury while carrying out assigned activities, the company would be vicariously liable for that action. The injured individual, however, would not be able to sue the shareholders because of the principle of limited liability.

Tax advantages gained through incorporation.

TAXES. Although integration was supposed to do away with the differences between the federal income taxes paid by sole proprietors, partners and corporations, because the system is so complex, there still may be advantages available to the individual taxpayer through incorporation. At the least, the shareholder can leave the funds in the corporation and use it as a vehicle of investment, thus avoiding some taxes until a later date. In addition, it should be noted that many provinces have not followed the federal lead; there may still be significant provincial tax advantages to be gained through incorporation. However, federal and provincial income tax laws are extremely complicated. It is possible that incorporation will backfire and that the process will lead to more income taxes rather than fewer. When a business faces potential losses, the taxpayer is better off if the business is not incorporated so that these losses can be applied directly against personal income. Great care must be exercised in the process of tax planning for any business and it is a prudent business person who seeks expert advice in these circumstances.

SUCCESSION AND TRANSFERABILITY. Because a corporation is a separate legal entity and a mythical person, it does not suffer from the normal frailties of human beings. A corporation will not die unless some specific steps are taken to end its existence. When a partner dies, the partnership will usually come to an end. The death of a shareholder, even a shareholder who owns 100 percent of the shares, will not affect either the existence or the normal operation of the company, assuming the shareholder was not personally involved in that operation. The share is simply an asset in the hands of the shareholder and is treated like any other asset the deceased may have. For example, if two people formed an incorporated company in which each owned 50 percent of the shares and both were killed in an airplane crash, the company would still continue to exist, the shares would form part of the estates and the heirs would become the new shareholders. If the two people were carrying on business as a partnership, however, the partnership would automatically be dissolved.

Since partners are responsible for each other's actions and since they play such a significant role in the management of a corporation, the process of one partner divesting himself or herself of interest in the partnership is complex and involves negotiating with and obtaining the consent of the other partners. Since a shareholder does not have similar rights and responsibilities, shares can be transferred at will without reference either to the other shareholders or to the corporate body. This free transferability of shares is one of the attractive features that led to the creation of the corporate entity in the first place and it provides an effective method for the contributors of capital to restrict their relationship with the company. Because free transferability of shares is not always desirable, it is possible to introduce a measure of control on this right by a shareholders' agreement or by provisions contained in the bylaws and incorporating documents. Share transfer restrictions can take many forms and are usually found in closely-held corporations.

No duty on shareholder in a corporation

OBLIGATIONS OF THE PARTICIPANTS. Another attractive feature of the corporation is that the shareholder is free of any obligation or duty to that corporation or other shareholders. Unlike a partnership where each partner is obligated to act in the best interests of the other partners, the shareholder has no such obligation. A shareholder is free to enter into business in competition with the corporation. The extent of this freedom of action can be illustrated by the activities of several environmental groups. They have acquired a few shares in some of the large corporations they consider a threat to the environment with the express purpose of using the special privileges available to shareholders, such as rights to information and to attend shareholders' meetings, to acquire information which can be used in the battle against the polluting corporation. Even when the interests of the environmental group are diametrically opposed to, and interfere with, the profit-making ventures of the corporation and other shareholders, they are under no obligation to act otherwise. Only when people acquire sufficient shares to be classed as insiders or when an individual has a majority of the shares are certain restrictions placed on their activities. These restrictions usually take the form of rules which prevent the shareholders from abusing their positions of power within the corporation and causing injury to other investors.

Separate management can be maintained

MANAGEMENT. In a sole proprietorship, the business is controlled by a proprietor; in a partnership, each partner has a say in the business decisions of the partnership; in a corporation, however, it is possible to separate the managers from the owners. The shareholders elect a board of directors who control the business. They in turn can hire professional managers who have the expertise to make sound business decisions on behalf of the corporation. The shareholders do not have to devote time or attention to managing but they can change the management by electing different people to the board of directors if they are unhappy with the decisions being made.

Disadvantages

A corporation is not always the best method of carrying on business. Many of the characteristics outlined above as advantages can just as easily become drawbacks. It is helpful to compare incorporation with partnership to illustrate some of the disadvantages of incorporation. Partners who wish to change important aspects of their partnership arrangement need only reach an agreement to that effect. In the case of a corporation, however, the incorporating documents themselves may have to be altered, which is an involved and expensive procedure. A partner may come to appreciate having the power associated with the partnership position when there is disagreement between colleagues. In a partnership, one partner can veto a proposal supported by ten others. A minority shareholder in a corporation can do little to alter unsatisfactory decisions and may not even be able to sell his or her shares. In some circumstances, mechanisms have been created to control the free transferability of shares, either through shareholder agreements or by limitations placed in the incorporating documents themselves. A shareholder in this type of corporation will often be required either to sell the shares to other shareholders or to acquire their consent before a share transaction can proceed. As with partnerships, the reason people organize themselves into a small, closely-held corporation is often because of the individual skills each shareholder brings to the company. These shareholders are usually employees as well, and their contribution to the operation of the business is often vital to its success. Free transferability of shares in such circumstances might be a significant threat to the corporation, especially if the shareholder withdraws his or her services when the shares are sold.

A corporation is the most expensive way to operate a business. Not only is the process of incorporation costly but the ongoing operation involves more expense than either sole proprietorship or partnership. There are more formal record-keeping requirements associated with corporations, and generally there is more government control exercised with a corporation.

Weak position of minority shareholders in corporations

Corporations more expensive than other forms of business

Termination of the Corporation

Corporations can be dissolved in several ways. Most jurisdictions include winding up provisions in their company law statutes, but some provinces have retained a separate winding up act. If the corporation owns sufficient assets, it may be worthwhile to follow this process. If something has happened to make a business unprofitable, however, usually it is not worth incurring the expense to go through the formal process of winding up the company. Dissolution can take place either voluntarily or involuntarily and the procedure can be induced internally by the directors or shareholders or externally by a creditor. On occasion, a court will order a company to be dissolved when a minority shareholder has been unfairly treated. If there are more debts owing to the creditors than the company has assets to cover, the common procedure is bankruptcy and the end result is usually the dissolution of the company. The process of distributing the assets upon winding up the company is set out in the various statutes and will not be dealt with here. It is important to note, however, that the directors have a considerable obligation not to allow any of the assets of the corporation to get into the hands of the shareholders until the creditors have been satisfied.

One of the commonest ways for companies, especially small, closely-held companies, to come to an end is for the principals simply to neglect to file their annual report. In a registration jurisdiction, such as British Columbia, after a few years without annual reports, the corporation is simply taken off the registered list of companies and that is the end of it. Some jurisdictions, notably Ontario and the federal government, have abolished the requirement that these annual reports be filed. In those jurisdictions, it is only necessary to report when changes are made in matters that were required to be filed in the original incorporating documents.

SUMMARY

A corporation is a fiction or a myth that has a separate status as a legal person from the shareholders who make it up. Registration, letters patent and articles of incorporation are the processes used in the various jurisdictions in Canada to accomplish incorporation. At law, the corporation is a separate legal entity and for this reason does not die. Nor are the shareholders liable for its debts (limited liability). In registration jurisdictions and where special statute corporations are involved, the capacity of that corporation may be limited.

Financing for the corporation is derived from the selling of shares (which may be common shares or shares with special rights and restrictions) or through borrowing (which involves the sale of bonds and debentures, secured or unsecured). Broadly-held corporations have more stringent government controls and greater reporting requirements than do closely-held corporations.

Directors and other officers of the corporation have a fiduciary duty and must act in the best interests of that corporation, avoiding conflicts of interest. The shareholders, on the other hand, have very few duties to the corporation or other shareholders unless they have sufficient shares to be classed as insiders. Since the duty of the director is owed to the company, a shareholder has no right to sue the director when he or she acts carelessly or wrongfully in carrying out his or her duties. In many jurisdictions, however, the shareholder can bring a derivative or representative action against the director on behalf of the corporation. A shareholder has no right to dividends.

The advantages of incorporation are limited liability, tax benefits, the ease of transferring shares, separate management and ownership, and the facts that the corporation does not die and that the shareholders are free of obligations to the company and other shareholders.

QUESTIONS

1. What is meant by a corporation having a separate legal identity?
2. Distinguish between companies that have been created by special acts of parliament, by royal charter, by registration, by letters patent and by filing articles of incorporation.
3. Explain the significance of the memorandum of association in a registration jurisdiction. Contrast it with the articles of incorporation and articles of association.
4. Describe the kinds of problems dealing with capacity associated with registration jurisdictions that are not present with other methods of incorporation.
5. Explain how the liability of a shareholder is limited.
6. What is meant by a "preferred" share? Contrast this with the normal "common" share. Explain why the term "preferred shares" is misleading.
7. Explain why the concept of a par value share is misleading and why they have declined in popularity.
8. Does a shareholder, whether preferred or common, have a right to a dividend? Explain.
9. What is the significant difference between a bondholder and a preferred shareholder who is entitled to a specified dividend each year?
10. Distinguish between a closely-held and a broadly-held corporation and explain these differences in terms of the provisions in place in your jurisdiction.
11. Set out the nature of the duties owed by a director of a corporation. To whom are these duties owed? Who else in the corporate organization owes a similar duty?
12. Explain any duties shareholders assume. Summarize the rights of the shareholders in relationship to other shareholders, the management and directors of the corporation.
13. Explain what is meant by a proxy and why proxies can be so important at a corporation's annual general meeting.
14. Explain the advantages of free transferability of shares and how and why this right is often modified by shareholder agreement.
15. Set out and explain some of the disadvantages associated with the corporate method of carrying on business.
16. How can a corporation be terminated?

CASES

1. Re *Graham and Technequit Limited.*
    Graham was one of four shareholders in Technequit and, according to the shareholders' agreement, he was a director and an employee as well. At one directors' meeting, the other three directors fired Graham from his position as director and from his employment. He retained only his status as a minority shareholder. What courses of action are available to Graham in these circumstances? Explain the likely outcome. How would your answer be affected by the knowledge that Graham was not adequately performing his duties as either employee or director and that the shareholders' agreement had a buy-out provision Graham could have implemented but chose not to?

2. *W.J. Christie v. Greer et al.*
    Greer was a long-standing employee of the plaintiff company, W.J. Christie, and had held the position of director and executive officer for ten year. Greer left W.J. Christie and went on to establish his own company, Sussex Realty and Insurance Agency Limited. In the process, Greer approached several customers of Christie and persuaded them to transfer their business to the new firm. In this action, W.J. Christie sued Greer for his conduct. Explain the arguments available to both parties and the nature of the compensation Christie would probably obtain if successful.

3. *Wedge et al. v. McNeill et al.*
    In this action, the appellants were directors and shareholders in the respondent company, Hillcrest Housing Limited, and as such had the right to vote at meetings of directors and shareholders. A bylaw of Hillcrest Housing Limited allowed the directors to vote in matters in which they had an interest after having made proper disclosure. The majority of the directors set up a company called Arcona Construction Limited which was fully owned by them. At various directors' meetings, after fully disclosing their various interests, they participated in the decision to direct considerable amounts of business to Arcona Construction Limited even though the directors representing minority shareholders, Richard and Mary Wedge, complained about this action and voted against it. Explain the nature of the complaint lodged by the Wedges, the arguments to be raised by both parties and the probable outcome.

4. *Heinhuis v. Blacksheep Charters Ltd.*
    Mr. Hanson agreed to sell Mr. Heinhuis some property for $200 000 cash plus a yacht. To avoid paying sales tax, Mr. Heinhuis incorporated a

company into which the boat would be transferred and then the shares in that company were to be transferred to Hanson. The shares were transferred to Hanson and as security the company was to register a chattel mortgage on the vessel back in favour of Mr. Heinhuis. The money was deposited, the keys were given to the new owner and several payments were made on the chattel mortgage. The company that was incorporated was called Blacksheep Charters Ltd. and eventually the payments stopped. Heinhuis made a demand for payment which was not satisfied and so took steps to seize the vessel. It should be noted that the arrangements to sell the property and the chattel mortgage were all done before the company was incorporated. It was only after the fact that the company was created and the shares transferred. Explain the legal position of the parties and give arguments.

5. *Rowe et al. v. National Wholesalers Limited.*
   The directors of a corporation decided to pay themselves director's fees at three times the normal rate. A minority shareholder took exception to this practice and sued. Explain the basis of the shareholder's complaint, the arguments available to both sides and the probable outcome. Indicate how and on whose behalf this action would proceed. Would your answer be any different with the added information that the directors claimed they were loaning their director's fees back to the company with interest so that the company's tax position would be improved?

6. *Marzatelli et al. v. Verona Construction Ltd. et al.*
   Verona Construction Ltd. was set up with the petitioners together holding 46 percent of the shares. The majority interest was held by one person. The company was set up initially to carry on business as a general contractor but this function ceased in 1973. Since that time, the company had done no general contracting except two insignificant jobs in 1974. The petitioners, who were formerly employees, had ceased their employment by the end of 1973. No directors or shareholders meetings took place after 1973. Although the company was used as a vehicle for some transactions, it was clear that the person who primarily benefited from the continued existence of the company was the president and primary shareholder. He voted himself a $50 000 bonus in 1975, acquired a Cadillac for $2800 for which the company had paid over $10 000 and the company paid over $5000 to put up a steel garage on his land. The retained earnings of the corporation diminished from $150 000 in 1973 to $11 000 in 1978. Explain what course of action is available to the minority shareholders in these circumstances. Explain the probable outcome of their action.

ISSUES

1. The two traditional methods of incorporation used in Canada (the registration system and letters patent system) have problems associated with them. For example, in a letters patent jurisdiction, corporations could not be incorporated as a matter of right, and in a registration system, a corporation had its capacity limited to those activities authorized in its incorporation documents. Do you feel that limitations on the capacity of a corporation to carry on business in specific areas is a drawback or an advantage to the registration system? Similarly, do you feel that people ought to have an unfettered right to incorporate? In several jurisdictions in Canada, a third system has been introduced (the articles of incorporation system) that is intended to overcome some of these difficulties. In others the statutes have been modified to give corporations full capacity. Indicate the types of problems associated with the first two systems and decide whether the new system or the modifications to the old system effectively overcome these problems.

2. It is one thing for a shareholder to experience limited liability for the debts of a corporation, but, in the *Salomon* case, Mr. Salomon was not only protected from liability to the creditors but in fact had first claim against the assets of the corporation ahead of those creditors. Do you feel that it is proper or just for a major shareholder in a corporation to be able to acquire such a priority position in relationship to the creditors simply because he gave himself such a secured position? In your response, consider the requirement of registration of such securities (as discussed in Chapter 8) and whether this requirement overcomes the problem.

3. Because of the concept of separate legal entity, the corporation has the characteristic of being eternal unless some steps are taken to bring about its dissolution. As a result, several corporations have been in existence for a number of centuries and in that time have acquired vast tracts of land and become very powerful. This problem is similar to the one experienced in feudal times when the Church acquired vast land holdings, causing considerable strife between church and state. Today there are many powerful corporations in existence long after the original shareholders have died. Does this characteristic of a corporation lead to abuse or excessive power? If so, what steps should be taken to overcome this power? Consider the arguments for both sides.

4. The directors of a corporation owe the same kind of obligation to a corporation as a partner does to the other partners. This fiduciary duty requires the director to act in the best interests of the corporation. Because the corporation is a myth, however, there is no person to decide to sue the director when that duty is breached. In fact, it is the directors themselves who make

such management decisions on behalf of the corporation. Thus, where a breach takes place, it is rare for the director to be sued. Many jurisdictions have incorporated provisions in their company legislation allowing the shareholders to bring an action on behalf of the corporation against the directors (derivative or representative action). Does this right solve the basic problem outlined above? While this problem is serious, it merely illustrates the much broader problem of the corporate myth. All parties owe a duty to the corporation, but those who make decisions on behalf of the corporation are merely servants of the corporation. In such circumstances, it is very easy for the decision makers to escape legal or moral responsibility for their decisions simply by stating that they were obliged to act as they did as part of their duty to the corporation. Discuss the problems associated with the separate legal entity of the corporation and whether the legislation that has been introduced goes far enough to overcome these difficulties.

5. Because the corporation is a separate legal entity, the shareholder is separated from the management of that corporation. The shareholder, as a result, has minimum access to records of the corporation and has only indirect control over the management. Since the shareholder is the effective owner of the corporation, do you feel that there should be any restriction on the right of the shareholder to have access to all the information and records kept by the corporation? Consider both the advantages and disadvantages to the shareholder having such access. In your answer, consider the problem this would cause for such large corporations as General Motors, IBM, and so on. As well, take into consideration the distinction between broadly-held and closely-held corporations and whether this policy should be the same for each.

LEGISLATION

Alberta
Business Corporations Act, S.A. (1981) c.B-15
Companies Act, R.S.A. (1980) c.C-20
Co-operative Associations Act, R.S.A.(1980) c.C-24
Securities Act, S.A. (1981) c.S-6.1
Societies Act, R.S.A.(1980) c.S-18

British Columbia
Company Act, R.S.B.C. (1979) c.59
Company Clauses Act, R.S.B.C. (1979) c.60
Co-operative Association Act, R.S.B.C. (1979) c.66
Securities Act, B.C. (1985) c.83
Society Act, R.S.B.C. (1979) c.390

Manitoba
Business Names Registration Act, R.S.M. (1987) c.B-110
Co-operatives Act, R.S.M. (1987) c.C-223
Corporations Act, R.S.M. (1987) c.C-225
Securities Act, R.S.M. (1988) c.S-50

New Brunswick
Business Corporations Act, S.N.B. (1981) B-9.1
Co-operative Associations Act, S.N.B. (1978) c.C-22.1
Corporations Act, R.S.N.B. (1973) c.C-24
Corporation Securities Registration Act, R.S.N.B. (1973) c.C-25
Security Frauds Prevention Act, R.S.N.B. (1973) c.S-6
Winding Up Act, R.S.N.B. (1973) c.W-10

Newfoundland
Co-operative Societies Act, R.S.N. (1990) c.C-35
Corporations Act, R.S.N. (1990) c.C-36
Securities Act, R.S.N. (1990) c.S-13

Nova Scotia
Companies Act, R.S.N.S. (1989) c.81
Companies Winding Up Act, R.S.N.S. (1989) c.82
Co-operative Associations Act, R.S.N.S. (1989) c.98
Corporations Miscellaneous Provisions Act, R.S.N.S. (1989) c.100
Corporations Registration Act, R.S.N.S. (1989) c.98
Corporations Securities Registration Act, R.S.N.S. (1989) c.102
Securities Act, R.S.N.S. (1989) c.418
Societies Act, R.S.N.S. (1989) c.435

Ontario
Business Corporations Act, R.S.O. (1990) c.B.16
Co-operative Corporations Act, R.S.O. (1990) c.C.35
Corporations Act, R.S.O. (1990) c.C.38
Corporations Information Act, R.S.O. (1990) c.C.39
Securities Act, R.S.O. (1990) c.S.5

Prince Edward Island
Companies Act, R.S.P.E.I. (1988) c.C-14
Co-operative Association Act, R.S.P.E.I. (1988) c.C-23
Corporation Securities Registration Act, R.S.P.E.I. (1988) c.C-26
Securities Act, R.S.P.E.I. (1988) c.S-3
Winding Up Act, R.S.P.E.I. (1988) c.W-5

Québec
Companies Act, R.S.Q. (1977) c.C-38
Companies and Partnerships Declaration Act, R.S.Q. (1977) c.D-1
Cooperatives Act, R.S.Q. (1977) c.C-67.2
Extra-provincial Companies Act, R.S.Q. (1977) c.C-46
Mining Companies Act, R.S.Q. (1977) c.C-47
Winding Up Act, R.S.Q. (1977) c.L-4
Special Corporate Powers Act, R.S.Q. (1977) c.P-16
Companies Information Act, R.S.Q. (1977) c.R-22
Securities Act, R.S.Q. (1977) c.V.1.1

Saskatchewan
Business Corporations Act, R.S.S. (1978) c.B-10
Business Names Registration Act, R.S.S. (1978) c.B-11
Companies Act, R.S.S. (1978) c.C-23
Companies Winding Up Act, R.S.S. (1978) c.C-24
Co-operatives (1989) Act, S.S. (1989-90) c.C-37.2
Non-profit Corporations Act, R.S.S. (1978) c.N-4.1 (1979)
Securities Act, (1988) S.S. (1988-89) c.S-42.2

Northwest Territories
Companies Act, R.S.N.W.T. (1988) c.C-12
Companies Winding Up Act, R.S.N.W.T. (1988) c.C-13
Co-operative Associations Act, R.S.N.W.T. (1988) c.C-19
Societies Act, R.S.N.W.T. (1988) c.S-11

Yukon
Business Corporations Act, R.S.Y. (1986) c.15
Societies Act, S.Y. (1987) c.32

Federal
Canada Business Corporations Act, R.S.C. (1985) c.C-44
Canada Co-operative Associations Act, R.S.C. (1985) c.C-40
Investment Canada Act, R.S.C. (1985) 1st Sup. c.28
Winding Up Act, R.S.C. (1985) c.W-11

13 NEGOTIABLE INSTRUMENTS

Objectives of the Chapter

- to examine the special nature of negotiable instruments
- to distinguish the various types and their purposes
- to describe how negotiable instruments are endorsed and transferred
- to discuss the rights and responsibilities of the parties

Mrs. Jordan was a bank clerk who had convinced her husband and Mr. Courage, the manager of the local branch of the Toronto-Dominion Bank, that she was a wealthy and successful business executive. In fact, she was using bank accounts of several relatives to move money from account to account to support her speculation in the stock market. Such a practice is known as "kiting" and involves drawing cheques on a succession of accounts to cover funds drawn from those accounts. Because there is a time delay in clearing the cheques and the final cheque covers the deficit caused by the first cheque, it is difficult to detect that there is an amount outstanding. Mrs. Jordan gave several gifts and benefits to Mr. Courage and involved him in some of her profitable speculations to encourage him to protect information regarding her transactions. Managers of two other banks had become suspicious of the activity in Mrs. Jordan's account and warned Mr. Courage that she might be kiting cheques. He ignored their warnings but pressed her to cover an overdraft in the amount of $350 000. Mrs. Jordan persuaded her husband to give her a blank cheque signed by him and drawn on the Teacher's Credit Union which she filled in for $359 000 and gave to Mr. Courage at the Toronto-Dominion Bank to cover the overdraft. This cheque was subsequently dishonoured and signalled the end of this series of transactions. The Toronto-Dominion Bank branch of which Mr. Courage was the manager then sued Mr. Jordan for the face value of the cheque drawn on his account. If negotiable instruments had not been involved, the bank would not have been able to collect on the debt any more than Mrs. Jordan could. Because of her fraud, she could not have collected. But because a cheque is a negotiable instrument, the situation is quite different. If an innocent third party acquires the cheque in good faith, it can be enforced against the drawer even if the intervening party has been fraudulent. This raised the question of whether or not Mr. Courage had acted in good faith. The court looked at his involvement with Mrs. Jordan and decided that, while he may not have been directly dishonest, he certainly had not acquired the cheque in good faith and, therefore, the bank could not enforce it against Mr. Jordan.[1] This complicated set of transactions illustrates the most significant characteristic of negotiable instruments—that is, their enforceability in the hands of third parties and the corresponding extreme vulnerability of those who make such negotiable instruments and allow them to be circulated. In this chapter, we will examine negotiable instruments and the rights and obligations of the parties to them.

Negotiable instruments are freely transferable and a substitute for cash

Cheques, bills of exchange (often called drafts) and promissory notes are all **negotiable instruments**. They are in common use today because of several characteristics that greatly facilitate the commercial process. Negotiable instruments represent the right to claim funds from a particular debtor or financial institution. They are used as a substitute for money and allow for its exchange without the necessity of handling large amounts of cash. They can be transferred between parties not associated with the original transaction without the requirement of any notice and without diminishing the right of the eventual holder to collect on the negotiable instrument from the original parties. Another important characteristic of negotiable instruments is their capacity to create creditor/debtor relationships. Since a negotiable instrument gives the holder a claim for the stated amount against the maker of the instrument, and sometimes the financial institution it is drawn on as well, the negotiable instrument represents a creditor/debtor relationship until the claim is satisfied. When the object of the instrument is merely to transfer funds, this relationship is an essential part of the process. Whenever a significant period of time is involved between the creation of the in-

They facilitate the advancement of credit

[1] *Toronto Dominion Bank v. Jordan*, [1985] 61 B.C.L.R. 105.

strument and its discharge through payment, the negotiable instrument becomes an effective method of advancing credit, with the added advantage of being freely transferable between creditors. Negotiable instruments can provide for payment by instalment and require the payment of interest. They have become a standard part of business transactions and it is important to understand the legal principles involved and to know the rights and obligations of the parties. The use of negotiable instruments today is in decline to a considerable extent because of the use of credit cards and electronic transfers of funds. While these inroads are significant, the study of negotiable instruments is still important because of their unique character.

NEGOTIABILITY

Essential Characteristics

Our discussion of contract law demonstrated that it is possible to assign contractual claims but it is necessary to notify the debtor of the transfer before the assignee can enforce payment directly. The element that makes negotiable instruments an effective substitute for money in many situations is their free transferability from one party to another without having to notify or acquire the consent of the original parties to the transfer. To facilitate their transferability, negotiable instruments have acquired a second characteristic that makes them unique in the field of special contractual relationships. As you will recall, a problem with the assignment of contractual claims from the point of view of the outsider or assignee is that the assignee is in no better position than the assignor. When the debtor has a good defence against the assignor, it will hold against the assignee as well, thus allowing the debtor to avoid payment. This possibility obligates the assignee to investigate and accept the risks associated with the dealings between the original parties since the assignee is subject to them. A negotiable instrument is unique because, when it is transferred through negotiation to a third party who meets certain qualifications, that third party may take the instrument free of any problems which may exist between the original parties to it. The holder of the negotiable instrument may have better claims than the person from whom it was received. Even if the debtor under the instrument has a good defence against the original creditor, it cannot be used against an innocent third party, who is called a **holder in due course**, and the debtor will have to pay. This is the essential prerequisite to making negotiable instruments freely transferable because it removes much of the risk and uncertainty that might otherwise interfere with their use.

A negotiable instrument can only be an effective substitute for money if the person using it does not have to worry about disagreements between the initial parties. For example, if you were to go to a movie and give the teller a $10 bill for your ticket, you would be very surprised if the teller demanded to know whether that bill had ever been involved in a breach of contract or a fraudulent transaction, the assumption being that, if it had, the teller could refuse it because it had lost its

Negotiable instruments are freely transferable

Third party acquires better rights than original parties

value. Of course, money cannot work that way but must stand on its own as payment, independent of any previous dealings. It must be clearly understood that money is legal tender created by special statute and must not be confused with negotiable instruments, and to say that negotiable instruments are a substitute for money is not to say that they are equivalent, as explained in Chapter 5. Money and negotiable instruments have, however, come from common roots, and money nicely illustrates the essential quality of negotiation. A negotiable instrument can only be an effective substitute for money when the party receiving it is not obligated to go behind the instrument and examine the dealings of the parties to it but need only be concerned about the instrument itself.

The primary factors to keep in mind when studying negotiable instruments are the following:

1. They are a claim for funds against the person designated on the instrument.
2. They are freely transferable.
3. They may be used as an instrument of credit.
4. They may bestow greater rights or claims on the bearer of the instrument than on the party from whom the instrument was received.

Historical Context

Although variations of negotiable instruments have been used for thousands of years, the antecedent of modern forms developed in the Middle Ages. As trade grew in Europe, it became impractical and dangerous for merchants to carry large amounts of gold and silver as they travelled from one trading centre to another. They began to deposit their money at financial institutions designed for that purpose. When it became necessary for one merchant to give another money in the process of trade, the merchant would instead present a document which ordered the financial institution storing the merchant's money to pay out a certain sum to the person indicated on the document. Since their primary objective was to transfer money, these documents became known as bills of exchange. Their use effectively reduced the risks associated with trading since promises were being exchanged rather than actual funds. The rules associated with negotiable instruments were originally developed by the merchant guilds and included in their body of law called the "Law Merchant." These laws were adopted by the English courts and became an integral part of the common law system.

Negotiation an outgrowth of trading guilds

Bills of Exchange Act summarizes common law

BILLS OF EXCHANGE ACT. As part of the general legal reforms that took place in Britain in the last half of the nineteenth century, the numerous cases dealing with negotiable instruments were codified into one cohesive statute by M.D. Chalmers and enacted as the *Bills of Exchange Act* by the British Parliament in 1882. This *Act* was adopted by most common law jurisdictions and the *Canadian Bills of Exchange Act*, which the federal government passed in 1890, contained only minor changes.

Negotiable
instruments
under federal
jurisdiction

The statute remains very similar today.[2] The *Act* simply codified already existing principles dealing with negotiable instruments and did not change much of the common law. However, because of some minor changes, the *Act* makes it clear that common law principles apply except when specifically contrary to the provisions of the *Act*. The fact that the common law still applies despite the legislation can be important. The *Act* deals with the bills of exchange mentioned above as well as with cheques (which are bills of exchange drawn on banks and payable on demand) and promissory notes (which are promises by debtors to pay creditors specified amounts). These, as well as other types of documents that are also considered negotiable instruments although they are not included in the *Act*, will be discussed in more detail below. In those areas where the *Bills of Exchange Act* is silent, it is necessary to refer to the old common law provisions even today. Since 1890, the only significant amendment to the *Bills of Exchange Act* has been a 1970 addition concerned with "consumer notes."[3] Under the *Constitution Act (1867)*, only the federal government has the power to pass legislation regarding bills of exchange and promissory notes. The provinces may have legislative provisions which indirectly affect them but the provisions governing negotiable instruments are uniform throughout Canada.[4]

TYPES OF NEGOTIABLE INSTRUMENTS

There are other
types of
negotiable
instruments

Although the *Bills of Exchange Act* deals only with bills of exchange (drafts), cheques and promissory notes, it must be remembered that the *Act* is merely a codification of the common law. In fact, under the common law other types of instruments can qualify as negotiable instruments or take on many of the characteristics of negotiable instruments. For example, bonds made payable to a designated person or to his or her order have been held to be negotiable instruments. Similarly, share certificates qualify as negotiable instruments in some jurisdictions.[5] The discussion in this chapter will be limited to bills of exchange, cheques and promissory notes, although it should be remembered that the principles discussed will also apply to all other types of negotiable instruments.

Orders and
promises

Negotiable instruments have two main functions. The fundamental nature of a cheque or a bill of exchange is that it is an **order** or direction given by one person to another to pay funds to a third. The nature of a promissory note, on the other hand, is primarily that of a **promise** that funds will be paid out by the maker at some future date. Negotiable instruments fall into the category of orders in the case of cheques and bills of exchange, and promises in the case of promissory notes.

---

[2] *Bills of Exchange Act*, R.S.C. (1985) c.B-4.
[3] *Bills of Exchange Amendment Act*, R.S.C. (1970) 1st Supp. c.4.
[4] *Constitution Act*, (1867) s.91 ss.18.
[5] *Business Corporations Act*, S.Q. (1982) c.4 s.53(3).

Bills of Exchange

Although not in common use today except in some particular businesses, the bill of exchange is important to understand since its features relate to the other forms of negotiable instruments discussed below. A bill of exchange is an order made by one person to another to pay an amount of money to a third; it is often called a draft. The person drawing up the instrument is called the **drawer**. It is the drawer who orders the **drawee**, usually a financial institution, to make payment to a third party, known as the **payee**. Normally, the drawer has already established some sort of business arrangement, such as a bank account, with the person or institution being ordered to pay. Otherwise, the order would simply be ignored. However, in some circumstances, a bill of exchange is used as a means of collecting a debt and then the drawer orders the debtor to make payment to a third party. The idea is that, if the debtor fails to do so, his or her credit rating will be harmed. Although the instrument is addressed to the drawee, it is physically transferred to the payee and the payee then presents the instrument to the drawee for payment.

If the bill is made payable on demand, the normal course of action is for the payee to present the instrument to the drawee as soon as possible for payment. However, when the instrument is made payable at some future time, the payee or subsequent holder of the instrument must wait until the bill reaches the date designated for payment before the funds can be obtained. If the bill has not yet matured or if the payee or subsequent holder wishes to delay immediate payment for some other reason, another option is available. It is still important for the holder of the instrument to determine whether or not the bill will be honoured when the date of maturity is reached. The holder of the bill has the right to take the instrument to the drawee, even before maturity, to determine whether or not the drawee will assent to the order given by the drawer. Thus, the drawee commits to accept the obligation to pay out on the instrument the amount specified at the date of maturity, indicating this by a signature, the date and the word "accepted" written on the bill of exchange. When the drawee has done this, he or she has accepted the bill and is referred to subsequently as the acceptor rather than the drawee. If the drawee refuses to accept the instrument, it is said to be dishonoured and the holder must then seek redress from the drawer. Redress can be sought immediately without waiting until the maturity date. But if the instrument is accepted, the drawee becomes primarily liable on the instrument and the drawer no longer has any control over the payment of the bill.

It is interesting to note that, before acceptance takes place, the drawee owes no obligation to the payee to honour the instrument since there is no direct relationship between the drawee and the payee or holder. It is only because of the relationship that exists between the drawer and drawee that the drawee is willing to accept the order and pay out to the holder of the instrument. The drawer retains control of the situation and can countermand the order. Providing the bill has not been honoured through payment or accepted by the drawee, the drawee will respect the countermand and refuse to honour the instrument. For example, if Garcia buys a boat from Saito and gives Saito a bill of exchange, payable three months later, drawn on Ace Trust Company where Garcia has an account or line of credit, it is quite likely that Saito

Bill of exchange is order instrument

Bill paid upon maturity

Once accepted—drawee primarily liable

Drawee has no obligation to payee before acceptance

would go to Ace Trust Company as soon as possible to find out whether Ace would honour the bill three months hence. Ace Trust Company would indicate their willingness to honour the instrument at maturity by their representative writing "accepted" across the instrument, accompanied by the date and the signature of the appropriate signing officer. If they refuse to do this, the bill would be dishonoured and Saito would then turn to Garcia, the original drawer of the instrument, for satisfaction. But if Ace Trust Company does accept the bill, Garcia can no longer issue any instructions to Ace Trust Company in relation to it. In effect, the primary debtor is now Ace Trust Company. Since they have assumed the debt and the obligation to pay, Garcia has lost control of the situation.

In fact, the *Bills of Exchange Act* states that the position of the acceptor is the same as the maker of the promissory note.[6] If Garcia were to discover that there had been some fraudulent misrepresentation on the part of Saito, Garcia could countermand the order to Ace Trust Company any time before acceptance. But once Ace Trust Company has accepted the bill and become the primary debtor, it owes an obligation to Saito to honour the instrument independent of Garcia and so are uninterested in any difficulties that exist between Garcia and Saito. If there has been fraud, Garcia has the right to sue Saito for compensation but cannot prevent Ace Trust Company from paying out on the accepted bill of exchange. It is possible for the "acceptor" of the bill to make a qualified acceptance. When the acceptance is qualified, as in "acceptable when car repair complete," the bearer of the instrument can submit to the qualification or treat the bill of exchange as dishonoured and look to the drawer for satisfaction.

Bills of exchange can be used to accomplish two purposes. First, bills of exchange are an extremely effective method of transferring funds between parties without the necessity of carrying cash, and, second, they can be used to create a creditor/debtor relationship. Demand drafts and sight drafts are usually used to transfer funds, the demand draft being payable when it is presented and the sight draft payable three days after being presented. A bill of exchange, payable at some future time, is called a time draft. Although the bill of exchange was traditionally the most significant type of negotiable instrument, its use in modern times has dwindled because of business people's increased reliance on another negotiable instrument, the cheque. However, the bill of exchange is still a valuable tool of commerce and there are many circumstances in which, because of tradition or the need for the unique qualities of this instrument, the bill of exchange is still in common use today.

Another way a draft (a bill of exchange) is often used is in association with a letter of credit. A letter of credit is used by importers, exporters and similar enterprises dealing with businesses in other countries to ensure that they are paid by their customers. The customer makes arrangements to have his or her own bank make the required payment. The customer's bank sends the letter of credit, usually to the bank of the exporter, called the advising bank. When that exporter can show that he or she has met all of the conditions set out in the letter of credit, establishing that he or she has performed his or her part of the contract, the letter of credit is

Order to pay can be countermanded before acceptance

---

[6] *Bills of Exchange Act*, R.S.C. (1985) c.B-4 s.186(2).

honoured and he or she receives payment. If a "draft" is used as the method of payment, the drawer is the importer, the drawee is the exporter's bank and the payee is usually the bank of the importer.

Cheques

A **cheque** is a bill of exchange drawn on a bank and payable on demand. Thus, a cheque must be viewed as a type of bill of exchange; it has the same general characteristics but is limited to situations in which the drawee is a bank and payment can be demanded immediately. It should be noted that the definition of "bank" for the purposes of the *Act* has been broadened by a recent amendment to include credit unions.[7] Since a cheque is payable on demand, its primary purpose is to exchange funds conveniently rather than to function as an instrument of credit. However, cheques that are postdated can be used to create a creditor/debtor relationship over substantial periods of time. Because a creditor/debtor relationship is inconsistent with a cheque being payable on demand, a postdated cheque does not acquire all of the characteristics of a negotiable instrument until the date specified on the instrument. As a result, a unique feature of postdated cheques is that the drawer retains the right to countermand it up to the stated date, even against an innocent third party, and anyone acquiring the instrument before that date takes it subject to that right. Thus, if on June 3, Robinson were to make a cheque drawn on his account at the Royal Bank payable to Devji postdated to June 10, and if Devji were to take that cheque to her own bank (the Bank of Commerce) on June 7 and receive cash for it, the Bank of Commerce would receive a negotiable instrument but would take it subject to Robinson's right to countermand. If Robinson were to countermand the cheque on June 8 because of some fraud, the Bank of Commerce would not be able to demand payment as a holder in due course from Robinson. Its only option would be to turn to its depositor, Devji, for repayment. Once the date has passed, the instrument can be further negotiated and the person acquiring possession will be in the position of any other holder of a negotiable instrument. However, it is important to note that, because the Bank of Commerce took the instrument with an irregularity on its face, it would be subject to the countermand even when it attempted collection after June 10, when the irregularity was no longer apparent. When a bank has sufficient funds in a customer's chequing account to cover a cheque drawn on it or has agreed to a line of credit, that bank has an obligation to honour the cheque. Whenever it fails to do so, the bank can be required to pay substantial damages to the customer because of that failure. If there are not enough funds to cover a cheque, the bank will not honour the cheque and the liability is in the hands of the drawer.

One important feature of a cheque set out in Section 167 of the *Bills of Exchange Act* is that the authority of the bank to pay a cheque drawn on it is effectively terminated when either of two events take place. When the customer who has drawn the cheque dies, the authority of the bank to honour that cheque is terminated as

---

[7] *Bills of Exchange Act*, R.S.C. (1985) c.B-4 s.164.

soon as it has notice of the death. The bank's authority to pay out on a cheque also ends when the customer orders a stop payment or countermands payment on the cheque.[8] Many banks require their customers to agree to reimburse the bank if the cheque is inadvertently paid after such a countermand.

CERTIFICATION. While founded on English legal principles, the banking system in Canada has borrowed many of its procedures from American banks. This dual heritage has not only caused confusion but has also created a significant legal dilemma because the Canadian banking system has adopted the American practice of certifying cheques. The *Bills of Exchange Act* is silent on certification so its legal consequences are still somewhat in doubt. Certification requires the certifier to take a cheque to the bank on which it is drawn and have the bank indicate on the cheque that they will pay the amount shown on the cheque to any holder. This procedure is somewhat similar to the acceptance of a bill of exchange.

A cheque can be certified in either of two circumstances. A cheque may be presented to the bank for certification by the payee or some subsequent holder of the instrument and the result is similar to a bill of exchange being accepted by the drawee. That is, the drawer of the cheque will lose control over the instrument and the bank will assume primary liability to pay the payee. If Nagy gives a $5000 cheque to Coghill for the purchase of a car and Coghill then takes the cheque to the bank and has it certified, Nagy can no longer stop payment. This would be true even if Nagy were to get home and discover that Coghill had fraudulently misled him about the condition of the car.

But a cheque is not usually certified in this way. Usually it is the drawer who takes the cheque to the bank and has it certified before it is issued to the payee. This sequence of events is clearly not the same as an acceptance of a bill of exchange. In fact, the cheque is not a negotiable instrument at the time it is certified because it has not yet been delivered to the payee. When a drawer brings a cheque in for certification to the bank, no direct relationship between the payee and the bank has been established. Thus, any obligation of the bank to the payee after certification in this way is indirect and should be conditional. Many take the position that the bank only has an obligation to honour the instrument if it can be demonstrated that the drawer has an obligation. The result of such a certification at the request of the drawer is that the bank guarantees that there are funds set aside which are available to the payee or subsequent holder. The bank should be in a similar position as a guarantor of a debt. In fact, in practice, the banks usually treat a cheque certified by the drawer as they treat one certified at the request of the payee or subsequent holder, that is, as an accepted bill of exchange. Several recent court decisions have adopted this practice as correct in Canadian law and, therefore, it is likely that a certified cheque, no matter whether it was certified at the request of the original drawer or by the payee or subsequent holder will be treated as equivalent to an accepted bill of exchange with the bank being the primary debtor and the drawer losing all control. To avoid this problem, some banks have adopted the practice of giving their customers a bank draft rather than certifying a cheque at the request of the drawer.

> When cheque certified by payee, it cannot be countermanded

[8] *Bills of Exchange Act*, R.S.C. (1985) c.B-4 s.167.

Promissory Notes

Promissory notes
are promises to
pay

Bills of exchange and cheques are orders to third parties but promissory notes fall into another category of negotiable instruments. They are promises to pay the amount set out on the instrument. The creator of the promissory note, the debtor, is referred to as the maker and the person designated on the instrument as entitled to the funds is referred to as the payee. Because only two parties are involved, the main function of promissory notes is not to exchange funds, as was the case with bills of exchange and cheques, but rather to advance credit. They are an important form of negotiable instrument used by financial institutions and are common in consumer transactions. Because they are used for the granting of credit, it is acceptable and quite common for promissory notes not only to bear interest but to be paid by a series of instalments. The abuses associated with this type of negotiable instrument in consumer creditor transactions led to the 1970 amendments to the *Bills of Exchange Act* which created consumer notes and which are discussed below.[9]

The maker of a promissory note corresponds to the acceptor of a bill of exchange.[10] When the drawee on a bill of exchange has accepted the instrument, the drawee has a direct obligation to pay the payee or subsequent holder. The maker of a promissory note also has a direct obligation to pay the payee when the promissory note comes due. The other provisions of the *Bills of Exchange Act* also apply to promissory notes and, therefore, can be negotiated to third parties who, if they meet the qualifications of a holder in due course, will acquire better rights under the instrument than the original payee possessed. It is this characteristic that makes promissory notes so attractive to institutions in the business of loaning money. Traditionally, a customer would purchase a commodity from a merchandiser and make arrangements to pay for the goods by instalment. This sale usually took the form of a conditional sale as described in Chapter 8, but, in addition to the conditional sale agreement, the customer would be required to sign a promissory note. The merchandiser would then sell or assign the conditional sale agreement to the third party credit institution and, along with that assignment, negotiate the promissory note to that same institution. That institution would then become an innocent third party or a holder in due course and could rely on the promissory note, independent of any problems between the merchandiser and the customer. If the merchandise proved defective, so that the customer would normally not be required to pay the merchant, this would not affect the position of the credit institution which could still demand payment. This particular advantage to the credit institution has been significantly reduced by the passage of the 1970 amendment to the Bills of Exchange Act dealing with customer notes which will be discussed below.[11]

Promissory notes
often used for
consumer credit

A simple IOU is not a negotiable instrument. A person who signs a document, "I owe you $500, (signed) J.B. Samra," has acknowledged a debt but has made no promise to pay. Use of the words "payable on demand," or if it is designated payable at some specified date, make the instrument a promissory note.[12]

---

[9] *Bills of Exchange Act*, R.S.C. (1985) c.B-4 Part V.
[10] *Bills of Exchange Act*, R.S.C. (1985) c.B-4 s.186(2).
[11] *Bills of Exchange Act*, R.S.C. (1985) c.B-4 Part V.
[12] *Bills of Exchange Act*, R.S.C. (1985) c.B-4 s.176.

NEGOTIATION

Bearer
instrument
negotiated
through transfer

Negotiation involves passing negotiable instruments on to people who were not original parties to the transaction. The process can take place in two ways depending on the method used to create the instrument in the first place. If the negotiable instrument was created as a bearer instrument, the negotiation of that instrument can be accomplished simply by transferring it from one person to another. A **bearer instrument** is created by the drawer making the amount specified payable "to bearer," and the bearer is the person in possession of the instrument at any one time. An **order instrument** is made payable to a specific person or his or her order. In this case, the person designated as the payee on the instrument (the person who is to receive payment) must endorse it before it is delivered to a third party. Negotiation of an order instrument is a two-stage process requiring both endorsation and delivery of the endorsed instrument to the third party. A negotiable instrument is endorsed by the designated payee signing the back of the instrument. The normal practice is for a cheque to be made payable to a specific person. For example, if Paquette draws a cheque made payable to Quon, Quon could negotiate that cheque to Naidu by signing the back of it and delivering it to Naidu. If this endorsation is only a signature, the cheque becomes a bearer instrument and Naidu could transfer it without further endorsation. If Quon not only signed his name but as part of the endorsement stated that the cheque is payable to Naidu or to the order of Naidu, then the instrument remains an order instrument and Naidu must go through the two-stage process of endorsing it and delivering it to some third party to negotiate it further.

Order instrument
must be
endorsed to be
transferred

In fact, there are many different types of endorsements which can be attached to a negotiable instrument, each of which is designed to accomplish a different purpose. An instrument that becomes a bearer instrument can be made an order instrument again by the bearer so stating with a "special endorsement" on the instrument. It should be noted that an instrument originally created as a bearer instrument cannot be made an order instrument through endorsement. The various types of endorsements and the liability of the endorsers are discussed below.

Requirements for Negotiability

The following is a summary of the general characteristics these instruments must exhibit to be negotiable:

Promise to pay
must be
unconditional

1. *Unconditional commitment.* Any instrument that requires an event to take place or qualification to be met before the promise to pay is binding on the maker of that instrument will not qualify as negotiable. These instruments must meet the obligation of being freely transferable so that subsequent holders do not have to look to the dealings of the original parties. If it were possible to make such instruments conditional, the holders would never know for certain if the condition had been met, thus defeating the purpose of negotiation. If Quon were to draw a cheque made payable to Paquette "if the barn has been painted" and Paquette

then transferred this instrument to Naidu, Naidu could not tell if the condition had been met from the instrument itself. Naidu would have to inquire of one of the original parties and, because this is inconsistent with the purpose of negotiability, the cheque would not qualify as a negotiable instrument.

Instrument must be in writing and signed

2. *Signed and in writing.* The instrument must be able to stand on its own. It must be in writing and the name of the maker or drawer must appear on the face of the document. Because the legislation does not require that the person signing the document be the one promising to pay, it is quite permissible to have it created and signed by an agent and still qualify as a negotiable instrument. The purported principal will not be bound, however, if the agent has exceeded both actual and apparent authority. Such an unauthorized agent would be personally liable on the instrument.

Instrument must have a specified time for payment or be payable on demand

3. *Payable at a fixed time or on demand.* An instrument can be made payable on demand by so stating on the instrument or by making no indication at all of a time for payment. A cheque is an example of a negotiable instrument payable on demand. The holder of the instrument is free to present the instrument for payment at any time during normal business hours. An instrument not payable on demand must be payable on some certain date or at some determinable time as specified on the instrument. Thus, if Quon were to make a note payable ninety days after his death, this would satisfy the requirement since his death is a certainty and so the date is determinable. However, care must be exercised because payment dates determined on some event carry considerable risk. For example, a note which is made payable ninety days after marriage is based on an event that is not a certainty. The note would be conditional and therefore not negotiable. In Canada, an instrument payable "at sight" is quite different from a note payable on demand or presentation. When it is made payable at sight, the payment is really due three days after it is presented, allowing the debtor three days of grace to gather the funds.

Instrument must be for a fixed sum

4. *For a fixed amount of money.* A negotiable instrument must be for a certain amount of money specified on the face of the instrument. It is possible that the payment of that money will be made in instalments and that interest may be added but the amount owing must be certain. Thus, a promise by Quon to pay his inheritance to Paquette is not a negotiable instrument because the amount owed is not specified. The amount to be paid must also be payable in Canadian funds if the instrument is to be presented for payment in Canada. It is possible to have the amount to be paid calculated in other currency but it must be possible to pay that amount in the equivalent Canadian funds. Thus, an instrument promising to pay $500 in U.S. currency will not qualify as a negotiable instrument but one promising to pay $500 U.S. will. Here the equivalent in Canadian funds can be delivered since there is no requirement that it be paid out in U.S. currency.

Instrument must be delivered to payee

5. *Delivery of the instrument.* Even if the instrument has been drawn up, it does not qualify as a negotiable instrument until it has been physically transferred to the payee. This first transfer to the payee is called the **issue** of the instrument and all subsequent transfers are called **deliveries**. If delivery has been induced by fraud or if the instrument was stolen before it was issued, the debtor is not

obligated to honour it. However, if the instrument gets into the hands of an innocent third party who qualifies as a holder in due course, such delivery will be conclusively presumed.

Partial claims not permitted

6. *The whole instrument must pass.* The entire claim specified on the face of the instrument must be passed to a subsequent holder for the instrument to remain negotiable. If the claim on a cheque is for $500 and the payee delivers that cheque to a third party but states in the endorsement that only $300 of the $500 claim is to pass, the instrument will not be a negotiable instrument in the hands of that third party. It should be noted that the third party will still have a claim against the debtor based on the assignment of contractual rights. This condition does not affect the right of the payee to discount the instrument. For example, if Quon were to transfer to Paquette all of the claim on a negotiable instrument made out for $500 for only $300, the instrument would remain negotiable since the entire instrument is passing. Quon has simply sold it for less than its face value. But if Quon transferred only part of the $500 claim to Paquette, retaining the right to collect some of the amount specified, this action would destroy the instrument's negotiability.

Only when all of these requirements have been met will the document in question qualify as a negotiable instrument. It is important to remember that even when the instrument does not qualify as a negotiable instrument, the claimants may still have significant legal rights under the principle of assignment discussed in Chapter 5.

RIGHTS AND OBLIGATIONS OF THE PARTIES

The right to enforce a negotiable instrument varies not only with the status of the holder of the instrument but also with the type of defence being raised. To understand the rights and obligations of the parties to a negotiable instrument, it is best to examine them from the point of view of the person seeking to enforce the instrument. The following is an examination of the position of a holder in due course, a remote holder and a payee.

Holder in Due Course

Throughout this chapter, the unique position of a holder in due course has been emphasized. We stated that a person who is not a party to the negotiable instrument but who acquires possession of it and otherwise qualifies as a holder in due course can actually acquire better rights or claims under that instrument than previous possessors held. Thus, if ever a problem such as misrepresentation or breach of contract existed between the maker of the instrument and the original payee, the

Holder in due
course acquires
better rights

holder in due course takes the instrument independent of any of these problems and will be able to enforce it despite their presence. The essential and unique nature of negotiable instruments is embodied in the person of the holder in due course. It is because of this special and privileged position that negotiable instruments are so attractive and useful as a medium of exchange and a method of advancing credit.

Qualifications of a
holder in due
course

Not all third parties to negotiable instruments are holders in due course. The qualifications which must be met to obtain the status of a holder in due course are set out in Section 56 of the *Bills of Exchange Act*. These qualifications can be summarized as follows:

—received
through
negotiation

1. A holder in due course must have received the negotiable instrument through negotiation and cannot be one of the immediate parties.

—complete and
regular

2. A holder in due course must have taken the instrument complete and regular on its face. If important portions of the instrument, such as the amount payable or to whom it is to be paid, have been left blank when the holder acquires possession of it or if the instrument had been obviously altered, for example, if the amount payable has been increased, the holder will not qualify as a holder in due course. If Dedrick fraudulently persuades Yoshida to issue a cheque with the amount left blank and Dedrick fills in $5000 and negotiates that cheque to Ramji, Ramji will be able to enforce the instrument if he otherwise qualifies as a holder in due course. If Dedrick fails to fill in the blank, Ramji will have acquired an incomplete instrument and will not qualify as a holder in due course and, therefore, will not be able to enforce it against Yoshida. However, assume Yoshida had given Dedrick a cheque for $500 and Dedrick added a zero making it $5000. If the zero which had been added to the instrument was not apparent to Ramji when he received it through negotiation, he would qualify as a holder in due course and be able to enforce the cheque against Yoshida but only in its original form for $500. If the alteration was obvious, Ramji would not qualify as a holder in due course because the instrument was not regular on its face. Similarly, if the instrument is marked paid or cancelled, the person who takes it in such a condition will not qualify as a holder in due course.

—acquired before
due and payable

3. The holder must have acquired possession of the instrument before it becomes due and payable. An instrument is overdue if the date specified on the face of the instrument has passed, whether that date is fixed or determinable. (A grace period of three days should be included in this calculation whenever applicable.) It is a little more difficult to determine whether an instrument is overdue or not if it is payable on demand. A bill of exchange which is payable on demand is said to be overdue when it appears on the face of it to have been in circulation for an "unreasonable length of time."[13] What qualifies as an unreasonable length of time is a question of fact. When a promissory note payable on demand is involved, the *Bills of Exchange Act* specifically states that the mere fact that the note has not been presented for payment within a reasonable period of time will not make it overdue when negotiated. The holder still qualifies as a holder in due

---

[13] *Ibid.*, s.69 s.2.

course. The difference in the way that demand bills and notes are treated illustrates an essential difference in their natures. When a cheque or bill payable on demand is drawn, a third party is expected to take payment quickly. But when a promissory note is involved, even if it is payable on demand, the original parties to it would not expect payment to be demanded immediately. A promissory note, bill of exchange or cheque becomes overdue as soon as it is presented for payment and refused. The status of a holder in due course is affected only if the instrument is negotiated in such a way that the holder should know that the payment has been refused. For example, suppose Dedrick holds Yoshida's promissory note which is payable on demand for $500 and is refused when Dedrick presents it for payment. If he then negotiates that note to Ramji at a significant discount and arouses Ramji's suspicions that there is a likelihood that Dedrick had previously tried to get payment on the note, then Ramji would not qualify as a holder in due course because he took delivery of it after it was overdue.

—without knowledge of dishonour

4. The holder must have acquired the instrument without knowing that it had been dishonoured previously. If the drawer of a cheque stops payment on it because of the payee's fraud, the payee cannot get around this by making a deal with an associate who hopes to enforce it against the original drawer as a holder in due course. Because the third party is aware of the countermand which constitutes dishonour of the cheque, he or she does not qualify as a holder in due course. On the other hand, if the associate who otherwise qualifies as a holder in due course is not aware that the cheque had been countermanded and is not in a position to have known, his or her status as a holder in due course will not be affected. The same principles apply when a bill of exchange or a promissory note is involved.

—without knowledge of defect of title

5. The holder must have no knowledge of any defect of title. A defect of title is some problem, usually between the payee and the original drawer of the instrument but also possibly between the payee or other holder, which affects the right to possess the instrument. A holder of the instrument who is aware that the person who negotiated it had a "defect of title" is not a holder in due course. Defects in title problems may result from fraud, duress, undue influence and some kinds of incapacity. For example, if Yoshida were drunk at the time of drawing up a promissory note payable to Dedrick and Dedrick was aware of Yoshida's condition, Dedrick's title to that negotiable instrument would be defective. If Dedrick then negotiated this promissory note to Ramji and Ramji was aware that Yoshida was drunk when the instrument was drawn up, Ramji would have notice of the defect of title and would not qualify as a holder in due course. Defect of title defences are discussed in more detail below.

—good faith

6. The holder must have acquired the instrument in good faith. There is considerable overlap between this requirement and number five, but essentially this one is broader because it requires honesty on the part of the holder in due course. The holder of an instrument who has no specific knowledge of a defect of title or other problem associated with the instrument but suspects that someone is being cheated would not be acting honestly by demanding payment. It is important to point out that Section 3 of the *Bills of Exchange Act* states that

the person is deemed to be acting in good faith when the act is honest but negligent. A person will not lose the status of a holder in due course merely because he or she has acted carelessly in taking possession of a negotiable instrument. It is for this reason that the bank in the example used to introduce the chapter could not claim to be a holder in due course and enforce the cheque against Mr. Jordan. The manager of the bank had been so involved with Mrs. Jordan that he could not be said to be acting in good faith. As a consequence, Mr. Jordan did not have to pay.

—for value

7. Value must have been given for the negotiable instrument. Value in this sense is defined in the *Act* as valuable consideration and has essentially the same meaning as it does in contract law. However, this definition also includes "an antecedent debt or liability" as consideration.[14] This exception is to avoid the problem of past consideration being no consideration when negotiable instruments are given for already existing debt or liabilities. It is not necessary that the holder in due course be the one to provide such valuable consideration. Section 54 of the *Bills of Exchange Act* clearly states that a holder is deemed to be a holder for value whenever value has been given for the instrument. Thus, if Yoshida issued Dedrick a promissory note for $500 in exchange for a motor vehicle and Dedrick gave this negotiable instrument as a gift to Ramji, Ramji's status as a holder in due course would not be affected by the fact that it was obtained as a gift because Dedrick had given valuable consideration for the instrument.

Real defences can defeat holder in due course

REAL DEFENCE. Only when these requirements are met can the holder claim to be a holder in due course, but even meeting these requirements does not ensure payment. The maker of the instrument has various defences available which can be raised against the different categories of holders seeking to enforce a negotiable instrument. A **real defence** is one which is good against any holder, even a holder in due course, because it involves a problem with the instrument itself.

Drawer not liable in cases of forgery

When the signature of the drawer has been forged or signed by an agent who has no actual or apparent authority to do so, the drawer or maker will not be liable on the instrument. A drawee is not liable for a forged acceptance nor is an endorser liable for an unauthorized or forged signature. It should be noted that, when the instrument has been endorsed, the person endorsing it cannot rely on a revelation of the forgery of one of the immediate party's signature before that endorsement as a defence against anyone holding that instrument. An endorsement encourages subsequent holders to believe the negotiable instrument is what it purports to be. Even when the signature is valid, if other material parts of the negotiable instrument, such as the amount, have been forged, this will constitute a real defence, although the original drawer will be liable to a holder in due course for the contents of the original unaltered instrument. When a signature is valid but has been given for another purpose (the drawer thought a letter was being signed), and someone subsequently forges a negotiable instrument around that signature, such forgery will constitute a real defence. Negligence on the part of the drawer in these circumstances will pre-

[14] *Ibid.*, s.52(b.).

clude raising the defence against an innocent holder in due course. It is interesting to note that, when the forgery is the signature on a bill of exchange or cheque and the drawee or bank pays out under the impression that the instrument is valid, it cannot then turn to the purported drawer for compensation. The drawee in such circumstances is the one who bears the loss.

A second type of real defence occurs when the instrument has been **discharged**. The discharge can take place in several ways:

Discharge of instrument is a real defence

1. Through payment in due course at the appropriate time which is apparent to the holder.
2. When the holder renounces in writing any claim to that bill (this only constitutes a real defence if the holder in due course has notification of this renunciation).
3. When the instrument itself has been cancelled in such a way that it is apparent on the face of it.
4. When the instrument has been materially altered without the consent of the parties in such a way that it is apparent on the instrument.

Lack of delivery of incomplete instrument is a real defence

Another real defence is lack of delivery of an incomplete instrument. The initial delivery is referred to as issuing the negotiable instrument to the payee. But when this has not taken place (if the instrument has been stolen from the drawer or if it has been delivered into the hands of the payee by someone purporting to act as an agent but without either actual or apparent authority to do so), the drawer would have a good defence against anybody except a holder in due course. Only when the instrument is incomplete as well as not being issued to the payee can the drawer claim a real defence and thus defeat even a holder in due course's attempt to enforce the instrument. If Rasmussen were to go to Cohen's office and notice a cheque on the secretary's desk made payable to him but with the amount left blank, and if Rasmussen took the cheque and later filled in what he considered to be the appropriate amount and then negotiated that instrument to Jaswal as an innocent holder in due course, Jaswal could not enforce payment. If the instrument had been complete with the appropriate amount filled in before Rasmussen took it, Jaswal would be able to enforce the instrument against Cohen because, if a complete instrument gets into the hands of a holder in due course, delivery is "conclusively presumed."

Incapacity is a real defence

Some forms of **incapacity** provide another type of real defence against a holder in due course. The *Bills of Exchange Act* makes it clear that what constitutes capacity in a given jurisdiction corresponds to the principles of contract law.[15] Essentially, if a contract is void because of the incapacity of one of the parties, a negotiable instrument will also be unenforceable against that incapacitated party. A negotiable instrument that has been drawn up by a minor is unenforceable because of his or her incapacity under contract law. Remember, however, that in some circumstances, infants are obligated to honour contractual rights. Thus, the holder of the instrument can sue the infant, not on the basis of the negotiable instrument, but on the basis that the contract was for necessaries. Of course the infant's obligation in such circumstances is to pay a reasonable price for the

---

[15] *Ibid.*, s.46.

necessaries which may or may not correspond to the amount set out on the negotiable instrument. When insanity or drunkenness is involved, such incapacity will not necessarily amount to a real defence and may not be available against an innocent holder in due course, unless the person has been declared insane under statutory power. Such a person would not be liable to even a holder in due course because the incapacity is absolute. The *Bills of Exchange Act* clearly establishes that a corporation with limited capacity in provinces using a registration system of incorporation or created by special statute will not be liable on a negotiable instrument drawn on it pursuant to a contract that is beyond its capacity to enter into.[16] Most provincial corporations now have full capacity but, as discussed in the previous chapter, some corporations created by special statute may have their capacity limited in this way.

It is important to point out that, when incapacity is claimed as a defence, it is only available to the person incapacitated and will not invalidate the negotiable instrument. Thus, a drawee who pays out or accepts the instrument and a payee or subsequent endorser will be liable despite the incapacity of the original drawer or maker of the instrument. If an infant has a bank account, draws a cheque on it and delivers it to a payee, that payee can present it to the bank and the bank is fully entitled to honour the cheque if there are sufficient funds on deposit. If the infant countermands the cheque, there would be no recourse against either the bank or the infant on the basis of the negotiable instrument. The liability of the infant would have to be established on the basis of a contract for necessaries. If the instrument is in the hands of a holder in due course, that holder in due course can enforce it against any endorser or against the acceptor, since once those parties have accepted or endorsed, they cannot claim the incapacity of the original drawer or maker as a defence.

Mistake can be a real defence

Under some circumstances, **mistake** can be a real defence. But this mistake must go to the nature of the instrument itself. That is, the purported drawer or maker of the instrument must have been under the impression that he or she was signing something other than a negotiable instrument when the signature was affixed to the document. This is an example of the defence of *non est factum*. This defence will not be available when the mistake was caused by the negligence of the drawer or maker. Since the principle puts an obligation on the drawer or maker to make an effort to determine the nature of the document being signed, it may well be that the only situation in which *non est factum* will be available as a defence on a negotiable instrument is when the drawer or maker has been actively misled about the nature of the instrument signed.

Apparent alteration prevents enforcement

Finally, any **material alteration** on the instrument will amount to a real defence, if it is apparent to the holder. Thus, a negotiable instrument with scratches on it or which otherwise indicates an erasure or alteration cannot be enforced at all against the original drawer or maker. Only when the alteration is not obvious can the instrument be enforced against the original drawer, and then only on the terms of the original instrument before any alterations. When such a real defence is available, the instrument cannot be enforced against the maker, even by someone who meets all of the other requirements set out for a holder in due course.

[16] *Ibid.*, s.46 s.2.

Other Holders

The holder of an instrument who is not an immediate party to it and fails to meet the qualifications listed above is known as a **remote holder**. But even a remote holder may be in a better position to enforce the instrument than was the original payee. Basically, a remote holder must not only refute any claimed real defences as listed above but must also establish that good title was held on the instrument. A defect of title defence (which is a problem with the way the instrument was acquired) can be effectively used against a remote holder. Many of the rules governing contracts are brought into play with this defence. Some examples of **defect of title defences** are as follows:

Real defences and defective title defences available against remote holder

1. When fraud, undue influence or duress is used to obtain the instrument.
2. When the consideration given for the instrument is illegal.
3. Some forms of incapacity. For example, if the person issuing the instrument is drunk or insane and when the person to whom it is issued knows or ought to know of the condition of that person, this constitutes a defect of title defence rather than a real defence.
4. When a complete instrument is not properly delivered. When an instrument is properly delivered but is issued in blank and completed by a subsequent holder, there is no difficulty since the authority to so complete is presumed. However, when the given authority to complete is violated, such as the wrong amounts or dates are put in the blanks, this constitutes a defect of title defence.
5. When the instrument has been discharged in such a way that it is not apparent to the holder of the instrument. Thus, if a promissory note is being paid by instalments and the last payment is made but there is no indication of this on the instrument and it gets into the hands of a third party, the fact that it has been paid is only a defect of title defence. Similarly, if the holder has renounced claim on the instrument, even when it is acknowledged in writing, it is a defect of title defence if it is not indicated on the instrument itself.

There is one circumstance under which a remote holder can obtain the same kind of rights as a holder in due course. If it can be demonstrated that someone has held the instrument previously who qualified as a holder in due course, then the remote holder who now possesses it will have all the rights and claims of a holder in due course, acquiring those rights from the holder in due course through assignment. In these circumstances, the holder is called a holder through a holder in due course and has all the rights of a holder in due course. The remote holder will only lose those rights if the holder actually participated in the fraud or illegality that is being raised in the defence.[17] When the payee deposits a cheque in her bank, that bank acquires the same rights as a holder in due course.

Payees

Immediate parties seeking to enforce a negotiable instrument have no better rights than are available in ordinary contract law. The contract itself governs the

[17] *Ibid.*, s.56.

Even personal
defences
available against
payee

relationship. It is possible to use not only real and defect of title defences against an immediate party but any other defence that would normally be available in contract law. These additional defences are called "mere personal defences," an example of which is the right of **setoff**. A right of setoff involves the person being sued having some other separate claim against the person suing that may not be related to the bargain involving the negotiable instrument at all. For example, if Nimmo were an employee of Deheer's Used Cars and bought a used automobile from Deheer for $1000 by issuing a promissory note to Deheer, Nimmo would be entitled to set off against that claim any amount Deheer may owe him as salary or commission. So if Nimmo were owed $800 in commissions from Deheer, the two amounts when set off against each other would result in Nimmo being required to pay only the remaining $200 to Deheer on the negotiable instrument. Thus, when a person is being sued by an immediate party to a negotiable instrument, setoff may be used as a defence.

Another typical example of a mere personal defence is when there has been a **partial failure of consideration**. Contracts require the exchange of consideration between the parties. When a negotiable instrument is involved, some consideration must be exchanged for it pursuant to the terms of the contract. If the parties fail to perform the terms of the contract properly, the drawer or maker of the instrument can use that failure as a defence against the person with whom the contract was made. This is simple **breach of contract**.

Endorsers

The unique features of negotiable instruments come into play when those instruments get into the hands of third parties. The process of transferring the instrument is through delivery to third parties. When the instrument is in bearer form, negotiation can take place through delivery only, but when it is made out to a specific person or order, negotiation takes place through delivery and endorsement. Endorsement is a notation on the back of the instrument or separate piece of paper which includes the endorser's signature. The general rule is that when a party affixes an endorsement to a negotiable instrument, he or she is obligated to see that it is paid. If an instrument, after endorsement by the third party, gets into the hands of a holder in due course who presents it for payment but is refused by the drawer or drawee, that holder in due course can then turn to anyone who has endorsed the instrument and demand payment. An endorser who has had to pay in this way can then enforce the instrument against the defaulting drawer. When it is a bearer instrument being negotiated through delivery, the person taking such an unendorsed instrument still has the right to seek compensation from the person who negotiated the instrument to him or her. The difference is the holder in due course can seek redress only from the immediately preceding party, not from a person who held the instrument and negotiated it without endorsement before the person who negotiated it to the holder in due course. Thus, if Burkholder made a promissory note payable to bearer and it was then passed to Sakich, Rahal, Diaz and Black, all without endorsement, if Black could not collect from Burkholder, he must then turn

Negotiation of
order instrument
involves delivery
and endorsement

Endorser is liable
if instrument is
refused by
drawer

to Diaz. Even if Black qualifies as a holder in due course, he cannot demand payment from Rahal who has not endorsed the note.

The liability of an endorser on a dishonoured instrument is only established when certain qualifications are met by the person seeking redress. As a general rule, the holder of the instrument is required to give **notice of dishonour** to any endorser from whom payment is sought and that notice must be given by the close of the following business day after the instrument has been dishonoured. Failure to give such notice in the prescribed period of time will eliminate that holder's right to sue the endorser of the instrument. In very limited circumstances (in Québec or if a negotiable instrument requires payment in a country different from where it was drawn), a more formal type of notice must be given called "protest" which is done before a notary public.

FORMS OF ENDORSEMENT. Other objectives are accomplished through the type of endorsement affixed to a negotiable instrument. As a result many different forms of endorsement have been developed. The following is a summary of the different forms of endorsement:

1. *Endorsement in blank.* This is a simple signature and will change an order instrument into a bearer instrument.
2. *Special endorsement.* This endorsement, in addition to the endorser's signature, also specifies the name of a particular endorsee; the instrument remains an order instrument.
3. *Restrictive endorsement.* This endorsement contains the endorser's signature as well as some restriction on the further negotiation of the instrument, for example, "Pay to B.R. Gatz only." This type of endorsement renders an instrument no longer negotiable.
4. *Qualified endorsement.* An endorsement which contains the words "without recourse" or their equivalent eliminates the normal liability associated with the process of endorsement. By including such words, the endorser is no longer liable in any way to a subsequent holder of the instrument if that instrument is dishonoured. At the same time, an endorser can remove the requirement that normally falls on a holder of a dishonoured instrument to provide notice of such a dishonour simply by including the words "notice of dishonour waived" or "protest waived." In such cases, the holder of a dishonoured instrument need not meet the technical requirements of giving notice in order to protect his or her right to seek redress from the endorser.
5. *Conditional endorsement.* Although the original negotiable instrument cannot be conditional in any way, it is possible for the endorser to make a conditional endorsement. Thus, if Jackson endorses an instrument, "Pay to J. Galati only if car properly repaired," this is a valid endorsement. If J. Galati negotiates the instrument to Jang, Jang is entitled to assume the condition has been fulfilled and can demand payment from either Galati or Jackson. If Jang does demand payment from Galati and the condition has not been met, Galati could not look to Jackson for reimbursement.

Holder must give notice of dishonour

Different kinds of endorsement

6.   *Accommodation endorsement.* Although the process of endorsement normally takes place in conjunction with the negotiation of an instrument, there are some circumstances in which it may be appropriate to have another endorser who has been neither a holder of the instrument nor a party to it add his or her credit. Such an accommodation endorser incurs all of the liabilities of an endorser to a holder in due course.[18]

There are two other situations in which it may appear that an endorsement has taken place. Often the drawee on a bill of exchange will be requested to pay out on the instrument without being certain of the identity of the person presenting it for payment. In such circumstances, a third party who is known to the drawee may be asked to verify that the person presenting the instrument for payment is who he or she claims to be. This third party then identifies the person presenting the instrument for payment by so stating on the back of the instrument. Although this may seem to be an endorsement, an "identifying endorser" is liable only if the identification proves incorrect. This identification by endorsement process can also have a role to play as the instrument is negotiated from one holder to another when the person taking delivery of the instrument is unsure of the identity of the person negotiating it to him or her.

A second situation that appears to be an endorsement is when the drawee bank requires the person presenting the cheque for payment to sign the back of the instrument in order to receive the money. This appears as a simple blank endorsement and has been mistaken as such by bank employees in the past. In fact, the holder of the instrument is presenting it to the bank for payment. Since this is not part of the negotiation process, the signature is not an endorsement. The signature is no more than an acknowledgment of receipt of the money. The bank when presented with such an instrument simply has the right to honour or reject it. If the bank, through its representatives, chooses to honour it, that is the end of the matter as far as the holder presenting it for payment is concerned. If it turns out later that the bank has a problem, they must look to their depositor, the drawer of the cheque, for compensation and not the holder of the instrument who presented it for payment, even though the signature now appears on the back of the cheque.

Acknowledging receipt of funds not endorsement

The Drawee

The person on whom a bill of exchange is drawn (the drawee) or in the case of a cheque (the bank) has no liability on the instrument. Since the instrument is made by the drawer or maker and issued to the payee directly, there is no relationship between the drawee and the payee or subsequent holder of that instrument. The only reason a drawee or a bank will honour such an instrument is because of prior arrangements made with their depositor, the drawer. When such arrangements have been made and the drawee fails to honour them by paying out on the instrument, they can be sued, but only by the drawer of the instrument. This is the reason why a drawer can stop payment on a cheque, and the bank does not hesitate to do so.

Drawee has no liability on instrument

[18] *Bills of Exchange Act*, R.S.C. (1985) c.B-4 s.54 & s.130.

However, if the drawee or bank pays out on a negotiable instrument because of its own error, it cannot look to the innocent holder of the instrument who presented it for payment for reimbursement but must turn to their depositor for compensation.

When drawee accepts, becomes primarily liable

The position of the drawee dramatically changes when a bill of exchange is presented for acceptance. Once the drawee has accepted the obligation on the bill of exchange, a direct relationship has been established between the drawee and the person presenting it for acceptance. Once this happens, the acceptor is personally liable for the instrument and must honour it, even if there have been problems or difficulties in the relationship between the drawer and payee. The acceptor cannot claim that the signature of the drawer is invalid, that there is not enough money on deposit to cover the debt or challenge the drawer's capacity to sign the document. Similarly, the drawee (now acceptor) cannot claim that the payee's rights in relationship to the instrument are in any way limited after acceptance. However, the act of acceptance on the part of the drawee in the case of a bill of exchange does not eliminate the responsibility of the drawer on the instrument. Although the acceptor has assumed primary liability to the holder of the instrument and must pay, the drawer of the instrument has guaranteed payment by the drawee, and the holder of the instrument can turn to the drawer for payment if the acceptor fails to pay.

Drawer remains liable after acceptance

CONSUMER BILLS AND NOTES

The fact that negotiable instruments bestow better rights on innocent third parties than on the original party has led to considerable abuse, especially in the area of consumer transactions. The problem developed out of the practice of merchandise being sold to consumers through a conditional sales agreement which included, as part of the transaction, a promissory note signed by the consumer. The merchant would then discount this right or claim against the customer to a financial institution who then would collect the payments. This arrangement poses no problems as long as there is no defect in the product, but if the customer is dissatisfied in some way he or she could not refuse to pay since the financial institution could demand payment on the promissory note as a holder in due course, despite any contractual dispute between the customer and the merchant. The *Bills of Exchange Act* was amended by the addition of a section dealing with *Consumer Bills and Notes*[19] to prevent this type of abuse. A consumer note is a promissory note signed by a person purchasing goods or services for a non-commercial purpose (not for resale or use in any business). A consumer bill is any bill of exchange or cheque given for the advancement of credit. In such a consumer transaction, a cheque postdated for more than thirty days is included as a consumer bill. In this way, a bill of exchange or cheque used just to transfer funds is not covered but one used to establish a creditor/debtor relationship is. This legislation is designed to protect consumers by requiring that all consumer bills or notes be stamped on the face as such. This removes the advantages of negotiable instruments

---

[19] *Bills of Exchange Act*, R.S.C. (1985) c.B-4 Part V.

in the hands of holders in due course. Even when the consumer bill or note gets into the hands of a holder in due course, the original drawer or maker of that instrument can raise most of the defences available in a normal breach of contract action.

While this amendment effectively curbs the abuse associated with the use of promissory notes and other forms of negotiable instruments in consumer purchases, it also interferes with the basic purpose of negotiable instruments, that is, free transferability without the need to look beyond the face of the instrument. Since the consumer bill or note must be clearly stamped on its face "consumer purchase," this problem is generally overcome. Any third party who might come into possession of a negotiable instrument used in this way has clear notice that it is a consumer bill or note with its attendant higher risk and can avoid problems associated with it simply by refusing delivery.

The *Act* makes it clear that negotiable instruments used for this purpose must be clearly marked "consumer purchase," but also recognizes that there may be circumstances in which this does not take place. It is possible for an innocent third party not to know that the instrument was used in a consumer purchase if the merchant fails to stamp the instrument as required. When a holder in due course has received no notice that the instrument has been involved in a consumer purchase, that innocent third party acquires all the rights of a holder in due course dealing with a normal negotiable instrument and can enforce it against the drawer, independent of any contractual dispute between the customer and the merchant. However, the merchant who has failed to stamp the instrument is subject to prosecution, the payment of a significant fine and is liable to compensate the drawer for any damages suffered.

The following example illustrates the operation of consumer notes. If Degraaf purchased a used car from Galer's Fine Cars Ltd. by entering into a conditional sales contract and signing a promissory note for $5000, Galer would have the right to negotiate that promissory note and sell the conditional sale agreement to Quinn's Finance Company. If it turned out later that Degraaf was the victim of fraudulent misrepresentation (in relationship to the purchase of the car from Galer's Fine Cars Ltd.), before 1970, Degraaf would still be forced to pay the $5000 to Quinn's Finance Company because Quinn was the holder in due course of the promissory note and took it independent of any problems between the immediate parties to the instrument. However, subsequent to the 1970 amendment, Galer would have been required to stamp "consumer purchase" on the face of the promissory note; this fact would be obvious and effective notification to Quinn that the promissory note did not convey with it the rights normally associated with a negotiable instrument. In such circumstances, Degraaf could not only sue Galer for fraud but could also refuse to honour the promissory note. If Quinn sued, Degraaf could raise the fraudulent misrepresentation as an effective defence. On the other hand, if Galer had failed to stamp the note "consumer purchase" and Quinn was not aware that it had been obtained in this way, Quinn would be the holder in due course of a normal negotiable instrument and would still be able to enforce payment against Degraaf. However, Galer would be subject to prosecution and would be required to pay a fine as well as being subject to an action to recover any money that had to be paid to Quinn to honour the promissory note.

SUMMARY

Negotiable instruments are freely transferable instruments, and are used effectively as a substitute for money and as a method of advancing credit. When the negotiable instrument gets into the hands of an innocent holder in due course, that person can acquire better rights than the immediate parties to the instrument had. The Federal *Bills of Exchange Act* regulates negotiable instruments. These instruments are promissory notes in which a maker promises to repay a payee; bills of exchange or drafts in which a drawer orders a drawee to pay a payee; and cheques which are bills of exchange drawn on a bank, payable on demand. A certified cheque is similar to an accepted bill of exchange in that the drawee or bank accepts a direct responsibility to the holder of the instrument to pay.

A negotiable instrument is negotiated by endorsement and delivery if it is an order instrument but by delivery alone if it is a bearer instrument. Several obligations must be met for the instrument to qualify as negotiable. It must be a signed instrument containing an unconditional commitment to pay a fixed amount of money at a fixed time or on demand. It is also necessary that the instrument be delivered and that the whole instrument pass. To qualify as a holder in due course, a person must have received the instrument for value, an instrument complete and regular on its face, through negotiation, before it was due and payable, in good faith and without knowledge of any defect of title or notice of dishonour. Only real defences can be used against a holder in due course whereas defect of title defences can be used against other holders. Endorsers of the instrument are liable on default by the original drawer only if properly notified of the default. Because of abuse it was necessary to amend the *Act* so that negotiable instruments used to extend credit in consumer transactions did not convey the same rights as regular negotiable instruments. Such consumer notes must be clearly stamped as such by the merchant.

QUESTIONS

1. What two important characteristics of negotiable instruments have led to their prevalent use in business activities today?
2. What is the difficulty associated with the assignment of contractual rights that is overcome when a negotiable instrument is used? Explain how the position of a holder in due course differs from that of an assignee of contractual rights.
3. Describe how negotiable instruments differ from money. Describe how negotiable instruments are similar to money.
4. Describe the *Bills of Exchange Act* and how it came about as a Canadian statute. Which level of government passed it and has jurisdiction in this area?

5. What is meant by a bearer instrument? Contrast this to an order instrument. Indicate how an order instrument can become a bearer instrument.
6. Explain what is meant by negotiation of a negotiable instrument and how this is accomplished. What qualifications must an instrument meet to be negotiable?
7. What is the difference between a bill of exchange, a promissory note and a cheque? Give an example of when each would be used and give examples of two other kinds of instruments that sometimes qualify as negotiable instruments.
8. What is the process of acceptance of a bill of exchange and the significance of acceptance? What types of bills of exchange would you probably see presented for acceptance? Explain the nature of the relationship before acceptance between the payee and the drawee. How does this change once acceptance has taken place?
9. What is meant by the dishonour of a negotiable instrument? What obligation falls on the holder of that instrument when such dishonour takes place?
10. When a payee presents a bill of exchange for acceptance to the drawee and it is accepted, how does this acceptance affect the position of the drawer of the instrument?
11. Under what circumstances will the authority of a bank to pay out on a cheque be terminated?
12. Will a bank honour a stop-payment order made against a certified cheque?
13. What is the primary purpose of promissory notes?
14. Distinguish between real defences, defect of title defences and mere personal defences. Indicate the circumstances in which these distinctions can be significant when dealing with negotiable instruments.
15. Define what is meant by a holder in due course, the characteristics this person must have to qualify and the significance of being so designated. Explain how the knowledge of a holder of a negotiable instrument can affect his or her right to claim to be a holder in due course.
16. When a person does not qualify as a holder in due course but acquires the instrument through a holder in due course, what defences are available to the original maker or drawer of the instrument?
17. Explain the significance of the 1970 amendments to the *Bills of Exchange Act* creating consumer notes.

CASES

1. *Royal Bank of Canada v. LVG Auctions Ltd.*
   Midway Motors purchased a Michigan Wheel Dozer and attachment for $9600 from the defendants, LVG Auctions Ltd., who were selling it on behalf of

Municipal Paving and Contracting Ltd. The $9600 was paid to LVG Auctions Ltd. by cheque. Only after the cheque was given did the person acting on behalf of the purchaser discover that the goods were defective (the cylinder had cracked). He advised LVG Auctions Ltd. that he was stopping payment on the cheque and had his accountant telephone the Royal Bank and make the appropriate stop-payment order. However, because of an error on behalf of the bank, the stop-payment was not put into effect and when LVG Auctions Ltd. put the cheque in for payment it was honoured. Explain the position of the Royal Bank, LVG Auctions Ltd. and Midway Motors. How would your answer be affected by the information that Midway Motors never collected the dozer and that it was returned to Municipal Paving and Contracting Ltd. as unsold by LVG Auctions Ltd.?

2. *Royal Bank of Canada Ltd. v. Pentagon Construction Maritime Ltd.*
Maramichi Glassworks Ltd. was a customer of the Royal Bank. It was in financial difficulty when it assigned any benefits flowing under a contract it had with Pentagon Construction Maritime Ltd. to the Royal Bank. Maritime was informed of this arrangement and made two cheques totalling approximately $20 000 payable to Maramichi Glassworks. Maritime made it clear to Maramichi that unless Maramichi performed the appropriate services contracted for, the cheque would not be honoured. Maritime also made this clear to the Royal Bank as well. Maramichi Glassworks did not live up to its contractual requirements and Maritime put a stop-payment on these two cheques. The Royal Bank tried to collect but the cheques were dishonoured. In this action, the Royal Bank sued Maritime for payment of the cheques. Explain the arguments of both parties and the probable outcome.

3. *Eastern Elevator Services Ltd. v. Wolfe.*
Wolfe was dissatisfied with his employment and discussed the possibility of working with an alternate employer, Pace. An agreement was worked out whereby a separate company, Eastern Elevator Services Ltd., would be incorporated and would employ Wolfe. But Wolfe had to give Eastern Elevator Services Ltd. a $5000 cheque to show how sincere he was, the understanding being that the cheque would not be cashed unless Wolfe failed to honour the agreement and did not take up his new position of employment. The deal fell through, Wolfe did not become an employee and he stopped payment on the cheque. Eastern Elevator Services Ltd. sought a court order that Wolfe be required to pay out on the cheque. Explain the arguments available to Wolfe as to why he should not be required to honour the cheque and more, why he should not be required to pay the $5000. Would your answer be any different if the cheque had got into the hands of an innocent third party who was a qualified holder in due course?

4. *Citizens Trust Co. v. Hong Kong Bank of Canada.*
A rogue purporting to act on behalf of Happy Auto Sales Inc. entered into a contract with Citizens Trust Co. for the purchase of gold and paid with a

certified cheque drawn on the Hong Kong Bank of Canada. In fact the signature of the signing officer of Happy Auto Sales Inc. was forged and the company knew nothing of the cheque. The rogue had taken the forged cheque to the Hong Kong Bank of Canada where it was duly certified and the rogue then presented the cheque to Citizens Trust in payment for the gold. Citizens then took the cheque and presented it for payment to the Hong Kong Bank of Canada. Hong Kong Bank then noted that the signature of the signing officer was forged and refused to honour the certified cheque. In this action Citizens Trust Co. is suing the Hong Kong Bank of Canada and demanding payment for the cheque. Explain which one of these two parties should be required to bear the $62 000 loss. Explain the position of Happy Auto Sales Inc.

5. *Stienback Credit Union Ltd. v. Seitz.*
   Mr. Seitz was a businessman in Winnipeg who agreed to provide bridge financing for the Winnipeg Lions Club to cover the expenses for a fund raising concert it was planning. He wrote a $100 000 cheque and gave it to the Lions Club which presented it to the Royal Bank for deposit. Before crediting the Lions' account with the money, the bank phoned Seitz's credit union to confirm that it would honour the cheque even though there were not quite enough funds in the account. The credit union assured the bank that the cheque would be guaranteed and that it was unnecessary to certify it. It turned out later that the concerts were a disaster and Mr. Seitz tried to stop payment on the cheque. Explain the arguments available to both parties.

6. *Canadian Imperial Bank of Commerce v. Burman and MacLean.*
   On May 4, 1979, the defendant, Burman, bought a car from the defendant, MacLean, for $3700. Burman made two cheques payable to MacLean to cover the price but both were dated May 6, 1979. About 6:30 p.m. on May 4, MacLean took these two cheques to the Bank of Commerce at Sydney River where he had an account. The cheques were drawn on the Bank of Montreal. The CIBC took the cheques and gave MacLean $3700 for them. It turned out that MacLean had fraudulently represented the nature of the vehicle. Instead of having 33 000 miles on the odometer it had 85 000 miles. Burman went to the Bank of Montreal and issued a stop-payment order before the bank opened on May 7, 1979. The CIBC in this action is seeking to force Burman to honour the $3700 cheques. Explain the arguments available to Burman, and explain the likely outcome.

ISSUES

1. One of the most significant features of a negotiable instrument is that the holder in due course can be in a better position to enforce the instrument than was the person from whom it was obtained. This is quite different from the law dealing with contractual assignments where the assignee takes the benefits of the contract assigned subject to any equities existing between the original parties to the contract. Thus, when a conditional sale agreement is assigned to a finance company, the original debtor on that conditional sale agreement can raise any defence against the assignee finance company that would have been available against the vendor. This is not so when negotiable instruments are involved. This discrepancy has been modified to some extent by the 1970 amendments to the *Bills of Exchange Act*. Do you feel that a subsequent holder of a negotiable instrument should be permitted to ignore the defences the drawer or maker of that instrument would have been able to raise against the original debtor? Do you feel that the advantages given to a holder in due course of a negotiable instrument ought to be given to the assignees of contractual rights as well, so that the assignee finance company of a conditional sale agreement would be able to enforce it against the original debtor independent of any rights or obligations existing between the original parties? In your answer, raise arguments for and against the positions presented here and consider whether the 1970 amendments go far enough or go too far.

2. There is considerable disagreement about the exact nature of the rights bestowed by a cheque certified at the request of the holder. Should a certified cheque be treated as an accepted bill of exchange in which the acceptor or bank becomes primarily liable on the instrument whether the cheque was certified by the holder or by the original drawer of the instrument, or should the drawer of the cheque always be able to countermand, whether or not it has been certified by either party? In your answer, consider how you would amend the *Bills of Exchange Act* to deal with the process of certification. Consider also the approach of some banks of substituting a bank draft for the cheque to be certified when the request comes from the drawer of the instrument.

3. In 1970, the *Bills of Exchange Act* was amended to include a section dealing with consumer notes. The effect of the amendment was to remove the advantages of negotiability for the creditor when a negotiable instrument is used in granting credit in a consumer transaction. Consider the nature of these amendments, the advantages and disadvantages of them and whether these provisions are consistent with the whole philosophy of negotiable instruments and the rest of the *Bills of Exchange Act*.

4. There are several real defences, such as forgery, which a drawer or maker of a negotiable instrument can raise even against the holder in due course. Do you think that the holder in due course ought to be able to enforce the instrument even when forgery is present? Should there ever be a defence that can be raised against a holder in due course? On the other hand, should real defences be expanded so that the drawer of the instrument would be able to raise defences such as fraud and undue influence against the holder in due course?

5. A person who endorses a negotiable instrument assumes the same obligations to the holder in due course as are imposed on the drawer or maker of the instrument. When the holder in due course cannot obtain payment from the drawer or maker, he or she can turn to the endorser for payment. There are some situations in which the endorser escapes liability, such as when the instrument is endorsed "without recourse." Similarly, if the instrument is a bearer instrument, no endorsement is necessary to negotiate the instrument, so no liability is attributed to the negotiator beyond the immediate party to whom the instrument is negotiated. Would it be more just to have recourse against anybody who negotiated that instrument to another party whether that party is an endorser or not when a holder in due course cannot get payment from the drawer or maker of the instrument? On the other hand, would it be more appropriate to deny the holder any recourse against any negotiator, including the endorser, except the person who negotiated the instrument?

LEGISLATION

Federal
Bank of Canada Act, S.C. (1991) c. 46
Bills of Exchange Act, R.S.C. (1985) c. B-4

CHAPTER

14 PERSONAL AND INTELLECTUAL PROPERTY AND INSURANCE

Objectives of the Chapter

- to define and distinguish between personal and real property
- to discuss bailment and its consequences
- to illustrate the different forms of intellectual property
- to discuss the statutory and common law protection provided for intellectual property
- to consider the purposes and various types of insurance

A young artist made two sketches of tall ships that he intended to have mechanically reproduced to sell to sightseers when two tall ships visited a neighbouring community. The job of reproducing the prints was given to a print shop where two employees ran off the requested fifty copies and then sixty more for themselves. The artist received his prints but decided not to sell them. The two print shop employees sold their copies of the prints and kept the profits. When the artist discovered this violation, he took the necessary steps to have them prosecuted. The court decided that the artist owned the copyright in the two sketches and that the actions of the print shop employees went beyond mere copyright infringement and amounted to theft under the Criminal Code. They were convicted. It is important to note that, although the artist retained the original sketches, reproduction of them without his permission was not only a violation of copyright but also amounted to theft. This decision has had considerable impact on the field of intellectual property.[1] Computer programs are often copied without authorization and without affecting the original. Similarly, it is common practice to copy compact disks or records onto cassette tapes. The protection afforded to the owners of intellectual property is one of the topics discussed in this chapter.

INTRODUCTION

Most people think of property as a physical object, such as a boat, car or land, but the term property more correctly refers to the relationship existing between the item and the individual who owns it. When a person owns a boat, it is said to be his or her property. Thus, the term property is more descriptive of the nature of the interest a person has in a particular item than descriptive of the item itself. It is helpful to keep this distinction in mind when trying to understand the nature of the different interests in property. The highest form of property rights is generally called ownership or the possession of title to a particular item. In our legal system, it is possible to separate ownership or title from possession. Thus, one person might be in possession of something that belongs to someone else. The rights that may be held in relationship to a particular item, such as land or a vehicle, can be restricted either by law or by simple contractual agreement.

Ownership and possession separated

Property interests can be divided into different categories. Traditionally, these categories have been real property and personal property. A third, called intellectual property, has been added recently and, in reality, is a division of personal property. The term real property means land and anything affixed to or constructed on the land including chattels that have become attached to the land in a permanent way. Real property is immoveable.

Things fixed to the land become real property

Personal property, on the other hand, is moveable and can be divided into two categories. Tangible property, also called **chattels**, consists of things which can be measured, weighed or otherwise identified as items. Intangible rights one person has in relationship to another, such as a claim of debt or compensation for performance of a service, are called a **chose in action**. (A chose in action arises when one person has a claim against another which is of some value.) A chose in action is a form of personal property and, in effect, is the right to sue. A claim may be based on debt or another type of contract.

Chattel—tangible property

Chose in action—intangible property

A special category of chose in action is now called intellectual property. Intellectual property includes copyrights that give authors the right to prohibit the unauthorized copying of their work; patents that give inventors the right to control the use, manufacture and sale of their inventions; trademarks that protect logos and other forms of names and designs identifying products or businesses; and

Intellectual property deals with ideas and creative work

[1] *R.V. Wolfe and Campbell*, 633-016. *Lawyers Weekly*, Dec. 19, 1986.

certain industrial designs and other private information that can be categorized as trade secrets.

The first section of this chapter is devoted to tangible personal property, the second to intellectual property. A discussion of insurance concludes this chapter. The topic of real property is discussed in Chapter 15, "Introduction to the Law of Real Estate."

PERSONAL PROPERTY

Personal property in the form of chattels consists of movables and personal possessions, such as baggage, clothes, radios, animals and boats. Even ocean liners and locomotives are examples of chattels. Real property, on the other hand, is land and things fixed or attached to the land. These fixtures may be affixed to the land by the owner, a tenant or some other third party, and concern about who is the rightful owner may arise. When a person buys and installs an item, such as a furnace or a hot water heater, in a house he or she owns, the item is a chattel that becomes a part of the house and thus part of the real property. Who has installed the item and the degree to which it has been affixed to the real property can be important factors in determining who has the rights to the affixed item. If Gauthier, who owns a house with a mortgage owing to Cembier, buys a new hot water tank, and if Gauthier loses the house because of his failure to pay the mortgage, the creditor would have no special claim on the water heater if it has not yet been installed. If it is not part of the real property, it is not available to satisfy the claims of secured creditors. If Gauthier had installed the water heater before the default took place and the mortgagee took action against him, then that water heater is a fixture or part of the real property covered by the security of the mortgage. Whether a chattel is a fixture or not usually depends on the degree of attachment to the land and the use to which the object is to be put. Of course, the owner of the land is free to remove a chattel that has become a fixture (severance) just as he or she was able to fix the chattel to the land in the first place. Difficulty arises when third parties become involved. For example, when property is sold or a mortgage has been defaulted, whether or not something has become a fixture can be vital in determining who is entitled to it. Similarly, when a tenant brings a chattel onto a rented property, it is important to know whether the chattel has become a fixture and what rights the tenant has relative to it.

Generally, when a chattel has been affixed to real property, it becomes part of that real property, but there are two situations in which it may be removed again. The tenant of a commercial property who has brought chattels onto the land and affixed them in such a way as to enhance trade or carry on business has the right to remove those trade fixtures when leaving unless they have been incorporated into the real property in such a way that they clearly are intended to stay, for example, reinforcing timbers set into the framework of the building to support heavy machinery.

In residential or commercial tenancies, non-trade fixtures attached for the comfort, convenience or taste of the tenant, can be removed, provided they have not been incorporated into the structure of the building in such a way that they cannot be removed without causing damage to the real property. Trade fixtures and domestic fixtures can only be removed during the term of the tenancy. When the tenant moves out at the end of the tenancy and takes mirrors, light fixtures, rugs and display cases installed by the tenant, the landlord has no complaint. If those items are left, and the tenant seeks their return only after the tenancy is surrendered and the landlord has retaken possession, the tenant is too late. Those fixtures have become part of the property of the landowner. Of course, any provisions in the lease to the contrary override these general provisions.

A finder gets
good title against
all but original
owner

FINDERS, KEEPERS. The rights of a person who finds goods are subject only to the prior claim and title of the original owner. If Cruz were to find a watch in a park and show it to his friend, O'Neil, who took it and then refused to return it, Cruz would be successful in regaining possession of the watch if he took legal action. The true owner, Gan, is entitled to demand its return from either Cruz or O'Neil. "Finders, keepers" applies only against subsequent claimants to the property, that is, a third party who acquires the item. As far as all subsequent claimants are concerned, Cruz, the finder, is the owner. Only Gan, the original owner, has a better claim to the watch.

Entitlement to "found" property sometimes depends on where the chattel is found. Who owns a chattel found on private property—the person finding it or the person who owns the property? If it is found on a part of the property frequented by the public, such as the sales floor of a department store or the lounge of a hotel, then the finder is entitled to it. If the goods are found in an area where the public does not go, such as the kitchen of a restaurant or the storage area of the department store, the owner of the store is entitled to it. If the item is found by an employee, the employer is entitled to the chattel whether it is found in a public or private part of the establishment.

BAILMENT

Bailment created
by giving goods to
bailee

When a person acquires possession of chattels through a voluntary arrangement with the owner, the relationship is called a bailment. One feature of bailment is that the bailee must be given possession of the chattel in such a way that it is clear that the possession is intended to be temporary and that the chattel is to be returned at the end of the bailment period. Another requirement for bailment to exist is that the goods be delivered to the bailee from the bailor. Determining whether the goods have been delivered is not as easy as it may first appear. When a car is left in a parking lot, has a bailment taken place or not? If the keys are left with an attendant or the car is handed over to a valet, a bailment has been created because those persons have been given control and possession of the car. But when a person drives onto a lot, parks the car and takes the keys, there is no bailment. Rather, the driver has acquired a licence to use the parking space and has not relinquished control and possession of the car. During this period of bailment, the title to the goods remains with the bailor and only the possession goes to the bailee.

Goods such as timber, oil and wheat are often placed in the care of another for the purpose of storage. They may be mixed with similar items being stored for others and become indistinguishable. Such goods are called **fungibles**. When they are returned to the owners, there is no obligation to return the exact goods deposited. The only requirement is that goods of a similar quality and quantity be delivered. This situation is still a bailment and is treated under bailment law.

The primary concern of bailment law is the liability of the bailee (the person in possession of, but not the owner of, the goods) for damage done to the goods in his or her care. Bailees are responsible for any wilful, negligent or fraudulent acts by themselves or their employees which causes injury or damage to the goods in their care. The standard of care imposed on bailees in determining whether they have been negligent will vary with the type of bailment created. The obligations of the bailee cannot be separated from the obligation of the bailor to pay for the service when such an obligation exists. In most common law provinces in Canada, the *Warehousemen's Lien Act* in place gives warehousemen not only a lien against the goods if they are not paid but also the right to eventually sell them to obtain compensation for their storage costs. Warehousemen normally sell the goods at public auction after giving the bailor sufficient notice of the intention to do so.

FOR VALUE. Bailments are either gratuitous or for value. Bailment **for value** involves a mutual benefit or consideration flowing between the parties. It may be based on a business arrangement, such as a repairperson repairing the goods, a warehouse storing them, a carrier transporting them, or the relationship might be merely domestic. When a friend stores goods for another in exchange for the right to use them, the standard of care imposed in such circumstances is simply the ordinary standard for negligence—that is, the amount of care that would be expected from a prudent person looking after his or her own goods in similar circumstances. Thus, the amount of care that should be exercised will vary with both the value of the goods and their nature. When delicate items are involved, such as china or an insect collection, more careful handling is expected from the bailee than is the case if a heavy-duty machine were being stored. Similarly, if a bailee were storing or handling diamonds, more care would be expected to keep them safe than if the stored items were rhinestones.

If the bailment is created on the basis of a business relationship, the provisions of the contract, as well as the customs and traditions of the industry, will be taken into consideration when establishing the degree of care the bailee must exercise in the circumstances. The normal practice in the car park business would have an impact on determining whether or not a car lot attendant was negligent in a particular situation. The standard imposed can vary with the contract created between the parties. Contracts of bailment may contain exculpatory or exemption clauses which limit the liability of the bailee. An example of such a clause is, "Any goods left on the premises are entirely at risk of the owner. The proprietor assumes no responsibility for any loss whether caused by damage, loss or theft of those goods." To be enforceable, such clauses must be brought to the attention of the customer at the time the contract is entered into.

Margin notes:

With fungibles the same goods need not be returned

Bailee has a duty to care for the goods

Bailment for value—both parties receive benefit

Duty—reasonable person caring for own goods

Duty may be determined by contract or common practice

Exculpatory clauses may limit liability

Two situations in which the standard imposed on the bailee is particularly onerous are with common carriers and innkeepers. Examples of common carriers are trucking and bus companies, railroads and airlines, and may even include pipelines. A common carrier must be distinguished from private companies or individuals providing transportation services only to a particular bailor. A private carrier is merely a bailee for a reward and has the obligation of a reasonably prudent person in the circumstances. The common carrier, on the other hand, undertakes the standard of an insurer. That is, if the goods are damaged or destroyed while in its custody, it is liable even when faultless, unless caused by an act beyond its control. If the goods deteriorate because of some inherent problem or because the packaging provided by the shipper is inadequate, then the common carrier is not liable. If an animal dies in transit because of a previously contracted disease or goods are destroyed because of spontaneous combustion, there is no liability. A common carrier can limit its liability by contract and may include such a term as, "not responsible for lost or stolen goods or damage over $500." Again, such a provision must be clearly brought to the attention of the shipper at the time the contract is entered into for it to be valid and binding on both parties. Common carriers are usually controlled by statutory provisions regulating the industry.

According to the common law, an innkeeper is responsible for the lost or stolen goods of a guest unless it can be shown that they were lost because of some act of God or negligence on the part of the guest. For liability to lie with the innkeeper, it must be established that the accommodation was an inn and the plaintiff was a guest of that inn. Only those establishments providing both food and temporary lodging for their patrons (transient type accommodation) are classified as inns and the innkeeper assumes the obligation of an insurer.

Because this obligation is quite onerous and the historical justification is no longer relevant, most jurisdictions have passed legislation limiting the liability of innkeepers and hotel-keepers.[2] This protection reduces innkeepers' liability from that of an insurer to that of a reasonable business person. Therefore, they are only liable when it can be proven that they or their servants have been negligent. This protection is only available to the innkeeper when the *Act* is properly complied with. Compliance usually requires the posting of copies of the *Act* in every bedroom, public room and the office of the inn or hotel. When this is not done, the common law liability of the innkeeper (that of an insurer) prevails, and the innkeeper is liable for lost, stolen or damaged goods whether or not there has been negligence on his or her part.

GRATUITOUS. The second major situation that creates a bailment occurs when one of the parties receives a benefit and the other does not. This is known as a **gratuitous** bailment. When the bailee is receiving the benefit of the bailment, as is the case when a neighbour borrows a lawnmower or a friend borrows a car, the standard of care imposed on the bailee is very high. The bailee is expected to show great diligence in the care of the goods and, therefore, is liable if the goods are

Common carrier has duty of an insurer

Innkeeper has duty of an insurer

Liability may be reduced by statute

Gratuitous bailment—when bailee benefits, duty high

[2] *Innkeepers' Act*, R.S.O. (1990) c.I.7

—when bailor benefits, duty less

damaged or stolen even when the bailee has been only slightly careless. Where the bailment is for the benefit of the bailor, however, the bailee is only liable if there has been gross negligence. An example of the latter situation would be when a person asks a friend to look after her violin while she is away on vacation. The provision of this service is without benefit to the bailee and so only imposes an obligation to be slightly careful in relation to the goods. At least this has been the traditional approach to such a situation; it must be emphasized, however, that the courts have been moving towards imposing the normal definitions and tests for negligence and standards of care, requiring a higher standard of care for the bailee even when the benefit of the bailment is for the bailor.

Finally, it should be noted that the onus of proof has shifted to the bailee. Normally, the person bringing the action is required to prove that the other person was negligent. In these cases, once the bailment has been established and damage to the goods has been shown, the bailee is obligated to show that he or she was not negligent towards the goods belonging to the bailor.

Involuntary bailment—duty low

INVOLUNTARY BAILMENT. Bailment can be established involuntarily. When goods are left at a home or place of business without the approval of the homeowner or business person, the care of such goods has been imposed and, therefore, the relationship is involuntary. Theoretically, for bailment to exist, the bailee must consent. Whether an involuntary relationship is bailment or not, there is still a duty on the holder of goods, if custody has been accepted. A person who sees a watch lying on the sidewalk has no obligation to pick it up. But if he does pick it up, he assumes the obligations associated with a gratuitous bailee for the benefit of the bailor. Thus, when a person exercises any control, even simply moving the item from one location to another, that person becomes the bailee of the goods and has a duty to take care of them. If a canvasser were to stop and chat with a person working in his garden and leave her coat on the fence, no bailment would be created until the resident moved the coat. By picking it up, the resident exercises control over it and thereby assumes the responsibility to look after the coat. One of the basic obligations of the bailee is to return the goods to the bailor. Generally speaking, if the goods are returned to the wrong person, the bailee is responsible.

INTELLECTUAL PROPERTY

Intellectual property law acts to protect results

Intellectual property law has as its purpose the balancing of two opposing interests. On one side is the protection of the product of a person's mental effort and, on the other, the free flow of new and innovative ideas which stimulate the advancement of the commercial environment. The law is intended to make ideas and information as freely available as possible while giving the creator the rights to develop, distribute and sell the results of his or her effort. Its primary focus is on the rights and responsibilities which exist between individuals in relation to ideas and information.

Although this topic has been included in a chapter devoted to property law, there are significant differences between the forms of intellectual property discussed in this section—copyright, patents, trademarks and trade secrets—and the other forms of property law discussed in this chapter. When a chattel is stolen or destroyed it is no longer available for the use of the original owner. When an idea is taken and used by somebody else, or confidential information is wrongfully communicated to another, the idea or information does not change. It is still available to the original holder but its value to the owner might be considerably diminished by the fact that others have free access to it. Because of the explosion in the amount of data and information available and the tremendous advances in methods of storing and transmitting information, intellectual property law has recently grown in importance.

Copyright

The term copyright refers to the right to copy or reproduce a created work. The federal legislation in place is intended to give the author or owner of the copyright a monopoly over the use of the created work. Such rights extend only to the work itself and are not meant to limit the ideas or thoughts which led to the creation of the work. A person may copyright the manuscript for a book but not the ideas expressed in it. To avoid a violation of copyright law, those ideas must be expressed in a different way and not be simply a reproduction of the original work. The power to make copyright law has been given to the federal government exclusively and the *Copyright Act* has recently been significantly amended.[3]

The work is protected, not the idea

MATTERS COVERED. It is not possible to copyright everything that results from creative or intellectual effort. To be copyrightable, the work must be original, that is, it must be the product of the artist's or author's own work or skill. There is no requirement that such a work be of high quality, only that it convey information and be instructive or entertaining. The work must also be preserved in some permanent, material, written or recorded form. Four categories of copyrightable material are set out in the legislation. Literary works include tables, compilations (books), and computer programs. Dramatic works include shows (movies, television and theatre) and mime performances, including the choreography and scenery. Musical works include written melody and harmony. Finally, artistic works include paintings, drawings, charts, maps, plans, photos, engravings, sculptures, works of artistic craftsmanship and architecture. One of the most significant changes in the 1988 amendments is that they provide copyright protection for computer software and hardware.

To be copyrightable, work must be original and preserved in some permanent form

CREATION. A copyright comes into existence in Canada automatically with the creation of the work itself and nothing more is necessary. In Canada, it is not even necessary that the work be published. However, a work can be registered if one chooses, and registration is an advantage, since it proves when the copyright came

Copyright comes with creation of work

[3] *Copyright Act*, R.S.C. (1985) c.42, as amended by R.S.A. (1985) (4th Supp.) c.10

into existence and also creates a presumption that the person named in the registration is the owner of the copyright. To extend copyright protection for a work created in Canada to countries which subscribe to the Universal Copyright Legislation Convention (including the United States), registration is necessary. Although not specified in the Canadian legislation, a notification of registered copyright generally takes the form of © with the word copyright beside it, followed by the year the copyright was first published and the name of the owner of the copyright.

For a person to obtain copyright protection in Canada, he or she must be a Canadian citizen, British subject or reside in one of the countries that adhere to the Berne Copyright Convention or the Universal Copyright Convention—international agreements that set out common rules of conduct in matters concerning copyright. Canada will also provide copyright protection to foreign nationals when the country of origin of that national would provide the same kind of protection to a Canadian citizen as it would to one of its own citizens.

OWNERSHIP. In general, copyright resides in the creator, but when a work is created as part of the author's employment, the employer owns the copyright unless there is an agreement between the parties stating otherwise. Once the copyright has been created, its owner can assign or sell it all or in part to someone else. Even when copyright is assigned, the author or creator maintains the right to be listed as such. Despite any assignment, the author will continue to have moral rights in the work. That is, when the copyright is assigned, the new owner cannot change the work in such a way as to degrade it and bring harm to the reputation of the author. In any form of dispute or litigation, in the absence of evidence to the contrary, the court will presume copyright is held by the creator of the work.

RIGHTS GRANTED. The copyright gives the owner of the work the right to publish it and receive any benefits from it. This right can be assigned, but whoever has copyright has complete control over the work except for the moral rights mentioned above. No one else can perform, copy, publish, broadcast, translate or otherwise produce the work without the permission of the owner of the copyright. (See Box 14.1, "Anti-copying war is escalating"). Generally, the period of copyright protection equals the life of the author plus fifty years. There are exceptions, however, such as photographs for which the protection is fifty years from the creation of the negative. A copyright infringement can take place when anyone tries to obtain a benefit from the sale, distribution, performance, broadcast or other commercial use of the work. It is an infringement of the moral rights of the author if someone else claims authorship or if the work is mutilated or modified in such a way that the reputation of the author is harmed. When the author's moral rights have been violated, he or she has the right to compensation even when the copyright has been sold to someone else, provided the author has not waived these moral rights.

There are, however, exceptions to this copyright protection. The *Copyright Act* states that when a work is reproduced for private study, research, review or newspaper summary, it is not an infringement of copyright. An important aspect of the 1988 amendment to the *Copyright Act* makes it clear that anyone who is in

Registration required for protection abroad

Copyright can be assigned but moral rights retained

Copyright holder has complete control over work for author's life plus fifty years

Exceptions

Box 14.1

Anti-Copying War is Escalating

The battle to protect authors' and publishers' rights to their books is heating up. Last month, the RCMP laid seven charges related to copyright violations against Laurier Office Mart, a copy shop near the University of Ottawa, where professors had been photocopying material for their courses without prior permission. Then, on Nov. 8, Ontario Court judge Madam Justice Marie Corbett granted CANCOPY, the Canadian reprography collective established to protect the rights of authors and publishers, its first-ever search-and-seizure order. This was unusual, because it is rare for a court to award a search order for a civil as opposed to a criminal offence. The order was granted against a copy shop near the University of Toronto, Copy Ink (its legal name is Ink Copy Inc.). Although copyright infringements against several titles were investigated, the application against the copy shop specified one text, *Computer Organization*, Third Edition, published by McGraw Hill Ryerson, written by three University of Toronto faculty members. The text cost $88 at the University of Toronto Bookstore. Students were buying photocopied versions at the outlet for about $20. Toronto police conducted the raid on Nov. 12 with officials from CANCOPY. The police and CANCOPY officials carried off evidence which will enable them to file a civil application against Copy Ink. The case has not yet come to court.

Source: Val Ross, "Anti-Copying War is Escalating," Globe and Mail, *Nov. 27, 1993, p. C1.*

lawful possession of a computer program can make copies of the program as long as only one of the copies is being used by that authorized person at any one time.[4]

REMEDIES. When a copyright is violated, the standard remedies available in a civil action are available to the copyright holder although they may take on a special significance in this kind of action. One of the most important remedies available is the **interlocutory injunction**. This form of injunction is obtained before the actual trial of the issue if the plaintiff can demonstrate to the court that there is a *prima facie* case supporting his or her claim of infringement. This means that the evidence presented must show that a copyrighted work has been infringed upon and that if the injunction is not granted, irreparable harm will be suffered that could not properly be compensated for by damages after the trial has been concluded. To be successful in such an application, it must also be established that the balance of convenience is in the plaintiff's favour. (Is the harm caused more than the good realized?) This means that an injunction will probably not be granted if a small business is asking the courts to issue an order to stop the production and sales of a much larger operation.

Interlocutory injunctions granted before trial

Another somewhat unusual remedy that may be available before the trial is an **Anton Piller** order. This in an order by the court that the works actually be seized from the offending manufacturer or distributor. This is an *ex parte* procedure in which the evidence must be seized by surprise before the goods or relevant docu-

Anton Piller order provides for seizure of goods

---

[4] *Copyright Act*, R.S.C. (1985) c. 42 s.17(2)(1), as amended by R.S.C. (1985) (4th Supp.) c. 10

mentation can be hidden or destroyed. The court will not make such an order lightly, and before it can be obtained there must be clear and compelling evidence of the infringement of copyright, the danger of significant damage to the plaintiff and some indication that surprise is needed to protect the evidence.

Once the trial has taken place and the plaintiff has obtained a favourable judgment, one of the most important remedies available is that of the **permanent injunction**. By court order, a permanent injunction prohibits the defendant from the production, sale or distribution of any of the infringing products. If the defendant is not aware that the product being produced is in violation of copyright, the only remedy available under the act is an injunction. Otherwise, damages or an accounting may be obtained. **Damages** are an attempt by the court to compensate the victim of the infringement for the losses suffered, including the lost profits which he or she would have earned had the copyright not been violated. An **accounting for profits** requires the defendant to pay over to the plaintiff any profits made from the sale or rental of the offending product even if this amount exceeds the damages suffered by the plaintiff. Such an accounting may be granted because of the difficulty encountered in assessing the actual damages suffered as a result of the infringement. In some very blatant infringement cases, the court may even award **punitive damages** to punish the offender rather than simply to compensate the victim of the infringement. In any case, it must be noted that the limitation period in which an action should be commenced is three years.

In addition to these civil remedies, the *Copyright Act* provides for criminal penalties. It is generally conceded that before the 1988 amendments these penalties were so slight as to provide little deterrent (for a summary offence the fine was up to ten dollars per copy and a maximum of two months in jail). The new legislation, however, expands these penalties so that they are significant indeed (up to one million dollars in fines and five years in jail for an indictable offence), making them a much more effective deterrent. The provisions set out in the *Criminal Code* may also apply to the infringement of copyright cases, such as those sections prohibiting theft and fraud.[5] The *Criminal Code* was used to impose the penalties in the example used to introduce this chapter. However, there is some question about the appropriateness of the *Code* in these types of cases. The need to resort to the *Criminal Code* provisions has been considerably reduced by the greater penalties included in the new legislation.

CHANGES. The most significant changes included in the 1988 amendments to the *Copyright Act* are those related to computer programs, moral rights and increased penalties. Another important change is a provision for the creation of a Copyright Board which will have broad powers. The board is entitled to handle disputes between individuals and otherwise regulate the industry. It is common for associations or corporations to be created to represent the owners of copyright in their dealings with those who would like to use their materials. These bodies usually enter into agreements (licensing arrangements) with the users, who pay royalties to reproduce or perform the copyrighted material. Under the new legislation, these bodies must file with the board copies of the copyrighted material and information regarding any

---

[5] *Criminal Code*, R.S.C. (1985) c.C-46.

Permanent injunction granted at trial

Damages compensate for loss

Accounting requires handing over profits

Punitive damages may be available to punish wrongdoer

Fine and imprisonment available for infringement

Criminal Code may apply

New bill broadens protection, increases penalty and creates board

agreements entered into as well as statements of royalties that have been paid. Summaries of these lists and the royalties are to be published regularly in the *Canada Gazette* (a federal government publication). These associations have the exclusive right to collect the agreed-upon royalties (or sue if they are not paid) if adequate statements of royalties have been properly filed with the board. The second phase of reforms to the *Copyright Act* has been unexpectedly delayed and since, at the time of writing, its implementation is in some doubt, they will not be discussed here.

Patents

Patent creates monopoly

Must be original invention to be patentable

A patent is a government-granted monopoly to produce, sell or otherwise profit from a specific invention. Once a patent is granted, no one else can use or sell the invention without the permission of the patent-holder. For something to be patentable, it must be both new and an invention. If a patent has already been granted to someone else, or the invention has been in the public domain for some period or has been the subject of a publication over one year before the application, a patent will not be granted. The subject of the patent must also be original and come from the inventor, and not be the product of the skill and labour of others. It must be novel in that it has unique qualities which separate it from other products. It must have utility, meaning that it must be capable of being constructed and used based on the information supplied to the patent agent upon application.

Theories, concepts or obvious improvements are not patentable

The idea is protected rather than the work

A patent cannot be issued for a scientific principle or abstract theorem.[6] Newton would not have been granted a patent for his development of the concept of gravity. Other things which cannot be patented include improvements to objects that would be obvious to someone skilled in the area, objects designed for an illegal purpose, something that cannot work, a new variety of plant or tree and, generally, those things covered by copyright law. Computer programs, as a general rule, cannot be patented because they are merely a set of instructions to the computer. The scope of patent protection is much narrower than the protection offered by copyright legislation. In contrast to copyright law, patent law is intended to protect an invention, that is, ideas and concepts rather than the expression of the work itself. In this sense, the protection granted is all-encompassing once the patent has been obtained.

Patent must be applied for and registered

CREATION. While a copyright exists from the point of creation of the work, a patent only comes into existence when registered. The inventor must take care to apply for the patent as soon as possible. Any delay increases the risk that someone else will invent and patent the same item, causing the original inventor not only to lose the right to patent but also preventing him or her from producing or otherwise using the invention. As was the case with copyright law, if the invention is developed by an employee, the employer has the right to obtain the patent. Similarly, if the inventor assigns his or her right, the purchaser has the right to obtain the patent. Joint patents can be obtained when two people have worked on the same invention.

[6] *Patent Act*, R.S.C. (1985) c.P-4 s.27 ss.3.

The process of obtaining a patent is complex and some lawyers have specialized in this area, becoming patent agents. To obtain a patent, the inventor acquires the services of such an agent who searches the patent records to determine whether a patent already exists for the invention, or one similar to it, and then submits documents along with a petition applying for a patent. If the patent office is satisfied that all the conditions have been met, it will grant the patent, although it is not uncommon for the process to take two or three years. If opposing applications have been made for the patent, the patent office will grant it to the person who developed the invention first. Difficulties can arise if an inventor outside Canada registers a similar invention independently. Pursuant to international agreement, once a Canadian patent has been granted, application can be made for patents in other jurisdictions. Even though there can be considerable delay in the granting of patents in countries where protection is needed, the application will be taken to have been made on the same day as the Canadian patent was applied for, thus establishing a prior right to a patent in those jurisdictions as of that date. Of course, the reverse is also true and the Canadian patent office will grant a patent to a foreign applicant who applies in his or her own country before the Canadian applicant applies here.

Once the patent is issued it gives its holder a monopoly in relationship to the product for a period of twenty years, provided the appropriate fees are paid to maintain it. In exchange for that protection, the inventor must publicly disclose the invention in its entirety so that someone inspecting the file documents, which are open to the public, could create a working model of the invention. Thus, patent law does not protect information; rather, it provides for its disclosure. The inventor gives up any secrecy associated with the invention in exchange for the twenty-year protection. After that time, anyone can produce the product. It is thought that this disclosure of information creates a stimulating environment for further invention and development while still protecting the position of the inventor and encouraging that inventor to develop and produce the product and engage in further invention. The granting of the patent gives the patent-holder exclusive rights to manufacture, sell and profit from the invention, and it even protects someone who merely develops a variation of the product.

Unlike copyright law, which protects the specific way an idea is stated, patent law is intended to protect the idea or principle behind the product. Another person would not be able to produce a simple variation of the product without breaching the patent. When an infringement of a patent has taken place (through some unauthorized person manufacturing, selling or otherwise dealing with or using the invention), the patent-holder is entitled to the same remedies that would be available in any civil action, including injunction, damages and accounting, which have been discussed under the heading of copyright. As well, as was the case with copyright law, the legislation sets out procedures of enforcement, and the normal civil remedies are also available.

It should be noted that an important amendment to the *Patent Act* was enacted in 1987. Drug manufacturers were given more exclusive control over the production and sale of their products, preventing competitors from producing much lower cost "generic drugs" by capitalizing on the research and development of the manufacturer. At the same time, a Patent Medicine Prices Review Board was established with broad powers,

Patents registered can apply internationally

Date of application determines priority

Patent grants monopoly for twenty years but requires disclosure

Remedies same as copyright

including the power to reduce the sale price of medicines covered by this legislation.[7] This period of exclusive control has recently been extended to twenty years.

Trademarks

Another type of intellectual property given protection is any term, symbol, design or combination of these that identifies a business or a product. These are called **trademarks** and are protected by the federal *Trademarks Act*.[8] Words such as Kodak and Xerox, symbols such as the arm and hammer design found on Arm and Hammer baking soda, and combinations of words and symbols, such as the apple logo found on computers of that manufacturer, are examples of protected trademarks. Even the distinctive design of a product container may be the subject of such protection. The purpose of the legislation is to prevent people from deceiving others by using trademark words or symbols for their own purposes, thereby profiting from the good will developed by others. As well, the value of the trademark might be diminished if consumers are led to believe that inferior products or services are produced by the owner of the trademark when, in fact, they are not.

A trademark must be registered to be protected under the statute. Such registration gives the owner of the trademark exclusive rights to use it throughout Canada and in other countries party to the International Trademark Agreement. This protection is granted for fifteen years and is renewable. The registration also establishes a presumption that the person so registered is the owner of that trademark, thus requiring a defendant in an action claiming infringement to produce strong evidence that the owner was not entitled to the trademark.

In general, any mark, word, design, symbol or packaging that distinctively identifies a business or product can be registered as a trademark. A sound or colour by itself cannot be registered as a trademark nor can something obscene or scandalous. There is also a general prohibition against anything that resembles the insignia, crests or other symbols of royalty, the government or government agencies, such as the RCMP, service organizations such as the Red Cross, or even names, portraits or signatures of individuals, without their consent. There is also a prohibition against using any marks, symbols or designs that have become well known and would lead people to believe that the registrant was associated with that body or with the products or services of that body. As a general rule, people can use their own surnames in their business without fear of violation of a trademark unless that name has become associated with another product such as McDonald's hamburgers or Campbell's soup. It is possible for trademarks to lose their status through common use. In effect, the trademark becomes a generic term to describe the type of product itself. Aspirin is such a generic term in Canada and can be used by any manufacturer to describe that type of painkiller. This is also the case with the term trampoline. The name Xerox has become so connected with the photocopying process that the term is also in danger of losing its trademark status.

---

[7] *Patent Act Amendments*, R.S.C. (1985) (3rd. supp.) c.33
[8] *Trademarks Act*, R.S.C. (1985) c.T-13.

Applying for trademark registration is a complicated process, and any one doing so should acquire the services of a lawyer specializing in that field. It should be noted that after registration has taken place, there is an obligation to use that trademark. Failure to do so can result in the loss of the trademark through abandonment.

Essentially, the purpose of trademark legislation is to prevent others from using distinctive marks that will confuse people into thinking they are dealing with the owner of the trademark when they are not and thus prevent one party profiting from the goodwill developed by another. To enforce that right, the owner must convince the court not only that he or she is the registered owner of the trademark but also that it is likely the public has been or will be confused by the wrongful use of the trademark. If successful, the types of remedies available are the standard ones discussed under copyrights and patents. It should be mentioned, however, that one of the more effective remedies possible (when circumstances warrant it) is an order giving the owner of the trademark custody of the goods that are infringing on the trademark. Although it is possible to bring an action for infringement of a trademark before the Federal Court when the trademark has been properly registered under the *Act*, it is also possible, and a more practical course of action, to bring the matter before the appropriate provincial court.

Although trademarks are covered by federal legislation, this is one area in which there are overlapping common law provisions. When a business or product comes on to the market and people confuse it with another product, it is possible to bring an action called a **passing off action**. It is founded in tort and prevents a person from misleading the public into thinking it is dealing with some other business or person when it is not. See Box 14.2, "Stink raised over restaurant's name". The person being harmed can request the court to order compensation or that the offending conduct stop. This remedy is also available when a trademark is involved even if it is unregistered. To succeed in a passing off action, it is necessary to establish that the public was likely to be misled. Therefore, the person who brings the action must be able to show that the offending party used the mark, name or other feature of the business and that it became associated with its operation. It would be an actionable passing off for an independent hamburger stand operator to put golden arches in front of his place of business or use the same colour scheme as McDonald's in such a way that people would assume his operation was part of the chain. But if a business person were to see an attractive logo which had been developed by another person but not yet registered or used and use it in her own business, the originator of the design could not sue on the basis of a passing off action because the logo had not become associated with any business.

Remedies same as copyright infringement

Common law passing off action gives similar protection

Industrial Designs

A design or pattern that distinguishes a manufactured article is not covered by copyright law. Protection is provided by registering a unique shape, pattern or ornament under the *Industrial Design Act*.[9] A Coca-Cola bottle with its distinctive shape

[9] *Industrial Design Act*, R.S.C. (1985) c.I-9.

Box 14.2

Stink raised over restaurant's name

What's in a name? Plenty, according to Stink Inc., a California company that operates "The Stinking Rose—a Garlic Restaurant" in the North Beach area of San Francisco.

The company believes a "Stinking Rose" restaurant, even when it's linked to any other name, represents an infringement of its registered trade mark in California.

And that's why restaurateur John Venditti, proprietor of "The Stinking Rose Italian Restaurant" in Coquitlam [B.C.], recently found himself in hot water, not to mention a bit of a stink.

Stink Inc. claimed in a B.C. Supreme Court suit that Venditti's use of the name "Stinking Rose" was an infringement of its California trademark.

The company said patrons of Venditti's 60-seat Coquitlam restaurant might be confused into thinking it is somehow connected with the San Francisco establishment.

The California company sought an interim injunction against Venditti using the name until such time as the trademark issue is decided in a full trial.

Justice Kenneth Houghton, who in his judgment gave Venditti a good review ("The food and service quality are said to be excellent"), refused to grant the injunction.

A happy Venditti, surrounded Tuesday by garlic in his restaurant, said in an interview he is puzzled by the San Francisco company's action, which could still go to trial.

Venditti, 39, who also runs Paesano's, a Richmond restaurant, said he got the name, "Stinking Rose," from a cookbook someone gave him on his last birthday.

He had never heard of the "Stinking Rose" in San Francisco.

Noting the cookbook said the phrase, "stinking rose" is the historical name for garlic, Venditti said he decided it would be the perfect name for his new Coquitlam restaurant...

Venditti's lawyer, Elizabeth Watson, said in an interview the California company's suit was based on an allegation her client was "passing off" his restaurant as being associated with the San Francisco business.

She said a claimant in such cases has to establish he has a reputation, through massive advertising, in the market in which he claims his trade mark is infringed.

Watson said a computer check to see if the San Francisco restaurant was often mentioned here in the media turned up far more references to "Stinking Rose" as being the historic term for garlic.

Agreeing, the judge said British Columbians, on seeing the name of Venditti's restaurant, would more likely think of garlic than of the San Francisco establishment.

Source: Larry Still, "Stink raised over restaurant's name," Vancouver Sun, Feb. 23, 1994, Section B2.

Industrial Design Act—reproduced artistic designs must be registered

would appropriately be registered under this *Act*. In addition to registration, each item must be marked with ®, the name of the registered owner and the date of registration. Registration must take place within one year of the design being published. Any product, with a few specified exceptions, with a distinctive shape or pattern, can be registered and will receive protection for a period of five years, providing all the requirements of the *Act* are met. This period is renewable for a further five years if desired. As with copyrights, patents and trademarks, the product involved must be original and not a copy of some product already on the market. In a case before the Exchequer Court in 1964, a uniquely designed sofa was deemed to be protected by an industrial design registration.[10]

[10] *Cimon Ltd. v. Benchmade Furniture Corp.*, (1964) 1 Ex. C.R. 811.

Confidential Information

Confidential information is information given to a person in circumstances in which it is clear that the information is intended to remain confidential and not be disclosed. Information cannot be classified as confidential unless it is not generally known and the holder of the information has not already disclosed it to others. Over the years, a common law duty has been imposed on different kinds of trust or fiduciary relationships making it unlawful for individuals in such relationships to use confidential information in a way that will harm the confider or personally benefit the confidant or the third party to whom the information was given. The duty not to disclose confidential information arises primarily from the relationship between the confidant and the owner of the information, such as between principal and agent, between partners, between employer and employee, or between officers and their corporation, or can be the result of other expressed or implied contracts between the parties.

Confidential information protected by common law

The largest settlement in Canadian court history arose when LAC Minerals Ltd. and Corona Resources Ltd. found themselves in such a situation. The case is very complicated but, to simplify, Corona had obtained land claims in the Hemlo District of northwestern Ontario. Representatives of LAC entered into discussions with the representatives of Corona with the prospect of entering into a joint venture or partnership. In the process of these discussions, LAC discovered that Corona did not own the surrounding gold claims but was in the process of negotiating for them. When those negotiations broke down between LAC and Corona, LAC independently purchased the surrounding claims and made huge profits from the resulting mines. The court held that this was a violation of the fiduciary duty imposed on LAC as a result of the special circumstances in which the information was obtained. A trust relationship had been established and the information gained because of it was intended to remain confidential. When the representatives of LAC used that information for LAC's gain at the expense of Corona, it was a violation of their duty of confidentiality.[11]

TRADE SECRETS. A trade secret is a particular kind of confidential information that gives a business person a competitive advantage. Customer lists, formulas or processes, patterns, jigs and other unique features unknown to competitors are trade secrets. Successful actions for the wrongful disclosure of trade secrets have been brought in such varied matters as recipes for fried chicken and soft drinks, formulas for rat poison, methods to flavour mouthwash, processes for making orchestral cymbals and even the techniques prescribed in a seminar to help people quit smoking. A trade secret has the additional requirement that it be valuable to the business and not readily available to any other user or manufacturer. Customer lists available through government publication cannot be classed as trade secrets, nor can a process involved in the manufacturing of a product that is plainly discoverable simply by examining or disassembling the product.

Duty of confidentiality covers trade secrets as well

---

[11] *LAC Minerals Ltd. v. Corona Resources*, as reported in *The Globe and Mail*, Toronto, Nov. 19, 1986.

It should be noted that it is the conveying of the private information that is wrongful. There is no proprietary right in the idea or information itself. If Deng operated a company manufacturing tiddlywinks and had a secret process by which they could be produced more cost-effectively, and one of Deng's employees were to give that information to a competitor, it would be a wrongful disclosure of a trade secret. But if the competitor were to develop the same or a similar procedure independently, Deng would have no complaint since he has no proprietary right in the idea or process.

While an employee may be required either expressly or by implication in the employment contract not to disclose trade secrets and confidential information that he or she acquires in the process of employment, the employee can use the general skills and knowledge he or she gains on the job in another employment situation. An employee working in a guitar manufacturing factory who acquires the skills of a luthier would not be expected to refrain from using any of those skills if she were to work for another manufacturer. In such circumstances, the best protection for the first guitar manufacturer is to include a restrictive covenant in the employment contract (a non-competition clause). If the covenant is reasonable in nature, it will be enforceable and the employee will be prevented from seeking employment at a similar company for a limited period of time and within a limited area.

From a practical point of view, the owner of secret information can best maintain its confidentiality by informing the other person that he or she is in a position of confidence and is expected to keep the information private. It is also important to specify what information is confidential and what is not. Even the most honest employee can disclose such information if he or she does not know it is confidential. No liability will be imposed for the disclosure of information if a person could not have been expected to know it was intended to be confidential. Steps should also be taken to minimize the number of people to whom the information is given or who have access to the information. A person cannot be accused of wrongful disclosure of confidential information if the information is no longer confidential. It should also be noted that while in Canada the law related to trade secrets is founded on common law and equity, in some parts of the United States statutes have been passed to govern this area (*Trade Secrets Act*). Whenever those jurisdictions are involved care should be taken to look at the statutes.

REMEDIES. To succeed in an action for wrongful disclosure, it is necessary for the plaintiff to show that the disclosure of the confidential information has caused harm. Whether the confidant used the information personally or passed it on to someone else who used it to the detriment of the first party, both offending parties can be sued. When trade secrets have been wrongfully disclosed or confidential information passed on, the remedies available are similar to copyright and patent discussed above. If it is clear that there is a real likelihood the information will be disclosed because of some new relationship the confidant is in, then an injunction can be obtained to prohibit the disclosure. The court, however, is very reluctant to grant an injunction that will prevent an employee from earning a living in his or her field. Damages or an accounting are also available when confidences have been breached in this way. Even punitive damages have been awarded.

Other protection for intellectual property— contract

Contract and tort law may be used to give increased protection to the various forms of intellectual property. There are often contractual provisions in service or employment contracts which prohibit the misuse of position or the misappropriation or disclosure of confidential information or trade secrets. When an employee or other contracting party breaches one of the terms, it is a breach of contract which is grounds for dismissal. The offender can be restrained from further disclosure and can be required to compensate the employer for damages suffered. Because the employee will probably not be in a position to pay such damages, the victim will often turn to others for compensation. When the information holder has been enticed away and persuaded to breach the contract by a rival business, it is possible to sue the competitor for the tort of inducing breach of contract. Although this tort was first developed to prevent one employer from hiring away the employee of another, it has been expanded to many different kinds of contractual relationships and even to some relationships not based on contract. To succeed in such an action, the plaintiff is not required to establish malice on the part of the defendant but it must be clear that the interference was intentional.

Tort—inducing breach of contract

—breach of privacy

Another remedy that may be available when someone uses another's name or photograph without permission is founded on breach of privacy. The courts in Britain and Canada have not recognized the right generally for a person to have his or her privacy protected, but the British courts have established such a right to a limited extent by indirect means. When a manufacturer of a chocolate product promoted it by using a cartoon of a famous golfer with the package of the product in his pocket, an English court held this action to be defamation because it communicated the idea that the golfer had lent his name to the promotion of the product which would have been a serious violation of his amateur status.[12] Such indirect protection, while interesting, is not likely to prove effective, and several provinces have passed privacy acts intended to supply remedies for this kind of improper invasion of privacy. The British Columbia *Privacy Act*, for instance, specifically makes such wrongful use of another's name or portrait to promote a product or service without permission an actionable tort.[13]

Injurious falsehood

Another example of an effective tort in these situations is injurious falsehood, often called trade slander. When a rival misleads a customer of another company about the nature or suitability of its product, an injurious falsehood has been committed and that person can be held accountable for the damage suffered. For example, if a person in the business of selling widgets were to approach a competitor's customer and suggest falsely that the competitor was going out of business or that its product was inferior or made with inferior materials, that competitor could bring a tort action demanding compensation for the damages done. Such damages might be calculated on the lost sales which would have been made had the false information not been communicated. The courts have also resorted to the provisions of the *Criminal Code* relating to theft and fraud to deal with people who have wrongfully disclosed information or personally profited from its use. Even a civil action for conversion has been used to discourage such conduct.

Crime—fraud

[12] *Tolley v. Fry*, [1931] A.C. 333.
[13] *Privacy Act*, R.S.B.C. (1979) c.336 s.3.

INSURANCE

When property in any of its forms is the topic of discussion, insurance is an important consideration. Insurance was designed to provide compensation for damaged, lost or stolen property. Insurance coverage has been expanded, however, to include non-tangibles such as liability and life insurance, as well as business interruption insurance. The purpose of insurance is to reduce the cost of loss by spreading the risk among many people. Premiums paid are based on a prediction of the total cost of losses that might be suffered by a particular group, plus an amount to cover administrative and operation costs as well as a profit for the insurance company. Vast sums of money are involved in this business and, because of the potential for abuse, the industry is closely regulated. Two federal statutes designed to control the insurance business in Canada are the *Canada and British Insurance Companies Act*[14] and the *Foreign Insurance Companies Act*.[15] This legislation requires that all non-provincial insurance companies be registered. All provincial jurisdictions have similar insurance legislation. These provincial and federal statutes can be viewed as a type of consumer protection legislation in the field of insurance.

Contracts for insurance are covered by general contract law, and although insurance companies use standard form contracts the actual wording used will vary considerably between companies. Government controls ensure that the terms do not give unfair advantage to the insurance companies although, as in most contracting situations, the parties are generally considered free to bargain as they wish. Many different types of standard form policies cover the specific kinds of losses that can be anticipated. It is vital for businesses to acquire adequate coverage. Fire insurance, for example, will not normally cover damages caused by nuclear contamination, war or insurrection and for such events to be covered under a fire insurance policy special provisions must be included. Similarly, burglary insurance would not cover shoplifting or theft by employees. Natural disasters, such as earthquakes or floods, are excluded from most standard form policies, at least in relation to some types of property loss. Most insurance contracts require insured parties to maintain certain safety and security standards to protect themselves against the risk of fire and theft.

Property Insurance

The predominant form of property insurance covers losses to buildings and their contents due to fire. Most fire insurance policies contain a co-insurance clause with reference to certain specific types of risks which require that the insured be covered to a minimum percentage of the value of the property involved (usually 80 percent). A person who fails to maintain the minimum insurance will be considered a co-insurer for the difference and will bear the responsibility of that portion of any loss suffered that corresponds to the amount he or she underinsured. If insured persons have too little coverage, they will be co-insurers for the difference and receive only partial com-

Insurance spreads risk

Industry regulated by statutes

Standard form contracts are used and must be carefully examined

Co-insurance clause may reduce coverage

[14] *Canada and British Insurance Companies Act*, R.S.C. (1985) c.I-12.
[15] *Foreign Insurance Companies Act*, R.S.C. (1985) c.I-13.

pensation. If they have too much coverage, they will be over-insured and therefore paying for coverage they cannot collect. It becomes important, then, for the insured to have coverage that is at least close to the maximum potential loss which could be suffered. This is especially true when the insurance coverage refers to one of those areas in which a co-insurance clause applies.

Over-insurance wasteful

Business Interruption Insurance

Another major form of insurance is business interruption insurance. Often, an ongoing business will find itself unable to function because of some unforeseen eventuality, sometimes caused by events covered by other forms of insurance. For example, if Rampal operated a plant manufacturing widgets and due to no fault of his own the plant burned down, fire insurance and other forms of property insurance would normally cover the loss. Such insurance would not, however, cover the loss of profits suffered because the business had to cease operation while the plant was being rebuilt. Business interruption insurance will normally cover not only lost profits but also any added expenses incurred to bring the business back into production. Essentially, these two forms of insurance, physical damage and business interruption insurance, are designed to put the insured in a position he or she would have been in financially had the fire or other damage never taken place.

Business interruption insurance covers lost profits

Life and Health Insurance

Life insurance is usually purchased as a method of providing security for dependants after the death of the insured. Life insurance is often taken out on key personnel in a business or on partners in a partnership to provide compensation for losses incurred from any disruption that may result from the death or illness of an executive or partner.

Life insurance in business used to cover key personnel

Death is inevitable and so the likelihood of the insurance company having to pay out eventually during the coverage period is considerable. This is not a difficulty, however, because premiums are calculated based on a prediction of how long a person of a certain age and health can be expected to live. There are various forms of life insurance to meet the needs of different individuals. Premiums paid for term insurance provide a simple cash settlement at the death of the insured while whole life insurance provides coverage in the event of death as well as investment potential and retirement income. These are just two of several different variations of life insurance available.

Other forms of insurance quite common today are medical and disability insurance which is designed to pay health care expenses and provide an income for a person who is unable to earn a living because of illness or accident. Medical insurance can be arranged individually or as part of group coverage. Health care services in Canada are funded through the government-sponsored medicare system which is simply a large group insurance scheme. In the United States, however, such coverage is not universally available and must be negotiated either as group or individual coverage with insurance companies, although at the time of writing the U.S. government is in the

Health and disability insurance usually part of group coverage

process of developing a medical scheme for the whole population. In most Canadian jurisdictions, disability insurance can be obtained on an individual basis with an insurance company but is more often acquired by large organizations as part of an employee compensation package.

Liability Insurance

There are many situations in which people may incur liability for their wrongful or careless conduct. Visitors to the homes or businesses of others can be hurt because of some condition on the property. When people carry on their professional or business activities, they often run the risk of causing injury to other people or their property. Driving an automobile is a risk-taking endeavour. Personal liability insurance and motor vehicle insurance go a long way towards protecting individuals from potentially devastating claims against them.

Liability insurance covers negligence by self or employees

Another source of liability in business is when an employee causes injury to some third party. Vicarious liability will impose responsibility on the employer for such conduct. Many people think that when they have insurance coverage for a personal liability, they are no longer responsible for their conduct. Liability insurance does not prevent the injured party from suing the insured directly. Once liability has been established and judgment has been obtained, then the insurance company, according to the contract, is obligated to reimburse the insured for the loss. Because the insurance company is interested in keeping insurance losses as low as possible, it will step in and conduct the insured's defence and will settle the matter out of court without judgment if it believes that this course of action is the least costly. It is also important to realize that the insurance company is only obligated to pay where it can be shown that the insured was at fault. If there was no negligence or other wrongful conduct on the part of the insured, he or she is not liable for the losses suffered and neither is the insurance company. Many people are under the false impression that, if there is insurance coverage, the injured party is entitled to payment whether fault is established or not. In these circumstances, the injured party will not be entitled to compensation. Many argue for no-fault coverage in these circumstances.

Coverage only when insured is at fault

Only to extent of coverage

Similarly, if the insured has not purchased sufficient insurance coverage, he or she will be responsible for any shortfall. If Jones has liability insurance for only $500 000 and causes a $750 000 loss, he will be required to pay the $250 000 not covered by insurance. Such liability insurance coverage has become so important in the operation of automobiles that several provinces have instituted compulsory automobile insurance coverage.

Insurable Interest

Upon consideration, it becomes clear that insurance has many of the characteristics of a wager. An insured makes a payment (the wager) and if the insured-against event then takes place (if, for example, the house burns down), he or she wins and receives a prize in the form of a payment from the insurance company. Of course,

Must be
insurable interest
to avoid illegality

this example illustrates the essential difference between insurance and a wager. That is, to win, the insured has to lose. Insurance is only intended to put the person who suffers a loss back in the original position he or she was in had the event not taken place. The contract for insurance is a contract of indemnity. Consequently, the insured person, with the exception of life insurance, can recover only what he or she has actually lost up to the limit set out in the policy. As long as there is a loss to compensate, the insurance transaction is legal. But when the payout becomes a windfall, the insurance agreement is void as an illegal contract.

To realize on a claim for insurance, the insured must demonstrate that he or she has an insurable interest in whatever has been insured. The insured will only be able to collect on the claim to the extent of the value of that insurable interest. The insurable interest, then, is the amount he or she stands to lose if the insured-against event takes place. If Nahanee owned a half-interest in a house worth $150 000, Nahanee would have an insurable interest of $75 000. If Nahanee carried an insurance policy of $150 000 on the house and it was destroyed by fire, Nahanee would only be able to collect $75 000 even though he had insured it for the higher amount. Any other result would give Nahanee a windfall instead of merely indemnifying or compensating the insured for losses suffered, and this is prohibited. It should be noted that when life insurance is involved, the insurable interest is defined as the amount of insurance coverage contracted for, provided there is some sort of family or business relationship at the time the insurance is taken out.

A problem arises when property owned by a corporation is insured by an individual shareholder. Technically, the property is not owned by the shareholder but by the corporation, and it can be argued that the shareholder has no insurable interest. The Supreme Court of Canada dealt with this issue and decided that it was not necessary for the insurer to actually have a legally enforceable interest in the property to insure it. It is enough that a relationship to the subject matter or a concern in it exists such that the organization would suffer a loss if the insured-against event took place.[16]

Since an insurance agreement is an utmost good faith contract, there is an obligation on the insured to disclose any pertinent information. Failure to do so, or silence, will be taken to be misrepresentation. Even after the contract for insurance comes into existence, the insured may have an obligation to disclose information to the insurance company. If material changes take place which will increase the risk of loss, those changes must be communicated. For example, when an occupied building is insured and then, subsequent to the creation of the policy becomes vacant for an extended period of time or when the use of the building is changed so that the risk to the insurance company is materially affected, the insured must inform the company of the changes.

Other Features

One important feature of insurance that must be mentioned is the considerable duty of disclosure imposed on the insured. A relationship of trust exists between the insured and

---

[16] *Kosmopoulos et al. v. Construction Insurance Company of Canada Ltd.* [1987] 1 S.C.R. 2 (S.C.C.)

the insurer. The insurer depends on the insured to inform it of any pertinent factors that might affect eligibility or the rates charged for insurance. When there has been an injury, disease or other health problems in a person applying for life, disability or medical insurance, these fact must be disclosed. Similarly, certain types of information must be disclosed when applying for property insurance, such as whether the property is to be used for business purposes or if it will be vacant for any period. The insurer has no way of determining such important information by itself and must depend on the honesty of the insured to disclose it. Failure to disclose such information, if it is relevant to the loss, may result in the loss being unrecoverable because of misrepresentation.

Another important feature of insurance law is the right of subrogation. After making a payment on a claim, an insurance company acquires all the rights of the insured in relation to that claim. In other words, the insurance company steps into the shoes of the insured. Thus, if the loss has been caused by the interference of some third party and that outside interference is actionable, the insurance company assumes the right to sue the third party. If this were not so and the insured could still sue, the existence of the insurance would create a windfall instead of indemnifying against the loss. Thus, if Kostachues has an insurance policy on her house against fire and a neighbour carelessly allows a fire to get out of control causing Kostachues' home to burn down, Kostachues can turn to her insurance company for compensation. Her insurance company will then turn to the neighbour and sue him for negligence as if the insurance company were Kostachues. This is an important feature of insurance law and is another reason why people should not assume that just because someone they are involved with in an accident has insurance coverage they are protected as well.

Insurer steps into shoes of insured upon payment

People quite often misunderstand the nature of an insurance contract when they acquire two or more policies on the same property. When they have a claim for $2000, they think they can claim against both polices and collect a total of $4000. This is not possible because of a principle called contribution. This principle means that each insurance company will merely pay a share of the loss so that the insured will collect no more than the total amount of loss suffered. This policy is consistent with the indemnification nature of insurance.

Insurance contracts will also usually permit the insurer to minimize its loss in other ways. For example, if a house or boat is damaged, the agreement will usually give the insurance company the right to rebuild, repair or replace it. If the company is in a position that it must replace the lost property, the agreement will give the insurance company the right of salvage, meaning that if anything of value is to be recovered from the building, car or boat, the insurance company is entitled to sell it and keep the proceeds.

Right of salvage

When personal property is destroyed, the insured is entitled to claim for whatever is lost. However, the claim is for the depreciated value of the goods, not the replacement value. Most personal household insurance policies today provide for the replacement of destroyed or stolen goods at their full retail value. When a loss does take place, there is a general requirement on the part of the insured to report that loss to the insurance company right away so that the insurance company can take steps to minimize the damage. There might also be an obligation to report the matter to the police if a crime is involved or if the loss resulted from an auto accident. It should also be pointed out that an insured is not permitted to profit from his or her own wilful misconduct. In addition

Replacement or depreciated value

to the prohibition against insuring against wilful misdeeds, such as theft and assault, even where coverage is in place, if the insured deliberately causes the loss, he or she will not be able to collect. Thus if Floaen burns down his own house killing his wife in the process, he will not be able to collect on the fire insurance and he will not be able to collect on his wife's life insurance.

Finally, when there is a situation of considerable risk to an insurance company, such as a large project that needs to be insured (for example, a new chemical plant), the company will often turn to other insurance companies so that the risk is spread among them all. This pooling of risk is called re-insurance and is very common in the industry.

Bonding

While insurance coverage is not generally available for intentionally wrongful acts such as assault, many business people insist on some protection against the people they deal with who act wrongfully. Bonding is available in these circumstances, and it takes two forms. Usually an employer will pay a fee to have an employee bonded against that employee's own wrongful conduct (fidelity bond). If the employee steals from the employer or a customer, the bonding company will be required to compensate the employer for that loss. It must be emphasized, however, that this insurance does not relieve the bonded employee of responsibility. The bonding company can turn to the employee and collect from him or her.

Bonded parties still liable

The second form of bonding (surety bond) occurs when the bonding is designed to provide assurance that a party to a contract will perform its side of the contract. For example, in a large construction project, the company doing the drywalling may be required to put up a performance bond that it will finish the job by a certain time. If it fails to complete or does not complete on time, the bonding company will be required to pay compensation.

SUMMARY

Personal property involves tangible movable property in the form of chattels and intangible property called a chose in action. Chattels can become fixed to real property but where they are trade or tenant fixtures they can be removed when the tenant leaves if this can be done without damage. A bailment involves property owned by one person voluntarily which is temporarily in the possession of another. The obligation imposed to look after that property depends on contractual terms or on who benefits from the bailment when there is no contract.

Both federal legislation and common law protect intellectual property. A copyright protects literary, artistic and dramatic works from being copied or used by unauthorized parties for the author's life plus fifty years. Producing the work creates the copyright, but registration ensures international protection. Remedies can include injunctions, Anton Piller orders, damages and an accounting of profits. The registered patent gives international monopoly protection on the use of an invention for twenty years. The registered trademark protects certain terms, symbols and designs associated with a business or product, preventing consumer deception and protecting goodwill. Where there is no trademark protection, the common law remedy of a passing-off action may provide similar protection. Industrial designs are also protected by federal legislation. At common law, an employee or associate under a fiduciary obligation is prohibited from disclosing confidential information including trade secrets; damages or an injunction may be awarded when such confidences are breached.

Insurance is designed to spread the risk of loss. To be valid, the insured must have an insurable interest in the subject matter and, except in the case of life insurance, the recovery will be limited to the extent of that insurable interest. Property insurance, business interruption insurance, life and health insurance, as well as liability insurance, are the primary forms of insurance available. With liability insurance, payment will only be made where the insured was at fault. When a claim is paid, the company is subjugated to the rights of the insured and can salvage the property or take over the insured's right to sue a third party.

QUESTIONS

1. Indicate the difference between personal, intellectual and real property. In your answer, give the different categories of personal property and discuss the nature of intellectual property.
2. Indicate how personal property can become real property and discuss why a determination of why and when this has happened may be significant.
3. What is a fixture, and under what circumstances can someone other than the owner of real property remove those fixtures?
4. Explain what is meant by the term "finders, keepers" in terms of who is entitled to property that has been found.
5. Discuss the different ways in which a bailment may be created and the nature of the duty imposed on the bailee in each circumstance.
6. Distinguish between the obligation placed on a bailee for value and that imposed on a common carrier or innkeeper.
7. What two principles does the law of intellectual property try to balance?
8. Explain how a copyright is obtained and the qualifications that must be met to obtain such protection.
9. What is the significance of the 1988 amendments to the *Copyright Act*?
10. Summarize the nature of the protection given to the holder of a copyright and indicate what remedies are available to enforce such rights.
11. Discuss under what circumstances an Anton Piller order would be given and indicate how this remedy might be more valuable than other remedies which might be available.

12. What is the purpose of patent law and why is registration required for protection?

13. What kinds of things are protected by the trademark legislation and how is that protection obtained or lost?

14. Industrial design is intended to protect what kinds of material? How is this protection obtained?

15. How does the duty of confidentiality arise and what protection or remedies are available to the confider?

16. Indicate how criminal law, tort law and contract law can be used to protect intellectual property. How effective are such alternatives?

17. Explain conceptually the purpose of insurance and why it is not void as an illegal contract. (See also Chapter 5.)

18. Distinguish between business interruption insurance and fire insurance. Why might a business person want to have both forms of coverage?

19. What kinds of things cannot be covered under a liability insurance policy? Indicate any other methods a person or business might use to insure that the people they are working with perform their jobs properly.

20. Discuss the similarities and differences between insurance and a wager.

21. What is meant by an insurable interest and how does it apply to the various types of insurance discussed in the chapter?

22. Explain what is meant by the right of subrogation and how this may affect not only the insured but the person who has caused the injury or damage. Also indicate what other means the insurance companies have to keep their damages as low as possible.

23. What is meant by bonding? In your answer, distinguish between bonding and insurance coverage.

CASES

1. *Hammill v. Gerling Globel Life Insurance Company.*
   Mrs. Hammill obtained a life insurance policy in which she stated that she had been a non-smoker for the past twelve months. In fact, this information was incorrect. It was clearly established that she had smoked considerably during this twelve-month period. She had taken out the policy in 1985 and was killed in an auto accident on February 2, 1986. Although her smoking in no way contributed to the accident, the insurer refused to pay the beneficiary under the policy. Explain the legal obligations of the insurer in these circumstances.

2. *Punch v. Savoys Jewellers Limited et al.*
   Mrs. Punch owned a very valuable antique ring which was in need of repair. She took it to Savoys Jewellers who then sent it by registered mail to Walkers, a

Toronto jewellers. By the time Walkers had repaired the ring, there was a postal strike in progress so they used Rapidex, a branch of the Canadian National Railway, to transport the ring back to Savoys Jewellers with their agreement. There was a provision on the bill of lading used by Rapidex limiting its liability for "negligence or otherwise" to $50.00. Walker put a $100.00 value on the bill of lading when in fact the ring was worth about $11 000. The ring was never delivered and Mrs. Punch sued Savoys, Walkers and CN for the loss. CN had no record of what happened and was not able to show whether the ring had been lost or stolen. Explain the nature of the duty owed by Walker, Savoys and CN to Mrs. Punch and the likely outcome of her action against them for the recovery of the value of the ring.

3. *Spiroflex Industries v. Progressive Sealing Inc.*
   Mr. MacDonald designed a new pump coupler (a device used in a circulating water pump) which he intended to produce and sell. But he could not produce a special spring used in the device and so had to turn to others. He produced free-hand sketches of the product as well as directions and specifications, and went to different manufacturers to have it made. He entered into an agreement to have the product marketed and provided a photograph of the device to illustrate a brochure. Once the device was on the market, several companies made copies of the coupler, including the people he originally asked to produce the device and some of those involved in the production of the brochure. Explain MacDonald's rights against those parties.

4. *Brisett Estate et al. v. Westbury Life Insurance Company.*
   Gerald and Mary Brisett purchased a joint life insurance policy with the amount of $200 000 payable to the survivor of the two. A little over two years after the purchase of the life insurance policy, Gerald Brisett murdered his wife and was eventually convicted of that murder. As the beneficiary of the life insurance policy, he made a request to the insurer for the $200 000 payment and it refused to pay. Explain the arguments that are available to the insurance company to support it in its refusal. How would your response be affected by the further knowledge that the estate of the wife brought an action for the proceeds, the husband giving up any claim that he might have to the estate.

5. *Thurston Hayes Devs. v. Horn Abbott.*
   The plaintiff was the developer of the board game, Trivial Pursuit, which had been on the market successfully for several years. The defendants brought out a new board game with the same approach but which involved a different subject matter, and called it Sexual Pursuit. The board used was essentially the same, the box the game came in was similar, and the games were even played in the same way. Explain the nature of the complaint the plaintiff has, any legal action that can be taken to protect his rights and the likely outcome.

6.   *Ciba-Geigy Canada Ltd. v. Apotex Inc.*

Ciba-Geigy had the right to manufacture in Canada the product Metoprolol, a drug used for treating hypertension and angina. Under the *Patent Act* then in place, other manufacturers could acquire a licence and manufacture and sell the product in Canada. These versions are known as generic drugs. Apotex and Novopharm both obtained licences and in the process produced a drug with the same appearance as that produced by Ciba-Geigy. They used the same shape, size and colour. Even the dosages were the same size. In fact, these drugs were interchangeable with the original product. Given the fact that these companies have the right to produce generic drugs that are similar and use-able for the same purpose, is there any complaint that Ciba-Geigy can use against these imitators? Would your answer be affected by the fact that only doctors and pharmacists are aware of the differences and the ultimate consumer would not notice the difference?

ISSUES

1.   It was always thought that the person buying an insurance policy needed to have an insurable interest in the subject matter of the policy. This requirement caused problems when a person incorporated a business because a shareholder in the company loses all claim against the assets of that business. The shareholder does not own the assets; the new company does. A business person might make the mistake of taking out insurance on the assets of the business in his or her own name and would not be able to collect on the policy because there was no insurable interest. Recently, however, the Supreme Court of Canada held that a direct insurable interest was not necessary; rather, a relationship was close enough. The issue is whether it should be necessary to show an insurable interest at all and, if so, do you agree with the approach taken by the Supreme Court?

2.   Most would agree that Canada's copyright legislation was in great need of change when the 1988 amendments were enacted. The changes provide greater penalties for copyright infringement and cover computer programs. Yet most people think that there is nothing wrong with tape recording music, photo-copying pages of books and articles in magazines, or making unauthorized copies of computer programs, as long as it is for their own use. Students and instructors in educational institutions often find it essential to make such copies. Does the new copyright legislation go too far? Should people be free to make copies of such things without any restriction? The issue for discussion, then, is just what kinds of exceptions should there be to the copyright protection given to such materials?

3. The stated purpose of patent legislation is to provide protection for the patent-holder while disclosing as much information as possible about the invention involved. The idea is that such disclosure encourages others to build on what has been discovered and this provides an intellectually stimulating environment. The issue to be discussed here is whether such disclosure really does stimulate others and at what cost. Is this approach in the best interest of the inventor? Would it not be better to have the information disclosed on patent applications remain secret so that the inventor alone can profit from his or her accomplishments?

4. Innkeepers and common carriers are two examples of a group of businesses which traditionally have been assigned special responsibilities with regard to the care they are required to exercise in relation to the property of others. When a guest brings personal property onto the premises of a hotel, the innkeeper is required to look after those goods to the extent that, if they are damaged or lost, the innkeeper is liable for that loss unless it can be demonstrated that the guest was actually negligent or caused the loss himself or herself. The innkeeper, then, is required to function almost as an insurer of the guest's property. In many jurisdictions, this obligation has been modified by statute. In areas where an *Innkeeper's Act* or a variant is in place, the innkeeper can modify his or her liability by properly posting a copy of the *Innkeeper's Act*, reducing the obligation to essentially that of an occupier.

   At common law there are three categories of obligations imposed on occupiers of real property to take care of people and their goods on the premises. These classes are invitees, licensees and trespassers. There are *Occupiers' Liability Acts* in place in most jurisdictions that eliminate these three different categories and impose just one basic obligation owed by an occupier to anyone on his or her property. This obligation is to take all reasonable steps to protect those people or their property.

   The issue, then, is whether or not there is any justification for these historical anomalies. Why treat innkeepers, common carriers and occupiers differently from others who would be subject to the reasonable person test as discussed in Chapter 2 and applied in this chapter? Is the legislation modifying these common law obligations the direction we should be heading (creating a unified approach to the problem) or are there good reasons for treating the types of businesses mentioned differently? In your discussion, determine whether the posting and placement of the *Innkeeper's Act* is consistent with the direction the law ought to be taking.

5. When employees leave their jobs with the restriction not to disclose confidential information learned during the course of the employment, they may find that they cannot get work in the industry in which they have experi-

ence. Employers will often have their workers sign contracts which require them not to work in a similar industry for a specified period of time, and there are general requirements in the law for an employee not to disclose confidential information. Unfortunately, this information may have become part and parcel of workers' skills and it is not possible to forget this information when they go to work for someone else. The issue is whether or not an employer should have the right to restrict an employee from using the information obtained in the course of his or her employment, whether that restriction is imposed in the terms of a contract or by the common law generally. Should the danger that confidential information might be revealed be considered a business risk? Is that approach not more consistent with the free market system applied to labour? In your discussion, consider the social issues and public policy problems associated with these kinds of restrictions on an employee's right to work. Consider also whether management should be treated differently in this regard.

LEGISLATION

Alberta
Alberta Health Insurance Act, R.S.A. (1980) c.A-24
Health Insurance Premiums Act, R.S.A. (1980) c.H-5
Insurance Act, R.S.A. (1980) c.I-5
Motor Vehicle Accident Claims Act, R.S.A. (1980) c.M-21
Workers' Compensation Act, S.A. (1981) c.W-16

British Columbia
Carriers Act, R.S.B.C. (1979) c.43
Insurance Act, R.S.B.C. (1979) c.200
Insurance Corporation Act, R.S.B.C. (1979) c.201
Insurance (Marine) Act, R.S.B.C. (1979) c.203
Insurance (Motor Vehicle) Act, R.S.B.C. (1979) c.204
Hotel Keepers' Act, R.S.B.C. (1979) c.182
Workers' Compensation Act, R.S.B.C. (1979) c.437

Manitoba
Workers' Compensation Act, R.S.M. (1987) c.W-200
Insurance Act, R.S.M. (1987) c.I-40

New Brunswick
Workers' Compensation Act, R.S.N.B. (1973) c.W-13
Crop Insurance Act, R.S.N.B. (1973) c.C-35
Insurance Act, R.S.N.B. (1973) c.I-12

Newfoundland
Automobile Insurance Act, R.S.N. (1990) A-22
Fire Insurance Act, R.S.N. (1990) c.F-10
Insurance Companies Act, R.S.N. (1990) c.I-10
Workers' Compensation Act, R.S.N. (1990) c.W-11
Life Insurance Act, R.S.N. (1990) c.L-14

Nova Scotia
Insurance Act, R.S.N.S. (1989) c.231
Workers' Compensation Act, R.S.N.S. (1989) c.508

Ontario
Health Insurance Act, R.S.O. (1990) c.H.6
Innkeeper's Act, R.S.O. (1990) c.I.7
Insurance Act, R.S.O. (1990) c.I.8
Marine Insurance Act, R.S.O. (1990) c.M.2
Occupiers' Liability Act, R.S.O. (1990) c.O.2
Workers' Compensation Act, R.S.O. (1990) c.W.11

Prince Edward Island
Workers' Compensation Act, R.S.P.E.I. (1988) c.W-7
Insurance Act, R.S.P.E.I. (1988) c.I-4

Québec
An Act Respecting Insurance, R.S.Q. (1977) c.A-32
Automobile Insurance Act, R.S.Q. (1977) c.A-25
Deposit Insurance Act, R.S.Q. (1977) c.A-26
Hospital Insurance Act, R.S.Q. (1977) c.A-28
Health Insurance Act, R.S.Q. (1977) c.A-29
Industrial Accidents and Occupational Diseases Act, R.S.Q. (1977) c.A-3.001

Saskatchewan
Automobile Accident Insurance Act, R.S.S. (1978) A-35
Saskatchewan Government Insurance Act, (1980) S.S. (1979-80) c.S-19.1
Saskatchewan Health Insurance Act, R.S.S. (1978) S-21
Saskatchewan Insurance Act, R.S.S. (1978) S-26
Saskatchewan Medical Care Insurance Act, R.S.S. (1978) S-29
Workers' Compensation Act, S.S. (1979) c.W-17.1

Northwest Territories
Insurance Act, S.N.W.T. (1975(3)) c.5

Yukon
Insurance Act, R.S.Y. (1986) c.91

Federal

Copyright Act, R.S.C. (1985) c.C-42 (Note 1988 Amendments)

Industrial Design Act, R.S.C. (1985) c.I-9 (Note 1992 Amendments S.C. (1992) c.1)

Insurance Companies Act, S.C. (1991) c.47

Patent Act, R.S.C. (1985) c.P-4 (Note 1987 amendment S.C. 1987 c.32)

Trademarks Act, R.S.C. (1985) c.T-13

15 INTRODUCTION TO THE LAW OF REAL ESTATE

Objectives of the Chapter

- to consider the nature of real property and ownership of land
- to discuss landlord and tenant relationships
- to examine mortgages and their effect on real property

Mr. Hill was a bad credit risk who had been turned down by Paramount Life Insurance Company when he tried to obtain a loan through a mortgage on the house he and his wife owned. He then sold the property to his business partner and had his partner arrange for a loan with Paramount Life Insurance Company on the basis of a mortgage on the property. This mortgage was granted. The problem was that he had not obtained his wife's consent for the sale but had forged her signature on the documents. Neither the business partner nor the life insurance company knew this fact. Shortly after this transaction Hill died. Because Paramount was not receiving mortgage payments, it foreclosed. It was then the Mrs. Hill found out what her husband had done. She fought the foreclosure action on the basis of her late husband's fraud, claiming she was entitled to the property. Because the court action took place in a land titles jurisdiction where the Torrens System of land registry was in place, and because the partner and Paramount were innocent of any wrongdoing, the court found that the business partner had obtained good title to the property and that the mortgage granted was good. The government, through

> the local Land Titles Office, had granted a certificate of title to the land to the partner. This certificate of title determines ownership against all other parties. Mrs. Hill was the victim of her husband's fraud and lost the property.[1] This case illustrates the significance of the difference between the land titles system of registration used in some parts of Canada and the system of land registry used in the rest of the country. In the land titles system, a certificate of title is granted which establishes ownership of the property. Such a certificate had been issued to the business partner in this case. This chapter explores real property interests which are created under these two systems as well as landlord/tenant and mortgage law.

The need to understand the law of real property (land and buildings) extends beyond business relationships because accommodation is one of life's essentials. Whether shelter is obtained through ownership, rental or even squatting, the relationships created are governed by real property law. The premises used to carry out a business activity must be owned or rented and a thorough understanding of the legal relationships involved is fundamental for anyone studying business law. A significant industry has developed to serve the property needs of business, that is, the provision and management of space and the purchase and sale of property. Many private individuals and corporate entities acquire property purely for investment purposes with the objective of making profits, either by renting or by reselling the premises. There are several ways a business person can become involved with the use, possession and ownership of real property. The material in this chapter is necessarily abbreviated but it will serve as an introduction to the most significant aspects of the law of real property: interests in land and their transfer, landlord and tenant relationship, and mortgages.

LEGAL INTERESTS IN LAND

Real Property

Real property is land or anything affixed to land

The term **real property** means land and anything affixed to or constructed on the land, including buildings and chattels that have become attached to the land in a permanent way. It used to be thought that such interest in land included an unlimited area above and below the land. Today, a right to the air space above privately owned land is limited, extending only to the area the owner can permanently use or occupy, and even this space will probably be restricted by local zoning regulations.

[1] *Paramount Life Insurance Co. v. Hill et al.*, (1987) 34 D.L.R. (4th) 150 (Alta. Crt. of Appeal)

A landowner has no right to sue for trespass when an airplane flies over the property, but a permanent incursion into this air space, such as power lines or overhanging portions of an adjoining building, would give the owner the right to take action against those responsible for such an incursion, unless this right had been taken away by the operation of a higher authority. Although property owners in Canada still have rights to the area under their land, most crown grants have reserved the mineral rights for the crown so that the sub-surface rights, beyond those normally occupied by foundations or wells, are no longer intact. The crown can grant these rights to others and the surface owner will have no claim to sub-surface mineral rights and no complaint about a mine tunnel under the property.

Interest in Land

All land owned by crown

The current law of real property is rooted in the legal system introduced in England after the Norman invasion by William the Conqueror in 1066. The feudalism of that time was a rigid and complex system in which people held rather than owned their land. All land was actually owned by the king who granted the privilege of use to his favourites. The right to the exclusive possession and use of the land was called an **estate in the land** and the nature of that estate or interest in the land depended on the type of relationship and obligation imposed on the land holder. This tradition has had a great influence on our present law of real property. The original estates in land have been reduced to a few significant types known today as estates in fee simple, life estates and leasehold estates.

Fee simple comparable to ownership

FEE SIMPLE. The greatest interest a person can have in land today is **an estate in fee simple**. Although the crown theoretically still owns the land and the person claiming it only has an estate in the land, the fee simple estate is the closest thing we have to ownership today. A fee simple estate gives the holder of that estate the right to use the land subject only to any local restrictions which have been imposed by agreement or legislation. An important aspect of an estate in fee simple is the right of the holder to freely sell an estate, thus transferring all rights of use and control. This free transferability is what brings an estate in fee simple closest to our idea of ownership. In Canada, a person who is said to own land really holds an estate in fee simple in that land.

A fee simple estate should not be confused with a **fee tail estate** which provides for the land being passed down from father to the eldest son. Although some jurisdictions still have provision for this type of land holding, because they can be easily transformed to a fee simple, fee tail estates are of no practical importance in Canada today.

It should be noted that even when a fee simple interest in land is present, the "owner" of the property is not free from any interference in relationship to it. Several different levels of government may regulate what the property can be used for, the nature and description of the buildings that can be erected on it and require that certain health, sanitary and appearance levels be maintained. The "owner" may not even be able to keep the property if a governing body decides to expropriate it.

Although these factors are significant limitations on the value of ownership of property, it may be best to view them as one of the costs of living in a social environment rather than as an aspect unique to property law.

Life estate divides fee simple

LIFE ESTATE. Another type of estate in land more restrictive than a fee simple is a life estate. Fee simple and fee tail estates can be inherited but a person who has an estate in land for a lifetime cannot will the property to his or her heirs. Upon the death of the life tenant, the property reverts back to the original owner of the fee simple or that owner's heirs. The original grantor of the life estate retains a **reversionary interest** in the property. If this right is transferred to a third party, that person is called a **remainderman** and has a right to the remainder of the fee simple after the life estate expires. Life estates are not particularly common in Canada but they are an important method of establishing interest in land. It should be noted that a grantor of a life estate can establish the duration of the life estate not on the lifetime of the person obtaining possession but rather upon the longevity of some other person. This introduces several complications, however, and so it is very unusual.

Life estates are generally avoided today because of the difficulties they create in dealing freely with property, but interests close in concept to life estates are created through the operation of law. Historically, a woman's right to act in relationship to property was submerged when she married and her husband obtained full use and control of all family property. The **right of dower** was created to protect the wife in these circumstances. This right allowed the wife to claim a one-third interest in the husband's land as a matter of right. There are many difficulties associated with these dower rights, not the least of which is the fact that they establish significant impediments to the free transferability of property. Another difficulty is that a divorce eliminates any dower claim since dower rights are founded on the marriage relationship. Dower rights have been modified to some extent in most provinces and in many cases abolished altogether. Some provinces have substituted similar rights called **homestead rights**[2] and some provinces have established a spouse's right to one-half of all family assets in the case of marriage breakdown.[3] An examination of the different approaches to the protection of spousal interests is beyond the scope of this chapter but the implications of the law in place in each jurisdiction can have important consequences to the business person. Students are encouraged to examine the legislation in effect in the particular jurisdiction in which they reside.

Dower and homestead right protect spouse

LEASEHOLD ESTATES. Fee simples, fee tails and life estates are described as **freehold estates** because a person has exclusive possession of the property for an indeterminate time. **Leasehold estates** are significantly different because, when a person grants a lease on land to another, it is for a definite period and the landowner reclaims the land at the expiration of that time. Although a definite time period must be involved, it is possible to convey an almost unlimited right to possess the land by granting a long term (ninety-nine years) lease. It is also possible to create a periodic

Leasehold estates determined by time

---

[2] *Homestead Act*, R.S.S. (1978) c.H-5.
[3] *Family Relations Act*, R.S.B.C. (1979) c.121 s.43.

tenancy. This means that there is no definite termination date but rather the term is an automatically renewable monthly or yearly tenancy. An example of periodic tenancy is when a person rents an apartment or house by the month without a specified lease period. If neither landlord nor tenant do anything to alter the periodic monthly tenancy relationship, the lease period will automatically be extended from period to period. To end such a relationship, one of the parties simply serves notice that the next period will be the last month of the landlord/tenant relationship. Legislation or agreement between the parties may impose a longer period of notice or other restriction on the tenancy. This topic of leasehold interests is generally called landlord and tenant law and will be discussed in a separate section of this chapter.

—but may also be periodic

Lesser Interests in Land

Freehold and leasehold estates are called estates in land because they give the person holding the estate a certain status in relationship to the land, that is, the right to exclusive possession of that land while the estate is in place. However, there are several different types of interest a person can have in land that do not convey the right to exclusive possession of the property. The most important of these lesser interests in land is an **easement** which gives a person the right to use a portion of another's land, usually for a particular purpose. **The right of way** is one of the most common forms of easement. This entitles the holder of the right of way to cross another person's land, usually to get to his or her own property or to reach another point of interest such as a lake or the sea. Once the right of way has been established, the owner of the property must honour the holder's rights to cross the property, but this right does not extend to allowing that person to stop or build some permanent structure on the property. For an easement to exist, there must be a property upon which the easement is imposed (servient tenement) and another property whose owner is deriving a benefit (dominant tenement). In most instances, these properties are side by side or in reasonably close proximity.

Easement gives right to use of land—not possession

Must be dominant and servient tenement

There are many situations in which people must surrender the use of a portion of their property to facilitate power lines, sewer lines and other public utilities. In these cases, there is usually no dominant tenement because no identifiable, specific, public land benefits by the power lines or sewer lines. These restrictions on the use of land are not easements in a true sense because there is no dominant tenement. They are created by statutes and impose similar rights and responsibilities, and are sometimes called public easements.

There are several other types of interests or rights a person can have in another's land in addition to easements. A **licence** which can be revoked at any time gives a person permission to use another's land. This use of land by permission over a period of time, under common law in some provinces, can acquire the attributes of an enforceable right. For example, an individual who, without interference, habitually crosses the corner of a person's property with the permission of the owner of that property, either expressed or implied over a number of years, will acquire a right to cross that property as a matter of right (a right-of-way) even though no actual grant

Property rights
may be obtained
by prescription

of an easement has been given. Acquiring such a right over property is called an easement acquired by **prescription**. The effect of such an easement is as significant to the landowner as any other form of easement. The landowner must periodically exercise some control over the portion of land in question to avoid the creation of an easement by prescription. For this reason, the owners of private property with public access will periodically block it off. A period of twenty years is usually sufficient to establish a right by prescription under the *Statute of Limitations* of most jurisdictions. A right to actual possession of land can be acquired in the same way. When a person has had possession of land for a number of years and possession has been tolerated by the actual owner, that owner may lose the right to reclaim possession of the land. This process is called acquiring a right to possession of the property through adverse possession. Several Canadian provinces have abolished both the right to an easement by prescription and the right to acquire land by **adverse possession**.[4]

Another interest in land may be created when a contract is struck between the owner of land and another person to come onto the land and use some aspect of the land for personal profit, such as the taking of trees, gravel, soil, peat or sand from a property. Such rights convey an interest in land that is quite different from an easement or a licence and are referred to as a *profit à prendre*.

Restrictive
covenant may
bind future
owners

Finally, a person can acquire a right in relation to another's property through the vehicle of a **restrictive covenant**. It is possible for a person granting an estate in land to another to place restrictions on the use of that land that will bind all subsequent holders. These are called restrictive covenants. These restrictions can take many forms but they are typically the following: restrictions as to the type of buildings that can be put on the property—their height, shape and style; restrictions as to how the property may be used—residential, commercial or light industrial; and restrictions as to who can own the property—adult-only facilities and even restrictions on the grounds of racial, religious or ethnic origin. Many of these last types of restrictive covenants are invalid because they are discriminatory in their nature and thus are prohibited by law.

These and other interests in land run with the land, meaning that they are tied to the property itself rather than to the owner of it. They are binding not only on the original purchasers of the property who granted the restriction, easement, or *profit à prendre* but are also binding on any subsequent owner. They are better viewed as an interest in land rather than as a simple contractual relationship and so the rule of privity of contract does not apply.

However, when a person covenants to do or not do something in relationship to the land, the covenant must be negative in its nature for the restrictive covenant to be binding on a subsequent purchaser of the land. For example, a requirement that an owner not place a building over three stories high on a particular property is a negative covenant and thus binds subsequent purchasers. But a requirement stating that a building be built within a specific period would be positive in nature and only binding on the initial purchaser. It should also be noted that when a large development has the same restrictive covenants in place on all of the properties, this

---

[4] *Land Titles Act*, R.S.B.C. (1979) c.219 s.24.

is called a **building scheme**. Building schemes take on many of the properties of zoning bylaws because the developers have imposed basic rules governing the construction and use of property in the development just as a municipality would normally do through zoning bylaws.

Tenancy in Common and Joint Tenancy

Owning property together may be joint or in common

Only joint ownership creates right of survivorship

It is possible for two or more people to hold property together in either of two ways, and it is important to distinguish between the two different methods. A **tenancy in common** is when two people share an estate in the same property with each owning a portion and having an undivided interest in it. This means that each can enjoy the whole property. If one of the parties dies, his or her share in the property goes to that person's heirs and either party can sell his or her interest to someone else without changing the interest in the land. It is also possible for two people to hold a joint interest in property so that if one dies the other will be left with the whole property. This is called a **joint tenancy**. In effect, both individuals own the entire property outright. When one dies, the essential nature of the other's interest does not change. He or she continues to own the entire property through right of survivorship. Joint tenancy avoids many of the problems associated with inheritance and estate taxes. There may be instances, however, when people who hold property in joint tenancy do not want the other party to acquire the entire property upon their death. In such circumstances, it is possible to "sever" the joint tenancy. Severance of the joint tenancy must take place before the death of the party wishing to sever and is accomplished by that party acting towards the property in some way that is inconsistent with the joint tenancy continuing. If a joint tenant sold his or her half interest in a property to a third party or in some provinces to him or herself, this would sever the joint tenancy. The relationship between the other joint owner and the new third party is a tenancy in common rather than a joint tenancy. When people hold property together and wish to avoid joint ownership, they should not use such words as "held jointly" or "joint ownership" in the title document since the use of these terms will create a joint tenancy. When such words do not appear, the creation of a tenancy in common is presumed.

Other Interests in Land

Option gives right to purchase

Several other typical types of interest in land are of significance to landowners. When a person makes an offer to sell property, the offer can be revoked by the offeror any time before the point of acceptance, unless some added consideration is given by the offeree that imposes on the offeror an obligation to hold that offer open for a specific period of time. When such added consideration is given, it is called an **option agreement** and when the property involved is land, it conveys with it significant rights. The offeree has acquired the right to purchase the property at a given price, and this right in and of itself can be of significant value and can be sold. Often, when a person leases land and makes improvements, the lease will contain an option to purchase, but this option agreement must be registered to be effective against outsiders who may subsequently purchase the property.

Security given through mortgage or agreement for sale

An **agreement for sale** illustrates another kind of interest in land. When the person selling the land is providing the credit for the transaction, the conveyance of the title will be delayed until the last payment is made. In the interim, between the time the agreement is entered into and the title is conveyed, the agreement for sale bestows a significant interest in the property on the purchaser, including the right of possession. Upon final payment, the purchaser has the right to force the completion of the transfer of the freehold interest in the property.

A more common way of financing the purchase of property is through a **mortgage**. Typically, a mortgage transaction involves some outside third party lending the purchaser enough money to buy property from a vendor. The title of the property is conveyed (transferred) to the moneylender to be reconveyed upon receipt of the last payment. The use of the mortgage as security is not restricted to the process of purchasing property but can be used at any time by the owner of property as a method of raising needed funds. Because the use of mortgages is so common and important, special rules have been developed which will be examined in more detail in a separate section of this chapter.

Transfer and Registration of Interest in Land

In the past in Britain, the most common method of transferring real property during the lifetime of the owner was by grant. The **grant** involved the act of the grantor (the person selling) giving the grantee title to the property. The document used to accomplish this transfer had to be under seal and was called a deed of conveyance, now shortened simply to deed. A major difficulty developed with this method of transferring property. Because of the time involved and the possibility of many different deeds, it was impossible to be certain that good title to the property had been transferred by the most current deed, without inspection of all of the past deeds. Two different solutions to this problem were developed and either one or the other has been adopted in different jurisdictions in Canada.

Grants gave title to property

Registration imposed to assist ascertaining title

In both cases, the solution required that the transfer of land be registered at a registry office. The distinction between the two systems is in the effect of that registration. In most jurisdictions in Canada, the registration process does not affect the rights of the parties under the documents registered but simply provides assurance that the parties dealing with the property will not be affected by any unregistered documents. The registry is merely a repository of the documents that may affect the title of the property. It is still necessary for the parties to examine the title documents and establish a chain of valid deeds to determine whether the seller has good title.

The western provinces, New Brunswick, and some areas of Ontario, Nova Scotia and Manitoba have taken the registry system one step further and adopted the **Torrens System** of land registry. Although both systems require registration, the essential difference between the normal land registry system and the Torrens System

Some provinces
guarantee title

is that, in the Torrens System, once registration has taken place in a central registry, a certificate of title is created and registered which is binding on all parties. The government guarantees that the information on that certificate of title is correct. This information includes the declared, registered owner of the property as well as any mortgages, easements or other interests which might be held by others in that property. The key to understanding the Torrens System is that the certificate of title determines the interest of the parties listed on it to the land specified. For example, in British Columbia, the *Land Titles Act*[5] states that the certificate of title is conclusive evidence in any court that the person named on the certificate is the holder in fee simple of that property and that is an end to the matter. For this reason, in the example used to introduce this chapter, Mrs. Hill was not able to retain the property. Even though she was innocent and her signature had been forged, a certificate of title was issued to Mr. Hill's partner and this certificate extinguished any claim she had to the property. In both systems, parties claiming an interest in land must register that interest to be protected from some innocent third party buying the property. However, in the normal land registry system, it is up to the parties to sort out the legal relationships derived from those registered documents. In the Torrens System, the certificate of title determines the interests. For this reason, the Torrens System is commonly called the **Land Titles System** in Canada.

Condominium Legislation

Because traditional real property law did not recognize the difference between the land and the buildings affixed to it, it was incapable of handling the modern practice of creating ownership in suites stacked vertically in an apartment building. As a result, most jurisdictions have passed legislation allowing fee simple interest in individual apartments in a condominium structure. But because condominium ownership is essentially a form of common ownership, many unique rights and responsibilities apply. Although individuals may own their separate apartments, all common areas such as the halls, reception areas and laundry facilities are owned in common.

Condominium
legislation allows
vertical title

Condominium
interest involves
some shared
property

The condominium association functions in a way similar to municipal or corporate bodies, holding regular meetings with each member (those owning apartments in the development) having a vote. Bylaws are passed and put in place that outline the rights and duties of members. The condominium association will also levy a fee on each member to pay for such things as repairs, the cost of management and other services. Each member of the condominium owns his or her own suite and the normal rules of real property apply; the suites can be sold, mortgaged or rented, but the interest the member has in the common area goes with that conveyance and so do the responsibilities associated with it.

Apartments can
be owned
through
cooperatives

A cooperative is another method of owning apartment buildings and other forms of accommodation in common. A cooperative is quite similar to the con-

[5] *Ibid.*, s. 33

dominium in that the members of the cooperative all have shares in the apartment building. However, their rights to their individual suites are based on the terms of the contract and the bylaws of the cooperative as opposed to a specific real property interest in the suite itself. In this case, the real property interest in all of the suites and the common areas is held by the cooperative which is a company composed of the members holding shares in it. There are some disadvantages to condominium and cooperative ownership, such as submission to the bylaws and the monthly fee, but there are also significant advantages. This form of ownership is the only viable alternative to renting an apartment. Condominium or cooperative ownership ensures a constant monthly cost since the property is purchased rather than rented. Rents can change whereas a purchase price is fixed. It must be noted that the monthly service fee can increase over the years and be a significant cost in the ownership of the suite. Residents can be required to leave if they violate the bylaws. For example, some of these organizations stipulate that residents be adults only. Couples who have children are required to sell their property. (This particular provision may violate human rights legislation.)

THE LANDLORD/TENANT RELATIONSHIP

Leasehold Estates

A leasehold estate in land is different from a freehold estate in that it is limited in its duration to a specific or determinable time. The lease for real property will usually be for a specific period or end on a specified date. The leasehold interest is similar to a freehold estate in that it bestows on the tenant the right to exclusive possession of the land and buildings during the period of the lease. This right to exclusive possession is a hallmark of an estate in land and must be distinguished from a mere licence in which the licensee may be only one of several people allowed to use the property. Such a licence can be based on contract or given gratuitously. There is no exclusive right conveyed with the right to come on the property in question when a licence has been granted. For example, if Jones were to take a room in a hotel for a week, the relationship established would normally be one of licence. The hotel-keeper would still have the right to come in the room, make the beds, clean the room, do any repairs and even move Jones to another location if it is deemed appropriate. On the other hand, if Jones were to rent an apartment on a lease arrangement for a week, Jones would have the exclusive right to use the premises and the landlord could not come in without Jones' permission. A lease arrangement is created by contract in which the parties can modify these rights and responsibilities. Thus, in the lease agreement, Jones could give the landlord the right to enter the premises under certain circumstances. However, in the absence of such

Tenant has right to exclusive possession during period of lease

Terms of lease can modify obligations

agreement, that apartment is the property of Jones for the duration of the lease and Jones is entitled to possess it exclusively.

The general requirements of contract law apply to leasehold estates because they are created by contract. As with any form of contract, it is a good idea for a contracting parties to put their agreement in writing. Although this is generally not required for a lease period of three years or less, the requirement that a lease for over three years be evidenced in writing is a provision of the *Statute of Frauds* or similar legislation in place in most jurisdictions.[6] The *Statute of Frauds* requires that written evidence support the agreement that specifies the premises covered by the lease, the parties to it, the consideration or rent to be given by the tenant, the duration of the lease and any other special provisions the parties may have agreed to. A lease may have to be registered as well where required by provincial legislation.

A leasehold estate is as much an interest in land as a freehold estate and when a landlord sells property, any lease arrangements that were entered into before the new owner took over the property are binding on the new owner. Similarly, when the landlord mortgages the property after a lease arrangement with a tenant has been entered into, the creditor is subject to the lease arrangement. If the landlord fails to make payments and the mortgagee is forced to take action against the property to protect his or her investment, either by seizing the property or by having it sold, the tenant has the right to remain on the premises until the lease expires. If a lease arrangement were based solely on contract law, the principle of privity of contract would prohibit this result, but since a leasehold interest is said to "run with the land," the tenant is able to insist on the right to exclusive possession of the property for the duration of the lease, even against strangers who have acquired the property after the creation of the lease.

Other contractual provisions also apply to the contracts that create leasehold estates. A landlord who contracts with an infant, a drunk or a mentally incompetent person runs into all the problems associated with incapacity discussed in Chapter 4 and the resulting contract may not be binding. Historically, the principle allowing a contract to be discharged because of some frustrating event that makes the performance of the contract impossible did not apply to land.[7] Many jurisdictions have introduced legislation changing this; if residential premises are destroyed or otherwise rendered unusable, the contract will be discharged by frustration and the tenant's obligation to pay rent will cease. There are many other examples of legislation which significantly modifies the common law relationship of landlord and tenant. This is especially true when the premises involved are used for residential purposes. Most jurisdictions have introduced special legislative provisions determining the rights and obligations of landlords and tenants in residential relationships. This legislation varies from province to province so no attempt will be made to make a comprehensive summary of these statutory provisions except to indicate some of the more interesting provisions in place.

---

[6] *The Statute of Frauds*, R.S.O. (1990) c.S.19 s.3
[7] *Paradine v. Jane*, (1647) Aleyn 26 (K.B. Div.).

Types of Tenancies

There are two main methods of holding a leasehold estate in property. The first is by having an agreement establishing a leasehold estate for a specific period of time such as "one year" or "ending September 5." When such an agreement has a set duration, it is a **term lease**, often called simply a lease. In the absence of a breach on the part of either party, the lease entitles the tenant to exclusive possession of the property for the specified period. During that period, the tenant may have the right to sell or sublet the lease to another party depending on the terms of the lease. If the lease is sold, the tenant gives up all rights and claims in relationship to the property. However, if the property is subleased, the tenant retains a reversionary interest. Just as the landlord who holds the fee simple estate in the property has the right to retake possession of the property at the expiration of the lease, a tenant also has the right to retake possession of the property at the expiration of the designated period when a sublease is involved.

The second common method of creating a leasehold estate is with a **periodic tenancy** which is a period-to-period rental with no specific time duration. The rental period is specific, but the parties have agreed that the lease period will be automatically renewed in the absence of notice to the contrary. The period involved can be weekly, monthly or yearly, but the most common is the month-to-month tenancy. The feature of a periodic tenancy which distinguishes it from a normal lease arrangement is that there is no specific identified time when the relationship between landlord and tenant will terminate. The dominating aspect of a periodic tenancy is the requirement of notice necessary for any modifications in the status of the relationship between landlord and tenant. If the lease period in the periodic tenancy is one month, no notice can be given to take effect during that period. It must be given before the commencement of one period to be effective at the end of the next. If Nilsson rents an apartment from Delgado on a month-to-month tenancy, the lease period begins on the day the rent is paid, usually the first day of the month unless otherwise agreed. If one month notice is required and Nilsson wishes to end the leasehold relationship on May 31, Delgado must be given notice before the beginning of the month period ending May 31, which would be on or before April 30. If Nilsson waits to give notice until paying the rent on May 1, it is too late to be effective for May 31 because the lease period has already begun. This requirement has caused considerable problems and is an area that has been modified by statute in many jurisdictions.

There are two other, less important, types of tenancies. A landlord creates a **tenancy at will** when he or she allows a purchaser to take possession of a property before the date specified for the exchange of title. Under such an arrangement, either party retains the right to end the relationship at any time and no notice is required. While the requirement of rent by the landlord may give rise to a periodic tenancy, it is possible to specify that the relationship remains a tenancy at will regardless of the rent. A **tenancy at sufferance** is created when a landlord has given the appropriate notice but the tenant fails to vacate, or when the set term of a lease has expired and the tenant remains in possession. While this is called a tenancy, it is simply an over-holding tenant who may have rights of possession in relationship to

Lease sets out rights of parties

Property may be subleased

Periodic tenancy usually month to month

Notice period is one clear rental period

outsiders but can be ejected at any time by the landlord. If the landlord accepts a further rental payment from an over-holding tenant, there is the danger that a periodic tenancy will result. It is better to view tenancy at will and tenancy at sufferance as special situations rather than examples of leasehold estates.

Rights and Obligations of the Parties

No distinction is made in common law between tenancies dealing with commercial property and residential property. Most provinces have created legislation that significantly alters the common law provisions relating to residential, and to a lesser extent, commercial tenancies. Some provinces have several different statutes dealing with landlord and tenant law.[8] Others have incorporated all of their landlord and tenant legislation into one general landlord and tenant act meant to cover all leasehold tenancies.[9] The following comments are directed to the landlord and tenant law in place generally and apply primarily to commercial tenancies. The unique provisions which have been introduced to deal with residential tenancies will be discussed under a separate heading. It is recommended that the reader refer to the specific legislative provisions in effect in his or her jurisdiction.

Since the primary relationship between landlord and tenant is based on contract, the terms in that contract can modify the traditional obligations of the parties. As the rights and responsibilities of the parties are discussed below, it is important to remember that these provisions should be regarded as binding on the party *unless they have agreed otherwise* in their lease agreement.

VACANT POSSESSION. The landowner has an obligation to ensure that the premises are vacant and ready for occupancy at the time agreed for the lease period to start. A failure on the part of the landlord to deliver vacant possession to a new tenant may be caused by several factors, such as failure to eject an over-holding tenant, an error in calculating the prior tenant's rights to stay on the premises, or construction or renovation. The landlord's liability and the compensation due the tenant in these situations will be calculated on how much it costs the tenant to find other accommodation in the interim.

QUIET ENJOYMENT. A landlord is obligated to give a tenant quiet enjoyment of the premises. This term is somewhat misleading because it does not mean that the tenant has to be happy or like the premises, only that the landlord must ensure that nothing happens to interfere with the tenant's use of the property. Suppose Cho negotiates the purchase of an office building from Rankin and, in anticipation of the completion of the deal, rents accommodation in that building to Coghlan. Then the deal falls through. Coghlan will not be able to occupy the office space since Rankin is still the owner of the property. Because this interferes with Coghlan's quiet enjoyment of the

Obligations may be modified by statute

Landowner must provide vacant premises

Landlord must not interfere with tenant's use of property

---

[8] *Rent Review Act*, R.S.N.S. (1989) c.398, *Residential Tenancies Act*, R.S.N.S. (1989) c.401.
[9] *Landlord and Tenants Act*, R.S.A. (1980) c.L-6

lease, Coghlan can take action against Cho for failure to provide quiet enjoyment. It is also possible for a landlord to fail to provide quiet enjoyment of the property by allowing something to physically interfere with the use of the premises. For example, if Coghlan rents office space in a building owned by Cho and one day discovers that the only entrance to his office is blocked because of construction or that blasting next door makes it impossible to stay on the premises, this would interfere with his quiet enjoyment of the premises and Coghlan could sue Cho for breach of the lease agreement.

No general
obligation to
repair

REPAIR OF PREMISES. The landlord has no general obligation to deliver premises that are clean or in good repair. The tenant takes the property the way it comes and if he or she wants it in better condition, the cost is the responsibility of the tenant. Only when the premises are in such disrepair that it amounts to a breach of quiet enjoyment can the landlord be held responsible. In the example above Coghlan would have no complaint if the premises are not painted or the carpet is threadbare when he moves in. If Coghlan is dissatisfied with the condition of the office, he should put a term in the lease agreement which requires the landlord to correct these problems. If the structure of the building is in such poor repair that it is no longer capable of supporting a wall or a floor and a resulting cave-in would make the office unusable, that would be a breach of the covenant of quiet enjoyment. Because the lease is contractual in nature, it is possible for the parties to modify the commonly accepted terms and care should be taken to do so. There are many situations in which the courts will imply into the contract obligations on the parties because of the circumstances. For example, when a tenant rents only part of a building, the court will assume that the landlord has an obligation to provide heat unless otherwise stated in the lease. But when the tenant leases the entire building, the obligation will be assumed to be on the tenant.

TERMINATION. If a lease for a specific period of time is involved, the lease is terminated at the expiration of the specified period. Of course, the parties can enter into a new agreement extending the lease. If the rental arrangement is ongoing (for example, month-to-month) the tenancy is terminated by either party giving proper notice. If the tenant fails to leave after the lease has expired or after being given the appropriate notice, a tenancy at sufferance relationship is established. In these circumstances, the landlord is generally entitled to compensation from the tenant in the form of payment. However, if a normal rent payment is made for this period and accepted by the landlord, there is a danger of creating a periodic tenancy which would require the landlord to give additional notice before the tenant could be ejected. The length of notice required to vacate the premises when a periodic tenancy is involved is generally equal to the length of the tenancy period. Periodic tenancies may be week to week, month to month or year to year, but one clear rental period must be given for notice. In most jurisdictions, the notice period has been extended when residential tenancies are involved.

FRUSTRATION. Historically, the doctrine of frustration did not apply to real property but many jurisdictions have modified this in their landlord and tenant

Frustration may
apply to
residential
tenancies by
statute

statutes. The effect of this modification is that the obligation of the parties to a lease may be ended by the destruction of the property or other conditions that make the performance of the lease agreement impossible. In Ontario, the *Landlord and Tenants Act* states that the doctrine of frustration will apply to residential tenancies and as a result the province's *Frustrated Contracts Act* will apply.[10]

Tenant must pay
rent

TENANTS' OBLIGATIONS. The most obvious obligation on the tenant in a leasehold agreement is to pay the agreed-upon rent for the premises at the appropriate time. This obligation is independent of any obligations that the landlord may have agreed to in the lease contract, such as a duty to make repairs. If the lease requires that the landlord repair the premises and the landlord fails to do so, the tenant cannot withhold rent until the repairs are made. The tenant must still pay rent and the landlord can use the courts to enforce the payment if there is a failure to pay. Failure to pay rent, although it may appear justified in these circumstances, would give the landlord grounds to evict the tenant. On the other hand the tenant would have the right to seek other compensation. The tenant also has an obligation to keep the premises in good repair, such as cleaning clogged drains and replacing light bulbs, but the tenant has no obligation for the normal wear and tear on the premises. If Coghlan rents an office from Cho and the rug on the floor wears out over the years, Coghlan would be under no obligation to replace it. But neither would Cho be obligated to replace it since the landlord is not required to provide premises of any standard of fitness for the tenant. Of course, the landlord and tenant can agree otherwise and in many lease agreements, the landlord assumes the responsibility for keeping the property in good repair.

Tenants not
responsible for
normal wear and
tear

A tenant who uses property for a purpose other than that for which it was originally rented will assume the responsibility for any undue wear and tear, and the landlord can require the premises to be vacated. For example, if Coghlan rents premises from Cho to be used as an office and instead uses it for manufacturing furniture, Cho would have the right to require Coghlan to leave regardless of the terms of the lease. Cho could also sue for any damage that might have been caused by inappropriate use.

A problem that often arises with rental premises is when tenants attach some item to the building and then wish to take it away when leaving. The attached item is called a **fixture**, and tenants are not permitted to remove fixtures which have been attached in such a way that suggests they were intended to remain a permanent part of the building. If Coghlan installed modern wiring and added a staircase to the second floor in his rented office, these fixtures would become permanent and he could not remove them when he left. Fixtures attached to the premises which are really meant to stand by themselves but are attached merely to facilitate their usefulness and can be detached without damaging the premises can be taken away by the tenant. Shelving, display counters, machinery, decorative artwork and signs go with the tenant who attached them. Where the removal of the item will cause significant damage to the premises, it has become a fixture and

Tenant can
remove his or
her fixtures
before
termination of
lease

[10] *Landlord and Tenant Act*, R.S.O. (1990) c.L.7 s.86

cannot be removed. If the tenant neglects to take fixtures and tries to regain possession only after leaving, it is too late since the fixtures have become part of the real property. A more detailed discussion of fixtures and personal property generally is found in Chapter 14.

Remedies

BREACH OF LEASE. If the tenant breaches the lease agreement in some way, such as by failing to pay rent, the landlord can sue for the overdue rent. The landlord also has the right to require the tenant to vacate the premises and can evict tenants who fail to do so. Legislation often limits the availability of this remedy and the services of a law enforcement officer, such as a sheriff, must be obtained to carry out the eviction if the tenant resists. This process can be costly and time-consuming. In these circumstances, and for other lesser breaches of the lease agreement, several other remedies may be available to the landlord. When the tenant abandons the premises, the landlord retains the right to payment of rent for the duration of the lease period. It should be noted that the landlord is not obligated to mitigate this loss, at least in commercial tenancies, by finding a new tenant until the expiration of the lease period. The landlord also has the right to seize any property left by the tenant and hold it until the rent is paid or to sell the tenant's property to pay the rent owing. This power to seize the tenant's property is called distress and is usually modified in residential tenancy legislation. Because the lease arrangement is primarily contractual, the landlord also has the right to sue for monetary compensation whenever the lease is breached. In most circumstances, compensation amounts to the rent due. However, if damage has been done to the premises, the landlord can seek compensation for the cost of repairs. Injunction is another important remedy available for both landlord and tenant when the terms of the lease are breached. When either party is acting in a way inconsistent with the terms of the lease, the courts will not tolerate a refusal to honour lease obligations and will issue an order that such activity stop. Thus, when a tenant is misusing the premises and causing damage to them, the landlord can get an injunction to prevent the misuse of the property.

The remedies available to the tenant for the landlord's breach of the lease are more limited. The tenant is generally entitled either to sue the landlord for compensation for any injury suffered because of the breach or to seek an injunction. The tenant is not entitled to withhold rent to force the landlord's compliance with the lease obligations. But if the landlord's breach is significant enough to qualify as a breach of a major contractual term, the tenant may be entitled to treat the lease agreement as discharged and vacate the premises voluntarily, thus terminating the lease. For example, if the lease agreement requires the landlord to provide heat and water and those services are turned off, this would probably be a significant enough breach for the tenant to terminate the agreement. In any case, the tenant always retains the right to seek a court order that the lease be declared as ended or the tenant's obligation to pay rent be reduced because of the landlord's breach.

Landlord can sue for compensation when lease breached

Landlord can seize tenant's property when lease breached

Residential Tenancies

In a residential tenancy, a tenant rents or leases premises for the purposes of acquiring living accommodation. The common law provisions are the same whether the tenancy is commercial or residential, but the majority of provinces have passed legislation putting in place unique provisions dealing with residential tenancies. In some provinces, such legislation is included in the general landlord and tenant act. In most provinces, one or more special statutes have been passed dealing with different aspects of residential tenancy, for example, in Ontario, the *Landlord and Tenant Act*[11] and the *Residential Rent Regulation Act*.[12] These statutes not only alter the rights and obligations of the landlord and tenant but in some cases also introduce rent controls and establish administrative tribunals in the form of a rentalsman or rent review commission to handle disputes which normally would fall under the jurisdiction of the courts. Generally, the removal of landlord and tenant disputes from the courts has been advantageous to both landlord and tenants. The rights of the parties before such administrative tribunals are discussed in Chapter 16. In many cases, the residential tenancy legislation restricts the number of rental increases that can be imposed to one per year and many acts restrict the amount of increase to a certain percentage of the normal monthly rent.[13] Such an interference with the free market system has drastic implications that affect not only the profits available but also the amount of residential accommodation available on the market.[14] Readers are encouraged to study the legislation in their own jurisdictions to determine whether rent control provisions are in effect and their nature.

Another important provision of residential tenancy legislation is the requirement that the tenant be given significant notice of any intention to increase the rent. Under common law, the period normally required would be one clear month, but the residential tenancy statutes usually increase this to three months.[15] Similarly, residential tenancy legislation typically increases the amount of notice to be given when the landlord wants the tenant to vacate the premises. This period is one month under common law, although some provinces have increased this to three months.[16] Many provinces have extended the notice period still further when the landlord requires the premises for some specific purpose, such as for personal use or for conversion to condominiums.[17] In most cases, the required notice the tenant needs to give is one month.

Residential tenancy statutes also significantly alter the general obligations of the landlord and tenant. Many impose an obligation on the landlord to keep the property in good repair, to live up to the local health and safety bylaw standards, and to maintain the services that have been provided, such as laundry facilities and parking. Legislation protects the privacy of the tenant by restricting the landlord's

---

[11] *Landlord and Tenant Act*, R.S.O. (1990) c.L.7
[12] *Residential Rent Regulation Act*, R.S.O. (1990) c.R.29, as amended by S.O. (1991) c.4
[13] *Residential Rent Regulation Act*, R.S.O. (1990) c.R.19, as amended by S.O. (1991) c.4
[14] British Columbia has dismantled its rent control legislation, *Residential Tenancy Act*, S.B.C. (1984) c.15.
[15] *Residential Tenancy Act*, S.B.C. (1984) c.15 s.18(2)
[16] *Residential Tenancies Act*, R.S.N.S. (1989) c.401 s. 10(1).
[17] *Residential Tenancy Act*, R.S.A. (1980) c.L-6 s.10

right to enter the premises even in the face of provisions in the lease to the contrary. The landlord can usually only enter the premises without notice when the tenant has abandoned those premises or in the case of an emergency. After giving the tenant notice, the landlord can enter for purposes of inspection or to do repair work, but even this access is restricted to normal daylight hours. Most residential tenancy statutes require that a tenant be given a copy of a written lease before its provisions are binding.

In recent years, landlords have started taking large security deposits from tenants to ensure that the rent is paid and that funds are available to repair damage done to the property. This practice can easily be abused and most provinces have introduced severe restrictions on the landlord's right to require security deposits. The amount of the security deposit is generally limited to the equivalent of one month's rent or less.[18] These statutes also require the landlord to pay out specific interest on security deposits in their possession. In some provinces, the security deposit is to secure the payment of the last month's rent rather than provide security for damage. In those jurisdictions the tenant obtains repayment simply by not paying the last month's rent after giving notice of leaving. When it is a damage deposit, however, the tenant must pay the last month's rent and apply for the return of the security deposit. Many provinces have also imposed an obligation on landlords to mitigate their losses when the tenant abandons the premises. In these jurisdictions, after abandonment by the tenant, the landlord is not free to let the lease period run out and then try to retain the security deposit or seek out the tenant for further payment. Rather, once the premises have been abandoned, a landlord must try to rent them so that losses are kept to a minimum. Landlords of residential premises in many jurisdictions are not permitted to seize the personal property of tenants for unpaid rent but may be allowed to take goods that have been left after the tenant has abandoned the property.

The tenant is required to maintain reasonable health and cleanliness standards and repair any damage caused. It may be possible for the tenant to assign or sublet the lease but the landlord is usually given the right to veto this course of action as long as the consent to sublease or assign is not unreasonably withheld. There have been significant changes to the common law in the field of residential tenancies. These changes seem to favour the tenant, but they should be viewed as a form of consumer protection legislation designed to prevent the serious abuses that have occurred in the past in landlord and tenant relationships.

Amount of security deposit restricted by statute

MORTGAGES

The purchase of real property usually involves significant funds which the purchaser often has to borrow to finance the purchase. To secure such a loan, the borrower will normally mortgage the property which involves temporarily transferring title in the property to the creditor as security for the funds advanced. Upon proper repayment, the creditor will reconvey the title. However, if there is a default, the

---

[18] *Residential Tenancies Act*, R.S.N.S. (1989) c.401 s.12(2).

creditor's title in the real property gives the creditor first claim on that property above other creditors. The terminology used to designate the parties to such transactions can be confusing. The person who conveys the title (grants the mortgage) is the one borrowing the money (the mortgagor). The creditor is on the receiving end of the transfer of the title and is called the mortgagee.

Originally, the mortgagee took the title and possession of the land. This was inconvenient for both the lender and the borrower, and the practice soon developed by which the creditor held title but the debtor retained possession of the property used as security for the loan. In the event of default, the creditor had the right, because of title, to take possession of the property as well. Still, problems were associated with the process. Since the mortgagees had title, they could take the land upon default, but the debtors still had to pay back the loan even though they had lost their land. Subsequent developments of the law of mortgages, especially in the courts of chancery, were intended to overcome these problems and have resulted in a unique body of law.

EQUITY OF REDEMPTION. The law relating to mortgages is a significant example of how the courts of chancery stepped in to relieve the harshness or unfairness of the common law. In this instance, a mortgagor's rights in relation to the property were completely extinguished by a failure to make a payment. The courts of chancery recognized that the mortgagor had a continuing claim or right in relationship to that property. This right consisted of a right to redeem the property by paying the money owed plus any expenses involved. This right to redeem became known as the **equity of redemption** and it bestows on the mortgagor an interest in the land which goes beyond the basic contractual responsibility established between the parties. Most business people use the term equity to describe the value of the interest they have in a particular asset after subtracting any money owed on it. Thus, if Nagai has property valued at $100 000 and owes $60 000 on it, Nagai would have a $40 000 equity in the property. Assume Nagai has property valued at $100 000 and has a mortgage from Dhillon for $60 000, and Nagai fails to make the appropriate payments. Although Dhillon will have the right to obtain the title to the property, Nagai will have the right to redeem that property by making the $60 000 payment plus any expenses and interest. Since the value of the property is $100 000 and the cost of redeeming it is $60 000, the value of this right to redeem is $40 000. This value is properly termed the equity of redemption, which has been reduced to the term equity in modern usage.

FORECLOSURE. The mortgagor's right to reclaim the land by making the appropriate payment even after default was unfair because no time limit was established in which the mortgagor had to exercise the right of redemption. Therefore, as long as the mortgagee held the property after taking possession, the mortgagor had the right to redeem the property by making the appropriate payments. This could be very disruptive to the mortgagee since, theoretically, it could be exercised twenty or thirty years later, leaving the mortgagee in an uncertain condition. The courts of chancery devised a simple solution to deal with this problem. The mortgagee simply went to the courts and asked them to establish a time limit within which the mortgagor's right to redeem had to be exercised. If the mortgagor failed to pay within that time, an order could be obtained from the court which forever foreclosed the mortgagor from exercising that right to redeem. The process of foreclosure consists of the courts imposing a time limit on the defaulting mortgagor within which action must be taken to pay off the debt and reclaim the property. Failure to do so within that time period forecloses the mortgagor from exercising a right to redeem. This combination—a right to redeem on the part of the mortgagor and a right to obtain foreclosure on the part of the mortgagee—has worked well and is the system in place in Canada today.

Mortgagee can foreclosure the right to redeem

The process of obtaining foreclosure has two stages. Upon default, the mortgagee goes to the court and asks the court for an order establishing the time limit within which the mortgagor can redeem (called an *order nisi*). This time limit will vary with the circumstances and from jurisdiction to jurisdiction, although it is usually not more than six months. If the property is not redeemed within the designated period, the mortgagee returns to court and asks the court for a final order of foreclosure (called an *order absolute*). This order, once obtained, prevents any further exercise of the equity of redemption on the part of the mortgagor. It should be mentioned that even then, in most jurisdictions, the court retains the discretionary right to reopen the redemption period if the circumstances warrant. Once the property has been resold to a third party or once the order absolute is registered and a new certificate of title has been issued in a land titles system, the original owner no longer has a right to redeem the property.

Foreclosure is a two-stage process

It is important to note that the form of registration of mortgages is quite distinct with a land titles system. The theory is that the actual title transfers from mortgagor to the mortgagee when a mortgage takes place. In a Torrens Systems jurisdiction, the actual registration process does not show this transfer. The certificate of title establishing the fee simple interest in the property remains in the name of the mortgagor. The interest of the mortgagee is merely noted as a charge against the property, as an easement or a leasehold interest would be. But since the nature of the charge indicated on the title document is a mortgage, the rights bestowed by such a charge in the event of default are those of a mortgage as established by the common law. Thus, the mortgagee (chargeholder) has the right in the event of default to start the foreclosure process. In the event of the property not being redeemed before the time limit specified, the mortgagee has the right to have a new certificate of title created with the mortgagee identified as the new holder of the fee simple on a certificate of title. In other words, while the method of recording the relationship in the land registry in the provinces using the Torrens System might be different, the effect is the same.

In Torrens Systems jurisdictions, a mortgage is registered as charge on title

THE SECOND MORTGAGE. Once the courts of chancery recognized a right to redeem on the part of the mortgagor, in effect they said that the mortgagor retained an interest in the property. This interest was something of value that the mortgagor could transfer or sell to others. Nothing prevents a mortgagor of property, even after a mortgage has been granted on it to another person, from granting a

Mortgagor can
use right to
redeem as
security—second
mortgage

second mortgage to someone else by transferring the equity of redemption. Since the title itself was transferred the first time the property was mortgaged and the right to redeem is an equitable remedy created by the courts of chancery, any subsequent mortgages after this first mortgage are called equitable mortgages. But even after a second mortgage is created, the mortgagor has a similar right to redeem by paying off the second and first mortgages. Thus, the mortgagor retains the right to redeem the right to redeem. In this way, a third, fourth and fifth mortgage can be created. The mortgagor always has a right to redeem any mortgage interest that has been created.

It should be obvious that the more mortgages involved, the weaker the security, so anything beyond first, second and third mortgages is rare. To illustrate, if Redekop buys a new home and finances the purchase with a mortgage, the title to the home would be conveyed to Johal, the mortgagee, as security for the loan obtained. If the house were valued at $150 000 and this first mortgage was for $75 000, Redekop would retain a $75 000 equity of redemption interest in the property. This amount might not be enough money to buy the property and Redekop might want to borrow more. Redekop could then go through the same procedure, this time transferring the equity of redemption to a second mortgagee. If the amount borrowed this time is $30 000, Redekop would obtain the $30 000 and the creditor would obtain a second mortgage as security against the property. But Redekop would still retain a right to redeem the property from the second mortgagee. The value of that right to redeem would be $45 000 ($150 000 − $75 000 − $30 000 = $45 000). In other words, Redekop's right to redeem the right to redeem, or the equity in the property, is valued at $45 000. There is no reason why Redekop could not grant a third or fourth or additional mortgage on the property if somebody was willing to take them.

Power to
foreclose
increases risk to
second
mortgagee

There is considerably greater risk associated with a second or third mortgage since the first mortgagee has the right to foreclose the equity of redemption upon default by the mortgagor. Remember that the second and third mortgages have been based on the equity of redemption and if the first mortgagee is successful in obtaining foreclosure, the second and third mortgagees will be stripped of any interest or claim they have against the property. The second and third mortgagees must be prepared to buy out any mortgagee whose mortgage comes before them in this process. In the example above, if Redekop gave Johal a $75 000 first mortgage on the property and Nelson a $30 000 second mortgage, Nelson must be prepared to pay out the $75 000 owing on the first mortgage to protect his interest if Redekop defaults. This puts any subsequent mortgagees in a very vulnerable position. As a result, higher rates of interest are charged for second and third mortgages.

In a land titles jurisdiction, the first, second and third mortgages are listed on the certificate of title as charges against the property and the order of priority is established by the order in which they have been registered. This priority between mortgage holders is established by the date of registration rather than by the date of creation of the mortgage. In other jurisdictions in Canada which require interest in land to be registered, the rights of mortgagees will also be determined by the time of registration of their interest at the appropriate land registry office. The prompt registration of mortgages is vital in both systems. The whole purpose of a registration system is to notify people who are acquiring interest in land of other claims against the property. Those other interests must be registered to be effective and a person who fails to properly register an interest in a property will lose priority to any person who acquires an interest in that property afterwards and does register it. If Redekop grants Johal a first mortgage against his property and then grants Nelson a second mortgage, Johal will have priority over Nelson if both have been registered. However, if Johal neglects to register his mortgage interest and Nelson is not otherwise informed about it, Nelson is said to be a *bona fide* third party and is not affected by Johal's unregistered first mortgage. Nelson would gain priority over Johal's interests in the event of Redekop's default. It is only if Nelson has notice of Johal's prior interest that she will not be able to claim priority.

Remedies Upon Default

The process of foreclosure is just one of the remedies available to the mortgagee when the mortgagor has failed to live up to the terms of the mortgage agreement. In addition to the requirement that the mortgagee make the specified payments, including principal and interest as set out in the agreement, the mortgagor has other obligations. Mortgage contracts usually include an obligation on the mortgagor to insure the property. A considerable amount of the value on any property is often tied up in the buildings attached to it which are susceptible to damage or destruction. To protect the value of the security for the mortgagee, the mortgagor must take out insurance so that there is adequate compensation to ensure repayment of the mortgage if the property is damaged.

Similarly, the mortgagor usually has an obligation in the mortgage agreement to pay property taxes. Legislation gives municipal governments the right to seize property and sell it to pay the back taxes when taxes are not paid. This would defeat the security of the mortgagee, so the mortgagee can insist that such tax payments are made, either by requiring that the mortgagor make the payments to the mortgagee and the mortgagee pay the taxes, or that the mortgagor produce proof that the taxes have been paid. Similar provisions require the mortgagor to keep any buildings on the property in good repair as well as refraining from doing anything to the land or buildings to reduce their value (called waste). Although the most common method of breaching a mortgage agreement is failure to make the appropriate payments to the mortgagee, a breach of any of these terms will constitute default and entitle the mortgagee to seek a remedy. The following is a summary of the types of remedies available to the mortgagee.

SUING ON THE COVENANT. As with other types of contracts involving security, a mortgage agreement contains a covenant to repay the amount borrowed; the creditor has the option to ignore the security and simply sue on that promise of repayment. This right to sue on the personal covenant is available in most jurisdictions, and the mortgagor must submit to the judgment of the court if the creditor chooses to exercise this right. It should be noted that in most jurisdictions the right to foreclosure is lost when the mortgagee follows this course of action because the two remedies are inconsistent. Once foreclosure has taken place and the mortgagee wants

Creditor can sue for breach of contract

to sue on the covenant, he or she must be prepared to reconvey the property back to the mortgagor. As well, this is the reason why the mortgagee cannot sue for a deficit when the property has been foreclosed and then sold for less than was owing. Because the mortgagee has sold the property, it cannot be reconveyed to the mortgagor. The most valuable asset of the mortgagor is usually the property that has been used as security. Although it is usually requested in the judgment, it is only when it is used in conjunction with a remedy such as claiming for the deficit still owing after a judgment sale that the remedy of suing on a person's covenant to repay will actually be pursued.

Contract usually provides for right to sell property upon default

POWER OF SALE. In almost all cases, the contract embodying the mortgage will contain a term giving the mortgagee the right to sell the property upon default without going to court first. The exercise of this power will often give rise to a dispute between the mortgagor and mortgagee which will affect the rights of the ultimate purchaser of that property. Realizing this problem, most purchasers insist on a court authorization of the sale. Although this power of sale is present in most mortgage agreements, it is seldom used.

Right to take possession upon default

POSSESSION. The mortgagee also has the right to ask the court for an order giving him or her possession of the property upon default of payment. The problem with this course of action is that any profits earned through the property must be accounted for and given to the mortgagor upon redemption. Nor is the mortgagee entitled to compensation for any expenses incurred in looking after the property, such as the cost of a caretaker. If any damage is done to the property while the mortgagee is in possession, the mortgagee is responsible to compensate the mortgagor upon redemption. The mortgagee will generally not seek an order of possession of the property if it appears that redemption is likely because of the responsibilities involved. Only where the property has been abandoned or is in danger of deterioration for some other reason will this course of action be used.

Foreclosure is most common remedy used

FORECLOSURE. This remedy was discussed earlier but it must be pointed out that its availability varies with the jurisdiction. For example, foreclosure is only available in Manitoba after attempts to sell the property by the court fail.[19] In other jurisdictions, the process of foreclosure is the usual course embarked on by the mortgagee in the event of default by the mortgagor. However, in the process, all interested parties including the mortgagor and second and third mortgagees must be notified of the foreclosure, giving them opportunity to seek other remedies, which usually results in a court-ordered sale rather than a foreclosure.

JUDICIAL SALE. This important but often misunderstood remedy involves an application to the court by the mortgagee for an order that the property be sold under the court's supervision with the object of assisting the mortgagee to recover as much money as possible. The actual procedure of the sale varies from province to province. In some jurisdictions, the property is sold at public auction. In others, the responsibility to conduct the sale will be given to the party who has the incentive to obtain the

---

[19] *Real Property Act*, R.S.M. (1988) c.R-30 s.138(2).

highest reasonable price, usually the second or third mortgagee, depending on the value of the equity. The property is sold through a realtor in the normal way and when a purchaser is found, the parties return to the court and the court gives its consent to the sale. It is important to understand the effect of this remedy. If the first mortgagee goes into court and asks for foreclosure, the judge will usually grant a six-month redemption period during which the mortgagor will have six months to redeem the property. The problem is that on the same day and in the same action the second mortgagee will usually ask the court for an order for a judicial sale, and an order will usually be granted if the market value of the property is high enough to allow some payment to the second mortgagee. This order is designed to protect the financial position of the second mortgagee since foreclosure will destroy any claim he or she has in the property along with the mortgagor's interest. Thus, the person who acquires the order for the judicial sale obtains the right to have the property sold, not in six months but immediately. The timing of the judicial sale varies with the jurisdiction and the process involved, but it must take place before the end of the redemption period. It is obvious that the effect of such a successful judicial sale is to shorten the period available to the mortgagor to redeem the property.

Court will authorize sale during redemption period

In some provinces, the only practical remedy available to the mortgagor is to ask the court to sell the property. In every province, the mortgagor has the right to sell the property during the redemption period as long as the purchase price is high enough to cover the amount owed to the mortgagee. If the property has been sold by judicial sale and the total amount of money realized from the sale is less than the total amount owing on the mortgages, including accumulated interest and other costs, the original mortgagor will get nothing and will be still liable to pay out any outstanding amounts. If the amount obtained is more than the total amount owing, including costs, the mortgagor will be given any excess. The remedy of foreclosure, on the other hand, involves the seizure of the property and obtaining title rather than the payment of compensation. When this remedy is used and the property is sold for more than is owing, the mortgagee is not required to pay over any excess to the mortgagor. For example, if Morelli were to buy a home and grant a mortgage of $100 000 to Holberg and a second mortgage of $25 000 to Deegan, and default on the payments, Holberg would probably foreclose. Deegan could either take over the payments and foreclose himself or ask for an order for judicial sale at the same time that Holberg first goes to court to begin the foreclosure process. If the property is sold and the total amount of the sale is only $120 000, then Holberg will get $100 000 plus any interest, charges and costs, and Deegan will get the remainder. Since the amount of the sale will not cover all the money owed to Deegan, plus interest and other costs, Deegan will then turn to Morelli and sue for any outstanding balance. Morelli will be required to pay Deegan, which may jeopardize any other assets he possesses. However, if the value of Morelli's property is $100 000 and he borrows $50 000 from Holberg secured by a first mortgage, and no second mortgage is involved, Holberg will likely initiate the foreclosure process if Morelli defaults. If the redemption period expires and a final order is obtained, and Holberg then sells the property for $90 000, he will not be required to pay any of this windfall profit to Morelli in most jurisdictions. To avoid this loss, Morelli will probably make

Where judicial sale takes place— mortgagee can sue for deficit

great efforts to refinance and redeem his title in the property or sell during the redemption period. In most situations, therefore, the property is either redeemed by the mortgagor or is sold under the supervision of the court. While the other remedies are available, they are rarely used.

SUMMARY

Real property is land and things attached to it. The right to exclusive use of the land is called an estate and the fee simple estate is comparable to complete ownership of the land. The right to use the land for life is a life estate and, for a specific period, a leasehold estate. Easements, restrictive covenants and, in some cases, licences, constitute lesser interests in land. When property is held jointly and one of the parties dies, the other takes the whole property by right of survivorship. In a tenancy in common, however, the separate interests remain apart even with death. The land registry systems provide a depository of documents that may affect the title and interested parties must search those documents to determine the state of the title. The land titles system of registration goes further. Where in use, the government provides a certificate of title that is conclusive proof of the interests affecting the title of the land.

Leasehold estates involve landlord and tenant relationships. Commercial tenancies, although provincial statutes are usually in place, are governed primarily by the common law. Residential tenancies, however, have been significantly modified by statute. Changes include the notice that must be given by the landlord to increase rent or terminate a lease as well as the obligations of the parties to repair or pay security deposits. Rent controls are in place in some jurisdictions.

A mortgage involves the title to the property being transferred to a creditor/mortgagee as security for a loan. The debtor/mortgagor retains a right to redeem the property. This equity of redemption can also be mortgaged, creating an equitable second or third mortgage. In the event of default, the creditor seeks a foreclosure order which forecloses or ends the mortgagor's right to redeem. The second mortgagee in such circumstances will usually seek an order for judicial sale of the property to ensure some payment before the operation of the foreclosure order takes effect.

QUESTIONS

1. What does the purchaser get when he or she buys a house?
2. Distinguish between personal and real property.
3. What is meant by a fee simple estate in land?
4. Explain the rights and obligations of reversion and remainder when discussing a life estate.

5. Explain and contrast life estates and leasehold estates.
6. What is meant by an easement? Give examples and explain why an easement is called a lesser interest in land.
7. Explain the significance of a dominant and servient tenement when dealing with easements.
8. What is meant by a restrictive covenant? Under what circumstances will such a covenant be binding on subsequent landowners? How does this relate to a building scheme?
9. Contrast a tenancy in common with a joint tenancy and indicate how one can be changed to another. Why is the distinction important?
10. How can failure to properly register a mortgage or deed affect the initial parties to an instrument in a registration jurisdiction? What happens when an innocent third party becomes involved?
11. How is a leasehold right different from the rights of a resident created under a licence agreement?
12. Under what circumstances must a leasehold interest be evidenced in writing? Why?
13. What is a periodic tenancy? How does it compare to an ordinary lease arrangement? What special problems come into play with periodic tenancies which are not present with term leases?
14. Explain what is meant by a landlord's obligation to ensure a tenant's "quiet enjoyment."
15. What is meant by mortgage, equity of redemption and foreclosure? Distinguish between the mortgagor and mortgagee.
16. Compare the terms "equity of redemption" and "equity in property."
17. What is mortgaged when a second or third mortgage is created? Explain how the risk of a second or third mortgagee is greater than for the first mortgagee.
18. How is the registration of mortgages handled differently under a land titles (Torrens) system of land registry as opposed to the registration system in place in the rest of Canada? Why is the time of registration of a mortgage significant in all jurisdictions in Canada?

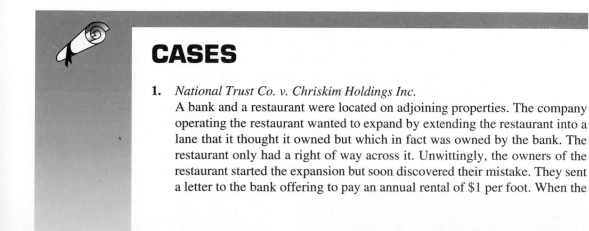

CASES

1. *National Trust Co. v. Chriskim Holdings Inc.*
    A bank and a restaurant were located on adjoining properties. The company operating the restaurant wanted to expand by extending the restaurant into a lane that it thought it owned but which in fact was owned by the bank. The restaurant only had a right of way across it. Unwittingly, the owners of the restaurant started the expansion but soon discovered their mistake. They sent a letter to the bank offering to pay an annual rental of $1 per foot. When the

bank did not accept this offer, instead of stopping, they continued with the construction. The bank sued. The restaurant counter-sued. It seems that a mistake had been made when the bank was built. It encroached slightly onto the property owned by the restaurant. The restaurant had been leasing the property since 1983 and had purchased it in 1987. Before this time, however, the former owner had used that right of way since 1952. The bank building had been at its location since 1967. Explain the obligations and rights of the parties to each other in these circumstances and the arguments available to each in defending their positions. Would your answer be any different if this had taken place in a land titles jurisdiction?

2. Re *Ramsay and Heselmann.*
   The appellant was the owner of a property consisting of twelve furnished rooms, one of which was rented to the respondent. Rent was paid weekly. The respondent failed to make proper payments and the appellant seized her clothing and personal effects as security for the non-payment of rent. (The *Innkeepers' Act* allows an innkeeper or boardinghouse-keeper to seize goods in this way. The *Landlord and Tenant Act* (RSO 1980 Chapter 232) does not allow a landlord a similar right.) The respondent has brought this action, applying for a declaration that her goods and personal effects have been wrongfully seized. Explain the arguments on both sides and the likely outcome of the case.

3. *The Toronto-Dominion Bank v. Faulkner et al.*
   Mr. Faulkner, a lawyer, owned property in the town of Goldbourn which he mortgaged to the Toronto-Dominion Bank as security for a loan of $50 000. Two years later Faulkner physically moved the house from this location to a piece of property in another town (West Carlton) which was owned by his wife. Faulkner and his wife mortgaged the second property with its relocated house to Crown Trust Company for $55 000. The problem here is to determine which of the two mortgagees is entitled to priority in relation to the house. Explain the legal position of the parties and the arguments to support the parties' claims.

4. *Hermanson v. Martin et al.*
   The plaintiff and her husband jointly owned the matrimonial home. The plaintiff moved away after their divorce and her husband sold the house to the defendant, Martin. To do this, he used a female accomplice to forge his former wife's signature on the transfer. Martin had no knowledge of this forgery. The transfer was appropriately registered and only then did the ex-wife find out about the fraud. Explain the courses of action which are available to her and any arguments which can be raised on either side. Where might she turn for compensation for any loss she incurs? These events happened in a land titles jurisdiction. Would your answer be different if this problem had arisen in a standard registration jurisdiction?

5. *Household Realty Corporation v. Michalow et al.*
   The defendant (the mortgagor) owned property which he had used as security for a first, second and third mortgage. He defaulted on the second mortgage and then made arrangements with the second mortgagee to overcome the default, thus bringing the mortgagor back to good standing in relationship to the second mortgagee. The third mortgagee relied on a provision of the mortgage contract which stated, "if the mortgagor makes default in the performance of covenants or conditions in any prior mortgage secured upon the said lands, then the entire unpaid balance hereby secured together with interest shall at the option of the mortgagee become due and payable without notice or demand," and commenced foreclosure action. Explain what defences are available to the mortgagor, the arguments which the third mortgagee will use in response and the likely outcome.

ISSUES

1. Most jurisdictions have passed condominium legislation which allows a person to own an apartment in a building. However, there are some distinct differences about this type of ownership. Such a unique approach to ownership was required because of the need to deal with the division of condominium units vertically rather than the more traditional method of dividing real property interests horizontally in relation to the land. Consider whether it is appropriate to apply such real property notions of ownership to condominium units. In your answer, consider the necessary relationships in the condominium organization that make it more like rental accommodation than ownership.

2. The traditional roles of landlord and tenant gave the parties the right to create almost any type of right in relationship to the premises through agreement and inclusion in a lease. Usually the parties created a periodic tenancy (month-to-month). Certain rules were imposed on the parties such as the requirement that one month be given for termination or rent increase, and that there was no obligation for repairs etc. Many of the provinces have passed legislation modifying these common law provisions dealing with residential tenancies. They usually include an imposition of a longer term of notice to vacate, restrictions on what grounds such notice to vacate can be based on, longer notice periods for rent increase and the control or prohibition of such rent increases. Are these changes in common law with reference to residential tenancies an unwarranted interference in the free market system? Would we be better off to stay with the common law provisions and let the

marketplace control the abuses? In your response, consider the changes which have been made, whether or not rent controls should be in place and whether the obligation to repair the premises ought to be divided between landlord and tenant. Consider as well the steps taken in British Columbia to repeal rent control legislation.

3. When the mortgagor defaults, the mortgagee has the right to foreclose against the property. This right exists even if the mortgagor has a considerable equity in the property. If the mortgagor resells that property after the foreclosure process is completed and makes a profit on the deal, in most jurisdictions he or she is not required to pay over any profit made to the mortgagor. Should a mortgagee ever be permitted to foreclose and obtain title to the property when the mortgagor still has a significant equity in it? Consider the arguments in support of both the mortgagee and mortgagor, as well as the fact that some jurisdictions have severely restricted the availability of foreclosure by not permitting foreclosure until after judicial sale has been attempted. Does this restriction solve the problem?

4. When the mortgagor begins the foreclosure process, the mortgagor is usually given a specific time in which to redeem the property, for example, six months. However, a second mortgagee will generally be able to obtain an order for a judicial sale of the property. The effect of this order is to put into place a mechanism whereby attempts are made to sell the property right away. The property can be sold within a month, requiring the mortgagor to vacate the premises long before the redemption period has expired. Much criticism has been levelled at this process on the grounds that it effectively shortens the period available to the mortgagor to redeem the property. Discuss the arguments which can be raised both for and against the remedy of judicial sale when the foreclosure process has been initiated. Consider the matter from the point of view of the mortgagor and both the first and second mortgagees.

5. Two major systems of land registry are in place in Canada today. One is the standard system whereby a registry is created to house the title documents of property. It is then left to those interested in the property to search the documents to determine the state of the title. Some provinces use the Torrens System which is a system of guaranteed title. That is, title is determined by the government agency. A certificate of title is issued and that certificate of title is a guaranteed summary of the state of the title of the property. Discuss the advantages and disadvantages of each system. The Torrens System of land registry was devised to overcome some of the disadvantages of the common law system of land holdings and the standard registration system that was introduced to augment it. Does it do a good job?

LEGISLATION

Alberta
Condominium Property Act, R.S.A. (1980) c.C-22
Dower Act, R.S.A. (1980) c.D-38
Family Relief Act, R.S.A. (1980) c.F-2
Land Titles Act, R.S.A. (1980) c.L-5
Landlord and Tenant Act, R.S.A. (1980) c.L-6
Landlord's Rights on Bankruptcy Act, R.S.A. (1980) c.L-7
Law of Property Act, R.S.A. (1980) c.L-8
Mobile Home Sites Tenancies Act, R.S.A. (1980) c.-18.5
Residential Tenancies Act, R.S.A. (1980) c.R-15.3

British Columbia
Commercial Tenancy Act, R.S.A. (1980) c.54
Condominium Act, R.S.A. (1980) c.61
Land Act, R.S.B.C. (1979) c.214
Land (Spouse Protection) Act, R.S.A. (1980) c.223
Land Title Act, R.S.A. (1980) c.219
Property Law Act, R.S.A. (1980) c.340
Rent Distress Act, R.S.A. (1980) c.362
Residential Tenancy Act, R.S.A. (1980) c.15

Manitoba
Condominium Act, R.S.A. (1980) c.C-170
Dower Act, R.S.A. (1980) c.D-100
Landlord and Tenant Act, R.S.M.(1987) c.L-70
Law of Property Act, R.S.A. (1980) c.L-90
Married Women's Property Act, R.S.A. (1980) c.M-70
Mortgage Act, R.S.A. (1980) c.M-200
Real Property Act, R.S.A. (1980) c.R-30
Residential Tenancies Act, C.C.S.M. R119 (passed in 1990-91)
Short Forms Act, R.S.A. (1980) c.S-120

New Brunswick
Condominium Property Act, R.S.N.B.. (1973) c.C-16
Easements Act, R.S.N.B. (1973) c.E-1
Landlord and Tenant Act, R.S.N.B. (1973) c.L-1
Land Titles Act, S.N.B. (1981) c.L-1.1
Married Woman's Property Act, R.S.N.B. (1973) c.M-4
Property Act, R.S.N.B. (1973) c.P-19
Quieting of Titles Act, R.S.N.B. (1973) c.Q-4
Residential Tenancies Act, S.N.B. (1975) c.R-10.02

Newfoundland
Condominium Act, R.S.N. (1990) c.C-29
Conveyancing Act, R.S.N. (1990) c.C-34
Family Law Act, R.S.N. (1990) c.F-2
Quieting Titles Act, R.S.N. (1990) c.Q-3
Registration of Deeds Act, R.S.N. (1990) c.R-10

Nova Scotia
Condominium Act, R.S.N. (1990) c.85
Conveyancing Act, R.S.N. (1990) c.97
Land Titles Clarification Act, R.S.N. (1990) c.250
Matrimonial Property Act, R.S.N. (1990) c.275
Overholding Tenants Act, R.S.N. (1990) c.329
Quieting Titles Act, R.S.N. (1990) c.382
Real Property Act, R.S.N. (1990) c.385
Rent Review Act, R.S.N. (1990) c.398
Rental Property Conversion Act, R.S.N. (1990) c.399
Residential Tenancies Act, R.S.N. (1990) c.401
Sales of Land Under Execution Act, R.S.N. (1990) c.409
Tenancies and Distress for Rent Act, R.S.N. (1990) c.464
Testators Family Maintenance Act, R.S.N. (1990) c.465
Vendors and Purchasers Act, R.S.N. (1990) c.487

Ontario
Certification of Titles Act, R.S.O. (1990) c.C.6
Condominium Act, R.S.O. (1990) c.C.26
Conveyancing and Law of Property Act, R.S.O. (1990) c.C.34
Land Titles Act, R.S.O. (1990) c.L.5
Landlord and Tenant Act, R.S.O. (1990) c.L-7
Mortgages Act, R.S.O. (1990) c.M.40
Mortgages Amendment Act, S.O. (1991) c.M.6
New Home Warranties Plan Act, R.S.O. (1990) c.Q.31
Partition Act, R.S.O. (1990) c.P.4
Perpetuities Act, R.S.O. (1990) c.P.9
Rental Housing Protection Act, S.O. (1989) c.R.31
Residential Rent Regulation Act, R.S.O. (1990) c.R.29
Short Forms of Lease Act, R.S.O. (1990) c.S.11
Vendors and Purchasers Act, R.S.O. (1990) c.V.2

Prince Edward Island
Condominium Act, R.S.P.E.I. (1988) c.C-16
Family Law Reform Act, R.S.P.E.I. (1988) c.F-3
Landlord and Tenants Act, R.S.P.E.I. (1988) c.L-4

Quieting Titles Act, R.S.P.E.I. (1988) c.Q-2
Real Property Act, R.S.P.E.I. (1988) c.R-3
Rental of Residential Property Act, R.S.P.E.I. (1988) c.R-13.1

Québec
Expropriation Act, R.S.Q. (1977) c.E-24

Saskatchewan
Condominium Property Act, R.S.S. (1978) c.C-26
Distress Act, R.S.S. (1978) c.D-31
Equality of Status of Married Persons Act, S.S. (1984-85-86) c. E-10.3
Homestead Act, S.S. (1989-90) c.H-5.1
Improvements Under Mistake of Title Act, R.S.S. (1978) c.I.1
Land Contract (Actions) Act, R.S.S. (1978) c.L-3
Land Titles Act, R.S.S. (1978) c.L-6
Recovery of Possession of Land Act, R.S.S. (1978) c.R-7
Residential Tenancies Act, R.S.S. (1978) c.R-22
Subdivisions Act, R.S.S. (1978) c.S-62

Northwest Territories
Condominium Act, R.S.N.W.T. (1988) c.C-15
Residential Tenancies Act, R.S.N.W.T. (1988) c.R-5

Yukon
Condominium Act, R.S.Y (1986) c.28
Distress Act, R.S.Y. (1986) c.46
Landlord and Tenant Act, R.S.Y (1986) c.98
Land Titles Act, S.Y. (1991) c.11

Federal
Land Titles Act, R.S.C. (1985) c.L-5
Residential Mortgage Financing Act, R.S.C. (1985) c.R-6

16 ENVIRONMENTAL LAW AND THE REGULATION OF CANADIAN BUSINESS

Objectives of the Chapter

- to describe the source and nature of government powers
- to outline the role of the courts in interpreting statutes
- to examine the government regulatory activities of taxation and licensing, securities and environmental control
- to explain the remedies available when administrative bodies abuse their powers
- to discuss methods used by legislatures to restrict judicial interpretation

The Bata shoe organization is a large company operating several different factories and facilities in southern Ontario. At one of these locations, inspectors from the Ministry of the Environment discovered metal drums leaking industrial waste into the soil. Tests were performed and it was discovered that the ground water had been contaminated. Despite the fact that Bata had shown a willingness to cooperate on environmental matters and that members of the family had made significant contributions to cleaning up the environment, charges were laid against the company and also against the individual directors who were in charge of the sites where the contamination was discovered. The ministry disposed of the offending material with the cooperation of the company and at company expense. Fines were imposed on the company as well as on the individual directors. These fines were reduced somewhat on appeal but the fines remained significant and had to be individually paid by the directors in question. In fact, when the company tried to reimburse the directors for the cost of the fines and legal expenses, the courts prohibited it from doing so. Since the successful action against the directors amounted to a conviction for a wrongful act or an offence, any employment provisions to reimburse them for such expenses were simply void and prohibited.[1]

Environmental concerns have great impact on business

Laws to protect the environment are significant and an important consideration in calculating the cost of doing business. As can be seen from this example, directors and officers of a corporation must carefully consider the risks and the potential costs associated with their positions. Some directors are extremely reluctant to serve on boards of companies where they may experience such exposure. This chapter will discuss the power of government, its regulatory agencies and the rights of people who deal with them.

REGULATORY ROLE OF GOVERNMENT

The commercial and industrial progress of this century has been matched by the growth of government agencies to regulate it. In the last few decades the size of government has expanded at an astonishing rate, intruding into the lives of its citizens, especially in their business activities, in an unprecedented way. Businesses face increasingly stringent government restrictions and regulations, and sometimes in the process government officials abuse their position or go beyond their authority. This chapter will begin with an examination of one of the areas in which government regulation has increased dramatically in recent years and then outline the recourses available to people when government or its agents have infringed on their rights.

Government consists of executive branch, legislative branch and judicial branch

As outlined in Chapter 1, government can be divided into three different functions: the judicial, the legislative and the executive branches. In the United States, care has been taken to keep these three branches separate and the law-making capacity of government is nicely balanced between them. Canada followed the British example of parliamentary supremacy and so, except for the division of powers between the federal parliament and the provincial legislatures, parliamentary bodies are supreme in their assigned areas. Parliamentary supremacy has been modified to some extent by the *Charter of Rights and Freedoms* which limits what parliament, the provincial legislatures and their representatives can do.

---

[1] *R. v. Bata Industries Limited*, (1992) 70 C.C.C. (3rd) 394.

There is little difficulty in distinguishing the judicial branch of government (the courts) from the rest of government activity. However, the legislative branch and the executive branch have become somewhat blurred in Canada. Parliament is the principal law-making body. From that assembly is drawn the prime minister (or premiers at the provincial level) and cabinet ministers. They are the chief executive officers or managers of the country. They are responsible for the various ministries and departments, the employees of which perform the work of government. When people have dealings with government, it is almost always with the executive branch of government and the civil servants who make up its bureaucracy. The executive branch is divided into categories based on primary functions: for example, service agencies such as law enforcement, education and welfare; administrative departments which include revenue, taxation and the internal management of government systems; and regulatory bodies concerned with such matters as the environment, product safety and human rights. There are many areas in which governments exert control over business, but regulations designed to protect the environment are typical of governmental intrusion and an important and growing area of concern for business people. We will begin our look at government regulation from that perspective.

THE PROTECTION OF THE ENVIRONMENT

Environmental concerns vast problem

Our society and the natural world are interdependent in a way that historically has not been recognized in either our economic system or our laws. The production of wealth is the underlining objective of the business world (which the economic system facilitates) and wealth is produced to a large extent through the consumption of natural resources. In the wake of economic progress, forests are stripped, fish stocks are depleted, minerals, oil and gas reserves are exhausted, and great scars are left on the earth in the process. Species of animal life are decimated as they are either directly consumed or their environment is destroyed around them. The by-products of this production in the form of waste materials are discharged into the atmosphere, into the seas and onto the lands, further degrading the environment.

The economic structures that form the basis of business and industry have traditionally not factored in these environmental costs. The range of problems contributing to the environmental crises is vast. From nuclear disasters to automobile emissions, from the disposal of chemical wastes to domestic sewage and from the depletion of the ozone layer to the depletion of the soil—all have serious consequences for the environment. Only recently have we been forced to consider the depletion of the environment as one of the important factors in the economic equation. The law has been even slower to react to these modern realities; it has only been in the last few years that our legislators have considered it necessary to create statutes which introduce some balance into the system. Such statutes have been enacted as the result of public pressure and the urgency of the problems, and in many cases fail to ensure the necessary balance between the production of wealth and the preservation of the environment. Most of the statutes are remedial in nature and are becoming increasingly stringent as the extent of the damage that has already been done to the environment is realized.

Common Law

Common law
protection

The rights of individuals to have property and person protected from pollution and destruction have been recognized for centuries in common law. Through such judge-made law, people who live near rivers are entitled to have the water come to them in undiminished quantity and quality, except for limited domestic usage such as washing, drinking and normal sewage disposal. Such entitlements are called riparian rights. These rights, however, can be overridden by a government permit that allows for the discharge of other waste materials into a river.

—riparian rights

—nuisance

Under tort law and specifically the tort of "private nuisance," people who have adjoining properties have the right not to have their enjoyment and use of their property unreasonably interfered with by their neighbours. Thus, if a person or industry carries on a polluting activity such as burning or operating a smelter which pumps toxic chemicals into the atmosphere or effluent into the land or waterways, the injured neighbour can bring an action for private nuisance against the polluting party. "Public nuisance" has even been used to support actions against those who pollute public waterways and the air. Normally only the Attorney General is able to bring an action for public nuisance but if an individual can show that she was harmed to a greater extent than other members of the general public, she can bring a personal action and seek a remedy such as monetary compensation or an injunction to stop the activity.

Strict liability
under *Rylands v.
Fletcher*

The torts of negligence and trespass can also be used to enforce a person's right not to be interfered with in this way by others, including municipal, provincial and federal government agencies which are to some extent liable for their wrongful conduct in tort law. One of the requirements of tort law generally is that some blameworthy conduct must be involved. That is, either the activity must be intentional or the person doing it must be careless or negligent. *Rylands v. Fletcher*, one of the most important cases in tort law, established that in some special situations people who bring dangerous substances onto their property that escape are responsible for any damages that ensue, whether or not it is their fault that the substance escaped. Such dangerous substances include stored water and chemicals. These torts are an important source of legal rights for people wanting to take action against those interfering with their property or person through pollution. Chapter 2 is devoted to a more in-depth discussion of tort liability. Some of the statutes that are designed to control damage to the environment give individuals the right to sue privately for compensation for personal injuries suffered because of a violation of the statute. In effect, these statutes create a statutory tort, but this is only the case when the statute makes clear that it creates a personal right to seek a remedy. (See, for example, the *Canadian Environmental Protection Act*.)

Statutory Law

Early environmental protection laws are all couched in terms of individual rights rather than a collective obligation not to pollute. An individual rather than the crown must sue and in doing so, he or she must be able to show some personal damage that others have not suffered and must bear the costs in the process. Quebec's civil law contains similar rights to those embodied in our common law, with the same problems of costs and the difficulties associated with enforcement. Because of these inadequacies, the great bulk of the law intended to protect the environment is found in statutes of the federal and provincial governments. One of the main features of these statutes is that polluting activities are generally prohibited. Other provisions allow government to enforce the statutes whether or not individuals have been harmed.

JURISDICTION. A discussion of statutory law must be preceded by an examination of the level of government which has the constitutional jurisdiction to pass environmental laws. Essentially, forests, minerals and fresh water are all local matters and under the jurisdiction of provincial governments. The federal government has power only when the activity becomes international or interprovincial in scope, takes place on federal lands or coastal waters, or when an area specifically assigned to the federal government is involved, such as the military. Of course, the federal government can exercise a considerable amount of control by requiring that provincial environmental projects satisfy federal standards to qualify for federal funding. Furthermore, if the activity becomes a threat to society generally, the federal government can use its power under the *Criminal Code* to declare the activity a criminal offence.

Businesses may face federal and provincial regulation

Both federal and provincial regulatory authorities become involved when businesses initiate projects and activities that have environmental implications. Corporations must receive permits and licences from various levels of government and must submit to environmental regulation. Federally incorporated companies may face regulations in both jurisdictions. Provincial companies engaged in activities that are local in nature deal only with provincial regulatory bodies. In fact, today there is movement towards considerable cooperation between the federal and provincial levels of government in environmental regulation. It is likely that in the future similar legislation will be put in place at both the federal and provincial levels so that one consistent system will prevail throughout Canada. Because this is not yet the case, we will now look at some of the environmental legislation that is characteristic of each jurisdiction.

PROVINCIAL LEGISLATION. All provinces have some form of environmental legislation. The standard type of legislation is a statute creating a ministry or government department which is designed to grant permits and establish standardized codes for the use of natural resources and the elimination of waste products. These departments have inspectors who enforce the standards and assess penalties for violations. In some cases, the rules and regulations are found in general environmental statutes such as the federal *Environmental Protection Act*, or the *Waste Management Act* and the *Environmental Management Act* in British Columbia. In some provinces, however, there are statutes designed to control specific activities such as the *Clean Air Act* or the *Clean Water Act*. Most provinces have also established laws stipulating that hazardous materials must be properly contained and when being transported must be carried in vehicles marked by icons that indicate the type of danger. The disposal of hazardous waste is a particular problem for industries. Even such seemingly innocuous substances as used oil from automobiles and tires can present a tremendous problem. The British Columbia government has established the B.C. Hazardous Waste Corporation to develop a comprehensive system for handling the disposal of hazardous wastes. In all provinces, a bureaucracy has been established to enforce the statutes and businesses must deal with these agencies. In many provinces, the department's mandate has recently been expanded to include the control and imposition of liability for oil and chemical spills.

Federal and provincial departments set standards, educate and enforce

Typically, government agencies concerned with the environment are divided into several different departments. One section requires that permits be obtained before engaging in an activity that causes pollution. Another section is responsible for research and development designed to establish the appropriate standards and identify possible future threats to the environment. A third section is devoted to prevention education, achieving compliance, investigation of violations and prosecutions.

Most provinces have followed the federal example and now require environmental impact statements, although the specific requirements vary from jurisdiction to jurisdiction. In Ontario, for instance, all public undertakings must submit to the assessment process unless they have been specifically exempted, but private undertakings are generally not required to do so unless they are "designated" by the environmental assessment advisory committee.

New tort rights created by statutes

The most recent trend in legislation, found in acts such as the Yukon Territory's *Environment Act* and the Northwest Territories' *Environmental Rights Act*, is the declaration that the people have the right to have their environment free from pollution. These *Acts* allow individuals to take action against the polluter to enforce those rights. The Northwest Territories Act, for instance, allows an individual to bring a private action when someone polluting the environment has committed a statutory offence. Quebec's *Environmental Quality Act* creates a right to a healthy environment which is bestowed on every person in the province and to the protection of living species.

FEDERAL LEGISLATION. The federal government has jurisdiction only in certain areas as set out in the *Constitution Act (1867)* but it has become involved through financing in environmental programs that primarily fall under the jurisdiction of the provinces. One of the purposes of the federal legislation is to help the provinces pay for their environmental programs. With such funding comes control; the federal government can stipulate how the funds will be used and, to some degree, control the extent of the environmental legislation in place in the provinces. The federal *Clean Air Act* controls air pollution throughout Canada. Note that it

Federal regulations control provincial areas through funding

does not prohibit pollution but it does set standards and its regulations must be met. The object is to reduce the maximums set in the regulations gradually to eventually eliminate pollution altogether. The federal *Environmental Protection Act* has become a model for other levels of government to follow. It is a comprehensive act meant to prevent pollution, provide for research and development, investigate and measure pollution levels, and monitor industry.

Another area of federal attention is the handling and disposal of hazardous wastes and material. The *Transportation of Dangerous Goods Act* controls the transport of dangerous chemicals and goods. The *Act* applies when goods are transferred between provinces or between Canada and the United States. Again at the federal level, the *Fisheries Act* with its 1970 amendments is very important because of its provision prohibiting the discharge of any dangerous substances into waterways, lakes and oceans. This *Act* has been used effectively to control the discharge of sewage from municipalities as well as effluent from pulp mills.

Extensive
enforcement
power

Federal and provincial environment statutes grant considerable power for enforcement to the government officials charged with the application of the various statutes, including the power to enter premises, to inspect, to seize documents, to take samples and in some circumstances to order certain activities stopped. But in most cases their power stops short of the right to use force. In fact, except in the most blatant cases of intentional dumping of waste, the enforcement branches find it much more productive to work with the offending business to help it live up to the standards rather than to punish it for failing to do so. Companies may be required not only to refrain from future activities that threaten the environment but may also face prosecution for past uncontrolled dumping and the costs of clean-up. It is not only the companies that face these responsibilities since the statutes often lift the corporate veil, making the directors personally responsible for the offences committed by the corporations they direct. Even secured creditors such as mortgagees and receivers can be held responsible for the cost of such clean-up. It is uncertain just how far this responsibility will go but it is clear that if such secured creditors realize their security by taking possession of the property, the responsibility to clean it up goes with it. Because of this responsibility, many lenders choose not to exercise their security in the face of default.

The penalties in environmental offences have been greatly increased. Under the federal act, fines range up to a million dollars and up to five years in prison. Either the ministers or the directors of the responsible government departments also have the power under these statutes to issue stop orders for any activity that violates the standards established in the regulation. In other circumstances, orders can be issued that direct compliance with the standards. These orders are control orders and are not quite so drastic. In some cases, orders can be issued that require an offender to repair any damage caused by the activity.

A NEW DIRECTION. Following the American example of the *National Environmental Policy Act (1969)*, the trend in Canadian legislation is to impose an environmental assessment review process on those wishing to undertake some new, potentially hazardous, project. The objective is to require the parties proposing the

Environmental
assessment
reviews required

project to file a report with a designated government agency which highlights its potential impact on the environment including any health risks. The government authority studies this report, seeks public input and holds a public hearing to air all of the various points of view. The government authority then decides whether to give its permission for the activity, withhold it or to grant the permit with conditions. Environmental assessment reviews were initially limited to public activities, but the trend is for environmental impact studies to be required for private industrial and resource-based projects as well. As this trend continues, producing such reports will mean a significant increase in the cost of doing business. Such reports are now required not only for large projects such as steel plants, pulp mills, hydro-electric dams and the like but also for smaller types of business activities that use specific types of chemicals or otherwise threaten the environment.

The new federal *Environmental Assessment Act*, proclaimed in September 1993, replaces non-legislated cabinet guidelines and imposes significant obligations of reporting on businesses dealing with the federal government. The proclaimed purposes of the *Act* are the following:

1.   to ensure that the environmental effects of projects receive careful consideration before any action is taken;
2.   to promote sustainable development and thus a healthy environment;
3.   to ensure that projects on federal lands do not cause adverse environmental effects to other lands;
4.   to ensure an opportunity for public participation.

The *Act* requires an environmental assessment for any project done on federal lands, any project the federal government finances, or any project for which it provides a permit or licence. The environmental review process consists of a comprehensive study of the environmental impact of the project, evaluation by a review panel and the implementation of a follow-up program where necessary. The panel also considers the purpose of the project, any alternative means that could be used and their environmental effect, and how renewable resources might be affected. Once approval has been given by the review panel, it issues a certificate and the project can proceed. To ensure public access and involvement, a registry is established to make available all information collected or submitted relative to the environmental review process for the various projects. The *Act* also establishes a federal environmental review agency which advises and assists the minister by administering and promoting the environmental assessment process, encouraging research, promoting uniformity throughout Canada and ensuring an opportunity for public input. In the process, the agency provides administrative support, training and information. This new *Act* is an important step towards establishing an comprehensive process for protecting the environment.

ECONOMY VERSUS ENVIRONMENT. The tendency by government towards increasing interference into business activities in relation to the environment may appear to be an unwarranted and unfair intrusion, but there is considerable justification for it. As our economy worsens and costs increase, businesses sometimes

Environmental
costs threaten
business

have difficulty surviving as profitable enterprises. Pressing bottom line concerns are bound to affect the attention given to environmental issues. As the environment is threatened, businesses become less economically viable and can less afford to take the steps necessary to preserve it. The increased attention that government is paying to the environment may be justified, but it is understandable that the imposition of more government regulation is not popular in business circles. It is usually in this regulatory arena that the clash between government bureaucrats, businesses and private individuals takes place.

The ongoing dispute between the environmental movement and various industries is forcing a reassessment of how government should deal with these matters; business people must not only concern themselves with a costly and interfering regulatory environment but also must contend with uncertainty and flux. Government regulatory officials impose standards, establish environmental screening processes and require reports when any new project is undertaken. An involved process of public hearings and submissions may be required before a licence or permit is granted. Once the project is under way, inspectors may measure compliance and, for industries that are considered dangerous, such inspections become routine. Industries must consider the costs of complying with environmental standards and the costs of prosecution when offences do take place. Even if a site was previously contaminated, modern statutes may require that it be cleaned by or at the expense of the polluter and that compensation be paid to those injured. These statutes may apply even when no regulations were in place at the time the pollution occurred or if the standards in place were lower than they should have been. It is enough to say that the trend is for government departments to become more and more powerfully involved in industrial and other forms of business activity. Almost any business decision must consider the environmental factors and the procedures that are laid down by the government agencies established to protect it, and that all businesses are subject to inspection and prosecution when their day-to-day activities pose a risk to the environment.

Regulations only
part of
environmental
costs

The controversy extends to whether development ought to take place at all—whether the forests ought to be cut down; rivers ought to be dammed; plants ought to be built. The recent example of environmental activists risking jail terms to stop logging in sensitive areas illustrates that the problem is more fundamental than waste disposal and pollution. The impact of these disputes can have a profound effect on businesses to the point of wondering whether they will be able to carry on business at all. A company recently applied to develop a considerable ore deposit in the Tatsensheny Wilderness area; the outcry and pressure were so great that in 1992 the British Columbia government stepped in, declared the area a national park and put an end to the project. The Old Man River hydro-electric project in Saskatchewan has run into many obstacles, all hinging on environmental concerns. Even when government has given approval, concerns and protests are not ended. On the west coast of Vancouver Island, the provincial government gave permission to MacMillan Bloedel to log in the Clayoquot Sound area, but the protests of environmentalists in the area (the arrests have gone into the hundreds) have put great pressure on the government to backtrack from its decision. As our population continues to grow and production grows, the pressure on the environment will increase. These conflicting interests will place greater pressure on businesses in the form of costs and restrictions. Government is the only body that can try to find a balance between these interests and it is hoped that our elected officials will be able to find some compromise or common ground.

Sometimes government officials through ignorance or because the law is uncertain will go beyond the power they have been given or will exercise it improperly. People affected by such actions can enforce their rights, and the methods available to them are outlined in the rest of this chapter.

ADMINISTRATIVE LAW

The relationship between business and the environment is just one of many areas of government regulation that businesses have to contend with. Consumer rights, taxation, competition, labour relations, securities and human rights legislation are other areas in which businesses must deal with government agencies. The resulting paper burden is another of the high costs of doing business. Government officials can and do make decisions that have far-reaching consequences. Not surprisingly, they sometimes make incorrect decisions or otherwise abuse or go beyond their power.

Challenging Government Regulations

Governments function through administrative bodies

As the executive branch of government has grown in recent years, the power of government departments and agencies such as the Unemployment Insurance Commission, the Workers' Compensation Board and the RCMP have been increasing at a significant rate. The officers and employees of government bodies are given the authority to administer their programs. In the process, they make decisions which affect people's lives. Generally, when a bureaucrat is simply making or implementing government policy, an individual's right to challenge the decision is limited unless it can be shown that his or her rights are directly affected. When the decision maker is functioning as a referee or judge, the decision, or the process by which it was arrived at, may be challenged in the courts. A typical example in business is a labour relations board deciding whether a particular union should be certified as the bargaining agent at a factory. Government decision makers are called **administrative tribunals** and the area of law that describes individual rights before them is administrative law. To determine whether the decision of a civil servant or administrative tribunal can be challenged, refer to the two basic principles that govern the actions of decision makers. The decision must be made within the authority of the government official or board and the process involved, as well, the conduct of the decision maker must have been proper.

The Authority of the Decision Maker

A fundamental aspect of the constitutional tradition we took from Britain is the **rule of law**. The rule of law holds that, even given the supremacy of parliament, neither parliament nor any government official representing parliament can act arbitrarily. Professor R.M. Dawson, in *The Government of Canada*, defines the rule of law as "the restriction of arbitrary authority in government, and the necessity for all acts of government to be authorized by reasonably precise laws as applied and interpreted by the courts."[2] This principle is effectively illustrated by J.A. Corry and J.E. Hodgetts in *Democratic Government and Politics*. The authors point out that government officials cannot rely on their status to interfere with the rights of a person but must rely on some empowering legislation to authorize the action. This proposition is summarized in these words: "This state can throw away the conscript's life but it cannot conscript him [or her] in the first instance on the plea of high policy or public expedience except as supported by law sanctioned by parliament."[3] This principle means that a government official or board must be able to point to some valid statute that authorizes the conduct, including any decision reached. If the decision maker has gone beyond this authority the decision can be challenged as being *ultra vires* and it will be set aside.

The first step in the process of challenging an administrative tribunal, then, is to examine the statutory authority and determine if the conduct in question was authorized under it. This statutory authority may be found not only in the statute itself but also in the regulations passed under that statute. While parliament and the provincial legislative assemblies create law primarily through legislation, the resulting statutes often give government institutions such as the Workers' Compensation Board the power to make further rules or regulations under that legislation. These regulations have the same force as the statute under which they were created. When the source of authority for the conduct complained of is in the regulations, it is important to determine not only whether the section relied on does authorize the conduct but also whether these regulations have been made within the statutory authority given to the body creating them. If the regulations have been properly passed as authorized under the statute, they are valid because that body has acted within its power (*intra vires*). But if the regulations were not properly passed, those regulations are invalid and the government body has acted beyond its powers (*ultra vires*). When the conduct complained of is not authorized under the statute or when the regulation itself is invalid, that conduct can be challenged, and the courts will have no hesitation in overturning the decision.

Government agents must act within existing law

Does administer have authority?

Statutory Interpretation

Rules of statutory interpretation

To determine whether a regulation has been properly imposed under the statute in question or whether any other aspect of the statute is being properly enforced, the courts will apply accepted rules of **statutory interpretation**. These rules have de-

[2] Dawson, R. MacGregor, *The Government of Canada*, (4th ed.), University of Toronto Press, 1966, p. 77.
[3] Corry, J.A., and J.E. Hodgetts, *Democratic Government and Politics* (3rd ed.), University of Toronto Press, 1959, p. 96.

Plain meaning of
statute

—golden rule

—mischief rule

veloped from three basic principles. First, if a provision of the statute is clear and unambiguous, and conveys a certain meaning that is not inconsistent with other sections of the statute, the court is obligated to apply the plain or literal meaning. If the statute is ambiguous, either because the provisions are inconsistent with other sections of the legislation or because the wording is capable of more than one meaning, the courts may apply either the golden rule or the mischief rule. The **golden rule** means a reasonable interpretation based on common sense will be used and that the literal meaning of the statute will be departed from only as far as necessary to overcome the ambiguity or inconsistency. The **mischief rule** means that the courts will try to give effect to the specific purpose for which the statute was enacted. Many statutes are passed to cure some defect or injustice in the common law or in some other statute. In applying the mischief rule, the courts look first at the original common law or statute with its defect and how the legislation in question was intended to overcome it. The court then imposes the interpretation that gives best effect to the original intent of the legislation. Thus, if there was a problem of interpretation with the federal *Young Offenders Act*, the application of the mischief rule would require that any ambiguity be interpreted to give effect to the intention of the *Act*, that is, to give the youth involved the same kind of rights and protection given to adults.

Another rule of statutory interpretation available to the courts is that a judge is not obligated to follow a statute unless it clearly and unambiguously overrules the common law provision. This is referred to as **strict interpretation of the statute**.

Statutes strictly
interpreted

Other specific rules have been developed to assist the courts interpret statutes. These rules may range from principles of grammatical construction to rules favouring one interpretation over another in different situations. The courts may also turn to similar statutes, both within and outside the legislative jurisdiction involved, as well as to the official translations of statutes and other publications such as dictionaries and academic articles. Each jurisdiction in Canada has passed legislation setting out general principles and specific rules judges must follow when determining the meaning of statutes or regulations. These rules are called interpretation statutes. Most statutes begin with a definition section which sets out specific meanings that must be applied to words used throughout that statute.

It is beyond the scope of this chapter to discuss statutory interpretation in any greater detail. However, it should be apparent that when faced with disputes over the meaning of statutory provisions, the courts have a cohesive framework of rules and guidelines to help them determine the appropriate interpretation. The interpretation eventually settled on by the court may affect whether the particular regulation in question was valid, whether the conduct complained of has violated a particular statute or whether the particular regulatory body or government agency had the power to make the decision or impose the control it did. Once this has been determined, the question remains whether or not the legislation itself was validly passed pursuant to the division of powers as set out in the *Constitution Act (1867)*.

As mentioned in Chapter 1, the powers of government are divided between the provincial and federal levels of government as set out primarily in sections 91 and 92 respectively of the *Constitution Act (1867)*. When a level of government that does not have the authority to do so under this division of powers passes the statute that

Division of
powers and
constitutional
authority

authorizes the conduct complained of, the courts will have no hesitation in declaring the statute *ultra vires* and the action of the decision maker improper. If a city council were to pass a bylaw prohibiting the sale of adult videos within the city boundaries, and the council, on the strength of that bylaw, were to deny such a business a licence to operate, the business could challenge that decision. Neither the province not a city deriving its authority from the province can pass such a bylaw because it encroaches on the federal government's criminal law powers. Since the bylaw was invalid, any decision made under its authority is also invalid and the courts would, upon application, declare the decision *ultra vires* and void. In the same way, the statute or regulation must be consistent with the provisions of the *Charter of Rights and Freedoms*, also discussed in Chapter 1. A statute which had the effect of discriminating on the basis of gender, religion or ethnic origin, or one which denied a person the right to a hearing, or restricted freedom of the press or religion could be challenged and a decision made under such a statute would be invalid.

PROPER PROCESS. Once it has been established that the decision maker has acted within the authority given under a valid statute or regulation, the question remains whether that authority was exercised in a proper way. Historically, the obligation of the administrator to act in a procedurally fair manner varied to a great extent depending on the function performed. When an officer was acting administratively and merely conducting the regular, ongoing business of a department implementing government policy, there was little recourse even when the actions were unfair (for example, a municipal officer distributing licences). However, when the administrator was involved in the adjudication of disputes, either between individuals or between the department and people being affected by the decisions of that department, or making decisions that affected the rights of individuals as opposed to mere privileges, the decision maker was functioning in a judicial or quasi-judicial capacity and had a greater obligation to conduct the process fairly. The distinction is less important today. Even when the decision maker is acting administratively there is an obligation to maintain at least a minimum standard of procedural fairness. If the issues being dealt with are important, the decision maker's function is to decide between competing parties or interests, or the remedies or penalties which can be imposed. These decisions can have a significant impact on the parties and the courts are much more likely to find an obligation on the decision maker to act fairly. These minimum standards of fairness have been imposed on the cabinet and ministers of the crown as well, although it should be noted that such obligations may be modified by statute. What constitutes fairness in these situations is determined by the rules of natural justice and what constitutes the minimum requirements of natural justice are set out below.

Administrator
must act fairly

Rules of Natural Justice

To determine what constitutes procedural fairness, one must first look to any governing statute and determine what obligations it imposes. Even if the obligations im-

Statute may
impose or modify
duty

posed by the statute are lower than the requirements of procedural fairness and natural justice, the statute will prevail if its provisions are intended to include all of the procedural requirements. Today, the process may be significantly affected by the *Charter of Rights and Freedoms* which requires that interference with one's life, liberty or security of person can only be done in accordance with "the principles of fundamental justice." The principles of fundamental justice have been taken to mean the same thing as procedural fairness.

FAIR HEARING. The most fundamental requirement of the rules of natural justice is that the party being affected by the decision of an administrator have an opportunity to a fair hearing. What constitutes a fair hearing will vary from situation to situation, but, essentially, the person being affected by the decision must have been notified that a decision is to be made and must have been given an opportunity to put his or her side forward. The courts have held that a fair hearing has not taken place when no notice of the hearing was given, or when the person was not informed of the nature of the complaint. Part of the requirement of a fair hearing is that all of the evidence that forms the basis of the decision be disclosed to the individual being affected by it. An individual must be given the opportunity to cross-examine witnesses who present material testimony or to refute any written declarations. Similarly, it is essential to a fair hearing that the individual be given an opportunity to present arguments and evidence to support those arguments.

All information
must be
disclosed at a fair
hearing

A fair hearing may extend to the right to demand an adjournment in certain circumstances. But there is no requirement that the decision maker follow the strict rules of evidence or even that the person affected have a right to counsel, although legal representation is a right if the proceedings might result in criminal charges. There is no general obligation on the decision maker to give reasons for the judgment, but many statutes do impose a duty on the decision maker to give reasons and often require that these reasons be put in writing. The test is reasonableness and an unreasonable imposition on the time of an administrator will not be tolerated. In some situations, the opportunity to present a case by letter is enough to satisfy the rule. Because of this flexibility in what constitutes a fair hearing, it is argued by many that the requirements of procedural fairness and the rules of natural justice are the same thing.

No obligation to
allow counsel or
follow rules of
evidence

HEARD BY DECISION MAKER. Another requirement of the rules of natural justice is that the decision must be made by the person hearing the evidence. If a board of inquiry is convened requiring five people to participate in the decision and something happens to one of them, that person cannot be replaced by another because the new person would not have heard all of the evidence presented. Similarly, the board of inquiry cannot proceed and make the decision with only four people because the statute requires five. It is permissible for the decision maker to use staff services to gather and summarize the evidence but the person making the decision must be the one who hears the evidence.

Decision must be
made by person
hearing evidence

IMPARTIALITY. A significant requirement of the rules of natural justice is that the decision be made in good faith and impartially. If it can be shown that the decision

Decision maker must be free of bias

maker is biased, the decision can be overturned. Because it is so difficult to establish a condition of bias, the courts have developed the principle that a reasonable likelihood of bias is enough to invalidate the decision. Bias is assumed when the matter being decided involves a relative, friend or business acquaintance of the decision maker. Similarly, if there has been an exhibition of bad feelings or hostility between the decision maker and the individual being affected by the decision, there is a real likelihood of bias and the decision can be challenged. Where it can be shown that the decision maker has an interest in the matter being decided or has already decided the matter, he or she will be disqualified from the decision-making process. A monetary interest in the subject matter affected by the decision will be grounds for challenge and the size of such an interest is not relevant. If Mueller participated on a rent review panel and was given the responsibility of deciding whether rents ought to be increased in a particular apartment building, the decision of the board could be challenged if it could be established by the landlord that Mueller had a brother living in one of the apartments. The decision could also be challenged if one of the tenants discovered that Mueller had a part interest in the property. Even if Mueller was merely one of several people on the decision-making panel, the presence of a bias on the part of one of the decision makers can disqualify them all.

Bias may be permitted by statute

Decision-making bodies are sometimes structured to incorporate a bias. For example, the statutes for labour arbitration cases require that each side appoint one of the arbitrators who together then choose a third. The two parties will probably appoint people who are clearly favourable to their position and thus are biased. The principle involved is that the bias represented by one side will be balanced by the bias of the other and the interests of the third arbitrator chosen by both will mediate between them. This emphasizes the point that the rules of natural justice are guidelines only. The courts retain a considerable amount of flexibility in the exercise of their supervisory jurisdiction as they ensure that the procedures involved are fair to all parties.

JUDICIAL REVIEW

Judicial review—inherent right of courts

Judicial review must be distinguished from the appeal process. Appeal is the process whereby the decision of an inferior court or tribunal is reviewed at a higher level. Judicial review involves the superior court's inherent right to supervise the judicial process. Whether or not an appeal is allowed, whether or not there are other courses of action open to the person affected by the decision, the courts retain the right to supervise and oversee the administration of justice. The courts have to correct the action of a decision maker who acts improperly. As a general rule, however, the courts require that all other remedies be exhausted before they will exercise their supervisory capacity in the form of judicial review. Generally, judicial review is available "where an administrative body has acted without authority, or has stepped outside the limits of its authority, or has failed to perform its duties."[4]

---

[4] *Judicial Review Procedure Act*, R.S.O. (1980) c.224.

The following is a summary of the situations in which a person affected by the decision of an administrator or administrative tribunal can go to the courts for relief.

1. When the decision maker has no authority to make the decision or has stepped outside of his or her authority in some way, that decision can be challenged in the courts. In determining whether or not the decision maker has the required authority, the courts must look not only to the contents of the statute to determine if the decision or act was authorized but also to the validity of the statute itself under the *Charter of Rights and Freedoms* and the *Constitution Act (1867)*. If the statute is valid, the decision can still be challenged on the grounds that the administrator was not functioning within the authority granted under the statute. For example, if a school board is required to review a dismissal application but appoints a committee of the board to hear the complaint because of the inconvenience of meeting over the summer, the decision of that committee is reviewable if the school board does not have the power to delegate its authority to a committee.

    Another such error can be made if the decision maker makes an initial decision which brings the matter in dispute under his or her jurisdiction. For example, if a labour relations board is given the authority to hear disputes between employees and employers and decides that a dispute between independent fishermen and the fish-packing companies they do business with falls within its jurisdiction, this primary jurisdictional determination can be challenged in the courts. Another type of jurisdictional error is when a decision-making body takes it upon itself to re-hear a matter after it has made a final decision. Usually, statutes will empower such a body to decide in the first place but not authorize them to re-hear the matter. Therefore, the second hearing is outside the jurisdiction of the decision maker. Although it is possible for such a body to cure a procedural defect in the original hearing by holding another hearing to overcome that defect, this is not a re-hearing since the first hearing was not valid.

2. The decision-making process itself is subject to the scrutiny of the court. There is a requirement of procedural fairness that must be followed whenever a decision is made that has an adverse impact on an individual.

3. If the decision maker is functioning within the proper jurisdiction and the process is procedurally fair, the courts are generally reluctant to interfere with the decision. But if the decision incorporates a remedy beyond the decision maker's power to grant, it will be reviewable on the grounds of jurisdiction. For example, under labour legislation, an arbitrator is given the authority to determine whether an employee was properly dismissed. If that arbitrator were to impose some other kind of consequence, such as a suspension from employment for a number of weeks, rather than simply deciding whether the dismissal was justified or not, the arbitrator would be assuming authority he or she does not have and that decision would then be invalid.

    Under rare circumstances, the court may find that there was not sufficient legal evidence for the administrator to reach a particular decision. The minimum legal standard requires that there must be at least some evidence to justify the

Authority of decision maker may be reviewed

Process must be fair

In some cases, the decision itself may be reviewed

conclusion reached by the decision maker before the courts can support that decision.

The courts have been willing to overturn a decision when the decision maker has committed an abuse of power. If a decision maker acts dishonestly, out of malice or with fraudulent intent in the exercise of his or her discretionary power, even though the decision may be within his or her power to reach, that decision is reviewable on the basis of abuse of power. The case of *Roncarelli v. Duplessis*[5] is a classic example of the abuse of power by a minister of the crown which was reviewable by the courts. In that case, a restaurant owner in Montreal supported Jehovah's Witnesses facing charges by paying their legal expenses. The premier of the province exerted his influence to have the plaintiff's liquor licence cancelled. This act was clearly outside the jurisdiction he had as premier and an abuse of his power. The court ordered the premier to pay compensation to the plaintiff.

The decision maker must consider all relevant matters and must not make a decision for an improper purpose. The exercise of the decision must be a genuine exercise. For example, if a decision maker with discretionary power merely follows the direction of a superior, that is an abuse of such power and reviewable in the courts.

4. Finally, and perhaps most significantly, the courts are willing to interfere with any decision that involves an error of law which is incorporated into the record of the hearing. The record consists of the decision, the reasons for it and any documents involved in the process of reaching the decision. A transcript of the proceedings can also be included as part of the record. Such an error of law on the record cannot be tolerated by the supervising judicial body and the decision will be overturned whenever such an error is substantial enough to affect the decision. Of course, an error of law must be distinguished from an error of fact. The decision maker is generally empowered to decide questions of fact and those decisions will not be interfered with. But when there is an incorrect declaration as to the law, this is of concern to the superior court and will not be tolerated. The error of law may be in misconstruing common law or statutes, a procedural error such as the refusal to hear evidence or hearing evidence that ought to have been excluded. The courts will not usually interfere with the decision merely because they do not like the decision or would have come to a different one themselves.

Abuse of discretionary power

Error of law on record

Methods of Judicial Review

PREROGATIVE WRITS. The courts have traditionally used the method of prerogative writs as opposed to the appellate process in exercising their supervisory power over administrative tribunals. These are ancient remedies traceable to the prerogative power of the crown. Four main prerogative writs are in use today, the best known of which is the writ of ***habeas corpus***. This is a court order to the custodial au-

---

[5] *Roncarelli v. Duplessis*, [1959] S.C.R. 121 (Supreme Court of Canada).

thority to present a person being kept in custody before the court and is used whenever there is concern over whether or not a person is being improperly detained. While this remedy is primarily used in criminal matters, *habeas corpus* is also used in immigration and child custody cases and when people have been institutionalized for mental health reasons. Many jurisdictions have passed legislation modifying the application of this judicial remedy, such as Ontario's *Habeas Corpus Act*.[6]

Certiorari overrules a decision

The other three prerogative writs, *certiorari*, prohibition and *mandamus*, play a significant role as the courts exercise their supervisory jurisdiction over administrative tribunals. A writ of **certiorari** renders the decision of the inferior body as having no legal effect. The granting of an application for *certiorari* nullifies an administrator's decision and eliminates any impact that decision might have on an individual. Prohibition is similar to *certiorari*. Its main distinction is when it is applied for in the decision-making process. For *certiorari* to apply, a decision must have been made that can be challenged. **Prohibition**, on the other hand, is used to prevent administrators or decision makers from using their power to make a decision in an unfair or otherwise inappropriate procedure. Prohibition is obtained before any decision and can be extremely effective in stopping an unfair or abusive process at an early stage.

Prohibition prevents decision from being made

Mandamus forces decision

Mandamus has quite a different application. When an individual is dealing with an administrator, delay in reaching a decision can be every bit as devastating as an improper decision or an abuse of procedure. A writ of *mandamus* can force the administrator to perform his or her duty. An administrator who has some discretion (the decision maker may or may not act) cannot be forced to reach a decision by *mandamus*. But an administrator who has a duty to reach a particular decision (usually imposed by legislation) can be forced to make the decision. However, it is possible that after being forced to reach a decision through the operation of *mandamus*, an administrator might be predisposed to decide in a way that is not in the best interest of the individual forcing the decision. Then other prerogative writs can be used to challenge the decision. If there is only one decision the decision maker can legally reach after applying the principles set out above, *mandamus* can be used to force that decision.

DECLARATORY JUDGMENT. Although the use of prerogative writs is the backbone of judicial review today, there are many situations in which this type of remedy is ineffective. They are available when a duty to act fairly is not met. They do not provide remedies when the impact of the decision has already been felt. For example, if Yamada owns property and builds a home on it that Adolfo, the city engineer, feels does not comply with the zoning regulations, and Adolfo then orders and supervises the demolition of the house, it would be little comfort to Yamada to go to the court, obtain a writ of *certiorari* and have Adolfo's decision quashed. The damage has already been done and a court declaration nullifying the decision will not undo it. Yamada needs monetary compensation to supplement the prerogative writ. To deal with situations in which there is no other appropriate action, the court has developed the concept of **declaratory judgment**. The court reserves the

---

[6] *Habeas Corpus Act*, R.S.O. (1980) c.193.

Court can make
declaratory
judgment

right to declare the law, assess damages and grant compensation in almost all situations. Declaratory judgments are available in situations in which prerogative writs are not and are often more effective in application. They have become an effective tool to assist the courts exercise their supervisory jurisdiction over administrators. The eminent English jurist Lord Denning went so far as to say, "I know of no limitations to the power of the courts to grant a declaration except such limit as it may in its discretion impose upon itself...."[7] It should also be noted that a special court has been established in Ontario to deal with these kinds of disputes. It is called the Divisional Court of Ontario.

Injunction stops
illegal conduct

INJUNCTION. Another remedy available to the courts to help them in their supervisory jurisdiction is the **injunction**. An injunction is simply an order by the court to an individual or body to stop breaking the law or otherwise interfering with another's rights. In the example above, an appropriate remedy for Yamada after the decision was made but before it was put in place, would have been to obtain an injunction to prevent the implementation of the decision. If the decision involved is merely the application for a licence, however, since no private rights of Yamada are being interfered with, an injunction would not be available. An injunction is somewhat limited in its application. In fact, there are many situations in which an injunction is completely inappropriate, such as when the damage has already taken place. In addition, there are limitations on whom an injunction can be obtained against. In many cases, the crown and servants of the crown are immune from the effect of an injunction.

Complex
requirements
modified by
statute

MODIFICATION BY STATUTE. While the declaratory judgment and the injunction are more straightforward than prerogative writs in their application, they are inappropriate in some circumstances and in some jurisdictions may not be available where *certiorari*, prohibition or *mandamus* are available. And the procedure to obtain a declaratory judgment or an injunction is quite different from that involved in obtaining one of the prerogative writs. Justice is often not obtained in administrative law proceedings because of the failure to meet technical requirements. Because of this, many jurisdictions have passed statutes incorporating these methods of judicial review into a consolidated and simplified procedure (for example, the Ontario *Judicial Review Procedure Act*[8] and the British Columbia *Judicial Review Procedure Act*[9]). The statutes go so far as to say that whenever an application for *certiorari*, prohibition, *mandamus*, declaratory judgment and injunction are applied for, that application will be deemed to be an application for judicial review under the statutes. The court then has the power to grant the relief available under the common law.

It should be pointed out that the process of judicial review as outlined in this section and contained in the modern statutes is available only when the decision maker is exercising a statutory power. When an individual is being subjected to the

---

[7] *Barnard v. National Dock Labour Board*, [1953] 2 Q.B. 18 p. 41 (C.A.).
[8] *Judicial Review Procedure Act*, R.S.O. (1980) c.224.
[9] *Judicial Review Procedure Act*, R.S.B.C. (1979) c.209.

decision of an administrator exercising a non-statutory power, such as a trade union, professional association, club or religious group, statutory judicial review will probably not be available and the individual will have to resort to the more traditional remedies such as breach of contract, tort or human rights legislation. It must be emphasized that one of the dominant elements present in the common law provisions has been carried over into statutory judicial review, that is, the discretionary power of the judges. The courts always reserve the right to refuse to grant a prerogative writ or declaratory judgment when it would be inappropriate to do so. This is an exercise of pure discretionary power and under the *Judicial Review Procedures Acts* of Ontario and British Columbia, this discretionary power has been retained.

Privative Clauses

Privative clauses attempt to prevent judicial review

Because the courts have always been protective of their role, they have been reluctant to give up any of their power to administrative tribunals. For this reason, many of the statutes contain provisions called **privative clauses** which attempt to make it clear to the courts that they are not to interfere with the decisions of tribunals. The principle of supremacy of parliament would lead one to believe that such a direction would be effective. However, the courts have resisted the operation of such clauses and often find ways to avoid them, causing legislators to develop better and more specific privative clauses. A typical example of a privative clause taken from the former Ontario *Labour Relations Act* is, "No decision, order, direction, declaration, or ruling of the board shall be questioned or reviewed in any court, and no order shall be made, or process entered, or proceeding taken in any court, whether by way of injunction, declaratory judgment, certiorari, mandamus, prohibition, quo warranto or otherwise, to question, review, prohibit, or restrain the board or any of its proceedings."[10] The intent of this legislation is obvious, but the courts have simply assumed that the legislature intended this to apply only when the board is acting within its jurisdiction. Thus, the original question as to whether or not the administrator has jurisdiction is still open to review. In fact, the way the courts have interpreted this type of privative clause varies with circumstances. It seems that if the courts wish to review a decision, they will find a way to do so despite the presence of a privative clause.

In addition to privative clauses which directly prohibit judicial review, the legislators have embodied in statutes other clauses which indirectly have the same effect. Legislative provisions which assign the right to review specific questions of law or other matters to a minister or other administrator can exclude the courts from this function. Other clauses try to define the nature of the power exercised as discretionary by using subjective wording: "the director may...," "Where the administrator is satisfied...," "Where it appears to be...," "Where in the opinion of...." It is difficult to tell when discretionary power is being abused when it is assigned

---

[10] *Labour Relations Act*, R.S.O. (1970) c.232 s.97.

in a subjective way. Subjective assignments of power are, therefore, quite effective in keeping the courts from reviewing a decision.

There are as many different types of privative clauses as there are drafters of legislation, but they are often not as effective as they might seem on first reading. It should not be assumed that judicial review has been excluded because a privative clause is present. The only way to be certain of the interpretation of a specific privative clause would be to find a case where a superior court has interpreted and applied it. The courts' right to interpret statutory provisions gives the courts the power of supervision over these administrative bodies. The result has been a contest between the courts and the legislature and this contest must be kept in mind when examining clauses which attempt to oust the jurisdiction of the court. The effect of such privative clauses must also be viewed as subject to the operation of the *Charter of Rights and Freedoms* which guarantees and enshrines the right to fundamental justice when a person's life, liberty or security is at stake. If these rights are interfered with by an administrative tribunal, the decision can be reviewed in the courts regardless of a privative clause.

Courts resist operation of privative clauses

Other Remedies

The powers and rights discussed in this chapter are largely extraordinary rights present when administrators or bureaucrats abuse their power or act incorrectly when making a decision that affects the position of an individual. In addition to the unique and special remedies discussed, the normal rights that arise when one individual has been injured by the act of another may be available. For example, if a contract is breached, all of the rights relating to breach of contract are applicable, even when one of the parties is the government or a crown corporation. Similarly, if the actions of the decision maker involve the commission of a tort such as negligence, defamation, trespass or even assault and false imprisonment, the injured individual has the right to pursue tort remedies against the administrator. However, there are some limitations to the availability of remedies under these headings. Until recently, an individual had no power to sue the crown under the premise that since the government was the source of the law it was not subject to the law and therefore could not be sued in its own courts. All jurisdictions in Canada have passed legislation making it possible to take the government to court and pursue judgment for breach of contract, tort, and so on. However, most jurisdictions have retained some of the crown's former immunity so it is difficult, if not impossible, to execute a judgment against the crown. For example, it is almost impossible to get an injunction against the crown although it may be possible against an individual bureaucrat abusing his or her power. Similarly, property of the crown will not generally be available to satisfy judgment. Once a judgment is obtained, the good faith of the government agency has to be relied on to satisfy that judgment. No force can be used to ensure payment. It should also be noted as a matter of common law that when an administrator exercises a statutory power properly, it will not give rise to tort action even if damage to an individual re-

Contract and tort remedies may be available

Enforcement of judgment may be difficult

sults from it. Some jurisdictions have extended this protection by statute. New Brunswick's *Protection of Persons Acting Under Statute Act*[11] is an example. The effect of such legislative protections may be to exclude a right of action in any given case and the student should be aware of any such local legislation.

A discussion of tort and contract law as well as many special rights and obligations created by statute are discussed in depth in previous chapters.

SUMMARY

Environmental law is one important example of government regulation of Canadian business. In common law, individuals have the right to sue others who damage the environment under riparian rights as well as the torts of nuisance and negligence. But these are inadequate to protect the general contamination of the environment and so controls have been enacted by federal and provincial statute. These statutes prohibit waste disposal except under prescribed standards and provide an enforcement body to investigate and prosecute violations. New projects which potentially threaten the environment are required to go through an environmental assessment process, sometimes requiring public hearings before permits are granted. The two objectives of government involvement are to penalize violation of environmental laws and to encourage good environmental practices.

When government bureaucrats make decisions affecting the lives of Canadians, they must act fairly, following the rules of natural justice. These rules require a fair hearing including adequate notice, that the decision be made by the hearer of the evidence and that it be made free of bias. When the rules are followed but the decision maker acts beyond the authority given under the statute or regulation, or when the statute or regulation is invalid because it violates the *Charter* or other constitutional provisions, that decision can be challenged in the courts and historical remedies applied. Governments often include provisions in legislation to restrict the power of courts to review the decisions of bureaucrats but such privative clauses are often ineffective.

QUESTIONS

1. Identify and describe the three different functions of government. Explain how the concept of supremacy of parliament affects how the three functions interrelate.
2. What common law provisions protect the environment? Why was it necessary to pass new federal and provincial legislation?

---

[11] *Protection of Persons Acting Under Statute Act*, R.S.N.B. (1973) c.P-20.

3. Is all pollution prohibited under modern environmental legislation? Explain.
4. What is the negative impact of these environmental statutes on business?
5. What is the extent of the power of the government officials who enforce these environmental laws?
6. Describe the principle of the rule of law. Explain how it affects the exercise of government power.
7. What is meant by the terms *ultra vires* and *intra vires* and how do they relate to federal and provincial legislation?
8. What is meant by the golden rule and the mischief rule? Under what circumstances can the courts apply these rules of statutory interpretation?
9. What is an administrative tribunal?
10. What obligations are placed on an adjudicative decision maker, even if not included in the legislation under which he or she is acting?
11. What three main elements constitute the rules of natural justice? Under what circumstances must a decision maker follow these rules of natural justice?
12. What requirements must be met for a person to receive a fair hearing?
13. Under what circumstances will judicial review be available?
14. Distinguish between *certiorari*, prohibition, *mandamus* and declaratory judgment.
15. What is a privative clause? How do courts usually react to them?
16. Give examples of three different types of privative clauses.

CASES

1. Re *Eastern Provincial Airways Ltd. and Canada Labour Relations Board et al.*
   During a labour dispute between the employer and the union, a series of events took place which led to charges by both sides of unfair labour practices. The Canada Labour Relations Board heard these complaints of unfair labour practices. The nature of the union's complaint was that the employer had failed to bargain in good faith, had interfered in the administration of a trade union, and had discriminated against, intimidated and threatened striking employees. The employer's position was that the union had failed to bargain in good faith, and intimidation and coercion were used to get people to join or quit the union. After the union had put its case and after the employer had presented some of its evidence, the board declared that it had heard enough evidence and decided in favour of the union. The employer brought this action to have the decision of the board overturned. Explain the nature of its complaint and the likely outcome. How would your answer be affected if the board gave the employer an opportunity to complete the presentation of evidence with the possibility that it might change its decision after the decision had been rendered?

2. Re *Young and Board of School Trustees of School District #47.*
    A parent wrote a letter to the district superintendent complaining about the conduct of a teacher. The conduct in question occurred when the teacher chastised the letter writer's son for bullying a classmate. The teacher made several remarks to the boy and the letter complained about them. When confronted with the accusation, the teacher said his comments were taken entirely out of context. *The Public Schools Act* (RSBC 1960 Chapter 319) states that the board is required to schedule a day in which a board or a committee appointed by the board would interview the teacher and the district superintendent. This date was scheduled and the teacher was notified. The teacher asked permission to bring a witness to testify and the request was denied. The teacher was suspended and brought a request to the court to have the decision overturned. Explain the nature of the teacher's complaint and explain the probable outcome.

3. Re *Saskatchewan Oil and Gas Corporation and Leach et al.*
    Mr. and Mrs. Leach, the owners of a property on which Saskatchewan Oil and Gas Corporation operated an oil well, had a dispute with the gas company over what Mrs. and Mrs. Leach ought to be paid as compensation for a well site and access roadway on their property. In Saskatchewan, the owner of surface rights to property does not own the mineral and gas rights. Saskatchewan Oil and Gas Corporation had the right to develop the subsurface minerals and oil and was only required to pay suitable compensation for the disruption of the surface rights. When such a disagreement takes place, the *Surface Rights Acquisition and Compensation Act* (RSS 1978) provides for arbitration. This legislation gives broad powers to the arbitrator and great flexibility as far as what evidence can be heard. A hearing was held and evidence presented, but after the hearing was finished, the chairman of the arbitration board wrote to a professional evaluator, Racine, for his opinion. Racine responded in the form of a letter. Neither the owners nor the operators were aware of the chairman's request to Racine nor of his use of the information in his response. The owner challenged the arbitration award. What is the nature of the complaint? Explain the probable outcome.

4. Re *Ottawa-Carlton Regional Transit Commission and Amalgamated Transit Union Local 219 et al.*
    The bus company known as Transpo operates a bus service in Ottawa. Part of that service consists of a route into Hull which lies across the Ottawa River in Québec. This route is a relatively small part of the overall bus services offered by Transpo. Transpo was involved in collective bargaining with its employees and took the position that a 1982 Ontario act entitled the *Inflation Restraint Act* applied and refused to bargain. Instead, it imposed a 5 percent increase in rates of pay for 1983 in accordance with the provision of that *Act*. The Canadian Labour Relations Board was hearing complaints into these matters when Transpo challenged its jurisdiction. The

board decided that it did have jurisdiction and rendered a decision that Transpo challenged. Explain the basis for its complaint and the likely decision of the court.

5. *Bailey v. Local Board of Health for Corporation of Township of Langley, McDonald and Attorney-General for British Columbia.*
    Mr. McDonald owned property in the Township of Langley on which he wanted to build. He brought an application before the medical health officer of the township (the petitioner in this action) for permission to build a conventional septic tank system. This request was turned down because of the disposal regulations passed under the *Health Act*. In October 1978, the council of the Township of Langley issued a building permit for the construction of a house on that property, providing McDonald obtained approval for the septic tank system from the medical health officer. He proceeded to build without obtaining approval. Instead, McDonald sought an appeal of the medical health officer's refusal before the local board of health which then held a hearing which took place over several sessions. An election took place and the makeup of the council changed after the first session. In subsequent sessions, some members were absent for part of the hearings but all members of the council participated in the decision at the end. The decision was to permit the septic tank system over the medical health officer's objections. The medical health officer than appealed this decision to the court. What is the nature of his complaint and the likely outcome of the action?

6. *Regina v. Canadian Pacific Limited.*
    The Canadian Pacific Railway Company is a transcontinental railway that falls under the legislative jurisdiction of parliament. Under the *Railway Act* the railway is obligated to keep its right of way clear of dead grass and other unnecessary combustible matter. To do so, on several occasions the railway instituted what is called a full burn. This procedure produces a considerable amount of smoke, including obnoxious odours which were offensive and caused discomfort to the people in the various towns along the tracks. The Ontario *Environmental Protection Act* prohibits such activities and the railway was charged with violating the *Act*. Explain some of the arguments that are available to the railway in its defence and the likely outcome.

ISSUES

1. The proliferation of government regulations and restrictions in the area of the environment has had a tremendous impact not only on the costs of carrying on business but also on whether certain types of business activities are permitted at all. On balance, is this interference in the way business has been traditionally carried out justified? In your answer consider forestry practices in British Columbia such as clearcutting and the current state of the east coast fishery.

2. The objective of recent environmental legislation is to limit the dumping of waste and other materials and lessen the impact of business and other human activities on the environment. Two methods have been primarily used to accomplish this end. First, regulations have been enacted whereby business activities are restricted and penalties are imposed when violations take place. Second, some jurisdictions are providing incentives to business, usually financial, to encourage them to engage in environmentally friendly business practices. Consider whether or not the basic objectives of environmental law are being adequately served by the statutes now in place in your jurisdiction and which of these two approaches is more likely to reach the desired end.

3. A significant trend in recent years has been the creation of administrative tribunals (administrative decision-making bodies that function like courts) which are given responsibilities to solve disputes between individuals in a given area, such as labour relations or landlord and tenant disputes. These bodies are typically created to be independent and not subject to any supervisory control by the courts. The courts have resisted this erosion of their power. Discuss the benefits derived from the creation of these bodies as well as any disadvantages arising from the courts being ousted from these areas of decision-making power.

4. When an administrative tribunal takes on the trappings and responsibilities that would normally fall to a court, there is little difficulty in identifying its function as quasi-judicial. However, there are many situations in which an individual decision maker who is acting as a bureaucrat or administrator implementing government policy makes a decision affecting a person. It is generally agreed that administrative tribunals acting judicially should act in a procedurally fair way, but is it necessary to place minimum standards of fair conduct on a decision maker who is merely carrying out an administrative function? The trend today is to require all administrators who make decisions affecting individuals to follow minimum standards of procedural fairness. Is this appropriate or should these administrators remain unfettered by the rules

and procedures that are being imposed on them by the courts? Consider the arguments for both sides and consider whether those minimum standards of procedural fairness ought to be the rules of natural justice or some lesser standard. Consider the different functions of various administrators from the clerk to the full-scale board of review and ask whether the same rules should apply to all.

5. Legislation creating administrative bodies often includes provisions which prohibit a court from interfering with or supervising the actions and decisions of administrative tribunals set up by the legislation. These privative clauses are often given lip service by the courts which then find methods of avoiding their application through their power of interpretation. This maintains the courts' right to review the decision of the administrative tribunal. Should a legislative body ever have the power to prohibit the courts from reviewing the decision of the administrative tribunal? On the other hand, should a court ever have the power to ignore the clearly expressed direction of a legislative assembly in this matter? Consider the problems which can arise from the adoption of either policy.

LEGISLATION

Alberta
Administrative Procedures Act, R.S.A. (1980) c.A-2
Arbitration Act, S.A. (1991) c.A-43.1
Environmental Protection and Enhancement Act, S.A. (1993) c.E-13.3
Proceedings Against the Crown Act, R.S.A. (1980) c.P-18

British Columbia
Commercial Arbitration Act, S.B.C. (1986) c.3
Crown Proceedings Act, R.S.B.C. (1979) c.86
Judicial Review Procedure Act, R.S.B.C. (1979) c.209
Waste Management Act in Bill 26, (1993)

Manitoba
Arbitration Act, R.S.M. (1987) c.A-120
Dangerous Goods Handling and Transportation Act, C.C.S.M. c. D12, amended by S.M. (1989) c.37
Environment Act, C.C.S.M. c.E125 amended by S.M. (1989) c.36
Ozone Depleting Substances Act, S.M. (1989) c.38
Proceedings Against the Crown Act, R.S.M. (1987) c.P-140

New Brunswick
Arbitration Act, S.N.B. (1992) c.A-10.1
Proceedings Against the Crown Act, R.S.N.B. (1973) c.P-18

Newfoundland
Freedom of Information Act, R.S.N. (1990) c.F.25
Proceedings Against the Crown Act, S.N. (1973) c.59

Nova Scotia
Arbitration Act, R.S.N.S. (1989) c.19
Proceedings Against the Crown Act, R.S.N.S. (1989) c.360

Ontario
Arbitration Act, S.O. (1991) c.17
Judicial Review Procedure Act, R.S.O. (1990) c.J.1
Proceedings Against the Crown Act, R.S.O. (1990) c.P.27
Statutory Powers Procedure Act, R.S.O. (1990) c.S.22

Prince Edward Island
Arbitration Act, R.S.P.E.I. (1988) c.A-16
Crown Proceedings Act, R.S.P.E.I. (1988) c.C-32
Environmental Protection Act, R.S.P.E.I. (1988) c.E-9
Environmental Tax Act, R.S.P.E.I. (1988) c. E-8.3
Judicial Review Act, R.S.P.E.I. (1988) c.J-3

Québec
Environment Quality Act, R.S.Q. (1977) c.Q-2
Expropriation Act, R.S.Q. (1977) c.E-24

Saskatchewan
Arbitration Act, R.S.S. (1978) c.A-24.1
Proceedings Against the Crown Act, R.S.S. (1978) c.P-27

Northwest Territories
Arbitration Act, R.S.N.W.T. (1988) c.A-5
Environmental Protection Act, R.S.N.W.T. (1988) c. E17
Environmental Rights Act, S.N.W.T. (1990) c. 38

Yukon
Arbitration Act, R.S.Y. (1986) c.7
Environment Act, S.Y. (1991) c.5

Federal
Canadian Bill of Rights Act, R.S.C. (1985) Appendix III
Clean Air Act, R.S.C. (1985) c. C-32
Environmental Assessment Act, R.S.C. (1993)
Constitution Act (1982) as enacted by the *Canada Act (1982)*, (U.K.) c.11
including the *Canadian Charter of Rights and Freedoms* and *Constitution Act
(1867)*. Formerly the *British North America Act*, R.S.C. (1985)
Appendix II

Index